THE PSYCHOLOGY OF VISUAL PERCEPTION

THE PSYCHOLOGY OF VISUAL PERCEPTION

SECOND EDITION

RALPH NORMAN HABER
University of Illinois at Chicago Circle

MAURICE HERSHENSON
Brandeis University

Holt, Rinehart and Winston
New York   Chicago   San Francisco   Dallas
Montreal   Toronto   London   Sydney

Library of Congress Cataloging in Publication Data
Haber, Ralph Norman.
  The psychology of visual perception.

  Bibliography: p. 408
  Includes indexes.
  1. Visual perception.   I. Hershenson, Maurice,
joint author.   II. Title.
BF241.H27   1980   152.1'4   80-12544
ISBN 0-03-020276-0

ACKNOWLEDGMENTS

Permissions by the following sources for reproduction of illustrations is gratefully acknowledged.

American Association for the Advancement of Science
Figure 3.11: G. Wald, Human vision and the spectrum. *Science*, 1945, *101*, 653–658. Copyright 1945 by the
  American Association for the Advancement of Science.
Figures 3.23, 3.24, 3.25: A. L. Gilchrist, Perceived lightness depends on perceived spectral arrangement. *Science*,
  1977, *195*, 185–187. Copyright 1977 by the American Association for the Advancement of Science.
Figure 13.12: A. N. Meltzoff, and M. K. Moore, Imitation of facial and manual gestures by human neonates.
  Science, 1977, *198*, 75–78. Copyright 1977 by the American Association for the Advancement of Science.
Figure 15.24: N. Weisstein, and C. S. Harris, Visual detection of line segments: An object superiority effect.
  Science, 1974, *186*, 752–755. Copyright 1974 by the American Association for the Advancement of Science.
Figure 17.9: M. I. Posner and S. W. Keele, Decay of visual information from a single letter. *Science*, 1967, *138*,
  137–139. Copyright 1967 by the American Association for the Advancement of Science.

American Psychological Association
Figures 6.22 and 6.23: B. G. Breitmeyer and L. Ganz, Implications of sustained and transient channels for theories
  of visual pattern masking, saccadic suppression and information processing. *Psychological Review*, 1976, *83*,
  1–36. Copyright 1976 by the American Psychological Association.
Figure 6.9: B. Sakitt, Iconic memory. *Psychological Review*, 1976, *83*, 257–276. Copyright 1976 by the American
  Psychological Association.
Figure 10.15: J. Hay and H. Pick, Jr., Visual and proprioceptive adaptation of the visual stimulus. *Journal of
  Experimental Psychology*, 1966, *71*, 157. Copyright 1966 by the American Psychological Association.
Figure 11.12: W. H. Eichelman, Familiarity effects in the simultaneous matching task. *Journal of Experimental
  Psychology*, 1970, *86*, 277. Copyright 1970 by the American Psychological Association.
Figure 12.3: M. A. Hagen, Influence of picture surface and station point on the ability to compensate for oblique
  view in pictorial perception. *Developmental Psychology*, 1976, *12*, 60. Copyright 1976 by the American Psycho-
  logical Association.
Figures 12.7 and 12.8: S. Coren, Subjective contours and apparent depth. *Psychological Review*, 1972, *79*, 360,
  363. Copyright 1972 by the American Psychological Association.

For Lyn and Amy

Acknowledgments (continued)

Figure 15.10: R. N. Haber, and M. Hershenson, The effects of repeated brief exposures on the growth of a percept. *Journal of Experimental Psychology,* 1965, *69,* 43. Copyright 1965 by the American Psychological Association.

Figures 15.17 and 15.18: F. Attneave, Some informational aspects of visual perception. *Psychological Review,* 1954, *61,* 183, 184. Copyright 1954 by the American Psychological Association.

Figure 15.19: J. Hochberg, and F. McAlister, A quantitative approach to figural "goodness." *Journal of Experimental Psychology,* 1953, *46,* 363. Copyright 1953 by the American Psychological Association.

Figure 17.7: J. R. Pomerantz, L. C. Sager, and R. J. Stoever, Perception of wholes and of their parts: Some configural superiority effects. *Journal of Experimental Psychology: Human Perception and Performance,* 1977, *3,* 427. Copyright 1977 by the American Psychological Association.

Figure 17.8: M. I. Posner and R. F. Mitchell, Chronometric analysis of classification. *Psychological Review,* 1967, *74,* 404. Copyright 1967 by the American Psychological Association.

Figures 18.5 and 18.6: M. Hershenson, Stimulus structure, cognitive structure, and the perception of letter sequences. *Journal of Experimental Psychology,* 1969, *79,* 329, 331. Copyright 1969 by the American Psychological Association.

Figure 19.3: K. Rayner, Eye movements in reading and information processing. *Psychological Bulletin,* 1978, *85,* 618–660. Copyright 1978 by the American Psychological Association.

Houghton Mifflin Company

Figures 8.21 and 8.26: J. J. Gibson, *The perception of the visual world.* Copyright (c) 1950 by James J. Gibson.

Figure 9.5: J. J. Gibson, *The senses considered as perceptual systems.* Copyright (c) 1966 by James J. Gibson.

Oxford University Press, Inc.

Figures 11.15, 11.16, 11.17, 11.18, 11.19, and 11.20: W. L. Laurence and R. B. Lawson, *Human stereopsis: A psychophysical analysis.* Copyright (c) 1976 by Oxford University Press, Inc.

University of Illinois Press

Figure 12.11: T. A. Ryan, and C. B. Schwartz, Speed of perception as a function of mode of representation, *American Journal of Psychology,* 1956, *69,* 66.

(Continued on p. 432)

/Preface to the Second Edition

The study of visual perception has advanced rapidly in the seven years since the publication of the first edition of this text. This advance is marked not only by a large number of experimental papers, but also by a sharpening of the theories and models, permitting us to understand many observations within a single conceptual framework. Our purpose in this edition, as in its predecessor, is to provide undergraduates and beginning graduate students with a broad and firm foundation for understanding visual perception within the contexts of current conceptual frameworks. Thus, the emphasis and the conception of the book has remained the same in both editions.

What has changed is our feeling about the field as a whole and the topics to be included or expanded. The reorganization of the three major sections of the text reflects the former—the section on *Visual Space Perception* now appears before the section on *Perception as Information Processing* to reflect our belief that an understanding of the way the visual system functions in processing symbolic information in perceptual and cognitive tasks requires an understanding of the way the system mediates perception and action in the real world. The addition of new chapters and the complete reorganization of others reflects our attempt to lengthen our discussion of important areas. For example, psychophysical measurement, eye movements, and binocular vision are treated extensively in separate chapters in this edition. The material covered in the chapters on *Perceiving the Layout of Space in Photographs and Pictures* and *Perceptual Components in Reading* is new to this edition.

Most of the topics covered in the first edition have been retained, but almost all have been rewritten or reorganized to improve clarity and to reflect recent changes in thinking. Examples have been added or updated; figures have been added or improved. We continue to include a summary and suggested readings at the end of each chapter in the belief that the student is aided by a review of the most important points in a chapter and by an indication of where additional information can be found. The suggested readings have also been updated.

Important terms are printed in boldface in the text. The number of the page that contains a detailed discussion of the term also appears in boldface in the index.

Many people helped in the production of this book at various stages, including several anonymous reviewers and many graduate students. Each helped us avoid errors and improve our ability to communicate ideas. The editorial and production staff at Holt, Rinehart and Winston has provided professional work of high quality and we thank them for it. We especially thank Brian Heald, who suffered through all the agonies but managed to keep up his good spirits and our momentum. Finally, it is clear that this revision could not have been accomplished without the love and support of our wives Lyn and Amy. To them we dedicate this book.

Chicago, Illinois   R. N. H.
Waltham, Massachusetts   M. H.

v

/Contents

SECTION ONE

PERCEPTION AS SENSORY ORGANIZATION

Chapter 1

Light, the Visual Stimulus, and the Visual Nervous System

The visual sense is important because, in the evolution of human beings and many other species, we have developed specialized neural tissue that responds selectively to a particular kind of energy we call light. This selectivity has, of course, also been true for senses other than vision—we have evolved a sense organ that responds to certain kinds of vibrations of molecules of matter (which we sense as hearing), to certain kinds of concentrations of ions in the air (which we sense as smell), to certain kinds of direct vibrations of nerve endings on the skin (which we sense as touch), and so forth. If it were not for these specialized receptors, we would have no direct way to pick up variations in light energy or molecular vibration or ion concentration.

In this chapter, we will first consider the characteristics of light as a stimulus; its source, how it is measured and specified, and how it reaches the visual receptors. Then we will look at the receptor systems themselves, and the pathways by which the initial information is transmitted to the cortex of the brain. Finally we will examine how light energy is transduced by a receptor into neural excitation.

THE VISUAL STIMULUS

Sources of Light

One form of energy in the universe is **electro-magnetic radiation**, which is emitted by any object that is heated enough to start its electrons vibrating. Our sun is the best example of a heated source, but the lowly candle also emits electromagnetic radiation, as does the filament in a light bulb when electric current is passed through it. Certain so-called fluorescent gases also emit electromagnetic radiation when electrically stimulated.

Physicists can describe electromagnetic radiation in two different but compatible ways: as discrete particles or quanta of energy and as waves of energy. Although physicists have worked out the relationship between these two conceptualizations, it has not been easy to describe electromagnetic radiation in these two ways simultaneously. Newton, in his work on electromagnetic radiation, described light as rays made up of discrete packages of energy—**quanta** in modern terms. For Newton, radiation is emitted from a source in all directions, each ray traveling in a straight line until it encounters some form of matter. From this point of view the amount of energy in a ray of electromagnetic radiation or the intensity of a source is specified by how many quanta are emitted and travel in each ray during some interval of time.

While Newton's description is adequate to account for many of the facts of electromagnetic radiation, it failed to explain demonstrations that rays of energy did not travel in straight lines. An alternative concept, that the energy traveled in waves, was required. For example, when experiments were designed to separate the energy emitted from a source so as to capture a single ray, unpredicted results occurred. It was assumed that a single ray could be isolated if the source was blocked by an opaque surface with but a single minute hole in it. By making the hole small enough one should be able to block all but a single ray from passing through it. However, as the hole was made smaller and smaller, the image of the light that passed through the hole first increased in sharpness and then, with very small hole sizes, becomes fuzzy and blurred. We now know that this is due to diffraction of light—a phenomenon that can be explained only by assuming that light travels in waves.

So electromagnetic radiation is both the radiation of packets of energy and, at the same time, an undulating wave of energy. Both of these properties are important for visual perception and our visual system has evolved specifically to respond to both of them. With respect to the rays of quanta, human beings are capable of detecting the presence of a beam of light aimed at the eye if it contains only a few rays, each of which has but one quantum that excites one of the photoreceptors in the eye. In this sense the human eye is the most sensitive light-measuring instrument possible. At the other extreme, the visual system can still function (though not for very long), if the number of quanta reaching the eye is so great that it burns the eye.

With respect to our ability to detect differences in the properties of light waves, the sensitivity of the human eye is far more restricted. Electromagnetic radiation varies in **wavelength** from waves so long that their peaks are separated by several kilometers (typical of some kinds of radio and television waves), to waves so short that billions of them would not measure a meter in length (certain types of X rays and cosmic radiation). Color plate 1 illustrates the electromagnetic radiation spectrum as a function of wavelength. For radiation at most wavelengths, human beings have no specialized receptors, so we are totally insensitive to the presence of such waves. For example, we cannot detect the presence of radio carrier waves using any of our senses. Nor can we detect directly the presence of very short wavelengths (microwaves), although prolonged exposure to some of them may damage tissue. The skin can detect energy of the middle wavelengths—called infrared radiation—which stimulate the temperature-sensitive nerve endings in the skin and are felt as heat.

The eyes of human beings are specialized organs, designed to detect a narrow band of rather short waves of electromagnetic radiation—from 400×10^{-9} to 700×10^{-9} meters in wavelength. Since 10^{-9} meters is one billionth of a meter, or a *nanometer,* the **visible spectrum** is frequently described as the wavelengths between 400 and 700 nanometers. By convention, electromagnetic radiation of wavelengths shorter than 400 or longer than 700 nanometers is not called light. Wavelengths shorter than about 400 nanometers are absorbed, primarily by the lens, thereby eliminating the possibility of harmful effects on the retina. Since these wavelengths never reach the receptors, the visual system can provide no information about such stimulation. Our response to the upper end of the spectrum is limited for a different reason. As we will see, the amount of energy in each quantum of radiation varies inversely as a function of its wavelength. While wavelengths longer than 700 nanometers can reach the retina, they are unable to excite the photoreceptors. We may feel this radiation as heat, and the thermal receptors throughout the body can respond to infrared radiation, but the photoreceptors in the retina are not sufficiently sensitive to such quanta to produce a photochemical reaction.

Reflecting Surfaces

There are relatively few objects in the universe that produce or radiate light. Although these sources are all important to human beings, they represent a very small proportion of the objects in the visual environment. Most things we see do not emit light, but reflect light from the sun or from man-made sources such as light bulbs or the gases in fluorescent tubes. Thus, the characteristics of light that reach our eyes are functions of the characteristics both of the sources of light and of the surfaces of objects that reflect it.

For our purposes, we can assume that quanta travel in straight lines and continue to do so until they interact with matter along the way. Objects placed in their path either absorb the quanta (in which case they disappear, usually being transformed into heat), reflect them in some other direction, or refract them through the matter and out the other side in a new direction. Light rays of quanta travel at such great speed that, at least on Earth, man is essentially in instantaneous visual contact with all objects, in a straight line, no matter how far away they are. Most objects in the path of quanta are **diffusely reflecting,** meaning that light is reflected in various directions that are largely independent of the angle of incidence of the light onto the surface. However, when a surface is very smooth, the dispersion of the reflected quanta is much narrower. In the extreme, a perfect mirror surface reflects quanta in only one direction, such that the angle of reflectance of the light from the surface equals the angle of incidence of the light to the surface.

In a typical visual environment, quanta from light sources fly and bound off objects in all directions, with some of them lost in the process through absorption. If an eye placed in this environment, every point in space in a straight line to the eye is, potentially, a pathway for a ray of quanta from that point to the eye. Thus, whereas light diverges from every point on every surface in space, from the vantage point of an eye, light converges from every point in space.

Imaging of Light in the Eye

With all these flying quanta, how can the eye capture any of them and make sense out of the patterns of energy they represent? We do not use our eyes simply to measure how much photic energy exists around us, as a light meter might. Rather, our visual senses allow us to collect information about the visual characteristics of surfaces and objects and the layout of visual space around us. To do this, the quanta that reach our eyes must represent or reproduce some of the properties of the surfaces that reflected them to the eyes.

It is easy to illustrate how some of this is done with a simple box camera, so, for the moment, imagine that the eye is a pinhole camera. Figure 1.1 illustrates such a camera, whose small pupil opening (the pinhole) is directed at a highly reflecting (white) stick that is lit by the sun. The background is a uniformly

nonreflecting (black) surface. Assume that the sun emits quanta in all directions, that the stick has a diffusely reflecting surface, and that there are no other reflecting surfaces around. The only light that can get into the camera-eye are those rays reflected from the stick directly toward the pupil of the camera.

Figure 1.1 shows that every point on the surface of the stick receives light from the sun and every point reflects light diffusely in all directions. From each such point on the stick, only a few of that infinite number of diverging rays can fit through the pinhole (the actual number depend on its size). Each of those rays continues through the pinhole and impinges on the back surface of the camera where photosensitive film is placed. The quanta in the rays that are absorbed by the film causes a photochemical reaction to occur. When the film is developed, each location where

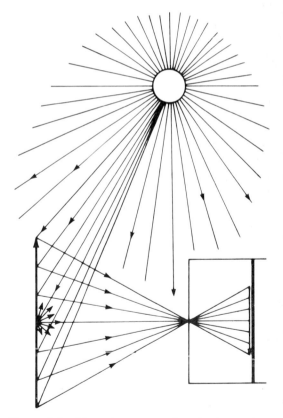

Figure 1.1 Schematic representation of a box camera, with a pinhole to admit light and an image surface on which film is placed.

quanta impinged is indicated by a change in the film density. Only part of the developed film shows these effects—only those places that are in a straight line through the pupil opening to the stick. An optical **image** of the stick is produced in this way on the film. That image is inverted. The rest of the film—to the sides of the stick's image—receives no quanta and therefore is unaffected.

In principle, the optical part of our eye or of any camera could operate like this—by forming an optical image of the surfaces reflecting light toward it, but such a device has one important drawback. Although each of the rays of light from the sun that reach the stick may contain enormous numbers of quanta per unit time, because the stick is diffusely reflecting, those quanta in each of the sun's rays are divided up into an enormously large number of new rays being reflected from the stick. Therefore, the quanta in any one of these new rays are far fewer than in each ray from the sun. Since the pinhole admits only a very few rays from each place on the stick, the number of quanta available from each point to form an image on the film inside the camera is quite small—so small in fact that, for typical film, no photochemical reaction would occur unless the camera were pointed at the reflecting stick for a long time—minutes or even hours. Consequently, the pinhole camera is a slow image-forming device, except under very high illumination.

One could try to solve the problem by increasing the size of the hole, as in Figure 1.2. The problem here is that the image projected on the rear surface of

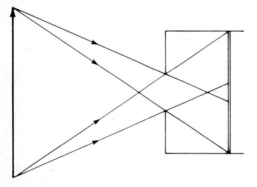

Figure 1.2 A box camera with a large opening in order to admit more light. This does not solve the problem, because the larger the hole, the more the image in blurred.

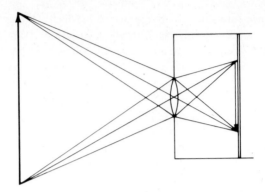

Figure 1.3 A box camera with a lens to focus the light rays onto the image surface.

the camera is now a hopeless blur, since from any given point on the stick a large number of different rays of quanta going in slightly different direction manages to get through the hole. Therefore any given point on the image surface may receive quanta from a number of different points on the stick and there would never be any way to sort them out. As the hole is enlarged the blur gets progressively worse, even though brighter. So, the bigger-hole procedure creates more problems than it solves.

The solution is to use a **lens** in the larger opening so that more rays can be captured from each point on the stick without their overlapping or blurring in the image (Fig. 1.3). Lenses capitalize on a property of light known as **refraction.** Light rays travel through the atmosphere in a straight line until they encounter a medium of a different density, such as glass. Although the glass is transparent (light can travel through it), the change in medium causes each ray to be bent so that it travels in a new direction. The amount of refraction depends, in part, on the difference between the density of the medium in which the light has been traveling and the density of the new medium that the light is about to enter.

A lens in air has a front and a back surface. Therefore light traveling through air is bent when it enters the lens and again when it leaves the lens. The curvature of the lens determines the amount of refraction. Figure 1.4 illustrates the amount of refraction for lenses of several degrees of curvature. Notice that because these lenses are convex on both surfaces each lens takes rays of light diverging from a point and bends them so

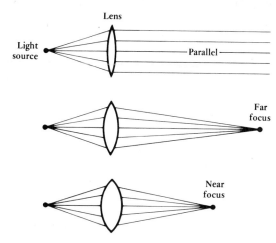

Lens

Light source

Parallel

Far focus

Near focus

Figure 1.4 Schematic representation of the convergence of light produced by the refraction of convex lenses. The greater the angle formed by the ray when it enters or leaves the glass, the greater the refraction.

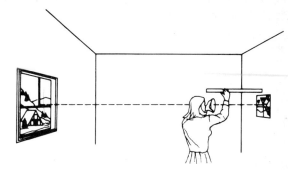

Figure 1.5 The focal length of a lens is the distance between the lens and the image of a distant object it forms. The lens has been moved back and forth until the image of the object is in sharp focus on the wall. The distance between the lens and the wall is then the focal length of the lens. (Adapted from Cornsweet, 1970.)

that they converge again to a point. The convergence provides the solution to the problem of a pinhole camera. Because the lens is large, a number of rays of light reach it from every point on the stick's surface reflecting light. These rays diverge from the stick so they impinge upon all parts of the lens. If the lens refracts each of these so that they converge exactly at the distance inside the camera where the film is placed, there is no blur. Each point on the object is imaged at a unique point on the film. Since many rays are at each image point the number of quanta in the image is larger, and the image appears brighter than in the pinhole camera.

If the lens is very thick through its center, relative to its diameter, the degree of refraction is great and the point of convergence is close to the exit side of the lens. The distance from the lens to the point of convergence is called the **focal length** of the lens.

Figure 1.5 shows that the focal length depends on two things, the shape of the lens and the distance from the lens to the source of the diverging light rays. Figure 1.5 illustrates this for one lens refracting light diverging from points at different distances. Therefore, for a lens of fixed shape the distance from the lens to the imaging surface behind the lens (that is, the film plane) has to be movable (a process called **accommodation**) to take into account different object distances. This is done in all photographic cameras, in which the focus adjustment moves the lens nearer or farther from the film.

A different solution is used for the human eye. The human eye has an outer covering, called the cornea, which provides most of the refraction of light. The shape of the cornea is relatively fixed and unchanging. Behind the cornea is a lens that is changeable in shape and provides a finer accommodation correction. The focal length for a typical human eye is about 17 millimeters. If the lens is fixed in shape and the distance between the lens and the retinal surface at the back of the eye is also fixed, then only objects at a certain distance would produce a sharp projection on the retinal surface. Since the diameter of the eyeball is relatively fixed, we can maintain clearly focused projections on the retina by changing the shape of the lens as objects move closer or farther away, or as we shift our attention from near to far ones. We will consider the accommodation control later in this chapter.

We have digressed at some length in the above comparison between pinhole cameras and cameras with lens in order to describe how light is imaged. Since the eye possesses many of the optical components and mechanisms that have become standard elements in the operation of cameras, many theorists have suggested metaphorically that the eye functions as a camera. While we have capitalized on this metaphor to describe how light is imaged in the eye, we reject the metaphor if it is used to suggest that perceiving has any relation to taking a picture. We shall return to the destructive uses of the **eye—camera metaphor** in Chapter 9.

REPRESENTATION OF VISUAL STIMULATION ON THE RETINA

We have considered, although briefly, how quanta flying about in a visual environment might end up in the eye, or more precisely, on the surface of the retina inside the eye. We shall see shortly how photoreceptors embedded in this retinal surface transduce the photic energy, first into photochemical events and then into neural signals. But before we can tackle that process, we need to examine some of the properties of the retinal image, especially in terms of the way it represents and preserves information about objects radiating or reflecting quanta. First we will see how changes in the intensity of light—the number of quanta from a particular direction—are specified in the retinal image. Then we will see how other characteristics of objects—their sizes or the sharpness of their edges and contours, and the uniformity of their surfaces—are represented. Another characteristic is the wavelength of the quanta. We will take each of these up in turn.

Intensity of Light

It is possible and often useful to measure the energy level of a source directly in terms of the number of quanta being emitted in a particular direction during a particular interval of time. Such measurements are usually not useful in the study of visual perception, however, because we rarely look at sources directly. Therefore we need a set of measurements that can specify the **intensity of light** at the eye in terms of the source, distance, and reflectivity of surfaces. These are called **photometric measurements**. To understand the various aspects of visual perception we need to specify the amount of light reaching a surface (or directed to the eye) directly from a source of light, the amount of light being reflected from a surface toward the eye, and occasionally the amount of light actually reaching the retina (Fig. 1.6). (To complicate matters, even these few measures of the amount of light can be expressed either in English units or metric

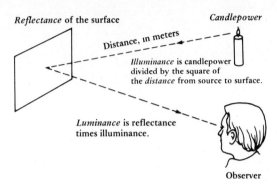

Figure 1.6   Measurements that specify the intensity of light at the source, at a surface being illuminated, and as reflected from that surface to the eye.

units. We shall use metric units throughout as they are increasingly becoming the international standards.)

Amount of Light Reaching the Eye from a Source—Illumination.

Visual science has defined a standard light source called a **candle,** in terms of a specific amount of light radiating from it in a particular direction per unit of time. The direction is specified by the solid angle formed by the rays radiating from the source. A source of one candle power emits a fixed number of **lumens** per second in each steradian (a measure of the solid angle).

If a surface is now placed in the path of all those rays, we can determine the amount of light that will reach any particular point on that surface. It is this value that we need—called the **illumination** of a surface from a source. Illumination depends on how many candelas are emitted and the distance from the surface to the source. To see why the latter is true consider Figure 1.7, which shows a segment of a surface at two different distances from a source. If the energy within the cone of light is fixed by the candle power of the source, then the farther away the surface, the smaller the proportion of the energy that illuminates it. Specifically, the illumination of a square meter of surface is equal to the number of candles radiated toward it divided by the square of the distance in meters: $I = c/d^2$. Distance has to be squared because the proportion of the cone of illumination that falls on a surface of a fixed size diminishes by the square of the distance as the surfaces move farther away. This meas-

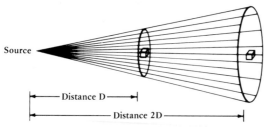

Figure 1.7 A schematic representation of light radiating from a source in a cone, in which an object of fixed size is being illuminated by the radiation at two different distances.

ure of illumination, described as candelas per square meter (cd/m^2) of surface, specifies the amount of light illuminating a surface from a source.

In terms of units one should have about 10 cd/m^2 on a desk surface in order to read comfortably. One cd/m^2 is adequate for normal street lighting at night. One could obviously increase the number of candelas per square meter illuminating the ground from a street light by shortening the pole on which the light is mounted. This increases illuminance on the ground around the base of the light, although to the degree that the light is focused downward, a shorter pole reduces the area on the ground illuminated.

Amount of Light Reaching the Eye from a Reflecting Surface—Luminance.

Illuminance tells us how much light falls on a surface, or on the eye when looking directly at the source. But most light that we see enters the eye after being reflected from surfaces rather than coming directly from a light source. How much light reaches the eye depends on how much of the incident light from the source is reflected from the surface to the eye. **Reflectance** is the ratio of light reflected from a surface to the light that reaches the surface. It is usually expressed as a percentage—100 percent reflectance signifying a perfectly reflecting surface.

The amount of light reflected is called **luminance** and is defined as the illuminance of the surface multiplied by the proportion of that illuminance that is reflected: luminance equals $R \times cd/m^2$. The unit specifying luminance is the same as that for illuminance: cd/m^2. Luminance is less than illumination to the extent of the amount of light absorbed by the reflecting surface.

Notice that luminance is not affected by the distance of an observer from the reflecting surface. The screen in a movie theater looks equally bright from the front or back row. However, the appearance of the screen changes dramatically if the projector is moved forward or back. If a light source radiated many quanta in one direction, it would be much more intense in that direction. Thus the solid angle over which the quanta are emitted also determines its intensity. So if you take the same number of quanta and concentrate them into a smaller area by focusing them with a reflector or a lens, the light will become more intense, as happens when a light source moves closer to the surface. However, this is not the same as changing the size of the portion of the surface that is reflecting light, as would happen when you move closer or farther away from that surface. Since this does not change the number of quanta being reflected from each point on the surface, the luminance of the surface is not affected. Thus, neither illuminance nor luminance is concerned with the area over which light is incident to or reflected from a surface.

Occasionally it is important to know not only how much light reaches an object or how much light is reflected from it, but how much reflected light actually enters the eye. This is proportional to the area of the pupil, and is called the **retinal illuminance.** Retinal illuminance is equal to the luminance times the area of the pupil, measured in square millimeters. This unit is called a **troland.** Hence, holding luminance constant, as the pupil opens, more light gets onto the retina, producing an increase in the number of trolands.

It should be obvious that if the eye looks directly at a point source of radiant energy, the intensity of light reaching the eye will be the same as if the light were first reflected from a mirror with 100-percent reflectance. Thus when the eye is looking directly at sources of light, the luminance of the light reaching the eye is the same as its illuminance.

Figure 1.8 presents some light levels found in normal environmental stimulation. As can be seen, there is a range of 10^{13} cd/m^2 over which the visual system can normally respond. This range is divided into a **photopic region,** increasing from about 1 (10^0) to 10 million (10^7) cd/m^2, and a **scotopic region,** descending from about 1/10 (10^{-1}) down to a lower limit of sensitivity of around $1/1,000,000$ (10^{-6}) of a *cd/m²*. Given this large range of sensitivity, it is usually not possible to plot graphs in luminance values directly. Instead, a logarithmic transformation is made, which, in effect, plots the exponents to the base 10 of luminance. Hence a luminance of $1 = \text{Log}_{10} \; 10^0 = 0$ in the log scale; a luminance of $100 = \text{Log}_{10} \; 100 = \text{Log}_{10} \; 10^2 = 2$ in the log scale; and a luminance of $1/10,000 = \text{Log}_{10} \; 1/10,000 = \text{Log}_{10} \; 1/10^4 = \text{Log}_{10} \; 10^{-4} = -4$ in the log scale. On this scale, the range of sensitivity is 13 log units. To say that sensitivity decreases by one log unit means that ten times as much intensity as before is needed to achieve the same perceptual effect.

	Scale of luminance in candelas per meter squared	
Sun's surface at noon	10^{10}	
	10^9	Damaging
	10^8	
Tungsten filament	10^7	
	10^6	
	10^5	
White paper in sunlight	10^4	Photopic
	10^3	
	10^2	
Comfortable reading	10	
	1	Mesopic
	10^{-1}	
White paper in moonlight	10^{-2}	
	10^{-3}	
White paper in starlight	10^{-4}	Scotopic
	10^{-5}	
Absolute threshold	10^{-6}	

Figure 1.8 The range of light levels to which the eye can respond.

Candelas, illuminance, luminance, and trolands all refer to physical measures of the amount of light present. Each is measured by physical instruments—the photographer's light meter being one. These measures are not concerned with the appearance of light. For that we use the term **brightness,** and its usage is determined by how light appears to perceivers. It is reasonable to assume that, as the luminance of a surface increases, its brightness increases, but the luminance–brightness relationship depends on many variables, and will occupy us for half of Chapter 3.

Spectral Composition of Light—Wavelength

Most natural light sources emit equal amounts of wavelengths over the entire visible spectrum, thereby making them appear white, but most surfaces do not reflect all those wavelengths equally. Suppose a surface is painted so that it absorbs all short wavelengths and reflects only long wavelengths. Such a surface appears red and not white (see Chapter 5). If it absorbs the long wavelengths and reflects only the short, it appears blue, since it is the short wavelengths that account for the perception of blue.

Size and Shape of Reflecting Objects

One can specify an object's size in space with a measuring instrument, such as a meter stick. Such measurements are useful if we are concerned with describing the environment. However, if we want to describe our perception of the environment, we need to know something about the size of the object as it is projected onto the back of the eye.

For simplicity's sake, we can again consider the eye as a camera, and draw lines representing rays of quanta from the edges of an object through the lens and impinging on the retinal surface at the back of the eye, as in Figure 1.9. An object of size S produces a **retinal image** of size s. If the real size S of the object is held constant, but it is moved farther away from the eye, s decreases in size. Consequently, the size of an object S in meters is not typically a useful measure.

Instead, it is possible to specify retinal size in terms of physical size and viewing distance. Since the angle made by the converging rays of light reflected from the extremities of an object is the same angle made by those rays diverging inside the eye to form the retinal image, there is a simple relationship between these variables and the size of the projection on the retina. The tangent of an angle is equal to the length of the side opposite the angle divided by the length of the adjacent side, when the two sides meet at a right angle. Therefore, in Figure 1.9 tangent $A = s/n = S/D$. Further, since $S, D,$ and n are all measurable, it is possible to compute s from $s = nS/D$. For the adult human eye n is about 17 millimeters or .017

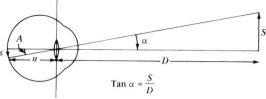

$$\text{Tan } \alpha = \frac{S}{D}$$

$$\text{Tan } A = \frac{s}{n} \text{ where } n \approx 17 \text{ millimeters}$$

$$s = \frac{17\,S}{D} \text{ in millimeters}$$

Figure 1.9 Schematic representation of the relationships between the physical size of an object (S) at a distance (D) from the eye, the visual angle (α) formed by rays of quanta reflected from its extremities, and the size of the retinal projections (s).

meters. Thus, a tree 10 meters in height at 100 meters distance, projects a retinal size of $.017 \times 10/100 = .0017$ meters or less than 2 millimeters.

It is often useful to know the **visual angle** formed by the extremities of an object or surface rather than the size of the retinal image it creates. This requires finding the angle whose tangent is S/D or s/n. In most experiments the size of stimuli presented to the eye is specified in a visual angle and not in physical size S or retinal size s.

Figure 1.10 presents some typical visual angles in relation to object sizes in the environment. Visual angles are reported in degrees, minutes, and seconds of arc. A complete circle is 360 degrees, and a right angle has 90 degrees. In each degree there are 60 minutes, and in each minute there are 60 seconds. Looking straight ahead with both eyes, we can see objects spread over about 200 degrees across the scene in front of our eyes.

Specifying the shape of surfaces or of objects is more complicated. While we can measure their physical shapes with meter sticks, a physical square or circle in space need not project that shape on the retina. The retinal size of a surface, as we saw, depends on real size and the distance of the object from the eye. The retinal shape of a surface, however, depends on its physical shape and the orientation of the surface to the line of sight. A circle, when it is perpendicular to the line of sight (Figure 1.11), projects a circular retinal image, but if the circular surface is tilted its retinal image is an elipse, whose eccentricity is proportional to the amount of tilt.

The relation of physical size to retinal size and physical shape to retinal shape is a concern of the **laws of perspective**—relationships first described by Eu-

---

Fovea is about 2° in diameter.

Your thumbnail at arm's length is between 1.5° and 2°.
   (D = 60 centimeters, S = 1.5 centimeters, Tan A = 1.5/60 = .025, $A \approx 1.5°$)

A four-letter word in this book held at 50 centimeters (20 inches) viewing distance is about 0.7°.

If you move the book to 25 centimeters, $A \approx 1.4°$.

Each letter is 0.16 centimeters wide, or about 12 minutes of arc at 50 centimeters.

One letter at 50 centimeters is 0.05 millimeters on the retina.

Sun and moon are each 30 minutes of arc. While the sun is nearly 400 times farther away, it is much larger, too.

A quarter coin at arm's length is 2°, at 85 meters is 1 minute, and 5 kilometers is 1 second.
   Under optimal conditions, an object the width of a quarter could be seen at 10 kilometers distance from the eye.

Figure 1.10 Some typical visual angles and retinal sizes of common objects at specified distances from the observer.

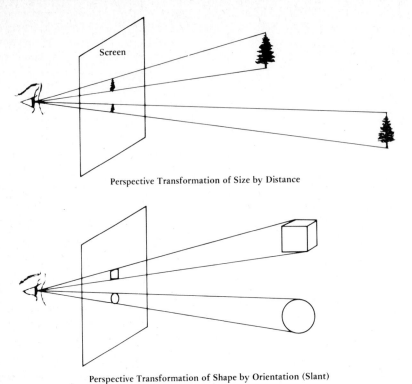

Perspective Transformation of Size by Distance

Perspective Transformation of Shape by Orientation (Slant)

Figure 1.11 Schematic examples of a perspective size transformation as a function of distance, and of a perspec-tive shape transformation as a function of orientation or slant.

clid in the third century B.C. When we begin the discussion of object perception and space perception we will consider the perspective transformations between real objects and retinal images in great detail.

Sharpness of Visual Edges

We have already considered the intensity of light reflected from an object, expressed as luminance, and the size of an object, expressed as visual angle. If we stopped here we would be assuming that the intensity distribution over an object was uniform and that the nature of the edges of the object was unimportant. However, these are of critical importance for perception, so we must consider how such changes can be described and how they are represented in the optical information reaching the retina.

As a useful analogy, consider what happens when the light output from a surface is measured with a photometer, such as a photographer's light meter.

When the opening that admits light to the meter is relatively small, the output of a photometer that is moved slowly in a horizontal direction along a picket fence seen against the sky is represented in Figure 1.12. Using the sky as a reference point of 100 percent, only 10 percent as much luminance is being reflected from the bars in the fence as from the sky behind it. Notice that the edges of the bars do not show up sharply, but are rounded off. Further, the bars themselves are not uniform in intensity, since the photometer picks up much more light near their edges than in their centers. While both of these characteristics could be due to a large opening in the photometer, it could also be due to gradual changes in luminance at the edges. The same measurements on a row of uppercase letter I's, such as might be printed on this page, would yield a distribution of light intensity similar to that of Figure 1.12, no matter how small an opening in the photometer was used. This is because

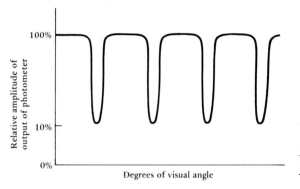

Relative amplitude of output of photometer

Degrees of visual angle

Figure 1.12 Hypothetical output of a photometer, measuring the amount of light reaching the instrument as it is moved slowly along a picket fence seen against the sky.

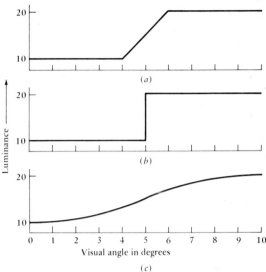

Luminance

Visual angle in degrees

Figure 1.13 Three luminance profiles, each of a different visual edge at the intersection of two surfaces reflecting different amounts of light to the eye.

the ink near the edges of the lines is not as dark as in the center of the lines.

A single homogeneous surface viewed against a nonreflecting void reflects the same amount of light (and the same luminance) over all parts of its surface. Similarly the surrounding void has zero luminance because its reflectance is zero. The only change in luminance across the retina occurs at the edges of the surfaces—the boundary of the surface and its background. Whenever two surfaces, or a surface and a background having two different reflectances, are adjacent to each other, the light reflected from them to the eye creates a **visual edge** in the retinal image corresponding to the physical edge separating the two surfaces. Visual edges occur whenever the amount of light reaching one part of the retina differs from the amount of light reaching an adjacent part.

Visual edges can also arise from a single surface if it is not homogeneous in its reflectance. A piece of pine board, for example, has much greater reflectance from the wood pulp than from the more pigmented grain lines. Light reflected from such a board to the eye projects a retinal image with many visual edges, each corresponding to changes in luminance across the projection.

Visual edges can be sharp or blurred depending on how much change in luminance occurs over a given retinal distance. The **luminance profile** of three different visual edges are shown in Figure 1.13 in which change in luminance is plotted against distance across

the retina in visual angle. It is obvious that other things being equal, edge (b) should be easier to notice than edge (c), with edge (a) somewhere in between. This is true even though the difference in luminance between the left-hand and right-hand sides of the edges is the same in each example. We would probably call edge (c) gradual or fuzzy, and edge (b) sharp or square. Edge (a) is often called a ramp. It would also be reasonable to expect that for edges of equal sharpness, those with a larger luminance difference would be more prominent or noticeable than those with a smaller difference.

While we can occasionally describe edges by name, or as sharp or fuzzy, we often need more precise and quantifiable means with which to specify edges. Two techniques are used, one very simple and the other complex.

The simple one is to specify the rate of change across the luminance profile of the edge, such as those shown in Figure 1.13. Thus, Profile (a) has a rate of change of 10 luminance units in 2° of visual angle or 5.0 luminance units per degree. Profile (c) changes the 10 luminance units in 10° or 1.0 luminance units per degree—five times more gradually. Profile b, if it is truly a "square" edge, has an infinitely large rate of change, since there is an increase of 10 luminance units over 0 degrees. In reality, such edges cannot be constructed. If the 10 luminance units changed in 0.1 degrees, then the rate of change would be 100 luminance units per degree.

Fourier Analysis & Visual Edges.

Another mathematical description of visual edges has become important because it appears to correspond to the way the visual system encodes edges. It is based upon the work of mathematician Charles Fourier showing that any curve, such as those in Figure 1.13 representing luminance profiles, can be described as the sum of a number of sine waves of varying frequency and amplitude.

Figure 1.14 shows several luminance profiles, each with the same **average luminance** of 15 units, indicated by the horizontal lines. Profiles (*a*), (*b*), and (*c*) are **sine waves,** that is, their *amplitude* (the difference in luminance from the highest to the lowest point) varies in a continuous and precise up and down way as a function of distance. Sine waves can have high or low **spatial frequency** depending on the number of cycles of the wave per degree of visual angle. Profile (*a*) has an amplitude of 10 luminance units and a frequency of 1 cycle per degree. Profiles (*b*) and (*c*) have amplitudes of 3.4 and 2.0 luminance units respectively and frequencies of 3 and 5 cycles per degree respectively.

To sum two profiles, a new profile is constructed whose luminance value at each point in space is the sum of the luminance of each component profile at that point. The sum of profiles (*a*) and (*b*) is shown as

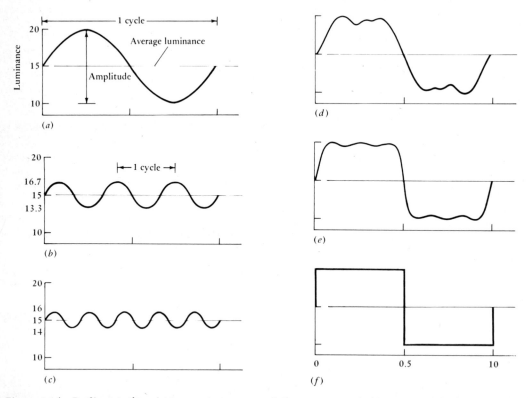

(a)   (b)   (c)   (d)   (e)   (f)

Figure 1.14 Profiles (*a*), (*b*) and (*c*) are each sine waves of the same average luminance (15 units) but whose amplitude decreases from 10 units to 3.4 units to 2 units respectively, and whose frequencies increase from 1 cycle per degree to 3 cycles per degree to 5 cycles per degree. Profile (*d*) is obtained by summing algebraically profiles (*a*) and (*b*), adding the luminance of each at each point along the abscissa. Profile (*e*) is obtained by adding profiles (*a*), (*b*) and (*c*) together. Profile (*f*) is a square wave of the same frequency, average luminance, and amplitude as profile (*a*).

profile (*d*), and if profile (*c*) is now added to (*d*) (equivalent to summing (*a*), (*b*), and (*c*) together), profile (*e*) is created.

Notice that in this example, that while (*a*) has the shape of a sine wave, (*d*) has a sharper increase and decrease in luminance, and (*e*) is beginning to look very much like a square wave in shape. Fourier showed that a square wave of a given frequency and amplitude can be constructed by summing together an infinite number of sine waves whose frequencies are the odd multiples (1, 3, 5, 7, . . .) of the frequency of the square wave, and whose amplitudes are the odd fractions (1, 1/3, 1/5, 1/7, . . .) of the amplitude of the square wave. Figure 1.14 used frequencies of 1, 3, and 5, and amplitudes of 10, 3.3, and 2. If we had continued to add in three or four more sine waves, the resulting profile would become more and more square. In theory, to be made perfectly square, as in Profile F, the sum has to include all of the component profiles up to infinity.

What has been illustrated is how to construct a square profile out of a number of **Fourier component** profiles, each the shape of a sine wave. Mathematically, this is equivalent to the statement that a square wave of a given frequency and amplitude contains within it a number of component sine waves of specifiable frequencies and amplitudes. Thus, we can describe the shape of a square wave by simply listing the frequencies and amplitudes of its component sine waves. That list defines its shape. (While in theory the list for a square wave is infinitely long, in practice it is rarely necessary to include more than about 10 components, and as we will see in Chapter 4, that large a number is necessary only for profiles whose frequency is very low.)

The example in Figure 1.14 shows the component sine waves in a square-wave luminance profile. Fourier worked out the mathematical procedures for listing the component sine waves in any profile of whatever shape.

We can make one final observation from these mathematics: The steeper the luminance profile, measured as rate of change, the more higher-frequency sine components are contained within it. The square wave has an infinite number of higher frequencies, the ramp relatively few higher frequencies, and the gradual profile has only one as it itself is a sine wave. In general, sharp edges have lots of high-frequency Fourier components whereas gradual changes in luminance can be described completely by their low-frequency components.

Although this may appear to be only a mathematical nicety, we will consider in subsequent chapters evidence to suggest that the visual system may be sensitive to these different sine wave frequencies. Hence, we may not respond to the sharpness of an edge directly, but rather to the frequencies of which the edge is composed. In that case our ability to see a sharp edge would depend on our sensitivity to high as well as to low frequencies. But the sharpest part of the edge depends only on the high frequencies. If we could not resolve high-frequency wave forms, then we would not be able to see a very sharp edge.

To recapitulate, in this section we have described four different aspects of visual stimuli and how they are imaged on the retina; the intensity of light, the wavelength of light, the size and shape of surfaces reflecting light, and the sharpness of the visual edges. These descriptions have all been made in physical terms—measurement of the energies and wavelengths in the light, reflectances of the surfaces, the geometry of retinal sizes and shapes of the surfaces projected, and the sharpness of the edges. Except for the effects of varying the exposure duration of the stimuli, the above list constitutes all the ways in which physical parameters of visual stimuli can vary.

THE VISUAL NERVOUS SYSTEM

We will consider three components of the visual nervous system—the structure and anatomy of the eye, the neural structure of the retina, and the visual pathways from the eye to the cortex.

Visual Anatomy

Figure 1.15 illustrates the principal components of each of the two human eyes. We will discuss them as we trace the path that light takes as it enters the eye. The components of greatest interest are the **cornea,** the **iris,** the **lens,** and the **retina.** We shall consider each of these in turn.

The Cornea The eyeball is about 25 millimeters in diameter. It is in part covered with an opaque layer called the **sclera**, the white of the eye that we see from the outside. The front of the eye is covered by a clear membrane called the **cornea.** The refractive power of the eye depends mainly upon the curvature of the cornea, since the index of refraction between the air and the cornea is greater than that between any other pair of media within the eye. However, while most of the refraction of the incoming light occurs at the outer surface of the cornea, the shape of the cornea is fixed so its focal length (the distance behind the cornea at which parallel light rays converge to a the sharp image) is also fixed. The cornea can become opaque with certain disease conditions.

The Iris. Behind the cornea is the **iris,** a sphincter muscle that can open and close, changing the amount of light that can enter the eye. The iris is the pigmented part of the front of the eye. The opening in the iris, called the **pupil,** is in part controlled

by a light reflex, whose effects are virtually identical to the intensity sensitivity function of the eye. If light can be seen the pupil contracts, and if the light changes in energy, the pupil changes in size. Figure 1.16 shows the change in normal pupil size as a function of retinal illuminance, specified in trolands. The normal range of pupil diameter is from about 2 to 8 millimeters, or about a sixteenfold change in area (about a 1.2 log-unit change). While the change in pupil size might be useful over small changes in energy, a 1.2 log-unit adjustment obviously cannot be very useful over the full visual sensitivity range of thirteen log units.

Notice that there appear to be two sections to the pupil-size function of Figure 1.16. The one at the lower illuminance level represents adjustments caused by light falling on those photoreceptors (rods) primarily concerned with perception under dim illumination (p. 19). The right-hand section of the curve represents further adjustments in illuminance from the light falling on the photoreceptors that respond only

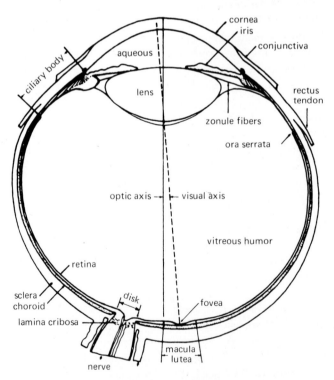

Figure 1.15 The principal anatomical components of a human eye. (Rodiek, 1973.)

to high illumination (cones). These two sections correspond to the scotopic and photopic aspects of sensitivity in the visual system, a characteristic we will notice in many functions.

If the iris mechanism is understood as only a device to adjust the visual system for variation in light intensity, then it would seem not to have much importance. The visual system is sensitive to intensity changes many billionfold (from 10^{-6} to 10^7 candelas per square meter), yet the iris can produce only a sixteenfold change. Further, adjustment in pupil size is quite slow, with initial adjustments requiring a half second and latencies up to ten seconds or longer for full excursion. It seems more likely that the iris serves a smaller yet still important function that is only partially related to the adjustment to light intensity. We saw that with a pinhole camera, the sharpest retinal projection occurs with the smallest pupil opening. This is true even with a lens in the opening. Further, the **depth of field** (the distance over which objects will be in sharp focus) is greatest with a smaller opening. Finally, given the various imperfections of the lens of the human eye, accurate focusing deteriorates sharply for those paths of light that enter the eye off-center. For all of these reasons, then, keeping the entrance part of the eye as small as possible will increase the sharpness of focus of the retinal projection. However, when the intensity of light drops too low, this sharpness must be sacrificed in order to capture enough quanta. It is then that a variable opening is needed. It is for this reason that much of the responsiveness of the iris is to low light levels, as seen in the left-hand portion of Figure 1.16.

There is also some evidence that the iris changes as a function of emotional and attentional variables, including those involved in thinking and problem solving. Although empirical relationships have been studied, their importance and possible cause-and-effect significance is not at all clearly understood yet (see Goldwater, 1972).

The Lens. After light passes through the pupil, it next encounters the **lens.** Although most of the refraction of light occurs as it passes from the air into the cornea, some remaining focusing is accomplished by varying the thickness and hence the refractive power of the lens. This process is called **accommodation.** The lens consists of a number of transparent crystalline layers arranged much like the layers of an onion. They are held in a sac that can be tightened or relaxed by the tension of the muscles holding the sac in place. If you close one eye and, while looking at your finger at arm's length, slowly move your finger toward your nose, you can feel the tension as the thickness of the lens is increased to keep the projection on the retina in focus. Focus breaks down for objects very close to your eye, and a blurred image results. In the normal eye, variation in lens

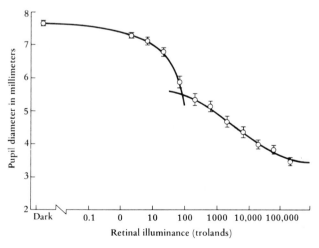

Figure 1.16   Change in pupil size as a function of retinal illuminance (ten Doesschat & Alpern, 1967.)

shape allows us to focus on objects from about 1/10th meter to about 5 meters. Rays of light reflected from surfaces more than 3 or 4 meters away are effectively parallel so that an accommodative response is not needed to maintain focus. The lens tends to harden with age and slowly to lose its ability to accommodate. Since the relaxed condition of the lens leaves it accommodated for far objects, aging results in a progressive loss of the ability to focus sharply on nearby objects.

The stimulus for accommodation changes appears to be retinal blur, but we do not yet know how this stimulus is picked up and signaled to the muscles. It is a relatively slow process, requiring nearly .8 of a second for a complete change from near to far accommodation. Further, the precision of the adjustment is relatively crude. However, given all the other imper-fections in the visual system, finer control of the refractive power of the lens does not appear to be needed.

The Retina. After the light exits from the lens it passes through the fluids in the center of the eyeball and is focused on the inside surface of the ball. The purpose of the fluids is to maintain the shape of the eye and to provide a medium with a similar refractive index to that of the lens, so that no further refraction of light occurs as the light exits from the lens.

The **retina** surrounds nearly 200 degrees of the inside the eye. Embedded in the retina are the photoreceptors and their neural support, as shown in Figure 1.17. The portion of the retina most sensitive to pattern is the **fovea,** shown as a small indentation at the

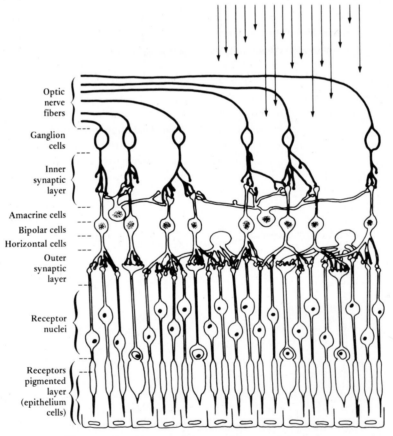

Figure 1.17 Schematic diagram of the neural interconnections of the retina. (Adapted from Dowling & Boycott, 1966.)

back of the eye. The blind spot, or optic disk, is an area of several degrees on the retina. It has no receptors because the nerve connections from the receptors exit from the eye at this point to form the optic nerve tract connecting to higher centers in the brain.

Neither the cornea nor the lens is a perfect optical instrument. This means that they are incapable of producing very sharp images on the retinal surface. Further, the fluids inside the eye lead to some refraction of light, scattering it around the inside of the eyeball. Not only is a substantial amount of energy lost in this way, but it reduces the contrast of the retinal projection. Further, the blood vessels supplying the nervous structure of the retina and all the nerve cells lie in front of the receptors, so that light must pass through them to get to the part of each receptor where a photochemical reaction can occur. Some light energy is absorbed by this mass, and more is refracted again. Consequently, only a small percentage of the light energy impinging on the cornea actually reaches the receptors, and that which does is no longer in sharp focus. We will consider this apparent paradox again in Chapter 4 when we describe our ability to notice very fine detail.

Retinal Structure

Figure 1.17 illustrates the arrangement of receptors and connective neurons in the retina. The two kinds of photoreceptors in the visual system are called **rods** and **cones.** There are about 120 million rods and nearly 7 million cones. Figure 1.18 shows the distribution of each type of photoreceptor across the retina. The center of the fovea, covering an area of perhaps 1 degree, contains only cones. The number and proportion of cones falls off rapidly and then levels off after 20 degrees with many fewer cones present beyond 10 degrees. On the other hand, no rods are found in the center of the fovea. They reach their highest density at about 16 degrees on either side, with decreasing numbers out to about 100 degrees at the edge of the retina. The density of cells also varies across the retina. In the center of the fovea cones are packed very tightly together, so that the center-to-center distance is about 22 seconds of arc, or .002 millimeters. In general, receptors are less tightly packed as one moves farther from the fovea. Figure 1.19 shows the high density over a portion of the center of the fovea.

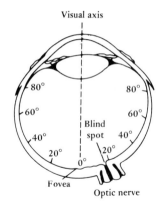

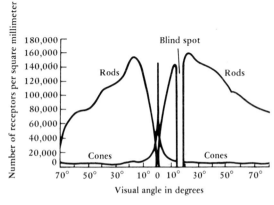

Figure 1.18 Density of rod and cone receptors across the retinal surface. (Pirenne, 1965.)

Each receptor is connected to a **bipolar cell** via a synapse. In the fovea, usually only one cone is connected to one bipolar. Outside the fovea there will be many receptors connected to one bipolar. This approaches a convergence of hundreds of rods onto one bipolar beyond 20 degrees into the periphery. This great pooling of receptors onto a single bipolar cell in the periphery means that activity in any particular bipolar cell cannot specify which of its many receptors had been stimulated by light. In the center of the fovea there is very little pooling.

Each bipolar cell is connected to a **ganglion cell** via a second synapse. The ganglion cell has an elongated axon that forms one of the fibers of the **optic nerve.** There are less than one million ganglion cells leaving the retina. Again, in the fovea each bipolar generally connects to one ganglion, whereas in the periphery a number of bipolars will converge on a single ganglion cell.

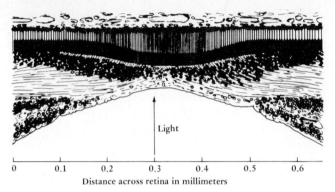

Light

Distance across retina in millimeters

Figure 1.19 Schematic representation of a microscopic section of the central portion of a human retina. The diagram covers about 2 degrees, equivalent to about 0.67 millimeter. (Polyak, 1957.)

Figure 1.17 also shows the interconnection among the bipolar and ganglion cells via **horizontal and amacrine cells.** While these interconnections are not on the direct pathway between receptor and cortex, they are involved in critical functions regulating the pattern of excitation in the retina, especially concerning inhibitory processes. We will consider some of these in detail in Chapters 3 and 4.

A few of the quanta traveling through the media of the eye are absorbed by those media, by the blood vessels, or by the neural tissues that lie in front of the receptors. A much larger number pass through these materials and also pass through the receptors themselves, and are absorbed by the dark inner lining of the eye. None of these quanta have any consequences at all for visual perception. Some other quanta are reflected off the back of the eye, pass back through the receptors again unnoticed, and bounce around inside the eye until they are finally absorbed by some of the media, by the lining of the eye at some other point, by pigment molecules in some other receptor, or exit back through the pupil and out into the world again. Of course, the degree to which any of this scattered light excites receptors represents substantial degradation of the retinal image.

Even under the most optimal conditions, only a small percentage of the quanta incident on the cornea actually have any effect on a photoreceptor. But it is these few that do that account for all phenomena of visual perception, for there can be no vision without quanta exciting receptors.

As shown in Figure 1.20 photoreceptors are elongated tubelike structures. A quantum has to enter the end of the receptor and travel down its length to the outer segment where it can be absorbed by photopigment molecules. Figuratively speaking, the tube acts like a light pipe, so if the path of the quantum is not directly down the tube it will reflect off the interior walls, bouncing back and forth down the length of the receptor. To facilitate the ease of travel down receptors, each receptor is oriented toward the center of the lens, that is, toward the most likely path of light approaching the retina.

However, rods and cones differ sharply in their ability to conduct light down their length when the light does not enter the receptor along its axis. Cones have a much smaller opening to accept the quanta, and, moreover, quanta bouncing down the tube will be more likely to pass through the wall than be reflected down it. Therefore light entering the eye in a direction other than through the center of the lens is much less likely to be absorbed by a cone receptor. Rod receptors, on the other hand, are less sensitive to the direction of light path. This effect, known as the **Stiles-Crawford effect,** has important implications for a variety of visual phenomena to be covered in later chapters.

As we will show in Chapter 3, the maximum sensitivity of the visual system requires that only about 10 rods absorb 1 quantum each for awareness that visual stimulation has occurred. But each rod has upwards of 4 million pigment molecules, each capable of absorbing quanta. The more of these that absorb quanta, the larger the output of the receptor.

Specifically, we know that some synapses are excitatory and some are inhibitory in their effects. Thus increasing the activity of a neuron may either increase or decrease the probability that the next neuron becomes active, depending on the nature of the neural transmitter substance released at the synapse. Further, we know that the more cells converging on a neuron that are active, the greater is the likelihood that the neuron becomes active. We should therefore expect spatial summation effects throughout the retina. In this sense, a many-to-one interconnection pools exci-

tation. Inhibition can also summate in the same manner, as we will see in Chapters 4 and 5.

For many reasons, all neurons show some activity, even in the absence of normally effective stimulation. Thus, retinal ganglion cells have a resting or **spontaneous rate of firing** on the order of several responses per second. Consequently, all measures of activity or effect of stimulation must be taken against a baseline of the spontaneous activity level. This is especially important because an increase in inhibition may be signaled by a decrease in the firing rate below that of the baseline rate.

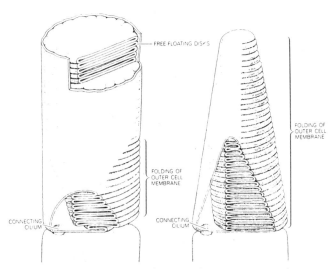

Figure 1.20   Schematic diagram of the components of a human rod (left) and cone (right). (Young, 1971.)

Visual Pathways to the Brain

Figure 1.21 shows the neural interconnections between each eye and the brain. Within each eye there are two synapses, one between the receptor and bipolar cells, and one between the bipolar and the ganglion cells. There are also cross-synapses with horizontal and amacrine cells. The ganglion nerves are several centimeters long and do not form their next synapse until they reach the **lateral geniculate** or the **pregeniculate nucleus** in each hemisphere of the brain.

The nearly one million fibers in the optic nerve are anatomically separated according to the side of each half of the retina from which they originated. This division results in a specific differential projection to the two hemispheres of the brain. Light arising from the left of straight ahead will be projected from both eyes to the right hemisphere of the brain and light arising from the right of straight ahead will be projected from both eyes to the left hemisphere of the brain. One can think of each retina as divided vertically through the fovea into two halves. In Figure 1.21

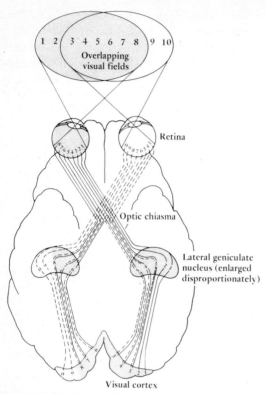

Figure 1.21 Schematic representation of the visual pathways from each eye to the visual cortex, via the optic chiasma and the lateral geniculate nucleus. The parts of the visual field represented at each level are indicated by tracing the numbers through the system. (Adapted from Lindsay & Norman, 1972.)

both eyes are fixated between points 5 and 6 in space (defined as straight ahead). The numbers 6 through 10 are to the right of straight ahead and will project on to the temporal (ear) side of the left eye and the nasal side of the right eye. The ganglion cells from these two sides all end up in the left hemisphere of the brain. Conversely 1 through 5 in space, all to the left of straight ahead, project to the nasal side of the left eye and the temporal side of the right eye. The ganglion cells from these two sides all terminate in the right hemisphere of the brain. While it may be difficult to remember which side of which eye has ganglion cells that cross over to the opposite hemisphere of the cortex, it is easy to remember that objects in space project to the hemisphere opposite to the side on which they are seen, just as nerve impulses from objects felt with a hand project to the hemisphere on the side of the body opposite to that of the hand. When the eyes are pointing straight ahead, light arising from surfaces that are themselves straight ahead will project on to both sides of both retinas and hence will be represented in both hemispheres.

From the lateral geniculate nucleus, **visual radiations** project out to the **striate cortex,** known as **area 17,** the primary visual cortex.

Not all the optic nerve fibers leaving the retina go to the lateral geniculate nucleus. A small percentage is separated out at the pregeniculate nucleus (not shown on Figure 1.21) and then project to other cortical and subcortical centers. The most important of these is the **superior colliculus** located in the midbrain. We now have substantial evidence that the superior colliculus provides the control for and the monitoring of most kinds of eye movements (Wurtz, 1976). We shall return to this center in Chapter 7 when we consider eye movements in some detail.

In spite of all the mixings and crossings, there is an approximate point-for-point representation between the retinal ganglion cells, the lateral geniculate nucleus, and the striate cortex. In the fovea this point-for-point representation continues all the way down to the receptor cells themselves, since they have one-to-one interconnections with ganglion cells. With only one million ganglion cells in each optic nerve, the majority of which are connected individually to single receptors in the fovea, the largest proportion of the striate cortex is taken up with foveal representations.

While these statements represent the results of tracing the anatomical path through the neural networks, they do not represent the functional organization of the retina-to-cortex interconnections. What is not appreciated in the structure is the importance of lateral connections made by the amacrine cells among the ganglions, and those of the horizontal cells among the bipolars in the retina. Further, a structural analysis does not specify whether a synapse is excitatory or inhibitory. As we shall see in Chapter 3, considering any part of the retina as having a one-to-one connection with the cortex is totally inconsistent with how visual stimulation is coded and transmitted. The best that can be said for a structural analysis is that most of the fibers that arrive in area 17 of the cortex represent activity from the central region of each retina, especially that of the foveas.

On the other hand, the pattern of interconnections between each part of the retina in an eye and the cortex is replicated in the other eye. For each receptor of the retina we can specify the structural path, the synapses, and interconnections between that receptor and its bipolars and ganglions, with horizontal and amacrine lateral connections, then to the lateral geniculate nucleus and to the cortex. If each receptor is assigned a set of coordinates corresponding to its location in its retina, then there is a receptor in the other retina in the corresponding location that has the same structural interconnections. Every location on one retina has a **corresponding point** on the other retina. This correspondence is carried up to area 17 in each hemisphere. As we shall see later, this anatomical correspondence is an important component in our perception of depth through stereopsis, for the correspondences, or lack of them, provide a way of comparing the similarity of stimulation of the two retinas. The discussion of the projection of stimulation within and beyond area 17 will be taken up in Chapters 3 and 4. The lateral geniculate nucleus and the striate cortex have their cells arranged in layers and in columns. Some of the importance of this will be seen in Chapter 4 on coding mechanisms, since the handling of pattern coding appears to differ from layer to layer.

The striate cortex projects to the association cortex, areas 18 and 19, which integrate other senses with memory and pattern. Other areas of the brain are concerned with language and symbols and these are connected to areas 18 and 19. The hemispheres are also interconnected.

Movements of the Eyes

Each eye is held and controlled in a bony socket by six muscles acting somewhat as three antagonistic pairs. One pair roughly controls up-and-down movement, another side-to-side movement, and a third rotational movement about the foveal-pupil axis of the eye itself. The muscles are coordinated by brain-stem centers, controlled by midbrain centers (see Chapter 7).

There are several types of eye movements of great importance to our perception of the world around us: three of them are **convergence movements** that keep both eyes pointing at whatever is our center of attention; **saccadic movements** that shift both eyes to a new center of interest; and **pursuit movements** that follow an object moving in space or maintain fixation on an object as we move in space. We will consider these three types of movements in substantial detail in Chapter 7.

If the position of the eye is precisely monitored by attaching a mirror directly to the eye and photographing deflections of a light from the mirror as the eye moves, it can be shown that the eye is almost continuously moving, even when the perceiver is attempting to maintain precise fixation on an object in space. Riggs, Armington, and Ratliff (1954) showed that the eye can shift by an amount equivalent to three minutes of arc during a one-second recording interval. During a one-tenth of a second interval, the excursion is nearly one-half minute of arc, about the distance between two cones in the center of the fovea. These movements are due to **physiological tremor,** and probably represent the irreducible minimum precision in trying to hold the eye in position with the balance of six very strong muscles pulling on it. As might be expected, the direction and distance of the tremors are independent over time.

In addition to tremors found during fixations, the eye also **drifts** off the fixation point quite slowly. After it has moved some distance, perhaps 10 or 20 cones, a **microsaccadic movement** will rapidly jerk it back toward the fixation point again. Figure 7.7 (p. 148) illustrates a brief sequence of tremors, drifts, and microsaccades.

It should be clear that given these small and somewhat independent movements, light imaged on the retinal surface by the cornea and lens is never stationary with respect to specific receptors. We shall examine the implication of this for sensory coding and visual acuity in several later chapters.

SUMMARY

The first half of Chapter 1 examines the nature of light as electromagnetic energy, both with respect to its intensive properties, specified in quanta, and its spectral properties, specified in wavelengths. These combine with the reflective properties of surfaces of objects to produce focused images of objects on the retina inside the eyeball, in much the same way as light is imaged on the film plane of a camera.

The retinal image of a reflecting surface in space is described in terms of four attributes. The first is intensity, which can be specified in terms of candelas, illuminance, luminance, or retinal illuminance (trolands), depending upon whether intensity is measured at the light source, at a reflecting surface, reflected from that surface, or reaching the retina.

The second is wavelength of light on the retinal surface, which is specified in terms of the selective spectral reflectance of light from the surface to the eye. The third is the size and shape of the retinal image in relation to the size and shape of the surface reflecting light. Retinal size is specified in the visual angle formed by rays of light from the edges of a surface, while the shape of the retinal image is related by the laws of perspective to the shape of the surface in space.

The fourth attribute of the retinal image is the sharpness of the visual edges, which can be specified either in terms of a luminance profile—the change in luminance across the retina—or in terms of the Fourier spatial frequency components of the edge.

The second half of the chapter examines the anatomical and neural components that make up the human visual system. The structure and function of the principal components of the eye are described, including the cornea, iris, lens, and retina. The retinal structure is examined in more detail, including the photoreceptors, bipolar and ganglion cells, their interconnections, and their pathways to the visual cortex. Finally, the principal types of eye movements are described.

SUGGESTED READINGS

At the end of each chapter, we suggest a few sources or references that can provide the interested student with more information or discussion on the topics of the chapter. A number of general or advanced textbooks, handbooks, and articles covers this chapter. For the physics of light, Monk (1963) provides a general introduction. Cornsweet (1970) has a good discussion of the representation of objects in space on the retinal projection. For the greatest detail on the neuroanatomy of the retina, Polyak (1957) is still the classic with Brindley's 1960 and 1972 books and Pirenne (1967), though difficult, providing a detailed discussion of most of the relevant topics covered in this chapter. The first section of Monty and Senders (1976) provides general information on eye movements.

There are several handbooks that contain useful sections or chapters on topics covered here. We will list several here, and they will come up in subsequent chapters. Davson's four-volume work (1978), Graham (1965), Woodworth (1938), Woodworth and Schlossberg (1954), Kling and Riggs (1971), Jameson and Hurvich (1972), and Carterette and Friedman (1973, 1974, 1975) have many relevant chapters, though usually at advanced levels. Stevens (1951), while older, is still quite useful.

For general texts on neurophysiology, including the visual system, see Stevens (1966) or Milner (1970).

Chapter 2

Psychophysical Measurement

The previous chapter described the properties of light that affect perception and the receptive mechanisms of the visual system. Up to this point, we have not made reference to perceptual processes themselves—the ways in which the patterned light stimulus is translated into the experience of seeing. The next four chapters begin this task, but before we can start it is necessary to describe how typical experiments in perception are conducted in order to measure the effects of light. This is the topic of Chapter 2. It is not only the experimental procedures that are important, but also the nature of the task, the kinds of questions asked, and the answers available from the perceiver about his experience of seeing.

Physical properties of light and the objects that reflect light can be measured using the instruments of physics. While it is tempting to associate the physical values of stimulation with their psychological counterparts, this relationship is rarely if ever simple. For example, doubling the number of quanta in a light source does not make it appear twice as bright. If simple linear relationships cannot be assumed, then the specific functions must be determined experimentally. To do so, we must first measure the physical variation and then measure the perceptions that result from these physical variations, a very difficult and

complex task. This produces functional relationships between the physical and the psychological domains.

The difficulty in making these measurements comes from the need to ask the perceiver questions about his experience. Each of us can describe how bright a light appears, or how red it is, or how beautiful a sunset is. But those descriptions are not precise because they reflect differences in the words we prefer to use, the care with which we attend to our experiences, our memories of past perceptions, and what we think the listener wants to hear. The primary task of psychological measurement in the study of perception is to eliminate these uncontrolled variables in the descriptions of our experience. This problem is the core of much of the study of perception and therefore we shall focus on it first in this chapter.

Classical **psychophysics** is the area of psychology that attempts to determine the functional relationship between a perceived or subjective magnitude and a physical magnitude. The most frequent form of psychophysical function studied deals with the relationship between perceived magnitude and stimulus intensity, such as perceived brightness as a function of the intensity of light. We have implied that the specification of the physical dimensions of stimulation is relatively straightforward. This is not always the case, and as we will see in several places in this book, the search for physical dimensions may be more complex than that for the psychological concomitants with which they are correlated. The perception of beauty is one example.

One major advance in psychophysical methods is to restrict the responses the perceiver is permitted to use to describe her experience. Thus, instead of asking her to describe what she saw, we can ask her whether or not two lights appear to be the same. Instead of asking her what a stimulus looked like, we can ask her whether she noticed a change. In these examples, the perceiver is asked to make rather simple discriminations, which by themselves are quite trivial. But we can infer the dimensions of perceptual experience from such relatively simple and restricted responses by following procedures that govern how we vary the physical dimensions while we ask for the perceiver's description of what she sees.

In the present chapter we shall describe both typical experimental arrangements—called **psychophysical methods**—and the tasks presented to the perceiver—often called the **response indicators**. This is done within two closely related contexts: detecting the presence or absence of a light stimulus and detecting a change in light from one condition to another. These kinds of questions have been linked to theoretical models of measurement and of the relationship between physical and psychological events. The present chapter does not elaborate on the models, but focuses on the empirical problems—how does an experimenter arrange an experiment, and what does he ask a subject to do? This supplies a background for subsequent chapters that describe the neural responses of the visual system to variation in intensity reflected from surfaces, to spatial arrangements of those surfaces, to variation in wavelength being reflected, and to variation in the duration of light stimulus reaching the eye. We make only occasional references to the theoretical problems and controversies underlying measurement.

FREQUENCY-OF-SEEING

Almost all experiments concerned with how perceivers react to light begin by determining a frequency-of-seeing function. For some methods and approaches

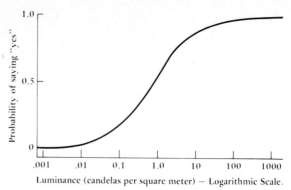

Figure 2.1 A frequency-of-seeing function, showing the change in the probability of saying "Yes" as a function of the luminance of the presentations.

this is the only determination needed, whereas for others it is only an intermediate step. A **frequency-of-seeing function** is a graphic description of the changes in the perceiver's detection response as a function of the physical variable being manipulated in the experiment. Figure 2.1 illustrates such a function, where the frequency-of-seeing, specified as the probability that the perceiver reports seeing the light, is plotted against the intensity of light, specified as luminance in candelas per square meter. From the graph we can see that the probability that the perceiver reports seeing the light increases as intensity increases. Further, from the shape of the frequency-of-seeing function, there is no energy value below which the perceiver never reports seeing the light, and above which he always reports seeing it. Instead, the graph suggests that each time a particular stimulus value is presented, the perceiver sometimes says "Yes" and sometimes says "No." What changes gradually over intensity is the relative proportion of "No" to "Yes" responses.

We run a frequency-of-seeing experiment in order to discover the variables that affect perception: in this example, the detectability of light. However, the frequency-of-seeing function is rarely useful as a final description of those variables: in this example, the energy of the stimulus. The reason it is not is inherent in the experimental task itself, a task in which perceivers have to make difficult decisions. When one is straining to "notice" a stimulus, particularly one of small magnitude, it is clear that there are two components to the process: the actual sensitivity of the receptor system to the particular properties of the stimulus, and the decision as to whether a stimulus change actually occurred. The decision process is important because there is **noise** inherent in any detection situation. Some of the noise is internal, related to the spontaneous activity level of the various neural processes. Some of it is external—variation in signal strength, light from other sources, and so forth. The internal sources are probably the more critical ones, particularly at very low energy levels. How can a perceiver tell whether the excitation being observed is a result of the stimulus superimposed on noise, or whether it was a result of noise alone? The inherent uncertainty that all perceivers feel in making responses in light detection experiments reflects these two components.

What does the perceiver do when he is uncertain? Some behave very cautiously, while others take risks. Figure 2.2 can be regarded as an example of what could happen in response to identical stimuli with a risk-taking and a cautious perceiver. Although the stimulus magnitudes are the same, the "risky" perceiver appears to have greater sensitivity. Since all that has been changed is willingness to take a risk, it is inappropriate to say that the perceiver has greater sensitivity, and yet equating sensitivity with the frequency of saying "Yes" implies just that. Thus, it is clear that one can bias sensitivity data by simply changing the perceiver's willingness to say "Yes."

The bias described here is an integral part of any decision process. One of the major advances in psychophysics has been the explicit inclusion of the observer's decision-making process in assessing psychophysical relationships. This model was initially worked out by Swets, Tanner, and Birdsall (1955, 1961), and described in more detail in Green and Swets (1966). As applied to measurement of sensitivity, this approach is called Signal Detection Theory.

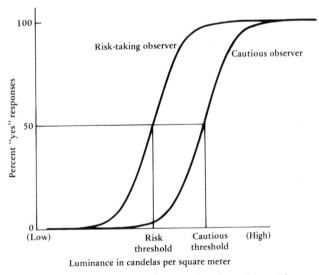

Figure 2.2 Frequency-of-seeing functions for a risk-taking and a cautious observer.

SIGNAL DETECTION THEORY

Signal Detection Theory stands for a set of procedures and analyses that is explicitly designed to measure perceiver biases and assess precisely their contributions to the measurement of sensitivity. To illustrate these procedures, let us start with a simple experimental example. Suppose you want to find out how an observer's sensitivity changes for four different intensities of light (say, 0.01, 0.1, 1.0, and 10.0 candelas per square meter). Consider first the light of 0.01 candela/square meter. Instead of simply trying to find the proportion of "Yes" and "No" responses, in a signal-detection-theory version of the experiment, blank or **catch trials** would be included in which the stim-

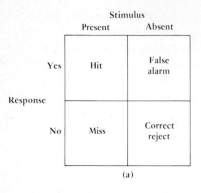

Stimulus

Present   Absent

	Present	Absent
Yes	Hit	False alarm
No	Miss	Correct reject

Response

(a)

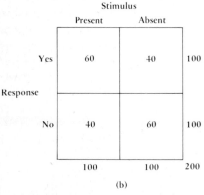

Stimulus

Present   Absent

	Present	Absent	
Yes	60	40	100
No	40	60	100
	100	100	200

Response

(b)

Figure 2.3 *Top:* A matrix that classifies the four possible outcomes of conditions in which the signal was presented or not presented, and the observer said "Yes" or "No." *Bottom:* Some raw data are tabulated.

ulus is not presented. That is, on some trials a stimulus of 0.01 candelas per square meter would be present and on other trials, identical in all other respects, the light would not be presented. Typically, half of the trials would contain the stimulus and half would be blank. These would be arranged randomly so that the observer would never know which was which, yet he would be required to respond "Yes" or "No" on each occasion.

Figure 2.3 illustrates the four possible outcomes of the series of such trials for each of the four stimulus-response possibilities: stimulus present or not and response "Yes" or "No." The labels in the top half describe the four outcomes. A **"hit"** occurs when the observer says "Yes" in the presence of the signal and a **"false alarm"** occurs when the observer says "Yes" in the absence of a signal. If the observer says "No" the response is scored as a "miss" if the stimulus is present and a "correct reject" if it is not present.

The bottom of Figure 2.3 shows hypothetical data based on 200 trials, 100 trials in which the signal is presented and 100 in which it is not. In the signal-present trials, this observer has a hit rate of 60 percent and a false-alarm rate of 40 percent. That is, on 60 percent of the signal-present trials, he says "Yes" and on 40 percent of the signal-absent trials he says "Yes." While the 40 percent false alarm rate seems to describe only the willingness of the observer to guess, the analysis of Signal Detection Theory indicates that the false alarm is a more complicated measure, based on a compromise between the perceiver's sensitivity and his willingness to guess.

Imagine that a perceiver is observing a screen on which he expects stimuli to be presented. First consider circumstances in which the trials are blanks. Even in this case, the perceiver's visual system will be spontaneously active, that is, "noise" will always be present because of spontaneous neural firing or variability of stimulus events such as background illumination. Thus, even though a signal has not been presented, there are some changes in the level of excitation that the observer has to evaluate in order to make a decision about which response to make. Furthermore, we can assume that the level of excitation occurring on a given blank trial will be variable—on some of the 100 blank trials the excitation is at a low level while on others it is quite high. The levels of excitation from noise alone is assumed to be a random variable with a normal distribution. This hypothetical distribution of the frequency of various excitation lev-

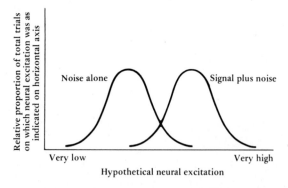

Figure 2.4 Hypothetical distribution of the frequency of sensory excitation that arises from many presentations of noise alone, and from many presentations of signals embedded in noise.

els that arise from noise alone is shown as the left-hand distribution of Figure 2.4.

But our sample experiment includes 200 trials. The second 100 trials also have noise in them but, in addition, there is a signal, which presumably increases the excitation to an amount proportional to the magnitude of the signal. Thus, the 100 trials that contain signal plus noise have a distribution of the same shape, but it is shifted to the right along the sensory-excitation axis in Figure 2.4. In our particular example, the magnitude of the signal (0.01 candela per square meter) is quite low. The two distributions of noise and signal plus noise therefore have a substantial overlap. As the excitation contributed from the signal increases relative to the noise, the signal-plus-noise distribution is shifted to the right relative to the noise distribution and there is less overlap.

On any one of the 200 trials in the experiment, the perceiver has available a single level of excitation. There is no way for the perceiver to tell whether the trial is a sample from the noise distribution or from the signal-plus-noise distribution. Yet the perceiver must respond either "Yes" or "No." In Signal Detection Theory, it is assumed that the perceiver sets up a **criterion** for her response, saying, in effect, that if the level of excitation exceeds some critical value, then she says "Yes," and if it does not exceed that value, she says "No." If the perceiver is very cautious, then she demands a relatively high level of excitation before saying "Yes," but if she is more willing to take risks, she says "Yes" on even a low level of excitation. The criterion is therefore shifted to the left or to the right in Figure 2.5 depending on whether the perceiver is cautious or is willing to take risks. The vertical line represents the criterion that divides the "Yes" and "No" choices.

The **criterion line** determines the decisions the observer makes in the course of the 200 trials. Since the two distributions overlap, the location of the criterion affects all four possible outcomes of the experimental arrangements sketched in Figure 2.3. Figure 2.6 shows the relationships between the criterion line and the two distributions separately. The signal-plus-noise distribution is divided into two segments by the criterion line. Since every excitation value covered by this distribution arose from the presence of the signal

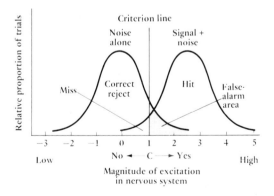

Figure 2.5 Noise and signal-plus-noise distribution showing position of criterion line dividing the amount of excitation into a range to which observer says "Yes" and a range to which observer says "No." The horizontal axis is marked out in standard deviation units from the mean of the noise source.

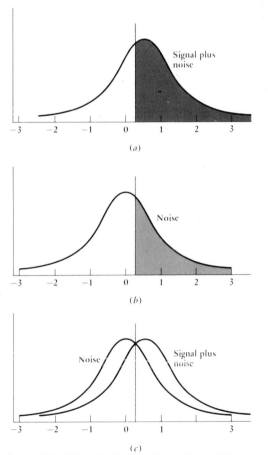

Figure 2.6 The distributions from Figure 2.5 shown separately.

embedded in noise, all the values to the right of the criterion line—the region where the observer says "Yes"—result in a hit. Conversely, all those values to the left of the criterion line result in a miss because the observer said "No" when a signal is present. In our previous example, the criterion line is positioned relative to the signal-plus-noise distribution so that 70 percent of the area (that is, trials) are hits and 30 percent are misses. This relationship is illustrated in part (a) of Figure 2.6. The similar relationships are illustrated in part (b) of the figure for the noise distribution, except that the criterion line divides it into different sized areas—40 percent false alarms and 90 percent correct rejections.

Part (c) of the figure shows these two distributions on the same axis. Given the separation of the distributions and the location of the criterion, we can determine the hit rate and the false-alarm rate by determining the proportion of the area of each curve to the right or left of the criterion line.

These distributions are hypothetical. The perceiver, of course, cannot tell on any trial whether the excitation arose from noise or signal-plus-noise. On the other hand, visualizing these hypothetical distributions, we can analyze the two principal parameters relevant to detection situations—the sensitivity of the perceiver and the criterion. The **sensitivity** is given by the degree of separation of the two distributions. If the distributions are far apart, there must be a strong signal relative to the noise. This parameter may be used in defining sensitivity. If the signal-plus-noise distribution virtually overlaps the noise-only distribution, then the sensitivity is minimal.

Sensitivity should be related to the intensity of the stimulus. Thus, holding other factors constant, as stimulus strength increases, the separation of the two distributions increases. The perceiver's criterion is shown by the location of the criterion line. Instructing the perceiver to be very cautious or to take risks should shift the location of the criterion, without shifting the location of the two distributions. Hence, from any experiment in which a hit rate and a false-alarm rate are available, we can arrive at a sensitivity measure and a criterion measure. Since these two parameters are independent, an experimenter can manipulate the perceiver's criterion without changing his sensitivity, or change signal intensity or the perceiver's sensitivity

without changing his criterion. Thus, signal-detection theory offers a means of providing information about the perceiver's sensitivity without it being confounded with his level of criterion.

Before examining the implications of this independence, let us go back to some data to see how the actual calculations are made. Since the two distributions are hypothetical and are themselves not directly measured in an experiment, we need to derive them from hit rate and false-alarm rate data. If the two distributions are normal and of equal variance (assumptions that are usually made in Signal Detection Theory) then, given the hit rate and the false-alarm rate illustrated in Figure 2.6, there is only one way the overlap can be drawn. That is, the hit rate and false-alarm rate define the degree of overlap of the two distributions. Since the degree of overlap reflects the observer's sensitivity, we can determine this value from the hit rate and false-alarm rate directly. To do so requires a table of the areas under different portions of the normal curve. Notice that the excitation axes of the figure are marked off in standard deviation units, starting at 0 for the mean of the noise distribution. Since the total area under the normal curve from its mean to the point that is exceeded only 40 percent of the area is located at 0.26 standard deviations from the mean, the criterion line must have been 0.26 standard deviations from the mean of the noise curve to produce 40 percent yeses to noise alone. Similarly, that same criterion line cuts off 40 percent of the area of the signal-plus-noise curve as misses. That occurs at -0.26 standard deviations from the mean of the signal-plus-noise curve. Therefore, the means of the two curves are separated by 0.52 standard deviations. This value provides a measure of the sensitivity of the observer—his or her ability to detect the presence of the signal magnitude (in this case 0.01 candelas per square meter) when embedded in the inherent noise of this psychophysical task.

The value of the separation of the two curves is called d' (read as "**d prime**") in signal detection theory. It can be calculated as outlined above with the aid of a table of the area under a normal curve. There are also tables of d' that can be used directly. Values of hit rates and false-alarm rates are listed and for each combination of the two a unique d' is tabled. Figure 2.7 contains a portion of such a d' table.

HIT rate \ False Alarm Rate	01	10	20	30	40	50	60	70	80	90	99
01	0	−1.04	−1.48	−1.80	−2.06	−2.32	−2.58	−2.84	−3.16	−3.60	−4.64
10	1.04	0	−.44	−.76	−1.02	−1.28	−1.54	−1.80	−2.12	−2.56	−3.60
20	1.48	.44	0	−.32	−.58	−.84	−1.10	−1.36	−1.68	−2.12	−3.16
30	1.80	.76	.32	0	−.27	−.52	−.78	−1.05	−1.36	−1.80	−2.84
40	2.06	1.02	.58	.27	0	−.26	−.51	−.78	−1.10	−1.54	−2.58
50	2.32	1.28	.84	.52	.26	0	−.26	−.52	−.84	−1.28	−2.32
60	2.58	1.54	1.10	.78	.51	.26	0	−.27	−.58	−1.02	−2.06
70	2.84	1.80	1.36	1.05	.78	.52	.27	0	−.32	−.76	−1.80
80	3.16	2.12	1.68	1.36	1.10	.84	.58	.32	0	−.44	−1.48
90	3.60	2.56	2.12	1.80	1.54	1.28	1.02	.76	.44	0	−1.04
99	4.64	3.60	3.16	2.84	2.58	2.32	2.06	1.80	1.48	1.04	0

Figure 2.7 Values of d' for various combinations of a hit rate and a false-alarm rate. Taken from Green and Swets (1966).

Figure 2.8 presents hypothetical hit rate and false-alarm rate data for the four separate luminance values of the experiment described earlier. As an example, using the d' table, it is possible to determine directly the four d' values for the four signal values. Thus, as signal strength increases so does d', the subject's sensitivity or ability to detect the presence of the signal when mixed with noise. These d''s are shown at the bottom of Figure 2.8.

The other parameter in a signal detection task is the observer's willingness to respond. Signal detection theory showed that the observer's willingness or criterion is independent of sensitivity. Therefore we need a measure of the criterion as well. Since the criterion line intersects both the noise and the signal-plus-noise distribution, the relative heights of those two intersections can be used as such a measure. Consider the four sets of curves in Figure 2.9. The separation of the noise and the signal-plus-noise curves (specifying the same sensitivity) is the same in each set, but the placement of the criterion line is different. In (*a*), the criterion line is set to the left—a high-risk setting. That

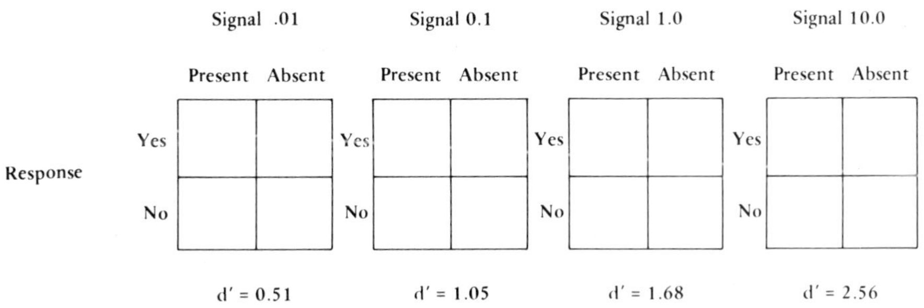

Figure 2.8 Hypothetical data from four conditions of a signal-detection experiment, in which each condition represents a different luminance value.

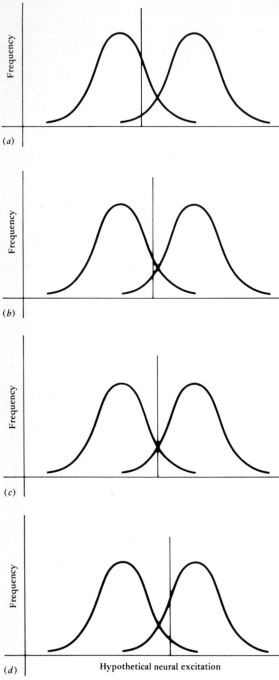

(a)

(b)

(c)

(d)

Hypothetical neural excitation

Figure 2.9 Hypothetical distribution of noise and signal-plus-noise from four conditions that differ only in the cautiousness of the observer, in which, from the top to the bottom panel, the observer increases the amount of neural excitation needed to say "Yes."

is, the observer says "Yes" even to small amounts of excitation—amounts that are much more likely to have been the result of noise than of signal-plus-noise. At this point the height of the signal-plus-noise curve at the criterion line is much less than the height of the noise curve and the ratio of these heights (signal-plus-noise/noise) is 0.2. In (b), the criterion represents a somewhat less risky attitude, though the ratio is still less than 1.0. In (c), the criterion is up to the point where the curves cross and the ratio of the two heights is 1.0. In (d), the height of the signal-plus-noise curve is greater than that of the noise curve, yielding a ratio of 1.5. If the observer became even more cautious the ratio would become very large indeed, as the height of the noise curve approaches the base line.

This ratio of heights can be calculated by reference to the height of the ordinate in a normal curve table. In signal detection theory, this value of the criterion is called β (**beta**) and there are also special tables in which the value of β is given for values of the hit rate and the false-alarm rate (Green & Swets, 1966). In Figure 2.8 the four sets of data yield the same β value even though sensitivity changes dramatically.

Receiver Operating Characteristics

It is easy to manipulate the sensitivity d', of an observer in an experiment: Simply vary the intensity of the stimulus. Each intensity value yields a different d'. But how can the observer's criterion be systematically varied so that we can examine how it changes? The procedure used most frequently is to vary the costs and benefits of each of the four types of outcomes in an experimental trial. The observer is told that he is paid according to a **payoff matrix** such as the one shown in Figure 2.10. For every hit that he makes he wins a penny and for every false alarm that he makes he loses a penny; similarly for the misses and correct rejects, regardless of the magnitude of the signal.

Referring back to Figure 2.9, we can see that if the observer sets his criterion cautiously (Figure 2.9 (d)), so that β is much larger than 1, he does not lose many pennies by making false alarms. He also wins little on the hits because he makes few of those, too. If he shifts his criterion to the left as in (b), his false alarm rate increases, but his hit rate increases even more, so that his net winning increases. But he cannot make

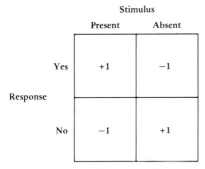

Figure 2.10 A payoff matrix indicating the costs and benefits of each of the four possible outcomes on each trial of a signal-detection experiment.

too many risky decisions—shifting the criterion past (*b*) to (*a*) causes the false alarm rate to increase more than the hit rate and the observer wins less. In fact, it can be shown that with the costs and benefits equal, and with an equal number of signals and blanks, the optimal strategy is to set the criterion at $\beta = 1$, where the two curves cross (at Figure 2.9 [*c*]).

If the experiment is now changed to a payoff matrix such as shown in Figure 2.11, the observer would shift his criterion leftward toward the risky end. Being more willing to make risky decisions, the observer produces relatively more false alarms than hits, but hits earn more than false alarms lose. It can be shown that in this case, the optimal strategy is to set the criterion at 0.5 to maximize winnings. Similarly, if the payoff matrix gives one penny for a hit but subtracts two for a false alarm, the subject would maximize his net winnings if he becomes more cautious: by using a criterion of $\beta = 2.0$.

Thus, varying the payoff matrix can cause a subject to change her criterion without altering her sensitivity. Much of the work reviewed by Green and Swets (1966) demonstrates that varying payoff matrices while holding signal strength constant produces changes in the relative rates of hits and false alarms, but that d' stays constant. Further, they have shown that the observer acts to maximize winnings—that is, she adopts criteria most suitable to the payoff matrix regardless of signal strength. This work is the basis for the claim that signal detection theory provides two independent measures of performance in a signal detection task, one of sensitivity and one of criterion.

These two performance measures are often plotted together to produce a set of functions that describe "**receiver operating characteristics**"—a description of how an observer operates for various combinations of sensitivity and criterion. To get a receiver operating characteristic function (or ROC curve), it is necessary to collect data at several signal strengths each under several payoff matrices. For example, suppose we had used four payoff matrices in our hypothetical problem along with the four signal values. We would now observe sixteen different combinations of hit rates and false-alarm rates. These are presented in Figure 2.12.

The sixteen different pairs of rates can be plotted against each other directly, as shown in Figure 2.13. They yield a family of four curves, each represented by a different d' value, increasing toward the upper left-hand corner. To get a score in the upper left-hand corner, the observer would have to have a high hit rate and a very low false-alarm rate. The only way that he can do that is for the signal-plus-noise curve to be well separated from the noise curve on the excitation distribution. The lowest d' curve, the one nearest the diagonal, is not very different from the diagonal, where, for every increase in hit rate (caused by relaxing the criterion) there is a nearly equal increase in the false-alarm rate, showing no gain in sensitivity. Each ROC curve, then, represents a single sensitivity value (corresponding to a single signal strength). The variation of hit rates to false alarm rates along each curve shows the effects of different criteria.

In most experiments, the investigator is not interested in the observer's criterion in itself. Instead, one wants to be assured that the perceiver does not

Figure 2.11 A payoff matrix designed to induce a less cautious criterion in an observer.

Payoff		Signal .01		Signal 0.1		Signal 1.0		Signal 10	
Hits	FA	Hits	FA	Hits	FA	Hits	FA	Hits	FA
+2	−1	85 $d' = 0.52$	70	88 $d' = 1.04$	55	90 $d' = 1.69$	34	95 $d' = 2.56$	18
+1	−1	60 $d' = 0.51$	40	70 $d' = 1.05$	30	80 $d' = 1.68$	20	90 $d' = 2.56$	10
+1	−2	20 $d' = 0.50$	9	43 $d' = 1.05$	11	67 $d' = 1.67$	11	85 $d' = 2.60$	7
+1	−4	7 $d' = 0.58$	2	24 $d' = 1.04$	4	50 $d' = 1.64$	5	80 $d' = 2.59$	4

Figure 2.12 Hypothetical hit rates and false-alarm rates for four different intensity values each presented under four different payoff matrices.

change his criterion from one condition to another. These curves also permit comparisons between different observers so that we can be sure that observed differences in sensitivity are not simply due to differences in their willingness to take risks. Typically, rather than varying payoff matrices over a number of values, the experimenter selects a single payoff matrix and uses it in all conditions. In Figure 2.13, the d' values corresponding to a single payoff matrix would be found by drawing a line from the corner to the diagonal, cutting across each ROC curve. Several such lines are shown in Figure 2.14, each illustrating the values that would be produced if only a single payoff matrix had been used.

We began this discussion by examining a frequency-of-seeing curve—the probability of an observer saying "Yes" as a function of signal strength.

We can now see that this ignores false alarms. The hit rate alone is inadequate as a measure of sensitivity unless we also know the false-alarm rate for each signal strength. If the experimenter does not want to study the effects of changing criterion, he need not manipulate it by varying payoff matrices. But he should have at least one payoff matrix so that he can get a false-alarm rate for each hit rate and can plot d'. Further, with a fixed payoff matrix for all conditions, the experimenter can more safely assume a constant criterion. Thus, a frequency-of-seeing curve based on a hit rate alone is not an adequate measure of a psychophysical relationship.

The best procedure is to provide an experimental arrangement in which the observer provides a hit rate and a false-alarm rate. To do this it is necessary to arrange the task so that the observer can make false

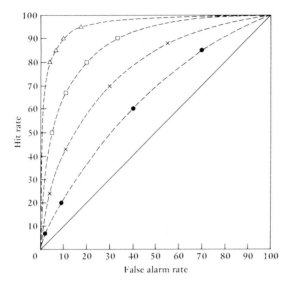

Figure 2.13 A family of Receiver Operating Characteristic (ROC) functions, resulting from plotting each of the 16 hit rates against their respective false-alarm rates from the data of Figure 2.12.

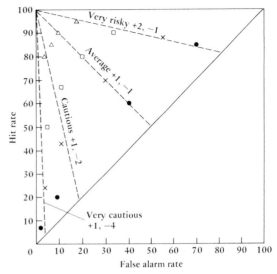

Figure 2.14 Each dotted line indicates the hit rate and false-alarm rate combination for each payoff matrix separately, corresponding to the separate rows of the data in Figure 2.12.

alarms—that is, say "Yes" in the absence of a signal. While the computation procedures to arrive at d' are simple, the experimental arrangements are not. To get a stable estimate of d' in each condition, there must be a sufficient number of signal-present trials and blank trials. Anything that increases the number of trials or the time that it takes to collect data increases the cost of the research, and its potential accuracy as well as subject fatigue become serious problems. Therefore, while signal detection theory is acknowledged to be the proper way to analyze data, a number of procedures have been developed to circumvent the demands of a complete analysis. These procedures permit control of the criterion while not having to specify what that criterion actually is. Since these alternatives still represent the majority of procedures used in experiments we shall describe the principal ones.

Forced-Choice Response Indicators

In all of the examples given thus far, the observer has been required to decide whether or not a signal was present. This decision is indicated by saying

"Yes" or "No," and consequently is called a **"Yes–No" response indicator**. Signal detection theory has been utilized primarily as a procedure to use "Yes–No" response indicators. An alternative, the **forced-choice** procedure described by Blackwell (1953), does not permit the observer to say "No" at all, and consequently the observer has no opportunity to bias the "Yes–No" decision. In this procedure, the experimenter tells the observer that a stimulus will always appear, but sometimes on the right and sometimes on the left.

The perceiver is not asked to tell whether he saw it, but simply to say on which side it appeared. If he truly cannot see anything, then his chance of reporting the location correctly should be 50 percent. As soon as his responses are significantly above 50 percent, we know that he must be seeing something of the stimulus. This procedure is called forced-choice since the perceiver is always forced to say "yes."

On logical grounds, the forced-choice procedure is not biased by the perceiver's criterion or willingness to say yes. No matter how uncertain he is as to whether he saw the light or not, he should still report the spatial location in which he thinks it was most likely to

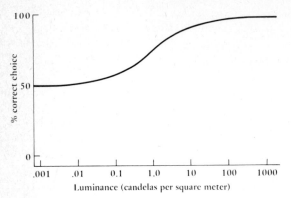

Figure 2.15 A frequency-of-seeing function obtained when using a two-alternative forced-choice indicator.

have occurred. He may think he is guessing wildly, but, presumably, will use whatever stimulus information he has.

Forced-choice procedures produce a frequency-of-seeing curve such as that shown in Figure 2.15 for two alternatives. The function begins at 50 percent because, even with his eyes closed, the observer can achieve that score by chance. As the signal strength becomes greater the probability of choosing the correct side increases until it reaches 100 percent.

The example above was of a two-alternative spatial forced-choice task. In many experiments, four alternatives are used and the observer is required to decide on which quadrant the stimulus appeared. This makes the probability of being correct by chance alone .25 as compared with .50 for the two-choice task. The main advantage of the four alternative forced choice task is the greater range over which the data can vary. In addition to spatial forced-choice tasks, the choice can also be made with respect to time. The observer can be told where the flash will occur, but that he has to choose in which of four time intervals it appears.

Blackwell (1953) has shown the advantages of a frequency-of-seeing curve based upon a forced-choice indicator over that of a "Yes–No" indicator. Green and Swets (1966) offered some comparisons between the d' measure based on signal detection theory and a frequency-of-seeing measure based on a forced-choice procedure. They showed that under the reasonable assumption that the observer picks the interval in which the observed excitation is greatest, the forced-choice

data reduces to the appropriate ROC curve. Thus, if it is possible to use a forced-choice response indicator in an experiment, the data are free of the effects of the subject's criterion shifts. The experimenter does not know what the observer's criterion is, but the shape of the frequency-of-seeing curve is not affected by the criterion, whatever its value is. In this sense, then, the forced-choice frequency-of-seeing curve plotted against signal strength, and the curve that relates d' to signal strength, with a constant payoff matrix, are equivalent descriptions of the way in which the sensitivity of the observer changes as a function of signal strength. These curves need not have the same shape (especially since the forced-choice frequency-of-seeing curve can be changed simply by changing the number of alternatives in which the subject must use his response), but they should describe essentially the same function.

Controlling Criterion by Instruction or Practice

What if the experimenter cannot afford the large number of trials that a d' analysis requires and for experimental reasons cannot use a forced-choice indicator? What does he do then? The techniques most frequently used to minimize the effects of criterion shifts, without either measuring the criterion or controlling it involve explicit instructions or practice. In many experiments using a "Yes–No" indicator, the subject is trained initially not to respond "Yes" unless he is *very certain;* otherwise to say "No." In effect, this procedure uses a verbal payoff matrix in which false alarms are penalized far more heavily than hits are rewarded. If the criterion adopted corresponds to a β of 3 or 4 or more, then slight fluctuations in the value of β do not have a pronounced effect on the hit rate, as least as compared to variations when β is around 1.0. Thus, telling the observer to adopt a very cautious criterion, but only measuring the hit rate does not produce an extremely biased hit rate as long as the observer responds very cautiously. Use of this procedure usually requires a long training period and often the use of professional subjects—those who serve in many experiments and are capable of following instructions and maintaining motivation throughout.

Unfortunately, many experiments use a "Yes–No" procedure without any criterion control except instructions and, since the subjects may not be experienced or practiced, serious questions can often be raised about the results.

THE CONCEPT OF THRESHOLD

We have described several different kinds of psychophysical functions that relate changes in the stimulus to changes in perception—the frequency-of-seeing curve, the family of ROC curves, the plot of d' against signal strength, the plot of percent correct forced-choice responses against signal strength. Each represents a continuous function relating the change in the psychological variable to changes in the physical variable. If the function is a straight line, then a linear equation describes it. More complex equations are necessary to describe more complex shapes. But there is no single point or range of points on the function that are unique or that could be said to characterize the entire function.

Classical psychophysical theory includes, as a major theoretical concept, a single point called a **threshold,** defined as the magnitude of the physical variable below which all detection or discrimination is impossible. Theoretically, this point is thought of as the beginning of perceptual experience. Below this point no awareness of stimulation occurs and, above this point, there is always some experience of the stimulus. Fechner's *Elements of Psychophysics* (1860) provided the foundation for much of this classical threshold theory.

Since there exist measurable amounts of energy that do not produce responses, it seemed reasonable to assume that such a threshold exists. The pattern of responses that would theoretically be produced when a perceiver is instructed to say "Yes" when he has a sensation and "No" when he does not, is shown in Figure 2.16, where the percentage of "Yes" responses is plotted as a function of stimulus intensity. This is a step function, with the percentage of "Yes" responses going from zero (all "No") to 100 percent (all "Yes")

at the threshold value. Notice that the threshold is defined in terms of physical stimulus magnitude.

Unfortunately, actual data collected in experiments designed to determine an absolute threshold never yield a step function. Experimental determinations of sensory thresholds always look like the function in Figure 2.1—the now familiar frequency-of-seeing curve, which is smooth, with the percentage of "Yes" responses increasing at some rate as a function of stimulus intensity. This function is produced because many variables enter into the processes that determine the sensitivity of the visual system, and therefore, measurements differ from moment to moment. Some of these variables result from the testing situation itself, some from variation within the perceiver, and some from the nature of the task the perceiver thinks is before him. For example, the stimulus energy may vary from trial to trial. The number of quanta in a very dim pulse of light may fluctuate substantially, even with the most precise stimulating sources. When fluctuation in energy occurs, the values along the abscissa in Figure 2.16 are impossible to repeat exactly from trial to trial. The errors produced make the results look like those in Figure 2.17.

In addition to the instability of the stimulus, there are substantial changes that occur in the perceiver that alter the sensitivity of the visual system being measured. For example, placing the perceiver in the dark for half an hour raises the sensitivity level of the visual system to its maximum point. However, once the testing has begun, each stimulus presentation changes the level of adaptation, thereby causing the eye to lose some of its sensitivity. Therefore, if the trials are spaced too closely together, later trials are testing a less-sensitive visual system. More energy is required and this, in turn, lowers the sensitivity still further. Sensitivity may change for other reasons, too, If a perceiver takes a coffee break in the middle of an experiment, the caffeine might affect some threshold systems; if he gets bored or fatigued, that might have other effects.

Finally, in most threshold experiments the responses are difficult to make. Usually the perceiver has some uncertainty as to whether he saw the stimulus. Whenever decisions are difficult, variables other than

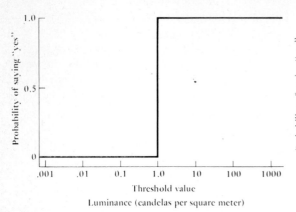

Figure 2.16 A theoretical absolute threshold function, illustrating changes in "Yes" response as a function of intensity, under the assumption of a true threshold.

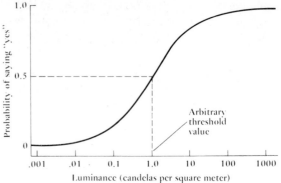

Figure 2.17 A more typically obtained absolute detection frequency-of-seeing function, showing a continuous and smooth change in percent of "Yes" responses as a function of stimulus intensity.

the energy in the stimulus begin to play a disproportionately large part. For example, if the perceiver is very confident of his judgmental abilities, then he may tend to say he sees the stimulus even when he does not. Conversely, if he feels that he should never say "Yes" unless he is absolutely certain, then he tends to withhold his reports of seeing, and appears to the experimenter as if he is very insensitive. Thus, the perceiver's bias in his willingness to make a positive report may enter into the measurement itself.

All of these variables are present in any detection experiment. They all interact and in many ways are impossible to assess. Usually, they are combined in unpredictable ways and, from the experimenter's point of view, create error. Their combined impact is that the empirical threshold functions obtained always look like that in Figure 2.17 rather than Figure 2.16. This second function shows clearly that the perceiver will sometimes say "Yes" to relatively low amounts of energy and sometimes will say "No" to relatively high amounts. Since the experimenter sees only the pattern of responses, he must accept this curve as a measurement of the threshold and base his definition on it. Consequently, the theoretical definition in classical psychophysics of threshold given earlier must be different from its empirical definition, for the latter must take into account the statistical property of the responses.

Thus, detection determination does not yield a

single point that can be identified directly with the theoretical threshold. For measurement purposes, some value has been arbitrarily selected to represent this value. This is usually the 50-percent point, the value of stimulus intensity for which the perceiver responded "Yes" half of the time and "No" half of the time.

Signal detection theory has demonstrated that there cannot be a single value of stimulus energy along a response function, below which all "Yes" responses are attributed to chance and above which all "Yes" responses are attributed to perception. If the distribution of excitation arising from noise alone exactly overlaps that from the signal combined with the noise, then d' is zero and there is no evidence that the viewer is sensitive to that stimulus. To whatever extent the presence of the signal displaces the signal-plus-noise distribution above that of the noise alone, d' is some value greater than zero and there is evidence for some degree of sensitivity. In this view, the response function is truly continuous and has no underlying theoretical step.

One simple demonstration of this is described by using a four-alternative forced-choice procedure. A step-threshold theory predicts that, if the observer is incorrect in picking the correct alternative, then the signal is below threshold and, if the observer is given a second guess, he would be at chance (one out of three chances to be correct since there are three alternatives left). A theory such as Signal Detection Theory that argues for a continuous psychophysical function with no theoretical cutoff predicts that a second or even a third guess would be above chance when first guesses are incorrect. The results of this experiment are clear-cut—second guesses and third guesses are well above chance when first guesses are wrong (Swets, Tannar, & Birdsall, 1961).

The logic of this prediction from Signal Detection Theory is straightforward. If the task is a four-alternative temporal forced-choice, then there is some excitation in each of the four detection intervals that the observer uses to make his response. He picks the interval with the greatest observed excitation level as being the one containing the signal. Since there is noise in all four intervals, the interval with the signal added to the noise has a distribution shifted to the right on the excitation axis. If the signal strength is very high, then the probability is small that the observed excitation in the three noise-alone intervals is greater than the excitation from the signal-plus-noise interval (the probability can be computed directly from the value of d'). But when d' is low, it is possible that the excitation from one of the noise-alone intervals exceeds that of the signal-plus-noise interval. In that case the observer chooses the noise-alone and is incorrect. But if the observer is now given a second guess to report which of the three remaining intervals contain the signal, he picks the interval with the greatest excitation of the three. Since the excitation of the signal-plus-noise interval is greater than that of the other intervals, over a number of trials, the chances of being correct on the second guess or his third guess is greater than pure chance (.33 or .5 respectively).

Given the results of the experiment, the basic premise of classical threshold theory has to be rejected. It is sometimes convenient for an experimenter to select an arbitrary middle point on the frequency-of-seeing curve or a d' curve to represent the entire function. But selecting such a point does not imply that there is an underlying threshold, below which no perception can occur. Precision is always an appropriate goal in science, but there should be no expectation that with greater precision the "true" threshold would be revealed as a step function.

The **experimental** definition of **threshold**—the midpoint or 50 percent point on a frequency-of-seeing curve—is used frequently in this book. But the major reason is that we need a way of representing psychophysical data—a statistical average of many observations. Consider the following experiment as an example. Suppose you want to study the changes in the sensitivity of the visual system as a function of a variable such as the amount of prior time in the dark. We know that the visual system becomes more sensitive to light the longer it is deprived of light. To demonstrate this psychophysically, we need to test an observer's sensitivity to a small flash of light after he has been in the dark. We expect the frequency-of-seeing curve for data collected after each minute in the dark to be progressively displaced to the left along an energy axis.

A typical procedure is to present a number of dim lights a number of times after the subject had been in the dark for one minute, each at a different luminance, and plot a frequency-of-seeing curve. Then, after two minutes in the dark, present another set of flashes of varying luminance and plot a new frequency-of-seeing curve. Presumably, if the subject is becoming more sensitive, the frequency-of-seeing curve will be shifted along the luminance scale as the subject is able to see more and more of the lower luminances.

Figure 2.18 shows what these curves would look like. There are four of them describing functions but they provide no way of summarizing the nature of this change.

One way to do this would be to take the average of each frequency-of-seeing curve—the luminance at which each reaches 50 percent "Yeses" based on all the measurements at each point in time. These average values can then be plotted as in Figure 2.19. We can see the average amount of luminance in each frequency-of-seeing function at a glance from this function and, even more importantly, we can observe that it decreases with time in the dark. Figure 2.19 is, therefore, a psychophysical or sensitivity function relating luminance to time in the dark. No assumption is made that the average represents an underlying cutoff threshold—only that it is a consistent way to characterize each frequency-of seeing curve.

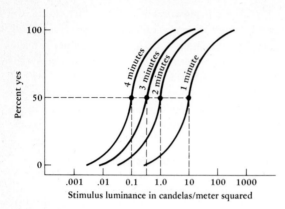

Figure 2.18 Four frequency-of-seeing curves, relating the observer's sensitivity (changes in percent "Yes") as a function of stimulus intensity. Each curve is based upon observations taken after different amounts of time in the dark.

Every example in this book that uses an average taken from a frequency-of-seeing curve is meant to be treated in this statistical way, with no assumption implied about a theoretical threshold.

PSYCHOPHYSICAL EXPERIMENTAL METHODS

This chapter has presented information on what a psychophysical function is, how to measure one, and how to control for the observer's criterion in order to obtain an independent measure of sensitivity. We have not described the experimental precedures used to collect the data that defines a psychophysical function. These are usually called psychophysical methods and for the most part originate with Fechner (1860).

Four decisions have to be made by an experimenter before he or she begins to collect data. First, what physical parameters will be varied—for example, the intensity of a flash, its size, the area of the light, the duration of the light, the amount of contrast? Second, is the response to detect the signal or to discriminate a change in the signal from some background? Third, what response indicators will the subject use? Fourth, how will the sequence of signals or signals plus blanks be organized for presentation?

Choice of Signal and Detection Versus Discrimination

Selecting the stimuli and determining whether the experiment concerns detection or discrimination is usually dictated by the purposes of the experiment. If the experimenter wishes to know something about how the visual system responds to very small amounts of signal, often trying to determine the lowest range of sensitivity, then a detection task is used. The signal is presented against a dark background. The psychophysical function is then some form of frequency-of-seeing curve.

But most experiments are concerned with discriminating changes in signal strength rather than with minimal signals. In such experiments, a split field of view might be presented, with a light of luminance L on the left and that luminance plus a bit more $(L + \Delta L)$ on the right: the observer is asked to report which half appears brighter. If ΔL is very small, the observer is usually uncertain. Such an experiment also lends itself to a frequency-of-seeing curve in which the response is now the percentage of trials in which the observer chooses correctly the side with the larger luminance. Magnitude estimation procedures considered below, are an alternative in which only a single stimulus is needed on each trial.

Choice of Response Indicator

Experiments that allow the perceiver to select his own indicator are rarely useful, because the experimenter has no way to classify the meaning of each response. Thus, an observer cannot be asked to tell the experimenter what the light "looks like." The questions must be restricted to predefined categories of responses, the definition of which the experimenter and the observer share.

We have already described the "Yes-No" and the forced-choice indicators, the two principal ones in use for psychophysical research. Since the "Yes–No" indicator is always sensitive to the effects of criterion bias, it should never be used without some kind of bias control—either a full signal-detection analysis using blank stimuli or one of the less satisfying but

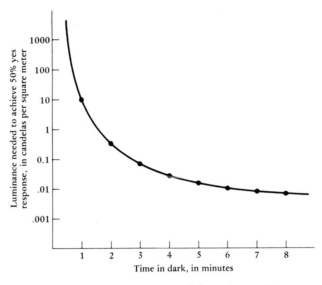

Figure 2.19 The luminance needed to achieve a 50 percent "Yes" response (the empirical threshold) as a function of time in dark. Data taken from Figure 2.18.

often sufficient instructional or training controls. Otherwise, a forced-choice indicator is to be preferred.

MAGNITUDE-ESTIMATION INDICATORS

Stevens (for example, 1971) has developed a psychophysics based on direct magnitude estimation of sensory experience. It is especially useful for suprathreshold tasks. Detection tasks, in which a single stimulus is presented, can be used to determine an empirical threshold as a function of stimulus magnitude or as a function of the interaction of two or more stimulus dimensions. For example, within limits a reciprocity exists at threshold between stimulus energy (specified as the number of quanta presented per unit of time) and the duration of the presentation. Thus, for a threshold stimulus, if the stimulus energy is doubled and the duration halved, the stimulus is still just at threshold. Given this finding, is reciprocity also found for supraliminal stimuli? Is a clearly perceptible light of a given intensity and duration the same brightness if energy and duration are reciprocally altered?

This question cannot be answered using a typical detection procedure (asking the perceiver whether she can detect the stimulus or not), since all presentations are clearly detectable by definition. One alternative is to present two stimuli in which both have the same product of energy and time but different values of each, and ask whether the two appear to be the same. Such a procedure was discussed in the previous section. While this is often an acceptable procedure, occasionally the presentation of two stimuli side by side (or one after the other) introduces undesirable interactions between them, and obscures the question being asked. It is also very time consuming.

A second alternative is to ask the perceiver to make a direct numerical estimate of the appearance of a single instance of the stimulus. In the above example, the perceiver is told that he will be shown a number of light stimuli. For each one he is to judge how bright it appears by assigning a number to stand for the amount of apparent brightness. When the first light is presented he is to assign whatever number seems most appropriate to represent the amount of brightness. Then for each succeeding one, he is to assign other numbers in proportion to their brightness.

If one light seems five times as bright as another, he should assign it a number five times as great. If the light seems one third as bright as another, he should assign it a number one third as large.

Such data are analyzed by computing the mean estimate (over repeated presentations of the same stimuli or over several observers of each stimulus) for each stimulus value. For stimuli that differ in luminance the magnitude estimates for brightness follow the solid line function plotted in the top of Figure 2.20. Marks (1974) has shown for nearly all magnitude estimation functions, regardless of sensory modality or dimension being estimated, that when the data are replotted on logarithmic axes, such as the solid line in the bottom of Figure 2.20, the function relating the stimulus magnitude to the estimated magnitude of the response is linear. If this is the case, then the function can be described mathematically as a **power function** of the form of $S = kI^n$, where S, the rated sensitivity, is equal to a constant times the physical intensity of the luminance raised to some power. The constant will be different for different perceptual modalities and ranges of values used in the rating. In Figure 2.20, the exponent n is equal to 0.6 for brightness, which shows that brightness first increases rapidly as the luminance increases, and then increases much more slowly at higher levels. The function actually levels off, so that observers cannot detect differences in brightness between two surfaces when they are very intense. The figure also shows functions for two other physical stimuli judged by direct magnitude estimation, in which the exponents are larger (1.0 for length and 1.6 for shock).

In many cases, magnitude-estimation procedures are the only ones applicable to supraliminal stimuli. Further, of the various psychophysical procedures, magnitude estimation is the easiest and fastest means of collecting data. Marks (1974) provides an extensive discussion of its applicability and reviews the evidence of the validity and reliability of these procedures in describing psychophysical functions. In this book, there are a number of examples of experiments in which magnitude estimation as a response indicator is used when supraliminal tasks are being studied.

Organization of the Sequence of Trials

To calculate a psychophysical function, the observer must be exposed to a number of different stimulus magnitudes. Each trial in the experiment consists of the presentation of one of these stimulus magnitudes, with the observer making a response to it. It is of paramount importance that the sequence of the trials be arranged to permit the proper construction of a psychophysical function. Some of the arrangements have been given specific names by Fechner or others; some do not have a formal label.

Sequences with Blank Trials   If you wish to find the sensitivity (d') associated with each of several signal strengths, you must define a payoff matrix and run each signal strength in a block of signal trials intermixed with blank trials. If you want to use four signal values, you need four blocks of trials. The observer is normally informed of the beginning of each block, shown a few examples of the signal, and then told the percentage of trials in that block that will be blank. If not told, the observer will not be able to determine the optimal strategy to use given the payoff matrix and his performance may be less than optimal (as defined by Signal Detection Theory).

If more than one payoff matrix is to be used in order to plot ROC curves, those also must be blocked (usually on different days) so that the observer is sure about what the costs and benefits are for each series of trials. There are no rules as to the order of the blocks although if several observers are being tested it is wise to use a different order of the signal strength and of the payoff matrices for the different observers. For each block of trials a d' (and a β, if desired) can be calculated that correspond to the signal strength and the payoff matrix of this block. If both signal strength and payoff matrices are varied in the experiment, a family of ROC curves can be plotted as in Figure 2.13. If only signal strength is varied and only one payoff matrix is used over all blocks, d' can be plotted against signal strength as shown in Figure 2.14. If more than one block at each signal strength is run, for each signal strength several $d's$ can be calculated and the plot in

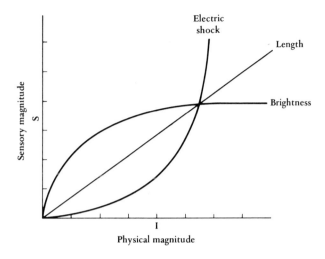

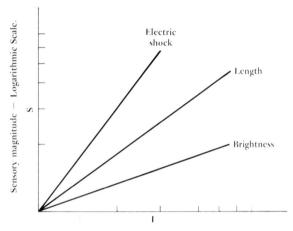

Figure 2.20 Three magnitude-estimation functions, one from brightness as a function of luminance, one for estimated length of lines as a function of physical length, and one for strength of shock, as a function of electrical voltage. In upper panel they are plotted on equal-interval axes. In lower panel they are plotted on logarithmic axes.

Figure 2.14 will be the average d' for each signal strength. If several observers are run, the d's can be averaged over the observers as well.

If you are not going to use blanks in the experiment, then more alternatives are available regarding sequential organization of the trials. Every trial contains a signal of some magnitude and a decision has to be made as to the sequence of those trials. Four principal methods have been described in the literature for

use with the "Yes–No" indicators; some can also be used with forced-choice indicators, although the magnitude-estimation indicators fit primarily the "Yes–No" type.

Method of Adjustment The
method of adjustment is often considered the simplest. The perceiver adjusts the luminance of the stimulus, changing it until he can see it. For example, he

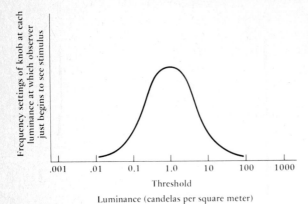

Figure 2.21 Distribution of detection responses using a method of adjustment procedure.

might have a knob that controls the output of the light source. A trial begins with the knob set at a very low level, and the perceiver turns it up until he can see the light. The experimenter then records the setting on the knob, resets it to zero, and asks the perceiver to do it again. This continues for a number of trials. When the settings of the knob are plotted as a frequency distribution, this usually yields data like that in Figure 2.21.

Occasionally these results are replotted as a cumulative function in which the ordinate is the frequency of seeing the signals. This looks like the familiar frequency-of-seeing curve, shown in Figure 2.1 (p. 26). The statistical threshold is given by the luminance at which the observer sets the knob 50 percent of the time. By definition Figure 2.21 and the cumulative plot yield the same threshold since they are mathematical transforms of each other.

Usually in such an adjustment experiment, the knob is also sometimes set at very high values, and the perceiver turns it down until he no longer sees the light. This occasionally gives a slightly different estimate and in such cases these trials are averaged together with those in which the adjustment is done in the opposite direction.

The method of adjustment is the quickest way to obtain a psychophysical function. It is subject to all the limitations of the "Yes–No" response indicator, and there is virtually no way to control criterion.

Comparisons across subjects are therefore nearly always confounded with criterion differences. Even within-subject comparisons can be confusing because the subject's criterion can be expected to shift with changes in condition, instruction, or even the difficulty of the judgments or discriminations. Even so, sometimes the method of adjustment is the best one to use.

Method of Limits
The **method of limits** is like the method of adjustment, except that the experimenter does the adjusting, and he does it in separate trials rather than continuously. Here he presents a flash of light to the perceiver at a very low energy level, and asks him if he saw it. The experimenter then increases the energy slightly, and gives another flash. The first few trials are chosen so that the observer rarely can see the flash. He continues this procedure until the perceiver says he saw it. The experimenter then records the amount of energy on the trial in which the perceiver changed from "No" to "Yes." The sequence is repeated, starting again at some low level. These values are also usually normally distributed, as in Figure 2.21 and can be cumulatively plotted, as in Figure 2.1. As with the method of adjustment, the experimenter can also start at higher values and decrease the energy until the perceiver says he can no longer see it.

The method of limits is probably the most generally used procedure. A major problem is that the perceiver always knows that the next trial will have more energy in it than the present trial. Consequently, his knowledge of the repetition procedure may interact very strongly with the responses that he makes (see Haber and Hershenson, 1965, for a discussion). It is for this reason that the next method is often used.

Method of Constant Stimuli
This is like the method of limits, except that the sequence of presentations is randomized. The experimenter decides which energy values to use. On the first trial he selects one at random from this set, presents it to the perceiver, and notes whether it is seen or not. On the next presentation, another energy value

is selected at random. In this way the perceiver cannot predict the sequence of intensities of the flashes. For each one, the experimenter notes whether the flash is seen or not. With this procedure, he can plot his data directly in the form shown in Figure 2.1. This method takes a long time and usually many more trials than the methods of limits or adjustment. On the other hand, the data are usually more stable and not open to the same types of criticism.

Neither the method of adjustment nor the method of limits is particularly useful with a forced-choice indicator, but the method of constant stimuli is ideal. On each trial the signal is presented, though unpredictable as to time or place. The magnitude of the stimulus is varied from trial to trial randomly, following the method of constant stimuli. The data can be plotted, as in Figure 2.15, in which the ordinate is the percentages of correct choice and the abscissa is the different luminances. Notice that the function will not begin at the origin but higher depending upon how many alternatives the observer has to choose from. Many advantages were noted earlier for forced-choice over "Yes–No" indicators even within the method of constant stimuli.

Staircase Method
Sometimes the experimenter is interested not in the whole psychophysical function from "never seen" to "always seen" but only in the middle of it, where the observer switches from saying "No" to saying "Yes." Therefore, most of the trials in the methods of limits and of constant stimuli are uninformative because the observer never sees the flash (or always sees it in a descending series). The staircase method concentrates on those signal values for which the subject is most changeable.

The standard procedure is to start at some low value and on each trial increase the intensity, and ask the perceiver whether he sees it. This is continued until the perceiver says he does. Whenever he says so, the energy is decreased by one unit. If he still says he sees it, it is decreased more, until he stops saying he sees it; then it is increased again. If one continues to adjust the stimulus specifically in terms of the perceiver's responses, then all the data collection will be

around the point at which he is changing from "Yes" to "No." This sequence of trials is continued until the perceiver has developed a relatively uniform rhythm. The statistical threshold now would be defined as the average of the intensities needed to change from "No" to "Yes," and from "Yes" to "No." Figure 2.22 illustrates the typical curve obtained by this method. One can also run the sequence starting at a high value and moving down. Typically, these curves overlap when threshold is found.

One of the systematic biases of the staircase method arises when the subject either knows the "rule" that the experimenter is following or fairly quickly figures it out. This permits the observer to set whatever threshold he wants simply by determining when he alternates the sequence of responses. To prevent the observer from doing this, the experimenter using the staircase method should violate the rules about 25 percent of the time. Thus, a "No" response usually causes the experimenter to increase the liminance, but on 25 percent of the trials following a "No" response he decreases the luminance; conversely, following 25 percent of the "Yes" responses the luminance is increased rather than decreased. This proce-

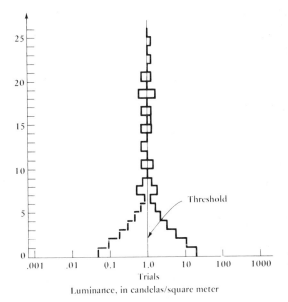

Figure 2.22 Hypothetical detection data collected using a staircase psychophysical method.

dure prevents the observer from developing a response strategy.

The method can be improved even further by running a simultaneous double staircase. The experimenter intertwines two sequences of trials, one that begins at a low luminance and increases until the subject says "Yes" and a second sequence that begins at a high luminance and decreases until the subject says "No." Each sequence separately follows the rules (often with a 25 percent violation principle added). The two sequences are intertwined so that, on any one trial, the subject does not know whether the flash belongs to the high-to-low sequence or the low-to-high sequence. The experimenter keeps them straight by having decided beforehand whether the trial is from the high or low sequence.

SUMMARY

The focus of this chapter has been on how perception experiments are run: the experimental procedures, the organization of the trials, the responses permitted to the observer, the treatment of the data, and the theoretical concepts used to describe the results. This is the topic of psychophysics, the area of psychology that describes the relationship between a perceived and a physical magnitude.

The most basic psychophysical function is described by a frequency-of-seeing curve, relating changes in the perceiver's detection to the various stimulus magnitudes presented. The curve shows a continuous increase in the percentage of stimuli detected as the stimulus magnitude is increased. Such a curve is rarely an adequate psychophysical description, however, because it is subject to a number of biases, especially those that arise from changes in the observer's willingness to respond. Signal Detection Theory describes both a set of procedures to specify these biases while at the same time providing an estimate of the observer's sensitivity to changes in stimulus magnitudes, independent of response bias.

Under a Signal Detection Theory design, some fraction of the trials are blank, permitting determination of both a false-alarm rate (the percentage of the blank trials to which the observer said "Yes"), and a

hit rate. Following assumptions about inherent visual and neural noise or random variation in any observation, Signal Detection Theory specifies a means to determine the observer's sensitivity and her criterion as independent values. It was shown how to determine both of these values from the relationship of the hit rate to the false-alarm rate, and how both of these are used to describe a receiver operating characteristic (ROC). A number of advantages are shown to stem from this description, but not all experiments follow the constraints imposed by Signal Detection Theory.

Several other techniques were described to help specify the observer's response bias. The main one is through the use of a forced-choice response indicator, in which the observer is not permitted to say "No." Rather the stimulus is presented on every trial, but in an unpredictable location in space or in time, and the observer is forced to respond with the location he thinks contains the stimulus. It is shown that this controls for response bias, and produces data equivalent to that under a Signal Detection Theory procedure. Response bias can also be controlled by instructions or training, though far less satisfactorily.

The concept of threshold has been used to describe the location on a frequency-of-seeing curve that represents the beginning of detection—the minimum amount of stimulus magnitude necessary to produce a response. However, both empirical evidence and theoretical arguments show that this notion of threshold is incorrect, in that psychophysical functions are always continuous and do not have an underlying discontinuity. Even so, specification of an experimental threshold, representing the mean of a frequency-of-seeing curve, is shown to have great practical usefulness in describing psychophysical data, without any claims to represent a theoretical minimum point.

The final section of the chapter reviewed the principal psychophysical methods that are used in conjunction with or in addition to Signal Detection Theory. Specifying the method requires the experimenter to decide whether he or she will measure detection or discrimination or magnitude estimation, what response indicator will be used, how the sequence of trials will be organized, and how he or she will plot the data. The direct method of magnitude estimation is described, in which observers assign numbers in proportion to their perception of the stimulus magnitude. These numbers are shown to describe a psychophysical function that is a straight line when both the stimulus magnitude and the response magnitude are changed logarithmically.

The methods of adjustment, limits, constant stimuli, and staircase are then described. Each represents a different way to arrange the sequence of trials as they are presented to the observer.

SUGGESTED READINGS

One of the best discussions of psychophysical measurement is by Galanter (1962). Torgerson (1963) has a complete discussion of scaling. Corso (1967) has an excellent discussion of the threshold concept and the psychophysical methods, which has been brought up to date by Gescheider (1976). We have already mentioned Blackwell's 1953 monograph, which covers many of the problems of threshold measurement, method, and indicators. Signal Detection Theory is presented by Green and Swets (1966) and Nachmias (1972), with an excellent discussion of many applications, especially in juxtaposition with more traditional threshold notions. The best general description of supraliminal techniques, especially magnitude estimates, is in Marks (1974). More advanced treatment of those topics is in the collection of papers by Moskowitz, Scharf, and Stevens (1974).

Chapter 3

Intensity, Luminance, and Brightness

This chapter and the next three describe the ways in which the visual system responds to the four major characteristics of light—intensity, spatial layout, wavelength, and duration. Normally all four of these aspects are present in every instance of stimulation by light. They can be separated only for analytic purposes. There may be occasions, therefore, in which we shall have to refer to information discussed in detail in later chapters, because we cannot fully describe responses to intensity without some reference to the other characteristics.

The present chapter considers the variables that affect the response of the visual system to changes in intensity. Nearly all research on these variables has assumed that the retina is uniformly illuminated over some large area, and has disregarded effects produced by the edges of the patches of illumination. The next chapter focuses on the coding of edges—discontinuities in luminance between two adjacent retinal areas. There we will be concerned with the ways in which we can specify edges, the effects of the sharpness or gradualness of an edge on its detectability, and the measurement of the fineness of detail that can be detected. Unfortunately, these effects occasionally produce changes in the appearance of luminance too, so that our analysis in this chapter will have to be qualified in

several important ways by the discussion in Chapter 4.

The Concept of Coding

A **code** is defined as a set of symbols that represent information and a set of rules that specify the selection and use of these symbols (Uttal, 1973). In this and the next three chapters we are concerned with how the principal properties of light—energy, spatial layout, wavelength and duration—are coded by the visual system. This requires an understanding of the nature of the representation of these properties by the visual system. How is variation in intensity or in wavelength represented? How is a visual edge represented? As an example, the representation of light energy (the information or message) is by a train of nerve impulses (the symbols) whose frequency is related to light energy logarithmically (the transformation rule). As we shall see this is not the only coding statement we can make about light energy. This one applies to the code at the level of a ganglion cell, but would be incorrect at the level of a receptor, where the symbols are graded electrical potentials, not impulses.

There is an important difference between this definition of coding and a more commonsense one based upon, for example, cryptology. Here we make no assumption about a decoder who translates the message back into its original form. As we shall show repeatedly in the book, the initial coding step, when light impinges on the retinal photoreceptors, is never the message to be decoded—we never need to or would benefit from being able to look at our retinal images. Rather the codes provide tranformation rules that relate the neural activity—the symbols—to the information in the light. Our subjective experience—the way the light appears—is a result of being able to identify the pattern of neural activity. This pattern does not have at some point to recreate the stimulus patterns in order for us to perceive the stimulus.

ABSORPTION OF QUANTA

Figure 1.20 (p. 21) shows the structures of a rod and a **cone** photoreceptor. Embedded in each of the membrane discs are photopigment molecules—about four million in each rod. In the rods each molecule contains a substance called **rhodopsin** that has the property of being able to absorb quanta of light. A molecule of rhodopsin that has absorbed one or more quanta is broken down into two substances, retinene and opsin. This process begins instantaneously with the absorption and continues (if no other absorptions occur) for about a second, by which time the molecule is said to be **bleached.** In the bleached state, the molecule cannot absorb another quantum. Retinene and opsin recombine spontaneously in the dark to reform rhodopsin, which is then able to absorb another incident quantum.

The recombination process usually takes about five minutes; that is, at the end of five minutes half the bleached molecules have recombined. By the end of ten minutes, half of the remaining molecules have recombined, and so forth. Approximately 40 minutes of darkness are necessary for all bleached molecules to return to the unbleached state, that is, to recombine to form rhodopsin and again be capable of absorbing quanta. This photochemically reversible process is the first stage of excitation of the visual system by light. By working out the fundamentals of this process over a twenty-year period, George Wald (1964) gained the Nobel prize in 1968.

The next stage in the processing is not at all as clear. All we can say with certainty is that one of the results of this breakdown process in the receptor generates a neural signal, which is then propagated across the synapse between the receptor and the neural units connected to it. The evidence that we do have suggests that there is a monotonic logarithmic relation between the number of quanta absorbed and the output of the receptor (Cornsweet, 1970). In other words, for every tenfold increase in quantum absorption, the output of the receptor doubles.

The receptor output is a **graded potential:** its output is described by the change of its voltage potential rather than by the frequency or number of times it fires. As we shall see, by the level of the ganglion cell, its activation is only in the frequency of its pulses, in which each pulse has the same voltage potential.

Absolute Limit of Detection

The minimum amount of photic energy that we can see is not a problem with great importance under normal conditions of perceiving. However, it is of theoretical interest because it can tell us a great deal about the nature of the visual system. An experiment by Hecht, Shlaer, and Pirenne (1942) attempted to make such a measurement. They maximized all conditions that would lead to the greatest sensitivity in their seven observers. The subjects were highly trained (through the use of both blank trials and instructions) to give virtually no false alarms, that is, to set a very cautious criteria for a "Yes" report. They were tested after having been in the dark for 40 minutes, enough time to have reached maximum sensitivity.

The stimulus parameters were selected so that a spot of light could be controlled in size, color, duration, and location on the retina. The spot, 0.17 of a degree in size, was presented 20 degrees to the temporal side of the fovea for one one-thousandth of a second (one millisecond), and was 510 nanometers in wavelength. Each of these values was determined on the basis of research that had showed these values to yield the greatest sensitivity. The bases for each of these decisions will be discussed later in the chapter.

A frequency-of-seeing curve was constructed by

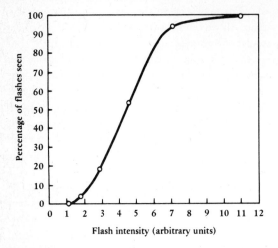

Figure 3.1 A frequency-of-seeing function for one subject in the Hecht, Shlaer, and Pirenne experiment (1942).

varying the average number of quanta in the flash, and asking the subject whether he saw the flash on each trial. Figure 3.1 presents the results for one subject (the other six are virtually the same). The 60 percent hit rate (a conservative choice) corresponds to about 100 quanta.

But that number specifies only how many quanta are delivered to the eye—not how many are absorbed by the rod system. To get that value, Hecht, Shlaer, and Pirenne made some further calculations. About 3 percent of the quanta incident to the cornea are reflected and do not pass through. About half the remaining quanta are then absorbed by the cornea, the lens, the optical media inside the eyeball, and the tissue of various neurons and blood vessels. This leaves about 50 quanta that actually make it to the retina. However, given the spaces between the receptors and the likelihood that a quantum passes through a receptor without being absorbed, they calculated that only about 20 percent of the quanta incident to a fully dark-adapted retinal surface are actually absorbed by photoreceptors. Therefore, of those 50 quanta, only about 10 were absorbed by the receptor cells in the retina to produce the 60 percent hit rate.

Hecht, Shlaer, and Pirenne then carried out a further analysis. The area of the retina where their spot fell contained about 500 rods. Given that 10 quanta are spread over the 500 rods randomly, the probability

that more than 1 quanta hit a single rod is very small. They concluded, therefore, that the 60 percent frequency of seeing can be obtained when only about 10 rods each absorb 1 quantum. Since a quantum is the minimum unit of energy, they concluded that a rod is capable of becoming sufficiently active—that is, of signaling a perceptual event—when it absorbs a single quantum. This limit is not determined by the receptors or the neural structure of the visual system, but by the fundamental nature of light.

Why does it take 10 rods—why not only one? The most likely answer is that receptors, like all neural tissue, occasionally become spontaneously active even in the absence of an appropriate light stimulus. This produces the neural noise that plays a central role in signal-detection theory. Although noise has not been measured at the level of the receptors, Cornsweet (1970) estimated that virtually all the differences among subjects in the Hecht, Schlaer, and Pirenne experiment could be accounted for by noise. Thus, subjects require about 10 rods to be active before they can respond with confidence that the excitation they have received came from a signal imbedded in the noise and not from the noise alone.

ADAPTATION

If the photoreceptors are suddenly deprived of quanta, the sensitivity of the visual system to subsequent stimulation increases. This process is called **dark adaptation,** the gain in sensitivity as the eye remains in the dark. This is a relatively slow gain, taking approximately 40 minutes to complete. **Light adaptation** is the loss in sensitivity when a dark-adapted eye is suddenly placed in the light. Complete light adaptation is much faster than dark adaptation, with much of its effect occurring in less than a second, and the whole process needing only several minutes.

Momentary Range of Sensitivity

The human eye has an overall range of sensitivity of 13 log units of luminance, that is, from 10^{-6} to 10^{7} candelas per square meter. At the lower end, 10^{-6} candelas per square meter is equivalent to 1 quantum per rod over only a dozen or so rods to produce a sensation of light under conditions of maximum sensitivity. However, at any moment the range of sensitivity rarely needs to exceed more than about two log units. Thus, in normal room illumination, with reflectances of surfaces rarely varying from no less than 10 percent to no more than 90 percent, the luminances reaching the eye might vary from, say, 1 to 100 candelas per square meter. If one is outdoors, the variation might be from 10 to 1000 candelas per square meter during the day or from .01 to 1 candelas per square meter at night. This represents the momentary range of visual sensitivity corresponding to the variation in reflectances of surfaces that one can expect when only a single source of light is available at any one moment in time.

When we are confronted with a sudden shift in luminance—larger than two log units, for example—the eyes become functionally blind for a brief period of time (the familiar experience of going from bright sunlight into a movie, or coming from a movie into bright sunlight). This represents a trade-off between the very large range in overall sensitivity and the relatively small range of momentary sensitivity. The penalties incurred with this processing trade-off between an extremely large total range and a small momentary range are normally not very severe, since in typical environments we rarely undergo sudden luminance changes of more than two log units.

This was especially true during most of the course of the evolution of the mammalian visual systems, in the absence of artificial light sources, where the principal change in illumination was the slow rising and setting of the sun.

Dark Adaptation

Adaptation is the process that accounts for the stability of this narrow momentary range and the way the visual system changes to a new momentary range. Dark adaptation refers to the time course of the increase in sensitivity of an eye when illumination is terminated. This is what happens when you walk into a darkened movie theater. The classic dark-adaptation function was obtained by Hecht in 1934. In a typical experiment, the perceiver looks at a fixation point at the center of a large screen uniformly illuminated at some value. Periodically a small increment spot is

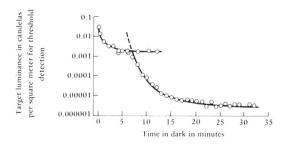

Figure 3.2   The time course of dark adaptation, as shown by the decrease in luminance threshold as a function of time in the dark after exposure to an intense light (Hecht, 1934.)

flashed on this background, and the perceiver indicates whether he saw it. The luminance of the spot is adjusted until it is barely detectable. Then the background light is turned off, and the increment spot is again flashed in the center of the now blank screen. The luminance of the spot is again adjusted so as to be just at threshold. Figure 3.2 shows the results—the amount of energy needed to see the small spot decreased rapidly over the first minute or so, and then more slowly after that, finally flattening out. This first ten minutes or so represents changes in the sensitivity of the cones and shows an increase of about 1.5 log units. We know this is a cone function since no change in adaptation over this time would have been found if the spot had been presented in the periphery—the relatively cone-free areas.

During this ten minutes, the rod receptors have also been increasing in sensitivity, although they do not start so fast as the cones. But this early portion of the rod adaptation function is difficult to show, since it is difficult to measure activity of the rods alone without involving the cones. Aguilar and Stiles (1954), using very exact procedures, have followed the early stages of rod adaptation without cone involvement, and they have measured the dotted portion of the rod function of Figure 3.2.

After about ten minutes, no further increase in sensitivity is possible for the cones. From then on, all further increases in sensitivity are due to changes in the rod receptors. They produce an increase of another 3 log units. After about 30 minutes, sensitivity has increased to its maximal value, given the size, wave-

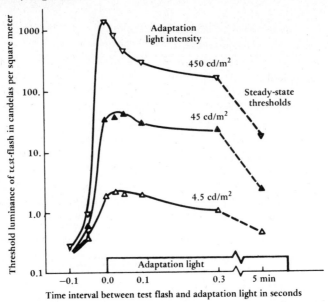

Figure 3.3 The time course of light adaptation, as shown by the increase in luminance threshold as a function of time of onset of an intense adapting light presented to a dark adapted eye. Each curve refers to a different intensity of the adapting light. (Adapted from Kandel, 1958, reprinted in Boynton, 1961.)

length, duration, and location of the increment spot. The overall change in the course of the 30 to 40 minutes is about a 10,000 fold increase in sensitivity.

Since the course of dark adaptation is very long compared to light adaptation, a dark-adapted perceiver loses his or her high sensitivity quickly if the lights are turned on, and has to remain in the dark again for a long period of time to regain that sensitivity. As a practical point, people who have to work in the dark but occasionally must turn on the lights have a serious problem in maintaining sensitivity. A typical example might be a soldier on patrol at night who must periodically glance at a map. Every time he turns on a flashlight to read the map, he becomes effectively blind for as long as ten to twenty minutes before he can again see in the dark. Since he is primarily concerned with seeing in the dark, it is the rods that he must protect from light adaptation. If the map is examined under long wavelength light, such as through red goggles, the soldier is able to see the map with foveal vision, which is sensitive to long wavelength light, while at the same time leaving the rods much less stimulated, since they are relatively insensitive to long wavelength light. When the light is turned off,

the rods are still quite sensitive and the perceiver does not have to wait for them to readapt. Of course, the soldier loses his foveal vision in the dark because the long wavelength light has adapted the cones. But since his cones are not useful for seeing in the dark anyway, he has had no actual loss.

Is dark adaptation a change in the photochemistry of the receptors, or is it a neural effect? We now know it is both, although up to the 1930s a photochemical effect seemed to be the whole answer. If each quantum bleached a molecule of photopigment, which then took up to 40 minutes to return to the unbleached state, this would account for the shape of Hecht's dark adaptation curve. This model of bleaching is very consistent and appealing, but it fails to account properly for the course of adaptation.

It is therefore necessary to look for neural determinants as well. There is now strong evidence that the sensitivity of the eye can be markedly reduced by presenting an adapting light to a dark-adapted eye even when the adopting light bleaches only a small proportion of photopigment molecules (Rushton, Campbell, Hagins & Brindley, 1955). Further, Brown and Watanabe (1965) measured the electrical activity within the eye and showed that, while the level of the activity of the neural components of the retina is reduced by the adapting light, sensitivity is reduced even with little reduction in the electrical potentials attributed to the receptors themselves—so they argued that the adaptation effects could not be attributed entirely to the receptors. Finally, the time course of adaptation and of photopigment bleaching are not identical. This is especially true for the much faster light adaptation.

For all these reasons some part of the dark-adaptation process must be mediated by processes beyond the level of photopigments in the receptor. Unfortunately, we do not have a definite answer as to what these neural processes might be. Several theories have been proposed, but as yet none can account for all the data of dark adaptation. We can say that photochemical processes establish an ultimate limit of sensitivity during the course of dark adaptation, but that neural processes may limit sensitivity during the adaptive process.

Light Adaptation

To some extent light adaptation is the mirror image of dark adaptation, except that it occurs very rapidly. It also has several other interesting properties. Figure 3.3, taken from Kandel (1958), shows the changes in luminance threshold for the detection of a brief test flash of light as a function of the presence of an intense adapting light. This is a typical detection experiment except that the presence of the intense adapting light terminates the state of dark adaptation. The three curves are for three different intensities of adapting light. By comparing the amount of energy needed to detect the brief test flash well before the adapting light is turned on (extreme left side of figure) with the amount needed when the adapting light is on, Kandel showed that the sensitivity of the visual system is reduced by up to four log units of luminance (a 10,000-fold change). This difference is what is called light adaptation.

There are three important characteristics to these functions. First, the threshold begins to rise up to 100 milliseconds before the adapting light is turned on. This is very puzzling, since it suggests that the effect of the onset of light acts backward in time to affect

events that occurred up to one-tenth of a second earlier. Second, there is the large overshoot; there is a rapidly occurring loss in sensitivity that is greatest when the light comes on, and then settles down to a lower asymptotic level. Third, the shape of the time course of light adaptation is virtually the same, regardless of the intensity of the adapting light. The more intense the adapting light, the greater and more rapid the loss in sensitivity and the lower the ultimate level of sensitivity after the transient effects have ended. But even with these changes, the shapes of the functions are similar. We will postpone most of our discussion of these effects until Chapter 6 because they have great implications for temporal processing, especially visual masking phenomena. The main point to note here is the rapidity of light adaptation.

To summarize the section on adaptation, we have seen that the response of the visual system to light depends very much upon the current state of adaptation of the retina. There is no single level of sensitivity. It can vary more than a millionfold simply by varying the amount of light to which the eye has been previously exposed.

Thus, we can still talk about the absolute threshold as the amount of energy needed to produce a response 50 percent of the time, even when conditions are less than optimal to produce maximum sensitivity. In fact, we might find that the absolute threshold for intensity is 1 candelas per square meter (one million times more than 10^{-6} candelas per square meter) for an eye that has been in daylight just before the test, or for a test stimulus that is red, or very small or very brief. Many of the graphs in this and later chapters plot absolute threshold data in which the threshold is considerably higher than 10^{-6} candelas per square meter. Thus, it is critical to specify precisely the adaptation state of the eye and the stimulating condition when talking about thesholds.

DETERMINANTS OF SENSITIVITY

In this section we consider variables other than adaptation state that affect the magnitude of the response of the visual system to light intensity.

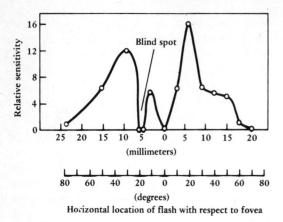

Figure 3.4 Relative sensitivity of the right eye for the detection of a brief flash at different locations on the retina (Pirenne, 1967.)

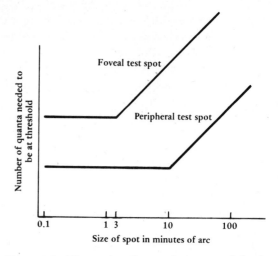

Figure 3.5 The number of quanta in a spot needed to be at threshold when those quanta are concentrated in spots of different sizes. The upper function is for spots presented to the fovea and the lower function for spots in the periphery of the retina.

Retinal Location

Figure 3.4 is a plot of the relative sensitivity of the eye to a small flash of light as a function of the location of the flash on the retina. It shows that the right eye is most sensitive to small flashes presented 16–20 degrees to the left of fixation (and conversely for the left eye). Hecht, Shlaer, and Pirenne (1942) picked 20° for the location of the test flash in their absolute sensitivity experiment as a result of data like those of Figure 3.4. Since the rod system is responsible for maximum sensitivity, it is interesting to compare Figure 3.4 to the distribution of density of rods across the retina (see Figure 1.18, p. 19). The match is sufficiently close to suggest that sensitivity variation to minimal amounts of light across the retina is determined primarily by the density of rods (Cornsweet, 1970). While we do not often have to look at or search for very dim lights, when we do, we are more likely to detect them by looking off-center than by looking straight ahead. Thus, to see a dim star at night, do not look at the star, but look 15 to 20 degrees off to the left of center with the right eye or the right of center with the left eye.

Retinal Size

Although it seems intuitively reasonable that we should detect a larger patch of light more easily than a smaller one, this is not always the case. If you look at a small, dimly illuminated spot on a screen at some distance from you and the retinal size of the spot is made larger (say, by moving the projector farther away), the detectability of the spot varies with its size (Fig. 3.5). When the spot falls on the fovea (upper curve in the figure), increases in size up to about 1/20th of a degree have no effect on the detectability. Further increases in size require more quanta in order to be detected. The result is the same for a spot in the periphery, except that the break in the function occurs for larger spots—about 1/6th of a degree.

Notice that the same number of quanta are involved as the spot is increased in size—they are concentrated over a smaller area of the retina on the left side of the graph and spread out more thinly over a larger area on the right of the graph. Thus, for either a foveal or a peripheral spot, detectability depends entirely on the number of quanta it contains regardless of how the quanta are concentrated as long as the spot is quite small. Once the spot exceeds some critical size, spreading the quanta out over a larger area lowers its detectability or, conversely, more quanta are required in order for it to be detected.

The experimental procedure can be altered so that the number of quanta per square millimeter of retina is held constant. Then, as spot size increases from some very small value, the number of quanta

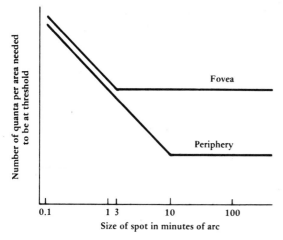

Figure 3.6 The number of quanta per unit area in a spot needed to be at threshold for spots of different sizes.

incident to the retina increases as well. Figure 3.6 shows the results. As size (and therefore total number of quanta) increases, the number of quanta per area of the spot can be decreased without reducing detectability. But this is true only up to a limit—the same limit noted above. Thus, for small spots, a reciprocity exists between the size of the spot and its luminance as they together affect threshold: $L \times A = k$, where L is the luminance required for threshold detection, A is the area, and k is a constant. This relationship is known as **Ricco's law** (1877).

These functions suggest the boundaries of the areas of spatial summation in the two parts of the retina. When many receptors converge on a single ganglion cell (optic nerve fiber), the activity level of that ganglion cell (assuming no inhibition) is the same whether all the quanta are absorbed by one of the rods or spread evenly out over all the rods in that convergence pool. This relationship is what the data at the left-hand portion of the function indicates. But once the distribution of quanta is larger than the pool of rods feeding to a common ganglion cell, then some of the quanta are lost to that cell and the total number of quanta affecting it is less. Hence, the lower detectability.

Direction

Rods and cones differ in the efficiency with which they absorb light as a function of the direction

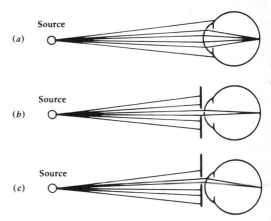

Figure 3.7 An eye forming a retinal image through different pupils. The natural pupil is shown in (a). In (b), a small artificial pupil is placed in front of the natural pupil and centered on it. In (c), the artificial pupil is displaced to the side so that the light enters the eye near the edge of the natural pupil. Note that even if the artificial pupil is shifted from its position in (b) to that in (c), the retinal image does not move with respect to the retina. (Adapted from Cornsweet, 1970.)

of the paths of light. Consider the situation illustrated in Figure 3.7 (*a*); light rays from a point on a physical surface in space are focused by the lens to a single point on the retinal surface. In (*b*) an artificial pupil (an eye patch with a small hole) is used to reduce the width of the path of light reaching the lens. This reduces the number of quanta reaching the retina and, if the artificial pupil is centered on the lens, only the light traveling in a straight path through the lens reaches the retina. If the artificial pupil is moved off center (*c*) only those rays that pass through the edge of the lens reach the retina. The image on the retina is not displaced as long as the eye remains focused on the surface. All that changes is the path of light through the eye.

Stiles and Crawford (1933) measured the amount of light needed for detection as a function of light path, that is, the location of the opening in the artificial pupil relative to the center of the lens. Figure 3.8 shows the **Stiles-Crawford effect**—a substantial loss of sensitivity for paths of light that enter the eye off-center. It has been shown that this loss is not due to optical effects at the cornea, lens, or optical media of the eye. Small losses do occur there, but they are far

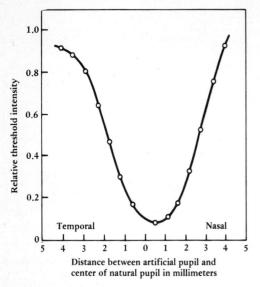

Figure 3.8 Relative threshold intensity as a function of displacement of an artificial pupil from the center of the natural pupil (Stiles & Crawford, 1933.)

too small to account for the substantial effects shown in Figure 3.8. Moreover, the effect has to be due to some property of the cone receptors since the Stiles-Crawford effect does not occur if only rods are stimulated.

O'Brien (1951) proposed that the orientation of the cone receptors is the critical factor. The end of the cone facing the lens acts as a funnel collecting quanta, and the sides of the cone act as a light pipe reflecting the quanta down its length to the end where the photopigment molecules are located. While rods act in the same way, O'Brien thought that the result is different for the different shaped receptors—if the quanta did not enter the cone on a path along its axis they are not reflected properly down its length. Enoch (1978) has now shown that this is exactly the case. This explanation is further supported by the fact that throughout the retina the cones are oriented toward the focal point of the eye. Light that enters the eye through the center of the lens from any direction in space is therefore imaged on the retina directly along the axis of the cones. Light entering off-center travels to the retina along paths that are not aligned with the axes of the cones.

The Stiles-Crawford effect has one important practical consequence. A substantial portion of the light entering the eye is reflected by particles in the optical media, by the blood vessels in the neural tissue, and by receptors that fail to absorb quanta. These reflected quanta are scattered all over the inside of the eyeball. If any of them are subsequently absorbed by receptors, their effect is to reduce the contrast of the retinal image. But the Stiles-Crawford effect suggests that the cones are unlikely to absorb any of that scattered light because the light paths rarely coincide with the axes of the cones.

Duration

It seems reasonable that the longer the duration of a test spot, the easier its detection should be. If we present a spot of light of a fixed number of quanta for different periods of time, we are changing the number of quanta per unit of time. The results of an experiment in which sensitivity to such stimuli is measured are shown in Figure 3.9. As long as the flash is shorter than about 100 milliseconds, it does not matter how the quanta are distributed in time. Even if they are all bundled together into one billionth of a second, the detectability of the flash is the same. However, once

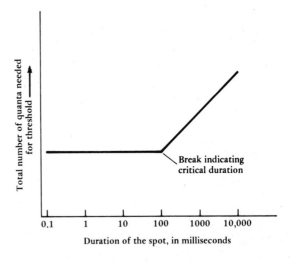

Figure 3.9 The total number of quanta in a flash of a spot needed for the spot to be at threshold, when those quanta are concentrated in flashes of different duration.

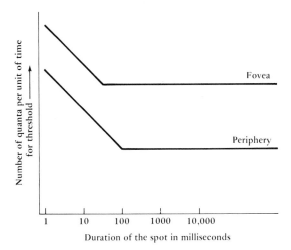

Figure 3.10 The number of quanta per unit of time in a spot needed to be at threshold for flashes of different duration.

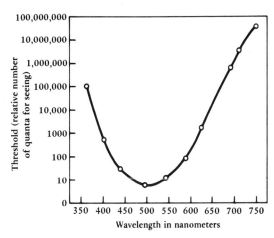

Figure 3.11 A spectral sensitivity function for rod receptors, showing the number of quanta needed for threshold as a function of the wavelength of the flash. (Data from Wald, 1945, as adapted by Cornsweet, 1970.)

the duration exceeds 100 milliseconds, more quanta are needed to detect the spot.

If the experiment is done so that the number of quanta delivered per unit time is constant and the total time is varied (so that longer flashes deliver more quanta), then the results are like Figure 3.10. As flash duration increased so that more quanta are delivered, the luminance of the spot can be reduced. This relationship is also one of reciprocity so that the product of luminance at detection threshold and duration equals a constant ($L \times t = k$). Notice that the reciprocity only holds for flashes up to 100 milliseconds for peripheral flashes, and about 10 milliseconds for foveal flashes. This reciprocity, called **Bloch's Law** (1885) will be discussed in detail in Chapter 6. But following the logic outlined for the reciprocity of luminance and area, Bloch's Law suggests that the retina summates quanta over time as well as over space.

Wavelength

Monochromatic light is light of a single wavelength or of a narrow band of wavelengths. Monochromatic light is used to determine whether the eye is equally sensitive to all wavelengths. Of course, such a test has to be done for the rods and cones separately.

Figure 3.11 presents the **spectral sensitivity function** for the rod receptors (Wald, 1945) for a

dark-adapted eye. It shows that the 510-nanometer (green) stimuli required the least number of quanta in order to be detected. The difference is sensitivity between 510 nanometers and very long or very short wavelengths is over a millionfold. Only one-tenth the number of quanta of 510 nanometer light is needed for detection as compared to 600 nanometers (red) or 400 nanometers (blue). It is clear that wavelength is one of the most important factors affecting the detectability of light.

The differential sensitivity to wavelength is related to the probability that the photopigment molecules of the rods absorb quanta. Once absorbed a rod does not respond differently accordingly to the wavelength of the quanta it has caught—the response of the rod is the same for any quantum once it has been absorbed. What the spectral sensitivity function indicates is that the probability of absorbing some kinds of quanta are better than for other kinds.

Scotopic and Photopic Vision

Nearly all the evidence we have considered in this chapter suggests that processing light at low levels is fundamentally different from processing light at high levels. Around one candela per square meter separates the lower part of the intensity range of

Scotopic		Photopic
Rods	versus	Cones
Night	versus	Day
Achromatic	versus	Color
Summative	versus	Discriminative
Low Acuity	versus	High Acuity

Figure 3.12 Some differences between scotopic and photopic processes.

10^{-6}–10^0 candela per square meter—the **scotopic** (literally low-light) range—and 10^0–10^7 candelas per square meter—the **photopic** range.

Almost everything in the visual system is different when the light levels switch from one range to the other. Figure 3.12 provides a brief list of the differences between scotopic and photopic processes. The most important change is that cones do not have sufficient sensitivity to function when luminance is below about 1 candela per square meter. Consequently, scotopic functioning almost exclusively depends upon rod receptors to collect the quanta. This means an absence of central vision (since there are no rods in the fovea), an absence of color discrimination (since that is mediated entirely by the cones), and a great reduction in resolving power of the visual system.

LUMINANCE AND BRIGHTNESS

Up to this point we have described how a receptor transduces quantal absorptions into neural signals and how these are transmitted to the brain. As an example, we studied an experiment that measured the lower limits of sensitivity to light. Since to carry out that experiment, the experimenters had to control all the variables that affect sensitivity, we considered each of these variables in some detail: the adaptation state of the eye, and the location, size, duration, and direction of the light on the retina. In each case we were concerned with the perceiver's ability to detect the presence of minimal amounts of light—the limits of sensitivity posed by each of these variables.

When studying the variables that affect detection of minimal amounts of intensity, experimenters rarely ask their observers what the light looked like.

In fact, in many cases, the observers are able to say that they saw something without being able to say anything about what they saw, even if they are asked.

But when we turn to the detection of changes in luminance, we are asking about lights that perceivers can clearly see without difficulty. We need to know what variables affect the appearance of such light. This requires that a distinction be made between **luminance**, the physical characteristics of light, and **brightness**, its psychological appearance. Luminance is always a physical measure, while brightness is always the term used to refer to its appearance.

Several different research procedures have been used to study sensitivity to changes in intensity. In some cases the perceiver is asked to specify the brightness of the light by magnitude estimation (Chapter 2, pp. 41–42); in others the perceiver is asked to detect a difference between two clearly visible lights, and finally, a number of procedures ask the perceiver to use a null response indicator, in which some property of one light is adjusted until it becomes indistinguishable from another standard light.

Since most of the research on sensitivity to changes in intensity has used a detection-of-difference measure, we shall consider the problem from this point of view. Other ways of measuring sensitivity to change in intensity produce very similar results.

Change in Intensity

We are rarely required to make perceptual judgments at or near our absolute threshold. We usually either respond directly to changes in intensity, or take changes in intensity into account when evaluating other characteristics of perception. Attempts to measure this type of performance do so by determining how small a change in intensity can be noticed.

Figure 3.13 illustrates two procedures for the presentation of stimuli in order to determine a difference threshold. With a **bipartite field,** one side may be at luminance L, and the other side at luminance L plus some additional amount, usually labeled ΔL. With the increment-spot procedure, the full field may be at luminance L, with the center spot at luminance $L + \Delta L$. It should be obvious that if $L = 0$, either of these would be an experiment to determine the abso-

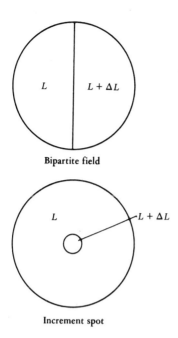

Bipartite field

Increment spot

Figure 3.13 A bipartite field and an increment spot procedure used for the determination of a difference threshold.

lute threshold. Usually in increment spot experiments, the diameter of the large field is on the order of a degree or two, with the increment spot being only a fraction of a degree.

A number of experiments have examined the minimal magnitude of ΔL needed for the perceiver to be able to say that he perceived a difference. From our earlier discussion, we know that the value of ΔL that results in the perception of a difference will depend on the value of L. This relationship is illustrated in Figure 3.14 for nine adapting levels. If the background L is dim, not much light has to be added to be seen as different. If the background is bright, then ΔL is larger. Thus, when the luminance is -1.45 log trolands, ΔL has to be $-.3$ log trolands to be detected as diffferent 50 percent of the time. If the background is made more intense, for example, with a luminance equal to 1.55 log trolands, then ΔL has to be $+.5$ log trolands to be detected as different 50 percent of the time.

These curves do not represent the sensitivity of the perceiver directly, but only specify the amount of change that is needed, ΔL, as a function of background luminance L. But it is possible to recompute these data so that they represent sensitivity to change. Weber (1843) noted that sensitivity to change could be specified for any stimulus magnitude as a ratio: $\Delta S/S = k$. He demonstrated the validity of this ratio for a number of dimensions. For example, he gave the subject a standard weight W to hold in one hand and a standard with an increment $(W + \Delta W)$ in the other hand, asking the subject to report which hand held the heavier weight. He found that for all W's, except for extremely light ones or heavy ones, the amount of change (ΔW) that was needed to be detected as different from W was always proportional to W. For weights, the **Weber function** is: $\Delta W/W = .02$ or 2 percent. That is, increments of 2 percent weight over the standard are detected 50 percent of the time. It did not matter if the standard was 10 grams, 100 grams, 1000 grams, or 10,000 grams, W was always 2 percent of the standard. Therefore, the ratio $\Delta W/W$ was a constant for all values of W.

To calculate the Weber fraction for detecting an increment ΔL added to a luminance L, the data of Figure 3.14 can be used directly. Each curve contains an L and a ΔL value at which the perceiver detected the presence of the increment 50 percent of the time. When values of $\Delta L/L$ are plotted for each value of L, as in Figure 3.15, it can be seen that the Weber fraction is not a constant at all.

When the background illuminance is low, a relatively large change in luminance relative to background luminance is needed to be noticed. Thus, when the light is 10^{-3} candelas per square meter, ΔL has to be ten times larger (a 1000-percent change) before it is noticed as different. At a normal reading level of around 10 candelas per square meter, a 10-percent change can be noticed, or 1 out of 10 candelas per square meter. At very high light levels a 1-percent change in luminance is detectable. Hence, small intensity changes are difficult to notice in dim illumination. But by the time the light level is fairly high, we can notice even a 1-percent change, which is a very small amount.

Notice the two components of the function in Figure 3.15. The component for the lower luminance

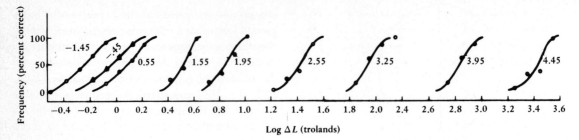

Figure 3.14 Frequency-of-seeing function as a function of the increment in retinal illuminance (log ΔL) in tro-lands, for each of nine adapting levels, also specified in log trolands (Mueller, 1951.)

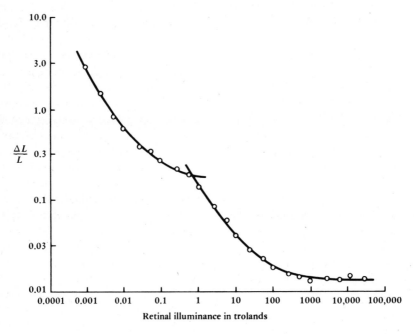

Figure 3.15 Brightness discrimination ($\Delta L/L$) as a function of retinal illuminance (Hecht, Peskin, & Patt, 1938.)

levels on the left, reflects the operations of the rod receptors and suggests that the rod's sensitivity to change in intensity of light is relatively poor. The cones begin to operate at about 1 candelas per square meter and they become very sensitive as luminance increases. Given the distributions of cones and rods in the retina, we should expect to find the highest sensitivity to brightness discrimination in the fovea. Thus, the peripheral rods are most sensitive to minimal amounts of light, whereas the fovea is most sensitive to changes in light intensity.

SUMMARY

In this chapter we begin the description of neural coding with a discussion of the way in which the intensity of light is represented in the visual system. The initial code is a transduction of quanta into a graded receptor potential through a process of bleaching the photopigment molecules in the receptors. To determine the absolute level of detection of quanta, we reviewed the experiment by Hecht, Shlaer, and Pirennne, who showed that only about 10 quanta, each absorbed by a different rod, are sufficient to produce detection of the presence of light.

A number of variables are then considered that affect the sensitivity of the visual system to light. These include the state of adaptation of the eye, the location of stimulation on the retina, and the size, duration, direction, and wavelength of stimulation.

Dark adaptation is the process by which sensitivity increases with time in the dark, whereas light adaptation is the loss of sensitivity due to the presence of light. While the limits of dark adaptation can be shown to be set by the photochemistry of the receptors, both dark and especially light adaptation also are limited by a neural component due to interaction among the neural units in the retina.

Retinal location affects sensitivity primarily as a function of the density of the rod photoreceptors, whereas the stimulus-size effect is limited by the area of the retina over which receptors pool their outputs onto bipolar and ganglion cells. Duration of stimulation also affects sensitivity, with the limit imposed by the extent of temporal summation. Both size and duration are reciprocally related to luminance below these limits of spatial or temporal summation.

The final topic concerned supraliminal effects of intensity. The sensitivity to detect changes in intensity is related to the intensity being judged, with the greatest sensitivity to change found for very high luminance levels.

SUGGESTED READINGS

The single best reference on sensory coding is Uttal (1973), with a companion collection of research papers edited by Uttal (1972). Brindley (1972) has an excellent discussion of adaptation. Cornsweet (1970) has good coverage of general problems of intensity coding, including that of the Hecht, Shlaer and Pirenne experiment. Hurvich and Jameson (1966) still has good coverage of the perception of brightness. Many of the handbooks suggested as readings at the end of Chapter 1 have chapters on brightness.

Chapter 4

Visual Edges—Neural Coding and Psychophysics

Chapter 3 described the coding of luminance information by the visual system. In this chapter we shall first discuss how discontinuities in luminance are coded in the retina and cortex, and then examine the variables that affect our ability to detect the presence of visual edges. We shall provide a general discussion of coding strategies found in the visual system, especially those that are utilized to code visual edges.

DEFINITION OF VISUAL EDGES

Visual edges can be defined in terms of the properties of space or in terms of retinal images. Both definitions are used, often interchangeably, but they are not the same. A **visual edge** in space is the locus of points that separate areas reflecting different amounts of light to the eye. The different amounts of light could be the result of different reflectances of two adjacent or overlapping surfaces (a **reflectance edge**), or the result of differing amounts of illumination falling on adjacent parts of the same surface (an **illumination edge**), such as that created by a shadow. The edges around a small black piece of paper lying on a white background illuminated by a single source of light are reflectance

edges, whereas the edge on a white card between the area illuminated by a lightbulb and that by a patch of sunlight is an illumination edge.

Both these types of visual edges in space have luminance profiles that can be measured and specified with a photometer. If we move a photometer across the border formed by two surfaces, the rate at which the photometer signals a luminance change is plotted as a luminance profile. Consider the profile of a black wire 2 millimeters wide whose reflectance is 2 percent, seen against a white background with a reflectance of 90 percent. If 100 candelas per square meter uniformly illuminate the background surface and the wire, then the profile might look like Figure 4.1(*a*). The sharpness of the edges in the luminance profile would be determined by the roundness of the wire and the size of the light meter's acceptance opening.

Imaging of Visual Edges on the Retina.

Visual edges can also be defined on the retinal surface: an edge is the locus of points separating two areas receiving different amounts of luminance. Normally, whenever a visual edge occurs in space it is reproduced on the retina. However—and this is the critical difference—the luminance profile of the retinal

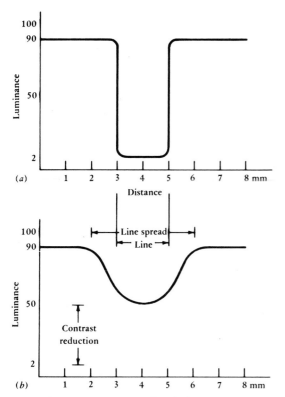

Figure 4.1 A luminance profile of a black line against a white background when measured by a photometer in space (*a*), and when specified across the retinal surface (*b*).

visual edge will always be different from that of the visual edge in space.

If the profile of the spatial visual edge shown in Figure 4.1(*a*) is measured on the retinal surface, it will look quite different, as shown in Figure 4.1(*b*) (Hecht & Mintz, 1939; Westheimer & Campbell, 1962). The area of low luminance reflected from the wire is spread out in width over the retina, and its contrast—the difference in luminance between the wire and the background—is markedly reduced. This spreading in width and reduction in contrast is specified by a **linespread function.** It is entirely due to the optical properties of the eye. All luminance profiles on the retina are wider and of less contrast than their corresponding profiles in space. If the illumination on a scene in space is high, and the differences across the scene in reflectance are large, then the differences be-

tween the shapes of the two profiles are small and not important. But whenever the overall light level is low, so that the contrast along the edge is low, then the two profiles can be quite different. In such cases, no matter how sharp the visual edge in space is, it is blurred on the retina, and the difference in luminances across the edge is greatly reduced.

One other important property of the linespread function shows up when the stimulus is a thin line as in Figure 4.1. Not only is the contrast on the retina reduced as the physical line is made narrower, but in addition, while the width of the profile of the wire on the retina also narrows it does so much less than that of the physical change in space. Further, once the wire reaches about two minutes of arc (1/30 of a degree), further reductions in width of the wire have no further effect on the width of the retinal luminance profile— only on the retinal contrast. Therefore, detection of very narrow lines depends upon their contrast on the retina and not on their width because the width of their luminance profile on the retina is a constant. It is also impossible to discriminate the differences in width between very narrow lines because, in fact, there is no difference in their retinal widths.

Having different luminance profiles for visual edges in space and visual edges on the retina does not matter much when light levels are well into the photopic range. But at lower light levels detecting and processing of visual edges is poorer than would be expected on the basis of the luminance profile of the edge in space.

CHANGES IN THE CONCEPT OF NEURAL CODES OF EDGES

The retinal image can be considered the first representation of the information about the visual world—the world of surfaces reflecting light to the eye. At any one moment, this image is a two-dimensional pattern of luminances. Until about 25 years ago, most theorists assumed that the pathways within the retina, and between the retina and the cortex, were designed to transmit an isomorphic or maplike representation of these luminance values to the cortex. If each receptor had a private line to the cortex there would be no difficulty in describing such a system. It was thought then (Polyak, 1957) that only the receptors in the center of the fovea had private lines, the rest of the receptors sharing party-lines, with more and more sharing the farther the receptors were from the fovea. The focus of research and theory was to understand how the private and party-line arrangement could account for the facts of visual perception.

One consequence of this analogy was to limit the function of the retina to that of a telephone relay station, and relegate all the interesting tasks of perception to the visual cortex and "higher" structures. It also suggested a conception of the visual system in which each stage of processing simply transmitted the point-by-point luminance information one step higher without ever "looking at it." Ultimately, however, such an approach requires an **homunculus,** a little person in the head, who looks at the pattern in the brain and "perceives" it. Of course, inside the Homunculus there must also be a retina and a cortex, and so forth and so on. Obviously, such an invention does not increase our understanding.

About twenty-five years ago evidence began to accumulate that the retina was not merely a relay station, but could respond to higher-order "features" from the pattern of luminances. The most interesting evidence was from Kuffler and Barlow working independently in 1953, that information about average luminance changes from one value to another could be "represented" by single cells in the retina, and that such a single cell represented the activity of hundreds or even thousands of receptors. Their work was rapidly followed by an explosion of research and theorizing that suddenly changed the conception of the retina from that of a transmitter to that of a major information processor. Kuffler's and Barlow's discovery did not reduce the cortex to insignificance. In fact, their work initiated a new view of the visual system—the coding that began in the retina continued at all stages and in the cortex. But more importantly, their work showed that because the absolute level of luminance was not very important, the visual system did not need to respond to it. This change also reflected the new

understanding of the visual stimulus: the realization that the critical features of the environment exist regardless of the particular intensities of the light present at the time (Barlow, 1972).

Kuffler's and Barlow's work did not end all controversy, even though it led to a fundamental redirection of thinking about visual processing. Their work suggested that different critical features of the environment were coded by the retina, especially the presence of visual edges resulting from borders between areas of different average luminance. But it turns out that there are several ways to describe a visual edge, and most of the theorizing today seeks to find the fundamental one. As we saw in Chapter 1, it is possible to construct an edge by summing a series of sine waves of different spatial frequencies. That is, the visual cortex or even the retina may code edges in terms of these spatial frequency components. If this is the case, describing the coding in terms of visual features such as edges obscures the more fundamental spatial frequency code underlying the edges.

It is possible that new discoveries or ideas will suggest new codes or new coding systems. At present most of the work is directed at discovering the fundamental codes in the retina and how that information is recoded and recorded by higher centers.

What Needs To Be Coded

We can begin by seeing what kinds of information must be coded. What are the qualities of visual stimulation that we need to know about in order to perceive the visual world? We must know something about the location of objects in space and whether they have moved. We need to know something about their sizes, shapes, and textures. We need to know something about the scale of space, the distances between objects and their relative sizes, and the organization of space. We need to know something about serial order, about what happened before and what is happening next. And we need some way to integrate across the successive retinal projections that occur when our eyes move.

It is obvious that the receptors themselves cannot give us any of this information. Let us look at the limitations of an individual receptor in providing even the simplest information about the light that falls on it. Where is the light source? From which direction in space did the light come? What is the light's intensity, wavelength, size? What is its duration? Of all these simple characteristics of light, only two can be partially specified by a single receptor—the intensity of the light and its duration. All other properties require more complex coding than that available in a single receptor.

As we noted in Chapter 3, the absorption of light energy is the only stimulus event relevant to visual perception. If there is no absorption, then there is no way in which the visual system can have any information about the presence of light and thereby about the visual world around us. But when a receptor absorbs some quanta, it can represent information about only two things—how many quanta it absorbed, and for how long. The number of quanta absorbed is coded by the output of the receptor, and the duration of the light by the time course of that output.

Even so, intensity coding by a receptor can at least start in the receptor itself. What about the other aspects? The problem is that once a quantum is absorbed, the receptor has no way of providing any information about that quantum. As we shall see, the photopigment in the rods is more likely to absorb quanta of 500 nanometers of wavelength than those of 600 nanometers. But once absorbed the result is exactly the same, and there is no way for the receptor to code the wavelength of the quantum. Likewise, the direction from which the quantum came, the path it followed upon entering the eye, is not coded. That path affects the probability of its being absorbed, at least by cone receptors, but once absorbed the same photochemical events are set in motion.

What about location on the retina—can a receptor provide information about its position on the retina? It cannot do this alone. The location of a receptor is specified only in terms of coordinates provided by a higher level combination of outputs of receptors. In order to specify that light hit the right-hand side of the retina, the output of at least one other receptor must be taken into account.

Without further detail it is obvious that a single receptor can produce a wide variety of responses, but

that by itself it is not very informative about even the simplest properties of the light that gave rise to those outputs. We have developed this point to show, first, that complex sensory coding is necessary before we can know anything about the light in the retinal projection, and second, that there is little reason to try to preserve the separate states of the separate receptors, since those states by themselves tell us very little. We should therefore be looking for coding processes that go beyond the states of individual receptors.

THE NEURAL CODES FOR EDGES

Spatial Summation and Spatial Inhibition

Virtually all the complex coding done by the retina and the cortex is based on the interplay of summative and inhibitive interconnections among neurons. We have described in Chapter 1 how synaptic connections between two neurons are either excitatory or inhibitory. If a group of receptors is connected to a bipolar cell with only excitatory synapses, the likelihood that the bipolar becomes active increases in direct proportion to the number of its receptors that absorb quanta. Likewise, if the interconnections among bipolars and ganglions involve only excitatory synapses, a further pooling of excitation occurs. Such interaction is called **spatial summation.** This process would be very useful in maximizing responses to light of very low energy levels. We have shown in Chapter 3 that, especially for small areas in the periphery of the retina, there is a reciprocity between area and intensity of stimulation. That is, the probability of detecting the presence of a light could be held constant even with a decrease in luminance if the area is increased by an appropriate amount. This is a very useful device for noticing the presence of small amounts of light.

Some of the connections between neurons include inhibitory synapses as well. In Figure 4.2 both receptors *A* and *B* have excitatory synapses with their respective bipolar cells, so that the bipolars show an

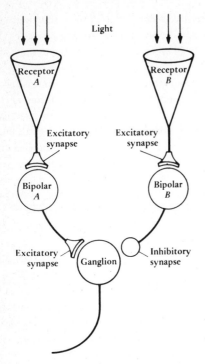

Figure 4.2 Schematic representation of excitatory synapses between receptors and bipolars, with one bipolar having an excitatory synapse to a ganglion and another bipolar having an inhibitory synapse to the same ganglion.

increase in activity when the receptors absorb quanta. But bipolar A has an excitatory synapse with its ganglion cell whereas bipolar B has an inhibitory synapse with the same ganglion. Therefore, when light falls uniformly on both receptors A and B they nullify the impact each has on their joint ganglion. Notice in this example that receptor A does not inhibit receptor B or vice versa. The response of each receptor is a function of the amount of quanta it absorbs, not the number of quanta its neighboring receptors absorb.

If any receptor in the periphery is connected into a neural network that has inhibitory synapses, the amount of spacial summation is greatly reduced or entirely absent. Therefore, for pooling of receptors to occur, either inhibition must be absent in the periphery or not involved during low-intensity stimulation. We now know that the latter is correct, and that inhibitory processes come into play only when light levels are quite high. Hence, we see an example of specialization—summation to capture small amounts of light, and inhibition to provide more complex coding when light levels are high.

The classic research on **lateral inhibition** by Hartline, for which he received the Nobel prize in 1970 (for example, Hartline & Ratliff, 1957), was performed on the horseshoe crab, *Limulus*. When he recorded from a single optic nerve fiber he found excitation to be roughly a logarithmic function of the intensity of the light falling on the receptor for that fiber. If a second spot of light stimulated other receptors, the output of the first receptor decreased as the second light moved closer or was made more intense. Each of these findings suggests lateral inhibition—the output of one receptor's ganglion cell was inhibited by the activity of another nearby receptor.

A schematic description of the inhibition in *Limulus* is shown in Figure 4.3. Light falling on receptors A and B excites ganglion cells A' and B', respectively, through their excitatory synapses. The outputs of the two ganglion cells travel to the brain. But those outputs each have two forks, one of which forms an inhibitory synapse with an adjacent ganglion cell. Consequently, as light falls on A it not only excites A', but also inhibits B'. If light also falls on B, B' is excited and A' inhibited. Thus mutual inhibition of A' and B' reduces the level of activity of both, well below what they would have been if A or B alone were absorbing quanta.

Lateral inhibitory effects have been found in every species studied. Except for man, most of the research has employed electrophysiological procedures in which a microelectrode records the activity level in a neural unit while light is applied to one or more receptors. In man psychophysical procedures have been used to supply similar evidence. Suffice it to say that there is overwhelming evidence for the presence of lateral excitatory and lateral inhibitory effects in man, as well as in other animals.

Figure 1.17 (p. 18) is a sketch of the neural units and their interconnections in the primate retina. Based on current knowledge, we believe that all the synapses shown are either excitatory or inhibitory. In fact, most of the interconnections between any two

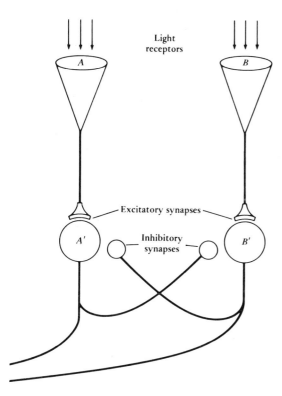

Figure 4.3 Schematic representation of excitatory synapses between two pairs of receptors and ganglion cells (bipolar cells have been omitted), with mutual inhibitory synapses between the two ganglion cells, as a description of the type of spatial inhibition found in *Limulus*, (After Cornsweet, 1970).

neurons have both excitatory and inhibitory synapses. In general, inhibitory synapses have higher thresholds—they need more activation of the presynaptic neuron to produce an effect in the postsynaptic neuron. This means that the output from a particular receptor produces differential effects in the neurons of the retina, depending upon the number of quanta absorbed and which other receptors are absorbing quanta at the same time. Variation in pathways is critical in the coding processes to be described. But it is also possible to describe pathways through the retina that have a relatively fixed structure. The most important aspect of structure is based on the concept of a receptive field.

Receptive Field Organization

The visual systems of many species are organized in such a way that collections of neurons act as functional units. When one attempts to determine the functional inputs to a particular neural unit, one is looking for the **receptive field** for that unit. If the visual nervous system were a completely noninteracting system, then there would be a different cell in the cortex for each receptor in the retina. Thus, the receptive field of each of the cortical cells would be a single retinal receptor. To locate the receptive field of one such cortical cell, **a microelectrode** could be embedded in the cortical cell, and a small spot of light moved over the retina until the receptor was found that would produce a response in the cortical cell being recorded. While this example is implausible, the principle is applied to the search for inputs to any neural unit.

Figure 4.4 shows the general procedure for mapping out a receptive field in a visual system by electrophysiological recordings. The methods are the same whether one looks for receptive fields of a ganglion cell, a cell in the lateral geniculate nucleus, a cell in area 17 of the cortex, or cells in other parts of the brain. For example, to locate a receptive field of an area-17 cortical cell, a recording microelectrode is placed in the cortical cell and light of a particular intensity and size is presented to some area of the retina. If the responsiveness of the cortical cell changes, this light can be considered to be stimulating part of the receptive field of that cortical cell, and so this light is a stimulus for that cell. The light is then moved to a new location, repeating the process, to find all areas of the retina to which the cortical cell responds. This provides a map of the receptive field of that cell for that particular pattern of light. The light can then be changed in intensity or size or shape or pattern of movement, and the process repeated until receptive fields for that cell are mapped out for all different stimulus characteristics. Usually, however, a particular cell responds to only one type of light pattern. When this mapping is done, the electrode is moved to another cell and the process is repeated. Note that this is a map of the retina, not of the cortex. It is the locus of all points of the retina that are capable of producing

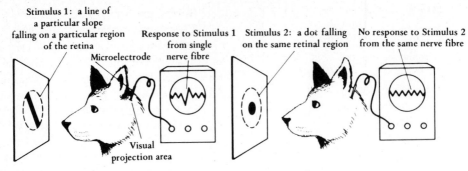

Figure 4.4 A schematic representation of the procedure for an electrophysiological mapping of a receptive field in the visual system.

response from the cortical cell from which a recording is being taken. Electrophysiological recording cannot usually be used with human beings, but it has been used with animals from frogs to primates.

Antagonistic Concentric Structures

Consider the receptive field of a mammalian ganglion cell for a small spot of light seen on an otherwise dark background. This field is mapped by recording the activity of a ganglion cell with a microelectrode while moving the spot of light around on the retina. When the ganglion cell's activity level changes, the receptors being stimulated are considered part of the receptive field of the cell. Figure 4.5 shows schematically an on-center, off-surround receptive field. Figure 4.6 shows the four hypothetical functions, illustrating the changes in activity level of such a cell. When one is recording from a cell of this type, a certain amount of spontaneous activity is found, even in the absence of stimulation. This is illustrated as function (*a*) at the top of Figure 4.6. If a small spot is presented to the on-center, the rate of firing initially increases (*b*) but then returns to the spontaneous level. Note that while no change in firing rate occurs as the light is left on, when it is turned off there is a brief inhibition. If a small spot falls only on the off-surround (*c*), there is a decrement in activity to the onset, and a brief increment to the offset. In each of these cases, the ganglion cell does not change its response to the steady state, when the light is either left on or left off. Further, if the spot of light is sufficiently large so that it falls on both the on-center and

the off-surround (*d*), the two parts of the field tend to cancel each other and the total change in response may be zero.

The particular receptive field illustrated in Figure 4.5 is called an **on-center, off-surround concentric field** because of the pattern of responses observed when it is stimulated by an increment of light. The opposite variety is also common, in which the surrounding part of the receptive field signals the onset of light with excitation. Notice that large stimuli

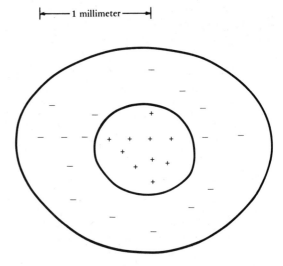

Figure 4.5 A schematic drawing of an on-center, off-surround concentric receptive field at the ganglion-cell level. Plus signs indicate that an elevation in activity of the cell is found when light falls on that portion of the receptive field, and minus signs indicate a decrease in activity.

would tend to produce no response from either of these types of receptive fields, because the light would fall on both parts, producing mutual inhibition. The most effective stimulus for this cell is an intense spot of light about the size of the on-center portion.

There are relatively few receptive fields that continue to signal the presence of unchanging light. As with *Limulus,* the mechanism of inhibition occurs

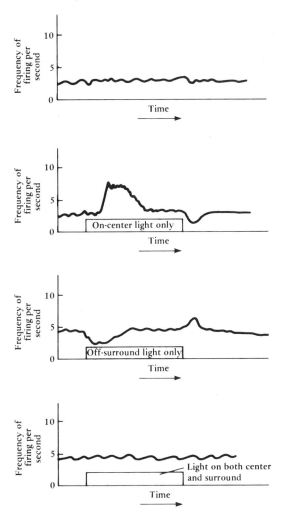

Figure 4.6 Four hypothetical functions illustrating the changes in activity level of a ganglion cell when (*a*) no light is present over its receptive field; (*b*) light covers only its on-center; (*c*) light covers only its off-surround; and (*d*) light covers the entire receptive field uniformly.

above the level of the receptor itself. Each receptor's activity continues to reflect the number of quanta being absorbed, but its effect at the ganglion level is changed, either being enhanced or inhibited, depending on the pattern of light and the shape of the receptive field.

There are three important characteristics of the on-off inhibitory mechanisms found at this level of the visual system. The first is that, when light falls only on an on-center, it tends to increase the level of activity in the ganglion cell above its spontaneous firing rate. When the light falls only on the off-surround area, it tends to depress the level of activity in the ganglion cell below its spontaneous firing rate. The center is an excitatory area and the surround is an inhibitory area.

Second, when light falls primarily on the on-center, there is an increase in the activity level of the ganglion cell at the onset of the light. The ganglion cell then returns rather rapidly to its spontaneous level, even if the light is left on. When the light is turned off, a brief opposite change in activity is found. If the light falls primarily in the off-surround area, there will be a rapid decrease in the firing rate of the ganglion cell when the light is turned on. When the light is turned off, there is a rapid increase in activity, which again rather quickly returns to baseline level, even if the light is left off. In this sense, then, the two parts of the receptive field are sensitive to the leading and trailing edges of stimulation over time, rather than to steady-state levels.

Third, the two parts of the receptive field are mutually inhibitory. Light falling on the on-center area tends to inhibit responses to light falling in the off-surround area and conversely. This effect does not show strikingly until light falls on both areas simultaneously, when we find a canceling effect, roughly proportional to the relative amounts of stimulation falling on each area. In this sense, then the on-center, off-surround receptive field is designed to be mutually inhibitory for large uniform illumination.

The type of ganglion cells whose receptive field has been described is a **spatially opponent** ganglion cell. This means it is primarily sensitive to luminance discontinuities between its center area and its surrounding area. The maximum positive response from an on-center off-surround ganglion cell is from an increment of light falling exactly on its center with no light falling on the surround. The maximum negative response (a reduction in the ganglion cell's activity below its spontaneous level) occurs when the surround is illuminated by light and the center is dark. The reverse occurs if the center of the receptive field is inhibitory and the surround is excitatory (off-center on-surround). Both types of ganglion cells are found in equal numbers throughout the retina. Both types give a negligible response to uniform stimulation over both parts of its area, whether the stimulation is an increment or a decrement over the overall illumination of the retina.

The antagonistic concentric receptive field appears to be the principal structure among the neural units converging on ganglion cells in the retina. Every ganglion cell examined has such a receptive field organization. The sizes of the receptive fields change, with the smallest being in the center of the fovea and the largest well out in the periphery (Robson, 1975).

Before going on to consider how the ganglion receptive fields are themselves organized by cells in the visual cortex, let us briefly consider the kinds of coding that ganglion-level receptive fields can handle. The most important of these are edge-enhancement processes.

Edge Enhancement
If the activity level generated in a ganglion cell by a particular group of receptors is lowered when receptors adjacent to it are also active, a unique property emerges, referred to as **edge enhancement.** Suppose we present a pattern consisting of two areas of adjacent luminance, one more intense than the other with a fairly sharp edge formed by the junction of the luminance differences. What will we see at the edge? Figure 4.7(*b*) shows the stimulus schematically, and photograph illustrates the appearance (*a*). Notice that there appears to be a brighter band on the bright side of the edge, and a darker band on the dark side. Hence, the brightness contrast at the edge is greater in our perception than it is in the physical intensity distribution itself. The edge has been **enhanced.** This is an ex-

ample of a **Mach band,** named after Ernst Mach, who first discovered and studied them in 1865.

Figure 4.8 shows how concentric antagonistic ganglion cells could produce such an effect. In the example only on-center cells are shown, although normally both on-center and off-center cells would be present. The area of the retina served by ganglion cell *a* receives many quanta, which are absorbed by both the center and the surround, leaving ganglion cell *a* about at the same level of activity before the edge is turned on. Cell *b,* whose receptive field is just to the intense side of the edge, responds quite vigorously because part of its off-surround receives few quanta and hence cannot inhibit the on-center. That is, the two antagonistic areas of the receptive field receive unequal stimulation. Thus, all the ganglion cells whose receptive fields are along the intense side of the edge, such as *b,* have more excitatory outputs than do the ganglions whose receptive fields are well to the center of the intense part of this stimulus.

The result is reversed on the darker side of the edge. Cell *d* is like cell *a*—both center and surround receive equal numbers of quanta, leaving its output unchanged. But cell *c,* just to the darker side of the edge, absorbs more quanta in its surround than in its center, reducing the activity of the ganglion below its spontaneous level. That is, the two antagonistic regions of the receptive field of *c* receive unequal stimulation. In other words, the ganglion cells whose receptive fields are just along the darker side are less active than those well inside the darker part, whereas those just inside the lighter part are more active than those well inside the lighter side. This corresponds to the picture seen in Figure 4.7. The result is that a response to an edge of a particular luminance difference is exaggerated at the place corresponding to the location of the edge—the edge is enhanced in coding. It has been suggested that this edge enhancement occurs to compensate for the spreading out of sharp edges in the retinal image.

If receptive fields *a* and *d* are at the same activity level, you might wonder why the right side looks so much darker than the left side. In fact, they do tend to look alike in brightness if the edge between them is the only edge in the scene. But the entire figure is

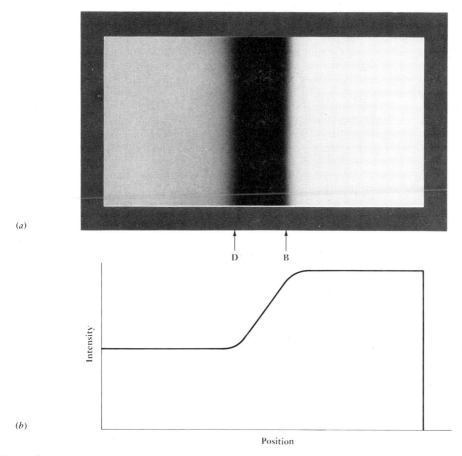

(a)

D   B

(b)

Position

Figure 4.7   A schematic representation of a ramp luminance profile (*b*), and a photograph showing the appearance of a Mach band (Cornsweet, 1970).

surrounded by a white background of the page, which forms another visual edge. That outside visual edge provides a greater luminance difference in contrast with the darker (that is the right) side, than with the lighter (left) side. It is those edges of different luminances that account for the overall appearance of the two parts. If the figure is made so large that its outer edges can not be seen, areas well away from the center edge do have the same brightness (Gilchrist, 1978).

The edge-enhancement processes can be seen in another way. Figure 4.9 sketches, in several steps, a luminous edge moving across an on-center, off-surround receptive field of a ganglion cell. In (*a*) the edge is well to the left of the cell; in (*b*) the lighter side of the edge is nearing the off-surround part of the recep-

tive field; in (*c*) the edge covers part of the off-surround but has not yet reached the receptors in the on-center, and so forth. Figure 4.10 shows the output of this ganglion cell as the edges move across it. In position (*c*) corresponding to Figure 4.9(*c*) above, the output of the cell shows inhibition because of the unequal stimulation between the two antagonistic regions, in this case more in the off-surround. In position (*d*) the two regions of the receptive field receive equal stimulation since the edge divided the receptive field exactly in half. By position (*e*), however, the two regions are again unequal, this time with more stimulation in the on-center than in the off-surround, and the output reaches a maximum. As the edge continues its progress across the receptive field, the output returns to its

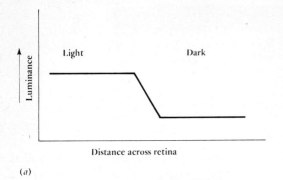

(a)

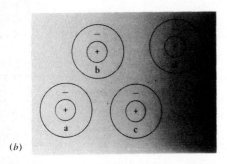

(b)

Figure 4.8 Illustration of how antagonistic center–surround receptive fields might account for Mach bands. In (a), a ramp luminance profile is shown as imaged over part of the retina. In (b) the antagonistic areas of fields (a) and (d) are equally illuminated and a minimal response occurs. In fields (b) and (c), the antagonistic areas are unequally illuminated, so that (b) should give a greater positive response than (a), and (c) a greater negative response than (d).

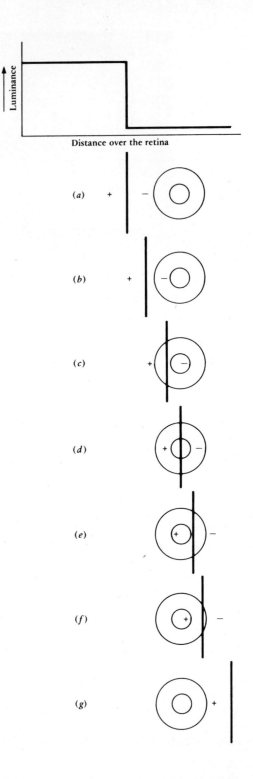

Figure 4.9 Seven successive alignments of a square luminance profile (shown in the top panel) as it moves from left to right across an on-center, off-surround receptive field. In (a), the edge is still entirely to the left of the field, by (c) the intense side of the edge covers part of the off-surround, in (d) the edge is centered on the field, by (e) the intense side of the edge covers mainly the on-center of the field, and by (g) the intense side of the edge completely covers the field.

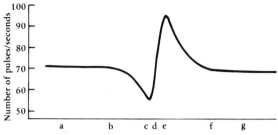

Figure 4.10 Measurements of the static response of an on-center ganglion cell to the movement of an edge across it. The edge is as in Figure 4.9, and the position indicated by the letters *a–g* refer to the successive frames of Figure 4.9. (Enroth-Cugell & Robson, 1966.)

spontaneous level as again the two antagonistic regions receive equal stimulation. Hence, the ganglion cell gives a double response to an edge as it sweeps across it, giving extra signalling to the dark side and to the light side. (If the ganglion cell in the example had been an off-center, on-surround or if the edge had moved in the opposite direction, the curve would have been inverted, but would have had the same shape.)

The visual system has another very important edge-enhancement process that also depends on inhibitory properties, especially of the type found in on–off receptive field organizations. Imagine a small spot of light that covers part of the center of a concentric on-center receptive field. This field provides a vigorous signal when the spot appears, and then returns to an activity level near its spontaneous rate. But as we know, the eye is not perfectly still. Drifts and micro-saccades shift the receptors of the eye relative to the retinal image by several receptors every 10 to 100 milliseconds. This change is irrelevant in the center of the spot of light, but at its edge it can move one side of the spot onto the antagonistic off-surround, which results in a sharp reduction of the activity of the ganglion cell whose receptive field is being stimulated. Of course, a few milliseconds later the eye moves back, creating a burst of activity in the cell in the opposite direction.

What these small eye movements do is to produce a continual signaling of the presence of the edge of a continuous spot of light even from a receptive field

organization that cannot respond to a steady state. These movements are very small, only on the order of a receptor or two, but they do provide a very powerful mechanism of edge enhancement.

Receptive Fields above the Retinal Level

The pioneering work in the discovery and mapping of cortical receptive fields has been done by two of Kuffler's students, Hubel and Wiesel (for example, 1962), using electrophysiological procedures with cats and monkeys. A number of investigators have demonstrated the existence of similar mechanisms in humans, using the psychophysical procedure of selective adaptation. Some of the results from each procedure will be described.

Ganglion cell receptive fields are nearly all concentric in shape, with the center excitatory and the surround inhibitory, or vice versa (Fig. 4.5). Such a receptive field is maximally sensitive to a small spot that falls entirely within the center or the surround without spilling over into the other part. Further, this type of field is summative, in that the energy in two spots that fall within the center are added together. But if one is in the center and one is in the surround, they may even cancel out, so the net response of the receptive field is zero.

As we have seen in Chapter 1, the next level in the visual system up from the ganglion cell is the terminus of the optic nerve in the lateral geniculate nucleus. When cells there have their receptive fields mapped, they have shapes and properties substantially similar to those at the ganglion level.

An optimal response from a ganglion or a geniculate cell usually depends only on the size, intensity, and location of a spot of light on the retina. If the spot is too large, the threshold for a response increases, but even diffuse light produces some response if the light is intense enough. This latter property is found less at the geniculate level, where the penalty for exceeding the critical size is more severe. But at both of these levels, only circular shapes have been discovered, and different directions of stimulus movement do not produce different responses. Thus, the specificity of the coding at these levels is not too great.

Most of the work of Hubel and Wiesel has been

with recordings of the receptive fields of cortical cells, and with these the patterns of coding are quite different. Cortical cells have been described as simple, complex, and hypercomplex, depending on the properties of their receptive fields. We shall briefly consider each type in terms of its shape and the types of visual features to which it is sensitive.

The **simple cortical cells** have antagonistic regions like the geniculate and ganglion cells, but their shapes are elongated rather than circular. Figure 4.11 shows several examples of simple cells. These, of course, respond to a spot of light anywhere within a single region, but the cell is obviously most responsive to an elongated stimulus, either an edge or a bar oriented in parallel with the axis of the receptive field of the cell. Thus, in cell (*a*) a maximal excitatory response occurs to a narrow lighted bar at 45 degrees to

the right, whose width matches the width of the on-center area. Cell (*b*) requires a dark bar on a lighted background. for an excitatory response. For most of the simple cells, misalignment by only 5–10 degrees no longer excites the cell. Notice that cell (*c*) is most sensitive to an edge separating two stimuli of unequal intensity. It does not matter what side is more intense, except that the polarity of the output is reversed. But the vigor of the response is the same.

All simple cortical cells respond to a moving stimulus, but the orientation of the direction of movement is critical and specific to the orientation of the receptive field. In most cases the direction of movement does not matter, except for a few fields that have some asymmetry in the flanking regions [cell (*d*)]. Some simple cells also have specificity with respect to the rate of movement. This occurs when there is

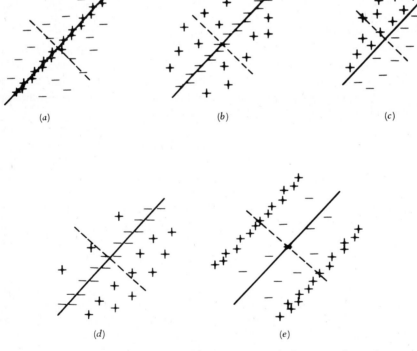

(a) (b) (c)

(d) (e)

Figure 4.11 Schematic representation of the receptive field shapes of several types of simple cortical cells. Plus signs indicate locations in the receptive field where stimulation increases the activity of the cortical cell, and minus signs indicate locations where activity decreases it. All examples are for diagonal orientation, but all other orientations have also been discovered.

marked variability in the width of the center region. For example, cell (*e*) responds more vigorously to a rapid movement because the three transitions from + to − and back to + are close together in time only with rapid movement.

It takes little imagination to describe these simple cortical fields as edge detectors and line detectors. They are sensitive to lines of specified widths and orientations, and edges of specified orientations. For most, the orientation and rate of movement is also specified. The sizes of these simple fields are relatively small, averaging about 2 degrees, with many as small as 15 minutes. They are found over most areas of the retina. Each field is specific to stimulation in its area—hence these can provide information about where a pattern is located on the retina.

While no direct physiological measurements have been made, several theorists (for example Robson, 1975) have suggested that the organization of the receptive fields of these simple cortical cells is determined by a combination of retinal ganglion cells feeding into them. Figure 4.12 illustrates one such suggestion. Simple cells, such as those in Figure 4.11(*a*), receive inputs from a number of ganglion concentric fields all with the on-center, off-surrounds antagonistic, all oriented in columns across one part of the

retinal surface. If a spot of light falls on any one of the on-centers, a small excitatory response occurs in the cortical cell. But the maximum excitatory response occurs if all of the on-centers are stimulated. This requires a bar of light at the proper orientation and at the proper width in that area of the retina.

The **complex cortical receptive fields** show two major differences from the simple cells. First, their fields are larger, averaging 5–10 degrees and often approaching 20–30 degrees. Second, while they are generally sensitive to the same kinds of features as the simple cells, it does not matter where in the receptive field the feature is placed. Thus, a field might be selective for a line 12 minutes wide at 45-degree orientation, but that line produces a large response when presented anywhere within the field. Such a field therefore remains a feature detector, but can specify only within a large latitude where the line appeared on the retina. As Cornsweet (1970) notes, the output of complex receptive fields directly codes slant, regardless of the location of the line on the retina.

The complex cells are also more responsive to movement than are the simple cells. Whereas simple cells do respond to a moving feature of the appropriate shape and orientation, they also do so when the feature is stationary. On the other hand, complex cells that respond to movement may not respond unless the target is moved (Hubel & Wiesel, 1968). Figure 4.13 from Hubel and Wiesel shows the orientation selectivity and movement selectivity of a complex cortical cell.

The **hypercomplex cortical cells** look as if they are the output of combinations of complex cells, in that they code combinations of stimulus features. For example, cells have been found that respond to the angles between two lines, rather than to the lines alone. Such cells are most likely to be found above area 17. These cells also are sensitive to the length of stimuli, since the response is often reduced when the line exceeds a certain length (Robson, 1975).

We have not said much about the obvious fact that mammals have two eyes. Hubel and Wiesel (1968) showed that most of the cortical neurons studied have connections from both eyes, though for simple cells one eye may dominate in influencing the ac-

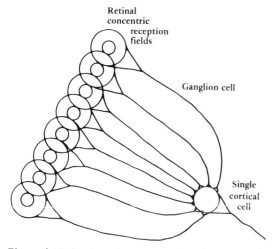

Figure 4.12 A schematic representation of how a number of ganglion cells might be connected to a simple cortical cell that would function as an edge or bar detector.

Retinal concentric reception fields

Ganglion cell

Single cortical cell

tivity of the simple cell. Moreover, Hubel and Wiesel (1970) have reported cells above the level of area 17 in the monkey that seem to be concerned with the similarity of the stimulation falling on the two eyes. Some of these cells respond only if the pattern on the two eyes falls on corresponding locations of each retina and do not respond if only one eye is stimulated, or if the patterns are not properly aligned. Other cells respond maximally only if the patterns on the two retinas are disparate—with different amounts of disparity producing maximum responses in different cells. This kind of coding could be the basis for binocular stereoscopic perception, as we will see in Chapter 11.

The receptive fields of cells at the ganglion cell level and at the lateral geniculate nucleus all tend to be circular so that they have no maximum response to one orientation of edge as compared to any other. At the cortical level, however, nearly all cells are orientation-specific. They respond less (or not at all) to some orientations of visual edges. Hubel and Wiesel (1968) showed that the cortical cells are arranged in columns, all the cells in a column responding to the same orientation, with the optimal orientation shifting in small steps from column to column. From this and other research, it appears as if the step size is about 15°, so that one column would be most responsive to lines of 30° off vertical, the adjacent column to 45°, and so forth. The data from Figure 4.13 earlier suggested that 15° is also about the range of sensitivity to orientation of a cell, so that its representation drops precipitously when the orientation of the luminance discontinuity is out of alignment by more than that amount on either side of its maximum.

Wavelength specificity will be the topic of central concern in Chapter 5, but it has some relevance here. In electrophysiological studies of the cat and of lower mammals nearly all the cells in the retina and in the cortex whose receptive fields have been studied give the same response to monochromatic light as to white light, and the pattern of antagonistic responses does not change much as the wavelength is altered. In the studies of monkeys—whose coding systems appear to be virtually identical to that of human beings—a substantial portion of the cells at the ganglion and geniculate levels, are selectively responsive to wave-

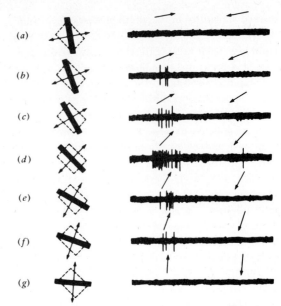

Figure 4.13 Responses of a complex cell in monkey striate cortex to various orientations of a black bar, as shown on the left. The receptive field is indicated by the dashed-line rectangles. The action potential records on the right indicate the number of spikes in a two-second interval. The arrow above each record indicates the direction the bar was moving during the period in which it was crossing the receptive field. Clearly, this cell is most sensitive to a bar in the orientation of panel (*d*), moving upward 90° to its orientation. (Hubel & Wiesel, 1968.)

length (DeValois & DeValois, 1975). At the ganglion cell level, the receptive field of the two antagonistic regions are each made up of cones with different spectral absorption functions. That is, they are selectively sensitive to quanta from different regions of the visible spectrum. As we shall see, this is the selectivity that provides the initial neural coding for color vision.

Since the visual system shows adaptation to light and, selectively, to color, one might expect that similar adaptation occurs for visual feature-detecting mechanisms. If this is the case, prolonged viewing of a stimulus consisting of a particular visual feature (lines of given widths, orientations, and so on) would render the visual system less sensitive to that feature in subsequent presentations. For example, Gilinsky and Cohen (1972) have shown that reaction times to a line of the same orientation as an adapting pattern are elevated by as much as several hundred milliseconds, compared to lines with different orientations. Comparable selective adaptation studies have been carried out for color-feature detectors (Harris & Gibson, 1968; McCollough, 1965) and for motion detectors (Sekuler & Pantle, 1967).

We have described receptive field organization as sets of structures tuned to certain visual features. There is a substantial amount of evidence for the existence of edge detectors that locate dicontinuities in luminance and may also respond specifically to orientation; line detectors, that can be specified in terms of their orientation and width; movement detectors for both edges and lines that describe the path of movement of a particular velocity and even acceleration. Binocular disparity may also be coded as a feature. In Chapter 5 we will see how color coding is handled by receptive fields of the lateral geniculate bodies. In addition, the location of a particular visual feature is indicated by the receptive field that signals it. Since receptive fields overlap a great deal, the same receptors are parts of hundreds of different receptive fields, each capable of representing a different aspect or critical feature.

The implications of these findings are that the activity of a single cell in the cortex can tell us about a retinal projection that represents the changing activity of millions of retinal receptors sampled over a long time. This type of specialization obviously represents a high level of complexity in coding, with an equally high saving in transmission load to the cortex.

Spatial Frequency Tuning

We mentioned in Chapter 1, (pp. 12–15) that a visual edge can be described either as a luminance profile of a particular steepness or as a composite of a number of underlying spatial frequencies—sine waves of different frequencies and amplitudes whose sum matches the shape of the profile. For the latter description to be useful, we need evidence, first, that the visual system is initially sensitive to the separate underlying spatial frequencies, and second, that the perception of a visual edge occurs because the separate spatial frequencies are then combined by the visual

system to reproduce the edge. We shall see that there is substantial evidence on the first point but virtually none yet on the second.

One of the most important experiments to demonstrate selective sensitivity to underlying spatial frequency is by Blakemore and Campbell (1969). They constructed stimuli consisting of alternating white and black bars in which the transition from black to white and back again was sinusoidal. Figure 4.14 illustrates two sinusoidal gratings. There are no abrupt transitions from white to black: rather the rate of change is specified by a sine function. The frequency of the grating is specified by the number of cycles (black–white pairs) per degree of visual angle. Viewed from 50 centimeters grating (*a*) has a spatial frequency of 20 cycles/degree, and grating (*b*) has a frequency of 3 cycles/degree. By way of comparison, grating (*c*) is a square wave grating, of five cycles per degree. Its transition from white to black is as sharp as can be drawn. The contrast of all three gratings in Figure 4.14 is the same, so that the difference in reflected light from the whitest part of the white and the blackest part of the black stripe is the same for each grating.

To demonstrate that the visual system is differentially sensitive to different spatial frequencies, Blakemore and Campbell ran an adaptation experiment. They reasoned that if there are separate neural networks—often called **channels**—in the visual system that encode each spatial frequency separately, then it should be possible to adapt selectively and thereby reduce the sensitivity of any one of those channels. To do this, they had subjects look at a very high contrast adaptation grating of a particular spatial frequency for several minutes. Following this adaptation, which in theory reduces sensitivity to that frequency, the subjects were shown brief presentations of several gratings that were very low in contrast, that is, the difference between the white and black was reduced so they were both barely different shades of grey.

Blakemore and Campbell found that after adaptation to a particular spatial frequency subjects needed more contrast to discriminate that spatial frequency from a uniform grey of the same average luminance. However, when tested on spatial frequencies that dif-

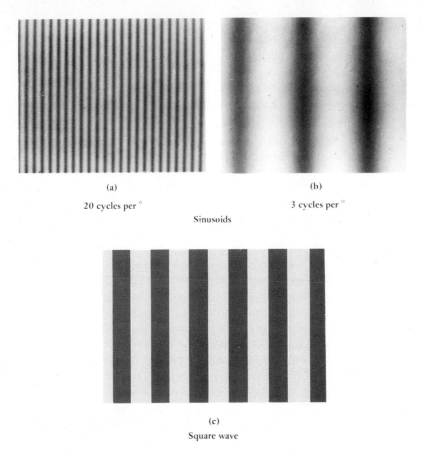

(a)

20 cycles per °

(b)

3 cycles per °

Sinusoids

(c)

Square wave

Figure 4.14 Examples of two sinusoidally varying gratings and one square-wave grating.

fered from the adaptation grating, subjects showed little loss in sensitivity. This was true for all the spatial frequencies they adapted.

This suggested to Blakemore and Campbell that a pathway of neurons is responsible for coding spatial frequencies of one cycle per degree, another channel for two cycles per degree, and so forth. If a channel is adapted, so that its sensitivity is lowered to subsequent stimulation, then a grating of that frequency has to have more contrasting light and dark areas to be detected.

It has also been shown that channels for spatial frequency are selective for orientation as well. If the test and adapting grid are of the same spatial frequency, but differ in orientation by more than about 15°, the adapting field has little effect on reducing the contrast sensitivity of the test field. It therefore ap-

pears as if there are channels specifically for each spatial frequency at each orientation.

Features or Frequencies In Chapter 1 we described how intensity discontinuities that make up edges and contours can be shown mathematically to be composed of a series of spatial frequencies. Are spatial frequencies another variety of visual features, or are they something different? The answer to this is not yet clear—again we are still too much in the middle of a rapid accumulation and change in research data to know the final story. There is rather clear evidence that the visual system detects bars of specific widths and orientations, and also that it detects grating patterns of specific spatial frequencies. It is possible that these are quite independent properties of patterns that the visual system is tuned to detect, but parsimony would suggest some relationship should be found between them.

We have much less electrophysiological evidence on the shapes of receptive fields for different spatial frequencies. Recordings taken by Robson (1975) from ganglion cells or at the lateral geniculate nucleus in cats indicate that some cells have receptive fields that are maximally responsive to a given spatial frequency and less responsive to both higher and lower frequencies. At these levels in the visual nervous system there appears to be no orientation specificity (Robson, 1975). It did not matter whether the bars making up the grating pattern were horizontal, vertical, or oblique. Presumably, this type of ganglion cell is responding to a group of concentric center-surround receptive fields in which the distance in any direction between the centers would give the frequency of the maximum response. Thus if a group of center–surround receptive fields are aligned so that their centers are 1 degree apart, then any ganglion cell fed by all these receptive fields respond maximally to a grating pattern in which the bars are one cycle per degree apart. Since the alignment might be in any direction, the orientation of the grating would be irrelevant.

However, Robson finds when recording from cortical cells that the orientation of the gratings is critical, just as we have seen from single bars or edges in the work of Hubel and Wiesel. Thus, he finds different cortical cells to have maximum responsiveness to gratings of different frequencies, but only when he has the orientation properly aligned. This suggests that the receptive fields for these cortical cells are alternating stripes of excitatory and inhibitory regions (Robson, 1975).

Robson mentions that the responsiveness of the cortical cell increases with the number of bars present in the grating, holding their spatial frequency constant. This suggests that for these cortical cells, the receptive fields are quite large, so that with more bars more excitatory and inhibitory stripes are covered, thereby yielding a larger response.

This work by Robson suggests the mechanism by which the visual system could code the spatial frequencies of luminance distributions in the retinal projection. The electrophysiological evidence from cats and monkeys strongly suggests that such coding takes place. Further, spatial frequency adaptation studies in man lend even stronger support.

What is not yet clear from the research to date is whether the visual system is triggered (a term suggested by Barlow, 1972) by certain visual features (that is, lines or motion) or by certain spatial frequencies, or whether these are simply different measures of the same thing. If the latter is the case, it has not yet been demonstrated. Further, while the trigger is based on frequencies, immediately present ecologically relevant aspects in the environment are picked up by the activities of a few cells in the visual system. Representation in terms of spatial frequencies would still require a spatial frequency analysis to construct the environmental features. There is yet no direct evidence that the visual system actually performs that kind of construction process.

Therefore, the argument that the visual system is a spatial frequency analyzer (Robson, 1975) is still speculative. Since the evidence continues to accumulate that cells in the cortex respond selectively to certain features and at certain spatial frequencies, it is inappropriate to choose between them at present.

THE PSYCHOPHYSICS OF EDGE DETECTION

Two principal techniques have been used to assess the resolving power of the visual system—its ability to detect the presence of visual edges in space (Thomas, 1975). The older one, called **visual acuity,** measures the smallest spatial pattern or detail that can be detected or resolved. The newer one, called **contrast sensitivity,** measures the minimal contrast needed to perceive a test pattern. We shall consider both in turn.

Visual Acuity

Figure 4.15 presents examples of the test patterns most used. In each case they are black on white with the contrast between the black and white areas made as large as possible. Typically this has been a reflectance ratio on the order of 95 percent to 5 percent, or about 20 to 1. To test the resolving power of the visual system, some relevant detail of the test pattern is made as small as possible to find a minimum

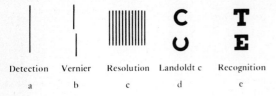

Detection	Vernier	Resolution	Landoldt c	Recognition
a	b	c	d	e

Figure 4.15 Examples of patterns used to measure visual acuity.

size at which it can just be resolved. This requires a frequency-of-seeing determination, and the threshold size is given as the visual angle of the detail that can be correctly detected 50 percent of the time. Figure 4.16 presents a frequency-of-seeing curve in which the threshold size, under these conditions of measurement, is 1.5 minutes of arc. If a standard nominal value is taken as 1.0 minute of arc, **visual acuity** is defined as the ratio of the standard size to the size obtained from a frequency-of-seeing-curve. In the case of the data in Figure 4.16, visual acuity is equal to $1.0/1.5 = 0.67$.

Figure 4.15 showed a number of different patterns. These correspond to different kinds of acuity tasks. Each of them will be described for the optimal condition of viewing to produce the best visual acuity.

Detection Acuity (Figure 4.15a)

The target is a thin black line seen against a white background under high illumination. The minimum

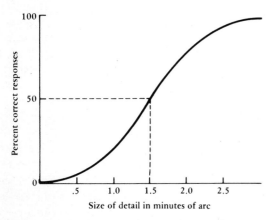

Figure 4.16 A frequency-of-seeing function for correct identification of recognition acuity targets.

width that can be detected and measured on a frequency-of-seeing curve yields the measure of acuity. Visual acuity reaches 120.0 using this method. That is, a wire ½ second of arc or 1/120 of a minute of arc can be detected 50 percent of the time (Hecht & Mintz, 1939).

Vernier Acuity (Figure 4.15b)

The perceiver is asked whether a line is continuous or offset. The threshold for perceiving the minimum misalignment approaches 1 second of arc so that visual acuity equals 60.0 (Berry, 1948). Since both detection and vernier acuity have such high scores—higher by a factor of 10 to 100 over the other measures of visual acuity—a very different kind of explanation for their effects is required.

Resolution Acuity (Figure 4.15c)

A grid of alternating light and black bars is used, in which the bars are varied in width. If they are too narrow the grid cannot be resolved and it appears a uniform grey. The threshold size of a single bar of a grid reaches 0.5 minute of arc for a visual acuity of 2.0 (Shlaer, 1937). It is possible to specify such a grid in terms of the number of alternating black and white bars per degree of width across the retinal image, that is, in terms of the spatial frequency of alternation. Using such a measure, if each bar is a 0.5 minute of arc at threshold, then 60 black/white cycles per degree can be differentiated from greyness at threshold or, put another way, the threshold is 60 cycles per degree.

The Landoldt Ring (Figure 4.15d)

The Landoldt ring is also used for resolution acuity. The target is a black circle with a gap so that the distance across the gap is 1/5 the outer diameter of the circle. The perceiver has to indicate by a forced choice indicator the position of the gap (north, south, east, or west) as the entire figure is reduced in size. The best visual acuity is about 2.5 for this pattern (Shlaer, 1937).

Recognition Acuity (Figure 4.15e)

This paradigm uses letters of the alphabet in which the width of the stroke, the length of the arm, or the gap between strokes, determines the feature sizes. These figures have gone through a number of standardizations (Sloan, 1951), the most common of which are used on the Snellen Eye Chart for clinical diagnosis of acuity. Visual acuity reaches about 2.0, that is, 0.5 minute of arc of detail with these measures (Ludwigh, 1941).

Recognition acuity is usually measured by the standard clinical eye charts used to assess the need for eyeglasses. It is not nearly so sensitive a test as detection, but it is much easier to administer and standardize, and is probably more relevant for the practical uses of visual acuity. Recognition acuity measures use a standard of a line 1.0 minute of arc, seen at 20 feet. This standard represents slightly poorer acuity than the very best (0.5 minute of arc), but for clinical purposes it is quite adequate. Acuity then is specified as the ratio of the standard distance (20 feet) to the distance of lines 1.0 minute wide that are recognizable. Hence, a very good acuity of 20/10 means that a line at 10 feet distance on a 1.0 minute arc, or 0.5 minute at 20 feet, would be recognized. This acuity is often stated as 2.0, or 200 percent. An acuity of 20/40 (or 50 percent) means that for you to see the line, it would have to be 1.0 minute at 40 feet, or 2.0 minutes at 20 feet. One is usually defined as legally blind with an acuity of about 5 percent, or 20/400. If your acuity is 20/30, you have a resolution of 1.0 minute of arc at 30 feet. An acuity of 20/10 is about the lower limit for recognition acuity in human observers.

Contrast Sensitivity

A second procedure for measuring the resolving power of the visual system is to determine the minimal contrast needed to perceive a test pattern. For example, instead of reducing the width of the bars in the grating in Figure 4.15(c), we could reduce the difference in luminance between the white and black stripes. The maximum contrast that is possible with a printed pattern of black on white is approximately 20 to 1, but if a positive transparency slide is constructed and light is projected through it, the range of contrasts possible goes up to 100 to 1 or more. A frequency-of-seeing function could be constructed for a grating of any spatial frequency by varying the contrast. The difference between the two luminances at

which the grid is resolved 50 percent of the time is considered the contrast threshold.

To have a measure of contrast that is independent of the actual luminances of light and dark bars Campbell and Robson (1968) defined contrast as the difference between the luminance of the white and black stripes divided by the sum of the two luminances. For example, if the white bars are 1000 and the dark bars are 100 candelas per square meter the contrast is 900/1100 or about 0.8. If the bars are 500 and 100 candelas per square meter then the contrast is 400/600 or 0.67. If the dark bars have zero luminance then the contrast is 1.0 for all values of the light bar.

Using this measure, Campbell and Robson (1968) found that for a grating of 1 cycle per degree, when the average luminance of the entire display was very high (500 candelas per square meter), the minimum contrasted needed to detect the grating was less than 1 percent. When the overall luminance level was four log units lower (0.05 candelas per square meter), then the minimum contrast needed to detect the grating increased to 2 percent. That is, the visual system was not as sensitive.

Figure 4.17 presents the results of the complete experiment. Each point on the graph presents the 50

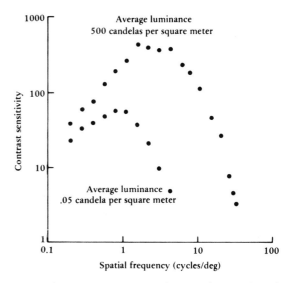

Figure 4.17 Contrast sensitivity functions for two values of average luminance. (Data from Campbell & Robson, 1968.)

percent point on one frequency-of-seeing function. These curves are called **contrast sensitivity functions.** They show several results. First, contrast sensitivity is greater for grids at intermediate spatial frequencies and decreases for either very coarse or very fine grids. There appears to be no way to resolve grids greater than about 60 cycles per degree no matter how great the contrast. Second, contrast sensitivity is greater for grids of high than of low average luminance. Third, when the average luminance is low, contrast sensitivity drops—especially for the very fine, high spatial frequency grids. Moreover, the peak sensitivity is now produced by coarser gratings.

Variables That Affect Sensitivity

Any factor that prevents sharp focus reduces acuity markedly. For individuals with poor accommodative responses, corrective lenses can usually be found to improve acuity.

All measures of acuity and of contrast sensitivity improve with increased luminance. In starlight (about 10^{-4} candelas per square meter), one can see the page of a book, but not whether it has letters on it or is blank. One can discern that there are letters on a page in moonlight (.01 candelas per square meter), but one cannot read those letters unless there are about 10 candelas per square meter. Figure 4.18 shows acuity as a function of luminance levels. There is relatively little change in acuity over the scotopic range of luminance levels, since not much acuity perception is possible with so little light. Only when the cones begin to function is there any improvement.

Pirenne (1967) has suggested two related reasons why an effect of luminance on acuity might occur. First, at low light levels, with quantal absorption quite low, the distance between receptors that actually absorb quanta is relatively large, making a rather coarse mosaic of active receptors. With high light levels, many more receptors are catching quanta, making the mosaic much finer. Since high resolution is helped by a fine mosaic of active receptors, higher luminance increases acuity. Second, given the convergence of receptors onto ganglion cells, when there are few quanta to be absorbed, only the ganglion cells with large re-

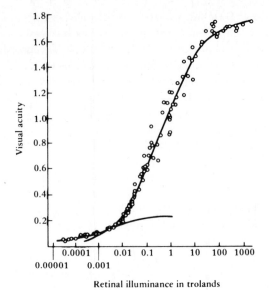

Figure 4.18 Visual acuity as a function of retinal illuminance, in trolands. (Hecht, 1934.)

ceptive fields are active since the smaller receptive fields do not catch enough quanta to excite their ganglion. At the higher light level, even ganglions with small receptive fields, that is, with few receptors feeding into them, become active. Under the reasonable assumption that small receptive fields are better for resolving fine detail, the higher luminances, which activate ganglions with smaller receptive fields, improve resolution.

One note about detection and Vernier acuity measures. Their limits are so much finer than that of the other measures that Hecht and Mintz (1939) argue that the detection is based entirely on the luminance discontinuity, without respect for the width of the lines—that is, their spatial frequency. They note that the linespread function does not decrease in width with progressively narrow lines; only the contrast is reduced. The minimum contrast between a black wire and a white background is about 1 percent, as estimated from the linespread function (Figure 4.1). As 1 percent is also the lower limit on the detection of a change in luminance ($\Delta L/L$), Hecht and Mintz argue that it is the latter process that limits detection acuity.

Figure 4.19 shows the sharp drop in acuity as a

function of retinal locus of stimulation—how far from the center of the fovea the acuity target is presented. Even within the fovea there is a significant reduction due to locus. This curve does not quite match the density of cones across the retina (see Figure 1.18, p. 19) nor the average size of receptive fields, though both variables must be involved. In any event, in a stationary eye, acuity is at a maximum only in the center of the fovea.

Pupil size produces several interacting effects. As the pupil increases in size, more light reaches the retina, which clearly improves acuity. Further, diffraction of light is much greater for very small pupil openings than for larger ones, so that larger ones produce sharper images. However, both of these benefits of large openings are offset by a degradation in the optical image due to spectral and chromatic aberration and errors of focus—all of which are far greater for light passing through the edges of the lens than through its center. A number of studies have shown that a pupil size between 2 and 4 millimeters in diameter (the smaller end of the overall range of 2 to 8 millimeters) provides the best acuity.

Eye movements affect acuity in two opposite directions. If the eye moves during the fixation on an acuity target, it blurs the retinal projection, thereby lowering the acuity. Conversely, if a luminance discontinuity that is produced by an edge moves back and forth over several cones, it helps to sharpen the dicontinuity, thereby increasing the chances of detecting it. Keesey (1960) stabilized the eye relative to acuity targets to prevent slight movements of the retina with respect to the edges of the targets. She found little change in visual acuity as compared to nonstabilized targets. It therefore appears as if these two effects cancel each other.

In sum, we have described five variables that are known to affect the ability of the visual system to detect luminance discontinuities: optical variables, intensity, retinal locus, pupil size, and eye movements. Some are related directly to neural coding processes.

CONTRAST—THE INTERACTION OF LUMINANCE AND EDGES

This chapter and the previous one have described the variables that affect detection of luminance and the

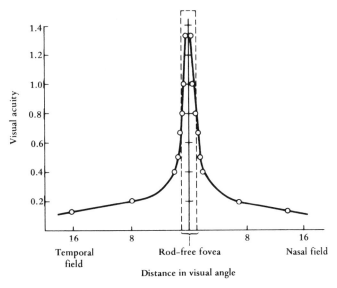

Figure 4.19 Changes in visual acuity for stimulation on different locations across a horizontal meridian of a human retina. (Alpern, 1962.)

variables that affect detection of edges. These two sets of variables interact in normal perception, however, in ways that are not predicted by the study of either alone.

The human visual system is not designed simply to detect the absolute values of luminance. Rather, it is most sensitive to changes in luminance, to edges that specify locations where the luminance level changes from one value to another. The **brightness** of the appearance of a surface in space is not determined by the absolute level of light reflected from it to the retina, but almost entirely by its relation to the amounts of light being reflected from surrounding surfaces. Brightness is determined by relationships between luminances, not by their absolute amounts.

The interactions do not end here. Edges are produced either when the retina receives light reflected from two adjacent surfaces in space, one with high reflectance and one with low, as in looking at a white wall with a black patch painted on it, or when looking at a uniformly painted white wall, half of which is in shadow from a light source illuminating the other half. Both edges are described in exactly the same way in terms of their retinal luminance profile. However, as Gilchrist (1977, 1979) has elegantly shown, these two types of edges, identical in their local properties on the retina, are treated on a vastly different way in our resulting perceptions. One tells us about the nature of the surfaces in the visual world and little about illumination, whereas the other tells us about the nature of illumination and little about the surfaces. As we shall see, the visual system has to have ways of telling the sources of these two kinds of edges apart.

Lightness and Brightness

One function of the initial coding of intensity may be to separate the information about illumination from the information about reflectance. The magnitude of illumination on the surface of an object varies in accidental and uncontrolled ways and is in no way predictive of the properties of the surface itself. On the other hand, reflectance contains information about the surface itself, irrespective of the momentary illumination that falls on it. The range of luminances due to reflection alone rarely exceeds about 30 to 1,

whereas the range due to illumination may be millions to 1. If the visual system rescaled everything in terms of the reflectances of surfaces, it would reduce the dynamic range of the signals needed to represent the visual world.

When we refer to the surface qualities of an object, especially the reflectances of its surface pigments, we need to measure its whiteness or greyness or blackness—all considered to be degrees of **whiteness** or **lightness.** A white piece of paper is whiter than a grey suit, which is whiter than a black lump of coal. The whiteness of an object is independent of the amount of illumination falling upon it—a white piece of paper should look white under dim illumination as well as under intense sunlight. Brightness, on the other hand, is a judgment made by perceivers about the appearance of the light that reaches the eye from a surface. As a judgment, it involves the effects both of reflectance and of illumination, whose product defines luminance (see Chapter 1, p. 9).

The receptors, as photodetectors, have no way to separate the luminance they receive into separate components of illumination and reflectance. Yet to make judgments about lightness—a characteristic of the reflectances of objects independent of the momentary illumination—the visual system has to discriminate the two. One way that has been proposed is to compare the luminance of a surface to the luminance of the background of the surface. Under normal conditions both are equally illuminated by any light source. If the surface has a reflectance different from that of the background or any neighboring surface, then a difference in luminance is due to differences in reflectances since the illumination is equal on each. In this way the differences in luminances (brightnesses) from different surfaces under uniform illumination specify the relative reflectances (lightnesses) of those surfaces.

We shall first consider the effects of a background upon the appearance of an object (contrast) and then use that process to understand the appearance of lightness independent of illumination.

Lightness Contrast

Contrast refers to the effects on the appearance of an object of neighboring objects. **Brightness con-**

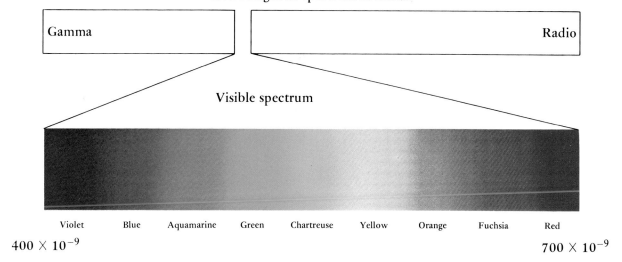

PLATE 1 The electromagnetic energy spectrum. The spectral hues associated with wavelengths in the visible portion of the spectrum are enlarged. A variety of color names usually associated with the perception of the different wavelengths is appended.

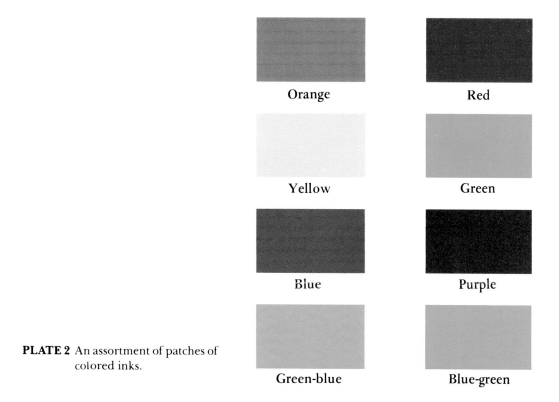

PLATE 2 An assortment of patches of colored inks.

PLATE 3 A circular arrangement of adjacent colored inks, grouped by similarity of appearance to each other.

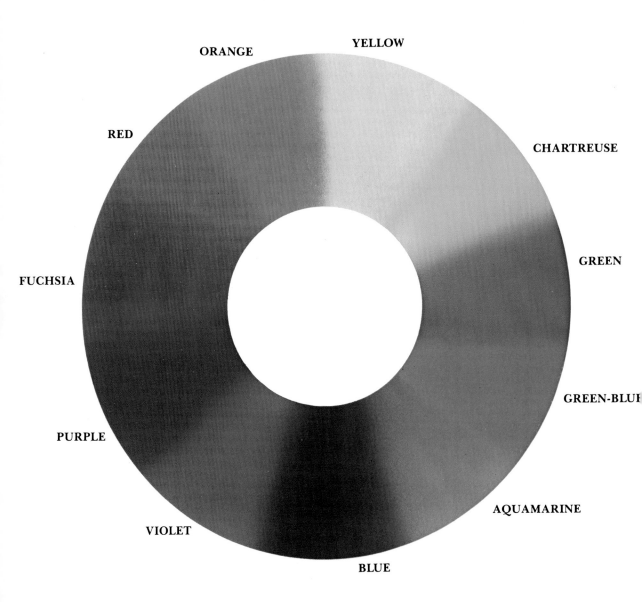

PLATE 4 A pointillist painting—Georges Seurat (1859-1891), The Bridge at Courbevoie. (Courtesy of the Courtauld Institute, London.)

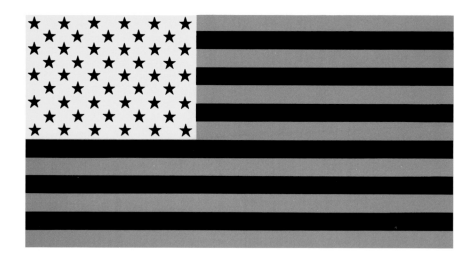

PLATE 5 Stare at the center of the red square, trying to hold your eyes still over the square as much as possible. After 30 seconds or more, move your eyes to look at a plain white surface. What do you see? Does it move when you move your eyes? Would you see it better if you stared longer at the red square? Now try this with the other two drawings on the plate. (See page 109 of the text.)

trast refers to the fact that the brightness of a surface is in part a function of the luminance of the background against which it is viewed. Thus, a piece of white (high-reflectance) paper viewed under fixed illumination appears brighter if placed next to a dark (low-reflected) surface than if it is seen against a high-reflectance background. Figure 4.20 shows an example of brightness contrast when one views a gray square against backgrounds of differing reflectances. Although the gray squares are all of equal reflectance, their brightness appears to differ substantially.

Wallach (1948) demonstrated this effect experimentally. In a dark room, a light source illuminated a white disk surrounded by a ring whose luminance was varied (Fig. 4.21). When the ring had a much higher luminance than the disk, the disk appeared black. As the ring's luminance was reduced, the disk's appearance increased in lightness until, when the luminance of the ring was set at a very low value, the disk appeared white. Wallach proposed a **ratio prin**-

ciple: the lightness of the disk is determined by the ratio of luminances of the disk and the surrounding ring. For example, a surface of a given luminance L_s appears whiter if the luminance of the background L_b is less, so that L_s/L_b is greater than one. If L_b exceeds L_s, L_s appears greyer or blacker depending on the magnitude of the ratio.

As a different kind of demonstration of contrast, Wallach presented two pairs of disks and rings to the viewer. The luminance of the left disk and ring was set so that their ratio was 2 to 1, a ratio that made the disk look fairly white. The luminance of the right disk was set at some other value and the perceiver had to adjust the luminance of the right ring until the two disks appeared to have the same lightness. Wallach found that the perceiver sets the variable ring on the right so that it has the same ring /disk ratio as the left pair. Thus, stimuli have equal lightnesses if the luminances are in the same proportion to that of the luminances of their backgrounds, irrespective of the absolute luminances.

The ratio principle of Wallach is important for the understanding of contrast effects. It shows that the four grey patches of Figure 4.20 appear to have different lightnesses because their luminance ratios with their respective backgrounds are different. But there are limits to the ratio principle. One limit is related to the appearance of the backgrounds. Each of the grey borders in Figure 4.20 is itself surrounded by white

Figure 4.20 An example of simultaneous brightness contrast when looking at a grey square against a lighter or darker background.

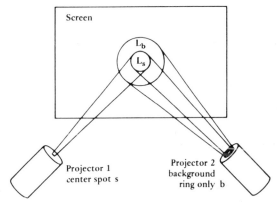

Figure 4.21 Schematic illustration of the procedure used by Wallach to study lightness contrast.

paper on several sides, and because there are no spaces between the four pairs of squares and surrounds, several of the surrounds are adjacent to surrounds of different luminances. Therefore, while we can measure the luminance of each surround, contrast effects work on them as well, so that their lightnesses are affected.

A second limitation is related to the way the illumination is presented. Katz (1935) presented a number of equally reflective grey papers to viewers, asking them to judge their lightness. The papers were on a background of fixed reflectance, but each paper was illuminated differently (Fig. 4.22). Even though the different illuminations produced different luminances, the ratio of the luminance of each paper to its background was constant, regardless of the absolute values of the four illuminations. As expected, the viewers judged each paper to be of the same greyness. However, when viewers were prevented from seeing the illumination on the background (viewing only the center of each paper through a peephole) so that they had no access to the luminance of the background, then the lightnesses judgments were really brightness judgments and were all different. They were determined only by the luminance from the paper. Therefore, lightness cannot be perceived as separate from brightness unless the background is visible and unless the viewer can see that the source of illumination on the surface in question is the same as that on the immediate background of the surface.

Both of these limitations restrict the usefulness of the ratio principle in explaining lightness constancy. This is particularly true when ratios other than those formed at the edge between the surface and its surround must be taken into account.

Contrast and Depth: The Coplanar Ratio Principle

Gilchrist (1977) has evidence that completely changes our concepts of contrast. In brief, he has shown that contrast occurs between two surfaces only if the surfaces are perceived to be at equal distances from the perceiver. If one is seen as farther away, even though still aligned with the nearer one, so that together they form a visual edge on the retina, no contrast occurs between them. Thus, contrast is not a property of visual edges on the retina but of visual edges in space. This is a distinction of fundamental importance.

Figure 4.23 shows the display that Gilchrist used. The subject looks through the peephole A through which he can see a dimly illuminated near

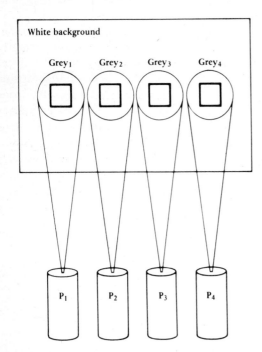

Figure 4.22 Schematic illustration of the procedure used by Katz to study lightness contrast.

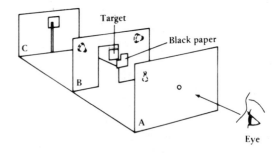

Figure 4.23 Sketch of apparatus used by Gilchrist (1977).

wall *B*. Through an opening in *B* he can then see an intensely illuminated far wall *C*. The target *T* of white paper is visible in the opening. The same type of white paper is also attached to the far wall visible through the opening in *B*. A piece of black paper is attached to the near wall next to the target. Figure 4.24 shows the appearance of the display to the observer when looking through the peephole. The target appears to be on the near wall beside the black paper and well in front of the paper on the far wall. However, on the retina the target is adjacent to both the black patch on the near wall and the intensely illuminated white patch on the far wall.

Subjects view the display and are asked to judge the lightness of the target by matching the lightness to one of a series of grey patches that differ in lightness from black to white. If contrast occurs between the target and the coplanar black patch the target should be seen as very light. But if the contrast is between a target and the very intensely illuminated white on the far wall, then the target should be perceived as dark grey. Gilchrist found in this condition that the target is matched to a patch of nearly the lightest white possible. Thus, a contrast ratio is computed across the coplanar reflection edge and ignored across the reflection edge in depth between the near target and the far wall.

In a second condition, the display is changed as shown in Figure 4.25. Notches are cut in the target so that it now appears to be at the same distance as the far wall, and not on the near wall. No change is made in the pattern of retinal intensities at all—only in the perceived depth, so that now the subject sees the target as next to the intensely illuminated white of the back wall. In this condition, the target is judged to be a very dark grey. Thus, a contrast ratio is taken across the other edge, which is now perceived to be a coplanar edge, and the reflectance edge between the target and the near wall is ignored.

Gilchrist argues from this study that Wallach's ratio principle applies only for surfaces perceived to be parallel and at the same distance, hence **coplanar**. This implies that the visual system first has to determine the distances and orientations of the surfaces, and only then is it able to interpret a visual edge between them on the retina. In other words, the visual edges on the retina are first used to construct a spatial map of the scene before the eyes (as we shall describe in Section II of this book). Only after this is done can the lightnesses of each of the surfaces in the spatial map be assigned as a function of the ratios of intensities of the surfaces at the same distances, but not according to the ratios formed by surfaces at different distances, or according to ratios across differences in illumination alone.

Lightness Constancy

If an edge on the retina is perceived to be an illumination edge, such as arises because of a shadow falling across a surface being looked at, then the luminance difference across the visual edge between them is ignored by the perceiver. No contrast occurs and the two areas appear to have the same lightness

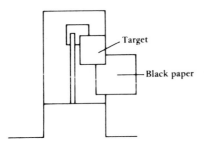

Figure 4.24 Appearance of the Gilchrist display when the target is arranged to appear to be coplanar with the near wall.

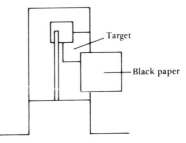

Figure 4.25 Appearance of the Gilchrist display when the target is arranged to appear to be coplanar with the far wall.

since they are in fact part of the same surface. When such perceptions occur we refer to them as examples of **lightness constancy:** regardless of the unequal brightness, the observer perceives equal lightness, so that the two parts of the surface appear to be the same.

However, when two surfaces of unequal reflection produce a visual edge, such as white paper on a grey paper background, lightness constancy requires that the unequal luminance is perceived as unequal lightness, so that the two surfaces appear different. If the illumination on both surfaces is perceived to be equal, then the lightness is determined by a ratio of the two luminances. This is the experimental demonstration provided by Wallach (1948). If the illumination is in fact not equal, but the viewer cannot determine that, as in Katz (1935—see p. 86), then he still pays attention to the ratio of luminances, which results in a misperception of lightness.

Until Gilchrist's experiments, all demonstrations of lightness constancy used displays in which the two surfaces meeting at the edge were coplanar, and where the edge in space was perceived to be a reflectance edge, whether it had been produced by papers of different reflectance or by different light sources projected on the same surface. Gilchrist's results now suggest that ratios of luminance across a reflectance edge occur *only* if the edge is perceived to be coplanar, but that no ratio is taken across edges at different depths.

The most important implication of this analysis is that lightness constancy cannot be explained simply by processes in the retina as they respond to a luminance discontinuity. As an example of such an attempt, Cornsweet (1970) has developed a model of brightness contrast leading to lightness constancy based upon lateral inhibition across areas of the retina receiving different amounts of luminance. He showed how it is possible for inhibition between adjacent areas to produce the equivalent of a ratio of luminances. The problem with his model, and all those like it that depend upon retinal mechanisms, is that the ratio-taking process occurs only for reflectance edges and not for illumination edges, and for reflectance edges only when the surfaces forming the edge are coplanar. Yet there is nothing in such models to indicate how those very peripheral inhibitory processes have access to in-

formation about the type of edge, and the depth differences in the layout of space. Therefore, it seems most unlikely that brightness contrast and lightness constancy are handled peripherally, as Cornsweet suggests. Ratio-taking may be the mechanism for lightness constancy, but only after edge information is processed.

Perception of Type of Edge in Space

We have distinguished four types of edges on the retina, depending upon whether they arise from a reflectance or illumination edge in space, and whether the two surfaces creating that edge in space are coplanar or not. While all four edges in space produce the same luminance discontinuities along the edge on the retina, they are perceived very differently in terms of the lightnesses of the two surfaces. How does the visual system tell these apart?

Two sources of information seem most important and most useful—information about the layout of space among the surfaces creating the visual edges, and about the pattern of intersection of the different edges that is presented at any one moment. The information about depth will not be discussed in detail until Section II of this book. We will show there that the perceiver has a great deal of information with which to determine whether any two surfaces in space are coplanar or not. In this way the two kinds of depth edges can be distinguished from the two kinds of coplaner edges directly. As we can see from the earlier discussion of ratio taking, if there is a difference in depth on either side of an edge, lightness can be determined from the luminances directly without taking the ratio across the edge. If the two surfaces on either side of the visual edge are parallel and coplaner, the edge may still be either a reflectance or illumination edge, so some additional information is needed.

The second source of information comes from the nature of the intersections of visual edges. Gilchrist (1977) has described in some detail how the intersection of coplaner edges differs depending on whether they are both illumination edges, both reflectance edges, or mixed. While the entire analysis has not been worked out yet, it seems likely that whenever intersections among several edges occur in a scene, no ambiguity would remain over which kind was which. In many laboratory experiments, such as those by Wallach (1948), there is no intersection information provided at all. Although there may be several edges, such as between a spot and a ring, and the ring and its background, none of these edges intersect each other. Apparently, without intersections, and without depth, perceivers cannot tell whether a visual edge on the retina arises from an illumination edge or a reflectance edge in space. Since normal scenes produce many intersecting edges, this ambiguity is removed.

A substantial research program is badly needed to demonstrate the ways in which the visual system does sort out these different kinds of edges. Trying to understand brightness contrast and especially lightness constancy by appealing to processing of luminance information in the retinas seems doomed to failure. Gilchrist's data strongly suggest that more complex mappings of edges are carried out before any absolute level of luminance is processed. We shall see this conclusion restated again in the next chapter on color, when we consider color contrast and color constancy. It will come up another time in the chapters on space perception, especially Chapters 9, 10, and 11, when we consider constancies of size, shape, and direction, There, too, we will see that local retinal luminance values play a very minor role in the perceptual outcome.

SUMMARY

A visual edge is defined both in space and on the retinal surface. While the visual system has access only to the latter, it is the former that is perceived. This chapter examined the ways in which visual edges on the retina are coded to perceive edges in space.

Two kinds of visual edges in space are distinguished; reflectance edges that arise from different reflectances of two adjacent surfaces; and illumination edges that arise from different amounts of illumination falling on adjacent parts of the same surface. Both of these create visual edges on the retina, separating two retinal areas receiving different amounts of luminance. The local projection along a retinal edge does not distinguish between the two kinds of edges in space, yet because those two kinds of edges provide very different information about objects in space, the visual system has to be able to tell them apart. The processes by which this is done concern this chapter.

Visual edges on the retina are degraded by the optics of the eye. This degradation is described by a line-spread function, showing both an increase in width of the edge and a decrease in luminance contrast across the edge.

Our concepts of the processing of edge information has undergone a revolution in the past 25 years. Before that time it was assumed that the retina encoded the retinal image point for point and transmitted that maplike representation to the cortex, where it was somehow decoded. But we now know that the retina does not create templates but is organized to extract detailed information from the image, particularly about the edges contained in it. This information appears to be both about specific visual features of the edges—orientation, width, length, movement and the like—and about the spatial-frequency components that make up the edges.

The basis for the newer concepts has been the discovery of how lateral or spatial inhibition interacts with spatial summation in the organization of the neural networks in the retina. We showed how inhibitory synapses co-occur with excitatory ones, and how their interaction provides a means to encode edge information. The basic unit in this coding is the antagonistic concentric receptive field of the ganglion cells of the retina. A receptive field is a map of those areas of the retina that when stimulated will produce a neural change. For the spatially opponent ganglion cells, the ganglion produces a different signal depending upon whether there is a decrement or an increment of light in the center as compared to the surround of its receptive field. It is this difference that produces edge enhancement and Mach bands.

Receptive fields of cortical cells have also been mapped. These are not concentric, but rather are generally elongated and larger than ganglion receptive fields. Furthermore, they appear to be specialized to respond to specific features of light patterns, especially movement, orientation, width, and wavelength. It has also been shown that they are sensitive to spatial-frequency components of edges, which are tuned not only to specific frequencies, but at specific orientations. Because there is sensitivity to both visual features and to spatial frequencies, we discussed evidence that the visual system detects and processes both, features and frequencies.

The most frequently used technique to study the psychophysics of edge detection is assessment of visual acuity—the smallest spatial pattern or detail that can be detected or resolved. A number of different acuity tasks have been developed, including detection and recognition. A second technique is to assess contrast sensitivity—the minimum luminance contrast between two areas in the pattern that can be detected. By this technique, the contrast-sensitivity function can be determined for patterns of different spatial frequencies and shapes. Edge detection, assessed by either technique, is affected by accommodation, by luminance, by retinal location and size of the acuity target, and by eye movements.

Evidence is presented that the visual system does not detect the absolute level of luminance, but rather is sensitive primarily to differences in luminance. But since a difference can occur as a result of an illumination edge or a reflectance edge, the resulting appearance of the luminance difference is not the same. The lightness of a surface of an object is independent of the amount of illumination falling on it, but rather is a property of the reflectance of the surface alone. To perceive lightness, it is necessary to compare the luminance of the surface against the luminance of a background illuminated by the same source. Wallach proposed a ratio principle to account for lightness, which involves taking into account the ratio or contrast across the edges.

Gilchrist, however, has shown that if the edges are perceived to be at different distances, no contrast occurs. Contrast ratios therefore cannot be determined at the retina, or at least not before the relative depths or distances of surfaces are determined. More specifically, whether the ratio principle is used or not to perceive lightness depends upon perceiving the nature of the visual edge in space—whether it bounds surfaces of equal or of different distances. Several techniques are discussed by which the visual system may be able to make these distinctions. The fact that these have to be done further illustrates the interactions of intensity and edge coding, and suggests the relative importance of edges in visual processing.

SUGGESTED READINGS

Two of the chapters in Carterette and Friedman (1975) are excellent resources: Robson (1975) and Thomas (1975). Cornsweet (1970) also has a fine discussion of inhibitory mechanisms. For more specific references on lateral inhibition, the two best sources are Ratliff's book on Mach bands (1965), and von Bekesy's book on sensory inhibition (1967). A more technical one is Fiorentini (1972). Dodwell (1971) has collected many papers on sensory coding of pattern, and many of the advanced chapters in Rosenblith (1961) are excellent, especially those by Boynton; Barlow; Rushton; and Lettvin, Maturana, Pitts, and McCollough. The best discussion on visual edge classification is in Gilchrist (1979) and Haber (1979). See Kaufman (1975) for discussion of contrast, as well as Rock (1977).

Chapter 5

Perception of Color

Color is a pervasive part of our normal perceptual experience. Color affects our ability to differentiate among objects, but in addition it changes our moods, feelings, and preferences, and influences our esthetic experiences as can no other single aspect of vision. Most people assume that "color" is synonymous with "hue"—the perceptual quality that differentiates the experience of red from green, yellow, blue, and so forth. As we shall see, there is more to the perception of color than the experience of different hues. But the perception of hue does represent the most important aspect of color perception. In fact, it is often the first attribute that we notice in our perception of objects, and it often appears to be more salient than size, shape, location, or function.

Color can be defined relatively simply as follows: "Any noticeable difference between two fields of luminance other than spatial, temporal, or intensity variation is due to difference in color." One can demonstrate this by presenting two different wavelengths of light in two halves of the visual field. If without changing wavelength there are no adjustments that a normal perceiver can make to either half of the field that make the two sides appear alike, we can say that two different colors have been perceived.

Most people believe that perceived colors originate in the pigments and textures of the surfaces of objects—that colors have nothing to do with the light incident to the surface or with the photoreceptors transducing that light reflected to the eye. In fact, it was not until Newton's discoveries, about 1700, that we had any knowledge of the role of light in the transmission of information about color. We now know that it is the property of light called wavelength that is the carrier of color information.

In this chapter we first consider the prerequisites for the perception of color. Using these prerequisites as a guide, we examine the physical dimensions of light and of objects that lead to the perception of color, and then the dimensions of that color experience. We devote substantial space to the receptor processes underlying color perception and color coding beyond the receptors. In the last section we examine a number of phenomena of color perception, including adaptation, contrast, constancy, and color-defective vision.

PREREQUISITES FOR THE PERCEPTION OF COLOR

Boynton (1971) distinguishes five prerequisites normally needed for the perception of color. First, the wavelengths of the light sources illuminating the visual world must vary. Second, the spectral reflectances from surfaces and objects must vary. Third, at least two receptor processes are needed that differ in their absorption of various wavelengths that comprise visible light. Fourth, the receptor processes must transmit information to the cortex in such a way as to preserve the spectral composition of light reaching the receptors. And fifth, there must be separate and unique perceptual experiences attached to this information reaching the cortex. We will discuss each of these prerequisites in turn, several of them in detail.

It seems obvious to the naïve observer that colors are on the surfaces of objects. To say that color is an experience in the visual system only seems meaningless. But we have already observed other visual properties of objects that are not part of the objects themselves. For example, the brightness of an object is at least in part a function of its reflectance—the proportion of incident light that is reflected to the eye. The light is not on the surface or in the surface. We can know nothing visually about objects except insofar as light is reflected from them and collected in our eye so that photoreceptors are excited. So it is with color. Red is not on the surface of an apple nor in the quanta of light themselves. Rather, it is a perceptual experience that arises as a function of particular properties of light reaching the receptors and selectively exciting different types of receptors whose responses are, in turn, encoded selectively.

Wavelength: The Stimulus for Color

We noted in Chapter 1 that physicists describe electromagnetic radiation in terms of its energy and its wavelength. So far we have focused primarily on its energy component, as specified in quanta. But all electromagnetic radiation can also be thought of as traveling in rays or waves. The waves have a frequency, specified by the distance from wavecrest to wavecrest, usually measured in meters. Color plate 1 shows the entire spectrum of electromagnetic radiation, with gamma and X rays at the short end and radio waves near the long end. Different parts of the human body are responsive to several sectors of this spectrum. Only the photoreceptors embedded in our retinas, however, have evolved photochemical sensors that produce a neurochemical response to a narrow range of electromagnetic radiation. This range is called the **visible spectrum,** or **light.** It is enlarged in Plate 1 to show the range more clearly.

The physicist Newton first reported evidence on the wave properties of light. He discovered that a very narrow beam of intense sunlight produced a rainbow of colors after passing through a wedge-shaped prism. Figure 5.1 illustrates Newton's demonstration, which can easily be repeated with a prism and a source of white light. If bright sunlight is directed through a narrow slit and then through the prism, the different wavelengths are differentially refracted, separating

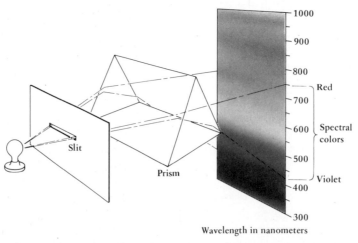

Wavelength in nanometers

Figure 5.1   Refraction of light by a prism into its component wavelengths.

the light of different wavelengths into different pathways. The result is observed by directing the light onto a screen. Without the slit, a number of partially overlapping spectra are produced and only their edges will show color. Another commonly observed example of the visible spectrum is the rainbow. It is caused by the refraction of sunlight through raindrops.

The colors seen are called **spectral colors.** They are separated because light waves are bent or refracted when passing from one medium (air) to another medium (the glass of the prism) of a different density. The angle by which they are bent is a function of their wavelength, with the shorter wavelengths bent more than the longer ones (Fig. 5.1). The separated wavelengths can be refocused by a lens so that they are recombined into light that again appears white (Fig. 5.2). The combination is accomplished by the same process—differential refraction as a function of wavelength.

Light from the sun contains radiation of all wavelengths in the visible spectrum as well as outside it at longer and shorter wavelengths. Other light sources differ in their spectral composition—they radiate different wavelengths depending on the method by which the radiation is generated. Mixing wavelengths of light results in properties that are different from other wave mixtures with which we may be familiar. In the case of white light, a physical device is always necessary to make the different wavelengths perceptible. No amount of practice or attention will permit us to see the different wavelengths in a mixture such as white light. In contrast, we can easily perceive the different wavelengths in a mixture of sound waves. The mixture is not a single sound but a chord, made up of perceptually separable tones.

White light can be separated into its component wavelengths and then recombined over and over again. This process is limited only by the precision of the refracting surfaces of the prisms and lenses and of the media through which the light travels. Mixing paint pigments is different, however. Pigments can also be mixed to form new colors, but once mixed, they can never be separated back into their original colors.

The optical **filter** is another means of separating wavelengths of light. It is a device that selectively passes some wavelengths while absorbing others. In principle, optical filters can be **monochromatic,** so that they transmit only a single wavelength of light. In practice, however, even the best filters pass a narrow band of wavelengths. Thus, the reference to monochromatic light in this chapter (and throughout the book) should be understood to mean light within a narrow range of wavelengths. For example, a 500-nanometer filter may pass wavelengths from 495 to 505 nanometers and no others. Since wavelengths within this band appear green, this is called a "green" filter.

Reflectance of Surfaces

We noted in Chapter 1 that virtually all the light that reaches our eyes is reflected from nonradiating surfaces. We observed that the luminance of a surface is a function of its reflectance. Different surfaces reflect and absorb different wavelengths of light in different amounts, depending upon the molecular structure of the surface. Some surfaces absorb most of the wavelengths that reach them. These surfaces appear black. But even the flattest, blackest surface will reflect 3 or 4 percent of the incident light. Usually any surface

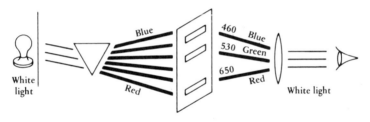

Figure 5.2 Illustration of a prism refracting white light into separate wavelengths, and a lens refocusing it into white light.

that reflects less than 10 percent of the incident light looks black.

Most surfaces reflect wavelengths differentially. Figure 5.3 shows examples of several different spectral reflectance distributions. The appearance of these surfaces can be predicted from these functions. A surface that primarily reflects long wavelength light (when illuminated by white light), appears red in color because the light that reaches our eyes is limited to those wavelengths that produce the perception of red. Thus,

surfaces "select" wavelengths, reflecting some while absorbing the rest. This selectivity determines the colors of surfaces.

We have now considered Boynton's first two prerequisities for the perception of color. Before turning to the remaining prerequisites we will briefly examine the ways in which our experience of color is described. This information is used to explain the effects of mixing different wavelengths.

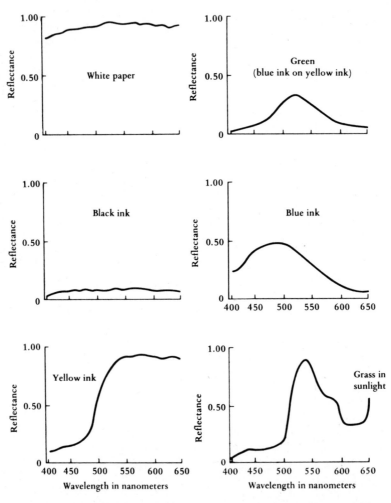

Figure 5.3 Several examples of spectral reflectance distributions that result when white light is reflected from different colored inks on white paper (Pirenne, 1967) and from grass (Cornsweet, 1970).

DESCRIBING COLORS AND COLOR PERCEPTION

Before we begin the formal description of color perception, let us consider colors from several different points of view. Look at the assortment of patches of pigments in color plate 2 and try to order them according to similarity. It turns out that almost all people (except those who are color blind—see below) order the pigments in the same way. For example, orange and red are treated as similar and so are placed next to each other: yellow is similar to orange so it is placed next to orange. But orange is more similar to red than yellow is, so orange is placed between red and yellow. By continuing these comparisons, green will be placed between yellow and blue, blue will be placed between green and purple, and purple between blue and red. This procedure generates the circle of pigments shown in color plate 3).

But the circle, so constructed, does not use up all our imaginary patches. What do you do with the pink or the brown? While viewers agree that pink is related to red, it is different from the red pigment because it looks less intense. The brown does not resemble any of the patches, nor does it appear to be a mixture of any of the colors. The royal blue is like the blue but somehow more intense. Finally, the pale yellow is like the pure yellow except that it looks less pure—as if a lot of white pigment had been mixed with the yellow.

These remaining patches of pigment can be represented along with those forming the circle by using two more dimensions. One way some of the patches differ is that they appear as if some white pigment had been mixed in, effecting what is called **saturation.** If all the colored patches in the rim of the circle represent the same amount of lightness, then the radius from the perimeter in toward the center can be used to represent decreasing amounts of saturation. The very center is that degree of greyness in which there is not even a hint of hue. The degree of lightness can be represented by different color circles stacked on top of each other. This creates the color solid illustrated in Figure 5.4. The position of each patch of pigment can then be described in terms of its hue, its saturation, and its lightness.

But our major concern is with light rather than with pigment, because it is light, not pigment, that reaches the eye. Fortunately the same kind of similarity ordering can be performed with lights of different wavelengths, intensities, and purities, so that the resulting color solid for light is the same as the one for pigments.

When intense sunlight is passed through a prism and imaged on a white screen, the hues in the spectrum of light are arranged in the order of red to orange to yellow to green to blue. The hues change continuously, that is, without discrete jumps or gaps. Nevertheless, we label certain places along the spectrum, as illustrated in color plate 1. For example, between yellow and green, there is a hue often called chartreuse. If the sunlight is intense, then all the hues are light. With a less intense light source, the hues are

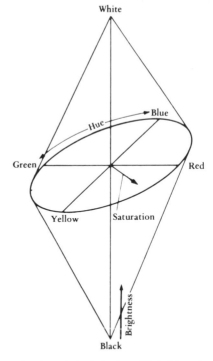

Figure 5.4 A psychological color solid (Judd & Wyszecki, 1952). Only one slice through the solid is illustrated, representing a color circle of intermediate brightness. On this one slice, hues vary around the perimeter, and saturation varies by the distance from the center.

darker. If some sunlight illuminates the screen directly, white light is added and each of the spectral hues look less saturated. In this way, the same dimensions that permitted the construction of a solid for pigments can be used for light—hues are distributed around the perimeter of each layer in the stack, each layer represents a different lightness, and the distance from the center to the perimeter on each layer represents the degree of saturation.

Luminance and Brightness

As noted in Chapter 1, the relation between luminance and brightness is not perfect, especially when wavelength is varied. There are two independant reasons for this. The energy in each quantum is a decreasing function of the wavelength of the radiation. Thus, each quantum of light from the short wavelengths has nearly twice the energy of a quantum from a long wavelength. Further, the photoreceptors are not equally sensitive to all wavelengths. Hence, both the energy in the quanta and the sensitivity of the receptors differ as a function of wavelength.

The sensitivity of the receptors to quanta of different wavelengths is described by a **spectral sensitivity function.** The procedure for deriving the function involves presenting a small bipartite field (usually about a 2-degree spot) that is divided in half, with each side illuminated separately. One side contains a standard energy value of a given wavelength. The perceiver adjusts the energy of the other side for each wavelength presented until the two sides look equally bright. The observer is told to ignore differences in hue or saturation in making his match. Figure 5.5 shows the average foveal spectral sensitivity function for a typical normal observer. (The function is an average over the three cone types that form an integral part of the mechanism for coding wavelength—see below.) The ordinate is the relative sensitivity of the eye to each of the wavelengths shown on the abscissa. The wavelength of the greatest sensitivity is given a value of 1.0 and all others are proportionally less. The cones in the fovea absorb light of all wavelengths in the visible spectrum, but they are most sensitive to wavelengths in the middle of the spectrum, around 555 nanometers, and are much less sensitive to wavelengths below approximately 500 and above 625 nanometers. For example, a light of 480 nanometers has only 20 percent of the luminance of a 555-nanometer light. To make these two wavelengths appear equally bright, five times as much 480-nanometer light has to be presented.

Figure 5.5 shows the sensitivity of foveal cones. Since there are no rods in the center of the fovea, this function is uncontaminated by the spectral sensitivity of rods. It is very difficult, however, to measure the spectral sensitivity of rods without some cones being involved, because no part of the retina is free of cones. Rod spectral sensitivity is measured by first adapting

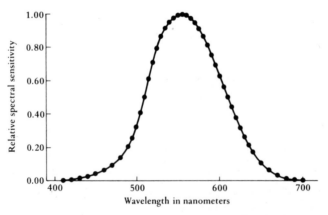

Figure 5.5 A foveal cone spectral sensitivity function for a normal observer.

the cones to high-intensity light, and then examining the rod spectral sensitivity function with low-intensity light that is below the cone threshold. The adapting light is directed through the center of the pupil, maximizing the probability of its being absorbed by cones. The light used to measure the spectral sensitivity of the rods is directed to enter the eye near the edge of the pupil, making it less likely to be absorbed by cones (because of the Stiles-Crawford effect—see p. 55).

Figure 5.6 presents the results of such measurements. The rods also have a spectral sensitivity function that covers the entire visible spectrum, but their greatest sensitivity is to wavelengths shorter than those of the cones. The entire rod function is shifted toward the shorter end of the spectrum by about 50 nanometers. Thus, the probability that a quantum is absorbed by a rod depends on the wavelength of that quantum.

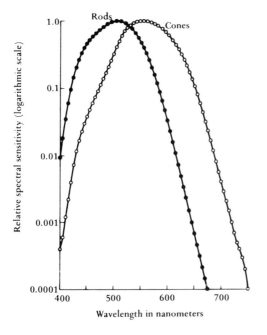

Figure 5.6 Spectral sensitivity function for rods in the periphery of the retina and for the foveal cones. The ordinate is plotted in the logarithm of relative sensitivity, which illustrates the sharp decrease in sensitivity to long and to short wavelengths.

One way of observing the difference between the rod function and the average cone function is to see what happens to the perception of the brightness of colors with rods and with cones. Since Purkinje (1825) first reported this effect, it is called the **Purkinje shift.** Select two wavelengths that look equally bright when viewed with cones, say a 500-nanometer (blue-green) light, and a 620-nanometer (red-orange) light. Both have a 40 percent relative spectral sensitivity (Fig. 5.6) for the cone function. If the overall luminance is lowered, so that the brightness discriminations are now being made by the rods, the 500-nanometer light looks much brighter than the longer wavelength light. Purkinje noticed this with flowers. In bright daylight a red and a blue flower might appear equally bright. At twilight, although both look less bright, the blue ones seem much brighter than the red.

Dominant Wavelength and Hue

In addition to the luminance–brightness dimension, light can be described in terms of its spectral composition and its corresponding hue. Whenever we name a color by its appearance, we are referring to its **hue.** When a number of wavelengths are mixed together, and the resulting light has no dominant wavelength, its hue is white or gray. As soon as one wavelength is more heavily represented than any other, the light takes on the appearance of color, or hue. For example, light of 650 nanometers has a red hue; while light of 450 nanometers has a blue hue.

What happens to the appearance of light when different wavelengths are mixed together? Most demonstrations and experiments in which lights of different wavelengths are mixed (called **colorimetry**) use selective filters that pass a narrow band of wavelengths of light. Such experiments have been known for centuries, but it has only been in the last 100 years that a rational scheme for their understanding has begun to develop. Nevertheless, no system of describing colors has been able to account for all the phenomena of the perception of colors (see Boynton, 1979, for a description of the principal systems).

Purity and Saturation

The final pair of descriptors is the purity of the spectral composition and the resulting subjective experience of saturation. A pure light is one with a narrow band of dominant wavelengths, with little white light mixed with it. This gives the appearance of great saturation. The spectral colors are the most saturated ones obtainable, but they differ from one another in their appearance of saturation even at their state of complete purity. Spectral red looks very saturated. If white light is added it looks pink. The more white light that is added, the more desaturated it becomes, until, with a sufficiently large amount of white, all traces of hue disappear. Much more white light must be added to spectral blue or spectral red than to spectral yellow to produce complete desaturation. Hence, spectral yellow is considered less saturated. In fact it is very difficult to get a yellow to be as saturated as red under any circumstances.

MIXING LIGHT

Newton was the first person to mix light of different wavelengths to see what hues resulted. He demonstrated that white sunlight was a mixture of all the visible wavelengths that could be perceived separately and that the light could be recombined with a lens to produce white light. He also noted that if light of three wavelengths that are fairly far apart (corresponding to hues of red, green, and blue, for example) is focused so that the three wavelengths illuminate the same area of a screen, the illuminated patch looks white or grey. In fact, by suitably adjusting the intensities of the three wavelengths, he could create any hue he wanted on the screen. Finally, Newton showed that there are certain combinations of only two wavelengths that yielded white or grey when mixed.

With these demonstrations in mind, the facts of mixing light can be described using the **color solid** of Figure 5.4. Figure 5.7 shows one slice of the color solid with the different hues arranged around the circle so that any two wavelengths exactly opposite each other produce white or grey when mixed in equal amounts. This is a psychological color circle.

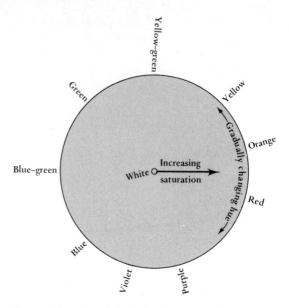

Figure 5.7 A psychological color circle, one slice from a color solid, such as shown in Figure 5.4.

Pairs of wavelengths whose mixture produces white and grey are called **complementary hues.**

When the hues are arranged around a color circle in this way, we can predict what a mixture of any two or more wavelengths will look like. As a general rule, mixing any two wavelengths results in a hue intermediate between them, but one that is less saturated than either. To determine the outcome more precisely, one can draw a line between the points on the perimeter representing the two wavelengths to be mixed (green-blue and red in the example in Figure 5.8). The resulting mixture of these two wavelengths is a color somewhere along the line connecting them, its precise location on the line depending upon the relative intensities of the two lights. If white light is passed through a red filter and a bluish-green filter, and these two lights are projected onto the same area of a screen, the hue on the screen is yellow, except that the mixture is much less saturated than a spectral yellow of the same wavelength. To get a perfect match with a spectral yellow of that wavelength, some white light has to be added to the spectral yellow.

If the mixture of red and blue-green contains more red than blue-green the mixture is much closer

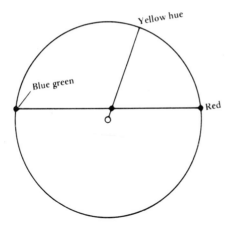

Figure 5.8 An example of how a color circle can be used to predict the appearance of an equal mixture of two wavelengths.

to red (Fig. 5.9). If the two wavelengths being mixed are opposite to each other, the line connecting them passes through the center of the circle; equal amounts of the two produce white or grey. If the mixture is unequal, the result has the hue of the more intense wavelength, but it is much less saturated than the lights being mixed.

If light of a third wavelength is added, the resulting hue of the mixture can also be predicted from the color circle. Connect the three wavelengths by lines as in Figure 5.10, to form a triangle. Any color located within the boundaries of the triangle can be

created by adjusting the relative amounts of each of the lights. Any resulting mixture is always less saturated than any of the hues on the rim of the circle. If the three wavelengths chosen are approximately equally spaced around the color circle, the triangle will include the center of the circle, so that mixing equal amounts of the three yields white light.

The gap in the circle between blue and red is labeled "purple," which is not a spectral color. It cannot be produced by refracting light through a prism, so it does not correspond to any particular natural wavelength. Yet we do see purple. The color circle shows why. Purples are produced by mixing blue and red of various proportions. Thus, in order to produce the hue complementary to green, red and blue must be mixed first.

The color circle, a slice from the color solid, is a means of describing hues and saturation. The descriptions based on these representations are quite accurate but not perfect—the predicted hue is often less saturated than the obtained one. This suggests that the shape of the perimeter of the color "circle" is not circular. There have been some very successful attempts to work out better shapes so that the predicted appearance of the mixture agrees with the obtained appearance (see Boynton, 1979).

The mixture of lights is an **additive color mixture**; the mixture of pigments is **subtractive**. The

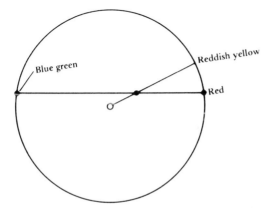

Figure 5.9 An example of prediction from a color circle when the mixture of wavelengths is not equal.

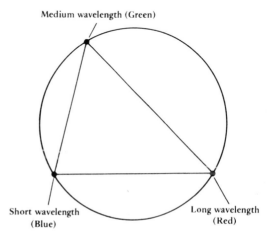

Figure 5.10 An example of prediction from a color circle using three different wavelengths.

hues associated with these subtractive pigment mixtures result from the light reflected from pigmented surfaces. When a surface painted with yellow paint is illuminated with white light, the surface absorbs most of the short wavelengths and reflects the long ones. The surface appears "yellow" because it is the hue resulting from the mixture of the green, yellow, orange, and red light that reaches the eye. Thus, in a sense, by absorbing the blue and blue-green wavelengths, the yellow paint subtracts them from the white light. Conversely, if white light is reflected from blue paint, it appears blue because blue and green are reflected and the long wavelengths are absorbed. (Figure 5.3 contains some spectral reflectance profiles from several different pigments.) If blue and yellow pigments are mixed, and a surface coated with the mixture is illuminated with white light, both the very short and the very long wavelengths are absorbed and therefore subtracted from the reflected light. The only wavelengths reflected are those in the middle, and the surface appears green. If we could construct a blue pigment that reflects only wavelengths from, say 400 to 460 nanometers, and a yellow pigment that reflects only wavelengths from 520 to 590 nanometers, a mixture of these two pigments would appear black because there is no overlap in the reflectances of the two pigments. All wavelengths would be absorbed or subtracted out. Such narrow reflective profiles are very difficult to produce. It is therefore difficult to make black by mixing paints.

Most artists use the subtractive procedure—that is, pigment mixing—to obtain the hues they need. However, there was a group of painters, the pointillists, who used additive methods. An example of a pointillist painting is shown in color plate 4. If you look closely, you can see that the painting consists of a collection of dots of pigments. Each dot reflects its characteristic hue—yellow dots reflect yellow light, blue dots reflect blue light. If you view the painting from a sufficient distance these two reflected colors are added and the area where the two are intermingled appears grey. The pointillist artist achieved a mixture that looks green by following the rules of color plate 3 and selecting hues on either side of green, but not so far away that they are complementaries.

CODING OF COLOR

Boynton's third prerequisite specifies that there must be two or more receptor processes that differ in their absorption of the various wavelengths. A photoreceptor collects quanta—any kind of quanta. It is a nonselective radiation detector in the sense that its response contains no information about any of the properties of the quantum that excited it. Its response is the same whatever the wavelength of the quantum. But quanta of different wavelengths have different probabilities of being absorbed. We saw this in the spectral sensitivity function in Figure 5.5.

Although the data in Figure 5.5 are based on a psychophysical experiment, they also represent the absorption function of a receptor, showing the percentage of quanta absorbed (or the probability of absorbing a single quantum) at each wavelength relative to the amount absorbed at the wavelength of greatest sensitivity.

If all receptors had the same absorption function, different wavelengths would produce only brightness differences, not hue differences. In order for receptors to respond differentially to wavelength, they must have different spectral sensitivity functions. Figure 5.11 is an example—two separate spectral sensitivity

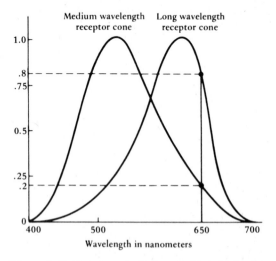

Figure 5.11 Two hypothetical spectral sensitivity functions: one for receptors maximally sensitive to long wavelength light; the other to medium wavelength light.

functions, one for a receptor system most sensitive to long wavelengths and another to medium wavelengths. Both curves extend over the entire visible range, but they absorb wavelengths in different amounts. As the wavelengths of the quanta change, there is a change in the relative output of the two receptor systems. For example, a quantum of 650-nanometer light has four times as much chance of exciting a long-wave receptor as it does a medium-wave receptor. Conversely, a 500-nanometer quantum is much more likely to be absorbed by a medium- than by a long-wave receptor. In the example here, the resultant hue is related to the ratio of absorption of quanta by the two receptor systems.

To encode differences in wavelength that lead to the perception of different hues, we have to have a comparison of two or more receptors that differ in their spectral sensivity function. If one receptor type is more sensitive to long wavelength lights and a second receptor type is more sensitive to short wavelengths, a quantum of long wavelength light is more likely to be absorbed by the first receptor than by the second. In this way the information as to what wavelengths are absorbed, is given by the relative activity of the two receptor types and not by the absolute activity of either. It is clear that we do not have receptors for specific bands of wavelengths. Rather, each of the few receptor types we possess responds to the entire visible spectrum. However, since the spectral sensitivities of the different receptor types are slightly different, subsequent neural mechanisms can compare the absorption of each receptor type and extract the wavelength information. In this sense the receptors are not color specific, but higher neural units are.

The intensity of the light is specified by the sum of the receptor activities—that is, the total receptor excitation. The simplest coding system is therefore made up of a small number of different receptor types, each with a different spectral sensitivity function, and in addition, a neural coding system that compares the outputs of the different types. The existence of each of these components of a system was first proposed in the nineteenth century—the former by Helmholtz (1867) and the latter by Hering (1877)—but it has taken over a century of research to show that both are required.

We now have direct evidence that human beings (and related species) have three varieties of cones, each with a broad band of sensitivity but differing in their peak sensitivities. The first evidence that there were at least two separable cone types was reported by Rushton (1958). In his experiments, he projected two small spots of light of differing wavelengths on nearby areas of the fovea. Some of the wavelengths were absorbed, thereby exciting those cones. More of the light passed through the cones and was absorbed by the lining at the back of the eye. But some was reflected from the back of the eye and passed back out of the front of the eye. Rushton measured the wavelength of reflected light, and by comparing it to the wavelength of the incident light, determined which wavelengths were absorbed. Then he adapted the photopigments with an intense light of a narrow band of wavelengths, bleaching the photopigments so that they now absorbed fewer quanta. Rushton compared the difference in relative absorption of each wavelength before and after bleaching with different wavelengths. With this procedure he was able to isolate two cone functions, one with a maximum absorption for light in the long-wavelength end, and one in the medium-wavelength region. He did not locate a third cone type, but his procedure was not appropriate to finding cones maximally sensitive to the short wavelengths.

Another technique isolates the photopigment of receptor cells and measures the amount of light absorbed at different wavelengths. The absorption spectrum of the photopigments of rods, measured in this way, is similar to the psychophysical spectral sensitivity function for rods shown in Figure 5.6. There are no comparable data for different types of cones.

A third procedure, microspectrophotometry, examines the absorption spectra of a very small number of cones in monkey and human eyes that have been removed for reasons other than retinal disease (Wald & Brown, 1965; Marks, Dobell, and MacNichol, 1964). This technique has proved sensitive enough to show three separable cone types. The absorption of different wavelengths is measured before and after the cones are adapted to intense monochromatic light. The difference between the absorption of each wavelength before and after the bleaching of the photopigment by the intense light provides a measure of the sensitivity of the photopigment itself. Figure 5.12 shows three cone functions with their peak sensitivities at about 450, 530, and 570 nanometers. When measurements were made on individual cones by this procedure, it was shown that each cone had only a single sensitivity function and hence probably contained only one photopigment. Thus the three receptor processes can be identified with three different types of cones.

DeValois and DeValois (1975) review several other procedures all of which yield evidence to support the pattern shown in Figure 5.12—spectral sensitivity functions for three cone types with peaks at about 440, 535, and 565 nanometers. Since these are all broad band receptors, they should not be named for the hues at their peak sensitivities, especially since two of them differ in their peaks by so little. Rather, we refer to them as cone types that are maximally responsive to long, middle, or short wavelengths, respectively. It is important to recognize that each of these sensitivities covers nearly the entire range of visible light.

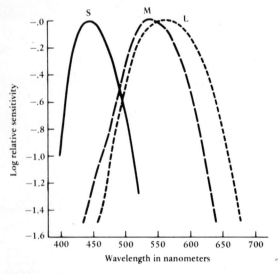

Figure 5.12 Normalized spectral sensitivity functions for the three cone types, labeled "short (S), medium (M), and long (L), found in the macaque monkey and human eye. Based on several different measurement techniques (see text) (DeValois & DeValois, 1975).

Neural Processes

Because receptors are not very color specific, there must be neural mechanisms that can contrast the relative amounts of absorption of the three cone types in order to code color. It should be obvious by now that the interaction of excitatory and inhibitory processes is an ideal mechanism to handle this comparison procedure and there is strong evidence that it is comparison of these excitatory and inhibitory inputs at each synaptic level that is critical for the coding of color.

Spatially Opponent Ganglion Cells

We have already described (see Chapter 4) Kuffler's and Barlow's discovery of the antagonistic concentric receptive fields of ganglion cells. A small white spot on a black surround, when centered over what Kuffler called the receptive field of an on-center gangion cell, produces a maximum excitatory response. A black spot on a white background produces a maximum inhibitory response. DeValois (1972) suggests that such a ganglion should be called a + white, − black cell since it is excited by white and inhibited by black. Kuffler also found ganglion cells with the opposite organization—they are excited by black spots on white backgrounds and are inhibited by white spots. DeValois calls these + bl − wh cells as they excite to black and inhibit to white. Both are called **spatially opponent cells.**

This class of cells is responsive to increments and decrements in light intensity, that is, to increases or decreases from the surrounding luminance. Moreover, they behave this way in response to monochromatic light of any wavelength as well as to white light. This is because the same cone types feed into the center and into the surround of these receptive fields; the centers and the surround areas have the same spectral sensitivity (Wiesel & Hubel, 1966). In this sense, these spatially opponent cells are spectrally nonopponent, for they do not differentiate among wavelengths (DeValois, 1972). Such spatially opponent cells are critically important for the coding of luminance discontinuties in animals in which color vision is absent or unimportant, as in the rabbit. The spatially opponent but spectrally nonopponent ganglion cells represent nearly all the ganglion cells in the retina in these animals, whereas in monkeys and man they make up less than 30 percent of the total number of cells.

Spectrally Opponent Ganglion Cells

A larger number of ganglion cells than the spatially opponent type in the human consists of one type of cone receptor connected to one part of the receptor field, and a different type of cone connected to the other part. These ganglion cells are excited by light of one wavelength and inhibited by light of a different wavelength. Since these cells respond differentially to different wavelengths, they carry color information.

DeValois and DeValois (1975) report four types of **spectrally opponent ganglion cells**, an example of which is shown in Figure 5.13. When the cell's receptive field is exposed to light of different wavelengths, the graph of the firing rate shows clearly that this cell is excited by long-wavelength light and inhibited by shorter-wavelength light. The DeValois's call this a "red excitatory–green inhibitory" or a "+ red − green" cell. The mirror-image cell, which is inhibited by long-wavelength and excited by middle-wavelength light (a "+ g − r" cell), is found equally often. A second pair of cells are those that respond differentially to the yellow and blue region of the spectrum, "+ yellow − blue" and "+ blue − yellow." Figure 5.14 illustrates the response record from these four types of spectrally opponent cells, together with

the two nonspectral cells, the "+ wh − bl" and the "+ bl − wh."

The best evidence to date (DeValois & DeValois, 1975) suggests that the different cone types are connected to the different ganglion cells in the manner shown schematically in Figure 5.15. Consider the four color cells first. The "+ red − green" cell receives excitation to its center region from long wavelength cones and inhibition to its surround region from mid-

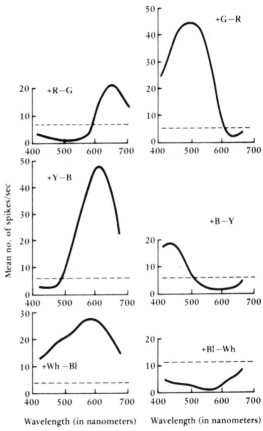

Figure 5.14 Plots of the average firing rates of a large sample of cells of each of the six lateral geniculate nucleus cell types in response to flashes of monochromatic light. The top four are spectrally opponent cells that fire to some wavelengths and inhibit to others. The bottom two are spectrally nonopponent cells. (It should be noted that these are responses to increments; the +Bl—Wh cells fire to decrements). (DeValois & DeValois, 1975.)

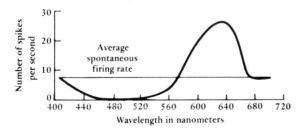

Figure 5.13 Example of responses to different spectral lights of a spectrally opponent cell. The number of spikes fired to each 10 nanometer section of the spectrum is plotted. It can be seen that this cell fires to long wavelengths (red) and is inhibited by shorter wavelengths (green). (DeValois & DeValois, 1975.)

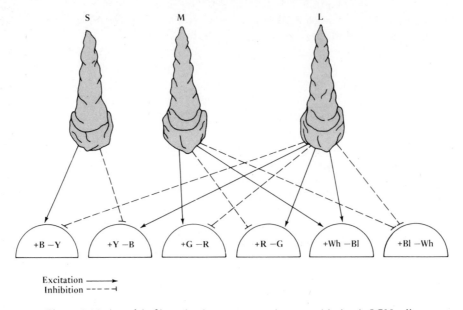

S   M   L

+B −Y   +Y −B   +G −R   +R −G   +Wh −Bl   +Bl −Wh

Excitation ⟶
Inhibition ----⊣

Figure 5.15 A model of how the three cone types interact with the six LGN cell
types (DeValois & DeValois, 1975).

dle-wavelength cones. The reverse is the case for the
"+ green − red" cell. Thus, both of these two cells
respond differentially to the changes in light in the
middle and long wavelengths but they do so in opposite directions. Of the two cells concerned with yellow
and blue the "+ yellow − blue" receives excitatory
inputs to its center region from long cones and inhibitory inputs to its surround from the short cones.

The two nonspectral cells are quite different. The
"+ Wh −Bl" cell receives excitatory inputs to its center region from two of the three cone types as well as
from the rod receptors, and receives inhibitory inputs
to its surround also from two of the three cone types as
well as from the rod receptors. The "+ Bl − Wh" cell
is the same, except that the inhibitory and excitatory
connections are reversed.

We began this section by arguing that a neural
component of color coding is needed to compare the
output of the three cone types, each of which has a
slightly different spectral sensitivity. Can the spectrally opponent cells be considered color specific? To
show why the answer is "Yes," consider Figure 5.16.
The solid lines are the spectral sensitivity functions for

the long cones and the medium cones, respectively. If
the "+ red − green" ganglion cells receive inputs
from both of these, one excitatory and one inhibitory,
this is the equivalent of taking the difference in the
output between the two cone types. Consider the "+
red" component of the "+ red − green" ganglion
cell. The greatest positive response, indicating maximum red, occurs for those wavelengths at which the
greatest excitation to the cell occurs in its center region and the least inhibition occurs to the surrounding
region. At what wavelength does this maximum response occur? The least inhibition would be found for
wavelengths at which the surround was not responsive
at all, that is, where the spectral sensitivity for the
surround showed minimum absorption of quanta. According to Figure 5.16 the medium cone function is
dropping sharply by 600 nanometers and has virtually
no responsiveness at all by 630 nanometers. Therefore, in this region, the inhibition to the surround is
minimal, but the excitation to the center is also dropping in this region, although the spectral sensitivity
function for the long cones is displaced above that for
the medium cones. The dashed line represents the dif-

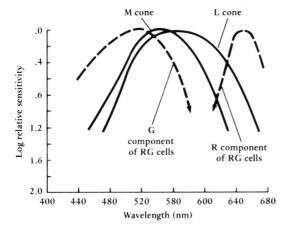

Figure 5.16 An indication of how the excitatory–inhibitory interaction between L and M cones in the red-green opponent cells leads to a narrowing of the spectral response curves and a shift toward the spectral extremes. The cones absorb all across the spectrum and both peak at middle wavelengths (greenish-yellow); the red-green cells, by differencing their outputs, respond to only narrow spectral regions, peaking at 500 nanometers (green) and 640 nanometers (red). (DeValois & DeValois, 1975.)

ferences between the two functions and has its peak for the "+ red" at about 640 nanometers. What this means is that while the long cone is maximally sensitive at 565 nanometers, (a hue of yellowish-green), the difference between the sensitivities of the long and medium cones, that which excites the "+ red − green" cells, is maximum at 640 nanometers (a hue that looks red).

A similar argument shows that the excitatory response to a "+ green − red" cell reflects a difference between the excitatory input from the medium cone and the inhibitory input from the long cone. The maximum difference between these two inputs occurs at 500 nanometers, right in the middle of the green range. What this shows is that even though the two spectral sensitivity functions for the two cone types nearly overlap, both with peaks in the greenish-yellow range, taking differences between these two functions produce peaks far apart, one in the green and the other in the red. Thus, while the two cone types are not color-specific, the output of a ganglion is.

The theory described above is a mathematical description of how the spectrally opponent cells code wavelength. Figure 5.14 presented the spectral sensitivity function for the four spectrally opponent cells, showing that they actually behave this way. DeValois, Abramov, and Mead (1967) also showed that human psychophysical color discrimination data (such as those reported by Judd, 1932) could be reproduced by direct recording from lateral geniculate cells. In other words, the accuracy with which psychophysical procedures can demonstrate the perceiver's ability to discriminate between adjacent wavelengths is equivalent to the discrimination function found by direct recording from the spectrally opponent cells in the lateral geniculate nucleus. The red-green cells account for our discrimination among the long wavelengths and the yellow-blue cells handle discrimination among the shorter wavelengths.

In addition, DeValois and Marrocco (1973) showed that the spectrally opponent cells register saturation differences. Figure 5.17 shows that the shape of the response function of a "+ red − green" cell does not change as white light is added to the monochromatic-pure wavelength but that the response to long wavelength light is increased as a function of the purity of the light at those wavelengths. While there are other components to the perception of saturation than wavelength, these data show quite clearly that the spectrally opponent cells are able to encode differences in purity.

It should now be easy to see how spectrally opponent organization of color coding can account for the color-mixing data presented earlier. Figure 5.18 shows where the radii through a single layer of the color solid are labeled by the two types of spectrally opponent cells corresponding to the complementary red-green and yellow-blue hues that were paired from color-mixing demonstrations. Just as before, it is now possible to predict the hue, brightness, and saturation of a color combination by the relative activities of the white/black, red/green, and yellow/blue cells as indicated by their location on the color solid. For example, if the + red − green and the + yellow − blue cells are both activated, the resulting hue is between red and yellow, that is, some variety of orange. If some

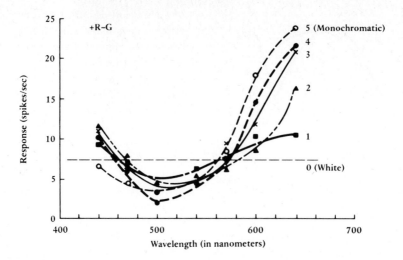

Figure 5.17 Saturation discrimination data from a sample of +R −G cells. Shifts were made from white light to various white-monochromatic mixtures, all equated for luminance. This was done at each of several spectral points. It can be seen especially clearly in the responses to 640 nanometers that the greater the purity (that is, the more monochromatic light in the white-monochromatic mixture) of the red light the more the +R −G cells fire (DeValois & DeValois, 1975).

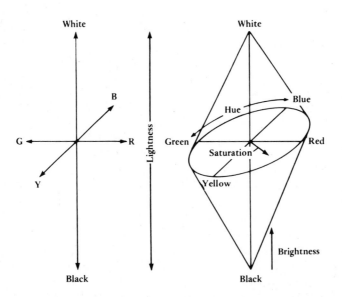

Figure 5.18   An example of how the axes of the color solid on the right can be described by the three pairs of opponent processes, shown on the left.

500-nanometer light is added to a 640 red, the excitatory activity of the + red − green is decreased so that the resulting hue is perceived as a red (or pink) desaturated by the amount of the 500-nanometer light added. If white light is added to a 640-nanometer (red) light it activates the + red − green ganglion cell and also results in a desaturated red. The success with which these mixing data can be understood by a combination of the spectrally and spatially opponent cells has increased the confidence with which these mechanisms are thought to represent the basic coding systems for color.

Spatial and Spectral Opposition
A spectrally opponent ganglion cell also has a spatially opponent organization. If a spot of light of any wavelength is placed in the center of the receptive field of the + red − green cells, that cell is excited because the long cones feeding to the center are excited by nearly all visible wavelengths. Similarly, a ring of light of any wavelength illuminating the surround inhibits the cell. Therefore, this + red − green cell maps luminance changes irrespective of wavelength in exactly the same way that a + white − black cell responds. The receptive field for a + red − green cell is shown in Figure 5.19. It is maximally excited by an incremental input to the center and a decremental input to the surround.

But what does a receptive field look like when illuminated by light equated for luminance but differing in wavelength? Here the answer is quite different. Since long-wavelength light produces the greatest excitation, the maximum excitatory response occurs if the long-wavelength light is in the center. But long-wavelength light also illuminates the surround, and that produces the least inhibition in the surround. If an equal-luminance green is put in the surround, it produces a lot of inhibition, cancelling the excitatory response coming from the red in the center. Consequently, the cell does not respond. So the receptive field for stimuli that differ only in wavelength is uniform and large, with no spatial opponency at all. Therefore, the spectrally opponent ganglion cells are spatially opponent for luminance differences but not for wavelength differences. If the light differs only in

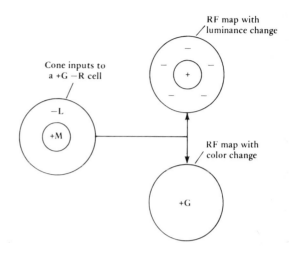

Figure 5.19 Receptive field map for a spectrally opponent cell that also shows spatial opponency. Such a cell responds to both luminance changes and color changes, but with entirely different receptive field maps for the two types of stimuli. When mapped with a luminance change, the cell shows a spatial antagonism and a receptive field like a +Wh −Bl cell; when mapped with a color change the receptive field is uniform in sign, the cell firing to a shift toward green (and inhibiting to red) anywhere in the field. (DeValois & DeValois, 1975.)

wavelength, then the optimal stimulus to excite a spectrally opponent cell is a large uniform patch of light filling all parts of the receptive field equally. In this way the same ganglion cell can be used to code luminance differences across space and to code wavelength differences regardless of space.

Color Coding in the Cortex
Thus far the description of neural coding has centered on the ganglion cell. The receptive field organization of lateral geniculate cells is so similar to that of the ganglion cells that all of the above applies equally to the lateral geniculate nucleus. In fact, most of the electrophysiological evidence for neural coding comes from recordings made at the lateral geniculate nucleus. Far fewer data are available on what happens in the cortex. DeValois and DeValois (1975) summarized what is known but, since this is an area of very active work, the story should become clearer in the next few years.

At present, it appears as if the spectral and spatial data remain integrated in some places in the cortex and separated in others. For example, Zeki (1973) found cells in area 20 of the visual cortex that respond selectively to wavelength and not at all to white light. Furthermore, the cells are arranged in columns that are selective for a narrow range of wavelengths. The cells within a column differ in terms of the form required—some respond only if the shape is proper for that cell, others respond to a green border in a particular orientation, while others respond to any shape as long as the wavelength is right. The cells in the neighboring column all have the same range of shape demands, except that the stimulus color is different. Presumably these cells receive the major inputs both from the spectrally opponent ganglion cells and from cells that code visual features from lower areas of the visual cortex. It may be that these cells in area 20 represent unique codes for the different wavelengths that are capable of being associated with specific perceptual experiences of color.

ADAPTATION OF COLOR PERCEPTION

Chapter 3 discussed light and dark adaptation to light considered without regard to wavelength. Does that picture change when the adaptation is to light of specific wavelengths? We can list several expectations concerning adaptation of rods and of cones.

In general, stimulating any receptor intensively with a large number of quanta both excites the receptor and reduces its sensitivity to continuing or subsequent stimulation. Figure 3.3 showed both a very transient, dramatic initial loss in sensitivity, and a less extensive but steady-state effect of a stable reduction in sensitivity proportional to the number of quanta incident to the receptor. We indicated in our discussion of the mechanism of light adaptation that the transient effect must be neural in character and probably is of an inhibitory nature, since the photochemical changes in the receptor caused by adaptation are not fast enough to account for the rapid transients.

On the other hand, the loss in sensitivity to more prolonged and intense light stimulation, such as would be normally encountered in bright sunlight, is due to the bleaching of the visual pigment in each molecule of the receptor. When the pigment of the receptor has been unstimulated for some time, it is in an unbleached state and is capable of absorbing quanta of the appropriate wavelength. As it is bleached, the pigment becomes transparent and the quanta pass through it without being absorbed. Very intense light applied for several minutes can almost completely bleach all the photopigment in a receptor, rendering it virtually incapable of responding immediately thereafter.

Figure 3.3 plotted the increase in sensitivity after the adapting stimulus is turned off. This function is identical to the regeneration of the photopigments observed in a test tube in the laboratory, so that we can be quite confident that it is the bleaching and regeneration of the photopigment that accounts for the nontransient effect of dark and light adaptation.

Rod Adaptation

Only one type of rod photopigment exists, and we know that it responds differentially to monochromatic light as a function of wavelength (Fig. 5.6). Hence, we should expect to find greater adaptation in rods to those wavelengths to which the rods are maximally sensitive. Thus, a 650-nanometer (red) light has relatively little impact on rods causing little bleaching, and does not lower the rod's sensitivity either to white light or to any narrow band of wavelengths. We have already observed that light adaptation can be attenuated in rods with the use of red goggles to preserve sensitivity at night. On the other hand a 500-nanometer (blue-green) light, to which rods are maximimally sensitive, produces very large adaptation effects, even at a moderate intensity.

Cone Adaptation

The expectations noted above apply to the cones as well except that the effects of adaptation are more dramatic, given the three different types of cones, each with a different spectial sensitivity function. Cone adaptation experiments provide further evidence for the three component systems of receptors.

The three spectral sensitivity functions of Figure 5.12 can be used to predict the differential absorption of quanta by the three types of cones to any particular adapting wavelength. If we present 600-nanometer (red) light, it lowers the sensitivity of the long-wavelength cones greatly, the middle-wavelength cones somewhat, and the short-wavelength cones little. Therefore, we have momentarily changed the relative heights of the three spectral sensitivity functions, though we have not changed their shapes. This means that a perceiver needs much more long-wave light than medium-wave light to match the brightness of a 600-nanometer (red) and a 550-nanometer (green) light following a 600-nanometer adapting light. As the effects of the adaptation wears off, the relative amount of long to medium wavelengths needed for equality gradually reduces until it reaches the ratio that existed before the adaptation occurred.

When the adapting light is white light, all three cone systems are affected in roughly equal proportions, and the relative heights of their spectral sensitivity functions are not changed. Thus no shift in sensation over the spectrum occurs after white adapting light.

Virtually all selective wavelength adaptation experiments have reported evidence consistent with these expectations. They therefore support the theory that the component receptor processes are made up of three different types of cones.

COLOR CONTRAST

Color contrast shares some properties with those of lightness contrast already described in Chapter 4. Contrast can occur simultaneously or successively. **Simultaneous contrast** refers to the case in which the contrasting surfaces are present at the same time. For example, the grey patch in color plate 5 takes on a reddish cast when seen against the green background. Although the simultaneous lightness contrast effects can be quite large, simultaneous color contrast is not nearly so pervasive. In **successive color contrast**, exposure to a particular hue produces the perception of the complementary hue when subsequently looking at a uniform grey surface. For example, if you stare at a red patch for half a minute, and then look at a large grey or white surface, you see a grey twinged with green [Plate 5(c)]. This phenomenon is also called a **negative afterimage** since adaptation to any wavelength produces its complementary color in the afterimage.

The opponent organization of receptive fields would seem to be the most obvious mechanism to invoke for explaining simultaneous color contrast. However, the relatively small sizes of the receptive fields compared with the relatively large retinal distances over which contrast effects can be produced, suggests that simultaneous brightness contrast can not be explained simply by reference to organization at the ganglion-cell level.

Further, as DeValois and DeValois (1975) noted, the spectrally opponent ganglion cells cannot account for simultaneous color contrast. In fact, the situation is quite the opposite. The + red − green cells will be maximally excited by a uniform red field covering its entire receptive field. Rather than producing contrast, a red patch on a green field is ineffective as a stimulus. Thus, the antagonistic center–surround arrangement of ganglion receptive fields makes them ideal for producing lightness contrast but not color contrast. DeValois and DeValois suggest that such mechanisms can be useful in explaining lightness contrast effects over relatively short retinal distances. But for longer retinal distances and for color-contrast effects, cortical-level mechanisms must be invoked. This is exactly the conclusion reached in Chapter 4 in dealing with lightness contrast.

A simpler mechanism—receptor adaptation—might seem to account for the effects of successive contrast. When one looks at a stimulus of a particular wavelength—say 650 nanometers—a greater percentage of long-wavelength cones are bleached than are short- or middle-wavelength cones. If one then looks at a uniform grey surface, all cones are stimulated equally, but the response of the long-wavelength cones has been diminished as a result of the adaptation. This diminution results in the perception of green, the complement of red. Although this explanation appears adequate at first glance, there are two reasons why this cannot be the whole story. First, successive color contrast can occur even with weak inducing stimuli that do not produce any significant bleaching. Second, the explanation in terms of adaptation requires subsequent stimulation of all cones in order to make manifest the changed sensitivity of the receptors. But the contrast effect can be observed as an afterimage that can be seen in the dark.

Thus, it may be that, in addition to receptor adaptation, a neural process plays a significant role in successive color contrast. One possible mechanism is the **neural rebound effect,** an inhibitory state manifest after prolonged stimulation. Given such a mechanism, if a + red − green ganglion cell is strongly excited by long-wavelength light, it switches to a brief inhibitory activity when the long-wavelength light terminates. The inhibition thus signaled is indistinguishable from stimulation by middle-wavelength light. Thus, the perceiver sees green. Since neural rebound is usually only a transient effect, such negative afterimages are brief. Neural rebound does not apply to receptors—they continue to produce after-discharges following termination of intense stimulation. This results in perception that is called **positive afterimages** (the opposite of contrast). The more intense the stimulation, the greater the after-discharge. The effects are minimal, however, except following intense stimulation.

DeValois and DeValois (1975) offer an interesting speculation about the purposes of the contrast mechanisms that we have been discussing. As we have already noted in several places, the visual world is made up almost exclusively of surfaces reflecting light to the eye, with virtually no self-luminous objects of any visual interest. Self-luminous objects emit a constant amount of light and can therefore be specified by their absolute intensity. If there were many self-luminous objects of importance to us we might have evolved a nervous system that registered absolute intensity information. But with the visual world made up exclusively of reflected sources of light, absolute intensity functions are useless. What we need to know is how much more light object A reflects than object B, a property of the two objects, and not how much light reaches the eye from each object. So we need

relative intensity or contrast in our visual world. Thus, to preserve object constancy we need a powerful contrast mechanism, which the opponent receptive field organization provides.

If we pursue the argument that color contrast is distinct from lightness contrast, the conclusion is different. Most light sources, especially the sun, are very broad-band, emitting light of all wavelengths. Since all wavelengths are present in incident light, the properties of pigmented surfaces are best detected by their absolute wavelengths reflected to the eye without modification by contrast. If the sun emitted only a narrow band of wavelengths that varied from time to time we would need a contrast mechanism to determine what the color spectral reflectances were. With all wavelengths available an absolute signal system for color would best provide object constancy with respect to their colors. Thus, it should not be surprising that the color-contrast effects are not nearly so strong as those for lightness contrast, and that in the presence of monochromatic light alone, perceivers have trouble determining the colors of objects, even when the light falls on backgrounds or on surrounding objects as well.

DEFECTIVE COLOR PERCEPTION

There are two general types of **defective color perception.** The first is represented by a group of perceivers who are missing one, two, or all three of the cone types. If a normal perceiver can match any wavelength of light by mixing different combinations of three wavelengths, then someone who is missing one type of cone needs only two wavelengths to be able to match any other wavelength. The color perception of such perceivers is called **dichromatic.**

Perceivers who are missing two or all three cone systems are called **monochromats,** since they match a particular wavelength with only one other, by simply adjusting its intensity. Monochromats may have all their cones functioning normally, except that each has the same spectral sensitivity function. But some monochromats have no cones at all, so that in addition to having monochromatic color perception, they also have poor visual acuity, poor central vision, and all the other defects that are associated with the absence of cones.

The second general class of defective color perception, and by far the larger, is composed of people called **anomalous trichromats.** Being trichromats, they need, just like a normal person, to mix three different wavelengths to match any particular wavelength. What is anomalous is that their mixtures may deviate from normal in several respects. They may act as if the spectral sensitivity functions of one of the cone types had been shifted along the spectrum. The largest class is composed of trichromats whose green functions are anomalous. When given a spectral orange and asked to match it with a mixture of three wavelengths, these perceivers add much more green to the mixture than does a person with normal color vision.

SUMMARY

Newton first demonstrated that the differences we perceive as hue are the result of the presence of different wavelengths of electromagnetic energy in the light that reaches the eye. He showed this by separating the wavelengths with a prism producing a full spectrum of colors. To be able to perceive these colors, it is necessary that the light source contains more than one wavelength, that surfaces of objects reflect more than one wavelength to the eye, and that the visual system have neural coding processes that can respond differentially to the different wavelengths. The chapter examined each of these requirements. The first one is easy to meet, since sunlight and nearly all artificial light emits wavelengths spanning the entire visible spectrum. The second is also easy, because surfaces are selective in the wavelengths they absorb and reflect. A surface appears to be a particular color because it reflects wavelengths that produce that perception and absorbs all other wavelengths, so that the colors of objects depend upon their selective spectral reflectances.

The appearance of the color of light can be described along three dimensions—its hue, its brightness, and its saturation. Hue corresponds to the familiar sense of colors we designate by different color names—red, blue, green, and so forth. The brightness of a color corresponds to the luminance of the light. The saturation of a color refers to the amount of white that appears to be mixed with it. Its physical counterpart is the purity of the light, specified in terms of how many different wavelengths are mixed together in the light. White light, the most desaturated light possible, contains a mixture of many different wavelengths and so is impure.

These three dimensions of the appearance of colors can be represented by a color solid in which hue, brightness, and saturation are along the three different axes of the solid perpendicular to one another. Each slice through the solid yields a color circle of a given brightness, relating hues around the perimeter, with saturation increasing as a function of distance from the center.

The relation of luminance to brightness is complex because the different wavelengths are not equal in the number of quanta they contain, and the receptors are not equally sensitive to the different wavelengths. The sensitivity of the receptors is specified by a spectral sensitivity function, found by asking a perceiver to adjust one side of a split field to match the brightness of the other side, when the two sides are illuminated by different wavelengths. The function peaks at about 550 nanometers for the cones in the fovea, and about 505 nanometers for rods, with sensitivity for both falling off for long and short wavelengths.

The relation of wavelength to hue is further described by examples of the mixing of lights of different wavelengths. The principles of color mixing are represented by the color circle, in which the hue and saturation of a light can be predicted by the placement around the circle of the lights that are mixed together. Mixing of lights is contrasted to the subtractive mixture of pigments.

The processes by which wavelength information is coded have two components. The first is based upon three different cone receptor types, each with spectral sensitivity functions whose maximum are in slightly different regions of the spectrum. Any quantum incident to the retina has a slightly different probability of being absorbed by each of the three cone types, as specified by these different spectral sensitivity functions. The second component is a neural coding process that relates the activity level of the three different cone types in an opponent fashion. This neural process is at the ganglion cell level, in which each ganglion has an antagonistic receptive field organization. The center of the field contains receptors of one type and the surround receptors of a different type. Since the center and surround are mutually inhibitory, the output of the ganglion cell represents the differancing of the outputs of pairs of cone types. It is this resolution that provides the color coding in the retina.

The evidence of the color-coding processes in the cortex is much sketchier, but what little there is suggests that spectral information and spatial information are separated in some cortical regions and integrated in others. In either case there are several candidates for cortical cells whose activity reflects the stimulation of specific wavelengths on the retina.

We briefly considered the effect of adaptation of color perception as a result of prolonged stimulation of one wavelength. The changes that occur can be nicely predicted by the two-stage coding process of different cone types connected in antagonistic fashion to ganglion cells. The most powerful evidence comes from findings that prolonged stimulation affects the three cone types differently, depending upon their respective sensitivities to the adapting wavelength. This then affects the sensitivity to any new wavelength because of the momentary relative changes in the three spectral senstivity functions.

Color contrast, like lightness contrast, describes changes in the perception of a light as a function of the light surrounding it in space, or following it in time. However, color contrast is not nearly as large an effect as lightness contrast, and the mechanisms by which it occurs are not as clearly understood. Given the nature of light sources, it was argued that color contrast is not nearly as necessary a mechanism in order to perceive the proper relation among surfaces as is lightness contrast.

In the final section we briefly reviewed the different kinds of color defects, often called color blindness. The differences are almost always due to abnormality in the distribution or nature of the three cone types, with some persons possessing only two, or one, or even no cone types at all.

SUGGESTED READINGS

In addition to Boynton's excellent chapter (1971), several textbooks on color perception are available. The most recent is also by Boynton (1979). Le Grand (1957) is now getting out of date. Several chapters in Graham's handbook (1965) are useful, but difficult, as are those in the Jameson and Hurvich handbook (1972). Cornsweet covers much of the color coding systems. Wyszecki and Stiles (1967) give a detailed and advanced coverage. The chapter by DeValois and DeValois (1975) comes closest to the point of view of the present chapter.

Chapter 6

Temporal Factors in Visual Perception

This chapter covers the basic time-keeping functions of the visual system. While vision is often considered a spatial sense, there are four important reasons to attend to its temporal properties. First, most visual stimuli vary in time—they do not occur in an instant to be gone forever. Rather, most events have a duration—a temporal extent. Furthermore, visual stimuli occur in succession—we are able to separate them into distinct events and can usually tell which came first, which second, and so forth. Since the environment has a temporal dimension, the visual system must be able to represent and respond to it.

Second, a temporal variation is imposed upon the stimuli by the movement of our eyes over an environment that includes stationary and moving objects. As a consequence of these movements, the brain is presented with information that varies with time. This variation is important for some kinds of perception.

Third, the study of temporal factors is important because perception itself takes time. It does not occur instantaneously with the onset of stimulation. Some stages of perception occur rapidly, while others are relatively slow. To know how perception of temporal events takes place, we must understand how long it takes each part of the visual system to respond.

Finally, temporal processing is important be-cause the visual system is easily overloaded with both spatial and temporal information. Over 100 million receptors are capable of responding at rates of many hundreds of times per second. The brain cannot come close to handling this bombardment of information. Therefore, in addition to the need for the reduction of spatial information, temporal coding of information must occur in order to make perceptual processing manageable. Several of these temporal resolution mechanisms were mentioned in Chapter 4, and others are discussed here.

As a first step in understanding temporal factors, consider how long it takes for the various neural events that we have described in the previous chapters to occur. Although it is not possible to make precise time measurements at all the functional levels of the visual system in humans, the picture is fairly complete. Light energy travels, for all practical purposes, instantaneously, from sources to the receptor surface of the eye. When the eye is dark adapted, the latency of the onset of receptor activity is effectively instantaneous, with a graded response to the light being produced within a few hundred microseconds of the onset of the flash. Not only does this initial response begin extremely quickly, but the output of a receptor follows a flickering stimulus at rates over several hundred cycles per second. In other words, at the receptor stage the eye is capable of very fine temporal resolution.

On the other hand, the temporal information reaching the brain is quite different. Using either electrodes placed on the scalp or microelectrodes located in selected cortical cells of area 17 to measure the response of the visual system, it is clear that this fine temporal resolution of the receptors has all but disappeared. Not only does 50 to 150 milliseconds elapse between receptor stimulation and area 17 excitation, but the resolution of temporally separate impulses of light requires the pulses to be spaced between 10 and 100 milliseconds apart, depending upon the state of light adaptation. This is at least a hundredfold loss of temporal resolution.

We know that most of this elapsed time occurs in the retina. For example, Woodworth (1938) reported that electrical stimulation of the ganglion cells produces a cortical response after only a few milliseconds in cats and in rabbits. Although we do not have direct measures of transmission time through the cortex, we do have some indirect evidence. For example, the simple reaction-time task, in which a perceiver must press a key as soon as he notices the onset of a light in a known location, yields data on the speed of transmission of information from receptor to fingertip. The fastest motor reaction time of a finger press to light onset is about 150 milliseconds. This high speed is found, however, only with very intense lights, and is usually much slower. The time needed for an efferent nerve impulse to leave the motor cortex and travel to the fingers is about 10 to 15 milliseconds, with another 30 milliseconds or so needed to move the key with the finger (Woodworth, 1938). Adding these times together leaves about 100 milliseconds of reaction time for events occurring on the retina and virtually none for those in the cortex.

If the reaction time involves a choice ("press the right finger if the right light comes on, and the left finger for the left light") another 200 milliseconds or so is added to the total reaction time. Presumably this addition involves cortical handling of the localization and decision processes.

We have already noted in Chapter 4 that the vis-

ual system is better able to process stimuli that differ across spatial domains than those that differ over time. Even so, we have just offered four good reasons why the processing of time is worthy of study. It is still true, however, that time is not treated with the same degree of accuracy as is space, nor is time as important in vision as it is in audition. Ecologically, these facts are not difficult to understand. There are relatively few physical events in the environment of humans for which fine temporal acuity is necessary. Natural light sources function continuously and when they do change, as at sunrise or at sunset, the changes are very slow. True, we occasionally see very brief flashes of lightning in an otherwise dark sky, but there is no reason to think that the human visual system evolved to process visual information during lightning storms.

Good visual resolution of time should be useful in the detection of motion. At some level in the visual system motion detection requires that a spatial pattern be compared at two different points in time. If the time intervals are large or unpredictably variable, detection of small movements would be very poor. Since objects that shift position in space have a great potential significance for human beings, being able visually to detect their motion seems quite important. We will see later that the visual system has evolved cells that are specialized for this purpose.

We shall also see that temporal processing is intimately involved with saccadic eye movement. Our eyes constantly make rapid saccadic sweeps that change the direction of gaze. Each movement produces a displacement of the retinal image. This should produce, in theory, a complete upheaval of signaling from the retina to the cortex. Yet none of that upheaval reflects information about movement in the visual world in front of the observer. In fact, in order to have a stable perception of a stable world it is critical that we do not perceive the movement of stimulation on the retina produced by our own movements. Yet we cannot simply suppress this stimulation or else we would never be able to perceive real movement. So we shall see another aspect of temporal processing that originates in the changes that occur around saccadic eye movements.

In general then, the message of this chapter is that the visual system is not very sensitive to variation in time. We shall find many instances in which spatial resolution has been enhanced at the expense of potential temporal resolution. Within this context, however, there are several specialized adaptations, particularly concerning detection of motion and control of saccadic eye movements, in which temporal resolution is quite accurate.

In this chapter we examine a number of temporal tasks, those involving both the perception of time and the time of perception. Unfortunately, because of the coding processes, the analyses of these two aspects are generally inseparable. We first examine several different lines of work on how the coding of time interacts with nontemporal processing, especially intensity and temporally contiguous events. Then we examine the time it takes perceptual events to occur, and how the processing of time is carried out.

Research Strategies to Examine Temporal Processing

Several approaches are used to assess the temporal resolution of the visual system, that each ask slightly different questions and often provide incompatible answers. One approach involves a neurophysiological level of analysis of the time course of excitation and inhibition following the onset and offset of flashes of light of different durations, and following multiple flashes with varying spatial and temporal separation. By recording the electrical activity of receptors, ganglion, or cortical cells, we can gain some insight into the way temporal variation and stimulation is coded and transmitted. Unfortunately, compared to electrophysiological evidence for the coding of luminance discontinuity and of wavelength, far less direct recording data has been reported for the coding of temporal variation in light.

The second strategy manipulates temporal variables psychophysically to determine their effect on threshold detection, on brightness, on discriminability of multiple flashes, on judgments of duration of stimulation, on successiveness, and so forth. The functions describe lawful relationships that can be re-

lated to or tested against the electrophysiological recordings made directly from the neural units in the visual system. It is expected that one set of laws describe all of the temporal coding effects.

What are some of the psychophysical effects to be described? For example, what is the shortest flash of light that can be detected? Is it a tenth of a second, a hundredth, a thousandth? The answer is surprising—there is no shortest flash. However short you make a detectable flash, it can be made still shorter if its luminance is increased. It is not the duration but the total number of quanta reaching the retina that determines the detectability. But this does not mean that we can perceive short flashes as short. No matter how brief the flash is made, as long as it can be detected, it is judged to be at least a twentieth to a tenth of a second in duration.

Another task asks a perceiver to discriminate two flashes of light, when both are presented close together in time to the same retinal location. A number of variations of this procedure have been used, including ones in which one of the flashes is made more intense than the other or covers a larger area in the retina or does not overlap the first one. In each case, the objective is to understand what determines whether separate events can be discriminated as separate.

TRANSIENT VERSUS SUSTAINED SIGNALING

As we saw in Chapter 4, Kuffler's description of the properties in nearly all ganglion cells indicates that they signal transient events. Figure 4.6 showed that typical ganglion cells exhibit an increase in excitation or inhibition to the initiation of stimulation, depending upon whether the stimulus falls on the center or the surround. It makes an opposite response when the stimulus ends. However, Kuffler found very few ganglion cells that continued to signal excitation or inhibition for the duration of a stimulus. Consequently, the antagonistic organization of ganglion cells tends to minimize the signaling of temporally continuous events and makes them sensitive mainly to changes in stimulation.

More recent work has shown that Kuffler's description is too narrow. Ganglion cells are now classified as **transient** or **sustained**, depending upon their response characteristics. Figure 6.1 shows an example from Enroth-Cugell and Robson (1966). The sustained cell responds to the beginning of stimulation and continues to respond until the stimulus terminates. The transient cell, however, responds only to the onset and offset of the stimulus (and primarily, in this case, to the decremental edge of the stimulus, since it is an off-center cell) but does not continue to respond to the continuation of the stimulus. It is the latter type of cell that Kuffler had found, although we now know that both types are present in the retina.

Besides the difference in signaling the continuation of stimulation, these two types of cells differ in other important respects. Since some of these are recent discoveries (for example, Dow, 1974) not all the data are yet in, but at present, it looks as if sustained cells have a longer latency before they begin to respond, are more responsive to stationary stimuli, have smaller receptive fields over the retina, are more concentrated in the fovea, and are more sensitive to high spatial frequency, to small patterns, to temporally steady or only slowly changing stimuli. Figure 6.2 lists these differences.

Hoffmann and Stone (1971) have shown that sustained ganglion cells project to sustained lateral geniculate cells, which in turn project to sustained cortical cells. They also showed the same parallel projections for transient cells. Thus, these two parallel sets of pathways from the retina to the cortex preserve the sustained–transient difference. It is on this basis that we will refer to a sustained and a transient channel from the retina to the cortex.

Judging from Figure 6.2, the transient channel is more appropriate for the detection of patterns moving over the retina or flickering rapidly, whereas the sustained channel communicates information about visual edges that are stable. Breitmeyer and Ganz (1976) suggested that the transient channels are designed as an early warning system that helps the perceiver orient and direct attention to locations in space that may contain moving or unexpected information. The transient channel is specialized for fast responding with high temporal but low spatial resolution. Once the warning has been heeded, usually with an eye movement to the target, the novel information can be analyzed by the slower, high-resolution, long tem-

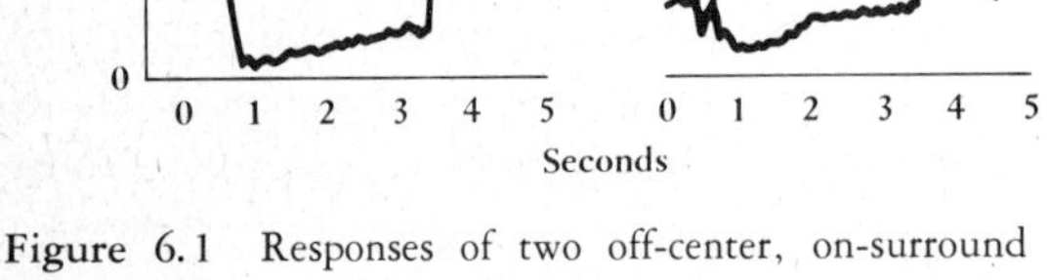

Figure 6.1 Responses of two off-center, on-surround ganglion cells, one a transient and the other a sustained cell, to a 2-second spot located either over the cell's center (providing an increment in excitation) or over its surround (decrement). (Enroth-Cugell & Robson, 1966.)

Transient channels

Short latency of response

Moving target

Large receptive field

Found more in periphery

Low spatial frequency resolution

Better for flickering stimulus

Can inhibit sustained

Not sensitive to blur or refractive error

Sustained channels

Long latency

Stationary targets

Small receptive field

More likely in the fovea

High spatial frequency resolution

Steady state

Can be inhibited by transient channels

Requires sharp focus

Figure 6.2 Some differences between transient and sustained channels.

poral-integrating, sustained channels, whose units are more concentrated in the fovea. All the properties of these sustained channels should facilitate good spatial visual acuity.

Although the sustained and transient channels project in parallel from the retina to the cortex, they do interact. Specifically, Singer and Bedworth (1973) showed that, following the onset of a brief flash of light, the transient channel (measured in the lateral geniculate nucleus) begins to signal with a latency of about 50 milliseconds. The sustained channel is inhibited initially by the transient channel. It is not just that the sustained channel has a longer latency—it is actively inhibited and can only begin to respond when released from inhibition. This inhibition can be seen in Figure 6.3, which shows a recording from a sustained on-center neuron to light onset. The spikes at the left represent the spontaneous activity level. After 35 milliseconds, there is a sharp drop in the voltage of the cell—that is, there is an inhibition of its output. After another 45 milliseconds, excitation potentials begin, as shown by the increase in voltage, but the

first excitation spike is not manifest until 110 milliseconds after light onset. Thus, inhibition precedes excitation by over 50 milliseconds. Breitmeyer and Ganz (1976) argued that this inhibitory relationship of the fast-acting transient channel over the slower sustained channel is found throughout the visual pathways. It is a major component of their explanations of masking effects discussed later in this chapter.

TEMPORAL SUMMATION

We have already noted in Chapter 4 that time and luminance are reciprocally related to visual acuity. The acuity obtainable from a short, intense flash is equivalent within specified limits, to that of a long, dim flash. This reciprocity is also generally true for threshold sensitivity and superthreshold brightness judgments. For example, suppose that a perceiver is asked to set a briefly flashed spot of light so that he can just see it. What happens if the flash is made longer or briefer? Below about 100 milliseconds of exposure duration, there is a trade off between the duration of the flash of light and the intensity of that flash (**Bloch's law**). Figure 6.4 shows two traditional ways of plotting these effects, both of which illustrate that below a critical duration, in this case about 100 milliseconds, the degree to which intensity (I) and duration (T) contribute to the total energy in the light flash is irrelevant as long as the simple product is held constant ($I \times T = k$).

Figure 6.4 (*a*) shows this when luminance—specified in this case as the number of quanta per unit

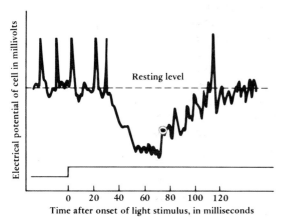

Figure 6.3 Demonstration of inhibition of a sustained LGN neuron by transient neurons. Recording is intracellular of a sustained on-center neuron. The five spikes on the left are due to spontaneous activity. After onset of the 35 millisecond light stimulus, a hyperpolarizing (inhibitory) potential starts and terminates about 100 milliseconds later. Excitatory potentials begin 80 milliseconds after light onset. Light-evoked spike activity begins only 110 milliseconds after light onset. Thus inhibition precedes excitations by 40–50 milliseconds. (Singer & Bedworth, 1973.)

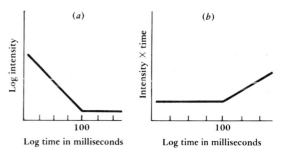

Figure 6.4 Two ways of illustrating Bloch's law, showing the range over which time and intensity are reciprocally related.

time—is plotted against time. Both scales are loga-rithmic and the slope of −1 shows the perfect reci-procity of luminance with time. In other words, all that matters for threshold detection is the total num-ber of quanta, not whether they are packed into an intense but brief burst or spread out more thinly over time. Figure 6.4 (*b*) illustrates the same result plotted differently. The ordinate is the product of luminance and time (equivalent to total energy). The flat portion of the function shows that total energy determines threshold detection, since it does not change as time increases.

The reciprocity specified in Bloch's law breaks down if the duration of a flash is too long. The upper limit of the reciprocity is called the **critical dura-tion**—the duration beyond which adding more time ceases to have any effect. For example, a very dim light may never become visible, no matter how long it is left on. The magnitude of the critical duration de-pends on a number of variables. For reciprocity at ab-solute threshold of a spot of light seen against a black background (that is, under scotopic conditions), the critical duration is about 100 milliseconds. Under photopic conditions—somewhat more relevant to the normal functioning of the visual system—the critical duration is shorter, more on the order of 10 to 20 mil-liseconds.

On the other hand, when the task is form dis-crimination based on acuity, such as being able to tell the orientation of a small gap in a circle (Kahneman, 1966), time and intensity are reciprocally related for

durations as long as several hundred milliseconds. Therefore, the nature of the task defines the value of the critical duration as an upper limit on the time over which reciprocity holds.

Block's law suggests that energy is integrated somewhere in the visual system—that intensity is av-eraged over time. This process is called **temporal summation.** Bloch's law states that the temporal composition of the flash is irrelevant, as long as the simple product of time and luminance is constant. For example, the response of the visual system to each of the flashes shown in the upper part of Figure 6.5 will be the same (Boynton & Seigfried, 1962; Davey, 1952; Long, 1951).

These summation processes obviously obscure much of the temporal specificity of stimulation. As we observed in Chapter 4, such summative effects are use-ful to aid responding under scotopic conditions. Thus, when light intensity is very low, any strategy that al-lows intensity to be integrated over longer periods of time improves the chances of detecting the presence of that energy. But the price paid for this is loss of tem-poral specificity. The visual system does not record whether the flash is long and dim, or brief and intense, or whether it is one long, dim flash, or several briefer but more intense ones. We also observed that, al-though this is a useful trade-off at scotopic levels, the same trade-off is found at photopic levels.

Figure 6.6 illustrates the change in critical duration as a function of the luminance of the back-ground against which the flashes of light are pre-

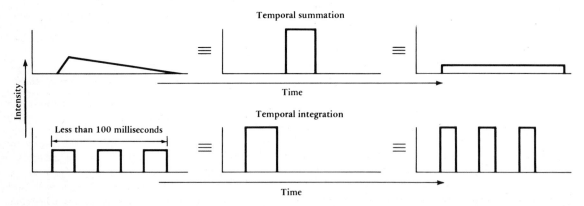

Figure 6.5 Schematic illustration of temporal wave forms used to study temporal summation and temporal integration.

sented. Notice that as the amount of light reaching the retina from the background decreases, the critical duration becomes longer. In a detection task, the critical duration may range from 100 milliseconds with a black background to about 10 milliseconds with very intense backgrounds. Thus, with high light levels, temporal resolution is much greater, but even 10 milliseconds of summation means the temporal resolution is still pretty coarse.

Where in the visual system do these summation effects occur? The evidence is now convincing that it is at the receptor level, the very first stage of process-

ing. For example, the continuation of electrical activity in the receptor continues for a much longer time than does the test flash itself (Fain & Dowling, 1973). Even a brief flash of light elicits longer periods of excitation in the receptor, exactly what would be expected by Bloch's Law. Furthermore, Whitten and Brown (1973) showed that, as the luminance of a test flash increases (holding duration constant) the decay following termination of the flash becomes much faster and sharper, exactly what would be expected by the reduction in critical duration with increased luminance. Figure 6.7 shows these results. While the onset of the receptive potential is virtually instantaneous at all luminance levels, the offset changes dramatically.

TEMPORAL INTEGRATION

So far we have referred only to presentations of a single flash. It might be expected that if time and intensity can be averaged, the number of flashes given would not matter as long as all of them occurred within the critical duration. In fact, this has been

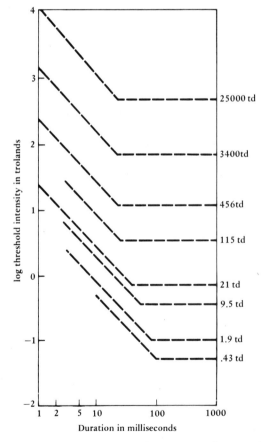

Figure 6.6 Change in threshold intensity as a function of duration. Each curve represents a different background intensity against which the spot is presented. Notice that as background intensity increases, the break in each curve, signifying the critical duration, occurs sooner. (Roufs, 1972.)

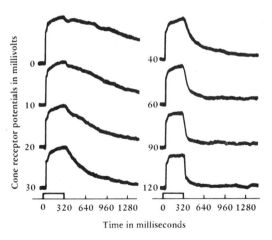

Figure 6.7 Cone receptor potentials from monkey retina following a 320-millisecond flash. Record 0 is obtained under dark adaptation. Records 10, 20, 30, and so on are obtained with successively more intense backgrounds. Note that the decay becomes more rapid as background level increases. (Whitten & Brown, 1973.)

shown to be the case, and is called **temporal integration**. As long as the offset of the last flash occurs within the critical period from the onset of the first flash, the response is a function of the total energy averaged over all the flashes. See the bottom of Figure 6.5 for some examples of equivalent stimuli.

Where in the visual system does the temporal integration occur? Boynton (1961) has suggested that, given the precision of this reciprocity relationship, one might be tempted to look for the integration at the very first stage, in the receptors themselves. However, Boynton offers three arguments to show that integration in the receptors is impossible, and that it must be a neural process occurring beyond the receptors. First, the receptors begin their response very quickly and continue to respond to closely spaced flashes. Because of the rate at which rhodopsin changes when exposed to very brief flashes (Wulff, Adams, Linschitz, & Abrahamson, 1958), Boynton suggests that, even within the critical duration, the speed of reaction of a photoreceptor is fast enough to allow two separate photochemical events to occur. If this does occur, then the receptor cannot be integrating over time.

Second, at threshold the chances that two or more quanta will hit the same receptor are negligible. Thus, a receptor is capable of responding to the absorption of a single quantum by only one of its millions of molecules of photopigment. If two or more quanta never hit the same receptor at scotopic levels, then the receptor cannot be integrating over time. Finally, temporal integration is just as effective if the two pulses fall on nearby receptors as it is when they fall on the same one.

For all these reasons, integration must occur beyond the receptor stage. At the receptor level there appears to be little if any integration over time.

One of the strongest arguments for a postreceptor focus of temporal integration is an experiment by Boynton, Sturr, and Ikeda (1971). They demonstrated both good and poor temporal resolution in the same experiment. They presented a train of flashes at a rate of 30 per second, so that each flash was on for 16 milliseconds with a 16-millisecond dark interval. At this rate, under the conditions they used, the flashes

appear fused—the perceiver sees them as one continuous light, not a rapidly flickering one. The perceiver was told that a 1-millisecond test flash of light would be presented periodically against this phenomenally fused background, and his task was to detect it. The intensity needed to make the test flash just visible—that is, to keep it at threshold—was varied. They found (Fig. 6.8) that, if the test flash occurred during one of the 16-millisecond dark intervals, it could be substantially dimmer than during one of the 16-millisecond flashes and still be detected. Hence, even though the perceiver could not perceive the flicker, the increment threshold was dependent upon these very small differences. This also implies that the fusion of a rapidly flickering light occurs higher in the visual nervous system than the processing of increment thresholds.

The experiment by Boynton, Sturr, and Ikeda does not tell us where integration occurs in the visual system. Boynton's arguments suggest that it is not at the receptor level. This experiment makes that even more certain, since if it were, how could the temporal precision noted in the increment threshold values ever be subsequently obtained? Thus, integration must be neural, but is it at the bipolar or ganglion levels, or in the lateral geniculate nucleus, or the cortex? We do not yet know for sure.

The temporal integration we have considered

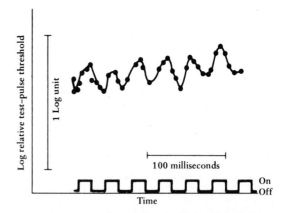

Figure 6.8 Changes in the detection threshold as a function of presentation relative to the cycle of a 30-cycle-per-second flickering light. (Boynton, Sturr, & Ikeda, 1971.)

used two or more flashes of light of the same size, presented to the same area of the retina. As we noted, their separateness is often lost. But what happens when the size and location do not precisely overlap? This creates a different type of interaction of profound importance for temporal processing. What is the apparent duration of a brief flash of light? How long is the shortest instant of visual time? In one approach to these questions, Efron (1967) presented a pair of very brief flashes, each of 1 millisecond duration, separated in space and time so that the perceiver could easily tell they were different events. On successive trials, one of the flashes was varied in duration while the other was held constant. The perceiver was asked to judge whether the two flashes appeared equal or different in duration. Only when the varied one reached 60 milliseconds or more did perceivers begin to report that they were different in duration. Therefore, Efron argued, the minimum duration of a stimulus that has temporal extent is around 60 milliseconds.

Visual Persistence   Measures of receptor activity in response to brief flashes of light such as in Figure 6.7 suggest that much of Efron's effect can be accounted for by **persistence of activation** of receptors beyond the termination of the physical stimulus. One reason to suspect the receptors is the finding that, no matter how persistence is measured, it is longer if the eye is dark-adapted. The termination of receptor activity after stimulus offset is most prolonged when light levels are very low (as in Figure 6.7). Furthermore, after-images following stimulation are prolonged if the eye is dark-adapted prior to the light flashes (Craik, 1940), and this effect appears to reside in the prolonged activity of the receptors themselves (Normann & Werblin, 1974; Sakitt, 1976).

A recent series of studies by Sakitt (1976) provides additional evidence of receptor involvement in persistence effects. In one study, she presented a brief flash of light to a dark-adapted observer who was asked to adjust the timing of a brief tone so that the termination of the light and the tone coincided. If the light persists, then the observer should set the tone to occur after the physical termination of the light. If the light

had no persistence, then the observer should set the tone and light offset so that they coincided physically. Sakitt wanted to find the amount of energy in the light flash necessary to produce a persistence of 0.5 second in the light. In other words, she wanted the observer to set the tone to occur 0.5 second after the light terminated. She argued that if the persistence effect was due to continued activity of the receptor, then the amount of energy needed to produce a 0.5-second persistence should vary with the spectral sensitivity function of the receptor. That is, if persistence is due to rod activity, then less energy should be needed at 510 nanometers than at longer or shorter wavelengths because that is the wavelength to which the rods are most sensitive. If it is the cone activity, then the minimum energy should be shifted to about 550 nanometers (see Figure 5.6, p. 97).

Figure 6.9 presents a typical result from Sakitt. The energy value needed to produce a 0.5-second persistence follows the spectral sensitivity functions for rods rather nicely. Sakitt argued, therefore, that the persistence measured by the tone–light-offset matching in the dark-adapted eye is due entirely to the persistence of rod receptor activity. She suggested that

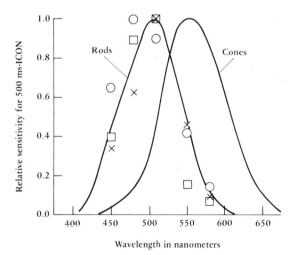

Figure 6.9 Spectral sensitivity functions for two normal observers (○, □) and one rod-monochromat observer (X). The complete spectral sensitivity function for rods and for cones, based upon normal observers (see Figure 5.5 or 5.6) are drawn in for reference. (Sakitt, 1976.)

cone persistence is also important but, because the light levels are so low in the experiment, the cones are not active at all. Sakitt then tested a subject who had only rods in her retina and no cones at all, and found the same pattern of results (also included in Figure 6.9). Since only rod receptors are available to this subject, it seems likely that it is the poststimulus continuation of rod activity that accounts for perceived persistence under dark-adaptation conditions.

Visual persistence under dark adaptation can be very long—many seconds, in fact, for intense flashes of light. What happens when the eye is not dark-adapted? A number of studies have shown that persistence following stimulus termination is much briefer. Because the receptor after-activity is also briefer, Sakitt has argued that all forms of visual persistence are the result of receptor after-activity—that is, that the perceived persistence of a brief light flash is due to processes at the very first stage of the perceptual processing.

In one study on persistence, Haber and Standing (1969) alternated two display fields. One contained an outline form drawn on a white background, and was presented for about 10 milliseconds. The other was a blank white field of variable duration. By changing the duration of the blank field, the time from the offset of the form to its onset in the next cycle could be systematically varied. The perceiver viewed a sequence of about ten cycles and judged whether the form had completely faded away before it reappeared (see Figure 6.10). The duration of the blank field needed to find such a persistence threshold was about 250 milliseconds. That is, it appeared as if the visual persistence of the brief intense pulse was about 250 milliseconds. When the background was reduced by 2 log units, persistence increased only a few milliseconds. When the blank field was turned off altogether, however, persistence increased to about 400 milliseconds. Since the background field provided the adaptation level, the latter condition produced dark adaptation, and the persistence nearly doubled.

As the matter now stands, therefore, visual persistence seems to be the result of after-effects of the receptors themselves. It is possible that neural events

beyond the receptors may also produce some persistence but, as long as the receptors themselves continue to signal after the stimulus is terminated, they affect all subsequent stages of neural processing.

It is interesting to speculate about the source of improvement in temporal resolution with higher light levels. One possibility is that neural processes are always temporally precise and that all that improves is the sharper receptor response to offsets when they are working at higher light levels (illustrated in Figure 6.7). An alternative possibility is that, in addition to the sharper offsets, the neural coding processes themselves sharpen up temporal resolution in much the same way that the antagonistic receptive field structures sharpen up the spatial coding by producing edge enhancement of the Mach band type. No one has yet demonstrated a "temporal" edge enhancement due to neural processes but it may turn out that such processes do exist.

One final note about persistence. If the effects of stimuli outlast their terminations, it should be possible for perceivers to use that time in order to have a longer "look" at the stimulus, the better to process it. In the last section of this book, we shall return to this notion of a brief visual storage of information that outlasts the termination of the stimulus (see Chapters 13 and 17).

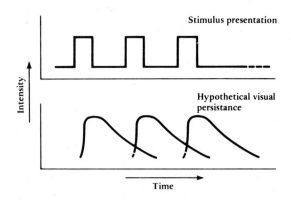

Figure 6.10 Schematic representation of a hypothetical persistence resulting from repeated stimulus presentations. (Haber & Standing, 1969.)

SIMULTANEITY, NUMEROSITY, AND TEMPORAL ORDER

If two stimuli are presented in different modalities or in different locations in the same modality, so that they are spatially clearly discriminable, how far apart do they have to be in time for the perceiver to tell that they are not presented simultaneously? Can he also tell which of the two comes first? From what we have seen already, if the perception of **apparent simultaneity** and temporal order requires only peripheral information, then a slight **asynchrony** in time should be immediately obvious to the perceiver. However, as it turns out, relatively large differences are needed before a perceiver can reliably perceive two stimuli as nonsimultaneous, and even larger differences are needed before he can tell for sure which one comes first.

Schmidt and Kristofferson (1963) presented two pairs of stimuli, made up of a click and a flash of light. One pair had their offsets physically simultaneous. In another, the click ended earlier than the pulse by an amount that varied from trial to trial. For each trial the perceiver had to indicate in which pair the stimuli had nonsimultaneous offsets. Figure 6.11 shows the results. If the asynchrony of offsets was less than about 10 milliseconds, they appeared simultaneous. From 10 to 60 milliseconds separation, performance increased in accuracy until by 60 milliseconds the perceiver could always tell which pair had nonsimultaneous offsets. While the particular values change slightly with changes in intensity or other stimulus parameters, Schmidt and Kristofferson's data are generally representative for the simultaneity-discrimination problem. The results are changed little when both stimuli are visual.

Apparent simultaneity judgment illustrates some of the losses in temporal resolution in the visual system. Ten to 60 milliseconds may not seem like much error. The auditory system, however, has a temporal resolution for asynchronies in time of arrival of sounds to the two ears on the order of millionths of a second. These are routinely used for spatial localization of the sound source. However, although time is measured in somewhat coarser units in vision, it is incorrect to say that time is imprecisely recorded.

Hirsh and Sherrick (1961) argue that the discrimination of order requires even more time than the judgment of simultaneity, suggesting that for some intervals of time, one may be able to judge that two stimuli are asynchronous, without knowing which is first. This interval, they suggest, is about 20 milliseconds.

If there is temporal summation in the visual system, or any other kind of process that limits the temporal discrimination of inputs to the senses, then the number of closely timed events that can be differentiated should also be limited. When events are presented at a rate of no more than five or six per second, perceivers have little trouble in perceiving and counting the number—a judgment of **numerosity**. Problems develop when the rate is faster. If a chain of

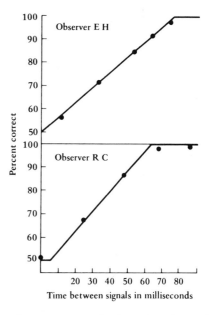

Figure 6.11 Percentage of trials in which the variable pair rather than the standard pair was judged to be more successive as a function of the time interval between the offset of a light pulse and a tone. Data are from two observers. (Schmidt & Kristofferson, 1963.)

flashes of 10 milliseconds duration each is presented at varying rates—10, 15, 25, or 30 per second—the number of flashes reported increases at a slower rate than the number presented. Further, the perceived rate appears to level off at about six to eight flashes per second (Cheatham & White, 1952; Forsyth & Chapanis, 1958).

Harter and White (1967) measured the evoked cortical potential with a scalp recording, and found that it corresponds to the perceived number of flashes, not the actual number of flashes. Hence the loss of information on number occurs before the information reaches the cortex. To support this, White, Cheatham, and Armington (1953) showed by recording of electrical activity at the retina that the stimuli were being followed at a rate of up to forty per second. The loss therefore has to be between the retina and the cortex.

THE PERCEPTION OF FLICKER

One set of experiments considered in the previous section asks the perceiver to count the number of flashes in a rapidly **flickering light**. There is a long history of research on the perception of flicker, but in most of those experiments the dependent variable is the rate of presentation at which the flashes become indistinguishable, that is, the rate at which the flickering light appears to be fused or continuous. This rate, often called the **critical flicker frequency**, represents one limit of temporal resolution of the visual system.

In flicker experiments the stimulus frequently consists of a flash of light of a given duration and luminance that is flashed over and over again, with the off-time between each flash equal to the duration of the flash. A temporal wave form of this type is illustrated in the upper portion of Figure 6.12. We can specify the frequency of the light as the number of on-off cycles per second. The intensity or amplitude of the flicker is the difference between the peak luminance and the average luminance of the wave form.

Often in early work, the luminance of the lowest part was zero, so that the light was being flickered on and off. The average luminance is the average of the light and dark intensities.

The perceiver looks at the objectively flickering light and indicates whether it is flickering or continuous. Other things being equal, better temporal resolution implies that the light has to be flickering at a higher rate before the perceiver is unable to notice its flicker. In this sense, the higher the threshold for **fusion**, measured as the rate of flicker for which the perceiver says the flicker is just barely noticeable, the greater the perceiver's sensitivity for this type of temporal resolution.

This paradigm has been used to discover a number of temporal characteristics of the visual system. The most important ones concern the effects of lumi-

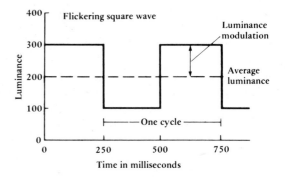

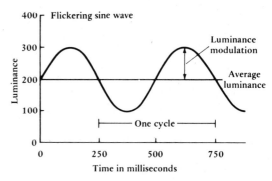

Figure 6.12 Two examples of wave forms used in studies of flicker perception. The top shows a square wave and the bottom a sine wave, both at the same frequency, average luminance, and luminance modulation.

nance on temporal sensitivity. The perceiver has greater temporal sensitivity as the luminance of the flicker is increased. This effect might be expected from the finding that relates the critical duration in temporal integration to luminance. When the luminance is very low, as in scotopic conditions, the critical duration approaches 100 milliseconds, but drops as low as 10 milliseconds under very high light levels. A critical duration of 10 milliseconds means that two flashes are integrated only if they occur within 10 milliseconds of each other. This suggests an upper limit on fusion of 100 flashes per second. Under scotopic conditions, two lights are integrated if they come within 0.1 second of each other, so that even 10 flashes per second are seen as fused.

The relation of the critical duration to the critical flicker frequency is a relative one. If you find the critical duration at which two flashes fuse, presenting more than two may produce some flicker. This is probably because of changes that occur in adaptation during the course of observing a flickering light. For example, if you are dark-adapted and then look at a flickering light, you gradually become light-adapted to the average luminance level of a flickering light. A reliable finding is that the temporal resolution of the visual system goes up with light adaptation (Lythgoe & Tansley, 1929), so that higher levels of flicker are needed to achieve fusion with light adaptation. As more cycles of a flickering light are observed, the eyes are adapted to a higher luminance level, thereby increasing visual sensitivity. Thus, two flashes are seen as fused, a third just barely, but by the fourth or fifth some perceptible flicker is noticeable.

Recently flicker perception has been viewed as a way to study more basic temporal factors in perception. Following the same principles of Fourier analysis and synthesis discussed earlier (Chapters 1 and 4) for spatial frequencies, it is possible to ask whether the visual system analyzes temporally varying light into its frequency components and then recombines or synthesizes these in later processing. A temporal luminance profile can be decomposed into a series of sinusoids made up of a **fundamental frequency** and integral multiples of that frequency (called **harmon-**

ics), just as with a spatial luminance profile. Figure 6.13 shows the fundamental sinusoid and harmonics that are the Fourier components of a square wave of flickering light illustrated at the top of Figure 6.12.

If the visual system is considered a system that analyzes any temporal waveform into its separate sinusoids, then it is possible to predict the sensitivity to any particular waveform of flickering light from a knowledge of the visual system's sensitivity to each of the separate sinusoids that compose that waveform. For example, if the visual system is sensitive only to sinusoids whose frequencies are 10 cycles per second or less, and cannot temporally discriminate the flicker in sinusoids of 30, 50, 70, and more cycles per second, then the sensitivity to the 10 cycles-per-second waveform in Figure 6.13 can be predicted entirely by the sensitivity to the sinusoid of its fundamental frequency. This is the logic of many recent studies in flicker. For example, Kelly (1961) varied the frequency of the flicker, its average luminance, and the **luminance modulation**—the luminance difference between the average and the peaks—in a flicker-discrimination experiment. The perceiver is shown a flickering field of a given frequency and average luminance and asked to adjust the luminance modulation until the flicker is just barely perceptible. This adjustment is comparable to varying the contrast between the black and white bars in the grating patterns used to study sensitivity to spatial frequency. In the case of temporal patterning, if the frequency of the alternation is such that the perceiver easily detects the flicker, then the amount of change in luminance can be reduced. However, if the flicker rate is such that the flicker is not detected, then a greater change in luminance is needed. In this sense, then, the amount of luminance modulation necessary to detect the flicker is a measure of the perceiver's sensitivity to the flicker—the less luminance modulation needed the more sensitive the perceiver.

Figure 6.14 presents Kelly's results for six different average luminance levels. Consider the top function, based upon a very low average luminance of .06 troland. If the frequency of flicker is low, only 2 cycles per second, then the luminance modulation has to be

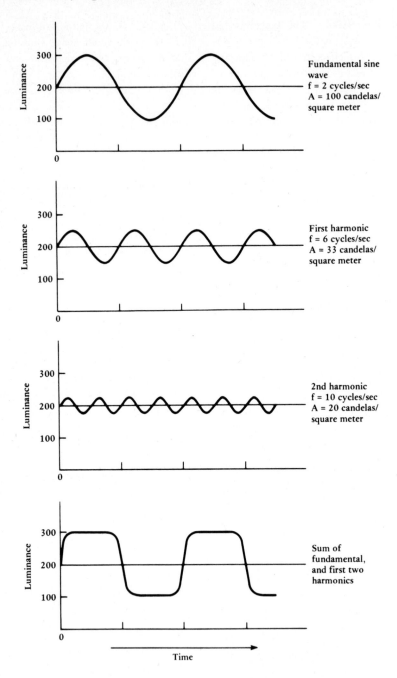

Figure 6.13 Sinusoid and harmonic temporal luminance profiles that are Fourier components of the square wave shown in Figure 6.12.

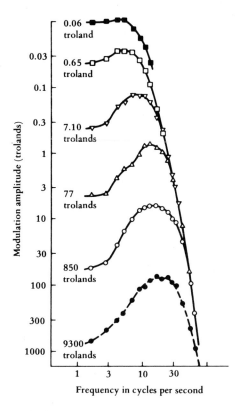

Figure 6.14 Modulation amplitude in trolands needed to keep a flickering light of different frequencies at flicker fusion threshold, for six different average luminance levels. (Kelly, 1961.)

.01 troland, a one- to six-fold difference, or about a 15 percent change for the flicker to be just noticeable. When the flicker rate exceeds 10 cycles per second, the luminance modulation must be larger. It cannot exceed .06 troland, which is the average luminance, or else its luminance will drop below zero when the flickering light is off. This means that, at this average luminance, the perceiver cannot find any luminance modulation that lets him see flicker above about 10 cycles per second. Thus, when the average luminance is very low, the visual system is most sensitive to temporal frequencies below about 10 cycles per second. Above 10 cycles per second sensitivity drops off rapidly.

Now consider the function obtained at the high

average luminance values. The greatest temporal sensitivity is found between 10 and 30 cycles per second. If the flicker rate is increased above 30 cycles per second, the luminance modulation increases sharply, and, by 60 cycles per second, no amount of luminance modulation enables the perceiver to notice the flicker. Thus, except for very low average luminance values, we are most sensitive to flicker between 10 and 30 cycles per second, with a rapid falloff in sensitivity above or below these rates of change.

Kelly's results provide us with estimates of the temporal sensitivity to sinusoidally varying light of different frequencies over a number of values of average luminance. One conclusion from these functions is that the higher-order harmonics in most temporal waveforms do not contribute to the sensitivity of the detection of the flicker. A square wave of 10 cycles per second has harmonics of 30 cycles, 50 cycles, 70 cycles, and so forth. Except at very high light levels, our sensitivity to even 30 cycles per second is so small that it cannot contribute and, of course, none of the higher-order harmonics contribute at all. In contrast, a square wave of low frequency, such as 1 cycle per second, has harmonics of 3, 5, 7 cycles per second, and so forth. Since we are sensitive to all these harmonics, the sensitivity to very low frequency square waves should be much higher than that to sinusoidal waves of the same frequency. Kelly verified this prediction (1972). Sensitivities to sinusoidal and to square waves are identical at all but the very low frequencies of flicker, when sensitivity to square waves is higher.

Kelly (1959) explored this in another direction. If a sinusoidal flickering light is a small spot seen against a dark background, then, in addition to the temporal luminance modulation within the test spot, there is also temporal luminance variation between the spot and the surround and spatial luminance variation around the edge of the spot. On the other hand, if the test spot filled the entire visual field, these additional temporal and spatial edges are not present. Figure 6.15 shows sensitivity functions, again measured by the amount of luminance modulation necessary to detect the flicker, for three different test patterns. As

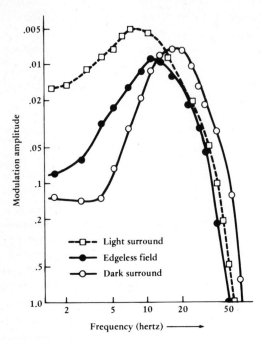

Figure 6.15 The effect of target size on sensitivity to flicker: (*a*) 2° sharp-edged target with steady surround; (*b*) 65° flickering target with blurred edges; (*c*) 4° sharp-edged target with dark surround. (Kelly, 1959.)

expected, there are no differences between the three functions when the temporal frequencies were high, supporting the hypothesis that the higher-order harmonics produced by the edges did not contribute to sensitivity. At the low temporal frequencies, however, the sensitivities differ substantially as a function of the different kinds of test patterns. Kelly's results (see Kelly, 1972, for a complete review of recent research on flicker perception) provide strong evidence for the notion that the visual system performs a simple Fourier analysis of temporally varying light as well as for spatially varying light.

Before leaving the topic of flicker, consider the possible reasons for the limitation on flicker sensitivity to very high and to very low frequencies. Kelly's lowest frequency is 2 cycles per second. What would be expected from even lower rates? If the flickering light is spatially homogeneous and very large, so as to preclude any spatial frequencies at the edges, then we should expect that sensitivity would approach zero as

temporal frequency approaches zero. In other words, the ability to detect the fact that a light is slowly changing in intensity should be very poor. This should not be surprising, since sensory coding mechanisms generally do not respond to steady states of excitation falling on the receptors. The issue will be discussed in some detail when we consider the effects of stabilized retinal images in Chapters 7 and 15. We will then see that the temporal sensitivity of the visual system becomes increasingly poorer as the rate of change in intensity over time approaches zero.

What about the limitation at the high-frequency end? Kelly's results (Figure 6.14) are most impressive. At each average luminance level, the functions appear to converge on a single line. With very high average luminance, the line indicates that flicker rates up to about 100 cycles per second can be detected. As the average luminance drops, the maximum rate drops too. Kelly (1971) believes this limitation is in the photoreceptors themselves, reflecting the rate at which they can change from one level of excitation to another. If he is correct, then the flicker research provides a way to measure psychophysically one of the basic temporal limitations in the visual system. We have already seen the same limitation at work in temporal summation. At high luminance levels, the critical duration over which summation occurs drops to about 10 milliseconds—the same limit Kelly finds. At low luminance levels critical duration in temporal summation is 100 milliseconds. The line in Figure 6.14, when projected upwards, is certainly in the neighborhood of 10 cycles per second or 100 milliseconds per temporal unit.

VISUAL MASKING

We have already shown that the increment in energy (ΔL) needed to detect a test spot depends upon the luminance (L) of the background. If the background is intense, the amount of light added to it has to be large in order to be detected. When we considered the relationship of $\Delta L/L$ in Chapter 3, the two fields being compared or discriminated are present continuously. Since we now know that the impact of brief flashes of light does not occur instantaneously, and, further, that they outlast the physical duration of the energy at the retina, it is reasonable that flashes that are not simultaneous interact with each other. Specifically, one flash coming after a previous one can still affect the perception of the earlier one under certain timing conditions. This effect is generally called **masking by light.** It refers to any situation in which the detection of a target is affected by a masking light presented before, during, or after the target in time. In this kind of masking the masking stimulus is a homogeneous light superimposed over the target.

Crawford first studied the effects of masking by light in 1947. The 0.5-second masking pulse is presented to a dark-adapted eye. The loss in sensitivity is tested by asking the subject to detect a small, brief target flash. Figure 6.16 shows the energy in the target flash required for threshold detection. Clearly the energy needed is greater during the simultaneous exposure of the masking field, increasing thresholds up to 4 log units (a factor of 10,000). What is intriguing is that the masking stimulus acts both backward and forward in time to affect the sensitivity of the visual system. Thus, while the masking flash began at time 0 as shown on the abscissa of Figure 6.16, the elevation in threshold showing the loss of sensitivity begins about 100 milliseconds before the masking flash begins. This has been called **backward masking by light** because the masking light appears to operate backwards in time to affect events that occurred earlier. Similarly, while the masking flash ends at 500 milliseconds, the threshold remains elevated for nearly another 1000 milliseconds before it returns to the base line. This is called **forward masking by light.**

Forward masking does not seem unreasonable, given that the after-activity of the larger and more intense masking flash continues for some time, making it difficult to detect the presence of a smaller, dimmer target flash. However, backward masking is not explained so easily. Crawford thought that the intense and larger masking flash travels faster to the central nervous system than does the smaller and weaker test flash. He referred to this as **neural overtaking.** There is some basis for Crawford's assumption of a differen-

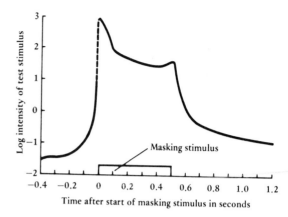

Figure 6.16 Masking by homogeneous light. A small circular target is presented very briefly at some asynchrony relative to a large masking field of 500 milliseconds duration. Log intensity of the test target at threshold is plotted against the asynchrony. Negative asynchrony represents trials in which the mask preceded the test; positive asynchrony represents the reverse sequence. (Crawford, 1947.)

tial latency. For example, simple reaction time in response to light onset is increased as the intensity of the light is reduced. However, a difference in latency of 100 milliseconds between intense and dim flashes is unlikely.

Boynton (1961) has mentioned a second component in addition to neural overtaking. He suggested that masking by light is related to the massive **on-discharges** caused by the masking stimulus. Figure 6.16 illustrates the on-discharges to which Boynton refers. At the onset of a large and intense masking stimulus, a dramatic increase in threshold occurs, lasting only about one-tenth of a second, after which the sensitivity gradually returns to a stable level (until the masking light is turned off, when another on-discharge occurs). We already reviewed electrophysiological evidence that these discharges are due to lateral inhibitory processes and the receptive field organization of the retina. Thus, the onset or the offset of a light produces a signal, whereas its steady state does not.

Boynton suggested that, when the adaptation level is low, the amount of on-discharge produced by the masking stimulus is especially large. Relatively little inhibition is present so that the temporal discontinuity is especially emphasized. Although the test stimulus also produces an on-response, the masking stimulus coming somewhat later overwhelms the visual system, preventing the response to the weaker test stimulus from being treated as a separate event. To demonstrate this, Boynton suggested that, if the overall level of adaptation is raised, the massive on-response to the masking stimulus is reduced, which in turn reduces the masking effect and lowers the test stimulus threshold. Thus, if the effect of the masking stimulus is reduced, even though the higher adaptation level reduces the overall sensitivity of the retina, the on-discharge produced by the masking stimulus is now not able to overwhelm the test flash, and the latter is seen. Boynton (1961) tested this prediction at several levels of adaptation, and found the effect he predicted.

Schiller (1968) provided some physiological evidence to support Boynton's proposal. He obtained single-cell recordings in the lateral geniculate nucleus in cats, and showed that the response to the test stimulus is entirely obliterated by the much larger response to the masking stimulus, whether the masking stimulus precedes or follows the test stimulus. Schiller's results are shown in Figure 6.17. The top panel shows the frequency distribution of spikes from a lateral geniculate nucleus cell plotted for the two seconds following the presentation of a small, dim target flash alone. The cluster of spikes is at about 60 milliseconds—the latency of the response of this LGN cell. The second panel shows the post-stimulus histogram for the masking flash. There is an initial larger burst of activity at about 25 milliseconds and a second and third less intense but more spread-out activity later on. The remaining panels illustrate what happens when the two stimuli are presented together—the target first and the mask second. At 300 and 100 milliseconds gap, responses to both stimuli are clearly evident, but when the masking flash comes within 50 milliseconds or less of the target flash, the response in the LGN cell to the target is obliterated. Presumably this also means that the cortex also does not receive the response. The masking flash is not perceived unless the test flash is made more intense. Schiller's measurements therefore provide direct evidence for the interaction of the two flashes, one acting "backwards" in

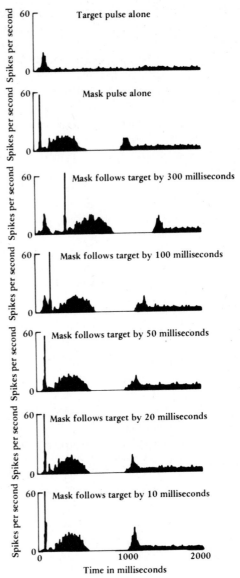

Figure 6.17 Masking by homogeneous light in single neurons of the lateral geniculate nucleus. Each record depicts spike frequencies as a function of time following the stimulus presentation. In the top record, a weak (.3 log above threshold) 1° disk is flashed briefly in the middle of the on-center, off-surround receptive field. In the next record a larger and more powerful masking disk (3 log units above threshold) is flashed, again centered on the receptive field. The records following show combined presentations at inter-stimulus intervals of 10–300 milliseconds. (Schiller, 1968.)

time on the other. His data also support Boynton's proposal that it is the larger discharges associated with the beginning of the masking flash that create the masking. Finally, Schiller's data indicate that masking by light occurs at a precortical level.

One procedure that is frequently employed to determine whether an effect is retinal or cortical is to see whether it can be produced across the two eyes as easily as within one eye alone. If an effect is entirely retinal, due to interaction at the receptor level or among the neurons in the retina, then simultaneous events in the other eye should neither diminish nor increase the effect. The research results reported so far have been **monoptic**—all stimuli have been presented to one eye, with the other eye usually covered. A number of masking experiments have included a procedure—called **dichoptic presentation**—in which both eyes are adapted to the same level and then the test flash is presented to one eye and the masking flash to the other eye. The general finding (for example, Battersby, Oesterreich, & Sturr, 1964) has been of a small, or often negligible amount of masking. To the extent that masking by light is minimal dichoptically, such masking can be attributed to processes in the retina and not to events that occur after the signals from each eye reach the cortex.

Masking a Patterned Target by Light

Although most of the research on masking by light has used homogeneous targets, such masking can also be demonstrated when the target field contains luminance discontinuities. The luminance and the duration of a pattern can be adjusted so that a perceiver can just report the presence of a line (or correctly identify its orientation). When the line presentation is followed, either immediately or after some brief delay, by a homogeneous masking field, the recognition threshold is elevated. This is caused by a reduction in the effective contrast of the line against its background, thereby making it more difficult to detect.

Contrast between two adjacent areas is defined as the ratio of the luminances of light being reflected from the two areas to the eye. Thus, if the retinal projection of the line has a luminance of 10 candelas per square meter and the background against which the line is seen has a luminance of 100 candelas per square meter, the contrast ratio is 1 to 10. This could arise, for example, if the illuminance was 200 candelas per square meter, the black ink of the line had a reflectance of 5 percent, and the background had a reflectance of 50 percent.

What happens to the effective contrast if, after the presentation of the target line has ended, a homogeneous lighted field is presented, covering the area on the retinal projection where the line had been? Given the properties of temporal integration, the energy from the presentation containing the line is integrated with the energy from the blank field following it, as long as it follows soon thereafter. This changes the contrast substantially (Fig. 6.18). For simplicity, let us set the masking flash luminance also at 200 candelas per square meter, of which half is reflected, so that it is as intense as the background against which the line is seen. Now the total amount of light falling on the retinal area where the line had been is 10 candelas per square meter from the line, plus 100 candelas per square meter from the second flash, or a total of 110 candelas per square meter.

For the rest of the field, the total energy is 100 candelas per square meter from the first flash and 100 from the second, making a total of 200 candelas per square meter. But now the contrast is no longer 1 to 10, but rather, less than 1 to 2. This means that the intensity of the area of the retina where the line fell is closer to that of its background, and hence far less discriminable. The more intense the masking flash is, the greater is the reduction in contrast.

This analysis, advanced in greatest detail by Eriksen (1966), nicely accounts for the masking of luminance discontinuities by light in a previously presented visual field. Eriksen refers to this as **luminance summation,** which leads to **contrast reduction.**

Notice that if the masking is done by projecting more light onto the scene, which is then reflected to the eye, there is no contrast reduction. Since the contrast ratio is determined by the reflectances of the line against its background, that ratio is unchanged regardless of the amount of illumination falling on the scene. Masking occurs not because the added light from the mask fell on the scene, but because it falls on

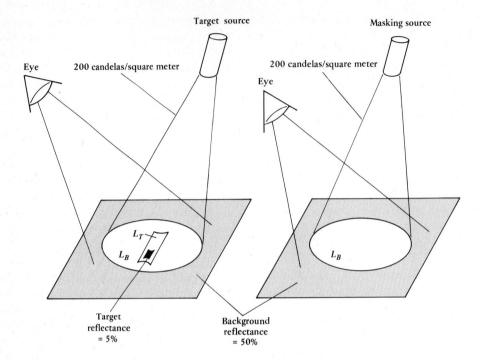

Figure 6.18 Schematic example of contrast reduction as a result of luminance summation. The viewer first sees the left side, on which a black line is displayed against a lighter background. Then that display ends and the eye is shown the right side, without a line. Combining the luminance to the retina over the background yields 100 candelas per square meter from each source, or a total of 200 candelas per square meter. The luminance on the retina where the line fell in the first display is 10 candelas per square meter-reflected for the first source and 100 candelas per square meter from the second, yielding a total of 110 candelas per square meter. Thus, the effective contrast, which would have been 100 to 10 = 10.0, from the first source alone, is reduced to 200 to 110 = 1.9, when the second source is added.

the same parts of the eye as the scene does but from a different light source.

It is for this reason that the contrast of a slide shown on a screen with a slide projector is reduced if the room lights are left on. Although the contrast ratios in the slide itself are unchanged, the added light is veiling the entire screen, adding equal amounts to the intense and dim areas, thereby reducing the contrast ratios between them. If the room lights are intense enough all contrast from the slide can be lost.

We have considered several aspects of masking by light. We have seen, in general, that it is a retinal effect. Backward masking is probably due to the interaction of large on-responses at the onset of stimuli in which the latency of the on-response of the more intense flashes is short enough to swamp the later and smaller on-responses to the target. Forward masking is probably due to the after-effects of the masking flash that swamp a target pulse that comes soon afterwards. In addition, if the target differs in contrast from its background, then the masking flash may reduce this contrast, thereby reducing the brightness or detectability of the contrast. This contrast reduction can occur in both the forward and backward directions.

Masking by Adjacent Contours: Metacontrast

Although the topic of metacontrast is often included under masking by light, the effects are sufficiently dissimilar to deserve separate treatment, especially because of the spatial component involved (Kahneman, 1968; Lefton, 1973).

Werner (1935) showed that if a briefly presented small disk is followed after about 50 milliseconds by a ring just circumscribing it, the perceiver is either unable to see the disk or he describes it as being much dimmer and with indistinct contours (Fig. 6.19). This is a backward masking effect, because the aftercoming ring interferes with the perception of the earlier disk. But now the effect is spatial as well—as the inner circle of the ring becomes larger in relation to the outer edge of the disk, the masking effect decreases. Werner stressed that a spatial contiguity is needed, arguing that contours take time to develop and that the ring interferes with this development.

In metacontrast a second stimulus appears to act backward to distort the perception of an earlier one. But unlike visual masking by light, metacontrast usually works with both stimuli at the same luminance and of the same general size. More important, it is dependent upon a precise spatial relationship, not one of overlap but of close adjacency of contours. Visual masking, on the other hand does not work well when the luminances or sizes are nearly equal, and it does not work much at all when the flashes do not overlap spatially on the retina. Further, the masking by light appears to be primarily retinal.

Metacontrast has been demonstrated many times

with different kinds of stimuli. (See Figure 6.20 for some examples.) In addition to a ring and disk, it is shown with a square as a test stimulus and two flanking squares as the masking stimulus. With an interstimulus interval of between 50 and 100 milliseconds between the offset of the test stimulus and the onset of the flanking masking stimulus, the test square is usually reported to be phenomenally absent (Fehrer & Raab, 1962). Letters or other simple visual forms have also been used as test stimuli, with a ring circumscribing one or more of the letters used as a masking stimulus (for example, Weisstein, 1966).

Alpern (1953) has reported the most detailed data for flashes of rectangular patches of luminance. He found that the amount of masking (as measured by the reduction in the brightness of the center patch) increases with the luminance of the mask. Further, the interstimulus interval for the maximum masking increases with the luminance of the mask. Thus, as the effectiveness of the mask increased with its luminance, it can be delayed later in time and still be effective. Masking is maximal when the borders of the mask are contiguous with the borders of the center square. Border contiguity appears to be crucial for masking since the masking effect drops off sharply as spatial separation increases.

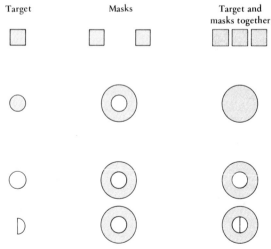

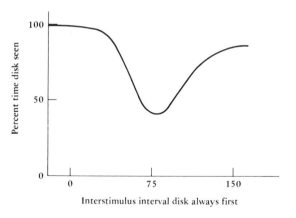

Figure 6.19 The accuracy of detecting the disk, as a function of the delay—interstimulus interval—with which the disk is followed by a masking ring. (Werner, 1935.)

Figure 6.20 Some examples of sets of targets and masks used in metacontrast experiments.

Metacontrast effects are almost always found to be as large dichoptically as monoptically. Thus, unlike masking by light, all the effect with metacontrast seems to be cortical. This implies that the appearance of this stimulus requires cortical processing. On the other hand, the reaction-time response to the onset of a stimulus appears to be initiated by information coming from the eye without complex analysis in the cortex. (Fehrer & Biederman, 1962; Fehrer & Raab, 1962).

Werner felt that metacontrast illustrated processes underlying the development of contours in the visual system. Thus, a second stimulus interferes with contour development in the first if it occurs during the critical time for that development. If it comes too soon or too late it has no effect. His argument is supported by the necessity for closely aligned contours, by the evidence that the effects are central and not retinal, and by the temporal pattern of metacontrast.

Since spatial adjacency is so critical, it appears that some kind of lateral inhibition effect must be involved in metacontrast, even though it is not the simpler types of retinal effects between adjacent receptors. Lefton (1973) has reviewed the arguments and evidence for an inhibition explanation to metacontrast. While the evidence is quite supportive, no single or general explanation for metacontrast is yet available, although some detailed models have been described (see especially Weisstein, 1966, 1972). It is obvious that temporal processes are involved in both, but not in any simple way.

Ganz (1975) has proposed that metacontrast can be explained by the same mechanisms that underlie simultaneous contrast. Heinemann (1955) showed that, if a target is surrounded by a more intense ring, the brightness of the target is sharply reduced (Fig. 6.21). However, very little reduction in brightness is found until the surround (the mask in the present context) is more intense than the target. Increasing the mask intensity above that of the target drops the target brightness sharply. Ganz pointed out that, if the mask luminance is greater than the target luminance when the mask surrounds the target, the brightness of the target is greatly decreased. Ganz described how this could happen when the target and mask are sepa-

rated in time. If the target and mask are of the same luminance and are presented simultaneously, the mask has little effect on the brightness of the target, as Heinemann showed. However, when the target is presented first, for a brief exposure, there is a persistent trace following its termination that decays in time. If, while the trace is still decaying, the mask now arrives, its neural effect is much greater than that of the decaying trace of the target. Thus, we have the conditions that Heinemann showed to be most conducive to the greatest brightness reduction: intense mask and less intense target. The differences in intensity in this case are in terms of neural activity, not in quanta at the retina, but the prediction is the same— reduction of brightness of the target. But what if the mask is delayed too long? While the differences in trace activity are greatest, it is also likely that the target is no longer represented in the visual system as a decaying trace. Most likely it would have been con-

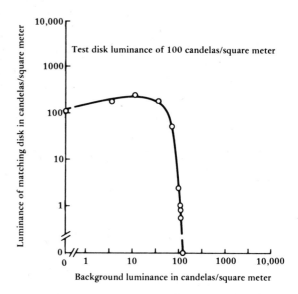

Figure 6.21 Changes in apparent brightness of a disk as a function of varying luminance of the background. Thus, when a test disk of 100 candelas per square meter is surrounded by a very low luminance ring, the test is matched to a comparison disk of about 100 candelas per square meter. However, as the background luminance increases to about the same as the disk, the disk appears much dimmer. (Data from Heinemann, 1955.)

verted into some form of information (see Chapter 15), making it impervious to subsequent visual masking. Thus, according to Ganz, metacontrast is greatest when the mask is delayed relative to the target, as long as the target is still represented only as a decaying visual trace. To test this, Ganz (1975) took data on target and mask persistence and coding time of the target from the work of Sukale-Wolf (1971). From each of these measures, he predicted the amount of masking that would occur when the mask followed the target by different delays. The predicted values matched the obtained values very closely (Ganz, 1975).

More recently Breitmeyer and Ganz (1976) have examined simultaneous contrast as a basis for metacontrast in more detail, and have replaced the notion of decaying traces with that of the differential activity of sustained and transient channels that are activated by the stimulus presentation. The transient channels respond first with a brief activation, which is then followed by the slower and more prolonged activation of the sustained channels (Fig. 6.22). These sustained channels differ among themselves in their latency and in their persistence, with those tuned to the very high

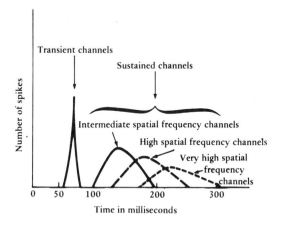

Figure 6.22 The hypothesized time-course of activation of transient and sustained channels after a brief presentation of a stimulus at time 0. Among the sustained channels, the activity of intermediate spatial-frequency channels, high spatial-frequency channels, and the very high spatial-frequency channels are differentiated. (Breitmayer & Ganz, 1976.)

spatial frequencies responding most slowly, most weakly, and over the longest time course. Breitmeyer and Ganz make use of one additional characteristic of the sustained and transient channels—the shorter-latency transient channels can inhibit the slower sustained channels when they are both activated. Specifically, they argue that, if both transient and sustained channels are activated at the same time, the transient channels inhibit the sustained channels, thereby preventing the information carried by the sustained channels from being processed further by the visual system.

To see the implication of this process follow the four timing arrangements of targets and masks illustrated in Figure 6.23. Keep in mind the experimental results in which the effect of the mask is strongest when it is delayed by 50 to 100 milliseconds after the target is presented. In Figure 6.23 (*a*) the mask precedes the target. The only inhibition that can occur is that the transient channels of the target inhibit the sustained activity of the mask—the inner contour of the mask is harder to see. If the target and mask are presented together in time (Figure 6.23 [b]) both sets of channels overlap and there is no inhibition. But when the mask is delayed relative to the target, as in Figures 6.23 (*c*) and (*d*), the transient channels activated by the mask occur at the same time that the sustained channels activated by the target are excited. The optimal delay of the mask would be to have the mask's transient channels inhibit the earliest set of sustained channels of the target, that is, those carrying the intermediate spatial frequency information that defines the edges of the target. If the mask is delayed for too long its transients inhibit only the very high spatial frequency sustained channels of the target. This may reduce its contrast or clarity, but does not seriously affect its detection.

This is a theoretical model of how metacontrast occurs. It is much more specific about the nature of the interactions among the neural units than is the earlier Ganz (1975) explanation based upon simultaneous contrast mechanisms alone. Moreover, it fits with what is known about neural coding. However, this is an active field of research and it may turn out that further work will show one or more of the as-

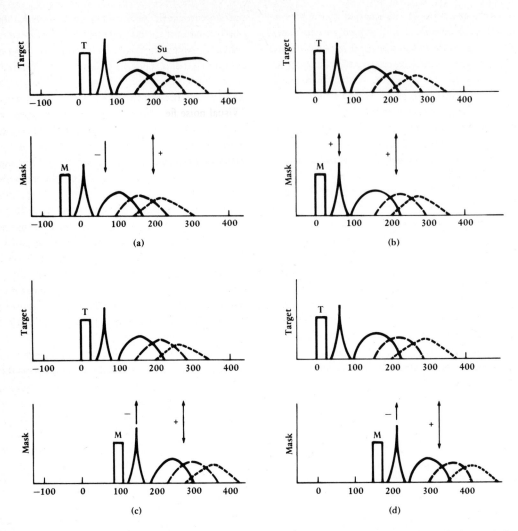

Figure 6.23 Each panel illustrates, for a different asynchromy of target and mask, how the time course of the transient and sustained channels activated by the target and the mask can interact. Within each panel, the vertical arrows indicate the nature of the interactions. (Breitmayer & Ganz, 1976.)

sumptions to be incorrect or superseded by other mechanisms.

Masking by Visual Noise

A third type of masking involves the temporal interaction between a flash containing a pattern and a following flash containing a random pattern of lines and squiggles. Such random patterns of line segments are referred to as **visual noise** (Sperling, 1963). A pattern of this sort may cover the entire visual field, being much larger than the test flash to be detected or reconized, or it may cover only specific areas of the visual field. When the masking pattern covers only the area upon which the test flash falls, it is still not considered simple metacontrast because it overlays the entire test presentation rather than only surrounding it. Usually the average luminances of the test and masking fields are equated so that the effects of masking by light and by visual noise can be separated. Masking by noise has proved very useful as an operation to study the more complex information-processing tasks that are described in the last section of this book.

When discussing masking by light, we noted that the perceptibility of a patterned stimulus is reduced when it is masked by light. A comparable effect is expected when the mask is patterned as by visual noise. Thus the background part of the visual noise field reflects light, and this light summates with that from the pattern, thereby reducing its contrast. Masking by light can be controlled by using an adaptation field before and after the pattern presentation. If the perceiver first sees a homogeneous background field of, say, 100 candelas per square meter, which is briefly turned off just when the pattern field is presented (also with a background luminance of 100 candelas per square meter), the effective contrast ratio of any pattern is reduced by the veiling light added over the entire retinal projection. Let us say that the adaptation field is on for several minutes, and then goes off for 10

milliseconds, during which time a field containing a line is presented, after which the adaptation field returns. This sequence is illustrated in the top two lines of Figure 6.24. Here Channel 2 is the background and Channel 1 is the array.

A test of the effects of visual noise asks whether a visual noise field produces more masking than does the background luminance alone. Such a test is illustrated in the bottom three lines of Figure 6.24. Virtually every experiment done in this way has shown that the masking effect is much greater from visual noise than from the lighted background alone (Lefton, 1973). Hence masking by visual noise must be more than simply creating luminance summation that leads to contrast reduction. There must be some impact of the additional contours being imposed upon the retinal projection of the patterned stimulus.

Under nearly all circumstances, masking by noise is maximal when the target and mask are simultaneous. If the mask is presented earlier (forward) or later (backward) the masking effect is reduced.

Sperling (1963) explained the visual-noise masking effect in terms of disruption of the representation

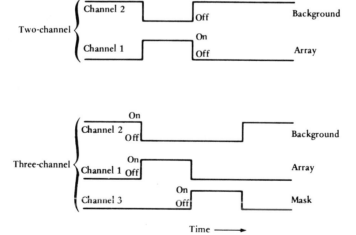

Figure 6.24 Schematic representation of the temporal sequence of a background and a letter array presentation in a two-channel tachistoscope (top), and with the addition of a masking pulse immediately following the array, using a three-channel tachistoscope (bottom).

of the luminance discontinuities after it reached the cortex. He suggested that the representation of the second patterned stimulus interferes with that from the previous one, replacing it, combining with it, or in some other way rendering it ineffective. Thus, until the arrival of the second pattern, the central representation of the first one is available for processing or information extraction.

Sperling based his argument on an experiment in which a test stimulus containing an array of letters was followed by a visual noise presentation after varying interstimulus intervals. Figure 6.25 contains his results. Sperling found that for each 10 milliseconds that the visual noise was delayed beyond the onset of the test stimulus, the perceiver could report one more letter. This suggested to Sperling that the visual noise is controlling the time that the test stimulus is available for processing, but not the adequacy of the test stimulus representation itself. This effect has been replicated by a number of other experimenters under a wide range of experimental conditions.

Sperling's interpretation is that the mask **interrupts** the processing of the target information so that no further processing is possible after the mask arrives. Others have argued that the neural code of the mask is **integrated** into the code of the target so that the two are combined. Thus, while the target information is not destroyed by the arrival of the mask it may no longer be separable from that of the mask. Breitmeyer and Ganz (1976) argue strongly for an integration mechanism based upon the summation of sustained channels from the target and the mask. The greatest integration occurs when the target and the mask overlap in time which is, in fact, the typical finding. One virtue of the Breitmeyer and Ganz model is that it predicts that the time course of masking is slightly different when intermediate spatial frequencies are used as compared to when very high spatial frequencies are involved. The former can be masked only if the target and mask are synchronized, since that is the only time when the intermediate sustained channels overlap and can be integrated. Given the slower and lower amplitude of very high spatial frequency sustained channels, however, they can be integrated with the mask's sustained channels at much longer delays of the mask.

Masking by visual noise has been used as a technique to control the time course of information processing as in the Sperling's (1963) experiment. By delaying the mask by various amounts of time, it has been possible to examine the amount of information that can be processed from a given target in a given time period. We examine this methodology in some detail in Chapter 18, especially in light of the assumptions underlying integration versus interruption by visual noise.

SUMMARY

Visual stimuli are described most generally by their spatial properties, to which we are very sensitive, but they also vary in time. This chapter describes some of the ways in which time is important in visual perception, and how the visual system codes and responds to those aspects of time.

Time is relevant because stimuli differ in duration, because even continuous stimuli are viewed discontinuously by saccadic eye movements, and because

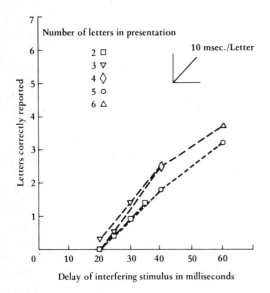

Figure 6.25 The number of letters correctly reported as a function of the delay between the onset of the letters and the onset of a visual noise field. (Sperling, 1963.)

even brief stimuli do not produce their effects instantaneously but take time to be processed.

Recent neurophysiological discoveries have shown that ganglion cells can be classified as transient or sustained depending upon their responses to onsets or offsets of light as compared to continuous stimulation. It has been suggested that these two types of cells are specialized to detect brief, flickering or moving stimuli as compared to fixed stimuli in which high spatial resolution is more important than high temporal resolution. The distinction between the two types of cells has been used to help understand several of the temporal processing tasks in this chapter.

The most fundamental concept is temporal summation, that is, up to some limit of duration, the visual system summates energy over time. This means that very brief intense flashes have the same effect as longer and less intense ones. The limit is called the critical duration, and it varies for detection of light, depending upon the adaptation level, from between 10 milliseconds at high light levels to 100 milliseconds at low light levels. For supraluminal tasks, the critical duration may be even longer. Temporal summation represents a loss of sensitivity to duration. It is primarily due to persistence effects of the photoreceptors themselves.

A related concept is temporal integration, in which very closely spaced flashes of light are seen as integrated into a single continuous flash. Unlike temporal summation, however, this appears to be a neural and not a receptor effect.

Many of these timing effects are related to or caused by visual persistence, especially of receptor activity after stimulus termination. Such persistence causes brief stimuli to appear as if they are more extended in time than they really are. This means that closely spaced stimuli flashes appear to be simultaneous when they are physically successive, and that the number of closely spaced flashes is underestimated.

Flickering light is often used to study the temporal sensitivity of the visual system. The frequency at which a perceiver cannot distinguish the separate flashes is called the critical flicker frequency. This frequency is greater the higher the luminance. Recent work has described flickering light in terms of its temporal waveform and applied Fourier analysis to determine the component sinusoidal frequencies. Research by Kelly has shown that the response to flickering light can be predicted by the responses to the component sinusoids. At low light levels, the visual system is most sensitive to light flickering at between 3 and 5 cycles per second, whereas at higher levels, sensitivity is greatest to flicker of around 10 cycles per second. Kelly's results in a series of experiments strongly suggest that the visual system performs a Fourier analysis of flickering light and this determines whether the individual flashes are detected as separate. Kelly's results also provide evidence about the limits of sensitivity to very high and to very low rates of flicker.

The last topic of the chapter concerned the different types of visual masking, in which the detection of one flash is affected by the presence of another flash. In masking by light, the detection of a dim, brief target is substantially reduced if it is preceded, overlapped, or followed in time by a more intense masking flash. When the masking flash follows the target, the backward effect may be due to the faster neural transmission time or to the massive on-discharges that the onset of any intense flash produces. Evidence is presented in support of both of these alternatives, especially the latter. In either case, masking by light appears to be retinal in origin and not due to interactions that take effect after the neural signals reach the cortex.

If the target is a patterned stimulus rather than just a uniform patch of light, then masking occurs because the light from the mask reduces the contrast within the light and dark areas of the pattern. This is also a retinal effect.

If the mask surrounds the target but does not overlap it in space, the reduction in detection of the target is called metacontrast. It only happens when the mask follows (backward) the target, and depends upon very close spatial alignment of the target and mask, suggesting that metacontrast is as much concerned with spatial as with purely temporal effects. Further, it appears to be cortical, in that the effect is unchanged when the target and mask are put into different eyes. While the explanation of metacontrast is not yet settled, it appears to depend upon processes underlying simultaneous contrast and the interaction of transient and sustained channels in the retina.

The last type of masking discussed is masking by visual noise, in which the target is a pattern to be discriminated, and the masking flash is randomly patterned. While some of this masking effect is due to the luminance of the mask, as in masking by light, some additional masking also occurs due to the patterning of the mask itself. Further, masking by visual noise is greatest when the target and mask are simultaneous in time. Several different explanations have been offered.

SUGGESTED READINGS

The recent chapter by Ganz (1975) contains many of the topics covered here. Since temporal factors usually are given some coverage in most handbooks on visual perception, many of the sources previously listed will be useful here, too. Specifically, several excellent chapters on temporal factors are found in Rosenblith (1961), Graham (1965), Kling and Riggs (1971), and especially Jameson and Hurvich (1972). This latter handbook contains chapters by Boynton on temporal integration and masking, Weisstein on metacontrast, and Kelly on flicker. Fraisse's book (1963) on the perception of time includes much material not normally covered in a chapter like the present one.

Chapter 7

Eye Movements

The preceding chapters have examined different aspects of the coding of information contained in light that is focused on the retinal surface of the two eyes. This analysis has been carried out under the implicit assumption that the retinas are fixed in space—an assumption that is clearly unjustified. The pattern of light focused on the two retinas is rarely unchanging or unmoving. Some of that change is the result of movements in the world around us, but most of it is caused by changes in the positions of the eyes resulting from movement of the eyes themselves with respect to the head, and movements of the head with respect to the environment. It might seem that a continuously moving retinal image would be a source of noise, whose effects would have to be ignored or overcome. However, visual perception is thoroughly dependent upon such movements. They provide the basis for perceiving the environment as well as information about the characteristics of the visual world around us.

Eye movements are classified in a number of ways, depending upon the kinds of analyses being made. We can separate those that are voluntary from those that are involuntary; those in which the eyes move in the socket from those in which the entire head moves; those that result in large displacements of the retinal image from those that result in small displace-

ments; and those in which the two eyes move in parallel from those in which they move in opposition. All of these are of interest, although we shall discuss them in terms more of their perceptual consequences than of the type of retinal image displacement that occurs.

MECHANISMS OF EYE MOVEMENTS

Figure 7.1 illustrates two of the three types of eyeball rotation that occur for an eye socket. These are defined with respect to a **line of sight**—a line drawn from the center of the fovea through the center of the pupil and out into space. If you imagine such a line projecting out of your eyeball, then a horizontal rotation moves the line horizontally back and forth, vertical rotation moves the line up and down, and a torsional rotation moves the eyeball in the socket without changing the direction of the line. Thus, in a torsion movement, the eye rotates around the line of sight.

Figure 7.2 is a sketch of the two eyes and the external muscles that control their positions. The six muscles on each eye can be thought of as three antagonistic pairs. The two muscles on either side of the eyeball (the lateral and medial rectus muscles) rotate

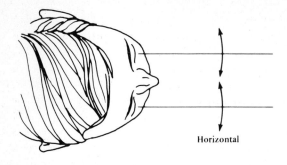

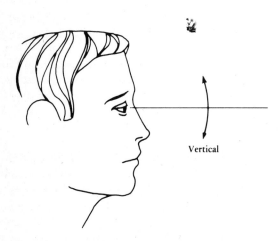

Figure 7.1 Sketch illustrating horizontal rotation and vertical rotation around the line of sight.

the eyeball so that the line of sight moves from side to side in a horizontal plane. The muscles on the top and bottom of the eyeball (the superior and inferior rectus muscles) rotate the eyeball so that the line of sight moves up and down in the vertical plane. The third set of muscles (the superior and inferior oblique muscles) also attached to the top and bottom of the eyeball, rotate the eyeball around in its socket.

When the eye is stationary and oriented straight ahead the three sets of muscles are under tension, each member of a pair in balance with its opposite. When a movement occurs along any one of these planes, one member of the pair contracts while the other relaxes. For example, if the eyes are to move laterally to the left, the tension on the lateral rectus muscle on the left side of each eyeball increases, shortening the muscle and pulling the eye around to the left, while the tension of the medial rectus muscle on the other side is relaxed, lengthening that muscle. When the eye comes to rest, it is now oriented to the left, and the tension on the two muscles equalizes again, except that the ones on the left are much less extended than those on the right. Keller and Robinson (1971) have shown that, when a movement begins, the antagonistic muscle (the one that has to relax) relaxes completely for the duration of the movement and then retenses exactly when the movement ends, effectively locking the eye in place. Most eye movements require reciprocal action of all three sets of muscles simulta-

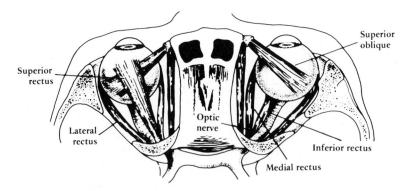

Figure 7.2 The oculomotor muscles of man as seen from above. On the left, a portion of the superior oblique has been cut away to reveal the inferior oblique; on the right, the superior rectus has been removed to permit a view of the inferior rectus. (Walls, 1942.)

neously. This, exact positioning of the eyes requires careful orchestration of the action of these muscles.

NEURAL CONTROL CENTERS FOR EYE MOVEMENT

We are still ignorant of all the neural mechanisms that control eye movements. Each of the three sets of muscles are innervated by different cranial nerves, which in turn are connected to separate motor neurons in the brain stem—one type of motor neuron for each set of muscles. Keller and Robinson (1971) showed that, when direct recordings are made from a motor neuron during the course of a horizontal eye movement, the motor neuron produces a sharp burst of spike activity corresponding with the onset of the movement of the pulling muscle. The motor neuron innervating the relaxed muscle shows a complete cessation of activity. The burst and cessation last for the exact duration of the movement itself, followed by a return to the resting level of activity of the respective motor neurons. So there is a nice specificity between activity in the appropriate motor neuron and movement of the associated set of muscles.

Fuchs (1976) argued that the source of stimulation to these motor neurons is in the pontine reticular formation in the brain stem, with different neurons there controlling different motor neurons. He presented evidence that the activity of neurons in the reticular formation is proportional to the size and duration of movement. But from this point inward the evidence is less clear. One center involved is the **superior colliculus**, since it has inputs from the retina and from the visual cortex (see page 22 in Chapter 1) and has outputs to the pontine reticular formation. Wurtz (1976) has shown that one area of the superior colliculus responds to novel stimuli (that move or suddenly appear) irrespective of their size, shape, content, contrast, or movements. He suggested that this is the location that determines which stimuli are looked at next. This anterior area of the superior colliculus becomes active preceding an eye movement (by 50–100 milliseconds), but not otherwise. Wurtz

suggests that it is the output of these cells that project to the brain stem to activate the neurons there that innervate the motor neurons to cause the muscles around the eyeball to change.

This is obviously not the entire story, however, and may only explain eye movements caused by the sudden appearance of visual stimulation on the retina. Eye movements that are the result of head movements have to be controlled in part by centers that keep track of the position and movement of the head in space. Melvill-Jones (1976) has shown a number of inputs from the **vestibular system**—the **semicircular canals** and **otoliths** of the inner ear that are responsible for detection of orientation in relation to gravity, and of acceleration in space—to the same motor neurons that move the muscles of the eyes, but we do not yet know how this **vestibulo-occulo-motor system** interacts with the eye movement initiated by unexpected stimuli.

TYPES OF EYE MOVEMENTS

Figure 7.3 lists the major types of eye movements. Some of these are more important for perceptual processes than are others and we shall concentrate on the former. **Saccadic movements** are very fast, jerky movements that move the eye in the socket to a new orientation. This is the principal movement used in visual search, in reading, in examining a picture or scene, or in noticing movement on the periphery of vision. **Smooth pursuit movements** are used to track an object moving across the field of view, as in watching an airplane take off or a bird fly by. These movements are smooth, rather than jerky, much slower than saccadic movements and require a moving object for them to occur. The third type of large eye movements are **vestibulo-occular movements**, in which the eyes rotate in the head to compensate for head and body movements in order to maintain the same direction of vision. Saccadic, pursuit, and vestibulo-occular movements each produce **conjugate movement**, in which the two eyes move in the same direction and by the same amount (with slight exceptions to be mentioned below). **Vergence movements**

Type of eye movement	Stimulus	Purpose	Speed
Smooth pursuit	Slowing moving object	To track slowly moving objects	Slow-up to 40 degrees per second
Saccade	Either peripherally detected motion or decision to change fixation	Examine new targets, visual search	Very fast-up to 1000 degrees per second
Vestibulo-occular	Head or body motion	Maintenance of fixation during head or body movement	Slow-up to 20 degrees per second
Vergence	Retinal disparity	To maintain convergence of both eyes on same fixated target	Very slow-up to 10 degrees per second
Drift	Failure to hold fixation	Random	Moderate-up to 100 degrees per second, and very small
Microsaccade (flick)	Prior drift	Reposition the eye with respect to previous fixation	Very fast-like saccade, and very small
Physiological nystagmus (tremor)	Irreducible muscle imbalance due to high tension	Random	Very fast and very small

Figure 7.3 A list of the characteristics of the various types of eye movements.

produce changes in the direction of the two eyes in opposition to each other that occur when we shift our gaze from a near to a far object (divergence) or vice versa (convergence), or when we move our body away from or toward an object upon which we keep our gaze fixed. While all of these movements can be either large or small, there are three types of movements that are always small—**drifts, micro-saccades** (often called flicks), and **physiological nystagmus** (often called **tremors**). Each type of movement will be discussed briefly below.

Saccadic Eye Movements

The typical stimulus for a saccadic movement is a sudden displacement of an object in the visual field. The eye then shifts to a new position that projects the object onto the fovea again. This is most probable when the object had been the center of fixation, but a saccade may also be initiated if a nonfixated object is suddenly displaced. Saccadic eye movements can also be considered voluntary since an observer can initiate

them when he wishes to look at some other part of a stationary visual field. This is the typical pattern in visual search. It is more difficult to study the temporal characteristics of the voluntary saccades, since we have no way of knowing when the command to begin such a movement is initiated.

The latency and speed of saccadic eye movements can be studied precisely (Alpern, 1962, 1971) by moving the fixation point and noting subsequent changes. The latency of movement is quite long— about 180 to 250 milliseconds elapse between stimulus displacement and the initation of an eye movement. However, if the perceiver has prior knowledge of the time and direction of the shift, he starts his movement somewhat faster. The estimate of one-fifth of a second is probably more representative of real life. Once initiated, the movement itself is very fast. For example, only about one-tenth of a second is needed for a 40-degree movement (400 degrees per second). Velocities are higher for larger movements, approaching 1000 degrees per second for a 90-degree shift. The movement time for a return sweep after reading a line of print is about 50 milliseconds, and is relatively independent of the length of the line.

Saccadic eye movements are **ballistic movements**—like those of bullets or rockets—in that their path and distance are completely determined prior to the actual motion. Just as the path of a bullet is specified by the direction in which the gun is pointing and the initial force of the propelling charge, the path of a saccadic movement is determined by a program that issues efferent commands to the muscles to move the eyes to a new fixation. Thus, once programmed, a saccadic eye movement proceeds to its destination unchanged, even if new visual information is added after the programming but before the movement starts.

This fact has been demonstrated by Westheimer (1954). He had a viewer fixate a spot which is moved to a new location and then returns to its original position after 40 milliseconds (Fig. 7.4). If saccadic eye movements are not ballistic, the return information could be utilized, and the eye simply remains where it is. However, Westheimer found that the eye moves to the new location 200 milliseconds after the light has begun to move, even though, by this time, the light has returned to its original position and has been there for 160 milliseconds. The eye remains at the new location for almost another 200 milliseconds (the latency of the next eye movement), and then returns to the original position.

It seems likely that saccadic eye movements are initiated by signals put out by the superior colliculus (Wurtz, 1976), as a result of detection of peripheral movement, of novel stimuli, or of a voluntary decision to move the eyes to a new line of sight. We know from the ballistic character of such movements that the superior colliculus signal is initiated up to 200 milliseconds before the movement begins. One reason why this signal may have to precede the movement by so long an interval is that the visual system uses that signal for another purpose. One theory to account for the stability of perception, given the changing retinal image, is that the superior colliculus signal is compared to the resulting retinal changes. If they match exactly, the retinal changes are cancelled or ignored (von Holst, 1954)—see Chapter 10, pp. 210–211.

Pursuit Eye Movements

Pursuit movements are those involved in tracking moving objects in order to maintain a stable retinal image of that object. Pursuit movements require that there be a moving object in the visual field. Figure 7.5 illustrates pursuit motion for four different speeds of moving objects, shown from the time an object begins to move. The 200-millisecond latency is

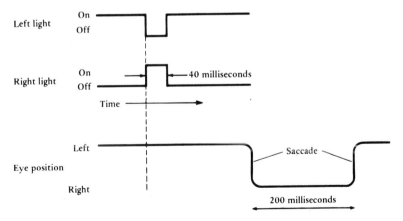

Figure 7.4 The upper panel shows the timing of the presentation of each of two lights, of which an observer had to fixate whichever one was illuminated. The lower panel shows the observer's saccadic eye movements to the onset of the two lights.

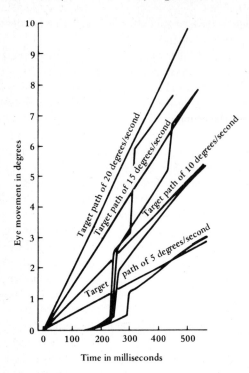

Eye movement in degrees

Target path of 20 degrees/second

Target path of 15 degrees/second

Target path of 10 degrees/second

Target path of 5 degrees/second

Target

Time in milliseconds

Figure 7.5 Displacement of the position of the eye pursuit movements as a function of time for four different speeds of moving objects. (Robinson, 1965.)

for the initial saccade. Then the eye matches the velocity of the moving object and tracks it smoothly, as long as the velocity of the object's motion is not high. Pursuit movements are distinguished from saccadic movements by their slower speed and by their smoothness. It is likely that completely different control systems underlie the two types of movements. Occasionally, pursuit movements are combined with saccades, as when an error in pursuit occurs. Then, a rapid saccadic movement may be made to correct the position.

Pursuit eye movements are virtually impossible to make in the absence of a moving target. If asked to imagine, say, a bird flying across the scene and to track it, the eyes actually make a series of saccades, not smooth eye movements (Robinson, 1976).

Vergence Movements

When the two eyes are fixed on a target located more than 100 meters away the lines of sight of the two eyes are essentially parallel. If the target is displaced closer to the observer, the lines of sight will converge in order to maintain the image of the object on the two foveas. If a near target is displaced farther away, the eyes diverge. The stimulus for vergence movements is retinal disparity (Westheimer, 1976), in this case when the stimulation on the two foveas is dissimilar.

The latency of vergence eye movements is approximately the same as that of saccadic movements. Vergence begins 200 milliseconds after disparity is introduced. The velocity of movement, however, is very slow, taking up to 500 milliseconds after it begins to bring the two foveas back onto the target. Also, unlike saccades, vergence movements are not ballistic in nature—if the target moves again before the vergence movement is initiated or completed, the movement is corrected for the new target position.

Vergence movements are different in another respect from saccades and pursuits—they move the eyes in opposition to each other rather than together. While the evidence is strong that the final neural pathways to the eye muscles are the same regardless of the type of eye movement, it is obvious that the programming of vergence movements must be quite different from those of saccades and pursuits. Westheimer (1976) points to several levels of evidence that the neural control for vergence is closely linked to those of accommodation and pupil constriction. While the latter two are pulled by muscles inside the eyeball rather than outside, all are concerned with changes in the visual system in order to perceive near objects—the eyes converge, each eye accommodates by thickening the lens, and each eye constricts the pupil opening. Westheimer has mapped out the neural pathways for these three processes, all beginning with a common center in the midbrain.

Vestibulo-Occular Movements

When a baseball outfielder runs to catch a fly ball, he has to "keep his eye on the ball" in spite of the incredible variety of head and body movements that occur during the few seconds of pursuit. Under less extreme circumstances, we frequently wish to maintain fixation on a target while moving our heads in space. Since we are rarely able to keep our head and body exactly stationary, we always need movements of the eye tied to the changes in position of our body. To do this, the eyes must rotate in their sockets to compensate for the displacements produced by motions of the head and body. Melvill-Jones (1976) has demonstrated that visual information alone is insufficient as a source of feedback to produce these compensations. It is not surprising, therefore, that there have to be direct inputs to the motor neurons from the semicircular canals of the inner ear to provide the compensations.

A brief digression into the mechanisms of the vestibular system shows how this works. Figure 7.6 illustrates one of the semicircular canals. The tube is filled with a viscous fluid. If the head is suddenly rotated to the left, the fluid is forced to the right in the opposite direction. This displaces the cupula located at the bottom of the canal. At the base of the cupula are nerve endings responsive to the amount of displacement. These nerve endings are connected to nerve fibers that terminate in the vestibular nucleus in

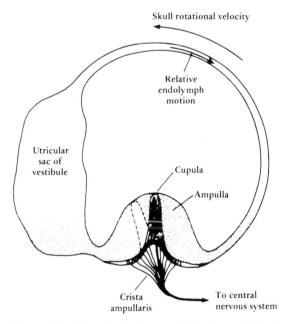

Figure 7.6 The principal anatomical and neurological components of the semicircular canals.

the brain. There are three such semicircular canals in man, each at right angles to the other, so that each records acceleration along one of the three axes of possible rotation of the head—side to side, back to front, and up to down.

Melvill-Jones and Gonshor (1975) have worked out the neural connections between the canals of the vestibulo-nucleus and the motor neurons to the eye muscles. They have shown how the outputs from the three canals control the antagonistic sets of eye muscles so as to move the eye to compensate for head motion regardless of the direction or acceleration through which the head is displaced.

Steinman (1975, 1976) argues strongly that most of our eye movements in the natural environment are compensations for head and body motion, which makes the vestibulo-occular system the most important source of control for eye movements. He supports this by showing how much better eye movements are predicted when head and body movements are also recorded. Thus, he feels that eye movements are designed primarily to provide a stable visual world by providing a stable retinal image while the observer moves about in space. Superimposed on this are voluntary pursuit and saccadic movements in order to look at something else.

The four types of eye movements discussed so far—saccade, pursuit, vergence, and vestibulo-occular—are all relatively large and all concerned with the perceiver's interaction with visual space. They each can be voluntary, although they each occur without any willing or intention as well. They each are in the service of exploring the visual world, keeping in touch with it and maintaining stability of perception in spite of changing retinal images. The next three types of eye movements are quite different.

Drifts, Flicks, and Tremors

Figure 7.7 shows a two-second record of eye movements while the perceiver maintains fixation on a small spot. Not shown are the very fine wiggles called physiological nystagmus or tremors of the eye. They are quite small, moving the eye less than a foveal cone on the average, and quite fast, occurring several hundred times a second. The two eyes wiggle independently so

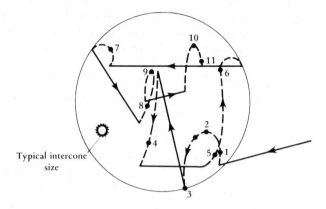

Figure 7.7 Changes in location of a point source imaged in the retina as a function of tremors, drifts, and microsaccades. The solid lines are microsaccades, and the dashed lines are drifts. Tremors are not illustrated but would be shown by a jiggle in all the lines of about the amount of the cone size shown. (Ditchburn, 1955.)

that the duration and timing of the tremor of the left eye does not match that of the right eye. All these facts suggest that the tremor in the normal eye is a result of mechanical tension—the massive simultaneous pull of the antagonistic muscles—and does not arise from neural instability in the higher centers. Further, because the tremors are very small, they appear to have no perceptual significance whatsoever. Perception would be no better or no worse if they were somehow removed or damped.

Not so for drifts and flicks. As Figure 7.7 shows, the eye does not normally maintain perfect fixation, but rather, the line of sight drifts across the fixation target. After the drift is pronounced, the eye makes a microsaccade or flick back to about where it had been before the drift began. This process continually reoccurs. Typically, such drifts and flicks cover about five to six minutes of arc, which shifts the image over perhaps ten to twenty cones. Drifts and flicks are correlated between the two eyes. This suggests that the cause must be neural and originate above the level of the muscles and their associated motor neurons themselves. This conclusion is supported by Steinman (1976), who has shown that normal subjects can minimize drifts and flicks by instruction and training alone. Even so, he finds an irreducible minimum around 2–3 minutes of arc, about half of what is found

without conscious attempts to minimize them. As we shall see below, perception depends in part for continuity and stability on the occurrence of drifts and flicks, for if they are prevented from occurring, vision fails altogether.

MEASUREMENT OF EYE MOVEMENTS

Several of the techniques used to measure the position of the eyes and head and assess the amount of movements that occurred will be described briefly. Detailed descriptions of these and other techniques can be found in Monty and Senders (1976) and Young & Sheena (1975).

Direct Photography

If enough light is present, high contrast motion or video-pictures can be taken of the eyes. Since the light from the scene being looked at is reflected off the cornea, the location of the center of the pupil in relation to the reflected scene provides an indication of the direction of gaze. Movement of the eyes can be determined by measuring the changes in the location of the center of the pupil from frame to frame of the movie sequence. It is difficult, however, to obtain very fine estimates of eye position and therefore of movement by direct photography. Because of the lack of resolution of the alignment of the scene and pupil, and because the curvature of the cornea produces errors of alignment the accuracy is rarely greater than 1°. Nevertheless, if you have the time to measure all the frames, this is the most direct technique and involves no interference with normal vision and no attachments to the observer.

Corneal Reflection Techniques

Instead of taking a photograph of the eye and then looking for the center of the pupil, it is possible to determine the position of the eye more directly. If the eyes are flooded with infrared light (which the observer cannot see), two photocells that are sensitive to infrared can be positioned to record the amount of light reflected from the eyes. The pupil opening reflects virtually no light, the iris very little, and the white sclera a large amount. Each photocell can be positioned so that it is focused on the sclera–iris boundary when the eye is looking straight ahead (see Figure 7.8(*a*)). If the eye is shifted to the right (see Figure 7.8(*b*)), the left cell is focused entirely on the high-reflectance sclera while the right cell is focused entirely on the low-reflectance iris and pupil. Thus, the large right–left cell difference would indicate a rightward movement. If the eye moved to the left, the difference between the two cells is reversed. The amount of the difference indicates how far the eye moved. Measurements of upward and downward eye movements are usually not as accurate with this technique. They involve adding the outputs of the two cells rather than finding their difference. Obviously, this technique can only measure where the eyes are directed relative to the photocells. It cannot tell the difference between an eye movement and a head movement, so the head has to be restrained. With voluntary head restraint, the sclera-reflection techniques yield accuracy of eye position to about 1 degree. Fixing the head, by having the observer bite on a dental impression plate that exactly fits his teeth, increases accuracy to 0.25 degree (15 minutes of arc) or less.

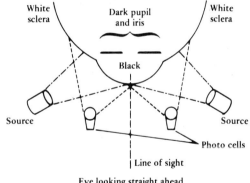

Eye looking straight ahead
(a)

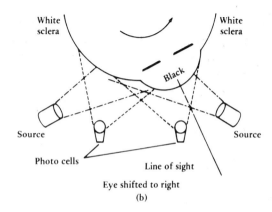

Eye shifted to right
(b)

Figure 7.8 Schematic diagram of the positioning of two photocells to pick up light reflected from the white sclera and the darker iris and pupil. In the upper panel, the two photocells are receiving equal reflections, whereas the rightward rotation of the eye in the bottom panel has reduced the input to the right photocell.

Optical Levers on Contact Lenses.

A contact lens can be fitted over the cornea and held tightly in place by suction. A short stalk that holds a half-silvered mirror can be attached to the lens (see Figure 7.9). As the eye moves, so does the mirror, and any light that is reflected from the mirror is imaged on a detector off to the side. The detecting surface is a photosensitive grid, on which the location of the spot can be monitored. Hadad and Steinman (for

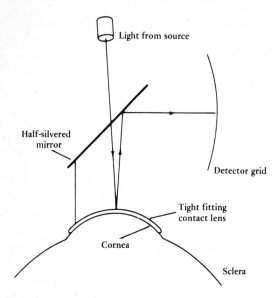

Light from source

Half-silvered
mirror

Detector grid

Tight fitting
contact lens

Cornea

Sclera

Figure 7.9 An optical lever holding a half-silvered mirror attached to a contact lens. As the eye rotates, the angle of the mirror changes with respect to the detector grid, which registers the position of the light that impinges on it.

example, 1973) found accuracy of about 3 seconds of arc (0.0008 of a degree) with such a device. However, the head has to be restrained with a bite bar and the contact lens has to be tightly fitting. Obviously the observer is aware that his eye positions and movements are being monitored.

These three types of measurements do not exhaust the techniques available, but they do give a brief idea of how some measurements are obtained. Which technique is chosen depends on the degree of accuracy needed, the amount of intrusion in the viewing situation, and the cost and the time available for scoring.

Several later chapters will emphasize different aspects of perception that involve eye movements, especially Chapter 10 on motion perception, and Chapter 16 on visual search. In the remainder of this chapter we will single out several aspects that are important for all these topics: visual sensitivity while the eyes are in motion; perception when all movements of the eyes are prevented; and how we maintain perception of a stable world even though the retinal image is so unstable.

VISUAL SENSITIVITY DURING EYE MOVEMENTS

It seems reasonable to expect some limitation on visual sensitivity while the eye is in motion. Indeed, the degree of visual sensitivity during eye movements should be different for different types of eye movements because the characteristics (and functions) of the movements differ greatly. For example, the rate of movement of a typical saccade is several hundred degrees per second, and the movement lasts only 0.03 second at best, whereas pursuit movements are only one-tenth as fast, but can continue as long as a moving object is present in the visual field.

Saccadic Suppression

Suppression of visual sensitivity during saccadic eye movements, called **saccadic suppression,** has been demonstrated by Latour (1962), who studied the percentage of light pulses that are seen at various times before, during, and after a saccadic eye movement. The test pulse is presented midway between two fixation lights that are oscillating irregularly. The perceiver is instructed to switch his eyes back and forth between the fixation lights when they change. Figure 7.10 shows Latour's results. Experiments by Volkmann (1962) and Volkmann, Schick, and Riggs (1968) confirm this pattern. Perception is not totally blanked out during a movement, but sensitivity is reduced substantially, not only during the movement itself, but for 50 milliseconds before the movement begins to about 50 milliseconds after the eye has settled in the new position. This suppression minimizes the perception of blur during the movement and provides continuity of perception between successive fixations to bridge the gap caused by saccadic sweeps (Volkmann, 1976).

It is important to note, however, that we are not blind during eye movements. Volkmann's (1962) data show a threshold rise during movements of little more than 0.5 log unit of luminance under the worst circumstances. This is not a great change, considering the total range of sensitivity of the visual system, but enough, perhaps, to reduce blur below annoyance levels. The change is probably enough to reduce sensitiv-

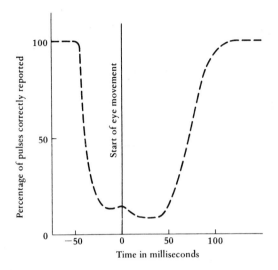

The y-axis is labeled "Percentage of pulses correctly reported" with values 0, 50, 100. The vertical line is labeled "Start of eye movement." The x-axis is labeled "Time in milliseconds" with values −50, 0, 50, 100.

Figure 7.10 Percentage of flashes detected as a function of the time of their occurence in relation to a concomitant saccadic eye movement. (Latour, 1962.)

ity to details that pass across the retina as the eye moves. This is further evidence of the ballistic nature of movement. Once planned, the eye movement cannot be changed, and for the 100 milliseconds before, during, and after the movement, the chances of noticing new information or fine detail is sharply reduced. Suppression can also be taken as evidence of interference between the directing and the identifying aspects of search, since the chances are reduced that the perceiver is able to identify targets passed over during an eye movement.

Three mechanisms have been suggested as possible causes of the suppression of visual sensitivity associated with saccadic eye movements: retinal smear, neural inhibition due to signals that initiate eye movements, and metacontrast masking. The most obvious cause is **retinal smear.** During a saccadic eye movement, details in the retinal image are smeared out across an area of the retina. Consequently, salient features of the image become blurred, contain less contrast, and are not as easily noticed. The strongest argument in support of the retinal smear explanation is that the greatest suppression occurs during the actual movement itself. However, suppression also occurs before and after the movement, so it cannot be

attributed entirely to retinal smearing. Indeed, targets that do not produce retinal smear nevertheless also produce suppression during saccades. For example, Volkmann (1962) flashed such targets and found that they require more energy for detection during the saccade than before or after it.

There is evidence to support both of the alternative hypotheses—neural inhibition and metacontrast masking. The demonstration that suppression can occur in total darkness supports the interpretation that suppression is caused by neural inhibition generated by the signal from the superior colliculus that initiates a saccadic eye movement. Observers trained to make saccadic eye movements between two fixation points 10 degrees apart continue to make saccadic movements between the two imaginary points when the lights are turned off. When brief stimuli are presented during the movements in the dark, thresholds are higher to the target during saccades than when the eyes are stationary (Riggs, 1976; Riggs, Merton, & Morton, 1974). Since there are no contours present to mask the target, the suppression must have been due to neural inhibition.

Several other studies have shown that visual masking resulting from an interaction among temporally and spatially adjacent contours can produce saccadic suppression. MacKay (1970) showed that a similar elevation in threshold occurs when the subject holds his eye stationary but the stimulus is moved by an amount equivalent to a saccade. The time course and magnitude of this "suppression" is sufficiently close to make the analogy very strong. Matin, Clymer, and Matin (1972) flashed a horizontal line during saccadic movements. The longer the line remained exposed, the longer its length appeared to be—apparently, due to smear across the retinal surface. However, as the duration is increased (especially after the saccade), the apparent length of the line is reduced, suggesting that portions of the line are masked by contours picked up after the eye came to rest.

Breitmeyer and Ganz (1976) have argued that masking in saccadic suppression is caused by the inhibition of the contour around sustained cells by the motion around transient cells. Since the transient channels are activated much more rapidly, this would account for suppression that occurs even prior to the beginning of the saccades, as well as continuing well after the termination of the saccade itself.

In sum, three independent processes can produce suppression of vision during a saccadic eye movement: retinal smear, neural inhibition produced by signals that initiate eye movements, and metacontrast masking. All three probably occur, although the first is undoubtedly the largest contributor in the natural world outside of the laboratory.

We have dwelled at some length on saccadic suppression because it may be implicated in several important perceptual phenomena. The most obvious is the reduction in the perception of blur. We are rarely aware of blurring in the retinal image despite the fact that it occurs several times per second. Second (a point made by Breitmeyer and Ganz, 1976), suppression prevents the contours perceived in one fixation from masking out those perceived in the next fixation. If such masking did occur, then much of the information picked up in each fixation would be lost because of forward masking by the previous array and backward masking by the following array. As a result of suppression, each fixation is isolated to a great degree, and, in a sense, stands alone so that the information it contains may be extracted with little interference from its temporal neighbors.

Sensitivity During Pursuit

Suppression has never been studied in the context of pursuit movements because the speeds are so much slower than during saccades. But pursuit movements do produce changes in acuity that are probably all due to retinal smearing effects. When the eye pursues a moving target, the visual image from the stationary visual world is blurred across the retina while the image from the moving target remains on the fovea. Mackworth and Kaplan (1962) studied the situation in which a perceiver is asked to track a target moving across a screen at velocities between 0 and 120 degrees per second (the zero-degree condition is for a stationary eye). An acuity test pattern is pulsed in the center of the screen, just when the target passes beneath it for 100 milliseconds. Figure 7.11 shows their results. When the stationary acuity pattern is

intense, acuity is not reduced no matter how fast the pursuit movement. As the pattern becomes dimmer, its stripes have to be increased in width to be seen, and the effect is more pronounced for vertical stripes (which are smeared with high speeds) than for horizontal stripes (which merely look longer). Although target velocities up to 120 degrees per second are used in this study, the eyes are unable to track them perfectly at those high speeds.

When the energy in the acuity target is held constant, but its duration and intensity were varied reciprocally, different effects are found (not shown in Figure 7.11). In a control condition with a stationary target and no movement of the eyes, perfect reciprocity is found. When the eyes are moving and the target is dim (less than 0.01 candelas per square meter) but long (100 milliseconds), increasing the velocity of pursuit takes its toll of acuity, especially for vertical stripes. However, when the target is intense but very brief (0.001 milliseconds), there is virtually no effect of the velocity of pursuit movements, nor of the orientation of the pattern. This finding is to be expected, since, even at the highest velocity, a flash that brief would not be smeared.

MAINTENANCE OF VISION IN THE ABSENCE OF EYE MOVEMENTS

While it is possible to ask observers to hold their eyes and head stationary so that no saccades, pursuits, vestibulo-occular, or vergence movements occur at all, voluntary means can never completely eliminate the drifts, flicks, and tremors. Are these small movements important and necessary for vision and what happens if they are optically eliminated? Their effects on visual acuity have already been described. We have also noted the impact of these movements on sensitivity to low-frequency flicker. In both contexts, we have implied that such movements are very useful in the enhancement of sensitivity of the visual system. In the early 1950s the technology became available to show this effect by essentially eliminating the small movements to produce a **stabilized retinal image** (Ditch-

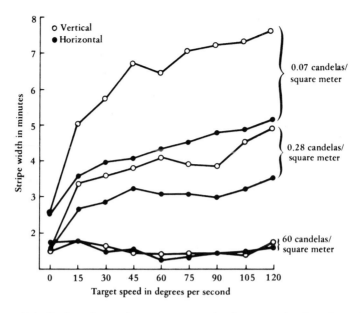

Figure 7.11 Minimum width of stripes of an acuity target that could be resolved when the eye was attempting to pursue a target moving at various speeds as a function of different luminances and orientations of the acuity target. (Mackworth & Kaplan, 1962.)

burn & Ginsburg, 1952; Riggs, Ratliff, Cornsweet, & Cornsweet, 1953). Two principal mechanical procedures have been used to study stabilized images. In one, a contact lens is fitted over the cornea. A stalk attached to the lens holds a miniature projector (see the right portion of Figure 7.12). Since the contact lens, stalk, and projector move with the eye, the image projected onto the retina does not shift over the retina as the eye moves. If the contact lens is carefully fitted, stabilization capable of eliminating the effect of drifts and microsaccades is possible. The left side of Figure 7.12 shows a second procedure, in which a mirror attached to the contact lens reflects projected light from an external source so that it moves exactly the distance that the eye moves, thereby producing a stabilized projection.

Heckenmuller (1965) has reviewed the procedures, results, and interpretations of much of the stabilized-image research. A general loss of perception of color and form occurs as soon as a stabilized projection is presented, usually within seconds, as long as the precision of the stabilization is within about 1 minute

of arc (no more than about 3 cones). Obviously, as fading progresses acuity for detail is lost. Most of the fading occurs in a "hazy" fashion—a fog comes over the field, beginning in the periphery and then moving centrally. The haze may have a periodic reappearance, as in some kinds of afterimages. The farther a stabilized contour falls in the periphery of the retina, the faster it fades. The presence of peripheral contours will speed up the whole process of fading. If only the center of a field is stabilized, the unstabilized peripheral contours continue to be seen and dictate what is seen in the center after the center contours have faded. This may help explain why we normally see the centers of large homogeneous fields, rather than having them fade out. The peripheral contours fill in the centers.

The general pattern of results provides very strong support for the thesis that variation in stimulation on the retina is needed for perception to occur. The stabilized visual image procedure removes temporal variation. When the identical pattern remains in the same location on the retina, perception fails rather quickly. It can be reinstated by movement, by

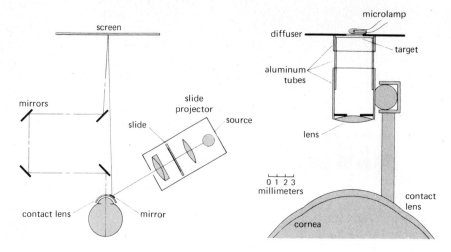

Figure 7.12 Two techniques used to produce a stabilized retinal projection. The right panel illustrates the apparatus used by Pritchard (1961), and the left one that was used by Riggs, Ratliff, Cornsweet, and Cornsweet (1953).

flickering the stimulus in time, or by changing its luminance, even while keeping it stabilized in space.

Tulanay-Keesey (1976) reviewed results of a number of experiments that have attempted to separate the different small eye movement components in these results. If stabilization eliminates drifts and microsaccades, but leaves the tremors, complete fading occurs. Therefore, the tremors are not responsible for the fading, and are probably not important in vision at all. If, after stabilization, the target is moved optically on the retina, the movement has to be at least 4–5 minutes of arc. The rate of movement is also important. Only if the movement is repeated slowly, approximately 5 times per second or less, is the fading prevented, regardless of the distance moved. Each of these results suggests that it is the slow, small drifts that account for the maintenance of vision. Finally, when the target is flickered in time rather than moved in space, maintenance of vision occurs only with slow rates of flicker, less than 5 cycles per second. This suggests that the drift components introduce temporal variation at each receptor site rather than move the stimulus over several receptors. Thus, the temporal modulation of stimuli seems to be the most important mechanism for the maintenance of vision. It is the slow drift component of the eye movement that best accomplishes this.

The disappearance may be due to the relative paucity of retinal receptive fields that respond under steady-state conditions. Most receptive field organizations require that either the retinal projection change in its luminance discontinuities, or that the projection shift its position relative to the receptors in that receptive field. When both of these are prevented, as when the projection is stabilized, then the receptive field cannot signal the presence of the projection and its output is indistinguishable from that produced from a homogeneous projection on the retina.

We briefly mentioned the periodic reappearance of the perceived form. The fading of forms is more complicated, since the fading also appears to be related to the integration of the form. Figure 7.13 shows several examples in which a form decomposed into component parts (Pritchard, 1961). These results have been replicated with a number of variations to control for response bias. If they are accepted at their face value, they complicate the explanation of stabilized retinal projections, as well as our understanding of the perception of form. If they can be shown to be artifacts of measurement or of response, then some parsimony can be maintained.

One interpretation has been to attribute the fading and reappearance of forms to slippage of the contact lenses over the cornea (which of course leads to

Figure 7.13 Several examples based upon perceivers' reports of the ways in which forms decomposed into simpler patterns during viewing under conditions of stabilized retinal projections. (From "Stabilized images on the retina" by R. M. Pritchard. Copyright 1961 by Scientific American, Inc. All rights reserved.)

some loss of stabilization), and consequent movement of the retinal projection relative to the retina (Cornsweet, 1966). Cornsweet (1970) notes that slippage not only explains the reappearance, but also the meaningfulness and simplifications ascribed to the forms. If a contact lens slips, it does so in only one direction, and for only a given amount. When this happens all luminance dicontinuities in the pattern parallel to the direction of slippage are unaffected, whereas those perpendicular to the slippage shift position on the retina and therefore reappear. In this way those aspects that reappear after slippage are both simpler (in the sense of having fewer components than the original) and more organized or meaningful.

Cornsweet (1970) also suggested that after-images may reappear from time to time for similar reasons. They are not perfectly stabilized because their intensity decreases continuously with the dark adaptation that follows the offset of the light that produced the afterimage. The after-images also spread somewhat over the retina with time (Brindley, 1963) and are sensitive to small changes in blood supply that could be produced by pressure changes due to eye or lid movements. Cornsweet concluded that there seems

to be no reason at present to reject the retinal slippage hypothesis for the reappearance effects, as well as for the changes in the reports of forms as they fade and reappear. In this way we can preserve the interpretation based upon receptive field properties and not have to invoke more complex central factors.

There is one other implication to this interpretation—the changes in the forms as they reappear allow us to learn something about the processing of visual features in the visual system (McFarland, 1973; McKinney, 1963; Pritchard, 1969). If the last component to fade or the component to reappear most often is a straight line, then this would imply that lines are a basic component of the visual system or a visual feature. The slippage explanation calls this interpretation into question, since it suggests that the line-segment content of the form that reappears will be a function of the direction of slippage of the contact lens and the direction of components in the retinal projection that are displaced when the slippage occurred. In this interpretation, the reappearance of line segments can tell us nothing about basic features. The order in which components fade might be useful for this purpose as long as it was not due to inaccuracies in the stabilization itself.

A similar critique can be made of studies of fading induced by prolonged viewing of nonstabilized patterns. Both McKinney (1963) and McFarland (1973) have reported that such perceptions also fade and reappear, with the reappearances becoming simpler in form. It is easy to induce such fading with blurred edges and low contrast between the high and low luminance values in the pattern. Even when the projection of the form is not stabilized on the retina, the gradual changes at the edges and the small overall changes due to the small contrast differences mean that minimal eye movements cannot produce much change at the output of the retinal receptive fields. Cornsweet (1969) demonstrated this by showing that targets with blurred edges faded out and reappeared while sharp-edged ones did not.

Given these explanations, it would seem unreasonable to assume that the pattern of fading and reappearance, even in the absence of stabilization, reflects basic visual features. Rather, it probably reflects the pattern of eye movements that occur during the fixation upon the pattern. With primarily horizontal drifts and microsaccades, vertical components will reappear more than will horizontal ones. If the movements are vertical, just the reverse should occur. When the movements are random, any pattern in the reappearance can be noticed, especially if a long enough time sample is taken.

In conclusion, then, the explanation of stabilized retinal projections based upon coding mechanisms sensitive to changes rather than to steady-state stimulation may be taken as evidence of the need for constant change in order to produce stability in perception. In addition to processing luminance discontinuities, lateral inhibitory mechanisms of the retinal coding systems actually enhance such discontinuities so that they stand out even more than they would in physical measurements. The presence of such enhancement can be considered further evidence of the need for luminance discontinuities to provide stable perception of form.

CONTINUITY OF PERCEPTION WITH SHIFTING RETINAL IMAGES

How do we continue to see the world as stable and continuous even with eye movements that produce massive and repeated displacement of the retinal image over the retinal surface? That the world remains relatively stable is obvious to everyday experience. That we can explain how it does is more complex. The explanation is also different for the different types of movements. In fact, it is really only saccades and pursuits that pose difficult problems. Vergence and vestibulo-occular movements are designed to keep the image stable in the presence of eye, head, and body motion. The tremors are irrelevant and the flicks correct drifts as a way to maintain fixation between saccades. With pursuits, a moving object is locked onto the fovea with a fixed background sliding across the retina. Our perceptual experience, however, is just the reverse. It is that of a moving target against a stationary background. With saccades, no moving objects are seen at all and all of the retinal displacement is attributed to the eye, head, and body movements and not to a unstable visual scene.

As has been clear from the discussion in this chapter, cancellation of retinal motion can occur with the efferent (superior-colliculus) signal to initiate the eye movement. This has been one important explanation of the stability of perception. But in Chapters 9 and 10 we will consider an explanation by Gibson who argues that no cancellation signal is needed at all. Rather, Gibson argues, a careful analysis of the retinal transformations alone will show that the changes on the retina are different for object motion as compared to observer motion. If this is the case, he argues, there is no need to keep track of self-initiated movements since visual information alone on the retina distinguishes the two sources of retinal motion.

A related question concerns the continuity of vision across eye movements. Why does not the visual scene look chopped up into separate "snapshots" rather than continuous? We see the visual world as if there were no eye movements at all. Further, while the scene we see is built up from information picked up in successive fixations, each in a different part of the scene, we seem to have this constructed scene all of the time and not only after a lot of movements. This will be an important problem for all the chapters on visual space perception and for Chapter 16 on visual search.

SUMMARY

Our eyes are never still, and are often moving very rapidly. Rather than making perception more difficult, however, most of these movements improve the quality of perception. This chapter concerns the types of movements and their effect on perception.

The position and movement of each eye is controlled by three sets of antagonistic muscles, corresponding to horizontal, vertical and tortional movements respectively. These muscles are controlled by different cranial nerves, activated by different neural centers, including the reticular formation, the superior colliculus, and the vestibular system.

Seven types of eye movements were distinguished according to their function, magnitude and velocities. Saccades are high-velocity ballistic movements designed to rapidly move the eye so that it is oriented to a new position in space. Pursuits are slow, smooth movements designed to permit the eye to remain fixated on a moving object across the field of view. Vergence movements, unlike the other two, move the eyes in opposite directions to each other, so that with changes in distance each eye can be oriented on the same plane in space. Vestibulo-occular movements are designed to permit continued orientation on an object in space in compensation for head and body motion. Given the amount of head and body movement present, these vestibulo-occular movements are critical to maintain a stable retinal image.

Three smaller eye movements also occur. Tremors appear to be very small irreducible random movements, spanning only a cone or two in magnitude, and do not affect perceptual processes. Drifts, on the other hand, are somewhat larger movements made while attempting to maintain steady fixation, in which the eye drifts slowly off fixation. Drifts are corrected by much more rapid microsaccades that move the eye back roughly to where it had been. If drifts and microsaccades are prevented, or overcome by optical stabilization of the retinal image, perception fades out, suggesting that the drifts are necessary to provide sufficient temporal and spatial changes in the alignment of the retinal image over the retinal surface. Without such changes, the ganglion cells in the retina cease to provide signals to the cortex.

Several techniques are described by which eye movements can be measured. These include direct motion photography of the eye, in which change in position of the center of the pupil can be measured from frame to frame. The corneal-reflection procedure focuses light on the boundary between the highly reflective sclera and the minimally reflective iris, and measures the amount of light reflected back from the eye. The third and most accurate technique is to attach a mirror to a contact lens worn over the cornea. Then a beam of light can be reflected off the mirror and picked up on a sensing grid, in which small changes in the eye change the angle of the mirror and therefore the direction of the reflected beam.

There are losses in sensitivity during the very high velocity saccadic movements, called saccadic suppression. Sensitivity to targets is reduced, not only during the movement, but for a brief time before and after the movement. Some of the loss is due to retinal smear, some to neural inhibition, and some to meta-contrast balance the patterns in the images on the retina just before and after the movement. Losses in sensitivity during the three types of eye movements do not occur unless the movements are all much higher than normal velocities.

SUGGESTED READINGS

Two recent volumes of collected research papers have summarized almost all the relevent topics on eye movements. The first by Monty and Senders (1976) and the second by Senders, Fisher, and Monty (1978) contain some 50 papers ranging from the neural control processes for eye movements to the role of eye movement in reading, search, and athletics.

SECTION TWO

VISUAL SPACE
PERCEPTION

Chapter 8

Monocular Stimulation

The task for a scientist trying to understand the perception of space is twofold: first, to examine the sources of information about the scene reflecting light to the eye, and second, to describe the processes by which that information is transformed into the visual image—the internal representation of that scene—

and ultimately into actions by the perceiver. The sources of information can be described using the laws of geometrical optics that govern the relationships between the distal and the proximal stimulus (Fig. 8.1). The **distal stimulus** consists of the objects and surfaces in space that reflect light to the eye. The **proxi-**

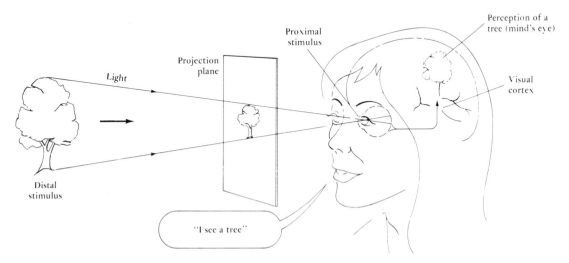

Figure 8.1 The different aspects of a perceptual event. The event includes the distal stimulus, the proximal stimulus, and the perceptual experience. It may include an overt

response indicating the occurrence of the perceptual experience.

mal stimulus is the representation of those distal objects in the pattern of light imaged on the retina. The relationships between distal and proximal stimuli have a special importance for an understanding of space perception because the visual system does not have a receptor for distance. Distance from the observer—the third dimension of Euclidean space—must therefore be represented by information in the proximal stimulus. Thus, in a sense, the visual system itself may be thought of as a receptor for depth. An analysis of the visual stimulus is designed to describe this information and the relationships that produce it. It is a task for geometry and for geometrical optics, and also requires an understanding of the optics of the eye.

Some stimulus analyses start with natural scenes and some start with simple line drawings of simple objects. Experimenters using simple stimuli have argued that it is reasonable to reduce the input to its fundamental components when studying a complex information system. In this way each property can be treated in isolation and analyzed. But this approach runs the risk of removing from the analysis precisely that kind of information most frequently used by perceivers. For example, there are different kinds of information—local information from circumscribed retinal regions and scaled information encompassing the entire retinal surface. It is likely that the dynamics of processing are different for these different kinds of stimuli. Restricting the information available about the environment may result in the observation of different processes in different laboratory experiments. If it is assumed that the highest level of information is processed when available, and that local information is used only if needed to reduce ambiguity, then the study of impoverished scenes in the laboratory may involve fundamentally different processes from those used when viewing natural scenes that are richly informative. For example, the degree of convergence of the two eyes may be used like a rangefinding device for specifying the distance of a single point of light in the dark (Gregory, 1966), but it rarely, if ever, contributes to the perception of the layout of a natural scene (Ogle, 1962). It is therefore empirically correct to call convergence a cue for depth, but it must also be

understood that convergence seems to be ignored in processing scenes that are rich sources of information.

The second task of the visual scientist requires a processing analysis. While geometry can specify the amount, kind, and veracity of information in the proximal stimulus, it cannot tell us how that information is transformed, sampled, or weighted to produce perception; and it cannot tell us whether the information is combined with information from earlier perceptions or from expectancies about the scene.

Probably the most important processes in space perception are those that maintain the constancy of the visual world. Clearly, the physical properties of the world around us are unchanging regardless of our viewing orientation, our viewing distance, and the momentary direction and content of the incident illumination present in the scene. Perceptual constancy is the perception of those invariant aspects of the world—the sizes, shapes, locations, orientations, and surface features of the objects and surfaces in the scene. These constancies are discussed in detail below, but it is helpful to give an example at this point. Size and shape are physical properties of objects and are not dependent on the presence of the observer, or on the observer's orientation or viewing distance. However, the orientation and distance of the observer alter the local properties of the pattern of light reflected to the eye from objects. In other words, the retinal size of an image of a tree is a function of how far away the tree is from the retina. Similarly, the shape of the retinal image changes with viewing orientation—a round plate will produce an ellipse on the retina if viewed from an angle. Size and shape constancy occur whenever the perception of objects in space remains constant despite changes in the position of the observer or of the object.

There are other aspects of change that must also be taken into account. Scenes are perceived by means of continuous successive samplings as part of brief discrete eye fixations separated by saccadic movements of high velocity. But we do not see the blur of the retinal pattern during these rapid shifts in eye position. Instead, we perceive a continuous stable scene. Neither are we conscious of the successive samples that are taken in brief fixations. In analyzing the stimulus on the retina, it appears as if the visual scene is broken up into small slices several times a second, separated by a complete blurring of the image as the eye shifts position. Yet none of this is reflected in our perceptual experience. Moreover, because of a number of optical factors, a sharply focused, high-contrast image is produced only over the center of the retina. Neural coding for fine detail, color, and contrast is concentrated in this area of central vision (see Figure 8.2 for a photographer's attempt to represent this stimulus). Yet the appearance of typical scenes is not of clear centers with fuzzy surrounds, it is panoramic and clear throughout. In order to construct such a panorama, multiple eye movements are required over a scene, with a substantial overlap between a large number of fixations (Hochberg, 1978). The panorama itself does not resemble any one of the retinal images, but is constructed from the sequence of them. Finally, when we look at a scene with two eyes, the retinal images in the two eyes are always in different positions in space. But we do not see two different views—we see a single image. That is, we construct a perception that uses the disparities between the two retinal images to create a third dimension over a third image. This "cyclopean" image does not duplicate either retinal image alone, but requires a comparison of the two of them.

All theories of perception treat the achievement of constancy as a fundamental. Beyond that statement, however, there is little agreement. Even the definition of the problem produces argument. Most of the research on processing takes the momentary retinal image to be the starting point, and asks what must be added, deleted, or transformed so that it can resemble or match the scene that gave rise to it. Thus, some researchers search for compensatory processes that act on the retinal image. At the other extreme, some theorists have argued that all the information is already contained in the retinal image so that no compensation is needed. Therefore, it is inappropriate to view the retinal image as a distorted picture which must then be transformed in order to reveal the true scene.

It should be obvious that neither a stimulus analysis nor a processing analysis is sufficient by itself. Consequently, they are treated equally in the discussion of visual space perception. This chapter contains a detailed description of the kinds of stimulation that reach a single eye.

STATIC MONOCULAR STIMULATION

In the seventeenth century, scientists began to appreciate the image-forming properties of the eye. It seemed natural to assume that this image in the eye is the source of perception. This view was reinforced by the invention of the *camera obscura* and, 150 years ago, of the photographic camera. The assumption was made that the eye functions like a camera—that the picture on the retinal surface was like the image in the photograph. This assumption was strengthened by the similarity of the optical mechanisms of the eye and the camera. Yet, despite these similarities, the analogy must be rejected as a model of perception. The retinal image should not be thought of as a picture, because then we have to ask how that picture resembles or differs from the real scene, on the one hand, and from our perception of the scene, on the other. The retinal image is not a template that must be matched to the scene. Braunstein (1975) has an excel-

Figure 8.2 A photographer's attempt to represent the loss of focus in the periphery of the retina. Even in this example, the blur at the edges is not as pronounced in the photograph as it would be on the retina. (Photo by *Life* photographer Herbert Gehr; copyright Time, Inc.)

lent discussion of the theoretical and practical pitfalls of the eye–camera analogy. Instead of thinking of the eye as a camera, it is more accurate to think of the retinal image simply as information. It would be better to pretend that we never heard of a camera—to think of light reflected from a scene and imaged on a photosensitive surface only as containing information about the nature of the scene before the eyes.

To study how we come to see a three-dimensional world containing objects that have stable sizes and shapes and are seen in particular locations in space, we must distinguish between two aspects of our experience of space—physical space and visual space. **Physical space** refers to the physical world studied by physicists and engineers. **Visual space** is the space of perceptual experience, the space that we, as psychologists interested in perception, will study in Section Two of this book.

Physical space is measured with straight edges, rules, and transits, following the rules of Euclidean geometry. These measurements are based on the assumption that an object may be displaced or rotated without deformation and without changing the relationships among its parts, and that objects can be assigned positions in a Cartesian (rectangular) coordinate system. These simple assumptions provide the foundation for our conception of a stable physical world.

It cannot be assumed that visual space can be described by the same geometry that describes physical space. The exact geometrical representation of visual space must be empirically determined. Indeed, it may be very different from the description of physical space because the perceiving organism must be taken into account. Therefore, it is necessary to speak of positions of visual points in a space centered on the perceiver. Such a space is best described using a **polar coordinate system,** where the perceiver is placed at the center (or origin), where measurements are given in terms of directions measured in angular deviations from the perceivers direction of sight, and where distances are measured as radial distance from the origin (Fig. 8.3).

What kinds of stimuli come to the eye that are informative about the layout of space? Let us review

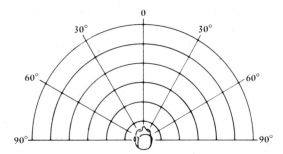

Figure 8.3 A polar coordinate system centered on the perceiver.

some of what we have already learned. Visible light radiates from light sources (such as the sun or lightbulbs) in all directions. Some of the rays strike surfaces and are reflected or absorbed. Most surfaces in the natural world reflect light diffusely so that the light rays spread in all directions from the point of incidence, regardless of the angle of incidence. In this sense, then, surfaces act as light sources themselves and, because every point on a surface reflects light in all directions, we do not have to know the location of the original light source.

If the cornea and the lens of the eye were optically perfect, all the diverging rays that reached the eye from a single point on a surface would be refracted so that they would all converge to a single point on the retinal surface at the back of the eye. In this case, the image of light formed on the retinal surface would be in one-to-one correspondence with the patterning of the light being reflected from the surface and traveling to the eye. In addition, surfaces are rarely uniform in their reflectances—some parts of a surface may reflect most of the incident light whereas adjacent parts may reflect little. If the scene in front of the eyes contains surfaces with high and low reflectances, the light reflected from each surface will contain differing numbers of quanta. This results in corresponding differences in the number of quanta reaching the different parts of the retina. In this way the pattern of reflectances in the scene is reproduced in the pattern of varying numbers of quanta in the retinal image of that scene. These differences provide the basis for the beginning of perception.

Relational Stimulation over the Retinal Surface

Surface Texture, Gradients

At every moment of waking time, an image is formed on the retina from light reflected simultaneously from all parts of the scene. That image contains a representation of the reflectances of different parts of the scene. The momentary patterns in the retinal image will differ as a function of the distance between the observer and the scene, and the angle at which the scene is being viewed. The relationship between an object in space and its representation in the visual image can be described by the principles of geometrical optics dating back to Euclid (about 300 B.C.; see Pirenne, 1970). Euclid noted that the image of an object will take up a smaller part of the retinal image if the object is far away than if it is near. That is, in general, the size of the retinal image of an object is an inverse function of its distance from the eye of the perceiver—the larger the distance, the smaller the size of the image.

Retinal image size is specified by the angle made by the rays of light reflected from the extremities of the object to be measured (see Figure 1.9, p. 11). The retinal size of objects whose images are projected onto the retina is usually measured in terms of this **visual angle** in degrees of arc. For example, the sun, although very large, is far away, and therefore subtends a visual angle of only 0.5 degree. A thumbnail at arm's length is small but very close and subtends nearly 2 degrees of visual angle (approximately the size of the fovea). The entire retinal image for one eye covers approximately 150 degrees of visual angle.

Most surfaces project images that are spread out over the retina rather than confined to a point, a line, or an outline shape. It will be easier to visualize this stimulation, therefore, if the outline shapes of the surfaces in space are projected onto a plane that is in front of the observer and perpendicular to the line of sight. Such a plane is called a **fronto-parallel plane,** a **projection plane,** or a **picture plane.** Figure 8.4 shows a solid pyramid in space projected onto a two-dimensional surface that is perpendicular to the viewer's line

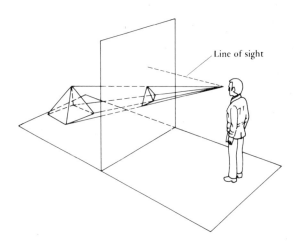

Figure 8.4 An object projected onto a plane that is perpendicular to the line of sight and in front of the observer. A plane of this sort is called a fronto-parallel plane, a projection plane, or a picture plane.

of sight when he is looking straight ahead. This projection is similar to the one on the retina. It has the advantage of permitting us to perform our analyses on an enlarged and upright view of the pattern. It should be clear, however, that substitution of a fronto-parallel plane for the retinal image is only a convenience—it does not imply that the retinal image is as clear or uniform as is the image on the projection plane in front of the eyes.

A visual scene is usually made up of objects on a ground. For any given scene, the surfaces that reflect light to an observer are those frontal and lateral surfaces of objects and of the ground that can be perceived. All surfaces in the physical world have a microstructure or "grain." This **texture** of a surface can be thought of as a series of structural units that are more or less the same size and are repeated over the entire surface. Thus, the units of texture are a fundamental characteristic of the surface and must also be represented in the information present in the retinal projections of the scene. Figure 8.5 shows some examples of textured surfaces from real life: (*a*) a coarse-grained texture found in a brick wall and (*b*) a fine-grained texture found in a grassy lawn. Much of the graininess in these pictures is randomly regular. For

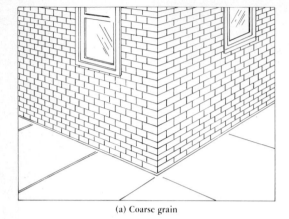

(a) Coarse grain

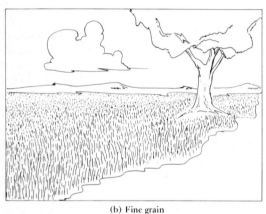

(b) Fine grain

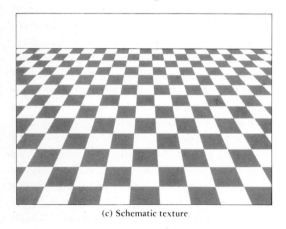

(c) Schematic texture

Figure 8.5 Some examples of surface texture showing (*a*) a coarse grain, (*b*) a fine grain, and (*c*) a schematic drawing of a textured surface with elements of the same size.

example, a lawn may have tall, short, and medium blades of grass, which also vary in width and color. Nevertheless, this random variation provides a fairly constant textural pattern or **texture density** over the entire surface. Thus, texture is one of the most distinctive characteristics of a surface. The figure also shows a schematic representation of a textured surface at a slant to the viewer (*c*). The elements of the surface are all exactly the same size and shape in the schematic representation, but they are only approximately the same in real-life surfaces.

If all the elements of the surface are effectively equidistant from the perceiver (when the surface is in a fronto-parallel plane), then the retinal projection of each of the units will be the same size. However, in the real world, the surfaces we encounter are almost invariably at a slant to our line of sight. Consequently, the units in the surfaces are projected onto the retina with sizes that differ according to the rules of perspective (see below). We therefore speak of the projection over the entire retina of texture elements that are gradually changing in size as a **texture gradient.** The fundamental rule governing these projections has already been described—the farther the object is from the observer, the smaller will be its visual angle and its retinal size. This rule is illustrated in Figure 8.6. In applying this rule to the elements of texture of slanted surfaces, one would expect that, in general, the elements in the nearer portion of the surface will subtend larger visual angles and the texture elements in the part of the surface that is farther from the viewer will subtend smaller visual angles. This should be true for both the height and the width of the texture elements. The changes can be visualized by imaging that you are looking down a railroad track (Fig. 8.7). The length of each crosstie is the same, but those farther into the distance subtend progressively smaller and smaller visual angles on the retina. The distance between ties is also the same all along the length of track, but, again, the farther this separation is from the eye, the smaller the projected visual angle. The consequence of these relationships is that the light reflected from the railroad tracks themselves will produce converging projections in the retinal image. These lines converge toward a vanishing point in the distance—usually at

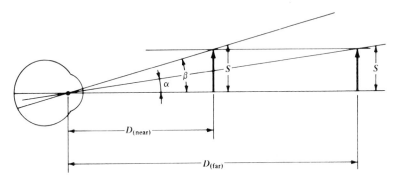

Figure 8.6 The relationship between physical size (S), physical distance (D), and the visual angles (α and β) when $\tan \alpha = S/D_{(far)}$, $\tan \beta = S/D_{(near)}$, and $\beta > \alpha$. An object of fixed size S will subtend a larger visual angle when near than when far.

the horizon. It is the convergence of lines such as these in the retinal image that form the basis for the study of **linear perspective.**

There are two rules that govern the differences in

Figure 8.7 Railroad tracks going directly away from the observer. The length of each crosstie is the same, but those farther into the distance subtend progressively smaller and smaller visual angles on the retina. The same changes occur for the distances between the ties.

projective unit size of texture elements, one having to do with the height or frontal dimension of the surface texture elements and the other with their width or longitudinal dimension. Consider the projection of the ground surface. This is the surface upon which a perceiver stands and which stretches away from the perceiver in all directions. For the sake of simplicity, assume that the ground surface is made up of square elements like linoleum floor tiles. Figure 8.8 shows these relationships for a viewer at point p looking down a row of elements whose projective size is shown on a fronto-parallel plane.

In order to make clear the two components of projective size change, consider the frontal dimensions of the squares. Figure 8.9 shows the rows of elements looking straight down on the surface. The projections (a, b, c, and d) of the frontal dimensions of the square elements (A, B, C, and D) decrease as the distance from the projection plane increases. Looking back at Figure 8.7, it should be clear that this change corresponds to a smaller unit size the higher the unit is in the projection plane (or, more precisely, the closer the element is to the horizon). This change in size in the projection of a unit also results in a change in the outline shape of the unit—the squares project as trapezoids because the projections of their far edges are smaller than the projections of their near edges. The sides, which are parallel in the physical world, are projected as lines converging toward the most distant point.

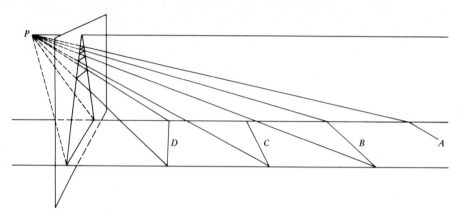

Figure 8.8 The perspective changes for square units of the ground showing the combined force of changes in frontal and longitudinal dimensions.

The longitudinal dimensions of the units are projected as the altitudes of the trapezoids on the projection plane. The altitudes are a negatively accelerated function of the distance and, therefore, this dimension is foreshortened in the projection—it is "compressed" in relation to the frontal dimension (Fig. 8.10). Thus, the change in texture and object size with distance may be analyzed into a **gradient** or gradual change of size and spacing of objects in space and of texture elements.

Since the gradient of texture is a function of the slant of a physical surface with respect to an observer, the density of the texture on the retinal surface varies with the distance from the observer. Consequently, the intersection of two surfaces, or the abrupt change

in slant of a surface, produces different gradients of texture. **A corner** is formed by the intersection of two planes with differing slants. This corresponds to an abrupt change in the gradient of the density of texture and gives the impression of a line across the field at the "corner." The stimulus for a corner is illustrated in Figures 8.11 and 8.12. An **edge** or a contour is specified by a change in the amount of density with the gradient remaining constant on either side of the change. This also gives the impression of a visual line (Figs. 8.13, 8.14). Corners lend solidity to objects and contours make them stand out from the background. Together they provide part of the basis for the perception of solid objects in space. In this analysis, properties of visual space are specified by changes in

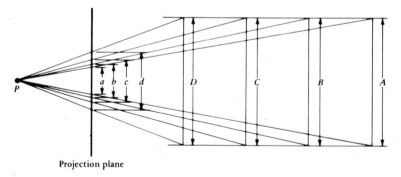

Projection plane

Figure 8.9 Top view of horizontal units of a surface showing changes in relative size of same-sized frontal portions of units when projected onto a fronto-parallel plane.

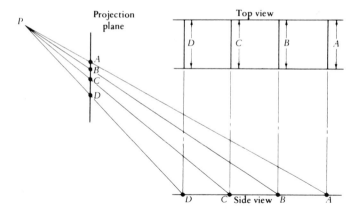

Figure 8.10 Side and top views of units of horizontal surface showing changes in the relative sizes of the longitudinal dimensions (altitudes) of units projected onto a fronto-parallel plane. These units show "compression."

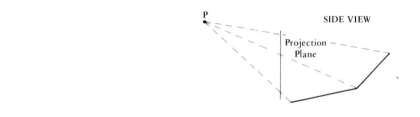

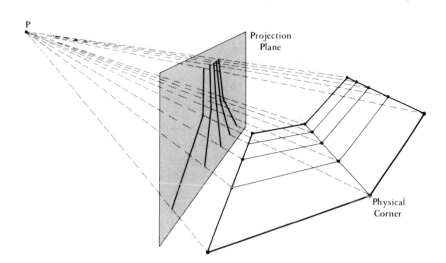

Figure 8.11 Perspective drawing showing the projection of optical texture from two planes with the same texture intersecting in a "corner" and the consequent optical pattern: an abrupt change in the gradient.

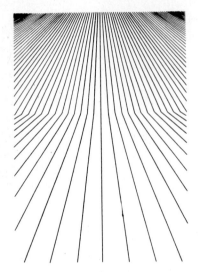

Figure 8.12 Fronto-parallel plane view of optical texture gradients provided by a surface changing its direction. This produces the perception of a corner.

the texture gradients alone, that is, without an edge or contour being present in the retinal projection. For example, there is no line defining the corner in Figure 8.12 or the contour in Figure 8.14, and yet we perceive these as if a line were present.

Linear Perspective

Whenever the scene being looked at contains objects and surfaces that are at different distances from the eye, the patterns of reflectances imaged on the retina contain perspective. It is the presence of perspective that provides information about the layout of space because it describes the lawful relationships between distances and sizes of objects in space and patterns of light on the retinal image. **Linear perspective** is the term used to describe these relationships. In general, linear perspective means that edges that are parallel in the real world project onto the picture plane as lines that converge to a vanishing point. Sets of parallel lines that are themselves not parallel will converge toward different vanishing points. The rate of convergence to-

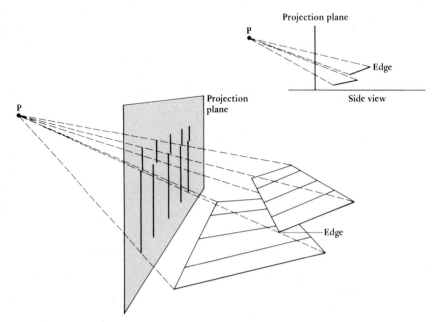

Figure 8.13 Perspective drawing showing the projection of optical texture from two planes, one in front of the other, and the consequent optical pattern: an abrupt change in the amount of density.

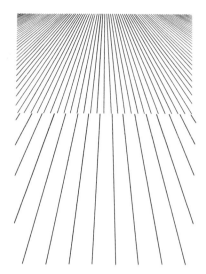

Figure 8.15   Drawing illustrating the relationships in linear perspective.

Figure 8.14   Fronto-parallel plane view of optical texture gradients provided by two surfaces, one in front of the other. This produces the perception of an edge.

ward the respective vanishing points will be directly related to the slope of the real edges in relation to the observer. These relationships result in a continuous decrease in the space between the projected lines on the picture plane—lines below the horizon converge as one goes up the picture plane and lines above the horizon converge as one goes down the picture plane (Fig. 8.15). Note, however, that this stimulus may be

described either as linear perspective or as a gradient of element size, depending on whether one focuses on the lines themselves or on the space between them. With attention on the edges of surfaces, the stimulus on the retina becomes an outline shape. The relationship between shape and slant has been studied in an otherwise empty field. Figure 8.16 shows that the projection of outline shape must be ambiguous when

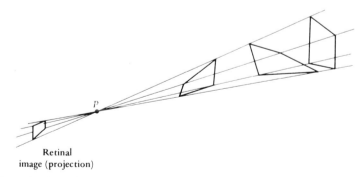

Retinal
image (projection)

Figure 8.16   A family of configurations that are equivalent in the sense that they could all produce the same-shaped projection on the retina. Given this retinal image as a stimulus, any member of the family—that is, any of these shapes—could be perceived.

treated in isolation—the three different shapes at different slants all produce the same retinal projections.

Gradients of Illumination

Brightness, shading, color, shadow, and aerial perspective all are capable of supplying some information about the relative depth of objects. All things being equal, bright objects appear to be closer than dim ones. Shading appears to be a strong cue for solidity—the shadow depending on the direction of the light source and the distribution of light. **Aerial perspective** refers to the fact that the retinal projections of distant objects are less sharp and less saturated in color than near objects. In general, the more the color of an object approximates the background, the more it tends to recede into it and to appear far away.

A gradient of illumination results from the relationship of the light source to the surface reflecting the light. The gradient does not vary with the distance of the surface from the source but with the degree of curvature of the surface. It provides, in the retinal projection, information that objects are not flat. Shading produces the perception of protuberances and indentations in surfaces as a function of gradients of illumination. Figure 8.17 shows how adding shading transforms ambiguous shape into clear three-dimensionality. A relief map correlates shading with the perception of protuberances (hills) and indentations (valleys) in a surface. The shading in one part of the map is related to shading in other parts by the

direction of illumination. All protuberances must be shaded on the same side and all indentations on the other or they will not result in proper perceptions. The gradient of illumination is similar to the texture gradient because they both describe a continuous change over the retinal surface as a function of the distances of the surfaces reflecing light to the eye. They are, in other words, both aspects of the transformation of retinal image size based upon distance from the eye.

Local Depth Cues

Whereas the gradients of texture and brightness provide information in terms of the relationships among the units spread over the retina, there are also sources of information about the relative depth of specific small portions of the field. These are called local depth cues—sources of information arising from intersecting visual edges in space.

Occlusion, Overlay, and Interposition

Objects on a textured surface will always **occlude** a portion of the surface—they will block part of the texture so that it will not be represented in the retinal projection. Occlusion supplies information about relative depth—what is in front and what is behind. The occlusion resulting from the juxtaposition of objects in space has been called **overlay** or **interposition**. This cue has been shown to be extremely powerful in determining the perceived relative distance of textureless objects in a

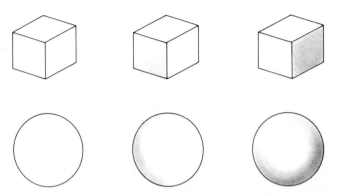

Figure 8.17 Rectilinear and spherical objects showing the impression of solidity resulting from gradients of illumination (shading).

textureless space. Figure 8.18 shows the relative positions of the borders for three arrangements of circles and rectangles. The figure with the continuous border is perceived to be an object in front of another object whose border is partially occluded. The occlusion occurs in such a way that the occluded portion of the more distant object corresponds exactly to the portion cut off by the front object. This is shown in the top of the figure.

The second row shows two figures in the same relative positions as those in the top row except that they now share a common border. In this case, the perception is of two objects at the same distance from the perceiver (see section on observer tendencies). The third row shows the force of the continuity of the border in determining which figure is perceived as the object in front and which is seen as behind. Even though the figures on the right side have a discontinuity in their borders, they are continuous at the point of intersection with the borders of the other figures. This continuity appears to be associated with the nearer object, but that is not always the case. The two configurations in Figure 8.19 illustrate a case where

interposition provides ambiguous information and does not predict the depth relations. Indeed, the basis for the information supplied by interposition is still unclear—Helmholtz proposed that the basis of depth information from interposition was continuity of edge, but Hochberg (1971) noted that it is easy to construct examples in which interposition helps us correctly perceive the spatial arrangements without continuity of edge (see Figure 8.19).

DYNAMIC MONOCULAR STIMULATION

If an observer moves in space or if objects move with respect to an observer, there is a flow of stimulation as the retinal projection shifts across the retinal surface. We usually move about in the world, move our heads and eyes, so that the stimulation on the retinas is constantly changing. Therefore, in order to understand how we perceive the three-dimensional world in these situations, we must learn something about the flow of stimulation on the retinas as a function of changes in object position and of eye, head, and body position.

One source of flow is derived from movements of the eye itself. When the eye turns in its sockets, two changes occur: first, the retinal image is displaced with respect to the retinal surface; and second, the part of the scene with maximum clarity and contrast shifts. The displacement does not produce a transformation in the pattern of the image. However, a portion of the initial image—an area on the side opposite

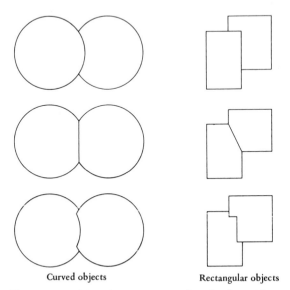

Curved objects   **Rectangular objects**

Figure 8.18   The relative positions of the borders of figures in the retinal image is a strong cue for relative depth. The figure with the continuous border is perceived to be in front of the other object.

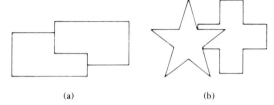

(a)   (b)

Figure 8.19   Examples of interposition information that is (*a*) ambiguous (Ratoosh, 1949) or (*b*) uninformative because both contours change direction at the intersection (Chapanis & McCleary, 1953).

to the direction of movement—will no longer fall on the retina and will, therefore, be occluded. Concurrently, a portion of the scene on the side toward which the movement was directed will become visible as the eye rotates toward it.

The effects of clarity are different. While there is no transformation in the retinal image from eye rotations, the part of the scene represented with sharpest focus shifts in accordance with the change in the direction of looking. Since only a small portion of the scene can be seen clearly when the eye is fixed, eye movements are an important component of visual search and an important way to build up an integrated perception of an entire scene.

Another source of flow is when the head or body moves. Changes in the retinal image due to head and body movements are much more complicated and provide a major source of information about the layout of space. In general, whenever the eye is displaced in this way, the pattern of discontinuities in the light on the retina undergoes a transformation: light arising from nearby surfaces is shifted in the retinal image more than light arising from far-away surfaces. The relationship between the relative rates of movement of the light patterns across the retina is a function of the differences in the distances of the objects. The visual edges created by the physical discontinuities in reflectances will be transposed, crossing each other as the observer moves. Thus, the relative rates of movement of the patterns of light across the entire retina can be described as a perspective transformation.

In order to understand the nature of these transformations, they must be separated according to the nature of the movement on the retina. Figure 8.20 shows a diagram of different retinal motions and the corresponding physical situations and perceptions, as developed by Gibson (1950). In the remainder of this chapter, we survey some of the kinds of information that exists in retinal motions of this sort.

Motions in Depth

Radial Movement
When an object moves directly toward or away from an observer's eye, or when an observer moves directly toward or away from a stationary object, we have the simplest case of **radial movement**. This situation is illustrated in Figure 8.21 for an object of size S at various momentary distances from an eye. The change in real distance of an object of fixed size (S) results in a change in retinal size S_1 to S_5. If we think of this as a continuous change, when the object moves away from the viewer or when the viewer moves away from the object, the retinal extent of the consequent stimulation decreases symmetrically. When the object moves toward the ob-

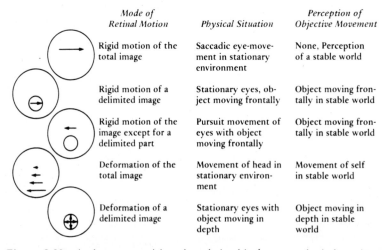

Mode of Retinal Motion	Physical Situation	Perception of Objective Movement
Rigid motion of the total image	Saccadic eye-movement in stationary environment	None, Perception of a stable world
Rigid motion of a delimited image	Stationary eyes, object moving frontally	Object moving frontally in stable world
Rigid motion of the image except for a delimited part	Pursuit movement of eyes with object moving frontally	Object moving frontally in stable world
Deformation of the total image	Movement of head in stationary environment	Movement of self in stable world
Deformation of a delimited image	Stationary eyes with object moving in depth	Object moving in depth in stable world

Figure 8.20 A chart summarizing the relationship between physical motion, retinal changes, and perception for several combinations of motion (Gibson, 1950).

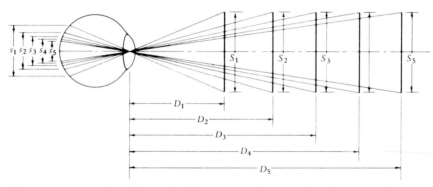

Figure 8.21 Schematic representation of the relationships between the momentary positions of lines of fixed size (*S*) moving away from (or toward) an observer and the corresponding retinal impingement. The physical change in distance is translated into an expansion and/or compression of the projected size.

server or when the viewer moves toward the object, the retinal extent increases symmetrically.

A pattern symmetrically increasing in size is perceived as an object of unchanging size moving directly toward a stationary observer on a "collision" course. Such an object appears as if it were "looming." If the observer is moving and the observer is stationary, the observer sees himself on a collision course. The converse is called "zooming," the object appears to "zoom" away from the viewer. If the increase in the retinal pattern is asymmetrical, the resulting perception is of an object of fixed size that is approaching the general direction of the observer or is being approached by the observer, but on a "miss" path. The degree of asymmetry will determine how much the path will deviate from collision (Ball & Tronick, 1971; Bower, Broughton, & Moore, 1970; Schiff, Caviness, & Gibson, 1962).

These relationships are illustrated in Figure 8.22. It should be clear from the illustration that the information at the retinal surface is simply a continuous change in the retinal extent of stimulation—that is, an optical expansion or contraction pattern. There is no depth in the stimulus, nor is any specific size specified by the momentary stimulation. Yet the perceptual system organizes such a stimulus in a way that results in the perception of an object of constant size that is changing its relative position in depth.

Motion Parallax The information provided by the relative movements of the projections

of objects on the retina as an observer moves laterally is called **motion parallax.** The extent and direction of these movements will depend on their relation to the point of fixation. This can be illustrated by analyzing the stimulus pattern on the retina for two objects in space, first when fixation is at an intermediate distance, and then when it is on a very distant object.

Figure 8.23 shows the former case. The observer moves his head, changing its location from point P_1 to P_2, while the observer maintains fixation on some point in space somewhere between a near and a far object. In this case the retinal pattern at P_1 will have all three points overlapping since P_1, the fixation point, and both objects are in line. When the head

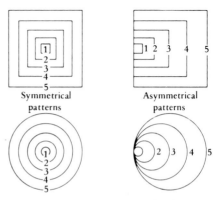

Figure 8.22 Successive momentary stimulus patterns for the perception of objects on collision paths (symmetrical patterns) and for objects on miss paths (asymmetrical patterns).

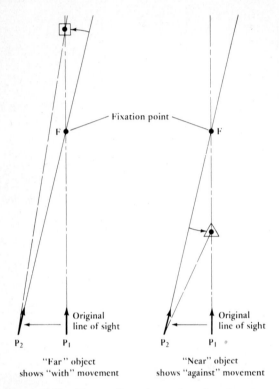

Fixation point

F

F

Original
line of sight

Original
line of sight

P₂   P₁

P₂   P₁

"Far" object
shows "with" movement

"Near" object
shows "against" movement

Figure 8.23   The transformation on the retina when viewing objects while moving from P_1 to P_2 and fixating at F.
Objects beyond the fixation point appear to move in the
same direction as the viewer ("with" movement) and objects
closer than the fixation point appear to move in a direction
opposite to that of the viewer ("against" movement).

moves the eye to a new position P_2, the objects and
fixation point are no longer in line but have moved
laterally in the visual field and in the retinal projection
in a particular way. The motion of the displacement
will be a direct function of the position of the objects
with respect to the fixation point and of the direction
of movement of the eye. The far object will be displaced in the same direction as the eye was displaced
("with" movement) and the near object will move in
the opposite direction ("against" movement).

With fixation on the far object, a different pattern of motion across the retina will occur. In this case,
the projection of the far object will not be displaced
on the retina, while the projection of the near one will
move against the observer's movement. If the eye is
fixated beyond the far object, then all objects will be

displaced in the direction opposite to the observer's
movement, and the nearer the object, the greater the
displacement.

This continuously changing situation is schematically represented in Figure 8.24, where a viewer
moves across a scene containing a man, a house, and a
tree while maintaining his fixation on the house. Five
momentary retinal fields are depicted at the bottom of
the figure. These show that, with fixation on the
house, the near object moves from left to right across
the retinal projection, the far object moves from right
to left across the field, and the house remains in the
same relative position. This apparent movement of the
world about the fixation point, the house, is perceived
as movement of the eye. If fixation were changed to a
distant object, say a tree on the horizon, all objects in
the field would appear to move in the same
direction—opposite to the direction of movement of
the observer, with the nearest object moving the fastest. It should also be apparent from the diagram that
occlusion is an essential aspect of parallax. The movement causes a shift in relative position in the projection and also causes occlusion and changes in occlusion.

Motion Perspective   Gibson
(1950, 1966) has described the flow pattern obtained
when a perceiver is walking along the ground. The
directions of flow of the optic array are illustrated in
Figure 8.25 for an observer moving forward. For this
observer, the transformations of the visual field appear
as projected on a spherical surface surrounding the
head. The horizon, stars, and field of view upward do
not move. However, the ground below him and the
world flow past him in a continuous stream. This flow
is a continuous transformation of the surface of the
earth, and no matter which way the observer looks,
the flow decreases upward in the visual field and van-
ishes at the horizon. In this sense there is perspective
in the flow. The rate at which an element flows, holding the locomotion constant, is inversely proportional
to its physical distance from the observer so that the
flow decreases as the stimulus objects move farther
away. The geometry of this decrease is the same as that
for stationary objects. In this sense the flow produces
a gradient or change in parallax.

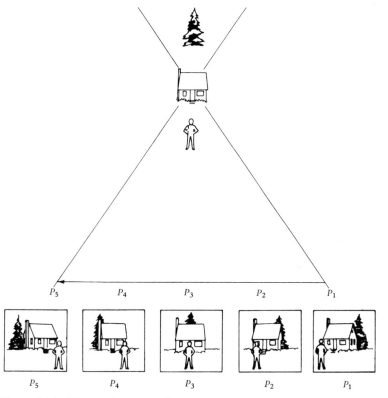

Figure 8.24 The transformations of the retina when moving through a sequence of positions while fixating a point of intermediate distance.

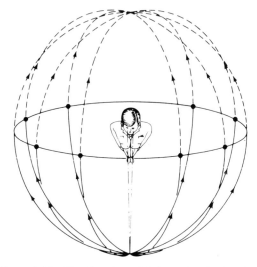

Figure 8.25 The directions of deformations in the visual field during forward locomotion as projected on a spherical surface around the head (Gibson, 1950).

The gradients of continuous transformation of angular separations of points in the field, which is a consequence of the movement of the perceiver, is called **motion perspective**. It is a transformation of pattern rather than a simple comparison of velocities as is motion parallax. Parallax arises when the perceiver moves his head from one position to another in order to obtain depth information. The relative velocities of the diplacement of two objects associated with such movements is conceived of as a cue. Motion perspective arises when a perceiver is locomoting in space and the retinal gradients of velocities are associated with the movement across the ground surface. Motion perspective is therefore the more general source of information.

The direction and speed of motion within this perspective flow vary independently. The direction of the flow as a visual impression depends on the physical direction of movement of the observer and the direction of regard. When looking ahead, the flow is downward, when looking to the right the flow is to the right, when looking to the left the flow is to the left, and when looking behind the flow is upward. The visual field ahead appears to expand outward from a focus, the focus being that point toward which the observer is moving. If he changes direction, the focus also shifts. In this sense the visual perceptual system always provides a "point of aim" for a perceiver who is moving in space. Thus the direction of movement is always present in the stimulation reaching the eye, even if it is sensed directly as change in body position rather than change in perceptual qualities.

Figures 8.26, 8.27, and 8.28 show the motion perspective for a moving perceiver when he looks forward, to the side, and in the middle distance, respectively. The gradients of velocity and direction depicted here are invariably concomitants of locomotion on the surface of the earth.

Figure 8.28 shows the relationship between the fixation point and the amount of flow and its direction. At the fixation point, the velocity of projected flow is zero, since the movement of the eye compensates for the movement of the physical world with respect to the body of the perceiver. All points above fixation in the projection plane flow in the direction of movement of the observer. All points below flow in the direction opposite to the perceiver. Once again the relationship to motion parallax is apparent. Thus, in perspective there is a gradual change in the rate of displacement of texture elements or of contours in the visual field. The change is from motion in the direction of the observer, through a line of no motion, to motion in the opposite direction.

When an observer or an object is in motion, there will be a continuous transformation of the perspective in the shape of the projection of the object on the retina. Figure 8.29 illustrates five time samples of the transformations that would occur in the retinal projec-

Figure 8.26 Motion perspective for a perceiver moving straight ahead down a country road and fixating at the horizon.

Figure 8.27 Motion perspective for a perceiver moving from right to left and looking to the right, fixating at the horizon.

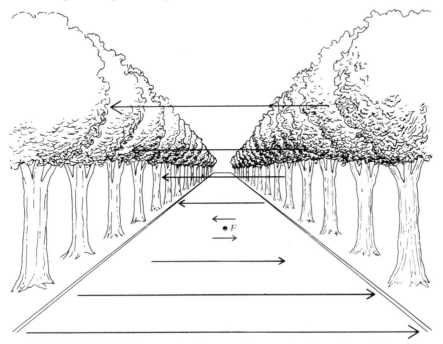

Figure 8.28 Motion perspective for a perceiver moving from right to left and looking to the right and fixating at an intermediate distance (point *F*).

Figure 8.29   Five momentary views of a table showing the perspective transformations that would occur in the retinal image when an observer walks by.

tion of an observer who was walking by a table. There is a continuous change in the size and shape of the projection of the rectangular table top. A similar pattern would be produced if the observer were stationary and the object were moving—as with a swinging door.

Rotational Motions

The rigid motions of objects in space about vertical or horizontal axes have been analyzed by Braunstein (1976) to uncover the possible sources of information. Each element in a pattern rotating about a vertical axis traces an elliptical path in the projection plane. Figure 8.30 shows perspective and top views of the stimulus configuration and projection-plane representations of the movements and path characteristics. If the rotation is divided into "near" and "far" halves depending on whether the element is in front of or behind the axis of rotation, then it is clear that the far half of the rotation is projected closer to the horizon than is the near half (panel [*a*] in Figure 8.30). Moreover, the far portion is curved more than the near portion. Panel (*b*) shows the effect of distance above and below the horizontal plane through the fixation point. The elements closer to the horizon project relatively narrower ellipses than the elements more distant from it. Thus, the farther the element is from the horizon, the shorter is the minor axis of the ellipse traced on the projection plane by its rotation. Panel (*c*) shows the effect of element distance from the axis itself. Elements closer to this axis have a shorter path—that is, smaller major and minor axes— than those more distant. All these changes are perspective effects in that

they reflect changes in the distance between the observer and the element, as the element moves through space.

There is another component to this motion that may also supply information—the relative velocity of the movement. If the motion is uniform such that there is a constant angular velocity—that is, if the angle subtended per unit time is constant—the position along the horizontal axis with respect to time can be described by the cosine of the angle through which it is rotated. This relationship is illustrated in Figure 8.31. The function $x = \text{cosine } \theta$ yields the horizontal position of each element and operates independently of the perspective effects.

Now it can be seen that the change in projected horizontal position of an element is determined by the product of the perspective factor and the cosine factor, that is, $x = \text{perspective factor} \times \text{cosine } \theta$. The change in vertical position is simply due to the perspective factor. The two factors carry different information about the element: the cosine factor carries information about angular velocity but does not indicate directionality; the perspective factor carries directionality information but not velocity information. Consequently, both factors are needed.

The changes in the retinal image when a textured plane is rotated around a vertical axis are illustrated in Figure 8.32. Once again we see a perspective effect— an expansion of the elements in both horizontal and vertical dimensions of the approaching side and a contraction of the elements in the receding side. The cosine factor is reflected in an overall compression of horizontal texture as the plane rotates away from the

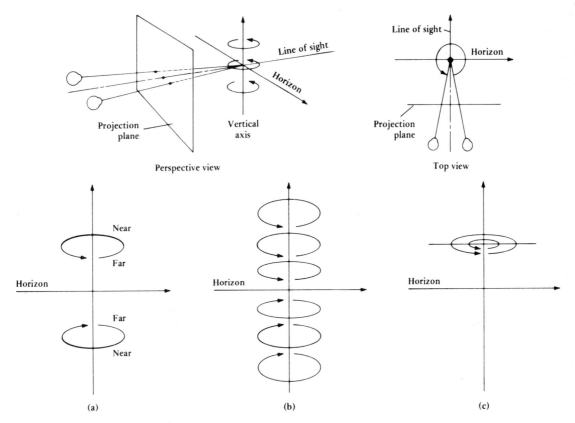

Figure 8.30 The transformations in the retinal image due to polar projection of element rotations about a vertical axis. Upper portion shows perspective and top views of the motion. Panel (*a*) shows the relative differences in the shape of the projected ellipses from near and far portions of the mo-

tion as well as the asymmetry of the "ellipses." Panel (*b*) shows the differences due to position with respect to vertical position, and panel (*c*) shows the differences due to element position with respect to horizontal position.

frontal axis, with maximum compression occurring when the plane is parallel to the line of sight. This overall compression is not related to the distance between the observer and the stimulus.

Kinetic Depth Effect

The question to be answered next is whether the perceiver uses this information. Perhaps the most direct and dramatic demonstration that observers make use of motion perspective information to perceive depth comes from the kinetic depth effect, first reported by Wallach and O'Connell (1953). Figure 8.33 illustrates the procedure. A cube made of wire is illuminated so that the wires cast shadows on a translucent screen viewed

by the observer. When the cube is stationary, the observer sees the pattern made by the wires—a two-dimensional rendering of a cube that looks two-dimensional. When the cube is rotated, the shadow cast on the screen changes in its perspective, that is, the rotation produces perspective transformations in the image on the flat screen. For example, as an edge of the cube is rotated so that it is closer to the light source (and, therefore, farther from the screen), its shadow on the screen lengthens and widens as it moves across the screen. Once rotated past the point closest to the light, the line continues to move laterally on the screen while becoming shorter and thinner.

Wallach and O'Connell (1953) found that the

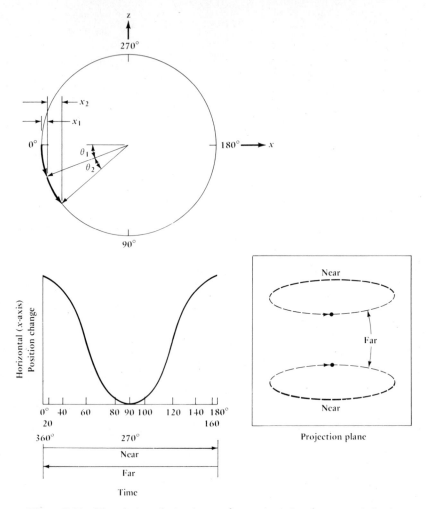

Figure 8.31 The relative velocity changes for rotary motion about a vertical axis. The horizontal (x-axis) position change with respect to time is described by the cosine of the angle subtended per unit time (θ). The velocity differences are also represented in a projection-plane view.

shadows of stationary objects were always perceived as two-dimensional. However, as soon as any regular rotation was introduced, observers always perceived the shadow as that of a three-dimensional solid object rotating in space. That is, the perspective transformation continuously displayed on the flat screen was always sufficient to produce the perception of depth.

Using the simplified stimulus of a moving point or pair of points, Johansson (1974) studied the perceptions associated with frontal-plane elliptical mo-

tions and motions that were computed as combinations of these. Figure 8.34 illustrates some of the stimuli used and the accompanying perceptual outcomes: (a) When only a single point was presented tracing an elliptical path in a fronto-parallel plane, the viewers simply saw a dot in elliptical motion in a frontal plane. (b) When a pair of dots were presented in coordinated elliptical motion in a frontal plane, they were perceived as the endpoints of a rigid rod rotating on a slanted plane. (c) When the two-dot

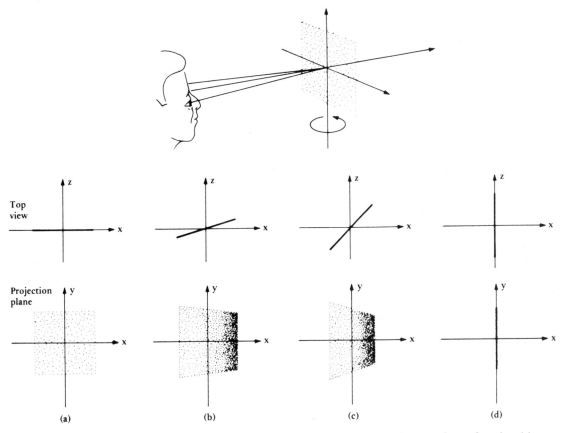

Figure 8.32   Rotation of a textured plane about a vertical axis. The projection plane changes are represented in panels (*a*) through (*d*) as the plane goes from a frontal position to a 90° rotation, with the left side approaching.

stimulus followed a complex frontal plane motion track (computed as a projection of a circular track on an oscillating plane), the resulting perceptual experience was of a rotating rigid rod, simultaneously describing a pendular motion.

Johansson concluded that the perceptual systems will produce a percept of a rigid object moving in space whenever it is possible to describe a continuous proximal change as a projection from a rigid structure. Such a situation produces perceptual shape constancy. Moreover, it is the perception of frontal figural deformations that is artificial—the perceptual system is organized to produce constant-shaped rigid objects in motion in three-dimensional space (Johansson, 1976).

SUMMARY

This chapter described the information available in the retinal image of a single eye. The information was analyzed for a stationary eye presented with a fixed stimulus and for dynamic stimulation in which the eye is moving, or objects are moving, or both are moving.

The static stimulus was analyzed in terms of the properties of surfaces—the texture in the stimulus that results from the elements out of which the surface is constructed and the gradients of texture that result from the angular relationships between the surface and the viewer. These relations also determine the outline shape of the surface and the linear perspective over the

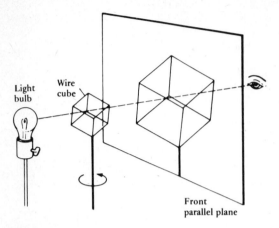

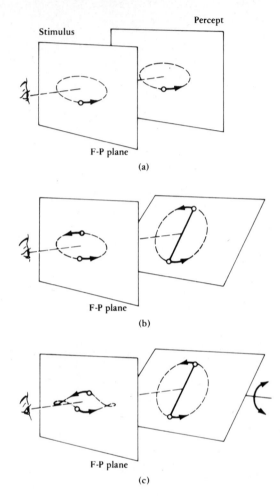

Figure 8.33 Shadow-caster like one used by Wallach and O'Connell (1953) and Wallach, O'Connell, and Neisser (1953) to study the kinetic depth effect. The wire cube is rotating as indicated. Its shadow cast upon a screen placed in the viewer's fronto-parallel plane is a two-dimensional pattern that shows a continuous and simultaneous change in length and angular orientation of sides. Such a stimulus produces the perception of rigid motion in three-dimensional space.

entire field of view. There is also local information in the stimulus provided by interposition or overlay when one object occludes the view of part of another.

The analysis of dynamic stimulation related movements of the observer and of objects to movement on the retina. Expansion and contraction patterns produce the perception of radial motion. Lateral motion produces motion parallax. Changes in the velocity and direction of portions of the total retinal flow are known as motion perspective which also includes continuous changes in outline shape. Rotational motions of objects produce expansion and contraction patterns that produce the perception of depth.

Figure 8.34 (*a*) Motion of a single dot in an elliptical path in a fronto-parallel plane produces a perception of a dot in a frontal plane moving in an elliptical path. (*b*) Coordinate motion of two dots in an elliptical path in a fronto-parallel plane is perceived as the endpoints of a rigid rod rotating on a slanted plane. (*c*) Coordinated motion tracks of dots computed as the projection of a circular track on an oscillating plane is perceived as a rigid rod rotating and simultaneously describing a pendulum motion (after Johansson, 1974).

SUGGESTED READINGS

Gibson's (1950) early book presents his analysis of stimulation. The visual cues are also presented systematically by Ittelson (1960). Braunstein (1976) provides a more recent analysis of the dynamic stimulus.

Chapter 9

Two Approaches to Perceptual Processing

The study of how the perceiver processes and uses information has generally been approached from one of two points of view. One view starts with an analysis of stimulation, sometimes describing characteristics of the actual physical object and sometimes those of the retinal projection. Such a view then asks whether the informational component that has been isolated correlates with various aspects of the resulting perceptual experience. This procedure has usually led to the conclusion that the retinal projection does not provide the information necessary for the accurate perception of objects in space. Therefore, other sources of information have been sought, either from other information simultaneously available to the organism or from memory, that may determine the perceptual experience. This approach has been called empiricism and is usually traced back to the philosopher Bishop Berkeley. Modern theorists sometimes prefer to identify Helmholtz, the great nineteenth-century physicist and physiologist, as the founder of a scientific empiricism. The empiricist view is discussed in terms of its modern versions, including both transactionalist theory (for example, Ittelson, 1960) and "algorithm" or "taking-into-account" theory (for example, Ebenholtz, 1977; Epstein, 1973, 1977; Rock, 1977).

The alternative view seeks to find correlates of visual space perception in the visual stimulus alone.

This is a psychophysical approach in its insistence on looking for correlates in the optical projections on the retinas that are sufficient to produce accurate perception. This view requires an exhaustive analysis of stimulation, including a complex analysis of stimulation over the entire retinal surface, before invoking other sources of information or resorting to memory or prior learning. The modern version of a psychophysical theory has its heritage in the relationism and nativism of the nineteenth-century physiologist Hering and in Gestalt psychology. This approach is currently represented by the "higher-order variable" theory of James J. Gibson (1950, 1966).

Since the views differ in some fundamental ways, they will be presented separately. We consider first their major premises, beginning with Gibson's approach and then describing both the classical and the modern empiricist approaches. We then compare the two approaches on a number of important issues.

THE GIBSONIAN (PSYCHOPHYSICAL) APPROACH

James J. Gibson (1950, 1966) argues that perceivers can extract information from the invariants in the optic array, and that the array is rich enough to provide all the information necessary for the perception of space, of object and perceiver motion, and for the control of perceptual-motor acts. Gibson focuses on transformations in the entire retinal pattern, transformations that, he suggests, can be uniquely related to particular patterns of the perceiver's perceptions and motions. For example, the textures of the surfaces of objects and the visual edges arising from the boundaries of objects both produce regular and predictable differences in the optical image over the surfaces in space that reflect light to the eye. In Gibson's theory, these gradual and continuous changes in stimulation over the retinal surface (gradients) are the stimulus correlates of the perception of surfaces at different slants, or, more generally, surfaces in depth. That is, Gibson suggests that a gradient of texture density is an adequate stimulus for the perception of continuous distance—it accounts for the perception of all parts of the surface simultaneously. If this is the case, then texture gradients can provide a scale for the perceptual world, a scale that defines a dimensionlity against which all other variations can be measured.

Gibson argues that the stimulus at the eye provides all the information necessary for perception of the physical world. To explore such a position, one performs psychophysical experiments, attempting to find psychophysical correlates that relate the pattern of information available in the retinal image to aspects of space perception. Study of the psychophysics of space perception is different from investigations of sensory psychophysics such as those discussed in Section One. In sensory psychophysics, there is little doubt about the stimulus variables to be correlated with aspects of perception such as brightness—obviously, we are interested in the functions relating stimulus intensity, duration, area, and the like, to perceived brightness. In studying the psychophysics of space perception, however, the initial task is to discover the physical variables. What are the variables of importance? What aspects of the stimulus pattern are correlated with our visual experience of space? This task is much more difficult.

There are several beliefs held in common by researchers who follow this approach. First, they are concerned with the information in complete natural scenes, not in components of scenes isolated one-by-one in laboratory analyses. Second, they believe that patterns of discontinuity in the light imaged on the retina should be considered as information about space and nothing more. Specifically, the pattern should not be thought of as a picture of space that perceivers look at and interpret. Third, they believe that the pattern of light on the retina contains so much information about the layout of space that the observer should rarely, if ever, have to use nonretinal sources of information such as information from prior experience, knowledge, or assumptions. Thus, from Gibson's psychophysical point of view, the visual system responds directly to higher-order variables of stimulation, variables that contain sufficient information to determine perceptual experience uniquely, without the aid of information from other sources, whether from other simultaneously available nonvisual stimulation or from representations of past experience in memory.

Gibson's psychophysics rests on a conception of physical space as one containing objects on surfaces, and it gives special recognition to a particular surface—the ground. Not only is the ground a surface that extends away from the observer in the third dimension, it also provides support for motor activity and is involved in the equilibrium of the body, in upright posture, and in locomotion in general. Moreover, since man is a terrestrial animal, the lower portion of the visual field is almost invariably filled by a projection of the terrain (Fig. 9.1), while the upper portion is usually filled with a projection of the sky separated from the terrain by a skyline. The ground projects an image that is spread out on the retina rather than confined to a point.

Figure 9.2 illustrates the advantage of conceptualizing the visual information at the eye in terms of surfaces rather than points and lines. Analyzing the retinal projections in terms of points of stimulation causes a major difficulty in assigning depth values to points in space when they are aligned, as are points A, B, C, and D. The distance along the line of sight could not be translated into differential stimulation on the retina by any means. With an emphasis on the surface below the eye, there is always a projection of an ex-

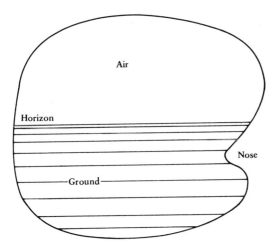

Figure 9.1 A typical visual field of one eye, showing the ground, the sky, the horizon or skyline, and the overall shape.

tended surface represented on the retina. Therefore, the points in the retinal pattern A', B', C', and D', which correspond to the points A, B, C, and D in the surface, are always discriminable on the retina.

Gibson's psychophysics of visual space analyzes the retinal projection of an object in terms of the surfaces that are in contact with the object in question. Perceptual constancy is, therefore, viewed as a direct consequence of the perception of textured objects on textured surfaces—the normal visual world. It would not be necessary to know the perceived distance of an object, to know what the object is, or to have come

into contact with it in the past, in order to perceive it as having constant size and shape. Constancy would be given in the particular relationships in the retinal image. It is the gradients and transformations in this projection that provide a constant scale for all of visual space. Within this metric, objects are perceived as attached to the underlying ground surface and thereby can be perceived in relation to its scale. It is scale, not the size of specific objects, that remains constant in perceiving objects in space.

Figure 9.3 illustrates the importance of scale provided by texture and perspective in determining the perceived size of the three objects. Each of the objects depicted subtends the same visual angle (you can verify this by measuring each of them). They differ in their relative positions with respect to the gradients on the projection plane. Therefore they intersect the scale provided by these gradients at different points. Since the scale provides the metric of size-at-a-distance, the point of intersection of the object with the surface will determine its relative depth and its relative size. The retinal projection intersecting the projection of the ground surface low in the projection plane does so where the texture, size, and perspective all indicate "near." The same projection near the top of the plane will intercept the surface at a point indicating "far." Since the texture size provides a constancy scaling as a decreasing size of the retinal projection, an unchanging size in the retinal projection will appear to be larger in the "far" position, and vice

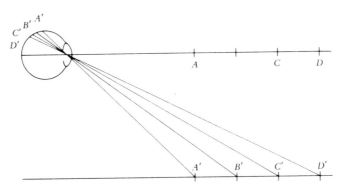

Figure 9.2 Two formulations of the problem of distance perception: one considers individual points on the retina and the other emphasizes the relationships among many points.

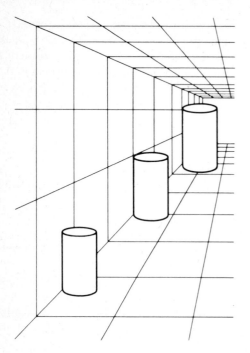 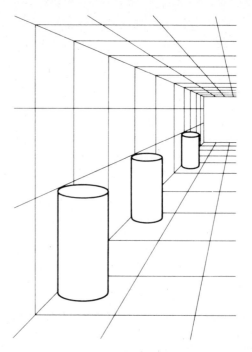

Figure 9.3 The "size illusion," showing the role of the scale provided by gradients of texture, size, and perspective in determining the perceived size of three objects subtending the same visual angle.

Figure 9.4 Perceptual constancy resulting from objects subtending different visual angles, but intersecting the ground plane at different levels and, therefore, scaled differently.

versa. Figure 9.4 shows what happens when the size of the retinal projection of the object decreases in the same proportion as does the gradient. Now the perception is clearly of three objects of the same size at different positions in depth.

Processing Retinal Flow

Gibson emphasizes the information available when the perceiver moves through space. It is clear that, regardless of what other information the perceiver may have, there is information in the changes in the visual input that is directly correlated with the characteristics of the visual world in which the movement is taking place.

The basic premise of the Gibsonian psychophysics of motion is that each variety of object motion and of observer motion produces a different and unique pattern of transformations over the retina. Therefore,

in order to perceive motion in the environment correctly, and never to confuse it with motion of the observer's eyes and body, all that is necessary is to attend to the differences in these stimulations. This analysis is again one of geometrical optics. Such an analysis is successful to the extent that evidence can be found that perceivers know these transformations, know how to use them, or use the differences to distinguish the source of motion on the retina. If such evidence is forthcoming, Gibson would have made a strong case that all the information we need for motion perception is contained in the transformation of visual information on the retina, and recourse to nonvisual sources of information is unnecessary.

If we look at a stationary scene that has no movement in it, and we hold our eyes, head, and body momentarily motionless a particular momentary pattern of stimulation is produced in the projection on the retina. We will consider this the baseline and discuss the transformations it might normally undergo. Consider first the change in which the entire pattern is shifted to the right. The extreme right-hand edge will disappear and a new part of the visual world will come into view on the left. Only one circumstance can produce this change—a movement of our eyes to the left without change in the position of our head or body, and without motion in the scene. In a psychophysical sense, then, this should be a completely adequate source of visual information to distinguish this type of movement from any other. Visual information alone should be adequate to tell us it was our eye and not the world that moved.

In another type of change, the baseline pattern remains stationary except for one part of it, which is displaced to the right. Only one reasonable circumstance can produce this change—an object in motion in an otherwise stationary visual world. Whenever there is a relative displacement of part of the pattern in the absence of any other changes, there must be something out there moving. Again, this is conveyed by visual information alone as a displacement in part of the retinal pattern of stimulation.

As another and more complex example, suppose that the pattern is shifted to the right, but different components in the pattern shift relative to each other at different rates. Thus some components are occluded sooner than others. There is only one set of circumstances that can produce this change—viewing a stationary scene with a moving eye. This is a common stimulus. It occurs, for example, when looking at a stationary scene out of the window of a train moving laterally to the left, without any movement of your eyes, head, or body. Another might be when you are walking or running while looking at a 90-degree angle to the path of motion. The specific circumstance depicted here is one in which fixation is on near space, a speck of dust on the glass window of the train, for example. The trees near the track will flash across our stationary retina at a high rate while distant hills will be displaced slowly.

The previous conditions can be made more complex by permitting some eye movement or head movement as well as bodily displacement laterally. The details become more complex but the principle is the same. Each particular type of motion, whether of specific objects, or of the entire visual world, or of the eyes, head, or body, or of any combination of these, produces a unique pattern of change in the stimulation in the retinal pattern. In other words, there is visual information that always is correlated with the perceived change in the visual world.

The point is that perceivers should never have any trouble distinguishing their own motions from motions in the visual world, and should be able to do this from information available in the changes that occur in the transformations within the retinal projection and in the displacement of that projection across the retina.

For example, according to Gibson, the motion of an object with respect to other objects is perceived when the retinal projection contains a perspective transformation associated with **kinetic optic occlusion.** As an object moves, it progressively covers and uncovers the texture of the surface behind it. The consequence of this motion in the retinal projection is described by Gibson as a "wiping out" of texture at the leading border, an "unwiping" at the trailing border, and a "shearing" of texture at the lateral borders. The perspective transformation is invariably associated with a break in the continuity of the texture of the background. This kinetic retinal projection is the normal stimulus situation. The kinetic occlusion specifies the existence of an edge, of depth at the edge, and the existence of one surface behind another. The apparent continued existence of the hidden surface may be a component of object constancy—the belief in the permanence of objects that momentarily disappear from view.

An object in motion produces transformation in its own perspective projection on the retinal surface and also relative changes with respect to its texture and that of the background. If the observer is stationary, the remainder of the optic array will be relatively stable. When the observer moves, however, the optic array becomes alive with motion. There is a flow of velocities of retinal points—a global motion parallax;

there is a perspective transformation of each form projected on the retinal surface; there is a displacement among the elements of texture; and there are breaks in the flow of texture as surfaces cut across one another. All of these changes in the retinal projection are related to each other and to the actual movements of the observer.

These systematic transformations in the retinal projection specify the perception of movement of the observer himself. For example, look back at Figure 8.25. It showed the directions of deformations in the visual field during forward locomotion. The flow in the retinal projection from the forward pole to the rear

pole specifies the locomotion of the viewer with respect to the world and, simultaneously, the layout of that world. The focus of optical expansion specifies the point toward which the movement is directed.

When moving from one place to another, the viewer changes his vista and new kinds of transformations are introduced that specify more complex kinds of environmental changes. For example, the successive transformations in the retinal projection of a person approaching a doorway are illustrated in Figure 9.5. The sequence of pictures illustrates the relationship between the movement of the observer and the changes in the array. As the observer moves forward,

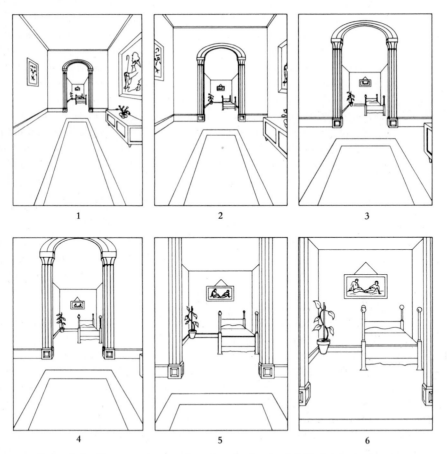

Figure 9.5 The successive transformations in the visual field of a single eye when moving from one vista to another (Gibson, 1966).

a number of objects will appear to emerge from behind the aperture. The doorframe will expand to uncover the array in the new room—another aspect of kinetic occlusion. All apertures in the visual world—doors, windows, spaces between objects—open on optically denser patterns. This ability to perceive openings and spaces as a direct correlate of properties of the retinal projection permits locomotion without collision.

What is the implication of all this? For Gibson, this tremendously informative (although complex) stimulation produces a scale for the visual world. The changes in this scale over the pattern and across time over changing patterns could arise only if the scale of the visual world were constant—the space between objects in the distance is specified in the same units as that between near objects. It is the recognition of this scaling as a consequence of the spatial and temporal patterning of the information at the retina that has led Gibson to argue that perception of space is given directly; that the "superstimulus" contains all the information necessary for direct perception of space and movement within it. It seems clear that motion and sequence are crucial aspects of the construction of a scale of space which provides the foundation for the perceptual world.

THE EMPIRICIST OR COMBINATORIAL (ALGORITHM) APPROACH

Historically, the empiricist view has been contrasted with the nativist view—the former proposing that perception is the result of learning to associate or integrate information from different sources in order to obtain a veridical (true to the stimulus) percept; the latter proposing that the ability to produce veridical percepts was part of the organism's innate capacity (Hochberg, 1962). Contemporary analyses have refined the distinctions between the major approaches, and it has become clear that the heart of the controversy is not so much the origin of the process as it is the source of the information used by the visual system (Rock, 1977). The modern versions of empiricist the-

ory continue in the position that the retinal representation of the stimulus object or stimulus quality is not sufficient for a unique, veridical percept. The perceptual outcome must therefore involve information from some sources other than the stimulus object.

The empiricist approach derived from Berkeley (1709) and Helmholtz (1850) may be classified as a "learning" approach. They stressed the learned associations between the optical input and nonvisual input such as movements of the body. Indeed, Helmholtz proposed that percepts are the results of a process that has the appearance of an **unconscious inference**. The **combinatorial/algorithm approach** assumes that the perceptual system generates veridical percepts by combining variables according to rules: specifically, those prescribed by the invariance hypothesis (see below). The variables include both *intrinsic* factors—the local retinal correlate of the distal property of the stimulus object that is to be discriminated—and *extrinsic* factors—those variables that contain information about organismic or environmental conditions (Epstein, 1977). Retinal size as measured by a visual angle is an example of an intrinsic variable, body position is an example of an extrinsic variable. The perceptual system is viewed as having access not only to the proximal stimulus, but also to the conditional events that change the visual inputs. The unique perceptual outcome is a joint function of the proximal pattern and of the conditional events, such that nonvisual events are "taken into account" (Rock, 1977). What is taken into account need not be limited to current visual stimulation—it can include efferent signals directing the movements of the eyes, or body motions, or stored information about comparable visual scenes seen at an earlier time. From this point of view, the visual world is perceived as stable even when the head and body are moving, because we take into account the intentions to make movements.

To appreciate this view, it is important to understand, as Helmholtz made clear a century ago, that one is not conscious of the operation of the visual system in carrying out these processes. Therefore, in describing the variables that may enter into the functions, it is necessary to distinguish between the *registered* (nonconscious) and the *perceived* (conscious) values of extrinsic variables. It is the registered values that enter into the algorithms. The experienced percept is seen as the result of unconscious processes operating on inputs that have no conscious counterpart.

The Role of the Stimulus

Equivalent Configurations and Stimulus Inadequacy
The empiricist analysis typically assumes that the physical world can be described using the laws of Euclidean geometry. Physical space is therefore described as consisting of lines and angles, with the fundamental property that parallel lines do not meet. This is the world that, presumably, extends outward from the eyes in a straight line and provides stimulation to the retinas. Under these assumptions, then, the size, shape, and direction of objects can be directly related to the configurations on the retinas, with the perception of distance and depth as the main aspects of space perception to be explained. In order to do this, the stimulus is isolated in the laboratory, and broken down into its components. Most of the research prompted by the empiricist view uses very simple stimuli—a single line or an outline shape projected on a screen, or a simple object such as a cube. The goal is to reduce the complex stimulus configurations reflected from a natural scene into its basic components.

The relationship between a simple object in space and the luminance discontinuities it produces in the retinal image has already been illustrated in Figure 1.9 for a line of size S at a distance D from the perceiver. The size of the projection on the retinal surface will be a function of the visual angle formed by the light rays from the extremities of the object. This angle supplies important information about the stimulus object, but it is not unique to this object. This particular object at this particular distance is clearly the only one that could give rise to the visual angle described. But is it the only object in space that could produce such a visual angle? Figure 9.6 shows that it is not. A number of objects of different sizes at different distances could give rise to an envelope of light rays entering the eye with the same visual angle. The-

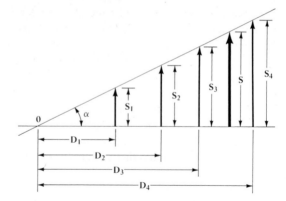

Figure 9.6 Four objects at different distances from the observer but at the same slant as S (perpendicular) that give rise to the same envelope of light rays as specified by the visual angle α. Theoretically, there is an infinite number of such objects.

oretically, there is an infinite number of such objects, since one could erect an object of the appropriate size at any distance. If the object is also allowed to be at a different slant, then the picture gets even more complicated. Figure 9.7 shows a number of objects with different slants all at the same (approximate) distance from the eye. These objects also subtend the same visual angle as the original object of size S at distance D. Once again, it is apparent that an infinite number of such objects could be erected at each distance.

All stimuli in space that could give rise to the same pattern on the retina are said to be members of a

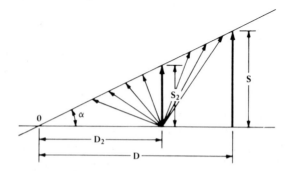

Figure 9.7 A number of objects at different slants, at the distance D_2, that subtend the same visual angle as does S at D. An infinite number of such objects could be constructed.

family of **equivalent configurations.** For example, all the arrows depicted in Figures 9.6 and 9.7, and the infinite number of arrows not shown, are members of the same family of equivalent configurations, because each could produce the same stimulus at the eye, the visual angle α. Figure 8.16 showed some members of a family of equivalent configurations for a two-dimensional surface. Notice that a single side of a particular quadrilateral corresponds to one member of a family of equivalent configurations that gives rise to a particular visual angle. Another member of the same family is represented as the corresponding side of a different quadrilateral. This relationship holds for each of the corresponding sides of the quadrilaterals in the figure. It should be clear, then, that an infinite number of such quadrilaterals could give rise to the two-dimensional configuration on the retina represented by the combination of visual angles corresponding to each of the sides. The concept of equivalent configurations implies that there is not enough information in the stimulus on the retina to determine a percept uniquely. Clearly, any member of the family of equivalent configurations could have given rise to this retinal pattern, and therefore it is not possible to tell which is the one out there, using the retinal information alone. If two or more objects can give rise to the same stimulus on the retina, and if the stimulus determines the percept, then clearly the perceiver would be unable to discriminate between these objects. The only conclusion possible is that additional information must be supplied from other sources to supplement the retinal information.

The Invariance Hypothesis

How, then, is stimulation processed into perceptual experience and how is the perceptual outcome to be described? One widely accepted answer is summarized by the **invariance hypothesis**, an attempt to translate the geometry of physical stimulation into a description of psychological events. In its general form, the invariance hypothesis states that, for a given stimulus configuration, the perceptual outcome must be a member of the family of equivalent configurations defined by the stimulus. For example, the invariance hypothesis predicts that,

given the visual angle specified in Figures 8.16 and 9.6, the observer will perceive one of the appropriately sized objects that project that sized line, or that sized and shaped quadrilateral on the retina. The hypothesis does not predict which one will be perceived—only that it will be one of those equivalent configurations.

There is, then, an infinite number of possible perceptions that satisfy the invariance hypothesis. However, there is one unique outcome in which the percept corresponds exactly to the particular physical configuration that actually produced the stimulus—in which the viewer actually sees what is really there. This outcome is given a special name—**perceptual constancy.** One of the major tasks of perceptual theory is to explain why almost all our normal perceptual experience is of this sort.

The invariance hypothesis has served two different functions in perceptual theory—it has been used both as explanation and as description. Since much of everyday perceptual experience is described by perceptual constancy, it should be clear that the invariance hypothesis describes perceptual experience fairly well (see, for example, Epstein, 1973; Epstein & Park, 1963; and Epstein, Park, & Casey, 1961). The use of the invariance hypothesis as explanation is to suggest that the perceptual system actually follows the rules (laws) or makes the computations prescribed by perceptual invariance.

The rules that are given by the invariance hypothesis represent algorithms that can be repeatedly applied to yield veridical perceptions. Ebenholtz's (1977) treatment of orientation constancy of objects is a good example of an application of this approach. **Orientation constancy** describes the situation where the perceived orientation or verticality of objects remains invariant despite changes in the proximal stimulus. Ebenholtz argues that, in order for orientation constancy to occur, the visual input must be processed jointly with information about body tilt. Without such information, the visual input is not sufficient to produce a veridical perception of gravitational orientation. Ebenholtz proposes an algorithm for calculation of apparent object orientation (AOO) in terms of registered body orientation (RBO), and the angle on the retina between the vertical retinal meridian and the image of the line target (α): AOO = α + RBO. Since this equation, describing a perceptual outcome, contains information from a nonvisual source (RBO), it supports an empiricist point of view.

Rock (1977) carries the argument even further, suggesting that the perceptual system operates under a set of rules that make it seem as if it were solving logical problems in a way that reflects the structure of the outside world. The algorithm-processing by the perceptual system is like a cognitive process in which conclusions are drawn from premises, except that the process is not conscious and the outcome is a percept and not a conclusion. Rock's illustration uses **size constancy,** the fact that an object appears to maintain a fixed size even though its distance from the observer—and consequently the proximal retinal size and visual angle—is changing. Rock suggests that the perceived extension on the retina correlated with the visual angle is interpreted by the perceptual system as signifying a particular objective size on the basis of information available concerning the object's distance. The steps would be like solving a problem in logic: (1) a particular extent is perceived based on visual angle, (2) the information that the object producing the visual angle is at a particular distance is invoked, and (3) the perceived size is deduced from the combination of these two kinds of information. The visual system must somehow "know" the algorithm relating visual angle and distance, and then utilize some other information in the function.

The Role of the Perceiver

Observer Tendencies Gogel (1965) has proposed that cues and other stimulus information are not the only factors that enter into the final determination of a perceptual outcome. There are **observer tendencies**—factors that affect perceptions but are not defined in terms of the conditions of stimulation. Gogel has described two observer tendencies, the equidistance tendency and the specific distance tendency. The **equidistance tendency** refers to the fact that, with relative distance cues limited, objects or parts of objects tend to appear to be at the same

distance from the viewer. The effectiveness of this tendency increases as the directional separation between the objects decreases (Gogel, 1965, 1973). This tendency is a factor in relative distance perception. The **specific distance tendency** refers to the fact that, with the reduction of absolute distance information, objects will tend to appear at a distance of about two meters from the viewer. This tendency is a factor in egocentric distance perception (Gogel, 1973; Gogel & Tietz, 1973). Each of these tendencies may be in agreement or in conflict with distance information from other sources.

The observer tendencies are important because information is not obtained uniformly from parts of the spatial array at different distances from the viewer—both the number and magnitude of distance cues are greater for a near than for a far depth interval. For example, for a depth interval extending about two meters in front of the viewer, all the absolute and relative distance cues will be above threshold. However, few, if any, of these same cues will be available for the same depth interval extending beyond thirty meters. Consequently, the information is reduced from "far" portions of the spatial array, but rather than perceiving an uncertain or ambiguous world, the observer tendencies operate in such a way that objects physically separated in depth will tend to be perceived at the same distance (the equidistance tendency) and at a distance near the observer (the specific distance tendency). All these factors must be taken into account in understanding how the perceptual system achieves constancy.

Expectancy Hochberg (1978, 1979) stressed the fact that perception almost always involves the integration of information from successive fixations. He described three characteristics of looking at scenes that must be taken into account: First, the retinal image is not uniformly clear—it has high contrast and sharp focus only in the center. Second, many tasks can be carried out only on the basis of information in central vision—information in the periphery can be used only if a subsequent shift in eye position places the information in the fovea. Third, in order to be able to perceive an entire scene, the information picked up by each of the successive glances over the scene must be integrated.

Combinatorial models provide little room for the perceiver as an active integrator. Hochberg carried the approach further by suggesting that repeated encounters with the structure of the physical world produces learned expectancies about the outcome of possible perceptual-motor acts. These expectancies permit us to perceive that object, event, or scene which would be most likely to have produced a given pattern of sensory stimulation. The mental structure forming the basis of this integration is a contruction of the scene that goes beyond any particular sample. It is a set of contingent expectancies as to what the perceiver will see as a result of particular sensori-motor movements. These mental structures are continually added to or modified as the perceiver tests his expectations about what he will see when he moves in such a way as to bring presently hidden or blurred parts of the scene into clear vision. Thus, perception is viewed as a process of sampling, testing, and construction based on knowledge, past experience, and guesswork on the part of the perceiver. We will return to the expectancy approach in considering the perception of form (Chapter 15) and of reading (Chapter 19).

Processing Spatial Information from Edges

Reflection and Illumination Edges

Since edges are important in visual processing, and since computers can easily locate edges in analyses of stimulation falling on banks of photoreceptors, many attempts have been made to use edges as the starting point for scene analysis by computer. A luminance discontinuity on the retina results from a difference in the amount of light reaching the eye from two adjacent areas in space. This is often referred to as a visual edge. If there were only one kind of arrangement of surfaces in the scene that could produce a visual edge, luminance discontinuities could be the basis for inferences about those surfaces. However, there are at least two kinds of visual edges produced by different spatial arrangements—**reflectance edges** and **illumination edges**. Illumination edges supply information about illumination, a characteristic that is not intrinsic to the scene and rarely reveals anything about the surfaces. The presence of shadows may help to find the direction of illumination and thus may help specify the layout of space, but the two kinds of edges cannot be distinguished by local properties along their edges.

Computer Processing of Scenes

Numerous computer programs have been developed to determine the spatial layout of a scene from information supplied by a bank of photoreceptors that produce an image on a display like a TV screen (Hanson & Riseman, 1978; Winston, 1975, 1977). While the goals of research on computer vision systems and on human vision systems usually are not similar, several proposals focus on some of the same processing problems. Many of the current systems designed for computer analysis of visual scenes use an intersection-of-edge procedure developed by Guzman (1969). Using line drawings of block forms (see Figure 9.8), Guzman identified different kinds of edge-inter-

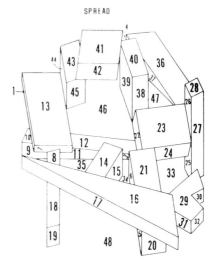

Figure 9.8 An example of Guzman's (1969) complex block figures.

sections. Figure 9.9 lists the types of edge-intersections he found and the properties that define them. Notice that by changing the angle c between the "fork" and the "arrow" intersections from one less than 180° to one more than 180°, surface c changes from one belonging to an object to one that belongs to a different object lying behind the first. Thus, the relative positions of the edges at the intersection can determine relative depth.

Figure 9.10 illustrates how such a classsification system might work for a single block figure. While the interpretation of each intersection is not unambiguous, contradictory interpretations can be resolved by weighting. For example, of the 26 intersections in the drawing, 15 involve adjacency of the background surface with one of the block surfaces. Intersection numbers 1, 3, 7, 21, 17, and 25 are all "L" intersections, dividing space into two surfaces belonging to different

objects. If the outer one is always called a, then it must be a single surface since there are no edges separating the different a's. While the "L" rule's specification of depth is not powerful, it does suggest that the surface bounded by the angle exceeding 180° is "behind" the other. In each case, the part of the background surface must be behind all of the others. Furthermore, intersections 2, 22, 23, and 26 are "arrows" and provide information that the a area is behind the other two, a consistent interpretation. Intersections 4, 6, 20, and 18 also include surface a, but because they are "T" intersections, they suggest that a belongs to the same surface as b. Consequently, 11 of the 15 intersections involving surface a provide information that a is different from all other surfaces and behind all of them, whereas four provide information that a is a different surface of the same object. The first tentative interpretation, with no other information from the intersections taken into account, would be that a is a surface of an object separate from all others, and behind all others. Analysis of other intersections may help to resolve any ambiguity.

Other schemes have been developed that depend on all of the features of edges, in addition to their intersections. Barrow and Tenenbaum's (1978) program locates edges in the image and classifies the surfaces bounded by the edges in terms of spatial positions on the basis of the relational properties around those edges. Thus, the first step arrives at a three-dimensional representation without first working on lower-order elements. Recent evidence in the psychological literature supports the primacy of depth perception. Gilchrist (1977) manipulated the apparent distances of light patches and their surrounds (see Chapter 4, pp. 86–87. He found that the traditional lightness-contrast effects were reproduced whenever the patch and the surround are perceived to be adjacent in space and coplanar. However, if the patch is perceived to be in front of the surround or behind it, then contrast does not occur—that is, the surround does not modify the appearance of the patch. This result has been reproduced in several different experimental situations.

Gilchrist's results make it impossible to explain brightness contrast solely in terms of inhibition

Type of intersection	Name	Most likely interpreted
	Fork	a, b and c are different surfaces of same object. Intersection is an outside corner
	Arrow	a and b are different surfaces of same object. c is surface of different object (often background), lying behind first object
	"T"	a and b different surfaces of same object. c is surface of another object occluding first object
		a, b, c and d are all different surfaces of same object
	"L"	a is surface of one object, b is surface of another object

Figure 9.9 Properties of edge-intersections found by Guzman (1969).

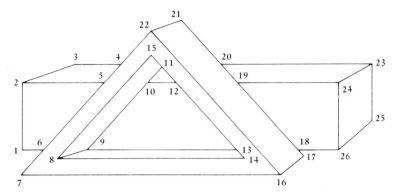

Figure 9.10 Block figure used in the analysis of edge-intersections. See text for a description of the sequential analysis.

among adjacent retinal areas since the retinal patterns were identical in all his experiments. Instead, it appears that interaction occurs only when the observer perceives the retinally adjacent surfaces to be spatially adjacent as well. That is, the observer has to construct the layout of space first, and only then can he assign the lightness (and presumably color) values to the surfaces.

COMPARING THE TWO APPROACHES

The Role of the Proximal Stimulus

One distinction that separates the empiricists from the psychophysicists is the role of the proximal stimulus in the perception of space. Gibson calls the proximal stimulus "the visual field" and contrasts it with the visual world. The **visual world** is what we perceive. It is made up of solid objects that look solid and of slanted surfaces that are perceived at their appropriate slant. The visual world has no boundaries; it is continuous, and it has a panoramic character. This world has no center and no differences in clarity among its parts. The visual world is perceived by scanning—it does not move when we move our head and eyes, it is stable and shows constancy of size, shape, and form. Thus the visual world is dependent on eye

movements rather than on a single fixation and, therefore, will require an explanation in terms of dynamic stimulus correlates, that is, correlates containing temporal patterning.

The **visual field** is the momentary visual stimulation that we usually do not experience. We may become aware of it by taking a special introspective attitude, for example, by fixating on a point and paying attention to the area that can be seen. Taking the sophisticated attitude of an artist will also permit one to observe the two-dimensional visual field. A typical visual field for one eye is made up of colored patches and surfaces divided by contours. It is bounded and is oval in shape, covering about 180 degrees horizontally and 150 degrees vertically. The visual field is sharp, clear, and fully detailed at the center but gets progressively vaguer and less detailed toward its boundary; that is, there is a center-to-periphery gradient of clarity. The visual field shifts as the eyes, head, and body move. Objects represented in the visual field show projective shape and, therefore, do not have constancy but change their size and shape when fixation changes.

This is a critical distinction for Gibson, and failure to acknowledge it imposes an insurmountable barrier to any theory of visual space perception. The visual world has continuity but we sample it with the motions of our eyes—eyes that move in a head that in turn is also moving in space. In the normal state of affairs, with our eyes, head, and body moving through space, the visual field is in a state of flux. Therefore the analysis of visual space perception must involve successive retinal stimulation from successive fixations. The successive stimulations of the retina do not fuse with one another but are integrated over time in the same sense that the successive frames of a motion picture film are not blurred one into the other, but simply supply the stimulus over time for the perception of continuous motion. It is therefore necessary to understand the geometry of transformations on the retina in order to explain why successive changes can correspond to various aspects of visual experience. Because the successive retinal images are not entities but simply represent temporal samples of a stimulus constituting change over time, the visual world cannot be perceived all at once. The perception of visual space is based not on a succession of images, but on a continuous but changing set of images.

This relationship is illustrated in Figure 9.5, which shows the optical transformations that occur as a perceiver enters a room. The information contained in a particular retinal pattern at any moment in time cannot be understood in isolation. It must be analyzed in terms of the effects of the motions of the observer and of the transformations produced by these motions. Chapter 8 described these relationships in detail.

Rock (1977) proposes an entirely different view of the proximal stimulus. He suggests that the role of the visual field has been underestimated and that Gibson merely distinguished between two modes of perceiving—the constancy mode and the proximal mode. The **constancy mode** is like Gibson's visual world—it is salient in experience and directly relevant in guiding behavior. It has an objective quality because it is a representation of the properties of things and spaces in the physical world. The **proximal mode** of perceiving corresponds to Gibson's visual field because it is not salient in experience and does not appear to be relevant to behavior. Indeed, it is frequently hard to describe, perhaps because it represents the experience of momentary conditions and of the relationships between objects and the self. But unlike Gibson, Rock suggests that proximal perception plays an indispensable role in the total perceptual process. Indeed, it is the proximal perception that can be registered and taken into account in algorithm theories.

The perception of size provides a good example of Rock's contention. Normally, when asked for size judgments, viewers match the objective size of the object, suggesting that they are functioning in the constancy mode of perception. Nevertheless, Rock argues that **perceived extensity**, the phenomenal correlate of visual angle, can be represented in consciousness. That is, we may be aware of the fact that a distant object does not fill as much of the field of view as it does when it is nearby, even though we are not attending to that fact at the moment. To support his contention, Rock cites a number of experiments in which perceived extensity was measured by asking observers to match the sizes of objects at different distances. In a dark field where no information about distance is available, observers produce matches close to visual angle size. Clearly the demonstration of proximal mode perception gives greater credence to their possible role in a perceptual process that computes algorithms or produces inferencelike outcomes.

Size-at-a-Distance

The relationship between physical size, physical distance, and visual angle that is frequently taken as a model for the relationship between perceived size, perceived distance, and visual angle is sometimes called Emmert's Law, although the original formulation applied only to the perceived size and distance of afterimages. Specifically, the **size–distance invariance hypothesis** states that a visual angle (or retinal extent) of given size determines a unique ratio of apparent size to apparent distance. Given these relationships, it is clear that retinal size (or visual angle) alone does not supply enough information to determine a unique percept. The perceiver only has enough information to determine a family of equivalent configurations defined by the ratio of perceived size to perceived distance. Since the perceiver usually reports seeing only one object at a single distance—and it usually is the actual physical distance of the physical object in space—empiricists have argued that other sources of information must be brought to bear. One source is **familiar size**—the sizes of objects that are learned as a result of our associations with the real, meaningful, and useful world. If the size of an object is known, then perceived size can be set equal to real size, and apparent distance is determined.

The algorithm approach views the size–distance invariance hypothesis as a model of the computations performed by the perceptual system. It is especially useful in explaining size constancy purely in terms of the local retinal stimulus—the retinal extent or visual angle. To accomplish this, the perceptual system must "take distance into account." But it is not physical distance that must enter into the computation, it is perceived or apparent distance. Thus the perceptual system must make use of whatever distance information is available to arrive at a value for apparent distance, and then must use this value according to the computational rule to obtain perceived size. If perceived distance is accurate, size constancy will result.

Rock (1977) described the operations in more detail, suggesting further that the process is like syllogistic reasoning: first, a given retinal extent (visual angle) results in a proximal mode perception of extensity. Then, information available concerning the distance of the object producing the visual angle is used to interpret the perceived extensity to produce (deduce) the perception of an object of a particular size. The visual system must somehow "know" how visual angle changes as a function of distance.

The classic experiment by Holway and Boring (1941) represents a prototype of experiments taken as support of the algorithm approach. In the experimental situation, the viewer saw one of two disks by looking in one direction or another down an L-shaped corridor. One disk was placed ten feet from the viewer and could be adjusted to match the size of a second disk placed at various distances from the viewer down the other corridor. The disks were constructed so that they each subtended one degree of visual angle at the respective distances. Viewers performed the matches in a number of different conditions: with full depth cues available using two eyes and using one eye; looking through an aperture that limited the field of view (reduction screen); and looking at the disk in an otherwise dark field. The results are shown in Figure 9.11. With either monocular or binocular viewing, size constancy matches were approximate only when full distance information was available. In the dark,

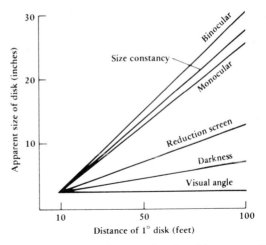

Figure 9.11 Perceived size as a function of the amount of depth information present. The full cue condition produces size matches that approximate size constancy, and the darkness condition produces matches that approximates visual angle size (Holway & Boring, 1941).

with no distance cues available, the matches approximated the visual angle of the stimulus. When partial distance information was available (reduction condition), the matches fell between the visual angle and constancy.

The experimental situation used by Holway and Boring was an attempt to isolate a single object of perception and to measure its perceived size. The fact that the darkness condition produced more visual angle matches suggests that there is not enough information in the stimulus—retinal extent alone without distance cues—to yield veridical size–distance perception. But suppose one additional stimulus object were added. Perhaps the relative information in the stimulus provided by two objects would be sufficient. Figure 9.12 shows the visual projection of two objects S_1 and S_2 at two distances D_1 and D_2, with their respective visual angles α_1 and α_2. If the perceiver can assume that the two objects have the same real size, through the use of other depth information, past experience, or by guessing, then $\alpha_1/\alpha_2 = D_2/D_1$. In this case, the object producing the larger retinal size will be perceived as closer. Similarly, if the perceiver can assume that the two distances are equal, then $\alpha_1/\alpha_2 = S_1/S_2$, and the two real sizes vary in the

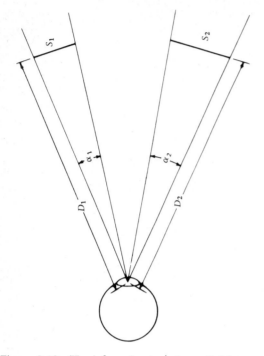

Figure 9.12 The information (α_1/α_2) supplied by two stimuli at different distances and in different directions.

same ratio as their retinal sizes. Moreover, now the equidistance tendency should operate to make the objects appear to be at the same distance from the viewer.

Objects in empty space therefore provide a monocular retinal projection that does not supply enough information to determine perceived size and perceived distance uniquely. However, when the object's surfaces have texture and when the objects themselves are placed on a textured surface, the information is greatly increased.

Surface-at-a-Slant

Epstein and Park (1964), in a review of the evidence pertaining to some of the psychophysical hypotheses, noted that the perception of surface and hardness was related to intensity gradients when looking at a Ganzfeld (see Chapter 15) or when looking at a coarse-textured plasterboard under full illumination (Gibson & Dibble, 1952). In both situations, perceivers reported seeing a fog—that is, no surface or form—with low illumination of the plasterboard or when

intensity gradients were absent from the Ganzfeld. Epstein and Park concluded, therefore, that texture was a sufficient stimulus for the perception of surface.

But Epstein and Park noted some limitations in the power of texture as a source of information. A number of experiments were found in which perceived slant increased as the texture gradient increased, but it could produce perception of a single surface at a particular slant only when supplemented by additional stimulus information. Moreover, a texture gradient alone was not so effective as outline perspective as a stimulus for perceived slant. Epstein and Park concluded that a gradient of texture density was not sufficient for veridical perception of slant.

But the research reviewed by Epstein and Park may not be appropriate to test psychophysical hypotheses in terms of the concepts developed in this chapter. It seems unlikely that our perception of objects in space is based on the processing of only one or a few cues, but rather depends on the generation of a scale of space from which all references are made. Since, in the natural environment there is a great deal of information about space, we probably make use of it all in an integrated fashion, rather than separately, cue by cue. What seems most unlikely is that cues are processed individually and then added together in some manner. It therefore seems unreasonable to conclude that texture is or is not a sufficient cue for slant, where the experiments are ones that add and subtract texture and other cues in isolation. The psychophysical argument is that slant will be perceived from information about the scale of space, a scale given in part by the texture gradients, in part by perspective changes in outline shapes, in part by the relative textures of object and background surface at their intersections, and so forth. None of these alone need be powerful enough, or consistent enough to define a perceptual organization such as the slant of a surface uniquely. This point of view is shared by Gogel (1977) even though he does not see texture gradients as differing fundamentally from other cues. His two-factor theory rests on a conception of the perceptual system as an integrator of information, with the output being related to a scaled or calibrated space.

If one pays attention to the edges of surfaces, the stimulus imaged on the retina from a surface at a slant is an **outline shape**. As seen in Figure 8.16 (p. 171), the projection of outline shape must be ambiguous when treated in isolation—the different shapes at different slants each produce the same retinal projection. But shape alone is not sufficient to specify the family of equivalent configurations—the visual angle must also be given. Within these limits, then, the shape–slant–distance invariance hypothesis suggests that (*a*) if shape or slant is known, a unique shape-at-a-slant is determined, but distance is indeterminate and (*b*) if size is also known, a unique shape-at-a-slant-at-a-distance is determined (Ittelson, 1960). It should therefore be clear why the empiricists' analysis concludes that the stimulus only provides enough information to specify a family of equivalent configurations—differently shaped surfaces at different slants at different distances—and why it is inadequate to specify a particular unique perceptual experience.

Braunstein (1976) noted that information about the slant of a surface may be used in making shape judgments. He suggested that it does not follow that the observer necessarily has conscious access to the information used in making judgments of the slant of a surface. Thus, slant information may be registered and used in an algorithm producing apparent shape, but it may not be available for apparent slant judgments.

The systematic foreshortening, perspective, and compression of area that accompanies the relative slant of a rectangle (or circle) in space is illustrated in Figure 9.13. When presented as isolated outline shapes, they specify only different families of equivalent configurations. But notice what happens as soon as a textured background is included and the outline shape is also given its texture. Figure 9.14 shows the five trapezoidal projections against a textured surface that provides a continuous scale of the visual world. Only shape *E* has a texture gradient that changes at the same rate as the surface—hence *E* is perceived as being on the surface, or parallel to it. Shape *A* has no texture gradient, and therefore it is perceived to be in a fronto-parallel plane, that is, standing upright on the surface rather than lying flat on it. With texture gradients added,

the slants of the shapes are determined by their relationships to the scale of visual space. The stimulus—that is, the entire stimulus—is now sufficient to specify a particular surface-at-a-slant. A similar argument could be made for size–distance. All the objects are perceived to be at the same distance because all of them intersect the surface at points where the textures of the surface are of the same density. The scale of space places these objects at the same distance from the perceiver even if he has to turn to see them all.

The psychophysical and empiricist views about the determiners of the perceived slant of a surface stress either the information in gradients (such as texture and the compression of shape) across the retina or the information in the outline of a single shape given by perspective or contour convergence. There has been a great deal of research aimed at assessing the relative contributions of these variables. The problem remains because, as noted previously, even a slanted, textured surface may not supply enough information when presented alone—a ground surface may be necessary to supply a scale of space.

A number of experimenters have demonstrated the effectiveness of texture gradients in producing judgments of surface-at-a-slant (see Epstein & Park, 1963, and Ericksson, 1967 for reviews). Gruber and Clark (1956) demonstrated that texture density affects slant judgments but size and shape regularity appear to be more important than distributional regularity in determining slant judgments (Flock & Moscatelli, 1964; Phillips, 1970). Attneave and Olson (1966) compared the effectiveness of the information from compression and form contour convergence by placing the information in conflict. Figure 9.15 shows displays in which (*a*) the compression and convergence information correspond and (*b*) and (*c*) where they conflict. Attneave and Olson found that the judged direction of slant was determined by convergence. Comparisons of texture gradients with contour convergence suggest that contour convergence was more effective than a texture gradient in slant judgments and that it was just as effective alone as it was when in combination with a texture gradient (Clarck, Smith, & Rabe, 1956).

If the slant of a surface is thought of as a rotation

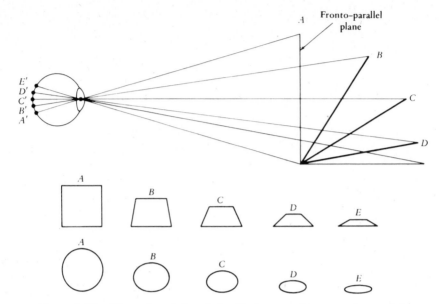

Figure 9.13. Illustration of the relationship between shapes-at-a-slant and the corresponding deformations of the retinal image.

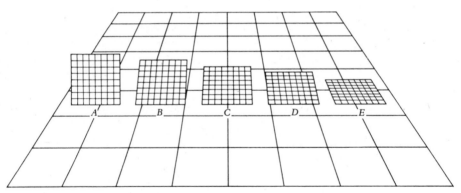

Figure 9.14 Textured shapes on a textured ground. The ground now provides a continuous scale of space and alters the perception of the shapes.

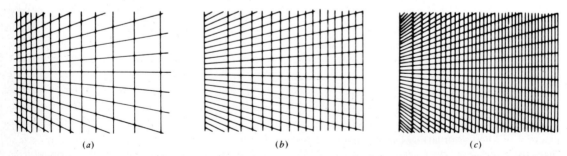

Figure 9.15 Regular line-grid patterns used to compare the effects of compression and contour convergence. In (a), both kinds of information correspond, whereas in (b) and (c) they are in conflict (Attneave & Olson, 1966).

about a horizontal axis, the angle of rotation is related to the relative changes in the horizontal and vertical positions of points projected onto the retinal surface. This rotation provides a potential source of slant information independent of perspective (this analysis also applies to rotation about a vertical axis). Braunstein (1976) defines this **form ratio** as the cosine of the slant angle measured from the vertical. This value is a ratio of ratios. It can be shown to be equal to the ratio of the vertical to horizontal distances of the slanted surface divided by the ratio of these distances in the frontoparallel plane. These relationships are illustrated in Figure 9.16. Note that, if the form ratio is used by the perceiver, the relative projections of h and v must be compared to the values these dimensions would have if the surface were unslanted. This requires some kind of knowledge on the part of the perceiver about the original spacing of the contours or other surface features. But, as Braunstein points out, some knowledge or assumption by the perceiver is also necessary for perspective or contour convergence to determine a unique percept. For example, the perceiver may seem to act under the assumption that the surface actually contains parallel lines and contours. Moreover, for the information supplied by a texture gradient to be effective, the perceiver must act under the assumption that the stimulus contains a uniform distribution of texture elements over the surface. With perspective and form ratio in conflict, more slant judgments are determined primarily by perspective, although form ratio also plays a role (Braunstein & Payne, 1969).

Which Approach Is Correct?

One of the great temptations of the psychophysical approach is simply to say that because all the information is provided directly by light coming from space, the observer does not have to do anything in

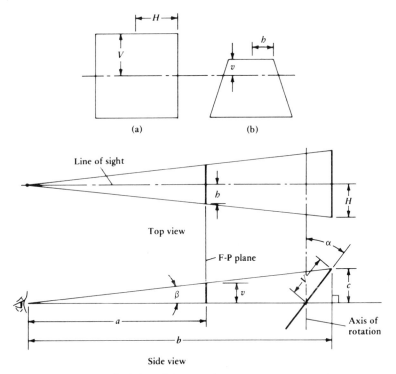

Figure 9.16 Relationships showing the deviation of the "form ratio," defined as the cosine of the slant angle, α, measured from the vertical. The dimensions of the surface are shown (a) when the surface is in the frontal position, and (b) when it is in the slanted position. The relationships to a fixed eye are also shown. The form ratio $=$ cosine $\alpha =$ $$\frac{v/h}{V/H}.$$

order to perceive the layout of space. In this sense, the psychophysical viewpoint has often been called a theory of the direct perception of space (Gyr, 1972; Turvey, 1977). Gibson's focus has been primarily on descriptions of the psychophysical relationships between the scene and the information available from it. He has said little about how the information is extracted and utilized. Indeed, one of the great virtues of the empiricists' approach is their attention to the mechanisms involved in the processing of visual information, and it is this attention to mechanism that has made their approach viable. On the other hand, the empiricists have chosen a narrow analysis of stimulation, minimizing the transformations described by perspective. By focusing on simple line elements as the basis for space perception, they have minimized how much information is provided from space.

In the past, the arguments between proponents of the two major approaches were clearcut. There were two main issues: (a) the innate vs learning issue and (b) the visual vs nonvisual information issue. The empiricists were necessarily committed to learning as the mechanism for supplementing the inadequate visual information. The Gestalt psychologists clearly espoused the view that the perceptual system is innately structured to process organized inputs into organized percepts. However, psychophysics in the form of Gibson's higher-order-variable approach does not require the assumption that the perceptual system possesses this ability innately and neither the modern algorithm approach nor Gogel's two-factor theory rests on the concept of learning.

The second issue—the degree to which the perceptual outcome depends on visual stimulation—remains an issue, but a somewhat diminished one. Indeed, there are some theorists who do not see a difference between the kinds of information Gibson sees as the determiners of perception and the cues identified by the empiricists. For example, Gogel (1977) suggests that gradients merely represent relative distance cues continuously distributed in depth. For example, the perspective cue may be thought of as formed by a distribution of objects of constant physical size extending out to the horizon and, therefore, can be regarded as an extension of the relative-size cue

to distance. Consequently, "gradients" are not considered to be qualitatively different from "cues" except that the overall perceptual effect of a "cue gradient" may be larger than that obtained in the minimal stimulus conditions defining the cue. Gogel concludes that there is no reason to assume that the basic processes in cues and in gradients are fundamentally different.

But one should not assume that the theorists agree that they are all saying the same things. Rock (1977) clearly attempts to argue that Gibson's higher-order-variable theory does not account adequately for size constancy whereas the taking-into-account theory does. He is suggesting, of course, that there is an important difference in the two approaches. What does the issue turn on? The fundamental question appears to be: Is there a new property—such as a scale of space—that emerges when information is represented over the entire retinal surface, or is this merely a collection of local events? That such structures do exist was demonstrated recently by Knudsen and Konishi (1978), who found a map of auditory space as an emergent property of the organization of higher-order neurons in the barn owl. They noted that this organization was different from all other maps that were direct projections of the information on the sensory surfaces. In other words, it is clearly possible that structures exist in the human visual system to produce the perception of the layout of space in response to higher-order stimuli.

SUMMARY

We have reviewed the two major approaches to the study of visual space perception. We have noted the major similarity in the attempt to isolate the nature of the information at the retina, and the major difference is either establishing that the information is inadequate or showing that it supplies sufficient information to yield the perception of a visual world without supplemental information. Historically, the empiricist approach has been represented primarily as a learning approach, emphasizing the associations between the proximal stimulus and information from nonvisual sources. The algorithm approach relieves empiricism of the burden of learning and association and substitutes simultaneous information from such sources as other aspects of perceptual experience or other sense modalities.

The psychophysical analysis of space perception assumes that the elementary impressions of the visual world have to do with surfaces and edges rather than points and lines. The search for stimulus correlates must take into account the fact that the visual world must be scanned in order to be perceived. Thus the retinal projection for a moving observer undergoes continuous transformations. The temporal patterning is an important part of the study. With scanning, the image becomes a continuous serial transformation that is unique, yielding the stable, panoramic, and unbounded visual world we normally perceive. The patterns of stimulation across the entire retinal surfaces may provide three separate but integral scales of space that may serve as the basis for the perceptual constancies.

SUGGESTED READINGS

Hochberg's (1962) chapter and the early chapters of Gulick and Lawson (1976) and Dodwell (1970) provide excellent historical reviews of these theoretical disputes. The earlier history may be found in detail in Boring (1942) and Pastore (1971). Two books by Gibson (1950, 1966) are essential for a further understanding of his position. The recent collection of essays in his honor edited by MacLeod and Pick (1974) describe recent developments from this point of view. Ittelson (1960) represents the transactional approach. Epstein's (1977) collection of summary chapters on the perceptual constancies contains an excellent historical review as well as a chapter by Ebenholtz on the algorithm approach, Rock's defense of "unconscious inference," and a comprehensive statement of Gogel's two-factor theory.

Chapter 10

Motion, Movement, Orientation, and Action

This chapter is concerned with the problems associated with movement—both the motions of objects in the physical world and the movements of our eyes, head, and body in space. How is it that we are able to perceive a stable world in which objects move and in which we, as perceivers, can move and perform physical acts with great accuracy? Is visual information sufficient for veridical perception of motion, orientation, and movement, or must it be supplemented by nonvisual information about our body position and motor activity?

What are the phenomena to be accounted for? Consider the visual world first: how do we perceive the motion of objects? When objects move, they may be seen moving against a stationary background—as when we see birds fly over a motionless stand of trees—or objects may be seen moving against a moving background—as when the leaves and branches of the trees are in motion. Thus, object motion poses the dual problem of perception of motion relative to the world as well as motion relative to the perceiver.

These phenomena become more complex when the perceiver's motion is taken into account. Since the perceiver is never motionless, the retinal image of stimulation from the visual environment will be constantly in motion—shifting, stretching, and trans-

forming its shape. Even sitting still, with eyes and head fixed, involves complex perceptual-motor coordinations. Together with the more complex and highly skilled perceptual-motor skills that human beings can acquire and perform with great accuracy (for example, walking, skiing, hitting a tennis ball), these acts require both planning, in order to perform the structured sequence of movements, and monitoring, in order to control the sequence in progress. Therefore, an understanding of motion, orientation, and movement must take action into account, suggesting that motion perception is fundamentally only a portion of a perceptual-motor act. Thus, the information necessary will include not only where the perceiver is now, but where the body will be in the near future.

MODELS OF MOTION PERCEPTION

Empiricists generally focus on the components of each process they study, and motion perception is no exception. They have attempted to describe the neural coding of motion, the basic stimulus that defines motion, and the way in which that simple stimulus is coded and represented in the visual system. They have described various sources of nonvisual information that may be important and how these are coded and represented. Finally, they have reported experiments in which the effects of various visual and nonvisual sources of information are compared, and their contribution to the resulting perception evaluated. Since these analyses lead to careful laboratory experiments, nearly all the displays used have been very simple, with rarely anything even approaching the natural scene considered by the psychophysicists.

One kind of theory sees the visual source of information used in the perception of motion as the successive stimulation of adjacent retinal points. Presumably, the visual system contains motion detectors that code successive changes across the retina as objects in motion. Indeed, there is strong evidence that structures exist to accomplish this neural coding. But this visual source of information is not sufficient because it cannot be used to distinguish changes over the retina produced by our own movements from those produced by objects moving in space. Therefore, we must also have information of a special sort about our own movements—either reafferent visual information or efferent nonvisual information. **Afferent information** about the position and movements of parts of the body is received from receptors in various parts of the body—in the joints, the muscles, skin, and tendons. **Reafferent information** is supplied by sensory events produced by self-initiated movements, that is, by observing the consequences of our own movements. The term "reafference" is used to emphasize the correlation between the changes in the visual input and the changes in eye, head, and body position. The **efferent nonvisual information** is obtained from the efferent commands issued by the central nervous system to induce the movements of our eyes and body. By knowing the ways in which we intend to move, we can distinguish between motion in the retinal projection that was caused by our own movements and that was caused by the movement of objects in the world.

Motion Detection

Light falling on a set of receptors at one instant, and on another nearby set in the next instant, and so forth, successively stimulates adjacent retinal points (loci). This sequence of events could be the necessary and sufficient source of information for a motion-detection system which signals that something was moving out there. All that would be needed is a coding device that could detect this change. Such a device is illustrated in Figure 10.1.

The discovery of cortical cells that respond to displacements in the retinal projection of the simulus has lent strong support to the view that motion perception is a result of the detection of successive stimulation on adjacent retinal loci. For example, in studying the visual system of cats, Hubel and Wiesel (1962) found cortical cells with relatively large receptive fields that were primarily responsive to movement. The cell did not respond when its receptive field was stimulated by a stationary bar of light. But if the bar was moved over that field, the cell did respond. Hubel and Wiesel found cells whose responsivity was specific to stimuli of a given width, length, orientation, direction of motion, and velocity of motion, although most cells were not specific to all of these variables simultaneously.

The evidence that motion-detection systems of this sort exist in humans is based in part on the study

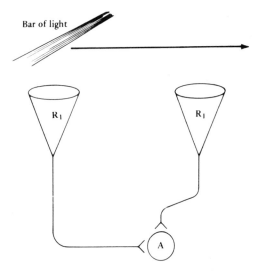

Figure 10.1 A diagram of a simple motion detector. As the bar of light moves from left to right across the visual field, it stimulates R_1 and then R_2 some time later. The unit A responds only when both R_1 and R_2 fire.

of motion aftereffects. **Motion aftereffect** is an apparent motion in the visual field that is induced by the prolonged viewing of motion. One example is the **waterfall illusion.** If you watch the water descending over a fall for a minute or two, and then look at a motionless visual field, the objects in the field will appear to be moving up—that is, in the direction opposite to the original motion. In the laboratory this is usually studied by viewing a rotating spiral disk, or the lateral movement of vertical bars rotating around a drum. For example, Spigel (1962) reported that after viewing a spiral pattern rotating slowly at ten revolutions per minute, all perceivers saw the spiral rotating in the opposite direction when the actual physical rotation was stopped. This aftereffect lasted nearly ten seconds on the average.

Sekular and Ganz (1963) had perceivers view stripes that moved in one direction for five seconds. They did this under stabilized retinal presentation (see Chapter 15) so that the only motion over the retina would be from objective stimulus movement, and not from eye movements. They then tested the luminance threshold for the movement of stripes when the stripes moved in the same direction or in the reverse direction. They argued that if motion was perceived because of a cortical motion detector, then viewing motion in one direction should decrease the sensitivity of that detector and elevate the threshold for that pattern of motion. Figure 10.2 shows a dramatic change in this threshold. In every case they found that the threshold for motion in the same direction as that of the previously viewed pattern was elevated. This finding strongly supports the argument that there are unitary motion-detecting systems in humans—systems whose sensitivities are momentarily changed as a function of stimulation.

Sekular and Ganz went to some effort to remove the effects of eye movements on motion sensitivity, so that their results would be due only to motion detectors sensing a displacement across the retina caused only by objective movement. Presumably under normal viewing conditions, we do not lose too much sensitivity to motion after prolonged viewing of motion, because our eyes are continuously in motion relative to the stimulus. This would shift the stimulus from one motion-detecting receptive field to another, assuming the eye movements were large enough. But to the degree to which motion aftereffects are found, and they are very common, some sensitivity loss is always occurring.

The discovery of motion-detector systems supports the view that motion perception is the result of detecting successive stimulation of adjacent retinal loci. But even before this evidence was available, this view had led to substantial research that explored the thresholds for motion. If the retinal projection of a luminance discontinuity moves across the retina too slowly, it will not be seen to move (although the perceiver might notice later that it is in a new position). If it moves too fast, the object moving will not be seen as anything except a blur.

These lower and upper thresholds for motion have been found to be a function of a number of variables—so many, in fact, that it would be misleading to imply that there is a single value for each. Under optimal conditions a minimum displacement threshold approaches the resolution acuity for the object itself. This means that if the thickness of the line

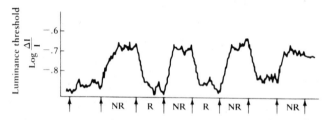

Figure 10.2 A continuous record of luminance threshold values during one session for both same (*NR*) and reverse (*R*) directions. Arrows indicate when directions were changed. (Sekular & Ganz, 1963.)

elements in the object are 30 seconds of arc wide, and if the object is displaced by as little as 30 seconds, the perceiver will say it has been moved. But it will not necessarily be seen as it moves—only that it is in a new position. Whether it will be perceived as moving or not will depend on its size, the illumination on it, its contrast, and the number of nearby objects. For example, any variable that increases the sharpness of the object will increase the chances of the perceiver noticing it moving—hence increases in illumination and contrast will lower motion threshold. Object size, however, has the reverse effect—smaller objects are easier to see in motion than larger ones.

Despite all this evidence, simple everyday observation will show that motion detection is not as simple as outlined above. Consider, for example, the role played by other parts of the visual field. It is very difficult to perceive motion of an object moving over a homogeneous or textureless field. If the object is seen through a window, it is much easier to notice it moving when it is near the edge of the frame than when it is in the center of the window, away from all other objects or contours. This clearly suggests relational properties to motion perception, comparing the change of position of one object to that of another.

The importance of the field in stabilizing stimulation is shown by the phenomenon known as **autokinetic movement.** If a small light is presented in an otherwise dark room, the light will appear to move about, usually in an unpredictable and erratic manner. The most common explanation has been in terms of eye movements. In the dark, the viewer has difficulty in maintaining orientation and cannot distinguish between eye movements and movements of the light. Since the eyes do move, and the observer has no visual frame of reference, some of the movement is attributed to the stimulus. Furthermore, it is nearly impossible to perceive real motion when such a light really does move in the dark. In the absence of a visual frame of reference, real movement is almost impossible to detect.

These examples show that even in the presence of stimulation of successive retinal loci without observer motion, object motion may not be perceived, or may be misperceived. Why should the absence of a frame of reference make motion perception more difficult? Should not the detector for motion over one part of the retina be independent of edge detection elsewhere? Of course, Gibson has an explanation for the need for a frame of reference, but the empiricists have looked elsewhere. In general, they have argued that nonvisual information is needed, especially when the visual information is impoverished. Specifically, a complete account of motion perception requires consideration of the correlation of visual and nonvisual information (especially motor information) at each moment in time.

Visual-Motor Correlation

Helmholtz (1867) attempted to solve the problem of differentiating observer from object motion by postulating some type of unconscious computation or feedback from eye position or body position, so that these changes could be subtracted from the retinal displacement. If there was a displacement of the projection on the retina of 10 degrees to the right, but there was also feedback from the eye muscles providing information that the eye had moved 10 degrees to the left, these two would be subtracted. The net result of zero would then be interpreted to mean that no object motion occurred. Other combinations would be interpreted in a similar manner.

Without denying that we potentially may have feedback information about the current position of our eyes, head, or other parts of our body, there are enough reasons to doubt the usefulness of this form of a perceptual-motor integration. Spigel (1965) reviewed some of this evidence, primarily noting that the position sense of the eye is not precise enough to provide the input needed for the type of computation proposed by Helmholtz. In addition, since the latency to initiate a saccadic eye movement is about 200 milliseconds, feedback from an actual change in eye position would be very slow, far slower than permissible given the precision of our movement perception. In a more direct test of this theory, Brindley and Merton (1960) covered the eye, and anesthetized its surface, so that only the muscles attached to the eye could provide feedback about the movements of the eye. Under such circumstances, perceivers could not tell that the eyes, singly or together, were being moved mechanically.

There is another sense in which Helmholtz might be correct. If instead of using the feedback from the eye position, one used the efferent or outgoing signals from the brain that control the eye, head, and body movements, then those objections would not be so serious. In addition, another troublesome problem of motion perception would be solved—how to account for the perceptual consequences of eye movements that were not self-initiated. If you move your eye intentionally over a stationary scene, you perceive it as a stationary scene—it does not shift or jump in any way. However, if you put your finger against the side of your eye and press it so as to rotate the eye back and forth, the visual world jumps around in correspondence with the externally initiated movements. This would not be expected if feedback from the eye position were being monitored, but it would be predicted if the efferent signals to the eye muscles were involved. When you press on your eye, there are no efferent signals (except to your fingers), hence the displacement is sensed as belonging to the world and not to the eye.

Von Holst (1954) reported experiments that support this observation and interpretation. First he replicated an experiment by Helmholtz (1867). The eye muscles of a perceiver were paralyzed so that the eye could not move in a given direction, and then the perceiver was instructed to move his eye in that direction, say to the right. This instruction, which presumably produces an efferent command but no resulting displacement on the retina (the eye could not execute the command), resulted in the perception of the visual world moving to the right. In a second experiment, von Holst moved the paralyzed eye mechanically to the right instead of instructing the perceiver to move it. In this case, there should be no efferent command, but now there is retinal displacement. Here also, the perceiver reported seeing movement of the visual world, but now he saw it moving to the left, as would be expected. In a third study, von Holst instructed the perceiver to move his paralyzed eye, and at the same time von Holst moved the eye mechanically in the same direction. In this case there

will be both an efferent command and a retinal displacement. The effects merely canceled, and the perceiver reported that the visual world was stationary.

As a consequence of these studies, von Holst (1954; von Holst & Mittelstadt, 1950) proposed a model to account for the stability in the perceptual world, given the movements involved. The essential feature of the model was a comparison between a copy of the efferent signal to the oculomotor system and reafferent visual signals from the eyes. Specifically, when an efferent signal is sent to the oculomotor system, a "copy" is sent to a comparator, a system that compares it with reafferent visual signals. The comparator could then determine which portion of the visual signal could be attributed to movements of the eyes and which could be attributed to the motions of external objects. If the reafferent signal could not have been predicted from the copy of the efferent signal, then the motion could be attributed to the object and motion would be perceived. If, however, the efferent copy matches the reafferent signal in terms of its predicted position, then the changes in visual input are discounted and motion is not seen.

In order to account for both the correlation between efferent and afferent information and the long-term effects of adaptation to distortion of the visual input, Held (1965; Held & Hein, 1958) added a correlation storage system to the basic model proposed by von Holst. In this model, illustrated in Figure 10.3

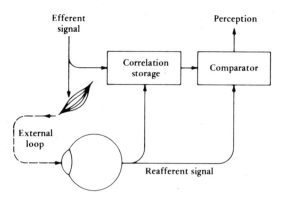

Figure 10.3 Schematic representation of Held's (1965) proposed model for the correlation and recorrelation of efferent signals with visual (reafferent) signals from the eye.

copies of the efferent signals to move the limbs activate a signal or trace of previous combinations of efferent and reafferent signals. One important consequence of implicating efferent commands is that they occur only in production of self-initiated movement—they are not involved in passive movement. The evaluation of these models and the questions of passive and active movements will be discussed below in the context of adaptation to distorted visual inputs.

The evidence of von Holst (1954) leaves little doubt that observers need nonvisual information—in this case efferent signals that initiate eye movements—in order to perceive the proper cause of the motion in the retinal image. The experimental conditions under which such experiments are performed, however, are quite different from the conditions described by Gibson. In nearly every study showing the need for efferent signals, the observer was looking at a two-dimensional display without texture or surface cues as to its distance or orientation. Consequently, most of the sources of information normally present were absent, and it is not surprising that ambiguity arose as to what moved. In the presence of such ambiguity, the assessment of efferent signals to the eyes would be needed to make the motion unambiguous. Therefore, the evaluation of the psychophysicist and empiricist interpretations of motion perception remains unclear.

REAL AND APPARENT MOTION

Real motion in the physical world is specified as the continuous displacement of an object from one location to another at a particular velocity and acceleration. If the perceiver's eye is stationary when observing real motion, a luminance discontinuity in the retinal projection will be displaced at the same angular velocity as the object in motion. But if the perceiver's eye is not stationary, the angular velocity of the projection of the object might be very different. It could even be zero if the eye is pursuing the moving object. In that case, however, the retinal projections of all the stationary objects in the visual environment would be displaced in the direction opposite to the

path of pursuit. Thus, in this case, displacement in the retinal projection occurs in the absence of physical motion in the visual world. Normally perceivers attribute such displacements to their own movements and not to object motion.

There are many common situations when observers perceive themselves as stationary and attribute motion to objects in the environment when, in fact, there was no movement at all. Such examples are referred to as the perception of **apparent movement**. We have already described one example—the waterfall illusion (p. 208)—in some detail. In that illusion, previous viewing of a continuous pattern of motion produces an aftereffect of motion, so that stationary objects appear to move in the opposite direction.

Phi-Apparent Motion

The motion we perceive in the flashing lights of theater marquees or "moving signs" is an example of **phi motion**. The motion we perceive when a series of separate scenes are flashed in rapid succession—as in motion pictures—is related to this phenomenon. The motion-picture projector presents a rapid succession of slightly displaced scenes. The visual system fills in the temporal gaps to produce the perception of continuous motion.

One important example of apparent motion was studied by Max Wertheimer (1912), and his observations played a major role in the development of Gestalt psychology. Apparent motion can be readily observed by alternately flashing two stationary lights that are not too far from each other. Depending on the distance between them, the duration of the flashes, and the interval between the flashes, different types of perceptions result. If the recycling interval is very long or very short, movement will not be seen—each light will appear to go on and off independently. However, for an intermediate range of temporal values, the viewer will report seeing a single light moving rapidly back and forth. That is, not only will motion be seen where there is no objective motion, but the light will be seen to move across the space where there is no stimulus object. If the recycling time is further increased, to an optimal level, the movement will be seen but the object will not be seen moving across the space between—the viewer will simply report the perception of partial movement or disembodied movement.

Wertheimer gave this perception a special name—the phi phenomenon—because he thought it represented a case of the perception of pure movement without a moving object. He suggested movement may be a separate experience, independent of object perception. Frisby (1972) has argued that phi motion might be interpretable in terms of motion detectors in the cortex. Just as real motion might be detected by a light moving over a receptive field at a particular rate, a cortical cell might be induced to fire if the light first fell on one region and then on another, without transversing the space between. As long as the same cortical cell responded to both cases, real and apparent (phi) motion would be determined in the same way.

The major problem for the perception of motion from this first viewpoint is to show how a perceiver differentiates successive stimulation of adjacent retinal loci caused by object motion as distinct from the motion of the eyes or body. Both will produce displacements of the retinal projection, yet we rarely attribute our motion to that of the visual world, or vice versa. Moreover, Rock and Ebenholtz (1962) have demonstrated that apparent motion can be perceived even without stimulation from different parts of the retina. They had an observer view two lights through two small apertures in two different directions. The observer had to move an eye from side to side to see the stimuli through the small holes. The observer first looked at one light when it was flashed on and off and then turned the eye to look at the other light flash on and off. Since the eye turned to look at the second light, and both apertures were small, both lights stimulated the retina in approximately the same place. When the two lights were flashed repeatedly, and the observer synchronized the eye movements with the flashes, apparent movement was seen—the light appeared to move from one position to the other. This observation suggests that the perception of motion requires more than a simple motion-detection device for adequate explanation. Moreover, Kolers (1963) has shown that objects seen in apparent movement do not have the same effect on other objects in

the field as do objects seen in real motion, suggesting further that the two types of perceptions may not be mediated by the same mechanism.

Kolers (1963) has shown that, under conditions that produce phi movement, apparent motion will occur even for pulsed targets that are more complex than the traditionally used spots. If the shapes are the same, the viewer reports that the shape is seen moving back and forth through the space between the two stationary positions. If, however, the shapes are not the same, as for example the circle and square in Figure 10.4, the observer reports that the shape of the target undergoes change as it moves. When the square is seen moving toward the circle's position, its corners begin rounding so that by the time the circle is pulsed, the square looks like a circle. The reverse happens to the circle as it apparently moves over empty space toward the square. Kolers's finding suggests that treating phi motion as a correlate of real motion, as Frisby (1972) implied, may be too simple an explanation.

Relative and Induced Motion

Relative motion refers to the perception of object motion with respect to the background or frame of reference. The term is used in the situation in which the stimulus object is actually moving while the background or frame of reference may either be stationary or moving. **Induced motion** refers to the motion perceived in an object which, in reality, is stationary. Frequently, the induced motion is produced by motion of the background or frame of reference.

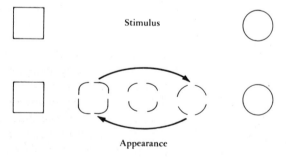

Figure 10.4 An illustration of the stimulus shapes and perceived shapes in Kolers's (1963) experiment.

The classical demonstration of induced motion perception was performed by Dunker (1929). The stimulus consisted of a luminous spot surrounded by a luminous rectangle in an otherwise dark field (Fig. 10.5). When the rectangle was moved slowly to the right, the observer reported seeing the spot move to the left while the frame appeared to remain stationary. Dunker concluded that relative displacement was necessary for the perception of motion and that the object surrounded by the frame will be the one that appears to move with respect to the apparently stationary frame of reference.

A more familiar example of induced movement is the misperception of the stationary moon moving through clouds on a windy night. While it is the moon that is actually stationary and the clouds that are moving, the movement of the clouds serves as a frame of reference because they cover so much of the visual field. Thus, they induce movement in the moon. This induced movement can be destroyed by viewing the moon and clouds through branches of a nearby tree. Now the tree becomes the frame and, if close enough and with enough branches, it will be seen as stationary, the clouds will be perceived as moving, and the moon will again be perceived as stationary.

While the psychophysicists have an easy time with the induced apparent movement demonstrations (because they can be easily explained by considering the relative transformations of all parts of the visual field), phi motion has been more difficult to explain

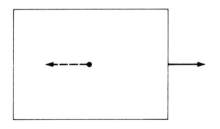

Figure 10.5 The stimulus arrangement for the perception of induced motion (Dunker, 1929). The luminous rectangular frame is moved slowly to the right. The stationary luminous dot appears to move to the left while the frame appears stationary.

from any viewpoint. This has been especially true following Kolers's work with different-shaped targets. Phi motion seems to be both clearly similar to real motion and clearly different at the same time.

ORIENTING TO GRAVITY

Balance and Stance

The analysis of balance and stance may be taken as the starting point for the study of movement and motion perception because, in a sense, balance represents the absence of movement. Indeed, when understood as a perceptual-motor control process, balance may be defined as the state of "zero movement."

In their study of balance and stance, Lee and Lishman (1975, Lee, 1977) noted that, when standing still, the body is pivoted about the ankle joints with balance controlled by the muscles determining ankle-foot position. The center of gravity is forward of the ankle joints, and approximately over the center of the support base. The position may therefore be maintained by a more or less constant torque applied to the ankles, primarily by the calf muscles.

There are three types of sensory contacts with the environment that could supply the information needed for perceptual-motor control of balance and stance: inertial contact through the vestibular system, physical contact through the feet, and optical contact through the eyes. These correspond to the three possible sources of information—the vestibular, articular, and visual systems—about the position, orientation, or movement of the body as a whole, or part of the body, relative to the environment. The vestibular system could, in principle, supply the information by means of the semicircular canals. The angular velocity and inclination of the body could be computed by an initial "fix" on the position of the canals with respect to gravity, and then by successive integrations over time. However, the effective sensitivity of this system is probably too low to account for the small angular accelerations that occur when standing.

The second possibility is the articular system—the system of receptors in the muscles and joints. If one is standing on a firm surface, the angular acceleration, velocity, and position of the body are accurately reflected in the changes in the angles at the ankles and in the pressures on the feet, which can be registered by the mechanoreceptors in the muscles, joints, and feet. But it is clear that this is the case only when the support surface is firm.

Finally, it is possible that, as Gibson (1950, 1958) has suggested, the information is obtained visually. Whenever the head is in motion, there is an optic flow pattern at the eyes. The spatiotemporal structure of this pattern depends on both the movement and the structure of the environment. Lee (1977) extended Gibson's analysis by suggesting that the optic flow pattern contains both information about the layout of space and the objects in it **(exteroceptive information)** and information related to the movements of the eyes, head, and body relative to the environment **(exproprioceptive information).**

Lee and Lishman (1975) performed two experiments to determine whether visual information is used for the control of balance. The apparatus they used included a "swinging room"—three walls and a ceiling suspended from ropes so that it could be swung back and forth (Fig. 10.6). The interior of the room was faced with floral wallpaper to provide a structured optic array. The visual information about body sway was manipulated by moving the swinging room about a person standing on a stationary base. Body sway was measured by a meter attached to the subjects' backs.

The first experiment investigated the role of visual information in controlling balance in stances that can be maintained without vision: normal standing, standing on a 25-degree ramp, standing on a soft surface, and standing on the toes. Subjects were tested inside and outside the swinging room and also with near and distant surrounds. The results showed that, when the swinging room was moved, subjects unconsciously and unavoidably "corrected" their posture and either swayed excessively or lost their balance. Moreover, the subject's body sway appeared to be driven by the visual input. Irregular movements of the room caused visual driving in all stances even when the subjects were forewarned, suggesting that misleading visual information could not be ignored. The

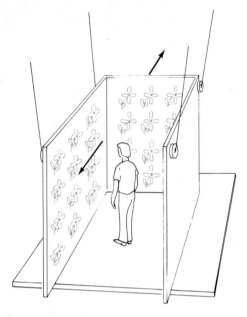

Figure 10.6 Schematic drawing of the "swinging" room of Lee and Lishman (1975). The walls are made of polystyrene foam on a steel frame. It is open at the bottom and at one end. The inside is faced with floral wallpaper to provide visual structure. See text for the various studies in which the room was used.

near-object–distant-surround comparison showed that balance control was finest when there was an object or wall close in front of the subject. Since the optical changes at the eye are accentuated by having an object close by, it seems clear that balance was improved by improving the visual information. Finally, comparing the different stances, it was clear that the effectiveness of visual information for balance control was a function of the degree of impoverishment of ankle-foot proprioception—the greater the impoverishment, the greater the visual control.

In a second experiment, Lee and Lishman studied three stances that are impossible without visual information: standing on a beam, a "Chaplin stance"—heels together with feet splayed out in line, and a "pinstripe stance"—standing on one leg with the other foot behind the calf, and the opposite arm extending sideways holding a weight (Fig. 10.7). The subjects stood in front of a paneled wall and practiced

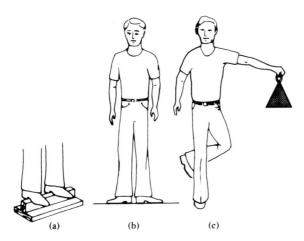

Figure 10.7 The three stances used by Lee and Lishman (1975) to determine the role of visual proprioception in balance with stances that are impossible without vision. (*a*) Standing on a beam, (*b*) the "Chaplin stance"—heels together, feet splayed out to form a straight line, and (*c*) the "pinstripe stance"—standing on one leg with the other foot behind the calf, and the opposite arm extended sideways holding a weight.

the stance for 30 seconds. They were then tested with eyes open and closed and finally in the swinging room.

All subjects could balance for 30 seconds with their eyes open; none could do so in any of the three positions with their eyes closed. The swinging room caused the subjects to sway or to lose their balance entirely. Indeed, their behavior was so directly determined by vision that Lee and Lishman described them as "visual puppets" whose balance could be manipulated by moving the surround, without their being aware of it. They concluded, therefore, that vision functions as an integral component of the control system for maintaining stance. In learning a new stance, visual and vestibular information are used to "tune up" ankle-foot proprioception and muscle control, with vision normally assuming the leading role.

Vertical Orientation Constancy—Knowing Which Way Is Up

Normally we work upright and we are quite accurate in judging whether objects around us are up-

right. But "upright" can be defined with respect to three different references—ourselves, gravity, or other objects. If we are the reference, we speak of **egocentric orientation.** If, for example, we are leaning, objects would be judged to be upright if they were also leaning by the same amount. A gravitational reference specifies the upright in relation to a line drawn from the center of the earth vertically out into space. Any object aligned with such a line is gravitationally upright. A relational frame specifies upright in terms of objects such as the walls of a room. Trying to straighten a picture hanging on a wall when one is leaning and the walls themselves are not straight is a situation in which the three references are not in agreement.

Normally, **vertical orientation constancy** is defined with respect to gravity. To exhibit constancy, perceivers should be able to detect a gravitational upright irrespective of their own orientation or the orientation of the nearby reference objects. For example, suppose you are shown a luminous rod standing roughly vertically in an otherwise empty space and you are asked to rotate the rod until it is upright with respect to gravity. In the simplest condition, you need to determine the angle that the retinal image of the rod makes with the vertical meridian of your retinal surface, and you need to know the angle that your body makes with the gravitational axis. You could obtain the latter information from perceived body tilt given by the output from the vestibular system. You could then compute the orientation of the object from these quantities.

Ebenholtz (1977) has proposed an algorithm from which to compute vertical orientation responses (see also p. 193), in which the apparent object orientation (AOO) equals the angle between the projection of the object on the retina and retinal vertical (α) plus registered body orientation (RBO): AOO = α + RBO. Constancy will occur if both α and RBO are accurately registered. Ebenholtz's interpretation is an example of an empiricist view of vertical orientation constancy. He isolates individual cues contained in stimulation in situations in which other aspects are not present and then proposes how the different relevant cues are combined. Because his model is tested in situations that do not include other visual information, the model provides no way to evaluate the possible role other sources of information may play.

ORIENTING TO THE ENVIRONMENT

Direction and Position Constancy

Ascertaining the directions and positions of portions of the environment and of objects arrayed in the environment about a perceiver is one of the most important functions of the visual system. And, as one might expect, the visual system can maintain the constancy of visual direction, perceiving where objects are in space irrespective of where the eyes or body are oriented, to a high degree of accuracy. There are two types of visual directions that have been studied in detail: oculocentric and egocentric directions. **Oculocentric direction** refers to visual directions with respect to the eye as center, with the fovea usually assumed to be the origin. **Egocentric direction** refers to visual directions with respect to the ego (self) as the origin (or center) of directional judgments. When the eyes move, oculocentric direction changes but egocentric direction does not. When the head and body move, both oculocentric and egocentric directions change.

There is a direction constancy associated with each of these visual directions. **Visual direction constancy** describes the invariance of apparent egocentric direction despite changes in oculomotor direction. **Visual position constancy** describes the invariance of apparent object position despite changes in egocentric direction (Shebilske, 1976).

In analyzing the relationship between eye movements and visual direction constancy, Shebilske (1976) concluded that both visual and nonvisual ("extraretinal") information is needed for judgments of static egocentric direction, whereas the evidence is inconclusive with respect to the dynamic component of visual direction constancy. Extra retinal information allows the observer to take eye movements into ac-

count—when the eyes move, the images on the retinas are displaced by an amount equal in magnitude to the movement. Thus, a simple computation could produce an invariant perception of egocentric direction.

The source and direction of this extraretinal information has been the center of a controversy. **Outflow theories** suggest that the position of the eye is registered by outgoing signals from motor centers in the brain to the eye muscles. **Inflow theories** suggest that the perceptual system monitors eye position by feedback from the extraocular muscles. There is some question about the availability of inflow information (Robinson, 1965; Naton & Stark, 1971), and most of the evidence seems to favor the outflow theory (see Dodwell, 1970; Howard & Templeton, 1966; MacKay, 1973; Matin, 1972 for reviews). Shebilske concluded that, although extra retinal signals provide eye-position information for static judgments of visual direction, the signals may not be synchronized with eye movements well enough to cancel out retinal motion signals.

With respect to visual position constancy, Shebilske noted that head and body movements must be taken into account for such a constancy to exist. He concluded that both higher-order visual information and extraretinal information are used by the processes underlying position constancy; however, there is no question that visual position constancy relies heavily on higher-order retinal information during body movements.

Investigatory and Performatory Orienting

Although it is clear that human beings can demonstrate the constancies of visual direction to a high degree of accuracy, orientation to the environment generally does not take place without some purpose—that is, it has a role in perceptual-motor acts that the perceiver performs for different reasons. Lee (1977) has described two such orienting activities that subserve two fundamentally different perceptual-motor functions: investigatory and performatory orienting.

Investigatory orienting refers to the repositioning of the perceptual system to obtain information about a particular part of the environment. Moving the eyes, or turning the head to look at something, or turning to face a sound are all examples of investigatory orienting. **Performatory orienting** involves a change in the position of the body with respect to the environment in preparation for the performance of an act. This type of orienting is involved in throwing darts, kicking a ball, or hitting a tennis ball.

Different kinds of orienting require different kinds of information. Investigatory orienting of the eyes means that the eyes must move in such a way as to bring the image of a stationary or moving object onto the fovea. Control of these movements requires visual information about the direction of the object relative to the eye. Moreover, since the eye is moving relative to the head, proprioceptive information is, presumably, also required about eye–head orientation.

Investigatory orienting of the head involves turning to face a stationary or moving visible object. Control of movements of the head requires visual information about the direction of the object of interest relative to the eye and proprioceptive information about the orientation of the eyes relative to the head. The proprioceptive information about the eye–head position may be related to the sight of the body parts or it may be due to receptors in the extraocular muscles or in tissues in contact with the eyeball. Lee cites the **autokinetic effect**—the apparent "wandering" of a stationary spot of light in an otherwise dark room— as evidence that nonvisual proprioceptive information is poorer than vision, in the sense that it is subject to considerable drift.

The information necessary for performatory orienting of the body is even more complex. In order for precise movements to be made, one must have proprioceptive information about the orientation of the head relative to the trunk and about the position and movement of the limbs relative to the trunk. This information could be obtained either from the articular system of receptors in the joints and muscles or from the visual system. Lee concluded that the evidence shows visual proprioception is more important and that it can dominate articular proprioception. This

evidence will be reviewed in more detail below when we discuss adaptation to distorted visual inputs.

BODY-CENTERED ACTIVITY

Body-centered action refers to those actions performed relative to the body or to a learned extension of the body, such as hitting a tennis ball, walking, playing a musical instrument, or scratching your head (Lee, 1977). Playing a musical instrument is an interesting example of actions in which the instrument becomes an extension of the body. Moreover, it represents a familiar model for the events taking place in acquiring most perceptual-motor body-centered skills. According to Lee, vision is normally used in learning such a skill by both watching the teacher and watching one's own body part while learning. Once the skill is learned, the control goes over to the articular system as well as to audition and touch. Once this shift is accomplished, the visual system is free to carry on its function of reading the music and planning the activity. However, the articular system tends to drift and must be kept in tune by vision. Hence, constant practice is required even for skilled performers. A similar analysis could be made for environment-related body-centered skills such as hitting a baseball or a tennis ball. Even the well-learned stroke must be constantly tuned by vision.

LOCOMOTION

Locomotion refers to the act of propelling and steering the body through the environment. These acts include not only direct propulsion of the body itself, such as walking and running, but also propelling the body in a vehicle such as an automobile. Lee (1977) suggested that visual information is used to steer the body and guide locomotor acts. The programming of locomotor acts is probably based on visual information about the layout of space—the timing of the act on visual information about "time to-contact." Moreover, this kind of information is, according to Lee, directly available in the optic array (Lee, 1974; Purdy, 1958).

Lee and Lishman (1977) have applied these ideas in a detailed analysis of the visual control of locomotion. Specifically, locomotor acts require control of body parts relative to each other so as to control the dynamic flow of the body as a whole relative to the environment. Three types of information are necessary: (*a*) information about the layout of the environment and about objects in it is necessary for planning a general route, as well as a specific path through the terrain; (*b*) information about the positions and movements of the body parts relative to each other is necessary for controlling bodily actions; and (*c*) information about the position, orientation, and movement of the body as a whole, or part of the body, relative to the environment is necessary for guiding the body through the terrain.

The role of vision is that of an overseer in the control of activity, developing patterns of action, and tuning up other perceptual systems and keeping them tuned (Lee, 1976). Indeed, these functions of vision are most obvious in controlling locomotion because the information from nonvisual systems provides very different patterns for different means of locomotion, such as walking, running, skiing, skating, cycling, driving, and flying. However, in all of these situations, the controlling visual information is constant.

Lee and Lishman proposed that all locomotor acts must be planned and directed by a program of action. This must necessarily be the case because locomotion presents problems that can be solved only by analysis of the entire temporal sequence of actions. The sensory input over time plays a vital role in the continual process of formulating locomotor programs, of monitoring their execution, and in continually adjusting to the changes made.

The major problems that arise during locomotion are the control of speed and direction of movement, and the control of the external forces acting on the body. The former is related to steering the body and stopping when necessary. The latter is related to such acts as securing adequate footing, and so controlling the dynamic flux of the body parts relative to each

other that the reactive forces from the ground can be efficiently utilized.

Stopping

Lee and Lishman analyzed stopping, steering, and footing separately. Stopping was studied in the task of driving a car, where a driver has to plan ahead in order to avoid collisions. Drivers must have information about potential future events in order to control them. Thus, in some sense, a driver must be able to "see" the potential paths and consequences of the present motion, before they occur.

Gibson (1958) has described the visual information involved in forward motion as a radially expanding optic flow field, with the center of expansion corresponding to the point toward which the viewer is heading. When an object, say another vehicle, lies in the path, its optic image will overlie the center of expansion. If the other vehicle is traveling at the same or faster speed, its image will be constant or contracting. But, if stopped or traveling at a slower speed, the image will be dilating. The change in the optic image of the lead vehicle, therefore, specifies whether or not the driver is on a collision course. The inverse of the rate of dilation of the image specifies the time-to-collision if the closing velocity is maintained. This information could be used by drivers when starting to brake the vehicle.

The three possible paths or action programs that could be used by the driver of a car are illustrated in Figure 10.8. The speed of the car is represented on the ordinate and the distance from the obstruction is represented on the abcissa. The solid line labeled "emergency braking" is the border between the safe zone and the crash zone. This line represents the maximum deceleration necessary to stop just short of collision. Safe drivers start braking before entering the crash zone and control braking adequately to stop before collision. The unsafe drivers could either start braking too late to stop in time or start early enough but do not brake strongly enough to stay outside the crash zone.

In Lee and Lishman's analysis, the driver needs information about the adequacy of deceleration so that the program for stopping can be adjusted when nec-

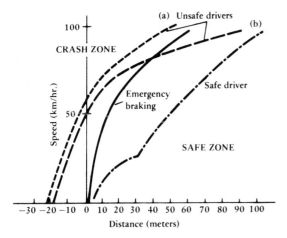

Figure 10.8 Analysis of action programs for stopping a vehicle. The safe driver starts braking before entering the crash zone and controls braking adequately. Unsafe drivers could either (*a*) start braking too late to stop in time or (*b*) start early enough but not brake strongly enough to stay outside the crash zone. (Lee & Lishman, 1977.)

essary. Moreover, the adjustments must be done early enough so that collision can be avoided. The information needed includes the closing velocity, the deceleration, and the distance from the obstacle. Lee (1974) has shown that all this information is available in the optic flow field. Thus, in principle, a driver could control deceleration simply on the basis of the rate of change of the visual variables that specify the time-to-collision if the closing velocity were maintained.

Steering

The analysis of the optical flow field for steering straight and along a curved path can be seen by projecting the pattern on a fronto-parallel plane. These flow fields are illustrated in Figure 10.9 for a driver going down a straight stretch of road toward a bend when (*a*) steering on course, (*b*) steering straight but off course, and (*c*) steering on a curved course. To understand how the straight flow lines in (*a*) and (*b*) were generated, think of the driver as stationary with the ground moving under the car. The points on the ground will be flowing along straight lines parallel to

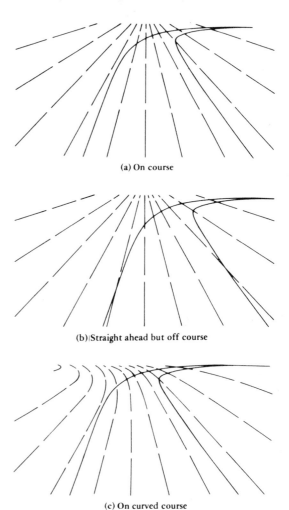

Figure 10.9 The fronto-parallel plane projection of a driver's optic flow field when driving down a straight stretch of road towards a bend: (*a*) steering on course; (*b*) steering straight but off course; (*c*) steering on a curved course. (Lee & Lishman, 1977.)

the direction in which the car is moving. The projections of these lines of flow onto the fronto-parallel plane give the straight optic flow lines.

To understand the curved optic flow lines in (*c*), consider the ground to be rotating under the stationary car about a vertical axis through the center of curvature of the path. The points on the ground will be flowing along concentric circles. The projections of these circles of flow onto the fronto-parallel plane yield the hyperbolic optic flow lines in the figure. A similar analysis of the optic flow pattern can be seen when entering a turn in the road and (*a*) steering on course, (*b*) correcting the steering angle, but making the adjustment too late, and (*c*) incorrectly steering. These patterns are illustrated in Figure 10.10.

When driving on a straight course, the center from which the flow radiates specifies the point toward which the car is moving. However, when driving on a curved course, there is no fixed point toward which the viewer is heading. But there are two properties of the optic flow field that could be used in steering, either on a straight or a curved course: (*a*) the locomotor flow line, and (*b*) the coincidence of road edges and flow lines. The **locomotor flow line** is the optic flow line that passes from view directly beneath the driver. According to Lee and Lishman, this line specifies the potential path, that is, the path that would be followed if the present forces on the vehicle are maintained. The coincidence of the road edges and flow lines refers to the fact that the images of the road edges and the optic flow lines coincide when steering on course. When steering off course, either straight or on a curved road, the locomotor flow line will not lie down the center of the image of the road, and the edges of the road will not coincide with the optic flow lines.

Turning must be planned before reaching the curve. The driver must change the locomotor program to one that will reduce the speed of the car to one appropriate to take the curve. This change must take into account the degree of curvature of the turn and the dynamics of the motion of the car. In other words, the problem of steering and of changing speeds appropriately is similar to the problem of stopping a car.

Footing

Walking, running, and other pedestrian means of locomotion entail special problems. The performer must secure adequate footing and control of the dynamic flux of the body parts relative to each other so that the reactive forces from the ground can be uti-

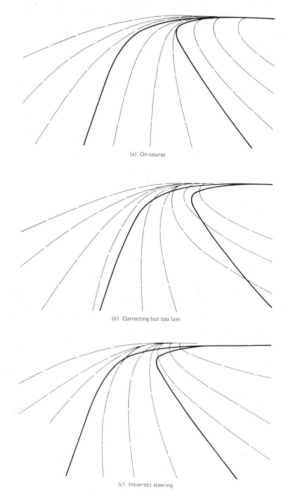

(*a*) On course

(*b*) Correcting but too late

(*c*) Incorrect steering

Figure 10.10 The fronto-parallel plane projection of a driver's optic flow field when driving into a turn of constant curvature with a sharp bend ahead: (*a*) steering on course; (*b*) steering at correct angle but making a late adjustment; and (*c*) steering at an incorrect turn angle. (Lee & Lishman, 1977.)

lized. The actor must plan where to place the feet, a plan that can utilize vision to obtain the necessary distance information. Precise information about the movement of the body relative to the environment is necessary for adjustments to the ongoing locomotor programs. According to Lee and Lishman, vision probably yields the most sensitive information about the layout of space.

ADAPTATION TO SYSTEMATIC VISUAL DISTORTION

One of the great difficulties in research on visual space perception is teasing apart the interplay within and between the different sources involved in perception of the layout of space. This has been especially true for visual-motor interactions, since there is no natural way to sever the connections in the brain between the motor and visual areas. The most important technique that has been used involves the alteration of the visual information reaching the eyes so that the normal relationships between the visual stimulus and motor responses are systematically distorted. For example, if perception of the straight ahead involves the integration of both visual information and information about eye position, that integration could be examined by having the observer wear prism spectacles that displace the light imaged on the retina, thereby altering the visual input. If the prism displaced the image 10 degrees to the right, and if visual information alone accounted for visual direction constancy, then the straight ahead would be permanently displaced 10 degrees to the right. Experiments that alter the visual input have represented the most powerful method available to analyze these interactions.

The visual input may be altered in a number of ways, using mirrors, prisms, and lenses. In this section, we first describe the studies performed at Innsbruck, since they demonstrate almost all phases of the adaptation phenomenon, especially when the distorting device is worn for an extended period of time. The remaining sections deal directly with the questions of the locus of adaptation and the role of the perceiver's own movements.

Research at Innsbruck

These studies describe the experiences of Erismann and of Kohler (1951), who wore distorting prisms and mirrors for extended periods of time. Their descriptions of the concomitant changes can provide the foundation for the more precise studies of each of the effects reported. These include the systematic variation in perception that occurs immediately upon introduction of the distorting device, and the gradual changes in perception that occur after wearing the distorting instrument for a period of time. These gradual changes are referred to as **adaptation** because the distortion in perception disappears. **Aftereffects** of the distortions also are found—distortions reappear in perception as a result of the removal of the distorting instrument.

In order to understand the effect of distorting the input to the visual system, the locus of distortion must be clearly pinpointed. In the experiments to be discussed here, the input to the visual system is systematically altered by placing a prism or a mirror in a pair of goggles and attaching the goggles to the head. In this way the change in input is introduced between the eye and the environment. This produces a fixed change between the light entering the eye and the position of the head; that is, since the goggles are attached to the head, this distortion is fixed. Both the eyes and the body may move with respect to the head and, therefore, with respect to the distortion. The light still carries information about the environment, but that information is biased in some way. Kohler and Erismann studied the long-term consequences of this bias.

In one set of studies, Kohler wore mirrors attached to his forehead in such a manner that he could only see the world in front of him by looking up into the mirrors (Fig. 10.11). Consequently, the stimulation coming to his eyes was inverted in the up-down direction. To imagine the kind of reversal this is, think of moving your eyes upward while the stimulation reaching your eye is that from moving your eye downward over the same scene. The pattern and flow are upside-down.

The results of this distortion of visual inputs were dramatic. The immediate experience was directly predictable from the distortion introduced— everything appeared to be upside-down. Errors were

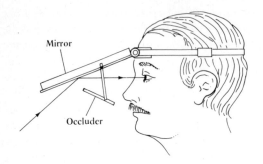

Mirror

Occluder

Figure 10.11   Mirror arrangement worn by Kohler to see the world ahead by looking up.

made in attempting to touch objects. The viewer felt unsure of himself and needed an escort in order to walk about. Even then his steps were halting. Over the first three days his behavior gradually became normal (or at least looked normal to another person). By this time, he was able to ride a bicycle without help, and on the sixth day he was again able to ski.

The perceptual effects as reported by Kohler are even more interesting. During the first few days, perceptions appeared to be right-side-up only sporadically. But this was not random. There were special cases when the perceptual world would right itself. Objects would appear in their proper orientation when they were simultaneously viewed and touched, or when a plumb line was present in the visual field, or when the object was in the perceiver's immediate vicinity so that he could see it in relation to his own feet.

When the mirrors were removed, objects immediately reverted to their previous upside-down position and for a few minutes, people and furniture appeared "suspended from the ceiling, head downward." After about half an hour, the aftereffects started to go away.

There were some interesting disturbances in eye–head coordination which resulted from wearing the mirrors. When they were on, the perceiver had to raise his head and eyes somewhat to see at all. As time went on and the perceptual adaptation took place, the kinesthetic sensations (of the head and eyes raised) were no longer felt to be unusual. After removal of the goggles, when it was again necessary to look in the actual

straight-ahead direction to look at the world ahead, the viewer felt that he was looking down, or that the floor was giving way under his feet. This aftereffect caused Kohler to maintain his head in a curiously crooked position, lowering his head by about 30 degrees to place his eyes in the previously "normal" position. Thus the orientation of the eyes and head involves the distortion not only of the accompanying perception but also of the felt position of the eyes with respect to the head and with respect to the objective straight ahead.

In general, the adjustment of overt behavior—the motor reactions—preceded the adaptation of perception. There were three main types of information that were essential in mediating the perceptual adaptation—touch, alignment with gravity, and familiarity. Whenever Kohler reached for and touched an object in his immediate vicinity, the object that was first seen as inverted suddenly appeared to be upright. This also occurred when the object was touched with a stick—essentially an extension of the arm. In general, the hands were the first objects to be seen as upright.

The second feature of information that corrected the inverted perceptual experience was information about gravity. A plumb line was seen in its correct direction as soon as Kohler held the string himself. Once this took place, he could use the plumb line to correct the perception of other objects. Whenever information about gravity was available, such as when he was driving uphill in a car, the world appeared upright. Specific objects would right themselves when appropriate gravity information was available. For example, a candle would appear upside-down but would change to its proper orientation when a flame was added. This would also occur with a cigarette, which could be perceived in any orientation until the smoke would supply information about gravity. Then the cigarette would be perceived in its proper orientation.

These comments and observations represent only a small segment of Kohler's findings, both upon himself and on other perceivers. The essential point is that complete perceptual adaptation can occur in a relatively short time when one is wearing inverting mirrors, so that the visual world comes to look perfectly normal, as long as the perceiver is permitted free, self-initiated movement. The importance of such movements will be evaluated below.

The up–down inversion just described is a gross change in the visual input. It represents some of the most dramatic evidence ever reported about the plasticity of visual-motor integration. While the initial changes are totally predictable by the alteration in the light path—in this case inversion—the subject wearing such mirrors is able to achieve normal perception of the visual world, as if the visual input had not been altered at all. Although these demonstrations with mirrors did permit the exploration of separate components of the adaptation, it appears as if the most critical factor was the opportunity to determine the visual consequences of movements of the eyes, head, and limbs. While the eyes received an altered input from visual space, they also received an altered input from the wearer's body, and of the consequences of his movements. He has a chance to learn a new set of relationships between his movements and the visual results of his movements.

In order to demonstrate the appropriate nature of these new perceptual-motor integrations, Kohler used some less dramatic visual alterations so he could examine the resultant changes more easily. In most of these experiments, wedge prisms were embedded in goggles. The distortion of the visual input caused by

prisms is different from that caused by inverting mirrors. Figure 10.12 shows a prism with base $ABCD$ and apex EF. When a viewer looks through the prism at a point in space, that point will be perceived as if it were in a direction closer to the apex of the prism than is the actual point, and slightly closer to the eye. This alteration in stimulation represents the simplest aspect of the distortion that takes place in a prism experiment—the distortion introduced into the retinal projection by wearing wedge prisms of this sort is much more complex. For example, contours appear to be surrounded by color bands because of the differential diffraction of light as a function of wavelength when it crosses from one medium to another. More important, however, is the complex distortion of shape. Figure 10.13 shows the type of distortion introduced when looking though wedge prisms with the base on the left-hand side. Notice the curvature introduced in the image—straight lines are no longer straight and right angles are no longer 90 degrees. In this figure, all of the vertical lines would have colored fringes. Figure 10.14 shows the distortion in more detail. It contains photographs taken through prisms and shows the distortion introduced when the prisms are placed in a position so as to simulate looking in different directions. The first plate (*a*) is a photograph of the stimulus configuration without prisms. This can be compared with (*b*) looking straight ahead

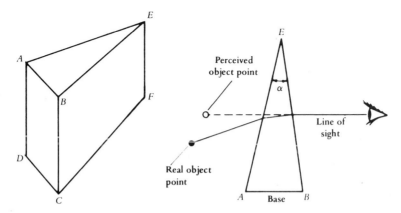

Figure 10.12 Displacement caused by a prism with base $ABCD$, apex EF, and apex angle α. The apparent position of the object point is displaced in the direction of the apex, and is closer to the eye.

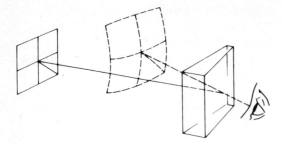

Figure 10.13 An approximate representation of the effect of viewing a pattern through a wedge prism. Displacement and curvature effects are shown. All lines with vertical components have color fringes if the borders of the pattern are black/white and are viewed in white light.

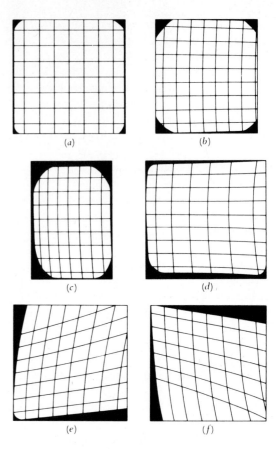

Figure 10.14 Systematic distortion introduced by looking through wedge prisms: (*a*) without prisms, (*b*) looking straight ahead, (*c*) contraction when looking left, (*d*) expansion when looking right, (*e*) looking up, (*f*) looking down. (Kohler, 1951.)

through the prism, *(c)* and *(d)* looking to the left and to the right, and *(e)* and *(f)* looking up and down. Less obvious but equally important are the curvatures of gradients, the warping of slopes, and the distortions of angles.

When an experiment is begun and the perceiver first puts on the wedge prisms, there is a close correspondence between the newly formed retinal projections and the perceptions accompanying them. The properties of objects change as the properties of the projections received from them change on the retina. Illusions of depth and distortions occur. The perceiver experiences the world as "rubbery" and feels "drunk" when walking on the street. Thus, the photographs in Figure 10.14 may be taken as fairly good representations of the momentary perceptual experience of a person who has just put on the spectacles containing the wedge prisms for the first time.

In the experiments by Kohler, a number of different kinds of prisms were used, varying in displacement from 10 degrees to 20 degrees in visual direction. In some experiments Kohler wore the spectacles for as long as 124 days. Once again we can divide the results into observations of the perceptual-motor behavior of the person wearing the spectacles, and the subjective reports of that person about what his perceptual experience is like. With respect to perceptual-motor behavior, all difficulties, such as the errors made in reaching for objects, disappeared within one day. Within six days, Kohler was skiing. The ad-

aptation effects took longer to begin. Within two days Kohler reported the disappearance of the apparent visual motion that he perceived when the spectacles were first put on. At this time, curved surfaces began to appear flat and figures looked less distorted than at first. After ten days, all surfaces appeared to flatten out and objects no longer appeared distorted.

When the spectacles were removed, aftereffects occurred immediately. Kohler reported the return of curvature and distortion in viewing surfaces and figures as well as the return of the apparent movement of the world. The experience was very similar to when the goggles were first put on. These aftereffects continued in general for four days and curvature aftereffects were noted for as long as twenty-three days.

Situational Aftereffects

The most striking discovery was what Kohler called the **situational aftereffect,** whose characteristic depended on a particular condition, such as on the direction of the line of sight. As an example, recall that the deflection of light by a prism is minimal when the viewer is looking directly through the center of the prism and that the distortion increases as one looks away from this position, both vertically and horizontally. The important point is that the quality of the perceptual change depends on the direction of vision, that is, on whether the observer is looking to his left or to his right to see the object. The same object would appear thin when viewed in one direction and thick when viewed in the other. Moreover, whether looking at the object to the left or to the right, the eyes turn in the head in such a way that the stimulation is falling, in general, on the same central portion of the retina. Thus the adaptation in some way corrects for the difference in distortion introduced into the projection when looking one way or the other. The situational aftereffects are a special kind of negative aftereffect because they occur only when the situation is the same as the one in which the prism-induced alterations originally took place. Consequently, after the prisms are removed, perceptual anomalies will occur whenever the head and eyes are moved. These anomalies will be opposite to the ones that occurred in the same head-eye posture when the prisms were worn. The effect is as if the perceiver were now wearing spectacles with prisms exactly opposite to the ones used in the original experiment.

Clearly the situational aftereffects raise a serious question for perceptual theorists. How can the same retinal projection arouse different perceptions when the ocular system is directed toward a different point in space? The answer cannot be in terms of isolated retinal projections or isolated retinal areas. The total stimulus situation must be considered and this must include the direction of regard, a motor component to be combined with the information from the visual sys-

tem. Somehow, the activity of the organism itself in directing the gaze must be taken into account in the ultimate perception. The following sections will illustrate some modern attempts to provide this type of explanation.

Visual vs Proprioceptive Change

The first step in attempting to understand the mechanisms involved in the perceptual-motor adaptation that occurs when the visual input is systematically altered is to pinpoint the changes taking place. Two major possibilities have been suggested. The adaptation may represent a change in the visual experience of the perceiver so that the object is seen differently, or it may represent a proprioceptive change so that the perceiver senses the position of parts of the body differently, and thereby sees the world from a different perspective.

The problem can be more easily understood when measuring adaptation in a simple pointing task. Figure 10.15 shows the apparatus used by Harris

Figure 10.15 Apparatus for testing visual perceptual and motor adaptation.

(1965) to measure visual and proprioceptive adaptation differentially. A perceiver viewed five upright pegs at the far edge of a horizontal plate of glass that was just below the level of her eyes. There were three tasks—pointing at visual targets, pointing at sounds, and pointing straight ahead. The viewer's normal performance in these tasks was measured before putting on the prisms. In this pretest, the glass was covered with a cloth so that the perceiver could not see her hand under the glass.

After the pretests, the perceiver wore wedge prisms for about three minutes, during which time she pointed repeatedly at the center target with the hand which was visible through the glass. Over the course of the three minutes, the direction of pointing, inaccurate at first, became accurate. The retest provided a measure of the effects of adaptation that could be compared to the pretest data. All retests were made without prisms. The results showed a large shift in pointing with the adapted hand, but little or no shift with the other hand for each of the three tests. Harris concluded, therefore, that the change involved in adaptation was in the felt position of the specific hand and arm that had been involved in the adaptation. He argued that the change could not be visual, or there should be no difference in direction of pointing between the two hands in the visual task and there should be no shifts in pointing to the sound—the nonvisual stimulus.

To determine whether the adaptation was a change in sensed position of hand and arm or a learning to correct motor responses, Harris (1965) performed some additional tests. In one test, he had the perceiver estimate the distance between his hands while he was blindfolded. These judgments were made before and after one arm had been adapted as before. However, the perceiver was blindfolded during the pretests and posttests and the experimenter moved the hand to the appropriate position. Then the perceiver was required to place his unadapted hand at a specific distance from his adapted hand. Thus he could only use information from the position sense to determine where his hand was. The results indicated that the perceiver felt his hands farther apart after the adaptation than before. Therefore, Harris argued, the

perceiver's position sense had been altered. Recall that Kohler had also commented in several of his experiments that, as adaptation occurred he changed the position or orientation of some part of his body. With the inverting mirrors, the orientation of the head was a principal component of the adaptation. Harris (1965) reviewed a number of instances of the proprioceptive component of adaptation, and showed how it would explain the reported visual experiences.

Hay and Pick (1966) studied the changes in reaching behavior that accompanied wearing wedge prisms producing a lateral displacement in stimulation. At first, each perceiver made many errors in reaching for objects, but within a few hours of active walking, they were able to reach for objects fairly accurately. In devising the experimental tasks, Hay and Pick reasoned that a change in reaching behavior or in proprioception of the hand should be manifest in reaching for nonvisual targets as well as visual targets. Therefore, if a perceiver who has adapted to wearing the prisms is asked to indicate the direction of a sound rather than a visual stimulus, they could tell whether the visual impression had changed or whether the felt position of the hand had changed. Furthermore, if the change was visual in nature, this could be determined by having the perceiver make a verbal indication of where an object was seen—for example, naming the position on a scale behind which a sound appeared to be located. Thus, while these investigators were studying the adaptation that took place in eye-hand coordination, they separated it into ear–eye coordination and ear–hand coordination in order to discover the major factor that had changed.

The results are illustrated in Figure 10.16 in which performance on the three tasks is plotted as a function of the duration of prism exposure. Changes in both ear–eye and ear–hand coordination occurred and these added up to the total change in eye–hand coordination. There is therefore evidence for both visual and proprioceptive adaptation. The two types of adaptation do not progress in the same way over time, however. The rate of proprioceptive adaptation increased rapidly during the first twelve hours and then slowly decreased until it leveled off at about seventy-two hours. The visual shift increased rapidly over the first twenty-four hours, then less rapidly until it too leveled off at about seventy-two hours. In other words, the immediate adaptation included both visual and proprioceptive changes, whereas later changes were largely visual.

Kornheiser (1976) reviewed the literature on adaptation to laterally displaced vision and noted that a number of studies repeated Harris's finding that there is no transfer to the unadapted hand. Since transfer is a major test of proprioceptive change theory, and a relatively few studies have reported transfer, Kornheiser concluded that there clearly is a change in the perceived position of the adapted arm during prism adaptation. Indeed, Kornheiser identified at least five loci of proprioceptive change: the wrist, hand, arm, head, and eye—suggesting that adaptation can take place at any locus at which two parts of the body can move relative to each other.

Thus far the studies have been concerned with the alteration of visual information about visual direction—the stimulus was displaced laterally by use of wedge prisms. Rock (1966) introduced a different kind of distortion—distortion of size and of shape—to test whether these kinds of changes might produce visual perceptual changes. The change in size was produced by a lens and the change in shape was produced by a cylindrical optical device that made the stimulus narrower. In the experiment on perceived size, naïve perceivers saw a one-inch white plastic square through the lens and touched it from below through a cloth

(see Figure 10.17). They could not see their hands. Three tests were used: (*a*) they were to draw the size of the square as accurately as they could; (*b*) they were to match the size from a series of visually presented squares, and (*c*) they were to match the size from a series that they could touch but could not see. The average size of the matched object or of the drawing was smaller when the vision and touch were in conflict than when touch alone was involved. The matched size was about the same when visual information was available and when touch was providing information in one case and not in another. Touch had therefore almost no effect on the visually perceived size of the object. In the experiment on shape in which similar conditions were involved, the information provided the perceiver with a rectangular visual object and a square tactual object. Once again the results showed that vision completely dominated the responses—not only did most of the perceivers say they saw a rectangle, but they claimed that the object felt like one also.

Active vs Passive Movement

The alteration which takes place during adaptation to the distorted input appears to be a realignment of the motor-kinesthetic portion of perceptual-motor acts. In order to reach, point, walk, run, or ski, the person wearing distorting goggles must have infor-

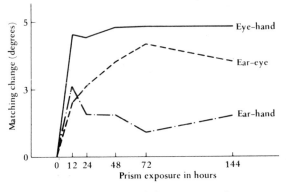

Figure 10.16 Magnitude of adaptive change for three intermodal comparisons as a function of length of prism exposure. (Hay & Pick, 1966.)

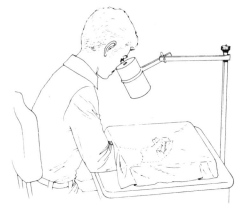

Figure 10.17 Apparatus used by Rock (1966) to provide conflicting visual and touch information about the size and shape of an object.

mation about the relationships of the systems involved and must readjust the internal correlation. This information can be provided visually by reafference—the visual consequences of movements of the observer initiated by the observer.

In the Innsbruck studies, the perceiver wearing the goggles was permitted free movement, almost entirely self-initiated. Such movement would be an important source of efferent and reafferent information. Is this movement necessary, or will adaptation take place with only visual input? Held and Hein (1958) compared performances of a perceiver wearing prisms for three minutes while he looked at his hand when it was stationary, when it was moved by a mechanical device that simulated real movements, and when it was moved by the perceiver himself. In pretests and posttests, the perceiver marked the position of the intersections of lines as illustrated in Figure 10.18. Clearly the active movement produced substantial adaptation—most perceivers showed complete adaptation within half an hour. No adaptation was shown by those receiving passive movement. Thus even though the visual information was the same in both conditions, there was no relationship between the efferent motor signals and the afferent sensory signals in the passive condition. This suggested to Held and Hein that contingent reafferent stimulation was the critical factor in adaptation to displacement. Similar results were found when movement of the entire body was involved (Held & Bossom, 1961; Held & Freedman, 1963).

A slightly different viewpoint concerning active movement asserts that the information obtained from a record of certain outgoing motor nerve impulses is available for use in adaptation. Specifically, this would mean that the perceiver would know the direction in which the eye was looking because it had a record of where the eye had been directed to go. For example, Festinger and Canon (1965) found that the accuracy of pointing at the location of a target was better when the target appeared suddenly than when the target moved slowly toward its destination. They took this as evidence that the efferent information was available and useful in judging target direction.

In this view, then, perception need not involve

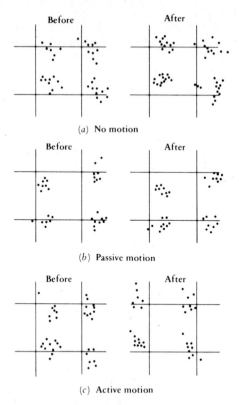

Figure 10.18 Before and after tests for marking the intersection of lines when wearing prisms and after looking at the hand when it was (*a*) stationary, (*b*) moved by a mechanical device, and (*c*) actively moved by the subject. (Held & Hein, 1958.)

the actual motor activity as much as the central concomitant of a readiness to activate a programmed efferent signal. The consequence of this view is that the visual information present in the psychophysicist's superstimulus must still be supplemented by nonoptic information of some sort for precise perceptual-motor behavior to take place. As Gyr (1972) points out, for adaptation to take place, the organism must actively confront the production and/or the reception of input from the environment. While the information need not be motor activity, or even its consequence in stimulation—reafference—an additional component must be present for adaptation—and, indeed, for perception—to take place.

A number of experiments have demonstrated adaptation with passive movement (Kornheiser, 1976), suggesting that self-generated movement is not necessary for adaptation. Consequently, a theory that makes viewing self-generated movement of limbs a prerequisite for perceptual adaptation is no longer tenable. Nevertheless, active movement is far more effective in producing adaptation than passive movement. Using an experimental paradigm that permitted independent manipulation of the apparent visual and apparent proprioceptive loci of external targets, Lackner (1973, 1974) demonstrated that adaptation does not occur unless a discordance exists between the visually and proprioceptively specified directions of the visual targets. The critical factor in determining whether adjustments will occur is the presence or absence of a discordance between the visual and proprioceptive locations of body parts or external objects (Lackner, 1977). Moreover, the discordance need not be consciously recognized in order for adaptation to take place. One reason for the greater effectiveness of active movement may be the greater accuracy of position-sense information about voluntarily moved limbs derived, in part, from muscle efferent signals.

SUMMARY

We have reviewed the three major views of motion and movement perception. Several tentative conclusions are possible. First, there is evidence that human beings possess cortical motion-detecting systems that respond to a displacement of a luminance gradient over a retinal receptive field. Second, evidence has been reviewed to suggest that relational qualities are critical for the perception of any kind of motion, real or apparent. Motion of an object on a textureless dark background is virtually undetectable, while such a stationary object will appear to move unpredictably. Gibsons's theory of motion and movement perception rests entirely on the relative displacements in the retinal projection. His explanation is internally consistent and possesses great power, especially in the analysis of action. Our understanding of the control of balance, stance, orienting, and locomotion are greatly enhanced by the analysis of the contributions of the visual system. Finally, it seems clear that nonvisual information may play a major role in adapting to distortion of visual input.

SUGGESTED READINGS

General coverage of the problem of perceived movement may be found in Spigel's (1965) book and human spatial orientation is thoroughly reviewed in Howard and Templeton (1966). Gyr's (1972) article contains a sophisticated discussion of the theories of movement and motion perception as well as reviews of the experimental evidence. A detailed discussion of the problems of adaptation to distortion may be found in Rock (1966), Kornheiser (1976), and Dodwell, (1970).

Chapter 11

Binocular Vision

Because the two eyes are slightly separated in the head, the two retinal images of a real scene are slightly different. If you look at a scene that has no depth to it (such as a picture), all parts are essentially equidistant from your eyes, and the two retinal images will correspond exactly over their entire extent. But if some parts of the scene are closer than others, the two images will not overlap perfectly. The degree of noncorrespondence will be proportional to the relative differences in distance (nearer or farther away) to the object on which you are fixated. If you change fixation, a new pattern of correspondence and noncorrespondence is created, but again, the disparity between parts of the images will be proportional to the relative distance of the objects in space. In this sense, then, the amount and location of the disparity between the entire two retinal images may be thought of as a third kind of perspective transformation (Haber, 1979). This chapter will be devoted entirely to the problem of seeing with two eyes. In the first part, we describe binocular stimulation in terms of corresponding and noncorresponding points in the two eyes. We then explore the consequences of such stimulation in terms of the perception of direction, solidity, and depth of objects in visual space. Finally, we describe theories of stereopsis.

The Problem of Binocular Vision

For a given fixation, the retinal images on the two eyes must be different because the eyes are in different positions in space. Yet the two different retinal images result in the perception of a stable world, filled with objects that are perceived as single and as having thickness, and that are positioned at different distances and in different directions from the observer and from one another. One of the early illustrations of this problem (Leonardo da Vinci—see Boring, 1942) noted the fact that the eye can "see around" and "behind" a near object, permitting more of the object and of the background to be seen. This has been called **binocular parallax** and is illustrated in Figure 11.1. The cylindrical object is placed between the observer and the background. The left eye sees the object's surface from c to d and moreover, this portion of the object occludes or covers a proportional part of the background from C to D that is not seen by the left eye when viewing alone. Similarly, the right eye sees the surface a to b and not the portion of the background A to B. Nevertheless, with binocular vision, the object is seen as a single, solid object, and the entire background is perceived as a continuous surface. The problem of binocular vision is to explain how this perception comes about.

Oculomotor Information: Accommodation and Convergence

Before beginning the discussion of binocular vision, however, it is necessary to discuss the relationship between the positioning and focus of the two eyes.

When looking at a scene, nonvisual information is available that may have usefulness for binocular vision. Receptors in the muscles that alter the position of the eye register the location of each eyeball in its socket. Consequently, they provide information about the orientation of each eye relative to the straight ahead, and about the amount of convergence between the two eyes. There are receptors in the ciliary muscles that regulate the shape of the lens in each eye, thereby providing information about the degree of accommodation of the eyes. The information may be repre-

sented by the afferent signals from the receptors themselves or by the efferent signals from the brain to those muscles that provide the movement.

Since the two eyes are separated and since they must converge in order to direct the foveas to a nearby, fixated target, it seems reasonable that the degree of convergence of the binocular system could supply information about depth. Indeed, one of the earliest theories of visual space perception proposed that the eyes act like a range-finding mechanism, informing the perceiver how far away an object is by calculating the angle of convergence necessary to fixate directly on the object (Boring, 1942; Gulick & Lawson, 1976). Similar logic also suggested that the accommodative mechanism supplies information used in depth perception.

The role of oculomotor adjustments in visual space perception is frequently demonstrated by the **"wallpaper illusion."** To observe the illusion, stand a few meters from a wall covered with wallpaper consisting of a regular, horizontally repeated pattern. The pattern may consist of vertical stripes or repeated figures. Face the wall squarely so that it lies in a fronto-parallel plane. Now fixate the tip of your finger placed at arm's length between you and the wall, but keep your attention on the wallpaper pattern. This procedure increases the convergence of your eyes while maintaining attention on a distant stimulus. Now you should be able to "fuse" different patterns from the wallpaper. They will appear smaller and nearer. Usually the wall will also appear smaller and closer (although sometimes it appears more distant). Refined versions of this demonstration have been used to argue that oculomotor adjustments clearly determine perceived size and distance (for example, Linksz, 1952). However, Ames has explained these effects entirely in terms of binocular disparities (Ittelson, 1960), suggesting that oculomotor adjustments play little role in space perception. The experimental evidence suggests that convergence alone provides relatively little depth information (Ogle, 1962), and that this information is not effective for stimuli beyond three meters (Gogel, 1977).

In terms of the geometry of light reaching the eyes, and the smallness of the distances between the

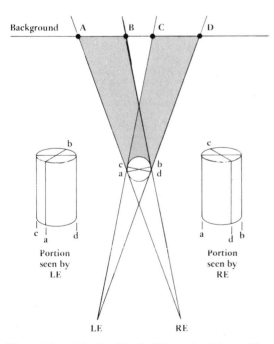

Figure 11.1 The "problem" of binocular vision as illustrated by binocular parallax.

eyes, convergence could not supply very accurate information about the space lying very far from the perceiver. But even within the geometrically possible range, the information value seems limited. Indeed, observers do not reliably use the information even when convergence is the only information available. When other sources of information about space are also present, convergence appears to be ignored altogether. Thus, convergence (and accommodation) provides an instance in which geometry and logic suggest a source of information that, in actuality, is not often used. The demonstrated existence of such a source underlines the necessity of determining empirically whether other sources of information actually are used.

BINOCULAR STIMULATION

The Geometry of Corresponding Points

The geometry of retinal correspondence compares the location of the retinal image in one eye to the location of the retinal image in the other eye. If it is assumed that the two eyes are spheres, then each will have a single point as its center (the spherical center), and the retinas may be represented as portions of the surfaces of the spheres. When the eyes converge and diverge, they rotate about a point. The point of zero velocity during horizontal eye movements is called the **center of rotation.** The center of rotation and the spherical center may be the same or different points. A set of coordinate axes can be applied to the surfaces of the spheres with the two foveas as origins (the reason for this will become clear later), and the coordinates of any point on the spherical surface can be identified. **Geometrical correspondence** occurs when a point on one retina has the same coordinates as a point on the other retina.

The overlap of the two monocular fields is called the **binocular field of vision.** The two monocular fields, superimposed and projected onto a fronto-parallel plane, are shown in Figure 11.2. All areas within the overlapping fields stimulate both eyes. The maximum width of the monocular field is between 90 de-

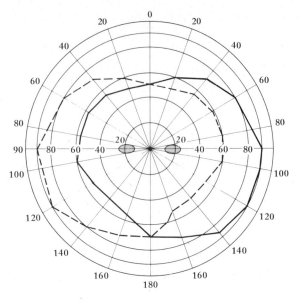

Figure 11.2 The binocular field of vision projected onto a fronto-parallel plane. The blind spots are represented by the elipses near the 20° marks.

grees and 115 degrees of visual angle, depending on the size of projection of the nose. The binocular field is flanked on both sides by a monocular field of about 30 to 35 degrees.

When these "spherical" eyeballs are converged symmetrically on a near fixation point, it is possible to pass a circle through the fixation point and the two points representing, for each eye simultaneously, the **optical nodes** (the respective centers of the optical properties), the centers of rotation, and the sperical centers of the two eyes, respectively. This circle is called the **Vieth-Müller circle** (V-M circle) after the men who first proposed that this geometrical relationship has a special place in the explanation of binocular vision. The assumptions underlying the geometry of the V-M circle are illustrated in Figure 11.3.

Figure 11.4 shows the geometrical relationships for two different points on the V-M circle—the fixated point (F) and a point that is not fixated (P). C_l and C_r are the centers of rotations, optical nodes, or the optical centers of the two eyes, respectively. Light rays emanating from the two points are shown passing through these points and intersecting the rear surface

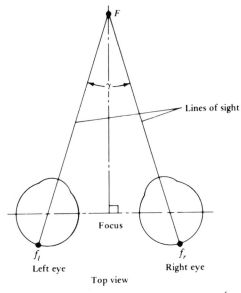

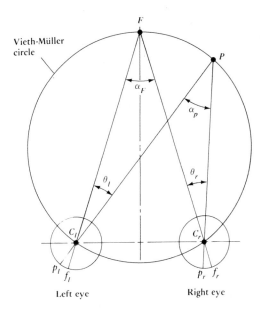

Figure 11.4 The geometrical relationships defined by the Vieth-Müller circle. Since P is on the V-M circle, the retinal points p_l and p_r are corresponding points.

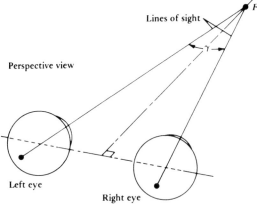

Figure 11.3 Diagrams illustrating the assumptions underlying the geometry of the Vieth-Müller circle. The eyeballs are assumed to be spheres, converging symmetrically on a near fixation point such that the lines of sight intersect the retinas at the respective foveas. For this to occur, it is also necessary to assume that the respective optical nodes, centers of fixation, and spherical centers all coincide. γ is the convergence angle.

of the spheres representing the eyes. This surface has been taken to represent geometrically the retinas of the two eyes. Rays from the fixation point, passing through the respective optical centers, intersect the eyeballs at points f_l and f_r, respectively. These points

are taken to represent the foveas of the two eyes. α_F is the convergence angle for point F.

The point P is not fixated but lies on the V-M circle. Rays from this point strike the retinal surface at points p_l and p_r. The convergence angle of this point is α_p and, since they lie on the circumference of the same circle and subtend the same arc of that circle, these two convergence angles are equal; that is, $\alpha_p = \alpha_f$. Moreover, since C_l and C_r fall on the circumference of the same circle and subtend the same arc of that circle, the angles θ_l and θ_r are equal. Therefore, the displacements of the points p_l and p_r on the two retinas are equal, and these two points are said to be **geometrically corresponding points**. It should be clear from this analysis that a given fixation point defines a V-M circle, and that the convergence angles for all points on that circle will be equal, that is, all points on the V-M circle stimulate geometrically corresponding retinal points. Moreover, if C_l and C_r represent both the optical nodes and the centers of rotation of the two eyes, it is not essential that convergence be symmetrical for these relationships to hold. If this were not the case, the optical transformations resulting from rotation of the eyes would be different for the two eyes, unless both eyes moved in a corresponding fashion.

An alternative way to think about corresponding retinal points is that the left- and right-eye images of a point are located at the same distance and in the same direction from their respective foveas. In this sense, when images are corresponding, they stimulate the same areas of each retina, using the center of the fovea as the common reference point.

Visual Directions

We noted in Chapter 8 that perceptual space is described using a polar coordinate system with the perceiver at the center. In this system, direction can be measured as angular displacement from the straight ahead and distance can be measured radially, that is, out from the center. This system is particularly useful in describing the perception of visual directions because perceived direction is almost invariably related to the perceived straight ahead.

First let us examine the visual directions associated with each eye separately. Think of visual lines that connect all points in space with various points on the retina. There is a line for each direction and there is an infinite number of points on each line, each at a different distance. We can single out one line for special consideration—the one that passes through the center of the lens and the center of the fovea. This line is called the **visual axis** of the eye. The subjective direction associated with the visual axis is called the **principal visual direction.** All other directions are experienced in relation to this direction. To say that we are fixating on an object means that the eye is oriented in such a way that the object is on the visual axis of the eye and that the projection of the object falls on the fovea.

This becomes a more difficult problem when we realize that we have two eyes, set about 6 centimeters apart. Consequently, what is straight ahead for on eye will be off to the side for the other, especially if the object in question is quite close. Both eyes can converge on the same fixation point, but then neither eye has its visual axis "straight ahead," at least in relation to the rest of the body.

But localization of visual direction does not occur for each eye separately. The directions from the two eyes are jointly referred to some kind of body image, so that directions arrange themselves in relation to the perceiver's "mind." Thus every object is seen in a single subjective visual direction. The directions of all points appear to be arranged about a definite center so that the bundle of visual directions appear to converge to a point between the two eyes. This point is called the **cyclopean eye.** Thus objects are located as if from a point located between the two eyes through which all visual directions pass. There is only one direction for each point in space with respect to the cyclopean eye. These directions are called **primary subjective visual directions** to differentiate them from the directions associated with each eye separately.

The relationships are shown schematically in Figure 11.5. The two eyes are fixating point F in space and the respective foveas are stimulated. The subjective visual direction is illustrated as a direction pointing straight at F from between the two eyes (D_f). Similar relationships are indicated for points A and B that are not being fixated. Their subjective directions

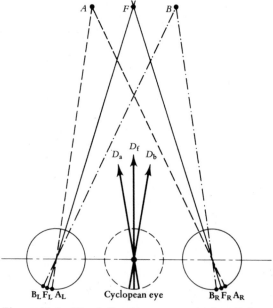

Figure 11.5 Visual directions are perceived as if there were a single "cyclopean" eye situated between the two eyes.

are also shown (D_a and D_b), and they suggest the cone of directions emanating from the cyclopean eye.

But this does not entirely solve the problem of defining visual directions. If both eyes are fixating a nearby object, there will be substantial disagreement between the two subjective visual directions given by each of the two eyes and the primary subjective visual direction emanating from the cyclopean eye in the middle. In such cases, the perceived direction corresponds to that of the cyclopean eye. The **law of identical visual directions** attributed to the nineteenth-century physiologist Hering, states that all objects lying on the two principal visual directions will be perceived in the same primary subjective visual direction, irrespective of their angular position relative to the observer. This law refers to other parts of the retina also—the subjective visual directions of other points will be determined relative to those that occupy the central portion of the retina. This relationship suggests that every retinal point in the binocular field of one eye has a partner in the retina of the other eye with identical directional value.

The law of identical visual directions can be observed by performing a simple experiment which Hering first described. Figure 11.6 shows two cases where the law operates, one for near fixation and one for far. For far fixation, the viewer looks through a pane of glass at some distant point. The glass is marked to correspond to the principal visual direction of each eye. Now clearly these two marks are separated laterally with respect to the viewer, but since they both fall on corresponding retinal areas of the two eyes, they will be seen in the identical visual direction. The same is true when with near fixation, two far objects are separated spatially but fall on corresponding retinal points. Figure 11.7 gives detailed instructions for reproducing Hering's experiment.

When corresponding retinal points are stimulated, the resulting perception is of a single point in a single visual direction from a point located somewhere between the two eyes of the observer. Thus the field is seen as if in cyclopean view. The views of the two eyes are said to "fuse" into one to form the single-appearing point. This holds for all points on the V-M circle. Figure 11.8 illustrates the relationships between corresponding points and their perceptual consequences. The corresponding foveal points f_l and f_r are stimulated by light emanating from the fixation point F. Point F is perceived as a single point in the direction D_f in the cyclopean field of view. Point P, a point different from F but on the V-M circle, provides stimulation for the points p_l and p_r on the left and right retinas, respectively. Point P is perceived as a single point in the direction D_p in the cyclopean field of view.

Because of this relationship between the geome-

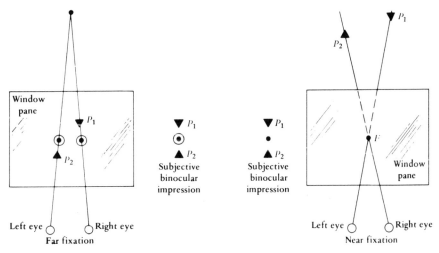

Figure 11.6   Hering's experiment showing the operations of the law of identical visual directions.

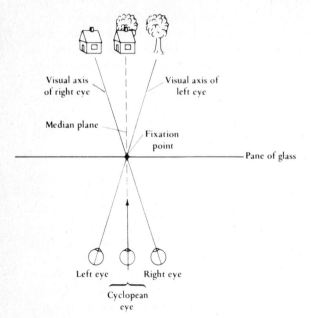

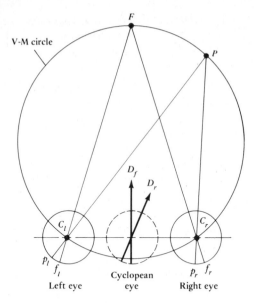

Figure 11.8 Perceptual outcomes for stimulation on corresponding retinal points. The stimulus points F and P are seen as single, and in the appropriate directions D_f and D_r, respectively, with respect to a single egocenter.

Figure 11.7 Instructions for the Hering experiment. (1) Stand in front of a window. Holding the head steady, close one eye (say, the right) and look at an object (say, a tree) in the distance to the right. While fixating the tree, place a small mark on the window pane so that it is in the direct line with the tree. (2) Now close the other eye and fixate the spot on the window pane. Then pay attention to some other object in the distance (say, a house and chimney) which is in line with the dot on the pane. (3) With both eyes open, and directed at the spot on the window pane, the house, chimney, and tree will all be seen in the same visual direction, and that will be the direction of the spot from the center of the two eyes.

try of the V-M circle and the perceptual outcomes associated with stimulation by points on that circle, early theorists codified the relationship into a single concept—the longitudinal horopter. The **horopter** was defined as the locus of all points in the binocular field seen as single. It was thought of as a mental line passing through the fixation point. The V-M circle was thought of as a "theoretical horopter." An alternative definition for the horopter was also proposed in terms of visual directions. It could be defined as the locus of points that give rise to the perception of identical visual directions.

There are a number of problems associated with this enticingly simple geometrical view of binocular stimulation. First, the eyes are not really spherical. Second, there is no reason to assume that the foveas of the eyes correspond to the origins of a coordinate system. Third, there is no reason to assume that the optical node, the center of rotation, and the geometrical center of the eye coincide. Indeed, Graham (1965) proposed a slight alteration in the horopter geometry of the V-M circle by assuming that the optical node and the center of rotation were located anterior to the geometrical center. Although this gave more accurate measurements, Gulick and Lawson (1976) claimed that it must also be rejected because the optical node is on the primary visual axis 17 millimeters in front of the fovea and the center of rotation is on the primary visual axis 11 millimeters in front of the fovea. Thus the optical node is approximately 7 millimeters behind the cornea, whereas the center of rotation lies virtually at the geometrical center of the eye. With changes in fixation, the problems associated with defining or determining the geometrical horopter get even more difficult. Gulick and Lawson conclude after a careful analysis of this problem, that since a single concept of the geometrical horopter cannot accommodate eye movements, the concept has no generality. We are left with the horopter as a concept that may help us to organize our thinking, but is of little additional use. Indeed, empirical measurements of the horopter show that it does not lie on the V-M circle, but between the V-M circle and the objective frontoparallel plane. The empirical horopter is concave at near distances, becoming more and more flat as it recedes, until it becomes slightly concave at greater distances. These changes in the shape of the horopter are known as the Hering-Hillebrand deviations.

Retinal Disparity and Stereopsis

Clearly there are many points in space that supply stimulation to the two retinal surfaces. The geometry of stimulation for these points, and their corresponding perceptual outcomes, are even more complicated than that for corresponding points. Figure 11.9 illustrates these geometrical relationships. With the eyes converged and fixating at the near point F, light from another point P', not on the V-M circle, stimulates the two retinas. Since the geometrical relationships described for points on the V-M circle do not hold in this situation, the light from point P' does not stimulate corresponding points that is, the retinal points p'_l and p'_r are noncorresponding points. Such points as P' are said to stimulate disparate retinal points, and this stimulation is referred to as **retinal disparity.**

Stimulation of noncorresponding retinal points may produce one of two perceptual outcomes: (*a*) when the disparity is relatively large, the viewer will see **double images** of the nonfixated point, with the visual directions of the two images different for the two eyes; or (*b*) when the disparity is relatively small, the viewer will see P' as a single point but at a different position in depth, that is, in front of or behind the plane of the V-M circle depending on the direction of the disparity. In other words, an object that stimu-

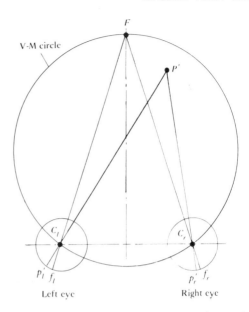

Figure 11.9 Geometrical relations that produce retinal disparity, that is, stimulation of noncorresponding retinal points. Since point P' is not on the V-M circle, retinal points P'_l and P'_r do not correspond.

lates corresponding points is seen as single and cannot be seen as double, whereas an object that stimulates noncorresponding points may be seen as single but at a different position in depth or as double.

Stereoscopic depth refers to the generation of the perception of relative depth solely from stimulation of disparate retinal points. This phenomenon was first demonstrated unequivocally by Charles Wheatstone (1838), who identified and defined the visual disparities produced by binocular viewing that produced both depth and singleness of vision. He invented a **stereoscope,** a device that permitted separate presentation of the right- and left-eye half-images. He was able to demonstrate that the visual disparity of importance in binocular vision was the lateral separation in the retinal images of fixated and nonfixated contours (Fig. 11.10).

The sign or direction of disparity will depend on the fixation point. By convention, we say there is "**un-crossed**" disparity when the nearer of two points is fixated and "**crossed**" disparity when the farther of

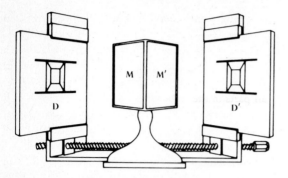

Figure 11.10 The Wheatstone mirror stereoscope. The disparate drawings *DD′* are seen by means of mirrors *MM′*. (After Boring, 1942.)

two points is fixated. Another way to organize these relationships is to realize that uncrossed disparities arise from stimulation by any point outside the V-M circle and crossed disparities arise from stimulation by any point within the V-M circle. The mechanism that produced stereoscopic depth perception must therefore keep track of both direction and amount of disparity.

As illustrated in Figure 11.11, these relationships can be readily observed. Place the index fingers of each hand directly in front of the nose, one behind the other and about 25 centimeters apart. Fixate the nearer finger tip but observe the far finger. The rear finger should be seen as double. Note also that the fixated finger does not appear to move when the eyes are opened and closed alternately. Thus, not only is

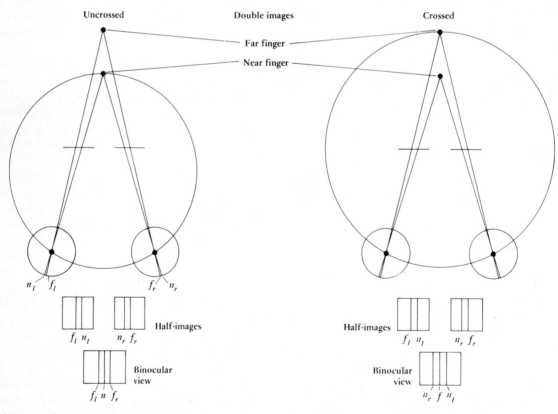

Figure 11.11 The geometry associated with crossed and uncrossed images when viewing two fingers at different distances from the head. Fixation on the near finger results in uncrossed images of the far finger; fixation on the far finger results in crossed images of the near finger.

the fixated finger seen as single, it is seen as in a single visual direction, that is, in the same visual direction for each eye. The double images of the far finger should appear to move when the eyes are opened and closed alternately. This is due to the fact that they are seen in a different visual direction for each eye. Close the left eye and observe that the right eye is seeing the image on the right side of the near finger. Now close the right eye and observe that the left eye image is on the left side of the near finger. These images are uncrossed. To see crossed images, change the point of fixation to the rear finger and repeat the operations.

Stereopsis occurs over the entire binocular visual field—it is not confined to the region about the point of fixation. It has been demonstrated in dim illumination and therefore works with rods as well as with cones. Because of the geometrical and anatomical relationships involved, stereopsis provides information for relative depth only for objects up to about 135 meters from the viewer. Stereoscopic acuity is greatest near the fovea and generally follows the decrease in visual acuity with peripheral angles.

Binocular disparity over the entire retinal surfaces provides a source of information about the layout of space. For example, if you look at a flat wall in the fronto-parallel plane, every point on the surface of the wall will be on the horopter. Light reflected from the wall will project images in the two eyes that fall on corresponding retinal points. There will be no disparity, crossed or uncrossed, and the wall will look flat. If you fixate on a point in space in front of the wall, then all points on the surface of the wall will create uncrossed disparities over the entire retinal surface. The retinal disparity between any two corresponding points will be the same for all pairs of corresponding points. The equal amounts of disparity over the entire retinal surface results again in a perception of a flat wall, although now it is seen as farther away than the fixation point.

Consider now looking at a natural scene, with surfaces and objects at various distances from you. If you fixate some particular point in the scene, say 3 meters from you, then that point will be represented in the center of each fovea with no disparity. All other points also 3 meters away will project onto corre-

sponding points and no disparity will exist between those parts of the images in the two retinas. All parts of the scene closer than 3 meters will be imaged with crossed disparity, with a greater amount of disparity the closer the part of the scene is to the eyes. Likewise, all parts of the scene farther away than 3 meters will create uncrossed disparity between the two images, with greater amounts of disparity the farther away the points are from the eyes.

If you now shift fixation to some other plane in the scene, the specific disparities from each point in the scene will be altered, but the same patterns will be preserved—points farther than fixation will have increasingly larger uncrossed disparities; there will be no disparity for points at a distance equal to the fixation distance; and there will be increasingly larger uncrossed disparities for points progressively closer to the eye than the fixation point. The same types of changes occur if you move to some other viewing place.

What has been described is a perspective transformation of disparity given by the direction and amount of disparity, referred to a zone of zero disparity at fixation. The magnitude of the disparity is proportional to the relative distances from fixation and the sign (crossed or uncrossed) indicates whether it is nearer or farther away. Whenever the eyes are fixed on a scene in depth, the disparities between the two retinal images are directly proportional to the relative distances of all visible parts of the scene, irrespective of the position occupied by the perceiver, or the place in the scene being fixated.

Panum's Area   The region about the V-M circle in which retinal disparity produces singleness of vision with an associated apparent depth difference is known as **Panum's area.** Specifically, what Panum (1858) found was that for every point in one eye, there is a corresponding "circle of sensation" in the other eye, such that, when corresponding circles of sensation are stimulated, the perception of a single object may result. That is, Panum found that the images of objects that fall within Panum's fusional areas give rise to the perception of a single object with one primary subjective visual direction, even though the images may fall upon different retinal loci within the two eyes. In the fusion of disparate images, either (a) one of the primary subjective visual directions disappears and the visual direction of the fused image is that of the other eye or (b) both primary subjective visual directions of the monocular images are replaced by a new subjective visual direction lying between the two. This shift has been called "directional difference," "lateral displacement," or "functional displacement." The question of whether displacement of direction invariably accompanies stereopsis or even causes stereoscopic depth will be discussed along with theories of stereopsis below.

The diameters of Panum's fusional areas have been measured as about 0.05 millimeters or the width of 15 to 20 cones. The dimensions of Panum's fusional areas as a function of peripheral visual angle are shown in Figure 11.12. It is clear that with increasing pe-

ripheral visual angle, the size of the fusional areas increases. Ogle also measured the limiting values for the three different kinds of stereo depth perception as a function of peripheral angle. Thus, with the discovery of Panum's areas, the horopter could no longer be conceived of as a plane from which all points are seen as single for a given fixation. Instead, it must have a certain amount of depth—with the size of the region of binocular single vision surrounding the horopter growing larger, the more the eyes approach a parallel position.

Figure 11.13, from Ogle, shows these relationships, suggesting that the character of stereoscopic depth perception changes directly with the magnitude of disparity and that the range of disparity values for any given type of stereoscopic depth increases with increasing peripheral angle. With small uncrossed disparities, viewers reported fusion and depth. As the magnitude of the uncrossed disparity was increased, the observers reported that the disparate object was seen as single and it appeared to move progressively behind the fixation point—fused "patent" stereopsis. As the disparity was further increased, the viewers re-

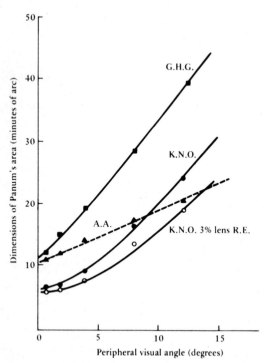

Figure 11.12 Dimensions of Panum's fusional areas as a function of peripheral visual angle for four subjects. With increasing peripheral angle, the size of the fusional areas increases. (Ogle, 1964.)

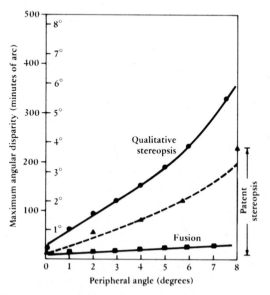

Figure 11.13 Maximum angular disparity as a function of peripheral angle for fusion, patent stereopsis, and qualitative stereopsis. (Ogle, 1952.)

ported a strong sense of depth, even though the disparate object appeared double and the separation between the double images increased with increasing disparity—"patent" stereopsis with double images. With still further increases in disparity, the viewers reported that the previously vivid depth impression disappeared, yet they could still report that the two images appeared unmistakenly behind the fixation point—"qualitative" stereopsis (Ogle, 1952). This experiment also clearly illustrated the point that fusion is not necessary for stereo depth to be perceived.

Contour and Stereopsis

Since the days of Wheatstone, it has been thought that stimulation by disparate contours was the necessary and sufficient stimulus for the perception of stereoscopic depth. This doctrine has been challenged recently by the demonstration that retinal disparity of dot patterns is a sufficient stimulus for stereoscopic depth.

Julesz (1971) used a computer to generate a textured pattern of "dots" within a two-dimensional matrix. Each cell of a 100 × 100 cell matrix was either filled (blackened) or left blank on the basis of a random sequence. This random-dot matrix served as a stimulus for one eye. The pattern for the other eye was identical, except that all the dots that fell within a central rectangular matrix were shifted one column horizontally. This procedure left the relational qualities of the dots unaltered within the submatrix and also within

the surround, while giving all the dots of the submatrix a one-column crossed disparity. A random-dot stereogram with a rectangular submatrix is shown in Figure 11.14.

Stereoscopic viewing of a random-dot stereogram of this sort results in the perception of a central rectangular surface at a different depth from that of the background. The surface is seen either in front of or behind the background depending on whether the disparities of the dots are crossed or uncrossed. The rectangular surface will have sharp contours separating it from the background. Stereoscopic depth can therefore be produced solely from disparities of texture. Contours are not necessary for stereopsis. It should be emphasized that, when viewed binocularly or monocularly, the two monocular half-images individually possess neither depth nor familiarity information—they contain no extended linear contours, meaningful patterns, or recognizable global forms. The identifiable form is perceived only when the stereograms are viewed stereoscopically.

Gulick and Lawson (1976) identified and studied a number of parameters of random-dot stereograms to see how they affected perceived depth. The two major parameters related to dot density were global density and matrix density. Global density is the number of matrix cells per unit solid angle, and matrix density is the percentage of cells filled. Figure 11.15 shows the frequency of reports of perceived surface depth when twelve observers viewed each of 24 random-dot

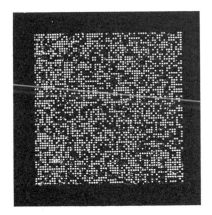 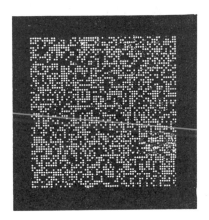

Figure 11.14   A random-dot stereogram with rectangular central submatrix.

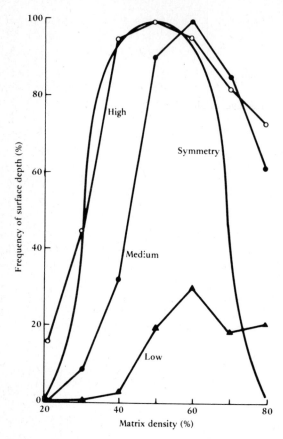

Figure 11.15 Frequency of perceived surface depth as a function of matrix density for low, medium, and high levels of global density—100, 400, and 900 cells per degree of solid visual angle. (Gulick & Lawson, 1976.)

stereograms five times as a function of matrix density for three levels of global density. It seems clear that the perception of surface depth reaches a maximum when the matrix density of 50 percent, regardless of global density of the stereogram. That is, the number of cells per unit solid angle is relatively unimportant in producing the perception of depth from random-dot stereograms. What is important is the proportion of cells filled (and unfilled). Presumably, the greatest amount of information can be carried by the matrix when half the cells are filled (and half empty). With different proportions, there is less opportunity for disparity information to be conveyed.

Another important parameter identified by Gul-

ick and Lawson is the degree to which the two half-images are correlated. Perfect **binocular correlation** is defined as that stimulus situation that produces a dot in one half-image analogous to a dot in the other half-image. The simplest example of perfect binocular correlation would be when the two half-images were the same random dot patterns. When retinal disparity is introduced by shifting a central submatix, the binocular correlation is not necessarily altered. It remains the same as long as each dot in one half-image has a dot in the other half-image with which to form a pair. Thus, binocularly correlated pairs can be presented with or without disparity. For example, in a random-dot stereogram like that illustrated in Fig. 11.14, the pairs comprising the surrounding matrix are all without disparity whereas the pairs of the control submatrix all have identical disparity.

Figure 11.16 shows what happens to the percep-

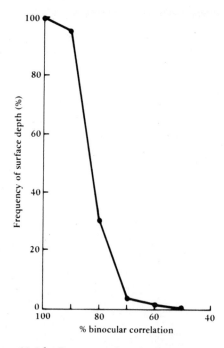

Figure 11.16 Frequency of reported surface depth as a function of the percentage of binocular correlation of dots in a random-dot stereogram with global density of 400 cells per unit solid angle and matrix density of 50 percent. (Gulick & Lawson, 1976.)

tion of surface depth when the percentage of binocular correlation is varied. With a moderate amount of global density (400 cells per degree of solid visual angle), and a matrix density of 50 percent, the degree of binocular correlation was manipulated, varying the percentage of dots in the submatrix that were shifted between 100 percent and 50 percent. As the percentage of binocular correlation decreased, there was a rapid decrease in the report of the perception of surface depth. Whereas a stable surface with sharp stereo-induced contours was reported when there was 100 percent binocular correlation, a reduction of as little as 20 percent in level of correlation resulted in a severe reduction in the perceived surface depth. The observers could report the shape of the central submatrix correctly, but the form had no surface properties or stereo contours. Subjects did, however, report many individual dots seen in depth. Even more interesting is the fact that the disparity of the individual dots was not always coded correctly. The dots in the stereograms were always shifted to give them a crossed disparity. But with less than perfect binocular correlation, the disparity was coded as either crossed or uncrossed depending on what was apparently random juxtapositions of the dots. This was most pronounced in the 50 percent condition, where observers reported that they saw dots lying in one of three planes—in front of, within, or behind the plane of the background. Apparently, the lowered binocular correlation did not result in the perception of surfaces in depth because the density of dots within each of the three planes was too low to define the forms.

With perfect binocular correlation, all the dots in the submatrix were seen in a single closer plane because they were all coded as having a single level of crossed disparity. Moreover, the density within the single plane was sufficient to allow the system to abstract a form and thereby facilitate the perception of surface depth. With low binocular correlation, the submatrix dots became spread in depth, with each of the three planes having about one-third of the density of dots. Since the density of dots in the stimuli was the same regardless of the level of binocular correlation, the density per depth plane—the cyclopean density—appears to be the factor of importance. Gulick

and Lawson therefore concluded that surface depth depends on the density of dots in a given stereoscopic plane, rather than on retinal density itself. This is a higher order variable, since cyclopean density is determined by global and matrix densities interacting with the level of binocular correlation.

Stereoscopic Contours In viewing random-dot stereograms, the central surface not only appears to be in a different depth plane from that of the background, but it emerges as a surface with sharp contours. Gulick and Lawson (1976) noted that the contours appeared to be between the rows and columns of the dots that showed a discontinuity in depth. These **stereoscopic contours** separated the depth planes functionally, although they appeared to be a part of (belonged to) the closer surface.

Gulick and Lawson proposed that these contours were of a class different from those produced by abrupt luminance gradients on the retina, because they occur in the absence of such gradients. In order to study the degree of contour perception they devised a procedure for establishing a subjective scale of contour sharpness individually for each observer. In establishing the scale, the observer first saw five rectangular areas, arrayed horizontally in a fronto-parallel plane. The leftmost rectangle had no contour within it and the rightmost had a very sharp horizontal contour dividing it in half. The subject's first task was to divide the middle rectangle in half with a horizontal contour that the subject judged to be halfway between the two extreme stimuli in contour clarity. This was accomplished by adjustment of the relative luminances of the two halves of the rectangle. Then, with the middle field set at the subjective halfway value, the subjects proceeded to bisect the two remaining intervals in a similar fashion. This established a five-point subjective scale for contour clarity. During the remainder of the experiment, the subjects could refer back to their subjective scale when making judgments about the clarity of the stereoscopic contours they were rating.

The subjects now viewed random-dot stereograms that varied in matrix and global density. The results showed that a contour was never reported in the absence of surface depth, but surface depth was seen in some cases when contour was not. The perception of stereo contours was facilitated by increases in both global and matrix densities, but low global contours never produced sharp contours. Medium and high global densities produced sharp contours when the matrix density was 50 percent or more. Gulick and Lawson concluded that there was a strong relationship between stereoscopically produced forms and stereoscopically induced contours. When the defining properties are weak, the disparate dots of the submatrix appear in depth but there is no surface depth or stereo contours. When the properties are stronger, the elements of the submatrix are all shifted into a single stereo plane different from the surround. This shift in surface appears to be a necessary condition for the perception of stereo contours. It does not appear to be a sufficient condition, however. The clarity of the contour increases as the ambiguity of the stereo match decreases.

Binocular Interposition

When a close object partially covers or occludes the view of a more distant object, we describe the information as occlusion or interposition (see Chapter 8). Interposition is usually listed as one of the pictorial cues to depth, suggesting that its function is purely monocular. But there also is a binocular interposition that, combined with disparity information, may be important in determining the perception of relative depth of surfaces.

Figure 11.17 shows a stereogram containing two squares of dots, one surrounding the other. The inner square of dots carries a crossed disparity relative to the outer square, but there is no interposition information present—that is, there is nothing in the stimulus to indicate that the inner square is covering or occluding part of the outer square. When viewed stereoscopically, only the inner square of dots appears in a closer depth plane—the surface enclosed by the dots does not appear in the closer plane even though this form is clearly defined and carries a crossed disparity equal to that of the closer dots (Gulick & Lawson, 1967). While the closer square of dots could have been seen on a nearer surface, there was no information in the display (that is, interposition information) that required the perception of surface to account for differences in the half-images. Clearly, then, retinal disparity is necessary for the perception of the relative depth of surfaces from stereoscopic stimuli, but it is not sufficient. Additional information is required in

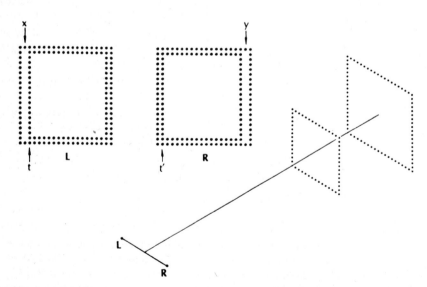

Figure 11.17 Stereograms of two square patterns in which the smaller (inner) square contains a crossed disparity relative to the larger, more distant, square, but no interposition information is provided. When viewed stereoscopically, only the inner square of dots appears closer in depth. (Gulick & Lawson, 1976.)

the stereoscopic display for surface depth to be perceived.

Figure 11.18 shows a stereogram containing the same disparity information as that of Figure 11.17 but with the addition of interposition information, that is, certain columns of dots are present in the left-eye half-image that are not present in the right-eye half-image, and vice versa. Stereo viewing of this stimulus results in the perception of a central square surface with sharp stereo contours interposed between the observer and a matrix of dots located in a single, more distant plane. The binocular alignment of the dot configurations that provides disparity information also produces interposition information. The only way to combine these different aspect of the stereoscopic view is in terms of occlusion of the more distant surface by the nearer surface.

Stereo Contours and Homogeneous Space

In all the stereograms illustrated thus far, the contours of the near surfaces followed closely the disparity information supplied, but there is no reason to believe that stereo contours are always determined in this way. Figure 11.19 shows a set of stereograms used

by Gulick and Lawson (1976) to study the factors affecting stereo contours. The first stereogram provides disparity and interposition information for the perception of a near, homogeneous square occluding part of a more distant dot matrix surface. The second provides disparity and interposition information for the perception of two concentric circular surfaces similar to the squares. There is nothing unusual about the fact that all viewers report the perception of interposed surfaces with sharp contours when viewing these stereograms.

The lower two stereograms in Figure 11.19 are somewhat different. They provide disparity and interposition information for only part of the near figures and surfaces. The visual system could conceivably produce perceptual outcomes in a number of ways, the two simplest being to finish the construction of a total "good figure" such as a square or circle, with the resulting perception being essentially the same as the two previous stereograms, or it could connect the endpoints of the disparate elements with straight contours that cross the homogeneous areas. All subjects reported the latter outcome—straight-line stereo contours were reported crossing the homogeneous field with a sharpness no different from that of the bounded

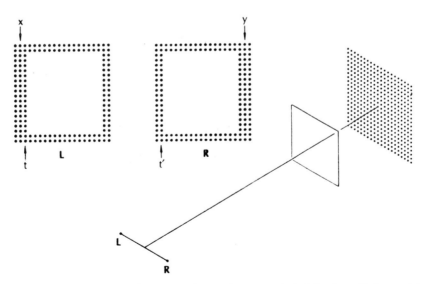

Figure 11.18 Stereograms of two square dot patterns in which the smaller (nearer) square carries a crossed disparity relative to the larger (more distant) square. The columns of dots are not included and provide interposition information, that is, the columns of the more distant matrix are selectively occluded. (Gulick & Lawson, 1976.)

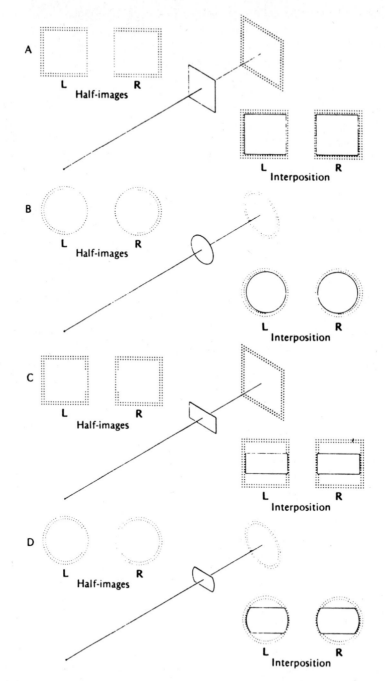

Figure 11.19 Stereograms for producing the perception of a homogeneous near surface occluding a more distant surface of dots. The perceptual experience of the observers is shown in perspective view and in fronto-parallel plane view. (Gulick & Lawson, 1976.)

contours produced by dot disparity. Thus, the shape of the binocularly perceived homogeneous surface can be different from the shapes of the homogeneous areas in the monocular half-images, as long as the outcome is consistent with the information in the half-images.

In a follow-up study, Gulick and Lawson varied the amount of structured curvature in the half-images and found that, except where the stimuli were ambiguous, straight-line contours were always perceived in homogeneous space. They concluded that straight-line contours are primary in the binocular visual system, even when they produce shapes that are more complex than those that would be produced by curved contours. Although this is an apparent contradiction of the Gestalt laws for figure perception, it may not be a contradiction of the rule of simplicity when the stereoscopic information is taken into account. When the information in the stimulus requires the perception of an interposed surface to account for the difference in the half-images, the lateral boundaries of the surface appear to be set in such a way as to minimize disparity.

An evaluation of the effect of curved contours produced by luminance gradients on the perception of contours produced by disparity was also performed using the stereograms illustrated in Figure 11.20. The upper part of the stereograms provide sharp disparate luminance gradients that produce the perception of a sharp curved stereoscopic contour. The lower part of the stereograms were dot patterns that provide disparity information that could be organized as continuations of the upper curved contours so that a complete configuration would be perceived. This stereogram produced the perception of a 180-degree arc on the top and a half octagon on the bottom, that is, straight-line stereo contours were perceived in the area where there were no luminance gradients.

THEORIES OF STEREOPSIS

Fusion

Fusion is clearly the most widely accepted theory of steropsis. As a simple general statement, **fusion** merely emphasizes the singleness of vision—of stereoscopic viewing—by suggesting that two points

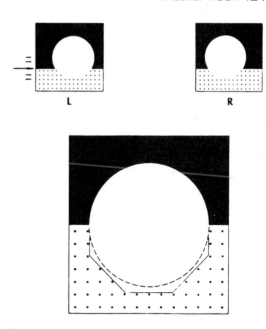

Figure 11.20 Stereograms for comparing stereoscopic contours with contours produced by luminance gradients. A representation of the perceptual outcome is shown below. (Gulick & Lawson, 1976.)

stimulating the two eyes are seen as one point—that is, they are fused. Fusion should not be confused with summation, the view that the resulting cyclopean view is simply due to the superposition of the two retinal images and a sum of these two images. **Binocular rivalry** shows that this cannot be the case. Suppose a vertical line is presented to one eye and a horizontal line to the other (see Figure 11.25). If the visual system simply summated these stimuli, the perceptual outcome would be of a cross consisting of each of the lines. This is never the case, however. Stimulating the eyes in this fashion produces binocular rivalry—the perception of one line or the other, but not both, in the area where the lines cross.

Fusion (as differentiated from summation) not only implies that there is an emergent object that results from stimulating the two eyes, but also that the visual direction of the object must be different from that of either of the eyes. Indeed, it is generally reported that the visual direction of a point seen stereoscopically is different from that of the point seen with either eye alone—a phenomenon that has been taken by some theorists as evidence for the occurrence of fusion.

Modern fusional theorists usually assume that there is an isomorphic relation between the perceptual event and a neurological event. They suggest that the fused image that is produced when stimulated by disparate retinal images is isomorphic to a neurological fusion that occurs somewhere in a projection field in the brain. For example, theorists such as Charnwood (1951), Linkz (1952), and Dodwell and Engel (1963)

assume that there is a point-to-point projection from the retina to the cortex such that some fixed pathways correspond to specific points on the two retinas. The theory asserts that these pathways meet somewhere in the brain where three-dimensional space is topologically represented.

Figure 11.21 shows a possible projection-fusion array suggested by Engel (Dodwell, 1970), but it is similar to almost all the fusional models proposed. The projection field contains a line of cells that signal when corresponding points are stimulated. Other

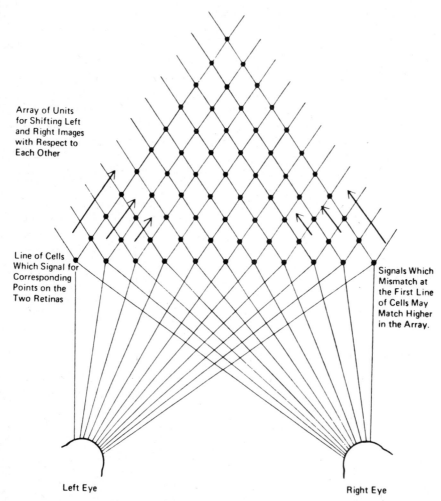

Array of Units
for Shifting Left
and Right Images
with Respect to
Each Other

Line of Cells
Which Signal for
Corresponding
Points on the
Two Retinas

Signals Which
Mismatch at
the First Line
of Cells May
Match Higher
in the Array.

Left Eye

Right Eye

Figure 11.21 A typical "projection fusion" array model to account for stereoscopic depth perception and temporal summation. This array was proposed by Engel. (See Dodwell, 1970.)

lines signal when a mismatch at the first line may match at higher levels. Dodwell (1970) improved on this type of model by providing a preprocessing unit to account for the locking of the eyes at a particular state of convergence. This model is depicted in Figure 11.22. The points on the receptor surface, A_1, A_2, ..., A_n and A'_1, A'_2, ..., A'_n represent similar receptive fields in the two eyes. The row of units α_1, α_2, ..., α_n represents a set of cells that are activated by the fields. These cells signal stimulation of corresponding points or elements to a higher unit that has inhibiting connections to the oculomotor system that controls the convergence of the eyes. Since the receptor units represent corresponding points in the two eyes, the system functions to bring the two monocular fields into registry in terms of congruent patterns on the two retinas. If the eyes are not correctly converged, the inhibitory system will continue to change convergence until one or more of the units inhibits it. This will occur when some pattern elements are congruent

for the two eyes at a given amount of convergence. If a number of pattern elements are in register, the output from the inhibitor system will be strong, and the eye will be "locked" into that convergence state.

Figure 11.23 shows Dodwell's (1970) model for a "binocular processing unit." Given that the stimulating elements such as A_1, A'_1 of Figure 11.22 are in register and that the system is locked, the system analyzes and evaluates the inputs of the a_{11}, ... a_{1n}, ... a_{nn}. These units detect contours that are congruent in the two eyes. Thus, a feature in the position a_1 is evaluated with respect to features over a much wider region, a'_1, ..., a'_n, in a similar part of the retina of the other eye.

Suppose a simple pattern like a vertical line is focused on a_1 and fires the set a_{11}, a_{12}, ..., a_{1n}. If there is no corresponding input from the other eye, the contour is detected at position a_1 in the direction corresponding to the monocular visual direction of a_1, and as at the same depth as the reference plane. If,

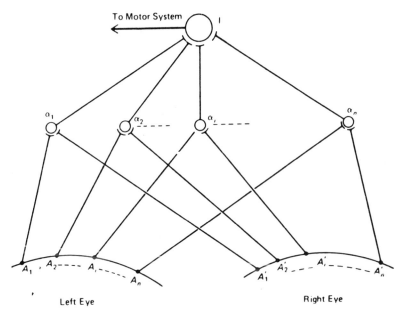

Figure 11.22   Dodwell's (1970) "convergence-locking" model. $A_1A'_1$, $A_2A'_2$, ..., $A_nA'_n$ are similar retinal receptive fields in corresponding parts of the two eyes. α_1, α_2, ... α_n are cortical detectors that signal stimulation of corresponding parts. Outputs from these units are summated

at I, which has inhibitory connections to the system controlling eye movements. When similar features are detected at the two eyes, the system locks, and processing stereoscopic depth can begin.

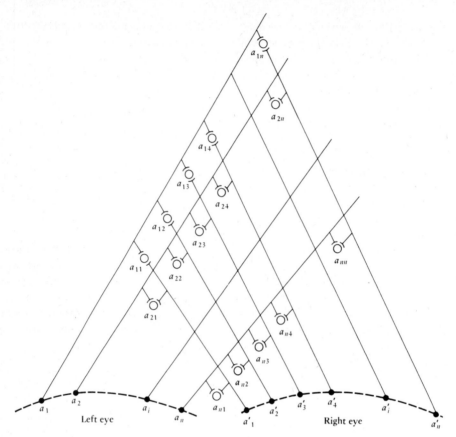

Figure 11.23 Dodwell's (1970) "binocular processing unit." Points $a_1, \ldots, a_n$ and $a'_1, \ldots, a'_n$ are similar retinal receptive fields in corresponding parts of the two eyes. $a_{11}, \ldots, a_{nn}$ are their cortical detectors. Maximum response from particular cortical units will be dependent on the degree of disparity between similar pattern elements on the two eyes.

however, there is a vertical contour that also stimulates the other eye in the region $a'_1, \ldots, a'_n$, it will signal "on" for the one unit of $a'_1, \ldots, a'_n$ being stimulated, and "off" for the surrounding neighbors that are in this same receptive field. Therefore, only one member of the set $a_{11}, a_{12}, \ldots, a_{1n}$ will be activated. All the others will be inhibited by mutually antagonistic responses for "on" and "off" portions of receptive fields for a single unit, even though the fields are in different eyes. Thus, the unit in the a_{ij} set with the greatest output provides information about differences in depth relative to the "lock" established by AA'. If it signals points that correspond, the depth is that of the reference plane; otherwise it is in front of

or behind the reference plane depending on whether the disparity is crossed or uncrossed (simply coded as the direction from the diagonal of the a_{ij} matrix). Dodwell suggested further, that the apparent visual direction will be a compromise between the visual direction of a_1 and whichever a'_i is activated. The output of this binocular processing unit provides an analog of the depth of pattern elements relative to the reference plane as well as a mechanism for mediating the change from monocular to binocular visual directions.

Now the binocular processing unit is indeed a simplification. But Dodwell suggested that if other contour elements in the visual field are processed in a similar way, the local stereoscopic depth processing of this type is consistent with what we know about Panum's fusional areas. Dodwell proposed further that these units are segments of an even larger array with these elements being understood as "pattern-element processors" or parts of a "primary detection" system. The larger arrays would process for different pattern features or for similar features in different parts of the visual field, and would require the parallel operation of these binocular processing units. These relationships are illustrated in Figure 11.24.

Although the predominant view favors fusion theory at the present, there are a number of reasons to remain skeptical. First, there is the existence of double images and the fact that stereopsis can be achieved even when double images can be seen. Thus, fusion may not be necessary for stereopsis. This point is given further weight by demonstrations of binocular rivalry where fusion does not occur but depth is still seen. Figure 11.25 illustrates a case of simple binocular rivalry. Orthogonal contours on corresponding regions

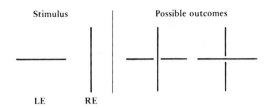

Figure 11.25 When the stimuli at the left are viewed stereoscopically, the result is invariably one of the two "rivalry" outcomes illustrated at the right. Frequently, the perception will alternate between the two. Part of the figure of the dominant eye seems to "suppress" the neighboring contour from the other eye.

of the two eyes results in "suppression" of one of the contours in the area of crossing. Frequently, the outcome will be an alteration between the two percepts, but a complete cross is never seen. Finally, there is the problem of the shift in visual directions. Whether or not this shift occurs and whether or not it invariably accompanies the perception of stereo depth is still an open empirical question.

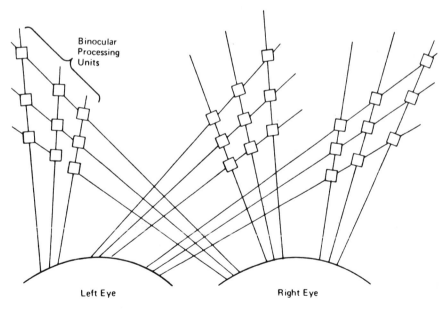

Figure 11.24 Hierarchical arrangements of Dodwell's "binocular processing units" into a projection-fusion array similar to that of Figure 11.21. Each unit now corresponds to an intersecting pair of transmission lines from the retinal output. Only three groups of units are shown, but a large number must operate simultaneously.

Suppression

These difficulties with the demonstration of some of the fundamental findings expected from fusion theory, have prompted some theorists to propose modern versions of **suppression theory.** Kaufman performed a series of experiments which suggested that a suppression explanation was more appropriate. In one, Kaufman (1964) constructed stereograms from matrices of typed letters by shifting a central matrix of letters one column laterally. Stereo depth perception was produced with these matrices, indicating that the pattern elements of the submatrix could vary in shape and still produce stereo depth. Using stereograms like these, Kaufman and Pitblado (1965) found that steropsis occurred in some cases even though the letters superposed were very different in shape. In this case rivalry also occurred, that is, at each moment, the perceptual outcome contained the letters from the stimulus to one eye or to the other eye. There was no fusion or summation for these dissimilar letters, suggesting that, at any given moment, one eye was dominant and suppressed the image from the other eye.

Simple suppression theory states that images near the reference plane are seen as single because input from one of the eyes suppresses the input from the other eye. This perceptual outcome is the same—singleness of vision—as that of fusional theory. The two theories differ, however, in their predictions with respect to visual directions. Suppression theory predicts that the monocular visual directions are maintained, whereas fusion theory predicts that the subjective visual direction of the perceptual outcome is a compromise of the fusion process. A more sophisticated version of suppression theory takes into account the receptive field structure of the visual system. In this view, the final binocular image is a composite of features—bits and pieces of contours—that may have originated in either eye.

SUMMARY

The addition of a second eye adds a great deal of information that can be obtained from the optic array. Stimulation of corresponding areas produces the perception of a single object in space at the same distance as the plane containing the fixation point. Stimulation of noncorresponding areas can produce the perception of either double or single images, and these can be seen either with or without an associated depth. Although contour disparities can play an important role in stereoscopic depth, they are not necessary for stereopsis to occur—depth can be obtained from a stimulus containing disparity among the elements of random-dot matrices. With the appropriate patterns, surfaces are seen at different relative depths, and contours belonging to these surfaces appear where none existed in the stimulus. Thus, surface and contour may be the result of stereoscopic depth rather than a cause. Finally, although the supression theory of stereopsis has gained some supporters, the consensus still appears to favor the fusion theory.

SUGGESTED READINGS

Gulick and Lawson (1976) provide an excellent review of the history of stereposis as well as detailed accounts of their experiments. They also give a detailed and lucid analysis of the horopter problem. Dodwell (1970) provides a good discussion of the theories of stereopsis, including the evidence from neurophysiology. Sekuler's chapter in the *Annual Review of Psychlogy* (1974) summarizes the more recent studies.

Chapter 12

Perceiving the Layout of Space in Photographs and Art

Pictures and photographs of scenes are clearly flat. They are "painted" on a flat surface and are often surrounded by a frame. We have no trouble perceiving them as flat. Even so, we also have no trouble perceiving the painted landscape, recognizing the objects portrayed, and perceiving the spatial arrangement of the objects as though we were looking at the scene itself. We shall refer to these two ways of perceiving a picture as its two realities: the **three-dimensional reality**—perceiving as if the picture were a window that opened onto a scene, and the **two-dimensional reality**—perceiving the picture as an object in its own right, as a flat surface with texture, solidity, surface colors, and a frame. Perceivers treat both these realities as commonplace and can alternate between them as their mood dictates.

This chapter explores the nature of these realities and contrasts them with the perception of natural scenes. It describes the kind of information contained in the light that is reflected from the flat surfaces of pictures and how that information is related to the information in light reflected from real scenes. We shall see how the notion of the dual reality of pictures can be used to better understand the rules for constructing representational pictures; why some pictures (but few natural scenes) create visual illusions in size

or orientation; and finally, what conventions are used to represent pictorially different kinds of realities.

STIMULUS ANALYSIS OF PICTURE SURFACES

In our previous discussion of the information reflected from real scenes to the eyes, we described the perspective transformations generated by objects at different distances and orientations, the motion perspective generated when we move our eyes or head when looking at a scene, and the binocular disparity between the images on the two retinas. These may be considered three scales of space because they provide information about space over the entire retinal surface (Haber, 1979).

Following the same type of analysis, consider the information from flat surfaces, including pictures. If you view a flat wall perpendicular to the line of sight, all three scales of space will indicate the flatness. The surface scale will be uniform—it will contain no perspective changes, no vanishing point, and no texture gradients. The motion scale will also be uniform—no matter how you move, there are no transformations indicating depth. Instead, all parts of the image of the wall surface move together. Further, the binocular scale shows no disparity anywhere—both retinal images will be the same because no part of the scene is at a different distance compared to any other part. Finally, all the non-scale sources of information about depth such as interposition, adjacency, or illumination gradients, will indicate flatness. In short, a great deal of information is present to support the perception of a flat surface.

What happens when, instead of looking at a wall, the flat surface is a photograph or a representational painting of a three-dimensional scene? To analyze this stimulus, we need first to digress slightly in order to describe the perspective rules a painter uses to create a representational painting. These rules were described in detail by Leonardo da Vinci in his notebooks (Richter, 1970) dating from the end of the fifteenth century.

Leonardo's rules are simple in principle. A landscape painter first chooses a vantage point from which to paint his picture. Then he places a sheet of glass between his eye and the scene so that he is looking through the glass (Fig. 12.1). He then traces the scene he sees through the glass onto the glass. The result is that nearby objects are painted in more saturated colors with sharper boundaries, coarser texture, and

Figure 12.1 A drawing from Dürer, showing an artist using glass to create a painting.

so forth. Far objects appear higher up on the glass and are relatively smaller, paler, and finer in texture. Lines that are parallel in the scene in a direction away from the painter are drawn as converging upward on the glass, toward a vanishing point. After the artist completes the sketch on the glass, he then reproduces it on canvas. The result is a two-dimensional representation of the three-dimensional scene. It represents the scene in the sense that the surface scale of space, entered on the glass as variations in perspective, in texture, and so on, reproduces the luminance and spectral discontinuities in the retinal pattern (except for blurring away from the center, which Leonardo knew nothing about).

Leonardo's rules do not end with the geometry of perspective. Filling in the texture and colors when the sketch on the glass is transferred to the canvas is not a simple process. Pirenne (1970) and Hochberg (1978) note, for example, that the scene reflects a far greater range of contrasts than can any set of pigments on a canvas. This has led to other painting rules involving induced colors, juxtaposition of shadows, and edge enhancement, to name only a few. But the principles are the same: all are used to produce a two-dimensional pattern that can produce the same retinal pattern as that reflected from the three-dimensional scene when viewed from the correct position.

A modern camera produces a print that also meets Leonardo's painters' rules, at least with respect to all its visual edges. The print will have far greater restrictions of intensity and spectral contrast than did the scene itself, though some film emulsions and development processes do a better job than others. Except for trick photography or special lenses, photographs are the same as representational paintings (see Rosinski, 1977, for a discussion of telephoto effects).

Given the geometrical exactness of Leonardo's rules, it should be possible to construct a two-dimensional picture surface that would reflect the same pattern of light to the eye as would the real three-dimensional scene from which the painting was made. If this is the case, then photographs and properly painted representational paintings would have a three-dimensional reality and would be confused with the scenes they represent. However, pictures are not confused with real scenes. If all that is seen is the picture surface itself, with no part of the surrounding wall or frame visible, and if only one eye is used, while the viewer is stationary and stands in the correct place from which to view the picture, then in theory, it should be difficult to determine whether one is looking at a picture of a scene or the scene itself. The degree of confusion should be determined by the degree of precision with which the picture or photograph reproduces the range of intensity and spectral contrasts.

Hochberg (1962) had subjects view real scenes with one eye through an immobile peephole covered with a piece of cellophane. He found that viewers could not tell whether they were looking at a real scene or at a picture of a scene. Hagen (1976) got the same result using a comparable procedure (see below). But we never look at pictures or at scenes in this way. Therefore, there must be additional information that can tell us that the picture is flat but the scene is not.

Information Regarding the Flatness of Pictures

There are three different potential sources of information about flatness: the flat frame and surround against which the picture is viewed, the picture surface itself, and the failure by the painter or photographer to match the surface information in the picture to that of the real scene. The picture frame and the flat wall on which it is hung provide indications that the picture is flat since all the surface information from the frame and wall is perfectly correlated with the information from the picture surface itself. The picture surface contributes a great deal of information of flatness. We can usually see the texture of the canvas or photographic paper. If you stand directly in front of the picture, it will project a zero gradient over the surface of the retina. If you view the picture from an angle, the gradient will exactly match that of the wall surface. (The effect of flatness from texture can be minimized if you stand far enough from the picture so that the textural surface information is below acuity threshold.) Finally, to whatever extent the construction of the picture fails to mimic perfectly the pattern of the light reflections from the scene it represents, it may look flat. Typically, the range of saturations of colors and the range of contrasts are much narrower in the light reflected from pictures than from scenes. Since such effects occur in almost all paintings and photographs, this is an important source of flatness information.

With the head fixed, moving the eyes while looking at a picture will shift the location of the pattern on the retina in relation to the retinal surface, with concomitant changes in the areas of maximum clarity. The part of the picture that had been imaged with maximal clarity will not be blurred and some new part, corresponding to the new center of fixation, will be clear. If the picture is large, some part of it may now be occluded because light reflected from it is no longer impinging on the retinal surface. At the same time some part of the opposite side may now come into view.

Three different changes occur when the head moves, causing the location of the eyes to be shifted in space. First, if the eyes remain fixated on the same point in a picture but are moved in space (as, for example, when one walks past a picture while looking at a particular part), the area of maximum clarity will remain the same, but the stimulus pattern on the retina will expand on the side towards which the head moved and contract on the other side. Such expansion and contraction will be proportional to the changes in the distance between each point on the picture surface and the eyes. However, when looking at flat pictures, no transpositional changes occur even with the expansion and contraction produced by head movement. The relations among the parts of the stimulus pattern remain the same. The absence of relative changes in the luminance and spectral discontinuities when the head moves is therefore a powerful source of information that the scene is flat.

Second, if you walk past a picture but do not hold fixation, not only is there an expansion and contraction as the pattern is shifted along the retina, but also a shift of maximal clarity. There is still no relative change in the position of the discontinuities in the pattern, because there is no "in front of" or "behind" in the scene—again, information that the picture is flat.

Third, a change on the retina occurs if you move directly closer to or farther away from a picture. This movement causes the entire pattern to expand or contract, with a maximum change occurring in the part of the pattern reflected from the nearest part of the picture. As with each of the other motion-produced changes, no relative transpositional changes occur in the retinal pattern with radial motion. Every variety of observer motion before a flat picture will reveal its flatness. There is no situation in which movement can produce information that a flat picture is a window opening into a scene.

When viewing with two eyes the story is like that for motion. When looking at a flat picture straight on, there will be no disparity between the two retinal images corresponding to any part of the picture. Since this situation occurs only when all parts of the surface are equidistant from the two eyes, it must be flat. If the picture is large relative to the viewing distance, then the edges of the picture will be farther away from the eyes than the center and there will be a slight difference in the distances to the center and to the edges. This will produce a disparity between the two images regardless of where the observer is fixating on the picture surface. However, this disparity is exactly consistent with the disparity of the wall and the frame. Hence, the surface of the picture will be seen as flush with the surface of the wall. Further, there are no local disparities over the picture surface. Because no part of the picture is farther away or closer to the observer than any of its neighboring parts, the picture yields a continuously uniform gradient of disparity, indicating a flat, extended surface. If the picture is viewed from an angle, a gradient of disparity will be produced that indicates the slant of the picture surface, but there will be no local disparities.

Consequently, a flat picture cannot provide information resulting in the perception of depth when the observer moves, or uses both eyes. However, if the observer holds his head still and uses only one eye, there is both flatness and depth information available.

It is this combination of information about depth and about flatness co-existing in the retinal projection from pictures that accounts for their dual reality.

THE DUAL REALITY OF PICTURES

It is the information in pictures themselves that results in the perception of a **dual reality.** Apparently, perceivers can see either of these realities and can go back and forth between them easily. The dual reality of pictures is clearest for so-called representational pictures, especially photographs of natural scenes. Perceivers have little difficulty recognizing or matching such two-dimensional representations to the natural scenes that were their subjects. Nor do they have much trouble correctly interpreting the object information and the spatial layout in such pictures.

The dual reality of pictures had been recognized and treated quite differently by theorists, painters, and perceivers. Since the presence of the "flat" reality presumably prevents pictures from being confused with scenes they represent, some artists have explored ways of constructing a painting that minimizes the flatness and increases the scenelike qualities—even to the point of confusion of a picture with its scene. Such a painting is called *trompe l'oeil*—literally "deceiving the eye" (Fig. 12.2). Indeed, it has occasionally been suggested that picture galleries should be designed to remove as many cues to flatness as possible (Pirenne, 1970). But *trompe l'oeil* paintings aside, the dual reality of pictures affects the perception of the scene depicted and the depicted scene affects the perception of the flat picture surface. The understanding of this interaction is the basis for understanding how we perceive the layout of space from pictures.

The Stationpoint–Compensation Hypothesis

Pirenne (1970) suggested that so long as a viewer can register both the three-dimensional and the two-dimensional realities of a picture, the correct station-

Figure 12.2 *Music and Good Luck* by William Harnett, Courtesy of the Metropolitan Museum of Art, Wolfe Fund, 1963, New York.

point can be determined and the viewer can compensate for any distortion on the retina produced by an incorrect stationpoint. While one might think that the flatness of pictures would detract from the perception of the depth that they represent, Pirenne argued that it is the ability to see the flatness that allows the viewer to align himself properly in order to see the depth correctly. It is only under free binocular viewing of pictures that both realities can be perceived, and it is only under such conditions that incorrect stationpoint distortions seem to be irrelevant.

The concept of compensation is based on the notion that the particular pattern of light on the retina at any one moment in time is never perceived as such. Rather it serves only as a source of information from which to construct a representation—a perception. In

and of itself, it is not a representation of space or anything else. Once this fact is recognized, it is not difficult to understand that the retinal pattern from a picture of a scene may differ from that of the scene itself, and yet both can contain the same information leading to the same perception.

Hagen (1976) tested Pirenne's explanation by testing its corollary: reducing the information for flatness should make surface information less useful and therefore less informative about depth. Subjects viewed a picture of two unlike-sized objects, one placed near and one far (Fig. 12.3), and had to point to the larger. A correct response required correct perception of the depth relationships. Viewing was monocular through a peephole, either from the correct stationpoint or obliquely from 40 degrees to the side. To manipulate surface information, Hagen used photographic prints that have high surface information, and rear-projected transparencies, that have low surface information. The subjects were 4 years old, 7 years old, and adults. Children were tested because Hagen assumed that the compensatory mechanism requires experience and practice with viewing pictures and so should be less developed in children.

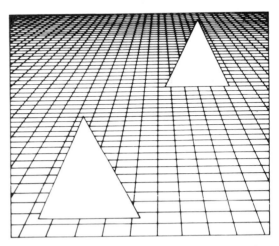

Figure 12.3 Stimulus pair in which the visual angle of the larger object is 70 percent of the visual angle of the smaller object. (Hagen, 1976.)

The results were consistent with Pirenne's hypothesis. Adults were better on slides than prints at the correct stationpoint, but not at the wrong one where the slide provided little surface information and could not help the perceiver compensate. For the 4-year-olds, accuracy was not affected by stationpoint when viewing slides but they were less accurate when viewing prints at the wrong stationpoint. Presumably this difference occurred because they could not compensate for the distortion. But Hagen's experiment did not give subjects much surface information about flatness—only the surface scale of space was available. The motion scale is probably the most powerful one both for depth in scenes and for flatness in pictures. If she had not used a peephole, but permitted free head movements, even the 4-year-olds should have been able to compensate for the oblique view of the print. Children even younger than 4 years old already have good perceptual abilities (see Chapter 13), so Hagen's results underestimate the rate of development.

What is lacking from Pirenne's hypothesis is the compensatory mechanism itself—what aspects of the surface are used to perceive depth correctly? Consider the more general perceptual compensation tasks routinely performed by perceivers: we move around while looking at a scene without the scene appearing to change, even though each successive retinal pattern undergoes massive changes. Perceivers must have ways of ignoring the particular retinal pattern of any instant in time and attending only to the commonalities of the successive patterns over time and over dif-ferent perspectives. The representations we construct of a scene or of the picture are not tied to, nor do they resemble, any one of the momentary retinal patterns that were projected from that scene or picture.

Limitations on the Dual Reality of Pictures

Leonardo's rules appear to depend on a critical picture-observer interaction. Failure to view the picture from the proper stationpoint results in a pattern on the retinal surface that is no longer isomorphic to the one on the hypothetical plate of glass. It does not contain the proper surface scale of space and local cues for the correct three-dimensional scene. Accordingly, failure of the observer to have his eye where the painter had his should lead to errors in the perception of the layout of the three-dimensionality perceived from the picture.

Farber and Rosinski (1978) have described the geometrical changes that occur under a variety of incorrect stationpoint observations. Figure 12.4 illustrates one example with a sequence of perspective drawings. The first shows the projection of light from a picture as it would be reflected to the retina when the retina is located at the correct viewing position in front of the picture. The next two drawings show how the retinal pattern changes when the retina is successively displaced to the right, so that the picture is viewed from a stationpoint to the right of the correct one. The various relationships among the luminance and spectral discontinuities become distorted—over-

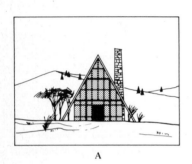

A

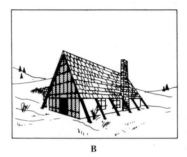

B

C

Figure 12.4 A series of drawings from progressively more oblique stationpoints.

lay is compressed, perspective is foreshortened, vanishing points of parallel lines no longer line up, and so forth.

The figure shows drawings that produce the distortions directly. The distortions are apparent. If you as viewer attempt to reproduce these effects by looking only at the first drawing in the figure and then move your own retina accordingly, the same changes in the pattern of light reaching your retina are produced as those of the successive versions of the first drawing. However, the critical difference is that you as viewer rarely notice the changes. Hagen (1976) has demonstrated experimentally that observing from the correct stationpoint is irrelevant for adults and for children when matching pictures to the three-dimensional objects they depict, and when rating the pictures for their naturalness or their pleasingness. Farber and Rosinski (1978) review most of the available evidence on the perceptual effects of viewing from the various incorrect stationpoints. Their evidence suggests that whenever the viewer is restricted to a static monocular view, what he will see depends entirely on the geometrical distortions created by the incorrect stationpoint. However, whenever the viewer can use two eyes, or move, the resulting perception often seems to be independent of the viewing point, and cannot be predicted by the geometrical distortions. Of course, if viewing is from a position that is far from the correct stationpoint, then the distortion may be obvious. Hochberg (1962) tried to make real scenes look like pictures by placing cellophane between the viewer and the scene and restricting viewing to one motionless eye. He found that when this kind of flatness information was provided, viewers could not distinguish the real scene from the picture which represented it. Hagen, Glick, and Morse (1978) showed that if you make a viewer think he is looking at a picture by adding irrelevant cues to flatness (a plate of glass, for example, placed between the viewer and the scene), the perceiver treats the new scene as if it were a picture of the scene and makes the same type of errors that he makes in looking at an actual print of the scene. Thus, not only does he confuse the modified scene with a picture of it (Hochberg's finding), but he perceives the depth relations in the modified scene and in the picture of the scene in the same way.

Developmental Evidence for the Dual Reality of Pictures

If the perception of depth in pictures follows the same processes as the perception of depth in real scenes, then presumably this aspect of perception develops and improves with age and with experience in perception, in parallel with the perception of real scenes. Similarly, the ability to perceive the flatness of pictures must also develop with age and experience. If these two abilities develop together, then children at all ages have access to the dual reality of pictures. But if one develops sooner than the other—for example, if children do not perceive the flatness of pictures until relatively late—then they will treat pictures and scenes in the same way and as the same thing. Such equivalence will lead to predictable types of errors in perceiving pictures. On the other hand, regardless of how children perceive depth in real scenes, if they are sensitive to the flatness information in pictures, then they should have trouble seeing the depth information in pictures. During the years that this is true, pictures will be perceived as flat surfaces only, and will not convey a layout of space.

Cooper (1975), as noted in Hagen (1976), studied children's ability to compensate for perspective distortion in pictures viewed obliquely. He found that 3-year-olds treated the projections on the retina from pictures as if they had come from real objects. The children's responses indicated a direct perception of three-dimensionality in a scene without recognition that the scenes were only two-dimensional. Similarly, Benson and Yonas (1973) investigated the development of the utilization of direction of illumination as a source of information about depth in pictures. They found that adults assume that illumination is always from the top of the picture even when the picture is turned upside-down so that the illumination pictured is from the bottom, but young children (3-year-olds) apparently assume that illumination is above their heads regardless of the orientation of the picture—

that is, they are not aware of the possibility that the picture and the illumination could be upside-down. The young children make many errors in distinguishing convexity from concavity whenever the picture is turned on its side, but not when it is oriented properly. Benson and Yonas interpreted these data as showing that the ability to see a picture as a flat object in its own right develops later than the ability to perceive the depth relation in pictures (or in real scenes). Hagen (1976) also found a developmental improvement from ages 5 to 20 in the utilization of shadow information in pictures to determine the direction of the source of illumination. Since Piaget and Inhelder (1967) showed that this process was fully developed for scenes in real space by ages 7 and 8, Hagen argued that there was a lag in perceiving the surface information in pictures beyond that of perceiving the depth information in pictures.

These studies all suggest that young children are not as good at perceiving the surface information, even at ages when they can perceive the depth information in pictures. For young children, then, pictures do not have a dual reality, and contain only the reality of a window opening out into space. The nature of this developmental process is not clear from these experiments. Young children must have access to the sources of information about flatness because these same sources define depth. It appears as if they do not apply such cues to pictures, but treat all projections on the retina as if they came from three-dimensional scenes.

Another series of developmental experiments manipulated the effects of flat surface information on the perception of depth relationships in pictures. These studies demonstrate the importance of flatness information in correctly perceiving pictures. Yonas and Hagen (1973) attempted to remove flatness information from pictures by eliminating motion parallax and using rear projected slides. When flatness information was removed, perceivers at all ages (3, 7, and 20 years) improved in their ability to perceive the depth relations in pictures. Accuracy did not reach the level found in real scene controls, presumably because the experiment could not remove all of the cues of flatness.

This evidence suggests that children develop the ability to perceive the three-dimensional relationships in real scenes and in pictures before they also perceive the surface qualities, that is, the flatness of pictures. Thus, for some period in normal development, pictures do not have a dual reality for children. This does not mean that pictures will look more vivid or be seen in "plastic depth" (to use Schlosberg's term, 1941). Rather, being less sensitive to the surface quality and the flatness of pictures will lead to qualitatively different perceptions from pictures. The differences will produce errors when pictures are viewed from the wrong stationpoint—that is, from a position in space other than the one where the painter or camera stood.

Making Pictures Look Like Scenes

Perceptual Constraints The
painter or photographer makes a conscious decision about where to stand when creating his picture. There are many esthetic criteria that can be applied to this choice, but there are also some perceptual criteria. Hagen and Jones (1978) have summarized these in a discussion in which they consider both the artist's rules for where to stand and the perceiver's preference for pictures made from different stationpoints.

Renaissance treatises generally suggest that the center of projection (that is, the painter's position) of representational pictures with linear perspective should be at a distance of about five to ten times the height of the principal objects being pictured. For example if a tree is the principal object and it is 3 meters in height, then the painter should stand between 15 and 30 meters from it. Hagen and Elliott (1976) tested this assumption by construction drawings of solids whose perspective created convergence at different distances; hence, the solids appeared as if they had been viewed at different distances when photographed. They found that, regardless of viewing conditions, children and adults selected the solid drawing whose apparent viewing distance was ten times its size as the one that looked most natural. Jones and Hagen concluded that there are perceptual constraints as to where a painter or photographer should place his stationpoint, though it is not yet clear what the source of these constraints is.

Techniques Hochberg (1978, 1979) describes a number of different techniques worked out by painters to put depth into their pictures. The major techniques involve contrast induction, the use of shadows, pairing of complementary colors on adjacent parts of the picture surface, and the use of additive rather than subtractive mixtures of colors. Ratliff (1965) also described a technique based on lateral inhibitory processes between adjacent areas that produce larger apparent contrasts in perception than are present on the canvas.

For the painter to produce a picture that reflects the same pattern of light to the eye as does the scene it represents, the painter has to distort the local color and brightness relationships. In other words, painting a picture that looks like a scene requires some cheating on the laws of perspective. The apprenticeship of a painter is in part a process of learning how to cheat and get away with it. Failure to cheat in a painting, or in a photograph, means that the resulting picture will look flatter than the scene it represents.

PICTORIAL ILLUSIONS AND THE DUAL REALITY OF PICTURES

Outline drawings that produce **visual illusions** have delighted both viewers and theorists for centuries (Fig. 12.5). It is generally believed that illusion-producing drawings produce illusory perceptions as a result of the operation of normal mechanisms of perception. Consequently, illusions have been used as demonstration for normal functioning.

A perception is called an **illusion** when a perceiver describes an experience that does not agree with a physical attribute of the stimulus. For the illusions illustrated in Figure 12.5, the lengths of the lines, or their degree of curvature, do not correspond to the way perceivers report seeing them. This definition of illusion, however, does not make sense when applied

to all two-dimensional pictures, photographs, or line drawings (Coren & Girgus, 1977). Consider first the problem with respect to representational paintings or phtographs. To the extent that a viewer perceives the three-dimensional scene represented by the picture, there is a mismatch between the picture surface and his perception. For example, a picture of a receding railroad track (Fig. 8.7, p. 167) contains unequal line lengths representing the railway ties, but these will be

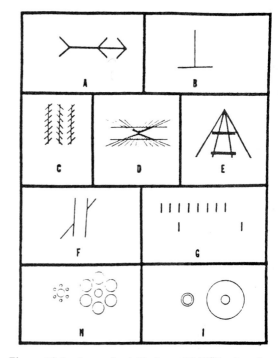

Figure 12.5 Some visual illusions: (*A*) Müller-Lyer figure, in which the two sections between the arrowheads are equal but appear unequal; (*B*) Horizontal-vertical illusion, in which the two lines are equal but appear unequal; (*C*) Zollner figure, in which the three vertical lines are parallel but appear unparallel; (*D*) Wundt figure, in which the two horizontal lines are straight and parallel but appear bent; (*E*) Ponzo figure, in which the two horizontal lines are equal but appear unequal; (*F*) Poggendorf figure, in which the diagonal lines are continuous but appear displaced; (*G*) Oppelkundt figure, in which the distance between the end bars in each row are equal but appear unequal; (*H, I*) The Ebbinghaus and Delboeuf figures, in which the two center circles respectively are equal in diameter, but appear unequal.

perceived as equal. In fact, every aspect, feature, or element of the picture surface will produce an illusory perception if illusions are defined this way. But no one calls such mismatches illusions—they are examples of size constancy. Now, perceivers might be aware of the fact that the picture is flat and that the railway ties are all different sizes on the picture surface. If they are, then they have two different perceptions—the two realities of pictures. Since the three-dimensionality of representational pictures and photographs is so powerful, even the cues to flatness are not sufficient to prevent the perception of the three-dimensionality of the picture, with its attendant constancy scaling. Normally, then, the three-dimensional reality overrides the two-dimensional reality.

Inappropriate Constancy Scaling

In the experimental literature, the term "illusion" is reserved for line drawings that manifest one of two defining characteristics: first, that the drawings were not intended by their creators to be representative of three-dimensional scenes, and second that the balance between the two realities of the picture has swung so far toward flatness that it is difficult to perceive their three-dimensionality. Perceivers looking at illusions act as if they were looking a flat drawing, but they perceive some of its three-dimensional reality. Since the artist had no intention of drawing a three-dimensional scene, such drawings are said to produce a misapplication or **inappropriate constancy scaling.**

This explanation of line-drawn illusions as an inappropriate constancy scaling was first proposed by Thiery (1896), but has more recently been identified with Gregory (1966, 1970). The theory states that perceivers use the two-dimensional information in outline drawings to construct a representation of a three-dimensional scene in the same way that they can construct three-dimentional space from fully representational pictures or photographs. It is a misapplication of constancy only because there is no three-dimensional scene denoted by the illusion-producing drawings. That is, while we, as theorists, insist the drawing should be treated as flat, perceivers treat it

like any other picture and construct a perception of it as if it represented a scene.

One problem with this otherwise reasonable theory is that perceivers often do not report perceiving the apparent depth relationships that the theory says are responsible for the apparent size changes. For example, in order to account for that apparent size differences, viewers of the Müller-Lyer illusion (Fig. 12.5A) should perceive the apparently longer line as farther away than the apparently shorter line. Yet many observers see the distances as equal (Worrall, 1974). It is easy to see why this might happen. The drawings are so impoverished that they appear flat. The two-dimensional information that specifies three-dimensionality may be registered but not perceived (see Chapter 9) because it is at variance with the clear flatness of the picture given by other sources of information. The registration is sufficient to produce the apparent size changes, but it does not result in perceived three-dimensionality. Gregory (1966, 1970) has shown that if the cues to flatness are reduced in the drawing, the illusory effect is increased and the depth becomes apparent to the perceiver.

Subjective Contours and Depth

There is a subset of illusory drawings that produce the perception of **subjective contours** (Coren, 1972). The contours are illusory because perceivers report seeing a contour when none exists in the stimulus. Coren described three such cases: (a) the edges perceived in stereoscopically viewed random-dot stereograms (see Chapter 11); (b) the edges defining objects when only the shadows cast by the objects are drawn; and (c) the edges of an unshown object seen overlapping a more articulated one (Fig. 12.6).

Coren argued that, in all three instances, the subjective contour is perceived because there is depth information in the drawings—their three-dimensional reality—that leads perceivers to stratify the entire configuration in several depth planes. Even if the contour is not drawn to separate the different planes, a contour is perceived because one part of the figure is seen in front of the other. In support of his argument, Coren presented data about each of the three types of

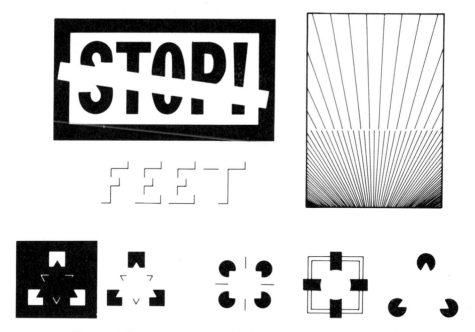

Figure 12.6 Some examples of subjective contours. (Coren, 1972.)

subjective contour examples to show that perceivers do see them in depth. Furthermore, when they are redrawn so as to eliminate the depth information, the subjective contours also disappear. Figure 12.7 shows an example of one of Coren's (1974) tests. If the white subjective triangle is seen in front of the black squares,

Figure 12.7 If the central white triangle is perceived as stratified in depth and, therefore, closer than the background, then the small ring in it will have to be perceived as smaller than an equal-sized ring on the background. (Coren, 1972.)

which are seen in front of the background of the page, then the small, black ring in the center will be perceived as closer to the observer than the comparison ring to the right drawn on the background. Since the two rings are physically the same size, they project the same visual angle to the eye. If the center one is seen to be closer because of the depth difference that produces the subjective contour, then, according to the size-distance invariance hypothesis, it ought to be perceived as smaller. Coren reports that observers perceived it this way. When the drawing is altered so that the subjective contour is destroyed, the two rings are perceived as equal in size.

THE ROLE OF LEARNING

Pictures and other two-dimensional representations are invented or constructed by human beings. Some theorists have assumed that perceivers would not have been able to perceive the layout of space or recognize objects portrayed in pictures without prior visual training or experience with pictures. According to the evidence already presented, however, the perception of pictures is mediated by the same mechanisms as the perception of three-dimensional scenes, and perception of the latter comes first. Therefore, whatever component of the perception of scenes is learned must also be learned in picture perception.

Experimental tests to determine whether learning is involved in picture perception are difficult to interpret. Since scene perception probably comes first, as soon as one aspect of scene perception can be accomplished, it can be applied to pictures. For this reason, the classic study by Hochberg and Brooks (1962) is open to two interpretations. They tested an 18-month-old child who had never been exposed to any two-dimensional representations, and found that he was as accurate in identifying familiar objects from pictures and from drawings of the objects as he was from seeing the objects themselves. This is a powerful finding, suggesting that prior experience with pictures is not necessary. But it does not rule out the possibility that object identification in three-dimensional scenes is learned.

Such logic can also be applied to the cross-cultural literature on picture perception (see Hagen & Jones, 1978, for a recent review). While there are cultures that do not produce or utilize two-dimensional representations, finding that aspects of their picture perception are accurate, even upon first exposure, does

not necessarily specify the acquisition process. On the other hand, finding differences in picture perception between people with no experience and those with lots of experience does suggest that experience is necessary. Deregowski (1972) tried to overcome these problems by using the device illustrated in Figure 12.8 to measure the apparent depth of objects on pictures. The half-silvered mirror allows the spot of light to be superimposed on the picture surface. By adjusting the location of the spot, it is seen in front of, on, or behind the picture surface. The viewer sets the spot so that it appears to be at the same distance as the objects in the picture being judged. This allows the perceiver to judge the apparent relative distance of different objects represented in the picture.

But several important assumptions underlie this technique. First, its use assumes that only the representational mode of the dual reality of pictures is evoked by the task. Otherwise the perceiver could simply say that all parts of the picture are equidistant because it is flat. To meet this assumption, all the cues to flatness have to be removed. Since the viewing device is monocular it removes many of the cues to flatness, but not all. Therefore, a control group with normal picture viewing experience should always be used in this same task, something that is rarely done.

Second, all the sources of information about the layout of space in the picture must be in agreement

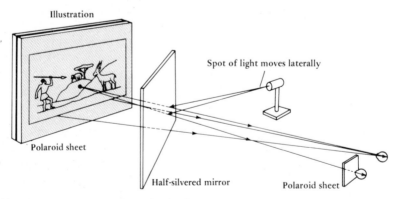

Illustration

Spot of light moves laterally

Polaroid sheet

Half-silvered mirror

Polaroid sheet

Figure 12.8 A device to measure the apparent depth of objects in pictures. The half-silvered mirror allows the spot of light to be seen superimposed on the picture surface. By adjusting the location of the spot, it will be seen in front of, on, or behind the picture surface. The viewer sets the spot so it appears to be the same distance as the object in the picture being judged.

with Leonardo's rules. If the picture does not reflect to the eye luminance and spectral discontinuity that correspond to those from the appropriate real scene, a perceiver's erroneous responses cannot be attributed to a failure to understand and use Leonardo's rules. It could be due merely to a confusion in the face of conflicting rules—rules that he understands perfectly well. No problems would exist here if properly made photographs were used as stimuli, but nearly all the work reported to date used outline drawings, all of which fail to follow some of Leonardo's rules and most of which treat others inconsistently.

Unfortunately, the stimuli that have been used in the cross-cultural research have been poor enough to weaken most reasonable conclusions. For example, Figure 12.9 contains two examples from Hudson (1960) that have been used in many subsequent experiments in Africa. While the evidence for naming objects from such pictures is generally consistent with

Figure 12.9 Two examples of stimuli from Hudson (1960).

the conclusions of Hochberg and Brooks, the data on extracting the layout of space suggests that many persons who had never seen pictures before had trouble doing it from Hudson's pictures. But this has been true both for African subjects and for Westerners. Hagen and Jones (1978) examined some of the stimuli in detail, and then used them to test subjects who were thoroughly familiar with pictures. They found that many of the Hudson pictures, as well as others used in the cross-cultural research, did not produce reliable responses even from experienced observers. This finding casts suspicion on all research with these pictures. Until we have better data, it is difficult to interpret any of the reported research as supportive of a learned component of picture perception. It is certainly not supportive of a learned process independent of space perception in general.

Canonical Depth Features

One objection to a perspective theory of picture perception is that it does not account for the perception of the layout of space in outline drawings, sketches, cartoons, and caricatures, or in pictures in which the perspective information is incompletely rendered. This objection actually constitutes a problem for any theory of picture perception. One part of the answer is that we may be able to perceive the layout of space without needing all the perspective information that Leonardo's rules provide. The concept of canonical depth features may provide a way around this problem.

Hochberg (1972, 1978) proposed the concept of **canonical form** to account for the easy recognition of objects from outline drawings, sketches, and cartoons. In his view, recognition does not depend on the full articulation of all the features and properties of an object, but can occur if only the object's essential characteristics or "distinctive features" are provided (see Chapter 15). An object's canonical form is the form that best displays its characteristic features—what might be called a prototype form. It would delete all ambiguous features, all features that the form shares with other forms (and therefore are not defining or distinctive), and all features that are irrelevant or noninformative.

This idea is illustrated in an experiment by Ryan and Schwartz (1956). They tested subjects on the recognition of single objects (Fig. 12.10) in a threshold identification task in which the exposure duration needed for correct identification was determined. They found that the photograph that supplies the most visual information was often the one requiring the longest exposure duration, whereas the cartoon or outline drawing often needed the shortest duration. Goldman and Hagen (1978) analyzed 100 caricatures of President Richard M. Nixon created by 17 different artists. They found great consistency within and between artists in the features selected for exaggeration, especially the jowls, the box-like jaw, and the length of the nose.

Haber (1979) has proposed an analogous concept—**canonical depth features**—the perspective features that can define all the possible three-dimensional relationships in a picture without requiring a full articulation of all perspectives and other depth information. The indication of a vanishing point is, perhaps, the single most important canonical depth feature. Figure 12.11 illustrates how the use of multiple vanishing points yields a strong depth effect. Canonical features of this sort would permit the correct perception of the layout of space from relatively

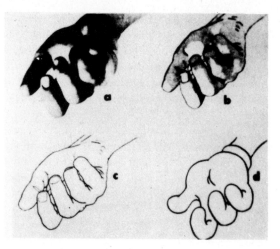

Figure 12.10 An example of one set of stimuli used by Ryan and Schwartz (1956). Each set involves a photograph, a shaded drawing, an outline drawing, and a cartoon.

incomplete drawings. They may also account for visual size and orientation illusions created by some two-dimensional drawings and sketches. If enough depth features are available to register the three-dimensionality but insufficient to cast the whole drawing into depth, then the two-dimensional features in the drawing could be misperceived.

Figure 12.11 Picture with three different vanishing points.

Pictorial Conventions

One of the most important conventions used to create drawings is the use of lines to represent edges or boundaries in space. Objects in scenes are not surrounded by lines, yet we have no trouble representing and perceiving objects in drawings simply by outlining their boundaries. Kennedy (1974) has argued that this convention is unlearned, and the data of Hochberg and Brooks (1962) support this view.

A second potentially unlearned convention has been demonstrated in the work of Benson and Yonas (1973). They showed that even young children assume that the source of illumination in a picture comes from the top. Since illumination defines shadows in relation to objects and therefore helps to locate those objects in space, this conventional assumption is an important way of specifying the layout of space.

Other conventions are clearly learned through interaction with pictures. Movement is one of the most important of these conventions, since pictures themselves are static. Movement of objects in a picture can be indicated by multiple representations of legs, by a smear drawn behind the object indicating speed, by blurring edges, to name just a few conventions. Friedman and Stevenson (1975) report evidence that these movement conventions are learned during preschool and early primary school ages. Examples of other types of conventions are drawing stars above someone's head in a cartoon to mean he is "seeing stars," or using big print in a cartoon balloon to mean the speaker is talking in a loud voice. The analysis of caricature by Goldman and Hagen (1978) is also one of conventionality.

Creativity and Convention

The creative artist's intention is rarely to render a painting or photograph so that it reproduces perfectly the spatial layout of the model scene. Leonardo's rules were not intended for painters to follow, but for painters to know so they could break them effectively. This creative breaking of rules is analogous to the creative use of language. One way to define a literary metaphor is as a violation of co-occurrence restrictions imposed by the rules of semantics or syntax. For example, many nouns and verbs in English can be classified as animate or inanimate. English has a rule requiring that an animate noun has to be used with an animate verb and an inanimate noun with an inanimate verb (Katz & Fodor, 1963). Consequently, the juxtaposition of "the clouds cried" or "the rocks laughed" in which inanimate nouns occur with animate verbs, is a violation that creates a metaphor. One detailed analysis of this kind has been reported by Kypriotaki (1972). Painters can, in effect, use the same technique in creative pictures: the violation of some of Leonardo's rules of perspective. Indeed, violation may be what makes pictures into art. Cubism, for example, shows many violations of perspective. There is extensive use of parallel perspective, so that the lines do not converge to vanishing points. Many objects are portrayed as transparent, so that interposition among objects does not occur and we have difficulty telling what is in front of what. We can even see the backsides of objects. Front and back ambiguity is further enhanced by inconsistent stationpoints in constructing the picture so that we can see around objects. These are all examples of visual metaphors resulting from the controlled violation of the rules of perspective.

SUMMARY

From some combinations of built-in mechanisms, maturation, and learned reactions, infants and young children are able to perceive the layout of space from the pattern of light reflected from such scenes to their eyes. When they encounter a picture, they perceive its layout of space from the pattern of light reflected from the picture in the same way as if the light had come from a natural scene. Such a perception will be undistorted if the picture is viewed from the proper stationpoint and if the picture was constructed using Leonardo's rules of perspective. To the degree that the young viewer is at the wrong stationpoint, the layout of space in a picture will be distorted because, at a young age, he does not yet know how to compensate through use of information about the distance and orientation of the picture surface. Such distortion will be overcome as the two-dimensional realities of pictures are perceived and then used to compensate for the incorrect stationpoint. To the degree that the picture is not based upon Leonardo's rules, the application of the three-dimensional perceptual processes from which the child is generalizing will be ineffective, and distortion may occur. This distortion will be overcome as the child learns or somehow acquires the canonical depth features that minimally specify the correct layout of space, or acquires knowledge of the cultural conventions used in representing space in pictures. Of course, some residual distortion of the layout of space may remain if the picture maker violates some of Leonardo's rules.

SUGGESTED READINGS

Pirenne (1970) has an excellent though technical presentation of the relationships of the laws of optics and of perception as they affect the appearance of photographs. Two recent volumes, one by Nodine and Fisher (1980) and the other by Hagen (1980), summarize most of the different points of view on picture perception. Coren and Girgus (1977) present a complete presentation of visual illusions.

Chapter 13

The Development of Visual Space Perception

It is natural to wonder about the origins of a psychological process—does it appear full blown at birth or does it develop in successively more sophisticated forms as the infant and child mature? Does it change with practice or experience, or is its growth independent of these factors? This chapter deals with some of these problems with respect to visual space perception. It begins with a discussion of the sensory and perceptual abilities of the human infant. We will see that the infant is capable of performing many visually guided tasks fairly well—certainly better than had been thought for many years. The perceptual experience of the newborn human infant certainly can no longer be described, as William James (1890) once did, as a "booming, buzzing, confusion." Following that, we review evidence that the infant demonstrates shape and size constancy, although possession of the latter ability is still a matter of controversy. Indeed, it is not at all clear when size constancy is completely present for greater distances. In the last section we suggest that the development of space perception involves the ability both to monitor our perceptual experience and to improve our utilization of it in making judgments over greater distances. It may be, then, that the scale of space is constantly being adjusted to the changing metric of our bodies.

SENSORY ABILITIES OF THE HUMAN INFANT

The close relationship between the structure of the visual system and perceptual experience has been noted many times in previous chapters. In studying perceptual development, it is even more important to ask, first, whether the organism possesses the basic anatomical and neurophysiological mechanisms necessary to produce the different types of perceptual experience, and second, whether the organism is able to produce responses that can demonstrate the existence of these processes. The latter question is frequently answered in terms of the ingenuity of the experimenter in using whatever responses or actions the young organism is able to make at different ages. The answer to the first question requires systematic evaluation of each stage of the visual system of the very young organism. This section constitutes a brief overview of the current state of this evaluation.

Maurer (1975) discussed the difficulties of assessing the anatomical and functional state of the infant's visual system. Nevertheless, it is clear that the retina of the newborn infant (one to five days of age) contains both rods and cones. However, at birth the macula is less mature than the rest of the retina—the cones are shorter, stumpier, and less numerous than they will be and there are layers of cells present which will move out to the periphery. This process is mostly complete by four months. Both the photopic and scotopic systems appear to be present and functional. The level of development of the central components of the newborn's visual system have been evaluated using the electroencephalogram (EEG) and visual cortical evoked potentials. The former is a measure of the ongoing activity of the brain and the latter is a measure of responsiveness to a discrete visual signal. These measurements indicate that at least some intact pathways exist at birth between the eye and the cortex. The functional consequences of these pathways are still a matter of controversy (Hershenson, 1967; Salapatek, 1975).

Accommodation The young infant's ability to respond to targets at different distances has been a puzzle since Haynes, White, and Held (1965) reported that, prior to about two months of age, infants can accommodate for only a single fixed distance. Studies of infant visual acuity (for example, Fantz, Ordy, & Udelf, 1962), had reported similar acuity values for targets over a wide range of distances. Salapatek and coworkers (Salapatek, 1975; Banks & Salapatek, 1974; Salapatek, Bechtold, & Bushnell, 1975) have proposed that the poor accommodation measurements may reflect limits on sensitivity rather than the accommodative process itself. They noted that infants under two months of age do not respond to spatial frequencies greater than about three cycles per degree, whereas adults respond to spatial frequencies up to 30 to 40 cycles per degree. Thus, the immature visual system of the infant may not be able to detect the high spatial frequencies utilized by more mature accommodative systems. Furthermore, since low-frequency spatial patterns are transmitted by an improperly accommodated eye, evidence of poor accommodation could be hard to demonstrate. It is clear, however, that by two months of age, the infant is able to accommodate fairly well. This is supported by visual acuity data indicating that the image is at least sharp enough to provide the infant eye with a fair amount of resolving power (loosely, about 20/200).

Eye Movements The evidence is clearer with respect to binocular fixation (convergence) and conjugate movement of the eyes. Newborn infants have been observed to follow a moving target with both eyes but, when looking at stationary targets, their eyes frequently appear to wander independently. In other words, while newborns can direct their eyes at a single point in space, it probably takes a compelling target to keep them there for any length of time.

Intensity Sensitivity to brightness has been measured in infants up to 113 days of age. The results show rapid development in the first two months of life (Doris, Casper, Poresky, 1967; Doris & Cooper, 1966). Differential visual preferences, as assessed by the number of fixations to three intensities of light differing by one log unit, have been found in human newborns in the first week of life (Hershenson, 1964).

Color There have been a number of studies of the infant's ability to perceive color using a variety of techniques. They seem to converge on the view that color perception is probably present in the two-month-old infant (Bornstein, Kessen, & Weiskopf, 1975; Dobson, 1976; Peeples & Teller, 1975) and similar to that of the adult by four months of age (Fagan, 1974; Schaller, 1975).

PERCEPTUAL ABILITIES OF THE HUMAN INFANT

It seems reasonable to assume that soon after birth the infant is able to extract and utilize complex visual information from the environment. This is not to say that perceptual abilities do not improve with experience, nor to deny that the developing organism is learning to use different kinds of information to supplement or replace its repertoire of innate mechanisms. It is quite likely that the visual discrimination of the adult and child is different from that of the infant. In this sense, perhaps Fantz (1965) was correct in his belief that perception is "innate in the neonate and learned in the adult." In this section, we will look at a number of different abilities, from simple to complex.

Simple Stimulus Features

The possible existence of feature analyzers in the human must be investigated by indirect methods since electrophysiological procedures cannot be used. One fruitful method, illustrated in Figure 13.1, uses photographs or television recordings of the eyes of infants in order to determine their direction of gaze. When markers are placed in the field, the fixations can be located fairly precisely (see Maurer, 1975, for a detailed discussion of the method).

In a study using photographic recordings, Kessen, Salapatek and Haith (1972) presented newborns with a single contour, either vertical or horizontal, located off the center of the visual field. Fixations on the blank control field were distributed fairly normally around the center of the field. The distributions of eye fixations for the horizontal contour were virtually identical to those for the blank screen. How-

ever, the vertical contours were clearly attractive to the babies—for the left-of-center contour, the distribution of eye fixations showed a sharp peak in the region of the contour. For the right-of-center contour, the distribution of fixations shifted to the right, and the peaking occurred to the right of the contour region. Thus, infants appeared to be attracted to those contours that could easily be crossed. These results suggest that some kind of excitation occurs when an edge is crossed and that this stimulation is implicated in the mechanism which maintains fixation around the contour. Like adults, it appears to be easier for an infant to move the eyes horizontally across vertical edge than vertically across a horizontal edge.

When figures are introduced into the visual field of newborns, a slightly different kind of visual behavior occurs. Salapatek and Kessen (1966) presented newborn infants with a large black triangle and photographed their eye fixations. Fixation points were plotted with respect to the real stimulus triangle presented to an experimental group and with respect to an imaginary triangle for the control group. Figure

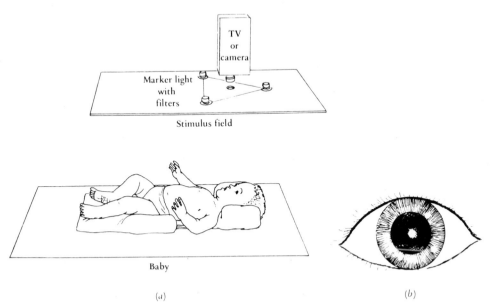

(a)

(b)

Figure 13.1 Schematic representation of method for obtaining pictures of the eyes of infants looking at forms on a screen, and of the type of pictures obtained. (a) Typical apparatus for observing the corneal reflex of infants. (b) Typical photo frame showing eye direction at one angle of a triangular stimulus, indicated by light reflected from marker lamps.

13.2(*a*) shows responses to a blank homogeneous field. Each point represents a fixation and these are connected in sequence. The eye moved almost every second, and much more in the horizontal than in the vertical direction. Figure 13.2(*b*) shows the response of a typical infant to the triangle. Eye movements were much shorter and the fixations tended to cluster around one of the three vertices. The infants appear to have responded to the angle rather than to the total form. In a subsequent experiment (Nelson & Kessen, 1969), three stimuli were shown to newborn infants—a complete outline triangle, only the sides of the triangle, and only the angles of the triangle. In this situation, the infants typically looked toward a single angle component—the angular elements attracted the infants' gaze whether the sides of the triangle were present or not. Taken together, these experiments suggest that the infants sought out those areas of greatest change or discontinuity—the angles in this case. Perhaps we could even argue that they were guided by the presence of angle detectors.

In an attempt to separate the important aspects of stimulation which were attracting the newborns' gaze, Salapatek (1968) varied size, angularity, figure-ground contrast, and figure type (solid or outline). The ocular response was subjected to detailed analysis by measuring the location of gaze, dispersion of gaze, number of shifts in gaze, direction of shifts, length of shifts, and time spent looking at the total figure, part of the figure, contour versus center of circles, and sides versus angles of triangles. Salapatek (1968, 1969) characterized the visually naïve newborn's response to patterned two-dimensional surfaces in terms of several salient aspects. Visual scanning was more dispersed in the horizontal than in the vertical dimension of the visual field under all stimulus conditions, whether a stimulus was present or not. In the absence of a stimulus, the broad automatic scan occurred reliably, in all infants and for extended periods of time. Introduction of a geometric figure into the newborn's visual field resulted in a decrease in the horizontal dispersion of visual scanning and a decreased difference between the horizontal and vertical dispersion of scanning. More specifically, newborns modified the pattern of visual scanning to fit the physical features of the stimulus.

Within a very short time after a figure or pattern was introduced into the visual field, the majority of newborns ceased their scanning and fixated the figure's contour, typically coming to rest on some limited segment or feature of the contour. Localization of fixation occurred for the majority of the infants within three or four seconds and often involved an eye movement across some portion of the figure. This pattern of behavior suggests that the newborn is able to discriminate pattern in its peripheral visual field, and that this

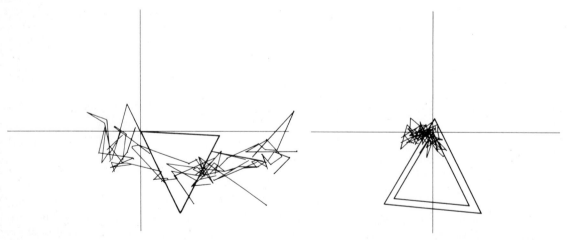

Figure 13.2 Visual scanning pattern of human newborn of (*a*) a homogeneous field and (*b*) a large black equilateral triangle. Each dot represents one time sample of eye orientation. (Salapatek & Kessen, 1966.)

determines the direction of eye movements. In this respect, angles appear to be particularly salient.

Salapatek (1969, 1975) followed the development of visual scanning through the first ten weeks of life. In the first experiment, two groups of infants were studied—one group ranging from four to six weeks of age and the other between eight and ten weeks. The stimuli used were a homogeneous field, a circle, a square, a triangle, a regular 12-turn shape, and a random 11-turn shape. With the homogeneous field, all infants either fixated the extreme portions of the visual field, became fussy, or fell asleep. When a geometric figure was introduced, infants rapidly fixated and scanned the figure for an extended period of time. In general, the scan was directed toward an angle, if one was present in the figure.

Of the two groups Salapatek studied, the younger infants concentrated most of their visual scanning on a small portion of the stimulus with a more focused scan as compared to the older infants, who directed their scan more loosely. Although all infants fixated the contour rather than the center of the geometric patterns, the younger infants limited their gaze to a very small segment of the contour (usually a single feature), whereas the older infants showed a more extensive scan and a tendency to direct some fixations toward the centers of the figures.

In summary, then, it seems clear that the human infant responds to elements or stimulus features from birth and that this response is specific to some types of elements selected for fixation or scansion. As the infant grows older, more and more extensive portions of figures are scanned actively. Thus, immediately upon being exposed to the world, the infant actively seeks stimulation rather than passively receiving it. As the infant matures, more and more information about the environment is sought and dealt with (Bond, 1972).

Complex Figures

Two different kinds of relationships occur between stimulus configurations and the meanings associated with them. The meaning could be an integral part of the configuration, not separable from it and, therefore, not arbitrary, or the meaning could be arbitrarily assigned to a configuration that may or may not have some natural significance. Faces are illustrations of the first kind of relationship, and letters and words are examples of the second kind. In this section, we shall discuss only the first kind of relationship.

The literature on human infants' responses to human faces is of great interest because the face is a recurrent and interesting stimulus for the infant. Haith, Bergman, and Moore (1977) measured infants' fixations on real faces each half second to reconstruct their scanning patterns. The apparatus they used is illustrated in Figure 13.3. It permitted the infants to ob-

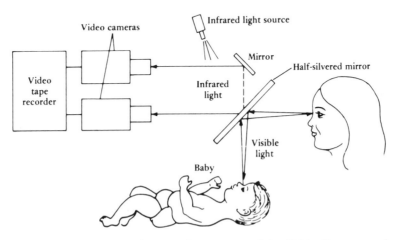

Figure 13.3 Schematic drawing of apparatus used by Haith, Bergman, and Moore (1977) to record eye contact and scanning of the human face in early infancy.

serve either their real mother or a stranger, who either remained still, moved slightly, or talked. The face was divided into four regions: eyes, nose, mouth, and "edges"—a category that included all other fixations on the face and head. Figure 13.4 shows the percentage of fixations for each age group on each of the features of the face. The youngest infants directed their gaze toward contours around the perimeter of the configurations, such as the hairline. At about seven to nine weeks of age, fixations were equally likely on internal contours, especially if their contrast was high. The internal fixations were directed to the eyes rather than to the contours and, while brief excursions were made to the mouth, they returned to the eyes when the mother spoke. There were no differences in looking patterns as a function of movement or the presence of speech. Maurer and Salapatek (1975), using a similar apparatus, also found that one-month-old infants spent more time looking at the outer contour of the face, usually looking at a single area (such as the chin, hairline, or ear) for long periods of time. Two-month-olds, on the other hand, invariably directed their gaze at one or several internal features of the face (the eyes or mouth). Typical scanning patterns are schematically illustrated in Figure 13.5.

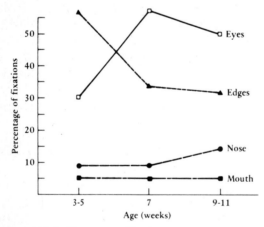

Figure 13.4   Percentage of fixations on eyes, nose, mouth, and "edges" (that is, all other parts of face) for infants approximately four, seven, and ten weeks of age. (Haith, Bergman, & Moore, 1977.)

There therefore seems to be a shift in visual attention from external to internal features of a face during the first two months. Is this shift peculiar to faces or does it reflect a more general change in the infant's visual search of complex stimuli? If it were only a change of responsivity to faces, it would suggest that the face had changed its status from a mere collection of elements to a meaningful entity or perceptual configuration. To determine the generality of this shift, Salapatek and Moscovich (Salapatek, 1969, 1975) presented one- and two-month-old infants with the stimuli shown in Figure 13.6. Schematic plots of visual scanning for each stimulus trial are also shown in the figure. It seems clear that the younger infants generally looked only at a limited portion of the external contour of a large simple or compound square. The older infants generally looked at the internal features of compound stimuli. Both age groups reliably fixated the internal element(s) when presented without a frame, so there was no doubt that the internal elements were above threshold.

Salapatek (1975) concluded that the pattern of results is consistent with the other findings on faces, but that it is not yet possible to tell whether they reflect a general property of perception in infants. It may reflect a change in the way objects are perceived, or it may reflect the maturation of different types of visual systems. Both Bronson (1974) and Karmel and Maisel (1975) have suggested that vision prior to two months of age is mediated by subcortical mechanisms followed by increasing involvement of the cortex.

While the developmental pattern shown by human infants in response to faces suggests that the configurational meaning is not manifest at birth, we should not generalize this result to include all possible meaningful configurational patterns. A remarkable experiment by Sackett (1966) with monkeys illustrates the fact that complex innate mechanisms may be involved in visually mediated behavior. Sackett raised monkeys in isolated cages from birth to nine months of age. On the fourteenth day of their lives, the monkeys were shown pictures of other monkeys in various activities and expressing various emotions. The pictures included monkeys in a threatening pos-

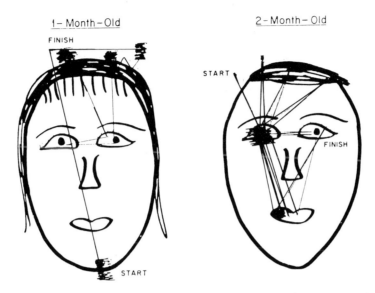

1 – Month – Old 2 – Month – Old

Figure 13.5 Schematic plots of visual scanning of a real head by a representative one- and two-month-old infant in the study by Maurer and Salapatek. (Salapatek, 1975.)

ture, in a fearful posture, playing with other monkeys, exploring, and having sexual relations. There were also pictures of other infant monkeys, a mother and an infant together, and monkeys just doing nothing. The responses to these pictures were compared with responses to control pictures of a living room, a sunset, an outdoor scene with trees, an adult female human, and various geometric patterns. Responses categorized as exploration, play, vocalization, and disturbance occurred most frequently to pictures of monkeys threatening and to pictures of other infants. From two and one-half to four months of age, the threat pictures produced a high frequency of disturbance level. If the monkey was given control of his viewing of the stimulus so that he could turn it on when he wanted, these picture were rarely looked at during this period.

Thus, pictures of infant monkeys and of threat appear to have nonlearned prepotent general activating properties for socially naïve infant monkeys. Pictures of threat appear to be able to release a maturationally determined innate fear response. These results suggested to Sackett that there exist innate recognition mechanisms which are species spe-

cific. (See also Chapter 12 on the development of picture perception.)

Natural Patterns of Looking

The research just reviewed used eye movements as a dependent variable when specific stationary geometric patterns were placed in the visual field. These results are difficult to interpret because the experimental situations were imposed upon the infants by the experimenters. We are just beginning to learn about the natural visual field of infants and their patterns of looking at it.

The natural patterns of integrated head and eye movements of infants between 3 and 15 weeks of age were studied by Tronick and Clanton (1971) using electrooculographic recordings of eye movements, and recording head position by measuring displacements of a light, free-moving gimballed harness. By combining these signals, accurate records of eye position, head position, and line of sight were obtained. Figure 13.7 is a schematic representation of the apparatus they used. The three objects in the field were brightly

1-Month-Olds

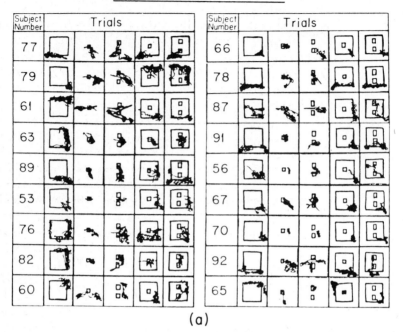

(a)

2-Month-Olds

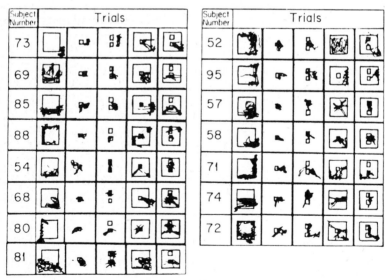

(b)

Figure 13.6 Schematic plots of visual scanning of fine and compound outline shapes by (a) one- and (b) two-month-old infants in the Salapatek and Moscovich study. (Salapatek, 1975.)

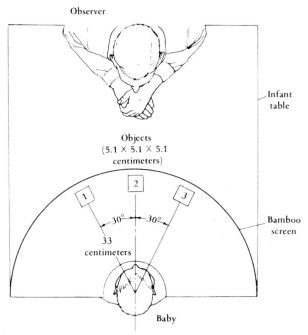

Observer

Infant table

Objects
(5.1 × 5.1 × 5.1
centimeters)

30°   30°

33
centimeters

Bamboo
screen

Baby

Figure 13.7 Apparatus used by Tronick and Clanton (1972) to study infant looking patterns.

colored cubes, two inches on a side, mounted on small motors so that they could be made to move.

Four looking patterns were observed in the records of these infants: First, the "shift" pattern, in which a saccadic movement of the eyes was integrated with a smooth and fairly rapid movement of the head. The lead of either the head or the eye did not appear to be related to the motion of the target. Second, the "search" pattern, in which a slow displacement of the head was coordinated with a series of eye fixations and saccades. These movements produced a steplike looking pattern that covered a large sector of the visual field. Third, a "focal" pattern, in which the head remained stable while a series of small saccades and fixations covered a limited portion of the visual field. In this pattern the eyes sometimes remained fixated for only brief periods, whereas there were many cases in which eyes and head remained stable for long periods of time. Fourth, the "compensation" pattern, in which the eyes and head moved slowly and continuously in opposite directions and then returned to their original positions. The resultant of the two movements was to maintain the line of sight without change.

In general, integration of head and eye movements was well executed by all infants. The movements were smooth and the looking patterns appeared better organized than either component alone. The major differences between the infants of different ages appeared to be quantitative, in that the fixations of younger infants were typically of smaller amplitude and there were longer periods in which no change of gaze occurred. The looking patterns indicated that infants even at 20 days of age possessed a visual system that is adapted for the exploration and extraction of information from the environment. The system appears to deploy attention to new loci, or to maintain attention at a particular locus, by shifting or stabilizing a visual line of regard with coordinated head and eye movements. The youngest infants explored less of the environment than the older infants. Their looks were of shorter duration and they looked to fewer places. The older infants were more skillful in the exploration of the visual environment, but this increased capability did not require a qualitative change in the patterns of looking.

The Visual Field of Infants

The effective visual field is a measure of how far a stimulus can be in the periphery and still register information for the control of exploratory fixations. If this effective visual field changed with age, it would have important consequences for our understanding of perceptual development. To study these changes, Tronick (1972) presented two- to three-week-old infants with fixation stimuli in the midline, and then with a stimulus at some position in the periphery. They were allowed 15 seconds in which to change fixation. The infants were tested weekly for nine weeks.

Figure 13.8 shows how far off midline a stimulus object could be to elicit a fixation, as a function of age of the infant, for four stimulus presentation conditions. Initially the infant's effective visual field was not much greater than 15 to 20 degrees on either side of his line of regard. When the fixation object was in motion and the peripheral object was stationary, the size of the field changed only slightly over the first ten weeks. In contrast, when the peripheral object was in motion and the fixation object was stationary, the vis-

ual field at ten weeks was 20 degrees larger than it was initially, and more than 20 degrees larger than it was in the reversed movement condition. At every age, the effective visual field was larger when the object in the periphery was moving. The other two conditions—both objects in motion and both objects stationary—fell between the two extremes. In general, the area of the effective visual field remained approximately constant until about six weeks of age, at which time it began to expand. This relationship was found in all conditions. Motion was a more effective stimulus for attention; it was more easily registered in the periphery, and was more compelling in the focal field.

The increase in the size of the visual field appears to reflect both an increase in stimulus control and a growing functional capacity of the infant. This developmental trend may also explain the change from an obligatory to a voluntary looking pattern in infants noted by some investigators (Hershenson, 1967). Now, rather than a transition, it may be seen as a result of a quantitative growth in the effective visual field.

THE DEVELOPMENT OF SPACE PERCEPTION

Binocular Vision

In their survey, Haith and Campos (1977) noted that we have only limited information about the developmental course of binocular vision. This lack of knowledge is due, partly, to the difficulty in specifying the point of fixation precisely for infant subjects. Nevertheless, binocular vision is probably achieved by at least five months of age, and perhaps even in the first week (Slater & Findlay, 1975).

However, there may be a critical period for the attainment of stereopsis; abnormal visual input early in life may affect the development of normal binocular vision. Banks, Aslin, and Letson (1975) claimed to have demonstrated the existence of such a sensitive period. They tested 24 subjects who once had convergent strabismus (a condition in which the visual axes are misaligned). To be selected, the subjects had to have had a reasonably well-defined age at which the

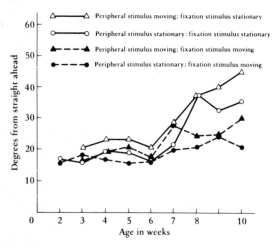

Figure 13.8 Looking patterns as a function of age for moving and stationary stimuli. (Tronick, 1972.)

strabismic deviation began and a well-defined age at which it was surgically corrected. All subjects were tested on the tilt-aftereffect, a measure highly correlated with stereopsis. Each person viewed with one eye an adapting field consisting of a square-wave grating rotated 10 degrees clockwise from the vertical. The test field, viewed with the other eye, contained a lower contrast grating of the same spatial frequency whose tilt the viewer could adjust. Presumably the degree of interocular transfer of tilt should reflect the degree of binocularity of the visual system.

By plotting the amount of transfer as a function of age of corrective surgery, Banks, Aslin, and Letson were able to show that people who were born with esotropia (convergent strabismus) and had early corrective surgery developed greater cortical binocularity than those who had later surgery. They concluded that the sensitive period for the development of binocularity—the prerequisite for fusion and stereopsis—begins several months after birth and peaks between one and three years of age.

These results agree with those from the literature on animals with experimentally induced visual deprivations—see Rothblat and Schwartz (1978) and Mitchell (1978) for general reviews. For example, Riesen (1975) reviews evidence that shows that cats deprived of patterned vision from birth to four months had permanent visual losses, whereas losses from deprivation at any time after four months were not permanent. Similarly Hubel and Wiesel (1965) raised kittens in such a way that they could never experience binocular vision. They alternately closed a different eye each day so that the kittens always had one eye open. Consequently, both eyes had full exposure to the natural environment, but at no time during the first four months were both eyes stimulated simultaneously. All aspects of visual performance were normal except those that required binocular perception. Furthermore, all cortical cells serving visual functions were normal except those with binocular inputs; they were greatly reduced in number. It is, presumably, these cells that account for the Banks et al. findings with children.

While it is clearly dangerous to generalize from animal to man, the pattern of results is quite consistent. It appears as if the cells in the visual cortex serving vision, especially those concerned with coding of specific features (those labeled by Hubel and Weisel as simple, complex, and hypercomplex—see Chapter 4) and of binocularity, do not develop normally if deprived of the appropriate stimuli during some critical period in their development. For human beings, this period is probably from birth through the preschool years. Any condition, especially extreme refractive error, astigmatism, or strabismus, which is present at birth and left uncorrected for the first several years, is likely to lead to permanent loss of visual function. Comparable conditions that begin after age five or so will have little permanent effect, so that after correction the visual system will return to normal quality.

Size and Shape Constancy

We have seen that the infant possesses a visual system that enables him to look around the visual world. Does this infant perceive a three-dimensional world of surfaces, edges, and solid objects? To test one aspect of this question, Bower (1964) trained infants 75 to 85 days old to turn their heads to one side to see an experimenter's head pop up above the table and say "peek-a-boo." Figure 13.9 shows a schematic representation of the apparatus and experimental arrangement used. The "peek-a-boo" functioned as a reinforcement for the infant's response of turning his head toward the stimulus—a 30-centimeter cube placed nearly one meter from the infant's eyes. This cube provided a standard against which the generalization tests could be compared.

The training and four generalization test situations are represented schematically in Figure 13.10. Two different sized cubes—one 30 centimeters and one 90 centimeters—were each placed at one meter or at three meters from the infants to provide the four test conditions in which projective size could be pitted against real size. After the infant had been trained to turn his head whenever the 30-centimeter cube was presented at one meter, generalization was tested by measuring the number of responses made to each of the four test stimuli. The first test stimulus was a 30-centimeter cube at one meter—the same stimulus as in training. In this case, therefore, both the real size

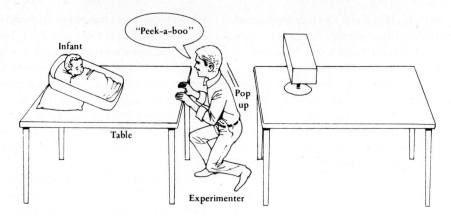

Figure 13.9 Arrangements in Bower's (1964) experiment with different-sized objects where experimenter pops up to say "peek-a-boo."

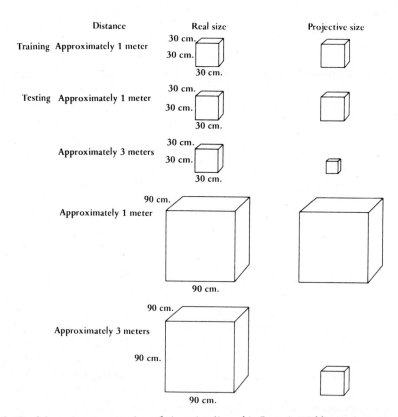

Figure 13.10 Schematic representation of the stimuli used in Bower's (1964) experiment on constancy.

and the projective size of the test stimulus was the same as the real size and the projective size of the training stimulus. The second test stimulus was the 30-centimeter cube placed at three meters from the infant. For this stimulus the real size was unchanged, but the size of the cube projected into the retina was very much smaller than when it was at one meter. In the third stimulus situation, a 90-centimeter cube was placed one meter from the infant. This test cube was much larger than the training stimulus in both real size and in projective size. The fourth stimulus was the 90-centimeter cube placed at three meters from the infant. While this cube was much larger than the training stimulus in reality, its projective size was now equal to that of the 30-centimeter training stimulus at one meter.

The number of conditioned responses in the four test conditions were 103, 66, 54, and 23 respectively, showing that, while the infants clearly responded less when any change was made, they responded more when real size was the same than when projective size was the same but real size was not. Thus, at least some of the information specifying distance and size-at-a-distance was received and used by the infants. Because they were not old enough to locomote and, therefore, had no opportunity for action in space, their discriminations of depth must have been made on the basis of information other than the learning associated with the projective size of objects displaced in depth. Because the infants responded to objects that were changed in their spatial positions in a manner independent of the spatial change, we may conclude that they showed a form of perceptual constancy.

In a subsequent study, Bower (1965) showed that motion parallax was the necessary stimulus for perceptual discrimination in infants between one and two months of age. These infants were also trained to turn their heads to one side to see the experimenter saying "peek-a-boo." There were three groups: a monocular group, a binocular group, and a group that saw only a projection of the real scene. All groups were able to make a discrimination based on changes in the size of the retinal projection. Only the first two groups, however, could discriminate among presentations where the retinal size was not changed. This response can be interpreted to mean that the infants could not only detect spatial position but could also detect size-at-a-distance, that is, they manifested size constancy. The ability to perceive size as invariant, with distance transformed, appears to have been based on information due to motion parallax. For both the binocular and monocular groups, head movements could produce relative displacements of objects and spaces in the visual field sufficient for the judgment.

In a similar experiment, Bower (1965) trained two-month-old infants to turn their heads whenever they were presented with a particular wooden block in a particular orientation. The infants were then tested for generalization with four different stimulus situations. In the first, the original block was presented in its original 45-degree orientation. This was simply a generalization test using the original stimulus with no change in orientation. The second test used the original block but now aligned with the fronto-parallel plane. This situation provided a stimulus with the same objective shape, but with a different projective shape and in a different orientation from the original. The third stimulus was provided by an object shaped like a trapezoid in the frontoparallel plane whose retinal projection was equal to that of the original block at 45 degrees. This object had a different objective shape from the original block but it provided a stimulus having the same projective shape as the original, although the orientation was different. The fourth stimulus was the trapezoid placed at 45 degrees. In this orientation, it provided a stimulus which had a different objective shape and a different projective shape from the original, but the orientation was the same.

The infants responded approximately twice as much to the original stimulus in the generalization test as they did to the stimuli that projected a retinal shape identical to it. They responded almost as much to the same objective shape in the different orientation as they did to the original stimulus. Bower argued that the infants had not learned to respond to a projective or retinal shape but to an objective shape which could be recognized in a new orientation. To this extent, they showed shape constancy.

Day and McKenzie (1973) found evidence for

shape constancy in infants 6 to 16 weeks of age, by measuring the rate of habituation of visual fixation to (a) a cube of constant orientation, (b) the same cube in different orientations, and (c) cutout photographs of the cube in different orientations. They reasoned that, if the infant has shape constancy—that is, if apparent shape is the same with variation of object orientation in depth—then little difference in rate of habituation with the cube in constant and different orientations should be seen. They found a decline in fixation time over trials for infants viewing a solid cube always in one orientation and for those viewing it when the orientation was changed on each trial. Thus, it seems as if the apparent shape was the same, regardless of orientation. There was no decline in fixation duration for infants viewing photographs of the cube in different orientations. Day and McKenzie concluded that the infants had demonstrated shape constancy.

Their data for size constancy were not as conclusive, however. McKenzie and Day (1972) maintained retinal size constant over four distances, 30, 50, 70, and 90 centimeters in one condition, and maintained actual size constant over the same distances in another. They reasoned that habituation would occur (a) with retinal size constant if the infants attended primarily to an object's projected size, (b) with actual size constant if they attended primarily to real size, and (c) would not occur if infants responded primarily to distance. They found no decline in fixation over trials under either condition, and concluded that the infants' attention was directed to varying object distance rather than to constancy of real or retinal size.

The fact that young infants display some degree of perceptual constancy suggests that distance information was not simply registered but was used appropriately in structuring space such that the perception of size and shape were reasonably unaffected by distance. Aronson and Tronick (1970) argued that perceptual structuring of this sort cannot be explained by assuming that distance perception develops within the first two months of life because, first, the reaching behavior that has long been the presumed learning mechanism for this accomplishment is not typically displayed before three months, and second, the infants would have had to learn to correlate distance infor-

mation with the changes in the retinal projection that are created by the same object at different distances, in addition to learning to perceive distance.

To see whether infants respond appropriately to objects with respect to changes in spatial position, Bower, Broughton, and Moore (1970) observed the adaptive responses of infants 6 to 20 days of age when an object approached them. This response consisted of the eyes opening wide, the head going backwards, and both hands coming up between the object and the face. The eyes generally remained straight ahead during the entire response.

In one experiment, they exposed infants to two foam-rubber cubes of different sizes moving directly toward the infants. The near-approach condition upset the infants sufficiently that the experiment had to be abandoned. Nevertheless it suggested that the infants were able to discriminate enough about the approaching cube to make an adaptive response. The next experiment used a visual expansion pattern projected onto a screen in front of the infants (aged 10 to 20 days). A red and black bulls-eye pattern initially attracted their gaze to the screen. On each trial an object moving away from the screen toward a point source of light produced an expansion pattern. Since the infants viewed the screen binocularly, they received the same pattern in both eyes—a situation somewhat different from the natural world where there would be binocular parallax associated with the stimulation to the two eyes. Figure 13.11 shows a typical shadow-casting device for producing an optical expansion pattern. Eight of the nine infants showed some avoidance responses to the expansion pattern. The responses were not as fully developed as when actual objects approached, although the same components were found. An additional experiment was performed to see whether the lower intensity of response was due to the lack of an air-pressure change. Four infants were exposed to air-pressure changes that approximated those produced by approaching objects. The air movement alone produced a response that was quite opposite to that produced by approaching real objects.

The adaptive response of infants to approaching objects was clearly demonstrated by Ball and Tronick

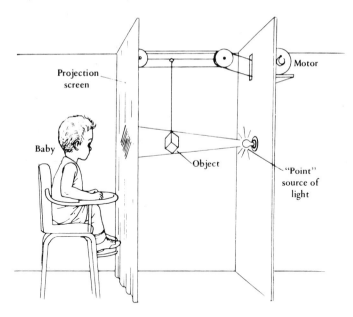

Figure 13.11   Typical shadow-casting apparatus for producing optical expansion patterns used by Bower, Broughton, and Moore (1970) and by Ball and Tronick (1971).

(1971). They found that infants 2 to 11 weeks of age responded with an integrated avoidance response and were "upset" when viewing symmetrically expanding shadows—the optical stimulus that specifies an approaching object. This response did not occur when the infants were presented with asymmetrically expanding shadows—the optical patterns that specify an object approaching but on a miss path. The response also did not occur for contracting shadows—the optical pattern specifying a receding object. These responses were observed in infants at all ages. In a second experiment, infants reacted defensively to the approach of a real object on a collision path, but not to one on a miss path. Apparently these infants were able to detect the direction and relative depth of approach, and could differentiate a collision path from a miss path, for both real objects and their optical equivalents.

These experiments show that the newborn infant displays a functionally appropriate avoidance response to approaching objects, and that visual stimuli control the response. While there are many experiments that show that infants can discriminate spatial variables, they do not show whether infants are perceiving objects-at-a-distance, or whether they are merely responding to proximal variables per se. For example, the demonstration that infants prefer to fixate solid objects rather than their two-dimensional representation does not differentiate between discrimination mediated proximally by information at the retinal or distally by the perceived spatial qualities of the object. That is, it cannot tell us whether the infants are fixating solids, as mediated by motion parallax and binocular parallax, or motion parallax and binocular parallax per se. This series of experiments on response to optical expansion found distally appropriate responses coordinated with distal variables—it was a response to the approach of an object, mediated by such variables as the optical expansion pattern. It was not merely a response to the proximal variables.

Perception and Action

A number of studies on infant perception utilized the fact that the visual system is involved as an integral part of specific acts. The most remarkable finding is the demonstration by Meltzoff and Moore (1977) that human infants under 21 days of age can imitate facial and manual gestures. The infants saw four gestures: lip protrusion, mouth opening, tongue protrusion, and sequential finger movements. Each infant's response to one gesture was compared to that for another similar gesture so the difference could not be attributed to mere arousal by oral activity of a dynamic human face. In two separate experiments, the judged behavior of the infants varied significantly as a function of the gestures seen (see Figure 13.12 for sample responses).

Meltzoff and Moore proposed that the neonate's imitation was based on its capacity to represent information visually and proprioceptively in a form common to both modalities and specific to neither—that is, "supermodal" representations. A comparison could then be made between the infant's own unseen action and the supermodal representation of the visually perceived gesture in order to construct the required match. In short, Meltzoff and Moore's suggestion is that the imitative responses observed were not innately organized and "released," but were accomplished through an active matching process, mediated by an abstract representational system. They conclude that the ability to act on the basis of an abstract representation of a perceptually absent stimulus becomes the starting point for psychological development in infancy—not its culmination. Indeed, they even report an observation of facial imitation in six newborn infants, one only 60 minutes old, to support their con-

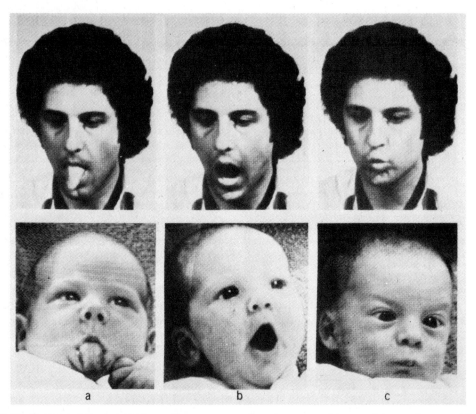

a   b   c

Figure 13.12 Samples of photographs from videotape recordings of two- to three-week-old infants imitating (*a*) tongue protrusion, (*b*) mouth opening, and (*c*) lip protrusion, demonstrated by an adult experimenter. (Meltzoff & Moore, 1977.)

tention that the use of intermodal equivalence is an innate ability.

Lee and Aronson (1974) showed that vision also plays an important role when an infant is learning to stand. To demonstrate the role of vision, they studied seven infants, 13–16 months old, who had between 1 and 22 weeks of experience walking. The infants were placed in the "swinging room" (see Chapter 10) and presented with optical flow patterns that would normally accompany either foreward or backward body sway. The infants' postural responses were recorded to determine whether they swayed, staggered, or fell, and the direction of change. Postural changes occurred on a majority of the trials and most of these were adjustments in posture to compensate for the visual information about body sway produced by the motion of the room.

That vision should play an important role in the early stages of locomotor development is suggested by the fact that the infant's body is changing rapidly during this period. The most sensitive information for standing is probably provided by the mechanoreceptors in the ankle, the associated muscles, and the soles of the feet. For the infant, however, the information from these receptors must be correlated with growth changes in lengths and weights of body parts. Indeed, few of the activities of the infant are capable of providing the constant practice or repetition needed for fine calibration of this system. Therefore, when the infant begins to stand, the mechanical proprioceptive system will afford only rudimentary and imprecise information. The visual system, on the other hand, is considerably more developed and reliable. Since this system should not be affected by skeletal growth, the infant should rely heavily on vision during the learning process. Later, vision can be used to keep the mechanical proprioceptive system in tune.

Space Perception in Children

A number of studies demonstrate that children and adults frequently do not produce similar judgments of size in a size-constancy experiment. The data of Zeigler and Leibowitz (1957) have been the basis for the argument that experience is an important factor in size constancy and, therefore, that size constancy improves with age. Before discussing all the ramifications of this position, it is best to describe the experiments.

Zeigler and Leibowitz had adults and children between seven and nine years old adjust the height of a comparison stick to match the height of a stick stimulus placed at different distances up to 30 meters from the viewer. The results are plotted in Figure 13.13. Adults were very accurate—their matches approximated the real size of the distant sticks. The children's matches were similar to those of the adults at the nearest distance (3 meters) but diverged progressively as distance increased. Zeigler and Leibowitz concluded that size constancy increases with age: that, through experience, the adult learns to utilize contextual cues to distance that provide the basis for a size-constancy correction. The child has not yet learned to use these cues effectively. Although the results from this study contradict some of the evidence from the infant literature, recall that Day and McKenzie's own work forced them to remark that the infant work is not conclusive with respect to size constancy. It is necessary, therefore, to examine other experiments with children.

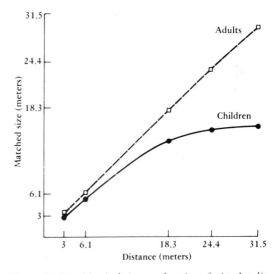

Figure 13.13 Matched size as a function of stimulus distance for children and adults. (Zeigler & Leibowitz, 1957.)

Rappoport (1967) tested children between 5 and 20 years of age by instructing them in two different ways. The "objective" instructions directed the viewer to judge the physical sizes of the test objects; the "apparent" instructions stressed how large the test objects "looked." Rappoport thought the increase in constancy with age may be due to "attitude" depending on instructions, an effect already demonstrated in adults (Carlson, 1960, 1962). She reasoned that "objective" instructions might encourage the subjects to compensate for distance and therefore show an increasing constancy function with age, whereas "apparent" instructions should not produce an age-related function. Each subject received both instructions and matched white triangles at 7.3 and 9 meters with standard stimuli at 2.5 and 3 meters.

Figure 13.14 shows the **point of subjective equality (PSE)** ratio for each age group tested, plotted separately for "objective" and "apparent" instructions. The PSE is the average of the size judgments when the viewer sets the comparison stimulus equal to the standard in accordance with the instructions. The **PSE ratio** is simply the ratio of the average size judgments to the size of the standard. Consequently, a PSE ratio of 1.00 would indicate perfect size constancy. Figure 13.14 shows that the size matches under "objective" instructions approached size constancy more closely the older the subject. Five-year-olds matched the stimuli at approximately 85 percent of their real size, whereas the matches of 15- to 20-year-olds was over 95 percent of real size. There was no increase with age under "apparent" instructions—the matches fluctuated about 90 percent of true size. Despite these overall differences, there was no effect of instructions and no age trend for the younger children (between 5.3 and 9.2 years old)—the differential response to instructions held only for children between 10 and 17 years of age. Rappoport explained these results as a reflection of the development of the ability to assume an "objective attitude" rather than an increase in their perceptual ability.

The importance of instructions in size-constancy experiments has been stressed by a number of investigators. The clearest demonstration of the effect of instructions, and of the interpretation of the problems raised, is the data of Leibowitz and Harvey (1967, 1969) who measured size matches under different instructions while varying other aspects of the experimental situation. In one experiment, adult subjects matched the size of human beings who stood in the

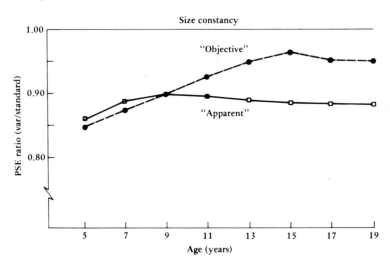

Figure 13.14 Size judgments under "objective" and "apparent" instructions for different aged subjects. (Rappoport, 1967.)

middle of a mall 104, 207, 311, 396, and 512 meters from the viewer. Three instructions were used: "objective" instructions, in which subjects were told to match size according to the "real size" of the stimulus object; "apparent" instructions, in which subjects were told to match size according to the way the stimulus object "looks"; and "retinal" instructions, in which subjects were told to match "projective" or "visual-angle" size.

Figure 13.15 shows the results, with the **Brunswik ratio (BR)** plotted as a function of distance. The Brunswik ratio equals $(PSE - VA)/(C - VA)$, where PSE is the point of subjective equality, VA is the size of a visual-angle match, and C is the size of a constancy match. The visual-angle match given by VA is the size the comparison would be set at if the viewer matched so that the comparison produced the same-sized stimulus extent on the retina as did the standard stimulus. A constancy match is when the comparison stimulus is set at the same size as the actual physical size of the standard. The Brunswik ratio transforms the PSE scale in such a way that visual-angle matches produce Brunswik ratios of 0.00 and constancy matches produce Brunswik ratios of 1.00.

"Objective" instructions produced fairly accurate constancy matches and did not vary as a function of distance. There was only a slight difference between the matches under "apparent" and "retinal" instruc-

tions, with the latter being closest to a visual-angle match. Both of these decreased slightly with distance. However, visual angle was never matched accurately—the ratios for "retinal" instructions fell between .09 and .18. It is clear that instructions are very important in size-matching experiments with adults. Different instructions could produce matches that were close to visual angle or to constancy depending on how the task is defined for the subjects. Moreover, Leibowitz and Harvey suggest that data obtained under "apparent" instructions are a first approximation to phenomenal size. In a second set of experiments, Leibowitz and Harvey (1969) used an unfamiliar test object (a 1.8-meter-high board) in an open mall, an open field, a field containing railroad tracks, and with all the variables combined. The results showed that the effect of instructions in a size-matching experiment was greater than that of any other single variable.

Tronick and Hershenson (1979) tested children between three and six years of age in a size-matching task in order to evaluate the role of instructions and of familiarity with the test objects. Prior to the experiment, each child was tested to determine what they understood about visual illusions—that is, whether they could knowingly separate illusory size from real size in the Jastrow illusion (see Figure 13.16). Although some children this age could separate their illusory experience from reality in the context of the two-dimensional illusion, none could respond differentially to "apparent" and "objective" instructions. All children produced fairly accurate matches of the objective size (size constancy) of objects at distances up to 3 meters, regardless of the instructions or of the familiarity of the test objects.

It would therefore appear that, judging from the infant and preschool data, size constancy is present in young children for near distances. The improvement with age may reflect the increasing ability to incorporate larger areas of space into an accurate constancy response. Moreover, older children begin to distinguish different modes of experience, and responses to these become more susceptible to control by instructions. Young children appear to operate only in a single instructional mode—that of objective size.

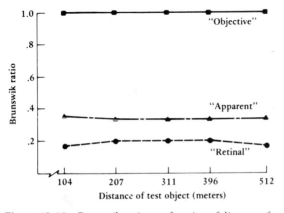

Figure 13.15 Brunswik ratio as a function of distance of test object (a human being) under Objective, Apparent, and Retinal instructions. (Leibowitz & Harvey, 1967.)

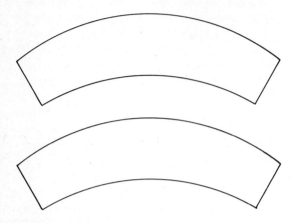

Figure 13.16   Jastrow illusion used to classify children in the Tronick and Hershenson (1979) study.

THE SCALE AND THE METRIC OF VISUAL SPACE

The data from experiments with human infants strongly support the psychophysical view described in Chapter 10. However, it is clear that perceptual development does take place—infants change their looking habits as they grow older and we suspect that they see things differently as a consequence.

One of the major developments that may be taking place during this period is the acquisition of a metric for the scale of space they already possess. This would explain the infant's ability to respond to the constancy of objects and would still leave room for the integration of information available to the infant only as a consequence of his own movements. The relational information provided by the retinal projection alone could be sufficient to produce perceptual constancy but it may not be sufficient to produce the exceptionally fine acts of perceptual-motor coordination of adults. Certainly the pinpoint accuracy in motor skills achieved by athletes in many sports—shooting in basketball and hockey, pitching in baseball, passing in football—requires more than the maturation of fine muscle control. The visual space we perceive must

have a very precise metric and that metric must be related to the size of our body and its parts.

A system that responded to relational information as a consequence of its structure, and to metric information as a consequence of development (learning, adaptation, or differentiation), would be precisely suitable to an organism gradually maturing and growing over a number of years. The basic spatial information—the ground with objects having constancy of size, shape, and position spaced out on it—would be available immediately and would provide a foundation for later development since it is based on those qualities of space that are permanent. The metric of this space would be changeable and could be continually modified as the organism's body size changes with age. At every age the organism would supply his own metric to the relational qualities of the scale of space, depending on his size within that space. In this sense, then, the perception of space is both innate and acquired.

SUMMARY

It appears that the human infant has a fairly well-constructed visual system but that his responses are mostly to aspects of stimuli (to features) rather than to entire forms. At an early age, the attention is directed to simple features of the environment. Moreover, the young infant appears to be able to respond to spatial information in a spatially appropriate way. Gradually the infant comes to respond to more global aspects of stimuli, to have his selective attention tempered by his past experience with objects, presumably because these objects acquire meaning. Perhaps his movements in space permit the infant to supplement the early experience of space with a metric that can be calibrated to the relative sizes of his own body. Regardless of whether these guesses about the precise course of perceptual developoment are correct, it is clear that the human infant is a pretty good perceiver in every sense of the term—the infant is active, selective, and a seeker after knowledge. His rapid acquisition of knowledge probably also rapidly alters his perceptual experience.

SUGGESTED READINGS

Details about the perceptual abilities of infants can be found in review articles by Hershenson (1967) and Bond (1972) and in a chapter by Hershenson (1971). Epstein (1977) covers many different topics in perceptual development in his book. Gibson's (1969) book is probably the most complete source for both theory and experimental findings. The two-volume work by Cohen and Salapatek (1975) provides a comprehensive and detailed view of the field.

SECTION THREE

PERCEPTION AS INFORMATION PROCESSING

Chapter 14

Processing Visual Information

This chapter begins a new section of this book—a shift to problems that contain a cognitive as well as a perceptual component. Naturally, much of our new interest is with meaningful stimuli—with how we perceive and come to understand figures, letters, words, and sentences as conveyors of meaning. The concepts to be developed in the following chapters may be applied to many of the problems discussed previously, although we will not do so explicitly. Nevertheless, we trust that the continuity between these sections will become apparent as we develop the principles of information processing.

We have already noted an information-processing emphasis in our discussion of the processing of information contained in the patterns of light focused on the retina in order to perceive the layout of space. Our focus is now on information about meaning, mainly meaning conveyed by symbols. How do we perceive, identify, recognize, and remember symbols whose meanings are arbitrarily assigned by convention, learning, or experience? The significance of an expression on a face, the message contained in a page of print, or the response to be made to a danger signal are all examples of what we achieve by processing information about meaning.

NATURE OF INFORMATION-PROCESSING ANALYSES

The information-processing approach to the study of perception did not arise as a reaction against other viewpoints. Rather, it was a reflection of new conceptualizations and methods applied to the study of perception. Along the way, however, some conflicts with older approaches have developed. For example, we usually express a **naïve realism** when describing our perceptual experience—we feel that what we see is a mirror of the stimulus. Moreover, this realism implies that seeing occurs automatically, immediately upon the onset of stimulation, and that it terminates with the offset of stimulation. These assumptions are clearly unwarranted (see Neisser, (1967), and the demonstration of their falsity has provided the foundation for developing the information-processing explanations of perception and cognition.

Assumptions

The major assumption of an information-processing approach is that perception is not an immediate outcome of stimulation, but is the result of processing over time. Neither the perceiver's visual experience nor his overt responses are immediate results of stimulation. They are consequences of processes, or of a sequence of processes, each of which takes a finite amount of time. Therefore, in studying a complex perceptual task such as visual recognition, this time interval may be divided into a number of stages or **processes,** corresponding to a series of transformations of the information contained in internal representations of the stimulus.

An information-processing approach also assumes that experimental operations can be devised to examine the contents of the representation of the stimulus information at every point in the sequence. Comparing the samples over time with the original stimulus projection provides the basis for inferences about the nature of the processing involved. The total time from stimulus onset to the occurrence of a response can be divided into intervals, each characterized by a different operation. Each process can be assigned (at least theoretically) a duration during which its characteristic operation is performed. The various juxtapositions of processes can be represented by a **flow diagram,** in which blocks are used to represent the processes occurring at different intervals. Each block is then labeled according to its operation. The blocks are connected to suggest the order in which the operations are performed. This approach makes explicit the operations, stages, or processes that occur in the time between stimulation and the observed response. It is the identification of the processes, along with the determination of their position and impact in the sequence, that provides the major task for information-processing theorists.

Storage or Memory

Information may be deposited and retained at various stages along the way in the sequence of processing. This property of an operation is called **storage** or **memory.** Frequently, different types of storage are separated according to their relative durations, as, for example, short-term or long-term memory. We can ask many questions about the nature of the contents of different storages. Since the retinal projection of the light itself cannot get "into" the organism, a represen-

tation of it, which we call **information,** is the content that we describe in our theories. When this information is stored, we want to know its relation to the information in the retinal projection of the stimulus. Is it in the same form, or has it been transformed? Is it coded in some way? We also ask about the nature of the storage. Is everything preserved in its original form or does the information decay slowly over time? Is it possible for information to be removed from this storage, and if so, how?

Processes

One assumption essential to an information-processing approach is that as information is used by a perceiver, operations may be applied that transform the information in many ways. Some of these operations have already been suggested. For example, in order to think about information being maintained in a memory, it is necessary to think about a process to place it there (a **read-in** process) and one to take it out (a **read-out** process). One such read-out process, called **scanning,** describes the procedure of going systematically from one portion of an information field to the next, and then to the next, and so forth. When a field is scanned, each item is treated in turn. This is called **serial processing.** An alternative procedure processes all the items of information at once. This is called **parallel processing.** Notice that these processes refer to internal representations and are not to be equated with visual search patterns in which eye movements are involved (see Chapter 16). Read-in and read-out processes represent the transfer of information from one place to another, usually between separate storage points. Frequently these processes involve the loss of information in transmission. Transfer may also involve **coding processes** that preserve a portion of the information in a more efficient form.

Information Processing and Information Theory

The approach just described is sometimes confused with **information theory,** the statistical specification and measurement of information in a stimulus and in responses (Attneave, 1959; Garner, 1962). This approach grew out of the early attempts to define and measure stimulation—a notoriously difficult task. Notice that even in this book on perception, we have not offered a formal definition of a stimulus, although there are many definitions by example. Part of the reason for confusion of the two approaches is that they have a common ancestry and frequently have been practiced by the same investigators (see Haber, 1973, for a general review).

Information was initially defined by Shannon (1948) as the amount of uncertainty reduction in a particular communication channel. This quantity could be calculated and was independent of the particular content of the uncertainty being reduced—that is, independent of the content of the stimuli, the responses, and the particular communication channel involved. This definition of information was applied to psychology in all areas in which psychological tasks were viewed as reducing uncertainty between stimuli and responses.

An example may help to clarify the concept of information measurement used in information theory. Suppose you are interested in measuring response time to the onset of light. You want to know whether the time it takes to react to the onset of a light is affected by the number of lights that could possibly be flashed. To test this, you vary the number of lights presented on a given trial, and the relative frequency of each. The subject is asked to name the light presented, or to press a key corresponding to the appropriate light, as quickly as possible. To calculate the amount of information contained in each trial, you have to take into account the number of possible lights and their relative frequencies of possible occurrence.

For example, if the subject is told that on the next trial the flash will be one of two lights, the probability that either will occur is 1 out of 2 or .5. This is a **binary outcome**—the result could be either one or the other of two events. This kind of situation (the *b*inary *it*em) is the fundamental unit of information measurement, and is called a **bit.** If there are four equally likely lights, the amount of information is two bits; if there are eight equally likely lights, the amount of information in the stimulus is three bits, and so forth.

To see how these values are calculated, consider the game of Twenty Questions. If the correct answer is one of two possible answers (A or B), you need only guess one to find the answer. If you guess "A" and you are correct, you have found the answer. If you guess "A" and you are incorrect, you have also found the answer, because you know that "B" must be correct. If, however, the answer is one of four possible outcomes (A, B, C, or D), and each is equally likely, the maximum number of questions you need to ask is never more than two. The first question divides the total set in half: "Is it A or B? The next guess divides the remaining set in half again to get the correct solution.

Following the same logic, if there are eight possible equally likely choices, then you need not make more than three guesses to find the correct answer. Thus, if the alternatives are equally likely, the amount of information in a single experimental trial before it begins is equal to the number of binary decisions that must be made to obtain a correct solution. This value is given by the power to which the number "two" must be raised to equal the total number of alternatives: $N = 2^i$, where N is the number of alternatives, (the number 2 represents the binary decision) and i is the amount of information in bits.

The alternatives do not need to be of equal likelihood in order to calculate the amount of information contained in a trial, but if they are not the actual probabilities of occurrence of each item would have to be included in the calculations. Consider trying to guess which letter of the alphabet is chosen if all 26 letters are placed in a hat and one is drawn at random. The information or uncertainty here is quite high: $26 = 2^{4.7}$ or 4.7 guesses on the average to get the letter chosen correctly. But suppose the letters are not drawn from a hat containing exactly one instance of each letter; that is, suppose the hat contains the letters in proportion to their frequencies of occurrence in English text. Instead of the probability of choosing any particular letter being 1 out of 26 or .04, it differs from letter to letter, with the probability for the letter E being about .12 and for the letter Z about .0001. The inequality of the likelihoods of the letters reduces their uncertainty and therefore the amount of information. For English letters occurring according to their distributional frequencies in print, the amount of uncertainty is not 4.7 bits but 3.8 bits.

Maximum uncertainty occurs when each item in a message is equally likely to occur. Guessing which letter is drawn from a hat containing each letter of the alphabet an equal number of times may be described as a maximum uncertainty task, the uncertainty being measured as 4.7 bits. In those cases where the uncertainty in the task is less than maximum, the total amount of uncertainty is divided into two portions—the observed uncertainty and redundancy. For example, if you know that the letters in the hat are selected according to their frequency in print, the uncertainty is less (about 3.8 bits). This is an observed uncertainty. Redundancy is defined as a percentage of maximum uncertainty. It is equal to the difference between maximum uncertainty and observed uncertainty, divided by maximum uncertainty and multiplied by 100. In the case of letters distributed according to their frequency in print, it is (4.7 − 3.8)(100)/4.7 or 19 percent redundancy.

If the letters are being drawn sequentially to form words, then determining the first letter of a word greatly reduces the number of possibilities for the second letter. For example, if the first letter in a word is a T, the only possible second letters in English words are H, R, W, Y, and the five vowels—not 26 alternatives but only 9. Of these nine, the letter H alone accounts for over 40 percent of the occurrences. This is a tremendous reduction in alternatives and, in fact, the amount of uncertainty in guessing letters when they are in words is only 2.3 bits. This yields a redundancy of about 50 percent for English letters in context.

Returning to our original example (the choice of lights), Hyman (1953) actually performed this experiment, getting the results shown in Figure 14.1. The time it takes to make a choice increased linearly with the information value of the stimulus. The larger the number of alternatives from which the stimulus is chosen, the longer it takes to respond. Notice that if the data are analyzed, not as information contained in the stimulus but more simply as the number of possible alternatives, the relationship to reaction time is more difficult to interpret (Fig. 14.2). Because the

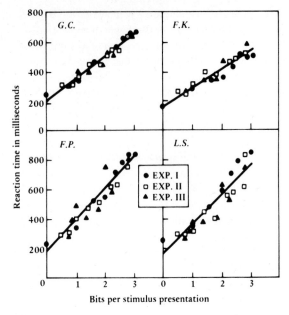

Figure 14.1 Simple reaction time in milliseconds to press a key to the onset of a light. Four subjects each served in three experiments, in which the relative probability of each alternative was varied. The horizontal axis is expressed in bits of information. (Hyman, 1953.)

information metric is linearly related to reaction time, Hyman suggested that the decision process is based directly upon the amount of information.

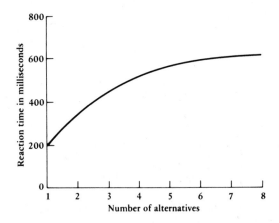

Figure 14.2 The data from subject F.P. in Figure 14.1 are replotted as a function of number of alternatives rather than bits of information.

Another reason for the use of information value rather than simply the number of alternatives is that the amount of information can be manipulated either by varying the number of alternatives or by varying the relative frequency of occurrence of the items. Hyman varied both of these and showed that, while each of these produce changes in reaction time, the relationship between reaction time and information is always linear regardless of how the changes in information are produced (compare the similarity of the different experimental values in Fig. 14.1). Thus, the one measure describes several different kinds of manipulations of the stimulus parameters.

Initially heralded as a major breakthrough, the promise of information measurement as applied to perceptual stimuli has not been fulfilled. Since it turned out to be relatively easy to calculate the amount of information contained in a stimulus or in a response, widespread use is made of this metric. But when the amount of information in stimuli and responses is correlated using different dependent variables, the relationships are not simplified. The amount of information in a pattern does not always correlate with ratings of complexity, simplicity, or similarity to other patterns, and does not always predict recognition, recall, speed of perception, threshold, or a number of other measures. Thus, the failure of information measurement in perception is empirical rather than theoretical. There are exceptions to this generalization in the literature (see especially Berlyne, 1973, 1974; and Garner, 1962) but in substance the metric fails to provide a useful description of form as a visual stimulus, and of recognition as a response. See Corcoran (1971) for a more recent review of this failure. The success with judgmental tasks is much better (see Garner, 1962), probably because the amount of information is computed over a number of different stimuli or the number of possible outcomes in a particular task. These situations are probably closer to the original application Shannon had in mind.

As a result, the refinement in definition offered by uncertainty reduction has had to be replaced by sophistication in experimental design, as well as a substantial amount of intuition. Rarely is information defined per se. Rather, the term simply refers to that aspect of the content of the stimulus that the experimenter is interested in studying or manipulating. By using a less precise term, we are able to speak more generally and to relate processes to one another that might otherwise be thought unrelated. In this sense, therefore, information is even less definable than stimulus. We do know that light impinges upon a perceiver, and we do know that something is processed and that we may label it information. It is part of the task of this approach to learn how to specify these terms more precisely.

THEORIES OF INFORMATION PROCESSING

Most researchers concerned with perceptual—cognitive functions agree with the descriptions of the assumptions and processes of the information-processing approach described above. In the 1960s, this general agreement resulted in a number of similar information-processing models. Figure 14.3 is a portion of a figure from the first edition of this book (Haber & Hershenson, 1973) showing a general model that reflects the ideas and data of the 1960s. Since then different models have evolved, many of which are discussed in later chapters within the context of discussions of specific processes whose functions they are developed to explain. Yet despite the many current alternatives, the model presented in Figure 14.3 still approximates what many theorists feel is a reasonable model of human information processing. At the least, it provides a clear set of conceptions with which other models may be contrasted. In the remainder of this chapter we describe briefly each of the components of this model. Some alternative conceptualizations are also presented.

A number of information-processing models have been proposed to account for many different psychological tasks (Atkinson and Shiffrin, 1968; Broadbent, 1958, 1971; Neisser, 1967; Norman, 1970; Posner, 1969; Sperling, 1963, 1967). The somewhat generalized version presented in Figure 14.3 owes much to the models suggested by these authors and others. It illustrates many of the general characteris-

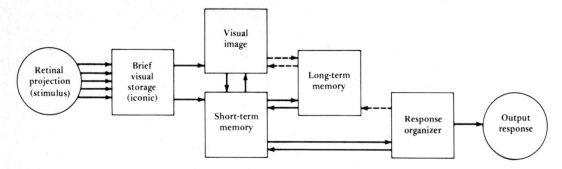

Figure 14.3 An information-processing model illustrates the more important stages, storages, processes, and channels. (Adapted from Haber and Hershenson, 1973.)

tics of information-processing models—stages, processes, storages, channels, and the interdependence of elements. While we do not discuss all of the data relevant to such a model of processing in perceptual tasks, we review some of this evidence.

The overall model may be divided into three parts: the luminance discontinuities in the light imaged on the retinal surface at any instant in time; the overt observable response made by the perceiver; and the nonobservable processes that form the heart of the model. Most models omit the first two parts, assuming that the distinction between observable and nonobservable phenomena is somehow to be understood. The model presented here makes explicit the difference between the retinal projection and the immediate internal representation of it. It also differentiates, at the other end, between the internal mental organization necessary to produce overt responses and the responses themselves.

The general shape of the model has some intuitive base, but it also derives from empirical evidence. If we start by analyzing what should (or, in some cases, must) occur to stimulus information to produce a relevant response, certain components of the model almost seem logically necessary. For example, the information defined by the luminance distribution in the retinal image must be internally represented in some way. Therefore, any model has to include this first storage. Second, it is clear that the overt responses require some prior programming and organization. Therefore, this fact must also be taken into account.

Frequently a substantial delay occurs between the first representation and the organization and production of a response. This suggests that the information is kept in some kind of storage for a period of time. The model in Figure 14.3 takes these considerations into account, while modifying them in accordance with experimental findings.

Brief Visual Storage

In the first stage, the information from the light impinging upon the retina is represented internally. This **iconic storage** is a neutral representation of the luminance discontinuities on the retina. It is therefore frequently described as "wholistic" and precategorical, meaning that it is an uninterpreted, unidentified copy of whatever is in the field of view (see Coltheart, 1975, for a detailed discussion of these characteristics).

The visual features that are the outputs of the receptive field organization of the cortex are prime candidates for the content of this representation. If the receptive field organization is the proper model for this information extraction, then we should show many arrows from the physical stimulus to the brief visual storage indicating that this analysis of features is a parallel process. This reflects a simultaneous coding of a large number of visual features from all parts of the retina.

Another view of this representation of the stimulus is simply to note that the stimulus information is coded "visually." This is the sense that Sperling

(1960) implied by labeling this first stage **visual information store,** and what Neisser (1967) had in mind when he called it iconic storage. The names "visual information store, "icon" or "iconic storage," and "brief visual storage" are used interchangeably in the following chapters.

The content of the iconic store appears to be related to the periodicity of saccadic eye movements. During the fixation time between saccades—a minimum of 250 milliseconds—the visual representations could be registered. When a saccadic movement occurs, the representations from the previous fixation are lost, due either to rapid decay during the eye fixation or to the suppression of visual sensitivity during the movement. (See Chapter 7 for a more detailed discussion of saccadic eye movements.) It is also possible that the new representation that arises from the new fixation erases the previous one. If the duration of exposure of the visual field is less than 250 milliseconds, then the persistence mechanisms discussed in Chapter 6 extend the duration of this brief visual storage to about 250 milliseconds. The quality of this representation deteriorates over this time and essentially fades away after .25 second.

Thus, in any perceptual task, the perceiver has little more than .25 second in which to process the content of this initial visual representation so that the information can be transferred to a somewhat more stable or permanent storage. Whether the content of the icon itself is affected by meaning, organization, or familiarity with the stimulus material before further processing has occurred remains a topic for research. These questions are discussed in Chapters 17 and 18.

The 1960s and 1970s produced much research on the role of iconic storage. Nevertheless, a separate iconic storage is not usually included as a central feature of recent information-processing models. Part of the reason for this is the work of Sakitt (1975, 1976; see Chapter 6), suggesting that the duration of the icon is simply a consequence of the persisting activity of the photoreceptors. Consequently, she saw no need for postulating the existence of a central process with properties distinct from retinal persistence. Another reason is the realization that, in typical perceptual tasks, the retinal image is continuously available during fixation pauses between saccadic eye movements. Thus, there is no reason to invent a storage device to preserve the information in the stimulus for a quarter of a second when stimulation normally remains for that period of time. The current usage of the term "iconic storage" simply refers to the fact that light imaged on the retina gives rise to neural codes that represent the information contained in the pattern of light.

Visual Image Representation

Two directions are indicated in Figure 14.3 for the processing sequence beyond the icon. It is expected that normally both channels are used in parallel. The upper one refers to the construction of a visual image representation that occurs soon after the onset of visual stimulation. This sequence indicates that stimulation is represented in a visual image—the conscious awareness or the experience of perceiving. Many perceptual theorists identify such a process as occurring after the original iconic storage and it is represented in our flow diagram in that position. It may be thought of as a constructed representation based on the content of the icon. If the representation is constructed, we would expect that it is integrated over time. Successive saccades introduce visual components that are combined with previous ones to build up an integrated image or picture. Such an image is by no means photographic, but rather follows the rules of perceptual organization (see Chapter 15).

The question of the duration of the visual image is also complex. If the visual image is a construction of the visual world, it contains more than the representations of the current fixation. Indeed, the entire visual scene has to be represented in the image since our eyes continually change fixation over the scene. In this sense, then, the visual image represents the entire visual world, not just that part seen with sharpest clarity in the center during the particular fixation. Since the visual image can be different from the specific content in the brief visual storage, the image may not be constrained at all by the one-quarter second duration of the iconic storage. If, after a visual construction has been established, the stimulus removed, and the visual field is blank, it is possible that the visual image persists. This is especially true if it is refreshed from short-term memory.

Since the greatest part of research on information processing has used verbal or symbolic stimuli easily coded into verbal representations, we know much less about how visual representations of visual scenes are constructed, stored, or remembered. Some of the work described in Chapters 8 through 13 appealed specifically to different models of how the information in light is processed into the perception of the scene before the eyes. But few of the researchers have translated their work on the perception of space into information-processing terms (an exception is Turvey, 1977).

Short-Term Memory

The second component into which visual information is transferred is called **short-term memory.** This sequence represents the encoding of the visual information into linguistic or conceptual representations that may occur either in parallel with the construction of a visual image or in series with it. The sequence might function as follows: When the stimulus is letters, the visual representations of the letters may be rapidly scanned in the icon so that they can be coded into the letter names. As we shall see, however, if the letters spell a familiar word, not all of the letters may need to be scanned separately. Only a few may be named, which, along with word shape and length, may be sufficient to derive the name of the word for storage in short-term memory.

There is evidence that the short-term memory representation is in the form of an **acoustic code.** The perceiver might literally name the letters when presented individually, or the phonemes comprising the word, as he scans them and transfers them from iconic storage to short-term memory. There may be a similar sequence for processing auditory stimuli. The acoustic signal is held briefly in an **echoic** (rather than "iconic") storage while its basic acoustic features are processed and encoded into phonemes that are then held in the short-term memory.

Short-term memory is not a permanent **storage.** Since it can store an auditory code (for example, letter and word names) it would require a duration sufficient to retain information until it could be encoded and stored in long-term memory, or used in an immediate response. For example, suppose you look up a telephone number and then need thirty seconds before you can use it by dialing the number. You cannot look at the telephone book during this time, but you are able to retain the information—the number has been residing in short-term memory. You may notice, moreover, that you are rehearsing it by saying the number to yourself over and over. A number of investigators have suggested that rehearsal of the auditory code is an essential feature of this type of storage. Without constant rehearsal, parts or all of the information may be lost. Rehearsal permits the information to be retained until it can be transferred to long-term storage, or used and forgotten. The duration of short-term memory is very much longer than that of the initial iconic storage. It certainly lasts several seconds without rehearsal, and may be much longer when rehearsal is used.

Long-Term Memory

The longest lasting information store is called **long-term memory,** with persistence measurable in decades. We do not say much about the properties of long-term memory in this book. Nevertheless, this system cannot be ignored, since its activities and contents affect both the contents of earlier stages and the types of transfers between them. The content of long-term memory may be images, or letters, or words, but is most likely to be some type of semantic representation that contains meaningful structure. Some of the properties of this system are discussed as they relate specifically to a perceptual problem or task under analysis in subsequent chapters. Many theorists now collapse short- and long-term memory into a single processing stage, and distinguish different levels of processing within it.

Output Processes

The last box in Figure 14.3 represents the outputs from the perceptual information-processing system. A spoken response requires a motor program to operate the articulatory apparatus. Written or pointing responses, or other behavioral indices reflecting perceptual activity, also require programs for their operation. This box therefore represents many possible avenues for output from the system, all of which are organized in some way.

Notice that the model provides no outputs from any other components of this information-processing system. There can be none from the visual image representation because there is no way that others can see our visual images. Nor is any output indicated from long-term memory, for the model assumes that the contents of memory first have to be translated into words or actions. Finally, no output is shown directly from the iconic storage. These assumptions of the model clearly require empirical evidence. Some already have strong support, but others do not. We shall discuss several of these further in subsequent chapters.

Interconnections

The interconnections between the processes in Figure 14.3 are specified by arrows that suggest the direction of action and influence. Arrows in both directions mean not only that information can flow in both directions, but that each process can influence the other. In general, the arrows represent the possible sequences for the processing of information. Thus, not only does the ordering of the processes supply conceptual hypotheses to be validated by research, but the arrows also suggest experimental problems.

The inputs to the iconic storage are shown in parallel, since light reflected from objects reaches all parts of the retina simultaneously. The two exits from the icon are assumed to be parallel and independent, although the possibility that they are serial is not yet disproved. There can be simultaneous naming of items represented in the icon along with a construction of their visual image representation. These are both information-extraction processes. It is supposed that the visual image construction always occurs, but the naming may occur only if the names are available. The contents of short-term memory (often influenced by long-term memory) may affect these two extraction processes. Hence, naming should occur faster if the material is familiar. Likewise, although we can construct a visual representation without prior experience

with the stimulus pattern, such familiarity might be capable of changing the visual image representation.

The arrows between the visual and short-term memory representations suggest that both can affect the other and either can be used to generate the other. For example, we can generate a visual image representation from a name even in the absence of concurrent visual stimulation. Similarly, we can name and describe our visual images even if we did not name the components when we initially processed them from the icon.

Long-term memory is reciprocally connected to short-term memory and to the visual image representation. The names of the components in the stimulus can be stored more permanently either as literal names, as when we rehearse and memorize a poem, or more typically as ideas or concepts. To retrieve these concepts later from long-term memory, names as words are regenerated. But these are paraphrases of the original text or representation, since the original itself is not stored. Notice also that visual image representations can be translated into long-term storage as concepts or ideas. It is not clear whether one can generate an image of stimulation directly from long-term memory, or whether one first has to go back through short-term memory.

The various stages (icon, visual image, short-term memory, long-term memory, articulation) can have substages within them. For example, the content of short-term memory can be maintained longer if it is rehearsed. This must be some form of repetition of the content, and must be conveyed by a self-feedback loop. It is possible that visual constructions can be rehearsed or refreshed internally without further inputs from the icon or short-term memory.

NEW CONCEPTS AND ISSUES

The general configuration of the process presented in Figure 14.3 still provides a satisfactory framework within which to discuss visual information processing. Naturally, some of the assumptions about the nature of the processes in different portions of the model have been questioned, and many of the interconnections have been the subject of intensive research. Indeed, some new concepts have been proposed that are not easily incorporated into a model like the one illustrated. Finally, some theorists have been less interested in a general model than in a more complete analysis of a single part. All these developments make the contemporary field of visual information processing much more complicated and less organized than it was in the recent past. We have already commented on the changes in the notion of an iconic stage of storage. This diversity is reflected in the large number of specific models presented in the remaining chapters. In order to provide some coherence, however, we conclude this chapter with a brief description and discussion of some of the newer concepts and issues. Many of them reappear in later chapters when different aspects of perceptual-cognitive functioning are examined in detail.

Channel Capacity

Experiments are not necessary to demonstrate that we do not notice everything before our eyes, that we cannot perform two tasks at once as well as either alone, and that we forget many things once learned. These facts suggest that information input is less than maximum, that central processing may be limited to one task at a time, and that memory or storage may have an upper limit to its capacity. A number of different concepts have been developed to describe and explain **channel capacity**, the limits or boundaries on the amount of information that can be processed. One idea is that the amount of information that can be processed, or held in storage, is determined by the limitations inherent in the nature of the process, or of the store. Or the limit may be due to the nature of the information itself. For example, it has been asserted that short-term memory can hold only seven plus-or-minus-two (7 ± 2)—that is, five-to-nine—independent items at a time (for example, Miller, 1956). If this is the case, then simultaneous visual presentation of a greater number of unrelated items would necessarily result in some of them not being reported because they could not be retained in short-term memory. What may have initially appeared as a limit on perception could now be understood as the reflec-

tion of a limit of a subsequent process, the short-term memory.

It is now recognized, moreover, that the limit may not be fixed, but may be altered dramatically by the way in which the information is encoded and processed. Even Miller, in noting the channel limitation, indicated that, if the items were organized into larger units (**chunks**), the limit may be raised. Craik and Lockhart (1972) have extended this idea by proposing the stratification of levels of processing, suggesting that information can be processed as single, unrelated items, or as items that have some associated relationship to each other, or as integrated components in an overall structure. The deeper and more complex the level of processing at the time of initial stimulation, the more items can be reported initially, and the more of them that can be remembered later. In this sense, then, the limit of capacity is not set by some aspect of the physical structure of the channel or store, but by the nature of the processing carried out on the information.

Control of Processing

One of the natural assumptions of an information-processing analysis is that the processing is adjusted to fit the demands of the tasks and of the information content. For example, when we read for content, we do it differently than when we proofread for errors; when we search for our roommate in a crowd, we do it differently than when we are looking for someone interesting with whom to share a cup of coffee. One of the advances attributable to information-processing analysis is the ability to map out alternative processing routes and alternative processing strategies. There has been a great deal of research in the past twenty years concerned with the ways in which perceivers adjust their strategies as a function of task and information demands.

Recently, this apparent flexibility has been questioned as a result of experimental findings that suggest that perceivers may not utilize all the flexibility the system appears to permit. For example, recent studies on proofreading tasks show that perceivers cannot abandon the normal reading strategy even though it is inappropriate, causes errors, and slows down the search when looking for errors (Schindler, 1978).

What we are coming to realize is that many information-processing tasks are well learned and well practiced. Consequently, perceivers utilize the learned strategies for all related tasks, even if they are less efficient.

The recent work by Schneider and Shiffrin (1977) and Shiffrin and Schneider (1977) have highlighted the distinction between automatic and controlled processes, and provided evidence of when each are used. For them, automatic processes result from overlearned and overpracticed responses to the same stimulus arrangements, such as learning the names of the alphabet, or knowing how to read. Once acquired, the appropriate stimuli engage the processing without taking up any processing capacity in short-term memory. This automaticity is at the expense of flexibility in that such automatic processes are inflexible and cannot be suppressed, even when the perceiver wishes to do elsewise. Controlled processes, on the other hand, do take up capacity, are relatively slow, and handle information item by item. But they are under attentive control, and can be altered or reprogrammed as the circumstances require. The great power of this distinction is the facility with which it can describe a variety of processing tasks within the context of a single information-processing model.

Effort and Attention

It has always been obvious that doing two things at once is difficult if not impossible. What has not been clear is why. In fact, this aspect of information processing has drawn more theoretical focus than any other single problem. The oldest and most developed idea is that attention acts like a perceptual filter (Broadbent, 1958) such that a switching or filter mechanism separates the inputs to be processed from those to be momentarily or permanently blocked from access to processing channels. When experiments began to show that the filtering was often not peripheral, new conceptions of the attentional process had to be developed. One of the most important of these is the concept of attentional effort (Kahneman, 1973). Kahneman assumed that any processing task takes mental effort and that the limit on processing is not due to channel capacity but to a limit on the amount of effort that can be invested at any one moment. This

approach is useful because we know that there are many complex tasks (such as driving a car) that appear to take little attentional effort unless an emergency arises. Kahneman provided some rules for determining how much effort is needed and when the effort can be divided among several tasks.

Allport (1971) also focused on the division of attention but tried to determine the similarity of the processing stages for different kinds of tasks. He argues that any two information-processing tasks can be performed simultaneously if they utilized different processing steps. Thus, for example, we can drive a car and listen to a conversation, or play a piano and listen to a conversation, but we can not listen to one conversation and type another at the same time.

Sequence

Flowchart models like that in Figure 14.3 make it easy to think of the system as a serial processor—first carrying out one step, then another, then the third; each in a particular order; each taking some time before the next one begins. This conception is useful, simple, and straightforward. Indeed, many experiments provide support for serial processing, but the results of other experiments suggest that certain tasks are performed in parallel that is, the information from different parts of the display appears to be processed at the same time. There is also evidence that a given system may process information serially or in parallel, depending on the nature of the information available and the way the task is understood. Moreover, it may be that, as often the case with simple conceptions, the serial–parallel distinction itself may not be applicable to the combined action of processes necessary to perform even the simplest visual tasks. If this were the case, no experiment could unequivocally differentiate between them (Townsend, 1971).

SUMMARY

This chapter introduced the section on perception as information processing. It provided an overview and introduced a new way of thinking about perceptual processes.

The information-processing approach is characterized by its focus on the information contained in the visual stimulus and on how this information is transformed into different representations or codes as it is used in different tasks. The codes may be visual, auditory, linguistic, or semantic, or take other forms. This way of thinking makes it clear that several stages or processes are involved, and that perceptual processes cannot be considered immediate or instantaneous.

The result of each process must be stored, or temporarily retained, suggesting that the information-processing sequence can be subdivided into stages, stores, and processes—each with its own internal sequences, time constants, and interconnections. Some of these processes are illustrated in a general model containing a brief visual storage, a visual image, a short-term memory, a long-term memory, and a response organizer. Each process, and its interconnections, is described briefly. New concepts and issues are also described relating to problems of channel capacity, the control of processing, the relation between attention and effort, and the sequence of processes.

SUGGESTED READINGS

Although this is a relatively new area in perception, a number of general discussions is available for further study. Haber (1973) has written a brief general introduction to information-processing approaches in perception. His collection of readings (Haber, 1969) on a variety of topics in this area provides a wide range of research and theoretical articles. Some other general models of information-processing tasks are developed and discussed in Broadbent (1971), Moray (1970), Neisser (1967), and Norman (1970), as well as in some of the more specific references given in the chapter. Leibovic (1969) provides a link to some of the visual nervous system components of these more complex processes. Comprehensive recent reviews can be found in Massaro (1975) and Rummelhardt (1977).

Chapter 15

The Perception of Form

THE PROBLEM OF FORM PERCEPTION

In Chapter 4 we presented what is known about the neural coding of visual edges, the boundaries between areas of different luminances on the retinal surface. At that stage we took for granted that if a particular pattern of visual edges on the retina arose because of a particular pattern of surfaces in space reflecting light to the retina, we would somehow come to perceive only that pattern of surfaces and none other. However, we noted there that the pattern of visual edges on the retina does not resemble the pattern of edges in space, that the retinal image is not a picture that resembles the scene in space before the eyes. Without reviewing all the evidence again, this fact suggests that what we perceive cannot be explained simply by examining the structure of the pattern on the retina. Rather, what we need is a set of organizational principles or rules that describes the relationship between stimulation and perception.

Figure 15.1 provides three simple examples. In the first we can perceive either a vase or the profiles of two people facing each other. Although those two perceptions alternate, there is nothing in the picture that changes. Since the alternation even occurs without eye movements, the changes in perception must be the

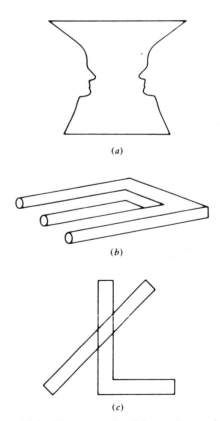

(a)

(b)

(c)

Figure 15.1   Three examples of figures that can be perceived in different ways.

result of changes in the perceptual system and not in the stimulus. In the middle example, the perceptual changes depend upon where you look. Here there must be something in the way the form is drawn that violates normal organizational principles. In the last example, we tend to see a letterlike figure with a bar across it. Logically, however, many perceptual organizations are possible, yet we see only one of them. What rules determine why that one is perceived and not some other? These examples are trivial, but the problem of explaining the organization principles that account for which visual edges are grouped together to form a perception is far from trivial. That is the topic of this chapter.

The term **form perception** can refer to the perception of three-dimensional objects that are represented in pictures or line drawings, or to the perception of symbols that have no existence in the real world. In the former case, a two-dimensional stimulus represents a three-dimensional object; in the latter case, a two-dimensional configuration simply represents itself or another two-dimensional configuration. An object in space is said to have a **shape** or a **form** determined by the outline of its outer surfaces. That is, when we say that an object is "round" or "boxlike" we mean, among other things, that the outer (visible) surfaces of round objects are curved and the outer surfaces of boxlike objects are flat. The study of shape-at-a-slant and shape constancy attempts to understand the perception of an object's shape in three

dimensions within the context of the perception of visual space.

However, form perception of objects can also be explored in two dimensions, the shape of objects projected onto planes. It is the study of the perception of the outline shape of objects as a single unit, of **configurations,** and of the fact that the shape itself involves parts that must be seen in a particular relationship to one another. For example, two eyes, a nose, and a mouth must be in particular spatial positions with respect to each other—for the total configuration to be perceived as a face. It is the study of this global perception of configuration that is the prototype for the study of the perception of form.

The term "form perception" is usually reserved for the perception of outline shapes in the frontal plane, whereas the study of the shapes of objects at slants to the observer is usually included under the heading "shape constancy" in a section on space perception (for example, Chapter 8, pp 180–183). The reason for this distinction can be understood by examining the kinds of stimulus transformations involved in the perception of shape in each case. Figure 15.2 illustrates the relationships between these two problems. Part (*a*) shows the outline shape of a bicycle in a frontal plane. The perception of this configuration as a whole and the recognition of this shape as a bicycle is a problem for study as a part of form perception. In panels (*b*) and (*c*) of Figure 15.2, the planes and the outline shapes have been rotated about

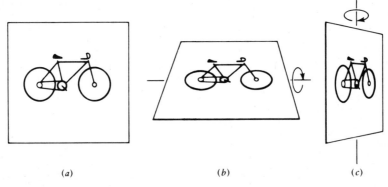

(*a*)   (*b*)   (*c*)

Figure 15.2   An outline shape of a bicycle (*a*) in a frontal plane, (*b*) in a plane rotated about a horizontal axis, and (*c*) in a plane rotated about a vertical axis. Perception of the

bicycle in (*a*) is a problem in form perception. The other two represent problems in shape constancy.

horizontal and vertical axes respectively. Both of these transformations are perspective transformations like those discussed in the chapters on space perception. The shape changes that occur are therefore all predictable from the laws of perspective. They do not alter the apparent shape of the object under normal circumstances where shape constancy prevails. The perception of shape in this situation is the product of whatever mechanisms produce shape constancy—the mechanisms already discussed in detail in Chapters 8, 9, and 10.

The uniqueness of the problem of form perception can be seen in the kinds of transformations that affect the perception of forms. Many years ago, the Gestalt psychologists showed that a form can be changed in its size, or in its position on the retina, without changing its perceived shape. This suggested to the Gestaltists that the geometrical relationships among the parts of the figures, rather than the elements themselves, provided the information essential for the perception of form. It was clearly demonstrated that perception remains unchanged if the relations are not altered, even when the elements are changed markedly. Figure 15.3 illustrates the stability of

shape perception over changes in size and in the elements comprising the shapes.

From this observation, it is possible to define form (or shape) by the pattern of invariant relationships. A particular form is specified if no change occurs in our perception of it even if its elements or component features are changed. It is the relationship among elements, independent of the elements themselves, that define a form.

Orientation and Form

In addition to geometrical relations among the parts of the figure itself, changing the **orientation** of the form markedly affects the way it is perceived (Rock, 1973). Changes in orientation involve rotations about a horizontal axis perpendicular to the plane of the figure (that is, rotation about the line of sight) that produce alterations of the up–down and left–right sides of the figure. These transformations produce marked changes in the perception of the figure (the way it looks) and in its recognition and identification. The influence of orientation in the recognition of form is illustrated in Figure 15.4. When the shape is presented in the orientation shown in the figure, it is usually not recognized. However, if the page is rotated clockwise 90 degrees, the shape is

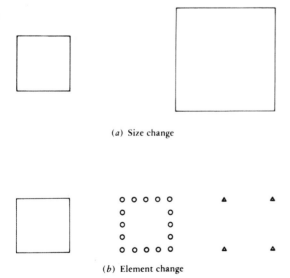

(a) Size change

(b) Element change

Figure 15.3 Illustration of stability in the perception of shape over transformations of size (a) and of the elements comprising the shape (b).

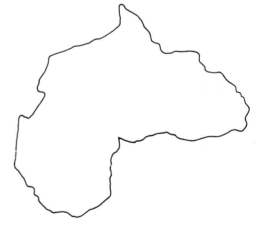

Figure 15.4 A shape that is usually not recognized in the orientation shown. However, if the page is rotated clockwise through 90 degrees, the shape should be recognized immediately as the outline of the African continent.

usually immediately recognized as the outline of the African continent.

Since orientation of a pattern changes the way it is perceived, then orientation has to be included in the definition of form. Specifically, the relationships of the elements to a gravitational upright is altered, as well as the relationship to the observer's own frame of reference.

Rock (1973) has studied the effects of changes in orientation on recognition of forms in the frontal plane. Figure 15.5 shows two of Rock's examples. The ambiguous shapes in (*a*) can look like a person's head with a chef's hat or, when rotated 90 degrees, like a dog. The outline shape in (*b*) can look like the profile of a bearded man's head or the map of the United States. Mach (1914) noted long ago that a square looks very different when rotated 45 degrees (Fig. 15.6). The two figures have identical sides and angles but the figures do not look the same. Even the angles of the diamond do not look like right angles. Orientation changes also affect recognition of complex pictures, as in Figure 15.7.

In studying the role of orientation, Rock identified two major changes that can occur when a figure is rotated in the frontal plane: (*a*) a change in the orien-

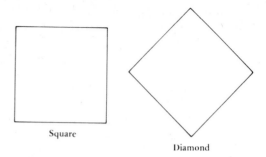

Square

Diamond

Figure 15.6 Although these figures have exactly the same elements in exactly the same relationships (all sides equal, all angles 90 degrees), orientation makes the shape on the left look like a square and the shape on the right look like a diamond. Indeed, the angles of the diamond do not look like right angles.

tation of the retinal image and (*b*) a change in the orientation with respect to the environment. The environmental changes include orientation both with respect to gravity and with respect to the visual frame of reference. In an early study, Rock (1956) showed that environmental orientation played the most important role (Fig. 15.4). In a series of experiments, Rock (1973) demonstrated that for an unfamiliar figure, change in orientation of the retinal image pro-

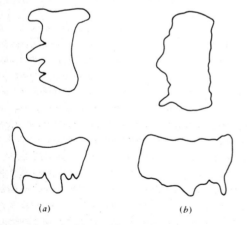

(*a*)   (*b*)

Figure 15.5 Ambiguous figures that are perceived differently depending on the orientation assigned to them. (*a*) can look like a head with a chef's hat or, when rotated 90 degrees, like a dog. (*b*) can look like the profile of a bearded man's head or like a map of the United States. (After Rock, 1956.)

Figure 15.7 Do you recognize this face? If not, turn the page upside-down.

duces little change in appearance of the figure. However, changing the orientation with respect to the environment alters the perception of the stimulus so that it is seen as a different figure. Indeed, in a recognition task, such an altered figure is rarely recognized.

Rock explained these findings by proposing that perceivers implicitly assign the directions top, bottom, left, and right to a figure on the basis of other information. This information may come from the visual frame of reference (Fig. 15.8) or from gravity. It is used by the perceiver to determine what is up and what is down in the environment. Rock differentiated form perception from contour formation—form perception is like an act of cognition in which the perceiver synthesizes a set of nonverbal descriptors of the figure. The set includes not only the features of the configuration and their interrelationships, but also the characteristics of the figure in relation to its top, bottom, and sides. This "description" of the figure determines what memory traces are judged similar to it and, consequently, whether the figure is recognized or not.

In this chapter we shall consider several sets of principles of organization that help determine which elements of a pattern are perceived together. The most powerful principle is based upon organization in

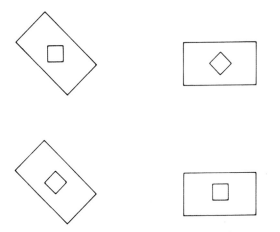

Figure 15.8 The importance of the frame of reference in figure perception. The upper figures appear to have diamonds in the frames while the lower figures appear to have squares within the frames. (After Kopfermann, 1930.)

depth. Visual edges on the retina are organized together if they can be perceived as belonging to the same object surfaces in space. This requires, therefore, that the three-dimensional layout of space be processed, as described in some detail in Chapters 8, 9, and 10. Three other principles are considered; one based upon figure–ground segregation, one based upon symbolic two-dimensional rules following Gestalt principles, and one based upon learned meaningfulness, familiarity, or predictability among the elements in the pattern. Since all these depend upon the presence of visual edges, we shall first examine what happens to perception in the absence of edges.

THE ROLE OF VISUAL EDGES

In Chapter 4 we described how luminance discontinuities in the retinal projection are transduced into neural information that reflects these discontinuities. It seems reasonable that the presence of borders, edges, and contours in the stimulus would provide the minimal information necessary for form perception, since they would provide the building blocks, the visual features, for the perception of stable, discrete portions of the visual field as figures and objects. Investigations concerning the perceptual effects of homogeneous stimulation in a Ganzfeld and of stabilized retinal projections relate directly to this problem.

Ganzfeld Research

Homogeneous stimulus fields, called **Ganzfelds,** are difficult to produce. An approximation of such a stimulus field was created by Hochberg, Triebel, and Seaman (1951), when they had perceivers wear caps over their eyes made from halves of Ping-Pong balls. Light was focused on the eyecaps, and red and green filters were used to provide color stimulation. Perceivers reported their visual sensations in a number of different situations. Under continuous red-light stimulation, they reported seeing a surfaceless field, sometimes described as "a fog of color," followed by total disappearance of color within three minutes. They reported then seeing a black or dark gray field, sometimes containing "hallucinatory shapes" and also sometimes containing what has been called a "flight of colors." The perceivers believed they ceased to see color because the illumination had been changed.

To determine whether the effect was peripheral or central, Hochberg et al. exposed only one eye and asked the perceiver to describe his perceptual experience as given by his unexposed eye. For example, the perceiver's left eye was exposed to red light until the color disappeared, and then both eyes were illuminated by red light. Most viewers reported seeing red after this sequence of stimulation. A few of them said they saw red in both eyes, but others reported seeing red in the right (unadapted) eye alone. The fact that the adaptation occurred predominantly in one eye suggested that the adaptation processes were peripheral rather than central.

The introduction of inhomogeneity further altered the perceptual experience. If, after the disappearance of color, a shadow was introduced over the eyecap by moving a finger vertically onto the central portion of the eyecap, the perceivers reported seeing a black shadow with a color halo around it in the background. These halos and the shadows quickly disappeared upon removal of the finger. If perceivers moved their eyes briskly back and forth from left to right, half of them reported the reappearance of the color, and half reported a quickly fading flash of color. If the light was interrupted for a two-second period, nearly all perceivers reported seeing complementary colors. The reestablishment of the stimulation yielded a flash of color. Thus, stimulation by a homogeneous chromatic visual field produced the loss of the perception of color. Inhomogeneity, or change in the stimulus field, was crucial for the maintenance of the visual experience.

Cohen (1957) explored the changes in perceptual experience of the texture and spatial characteristics of the Ganzfeld in a series of experiments in which the stimulus field was more precisely controlled than in the Hochberg experiments. The apparatus consisted of two 1-meter-diameter spheres that were joined together. Their inner walls were highly reflecting and showed no visible texture (Fig. 15.9). A hole in one sphere allowed monocular vision perpendicular to the plane of the aperture between the spheres, enabling a viewer to see partially into both the spheres. Two projectors were used to control the illumination, one for each Ganzfeld. When the Ganzfelds were equal in luminance, a homogeneous luminance distribution was presented to the eye. This resulted in the perception of a homogeneous field, that is, the aperture between them ceased to exist in the perceivers' experience. They reported seeing a foglike field, close at hand, but extending for an indefinite distance in front of them. The perceivers felt as if they were in the midst of a fog. After three minutes of adaptation, 15 of the 16 perceivers even reported complete cessation of all visual experience—that is, they did not even have the experience of blackness.

When the two spheres differed in luminance, perceivers reported seeing a simple inhomogeneity in an otherwise uniform field. This tended to reduce the density of the fog and increase its distance. For greater inhomogeneities, the aperture between the spheres was seen as a figure on a background. The appearance of a surface was related to the definiteness of figure–ground segregation, which was, in turn, related to the sharpness of boundaries. Chromatic gradients alone produced an indefinite figure; intensity gradients produced definite segregation of figure–ground, with the disappearance of the fog.

Cohen concluded that spatial inhomogeneity and temporal change are crucial for the maintenance of even minimal perceptual experience. Inhomogeneity in a field created figures and grounds and stabilized

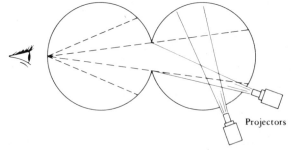

Projectors

Figure 15.9 Schematic representation of the arrangement of two spheres used by Cohen (1957) to produce a *Ganzfeld*.

the colors and the distances of the backgrounds. Figures therefore depend on inhomogeneity in the stimulating environment and, as is shown below, the presence of a figure is essential for the maintenance of the ground from which it emerged.

Microgenetic Development of Contours

Our discussion of temporal processes made it clear that all perceptual events take time, but relatively little work has been done on the phenomenological characteristics of these temporal events. In their microgenetic theory, Werner and Wapner (1952) argued that contours should take time to be perceived and that this development can be observed. They also suggested that the development can be interrupted if other contours are presented at about the same time. Several interesting experiments demonstrate this.

Cheatham (1952) tried to determine how long it takes a stimulus to be perceived, and how the contours develop during that time. He presented a stimulus field that contained a circle, a triangle, a square, or a diamond for 100 milliseconds, followed by a large masking field, presented some time later, also for 100 milliseconds. The response measured was transition points between three zones of phenomenal development. The first was the time for the perceiver to report the change from a simple brightening in the central part of the field to the appearance of the first part of a contour. This latency measured how long it took from the onset of the stimulus to the first inkling of contour that the perceiver could discriminate. The second was the latency of the change from a partial or incomplete contour to a complete or total contour (the figural development time). The results showed that latency and development time were inversely related to the luminance of the first stimulus field. The latency of the initial appearance of contour did not vary as a function of the shape of the stimulus, but shape was important for the development of complete contour: the circle, and the square were perceived more rapidly than the triangle or diamond. The perceivers reported that the sides of figures appeared before the angles and that hue was not perceived until the complete contour was formed. This is a simple demonstration of the sequence of events in the perception of simple forms, and supports the assumption that perceptual processes take time.

Simple interactions have also been shown for figural stimuli such as a disk and ring, as in metacontrast (Chapter 6, p. 133). If a black disk is presented in a white field for approximately 25 milliseconds, followed at various interstimulus intervals by a black ring that surrounds the disk, most perceivers report that, for some critical interstimulus interval, the ring has a light rather than the dark center formed by the disk. In explaining this phenomenon, Werner (1935) suggested that the perception of an object takes a finite time to develop. If the contour cannot be formed during that time, then the figure is not perceived. If, in the above situation, the process of forming the contour of the disk is still occurring when the ring is presented, the (outer) contour of the disk is used in constructing the ring. Therefore the outer contour of the disk is "usurped," so to speak, by the ring. Consequently, the center of the ring is identified with the background and seen as white. Werner used the notion of contour development to explain why maximum metacontrast masking occurs with a delay of about 50 milliseconds rather than with simultaneous presentation of disk and ring. If the ring comes at the same time as the disk, the inner contour of the ring does not develop at all and the entire area is black. Thus, there must be some development in order for interference to occur. If the ring comes first, the contour can develop and the disk cannot interfere with it.

Repetition Effects A topic related to microgenesis concerns the **repetition effect.** In a series of studies, Haber and Hershenson (1965a, 1965b; Dainoff & Haber, 1967; Haber, 1965; Hershenson & Haber, 1965) showed that if a pattern is initially presented sufficiently dimly and briefly so as to produce nothing more than a fleeting awareness of a flash and if it is presented repeatedly at the same energy value, it becomes progressively more visible, perceptually clearer, and eventually clear enough so that the perceiver can see and identify all the elements of the pattern. Figure 15.10 presents the results of a typical experiment. Since the intertrial intervals are as

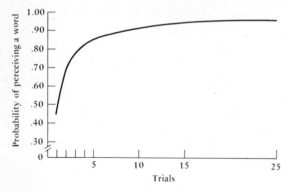

Figure 15.10 Increase in the number of letters clearly seen as a function of repetition of presentation. (Haber & Hershenson, 1969a).

long as 10 seconds, and can be even longer, the repetition effect cannot be explained by temporal integration, as the latter effects extend over no more than a few hundred milliseconds at best.

While there have been many demonstrations of the repetition effect (see Uhlarik and Johnson, 1978, for a review), so that its validity is well documented, its explanation is less clear. To say that there is some storage and accumulation of information from presentation to presentation does little more than restate the results. Haber and Hershenson postulated the successive development of a percept, with each flash being inadequate to establish a full percept, but adding to the accumulation of the previous ones. Doherty and Keeley (1972) argued to the contrary that each flash produced an inadequate but independent effect, and that the perceiver remembered what came in each in order to make a composite and therefore accurate guess about the entire stimulus pattern. This hypothesis seems unlikely to be the entire answer, since Haber and Hershenson (1965) showed that the repetition effect is unaltered even if the perceivers are shown the pattern ahead of time so that they are thoroughly familiar with it. If they are merely guessing, they should have been perfect on the first trial. Further, Standing, Sell, Boss, and Haber (1970) showed that the magnitude of the repetition effect is increased if the subject images the same pattern, but is decreased if the subject images a different one during the pre-

sentations, in both cases with full knowledge of what the pattern contained.

ORGANIZATION OF FORM FROM DEPTH

Perceiving which visual edges belong together often is the result of perceiving an organization in depth. If a visual edge is seen as a boundary of a surface, it is perceived as belonging to the other edges of that same surface, and different from boundaries of adjacent surfaces, or of surfaces nearer or farther away. Fundamentally this requires an analysis of which visual edges on the retinal surface are reflectance edges (see Chapters 4 and 9), since only reflectance edges provide potential information about the layout of space. Any available information that specifies that two visual edges are at different distances from the perceiver also specifies that those two edges belong to different surfaces or to different objects, and therefore are not to be organized together in perception.

We have already considered the various kinds of information available that specify the layout of space. In Chapter 12 we described how flat pictures (and even line drawings) can convey information about depth, and we suggested that such two-dimensional pictures are always treated as if they were pictures of three-dimensional scenes. In this sense then, the use of depth information to perceive the layout of space, and therefore the organization of the visual edges into the proper combination of surfaces and objects, is the primary way in which perceived organization occurs. This was especially highlighted by the analysis of visual illusions and subjective contours (Chapter 12, pp. 261–263), in which we ascribed many of these examples of misperceptions to the presence of inappropriate information about depth.

As we noted in the introduction to this chapter, the perception of form is equivalent to the perception of shape when looking at a three-dimensional scene. It is when looking at two-dimensional representations that form perception is more interesting in its own right. Yet, as we argued in Chapter 12, there is sufficient information about the layout of space in a picture of a scene to correctly perceive the scene itself. Therefore, perceiving the forms in a picture of a scene is equivalent to perceiving the shapes in the scene itself. It is only when the two-dimensional representation becomes symbolic or abstract, or where the depth information is improperly rendered, that form perception becomes unusual. Thus, if the information in the drawing is ambiguous with respect to depth, the form perceived may be unstable or ambiguous as well. In the absence of depth information, some of the other organizational principles can come into play. We shall briefly consider two of these that refer almost exclusively to abstract or symbolic two-dimensional representation: figure–ground segregation and Gestalt rules of organization.

FIGURE–GROUND SEGREGATION

A discontinuity of luminance in the retinal image leads to a perceptual segregation of the field into one part called a **figure** and another part called a **ground.** These parts are usually separated by a **contour** that may be said to divide figure from ground, although the contour seems to belong to the figure. Generally, only one of two homogeneous parts of a field may be seen as the figure and the other as the ground; it is the rare case where both would be experienced as figure on ground.

The features of **figure–ground organization** were first studied in detail by Rubin (1921), who noted that the figure has form or shape, whereas the ground is formless. The ground may have form properties but these are weaker and less definite. Thus, the figure has "thinglike" qualities whereas the ground appears uniform. The figure appears to be nearer than the ground, and the ground appears to be extended unbroken behind the figure. The figure is more easily identified; its color is more impressive; it is more easily connected with meaning, feeling, and esthetic values. The reason camouflage works is that it breaks down the figure–ground relationships that carry the meaning.

Rubin and the Gestalt psychologists proposed

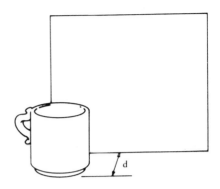

Figure 15.11 Hochberg's (1971) explanation for the learned figure–ground organization rests on the fact that in real three-dimensional situations, looking across the edge of an object (the cup in this case) results in an increase in distance (d) to the next surface on which attention might fall.

that figure–ground segregation represented a spontaneous organizing property of the visual system. They argued that this organization reflected a fundamental and innate aspect of visual physiology.

While the perceptual segregation of configurations into figures and backgrounds seems automatic and primitive, several kinds of evidence argue that this segregation cannot be the initial processing before anything else is perceived. *First,* if the form is large, it requires several glances before all the visual edges defining the figure can be registered clearly. Therefore there has to be some way of perceiving those edges prior to the figure–ground segregation. Some figures, of course, can be seen in a single glance, or with very brief exposures, but not if they are so large that scanning movements are necessary. *Second,* when scanning eye movements are made, these movements must be planned prior to their execution (the planning based upon information picked up in peripheral vision about places to look at) and upon the perceiver's expectation about the stimulus. Therefore both peripheral processing of information and the viewer's expectations have to occur before figure–ground segregation.

Third, it is possible to show that even local depth cues, those seen clearly in a single glance, can be insufficient to properly segregate figure from ground. Look back at the second example in Figure 15.1. With your eyes on any one part of this Devil's Pitchfork, it is easy to see which parts belong to the figure and which to the background behind it. But as you shift your eyes along the "figure," it can become "ground," and vice versa. There are many examples of this type of drawing, with the artist Maurits Escher bringing such effects to the level of art (see Teuber, 1974, for an analysis of the perceptual structure of his etchings).

For these reasons, it seems unlikely that the organization of figure from ground is primitive, innate, and unlearned. It is still a very important process, however. Hochberg (1971) proposed an alternative analysis beginning with events that take place while looking at a real three-dimensional object. When the eyes move across an object, they cross an edge of the object. As they cross, there is an abrupt increase in the distance from the surface of the object to the surface beyond the edge (see Figure 15.11). As long as the eyes move within the bounds set by the contours of the object (the cup in Figure 15.11), proper accommodation and convergence is maintained and a clear image reaches the retina. Outside the contour, the image is unfocused and blurred.

Because of these relationships of spatial viewing and because eye movements must be guided by some expectation of what the fovea will confront, Hochberg suggested that the properties of two-dimensional figure–ground segregation are learned and that they represent expectancies about the consequences of head and eye movements. Hochberg sees figure–ground phenomena as the result of carrying over the perceptual habits formed in looking at objects in the three-dimensional world to the perception of lines on the two-dimensional surface of a piece of paper. We shall discuss the role of expectancies in form perception in some detail below.

CONFIGURATIONAL STRUCTURE IN FIGURES

Sometimes the perception of two-dimensional figures seems to depend entirely on the relationships among the elements from which it is made. The features seem to be grouped in some way, with some seen as going together while others are perceived as part of larger structures. This superordinate organization seems to take place spontaneously. It is these relationships that are codified into the **Gestalt laws.**

Gestalt Laws

The Gestaltists proposed a number of laws of organization to describe perception as the result of the organizational processes of the brain and the relationships among the elements making up the stimulus. More precisely, they argued that the perceived organization arose from the impact of these elements on the representational processes within the nervous system, which the Gestalt psychologists saw as a field of forces with properties similar to those of electrostatic or magnetic fields in physics. This neurological model has fallen by the wayside, but their guiding principles are still important to our understanding of form perception.

Figure 15.12 illustrates the major organizational laws of Gestalt theory (Koffka, 1935). These include

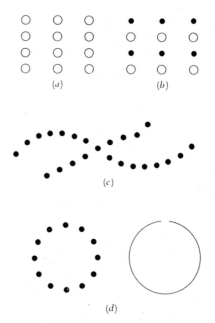

Figure 15.12 A number of examples of Gestalt laws of perceptual organization (see text for a description of the laws).

the laws of proximity, similarity, continuity, common fate, and closure. The law of **proximity** says that groups may be formed from elements that are spatially or temporally closer to one another than other elements. Thus, in part (*a*) of Figure 15.12 we perceive three vertical arrays of dots because the vertical spacing is less than the horizontal. The law of **similarity** says that groups may be formed from elements that are similar to one another. Thus, in part (*b*) of Figure 15.12 we see horizontal rows because, even though the elements are equally spaced, the elements in the horizontal rows are similar while those in the vertical columns are not. The law of **good continuation** says that a vector of a set of elements determines the direction of the next element. This can be seen in part (*c*), where there is a particular direction in which the next element is considered "good" and other directions that are not considered "good." The law of **closure** says that parts of a figure not present are filled in to complete the figure. This is seen in part (*d*). This law is similar to good continuation, although it adds the property of "filling in." It also suggests why we can denote a continuous line by closely spaced dots, as in part (*c*) of the figure. The law of **common fate** says that objects which move or change together are seen as a unit, that is, as having a "common fate." The law reflects the great power of relative movement as an organizing force for perception.

The laws of continuation, closure, and common fate are often grouped together as laws of good figure, or as examples of the **Prägnanz** principle (Koffka, 1935). All these laws predict that certain perceptions occur rather than others. For example, we may organize the lines in the top of Figure 15.13 in a number of different ways, only one of which satisfies the Gestalt laws. While other organizations are logically possible, we usually see it as it is shown in the middle figure.

The problem with the law of good figure (and to a lesser extent with the other laws) is the lack of adequate means to specify the variables that underlie the organizations predicted by the laws. The laws appear to be descriptions rather than laws of perception. Nevertheless, they make intuitive sense, and they appear to have direct practical applications, as in the construction of camouflage or embedded figures. Beck

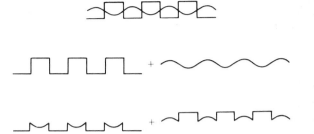

Figure 15.13 An example of the organization properties of a pattern. Although several organizations are logically possible, only one is perceived.

(for example, 1967, 1972) studied the determinants of perceptual groupings, especially those concerning the similarity among elements. He used relatively simple shapes, such as those shown in Figure 15.14. When a perceiver is asked to count the number of V shapes in the top panels, or ∪ shapes in the bottom, any process that facilitated the organization of Vs or ∪s as different from the rotated shapes speeded up the counting process. Beck showed that speed of counting (and therefore, by assumption, grouping) was fastest on the left and slowest on the right for the displays in Figure 15.14. This implies that organization is a function of the similarity of the slopes of the line elements.

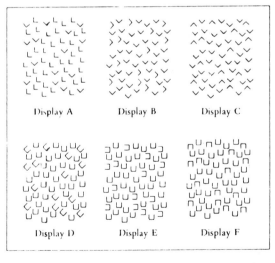

Figure 15.14 An example of a stimulus display used to study the role of form similarity. (Beck, 1972.)

Beck also argued that this property of slope difference is picked up in peripheral as well as central vision, as a function of the discrimination of stimulus differences prior to a narrowing of attention. This makes perceptual grouping primarily an acuity task—possession of the ability to notice differences throughout the visual field that helps organize the forms. Anything that increases peripheral acuity helps in this organization. Apparently slope differences among the constituted elements are more easily noticed than the overall orientation of the forms.

In one test of this hypothesis, Beck (1972) presented four forms, one at each of the corners of an imaginary square about five degrees on a side. One of the forms was different, and the perceiver had to locate and describe the odd one. As would be expected, the perceiver was best at this when the odd one differed in slope from the other three. Here the perceiver must direct his attention to each of the forms, and he has no way of foreknowing the location of the odd one. In another condition, only one form was presented at any one of the four locations. No difference in accuracy of describing the form was found. Beck argued that in this case the luminance discontinuities directed the attention to the form, since there was nothing elsewhere in the visual field. No further segregation was needed, and no difficulty was encountered in naming the form. Beck believed that grouping occurs over the entire retina before any detailed analysis of the elements is carried out. This distinction between peripheral location of figures and a central identification of them occurs again in the next chapter, since it plays a crucial role in visual search processes.

Perhaps the greatest contribution of the Gestalt psychologists was their isolation of a unit of analysis. The name *Gestalt* comes from the notion of the "Whole," that which is given by the relations of the elements. In this sense, the whole has unique properties, ones that are not merely given by the sum of the properties of the elements. Moreover, frequently the properties of the whole have no relationship to those of the elements and cannot be predicted from them (and vice versa). For example, the black triangles in Figure 15.3 have no squareness in them, yet together, and in a certain relationship to one another, they make

a square. That the units making the square may be triangles or circles does not change the squareness. It is the patterns or relations of the parts that constitute the essential quality of the whole. The crucial test of a Gestalt quality, therefore, is **transposition**—the possibility of replacing the elements with other elements while retaining the quality of the whole. If transposition is successful, the relationships are independent of the elements. The square is an example of transposition in the spatial domain. In the temporal domain a melody can be transposed into a key in which all notes are changed although the melody remains the same. Zakia (1974) provides a well-illustrated and useful application of the Gestalt rules to photography and to design problems in general.

As with figure–ground segregation as a principle of organization, the Gestalt laws are superseded by depth information whenever such a formation is available. These laws are therefore useful descriptors in accounting for perceived organization only for two-dimensional symbolic or abstract representation. This makes them much more restricted in their applicability than their discoverers intended.

INFORMATION AND MEANINGFULNESS

Another set of principles to help explain perceived organization assumes that we organize visual edges so that they make sense. "Making sense" can be defined in terms of familiarity, or in terms of meaningfulness, or in terms of predictability or expectation. We shall consider aspects of all of these in this section.

Information in Figures

One attempt to advance beyond the descriptive level of the Gestalt laws is in experiments aimed at specifying and quantifying the informational aspects of figures. This attempt was based on the assumption that certain parts of figures supply more information than other parts. The parts that supply little information are usually those parts that tell the perceiver little more than has been learned from their neighboring parts. When this occurs, we say that the information from this part of the stimulus is "redundant"—that portions of a figure are predictable from other portions. Moreover, it is assumed that this predictability is related to the organization perceived in figures and configurations.

This point is illustrated by looking at Figure 15.15, a computer-constructed picture of a famous person. The picture is made up of large squares of different shades of gray. The array of squares carries enough fundamental information to make the recognition of the person portrayed almost certain. It is the specification and quantification of information of this sort that was a major goal of the theorists who applied information analysis to form perception.

Attneave (1954) demonstrated the different ways that information can be carried by figures with the

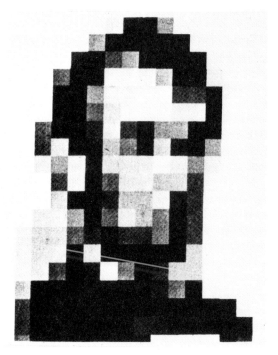

Figure 15.15 A computer-constructed picture, using only squares of different shading to represent a familiar face. If you have trouble recognizing it, hold it back, or defocus your gaze somewhat. If you still cannot recognize him, solve the anagram NNLLCIO. (Courtesy of Bell Telephone Laboratories.)

following experiment. Suppose a picture is divided up into a very large number of cells (see Figure 15.16), and suppose that a perceiver is told that a cell could be either white, black, or brown. The perceiver's task is to start at any cell, note its color and that of the preceding cell(s), and then guess the color of the next unit. The task is to describe the picture in a temporal sequence, cell by cell and row by row, and, therefore, is similar to a scanning process. If the perceiver's score in guessing the colors of cells is better than chance, it may be assumed that his or her responses took into account information supplied by the picture elements already available.

The simplest way to understand the task is to follow a typical perceiver as she performs. She starts in the lower left-hand corner and guesses whether each cell is white, brown, or black. First she may go across the bottom row, then up to the next row. We can keep track of the errors she makes. The first guess in the lower left-hand corner is, of course, at chance since she does not know what color to start with. But then when she guesses white and finds out it is correct, she will probably continue to guess white until she hits the first brown cell. After an initial error or two, she will continue to say "brown" and be correct. Now she may assume that the second row is similar to the first. The response pattern will be similar except that the origi-

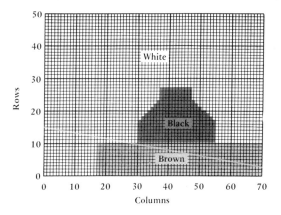

Figure 15.16 An example of redundancy in pictures (Attneave, 1954). See text for an explanation of experiments for determining the information content of various portions of figures.

nal "white" error will disappear. We find that errors pile up only in the first two rows and that gradually the perceiver is correct for the white–brown transition until she hits the corner, when she begins to make errors again. The occurrence of errors indicates an area of the picture that supplies important information—information that is not redundant.

According to Attneave, this demonstration shows that redundancy results both from an area of homogeneous color or brightness and from a contour of predictable direction or slope. Thus, information or uncertainty is concentrated along contours—regions where color or luminance changes abruptly—and at those points in the contour at which direction changes most rapidly—at angles or peaks of curvature. Objects that are similar in contour but unlike in other ways may nevertheless appear remarkably similar. This may be related to a Gestalt quality and is illustrated by the fact that artists can sketch the essence of a thing with very few lines. To demonstrate this point, Attneave asked perceivers to place a small number of dots along the contour of a figure at those points they would most want to remember if they had to reproduce the figure some time later. He found that most points were placed on regions where the contour differed most from a straight line, that is, the concentration of information was at points where the contour changes were most rapid. The results of this task are illustrated in Figure 15.17.

Now to return to Figure 15.16. Suppose we know that the figure contains a black ink bottle on the corner of a brown desk in front of a white background. If we continue to follow the perceiver making guesses,

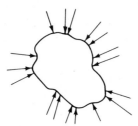

Figure 15.17 The high-information locations of an irregular form as defined by where perceivers place dots to specify defining points. (Attneave, 1954.)

she makes some errors at the edge of the ink bottle but soon learns the pattern. This suggests that there is redundancy in the pattern also. The step pattern is symmetrical, so that the right contour is predictable from the left contour by simple reversal. The perceiver ceases to make errors on the right-hand side, given her knowledge of the left-hand side. This is another type of redundancy.

Many of the Gestalt principles of perceptual organization pertain essentially to the distribution of information in the picture. For example, a "good" figure is a figure with a high degree of internal redundancy. Any given part is predictable from previously seen parts. The grouping laws, such as similarity, good continuation, proximity, and common fate, all refer to arrangements of elements that reduce uncertainty. In this sense, the perceptual system groups those portions of the input that share the same information. As a general statement, one may say that any source of physical invariance constitutes a source of redundancy for a perceiver capable of abstracting the invariance and utilizing it properly.

Hochberg and McAlister (1953) took a similar approach in analyzing the information content of figures that could be seen in either three or two dimensions. They proposed that the perceptual organization of a stimulus was related to its information content. If more than one organization is possible for a given stimulus configuration, the one most likely to be seen is the one which requires the least amount of information to describe. To put it another way, the figural organization perceived is the one that contains the greatest redundancy. Thus, in this formulation, the configuration in Figure 15.18 is seen as two overlapping rectangles because less information is required to specify that organization than any other. For example, to specify two rectangles, one needs eight line segments and points of intersection; eight angles and angles of intersection, or two line segments plus regularity, plus the angle of interconnection and the point of intersection. To specify it as 5 figures, one needs 16 different line segments and 16 angles.

In order to test these notions, Hochberg and McAlister performed an experiment in which perceivers were shown the four outline drawings in Figure

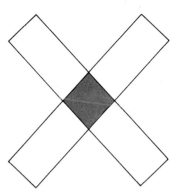

Figure 15.18 An example of how figural information may determine which of several possible organizations will be perceived. (Hochberg & McAlister, 1953.)

15.19. They viewed each of the figures separately, and, while they looked, signal tones were presented at random intervals. When the tones sounded, the perceiver has to decide whether the figure was seen more as two dimensional or three dimensional. The figures that were most symmetrical (for example, figure Z) were seen least often as three-dimensional patterns.

Hochberg carried this analysis further. Neither his earlier work nor Attneave's provided quantification of the Gestalt laws into statements that predicted perceptual organization from physical measurements of the stimulus. Since the most important of the Gestalt laws is that of Prägnanz, Hochberg followed up on the work of Kopfermann (1930) by developing what he called a **minimum principle**: of two possible organizations, the one seen will be the simpler one.

In one application, Hochberg and Brooks (1960) attempted to predict the perceptual outcomes for some simple line drawings (Fig. 15.20)—would they be seen as two-dimensional or three-dimensional? A group of perceivers first looked at a number of figures and rated whether they appeared more two-dimen-

sional or three-dimensional. Hochberg and Brooks then examined a number of physical measures of these drawings, such as the number of lines, angles, discontinuities, crossings, and inside corners. They found a good fit between the perceivers' reports and a formula that took account of combinations of number of angles, lines, and discontinuities. Thus empirically, as the complexity of a two-dimensional picture increased, it was more likely to be seen as a three-dimensional rather than a two-dimensional picture. To demonstrate that this was not simply a post hoc analysis, they then showed a new set of pictures to a new set of perceivers and used their formula to predict the perceived organization. Figure 15.21 shows that their results with the new set of pictures clearly supports their interpretation.

Most of the examples above have been of informational redundancies that result from structural properties of the stimulus. Information is concentrated at visual edges, where change occurs. And even at an edge, the information is reduced if there are structural predictabilities in the pattern, such as symmetry or repetition. These predictabilities or redundancies are not dependent upon prior knowledge by the perceiver about the pattern, but are conveyed by the pattern itself. Information content affects perception according to the minimum principle of Hochberg—we see the perceived organization that is most redundant—that which requires the least information. We will now consider examples where information is affected by prior experience.

Schematic Maps and Expectancies

Hochberg (1968, 1971a, 1971b) has provided the clearest theoretical position on how expectancies guide perception of form. We have already discussed

W   X   Y   Z

Figure 15.19 Stimulus forms that would be seen as two-or three-dimensional figures. (Hochberg & McAlister, 1953.)

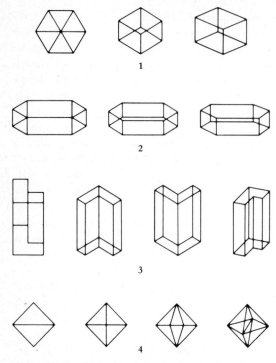

Figure 15.20 Examples of stimulus forms that can be seen as two- or as three-dimensional figures. (Hochberg & Brooks, 1960.)

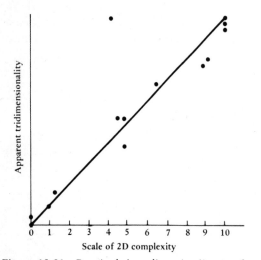

Figure 15.21 Perceived three-dimensionality as a function of the simplicity of the two-dimensional representations. (Data from Hochberg and Brooks, 1960.)

his work on expectancy guidance of the perception of space (Chapter 9, pp. 194–195). The extension to form perception is straightforward. Hochberg says that figural and object perception is a structure of expectancies—a successive accumulation of predictions about what visual edges mean, that is with what surfaces they go.

Within the center of each glance, the intersection of edges and other local depth information helps define potential regions that go together. The perceiver also has less clear information in the periphery of the retina—the edges there are blurred, and intersections are not as specific. Normally there is enough information to get some general idea of the overall structure of the pattern of edges, and especially to decide where to look next in order to pick up the most important information. So successive glances are tied together by expectancies of what will be clearly seen if the eye moves to specific locations.

What is emphasized in this description is that the pattern of visual edges on the retina is not at all random. Since they are the result of light reflected from a specific scene, if the perceiver has an expectation about what that scene might be, then he can predict what kinds of edges he will see, and what function those edges will play. If all the edges on the retina at any one moment are unrelated, the perceiver would have no way to arrange them, and he certainly would never remember them.

The structure of expectancies—Hochberg calls it a **schematic map**—is a meaningful organization of many separate elements, especially visual edges, into larger units or chunks, in which each element belongs because of the redundancy or predictability among them. In each glance, there are many clear visual edges around the center of the retinal image. These can be organized into a pattern of expectancies about what is being looked at, what the shapes or forms might be. The expectancies also include what is seen more vaguely in the periphery, and take the form of what to expect to see clearly if the eyes move to those different peripheral locations. So the structure of expectancies includes both clear, centrally perceived, edges and less clear, peripherally seen, edges. Obviously, if there is no redundancy, there can be no expectation. If there is no way to predict from one element to another, then each has to be treated separately, remembered separately, and there can be no perceived structure.

As an example, Hochberg (1970) showed subjects a simple form through a peephole that permitted only central vision. The form was moved around behind the opening, so at each moment a different view was obtained (Fig. 15.22). When the motion was predictable and regular, the perceiver could construct a structure of expectancies that allowed him to predict what the next view would look like. He could then identify the whole form even though he could see only a small piece of it at a time. Further, when the movement was regular but one view in the sequence was omitted, the viewer perceived a jump. This shows that an expectation had been built up which was disconfirmed by the irregularity of the viewing sequence.

Expectations can be built up because of structural redundancies, such as symmetry or repetition, in the pattern, even with forms never before experienced. But expectations can also arise from familiarity. Hochberg illustrated this with the examples in Figure 15.22, in which the same effects as with a regular pattern of movement were produced with an irregular pattern if the viewer were shown the form ahead of time. Both sources of redundancy normally would be available to perceivers.

This approach to form perception is an example of an **analysis-by-synthesis** model. It has been worked out in greatest detail as applied to problems of speech perception (for example, Fodor, Bever, & Garrett, 1975), as well as in perception and congnition (see Neisser, 1967, for the fullest treatment). In the context of form perception, the analysis of the form proceeds by a synthesis or putting together of visual elements picked up by the retina plus expectancies about elements not seen clearly or not seen at all. The organization of the construction has to be based upon perceived features together with expectancies or rules both for their organization and for filling in missing or not-yet perceived ones. Neisser suggests the analogy of the paleontologist, who can construct an entire dinosaur from only a few bone fragments, because of the rules he knows for the necessary character of the missing bones.

Analysis by synthesis requires the interplay of the visual features detected—such as visual edges—with expectancies about the surfaces in space that have given rise to that particular sample of edges. Expectancies are the rules that describe the perceived organization. Rules reduce the number of alternative features or stimuli and thereby permit "chunking," which reduces the number of separate elements to be remembered and organized. If there is no redundancy there can be no expectations. Then perception requires the careful analysis of each feature, one by one.

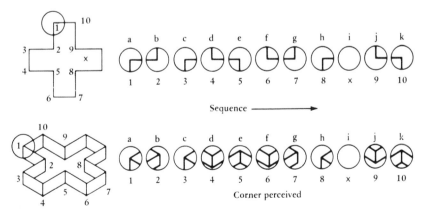

Figure 15.22 Two large shapes represented as they would appear in successive viewing of specific small portions (after Hochberg, 1971). The perception of the figure as a whole may be constructed from the "schematic map" represented by the content and sequence of the specific views.

If redundancy is very high, only a few features are needed in order to create an entire perceived structure. Thus in all perception there is a constant interplay between features and expectancies, with one being traded off against the other. We shall consider this trade-off in detail again in Chapter 19 on reading, another analysis-by-synthesis process.

We have now considered four general bases to account for perceived organization of form: depth information, figure–ground segregation, configurational rules, and expectations. Of these, the first and the last seem the most general and useful, with the other two confined primarily to abstract forms. We conclude this chapter by a brief consideration of how we recognize or identify familiar forms.

RECOGNITION AND IDENTIFICATION OF FORMS

This is a vast topic, and we can consider only a few aspects of it. There have been three general models of form identification, which differ in the specification both of the way a previously viewed form is stored, and of the way that stored representation is compared to current presentation to determine if it is familiar or to identify it. More detailed presentation of these models can be found in Gibson (1969), Lindsay and Norman (1971), Neisser (1967), and Sutherland (1973).

Models of Form Perception

The **template model** of form perception assumes that the representations of pattern in memory are structurally identical or congruent with the stimulus patterns on the retina. Recognition consists of matching the internal representation of present stimulation with templates stored in memory to find the one that is the closest match. Early attempts to explain pattern recognition with template models (for example, Selfridge, 1959) had trouble in accounting for the ease with which patterns can be recognized despite changes in retinal position, size, brightness, and color. To do this, it was suggested that the input first be processed so as to present the pattern in **canonical form,** that is, in one particular size and orientation. But this task requires another mechanism—a "preprocessor"—that has to recognize the top and bottom of the pattern as well as its proper size. This, in itself, became a problem and suggested that perception of patterns involves more than simply matching templates.

Visual-feature models have grown in popularity, in part because of the failure of template models, and in part because of the conviction that patterns are identified by their "attributes" or their unique "features." Simple feature-analyzer models suggest that the first stage of visual processing is composed of feature detectors that respond only when stimulated by specific configurations, such as those discussed in Chapter 4. These features may be line segments, angles formed by line segments, lines in particular orientations, curve segments of particular concavity, and so forth. Presumably, mechanisms that detect such features act simultaneously and are distributed over the entire visual field. In very simple models, these features may be thought of as stored in lists and compared with lists in memory. When the lists match, recognition has been accomplished. More complex models propose that higher-level structures are built from these feature elements. The higher structures, like letters or words, may then be translated into other kinds of codes, such as an auditory code, to be compared with auditory representations in memory.

Another form of visual-feature model suggests that the input is represented internally in a wholistic way, and that it is then analyzed into **distinctive features.** If complex visual forms of objects are identified by collections of properties, these properties must be simple but distinctive aspects of that visual form. Thus, sets of distinctive features consist of those features that set a particular stimulus apart from the other members of its class (see Jakobson and Halle, 1956, for a description of a system of distinctive features that successfully distinguishes among units of speech or "phonemes"). E. J. Gibson (1969) has extended this analysis to the recognition of letters of the alphabet. She suggested that printed capital letters of English can be described in terms of twelve features (for example, vertical line segments, horizontal line segments, and closed loops—see Fig 18.4, p. 371). For recognition to occur, a stimulus letter must be analyzed as to its feature content, and this list checked against all 26 letters until the best match is found.

Although visual-feature models can account for many aspects of form perception and recognition, most of the feature systems do not include a description of the relationships among feature elements. Moreover, for the feature-list system to be useful, the number of different features must be finite. It is critical, therefore, that information about the relationships between features be coded and retained, and used in later processing.

Constructive models also grew out of the failures of template models. These models usually describe the perception and recognition of forms as an active process. In general, constructive theorists (for example, Hochberg, 1968, 1970; Kolers, 1970; Neisser, 1967) propose that the perceiver forms an abstract representation of the stimulus pattern, guided by the organizational properties of the stimulus. The perceiver then makes hypotheses based on expectancies about what the stimulus might be. The hypotheses take into account the current stimulation in terms of visual features as well as the rules of similarity, redundancy, and probability that the perceiver has formed in past experience with the visual world. In the construction process, one particular pattern of segmentation might be tried and rejected when it results in an inconsistent, incomplete, or improbable representation. Then other hypotheses or constructions would be tried until one is found that matches most of the incoming information. The one that works best will be the abstract construction that is then stored as a representation of the stimulus. The act of forming hypotheses and constructions (or constructed images) is the act of perceiving and recognizing patterns.

Several brief examples of the role of expectation based upon redundancies illustrate these models, es-

pecially the last one. When chess players were given a brief look at a chess game in progress, chess masters could easily remember the location of each of the 20 to 25 pieces on the board. However, novices could place only 6 to 8 pieces correctly. When pieces were placed on the board at random, neither master nor novice could remember more than 6 to 8 positions (de Groot, 1965). Chase and Simon (1973) investigated these differences and concluded that the immediate perceptual processes are more important to the chess master than logical deductive thought processes. They suggest that the master was responding to learned patterns of perceptual structure, such as pawn chains or particular types of clusters. Visual properties like color and spatial proximity may be important elements in these structures, but the overall configuration based upon the identity of particular pieces was most important. The years of practice that are required to become a master involve the creation of these structures of expectancies so that the master no longer has to remember and keep track of each piece as if it were a separate and unrelated feature.

A second example concerns what is called the **object superiority effect** (Weisstein & Harris, 1974; Williams & Weisstein, 1978). They showed that a line segment was perceived better when it was part of a drawing that appeared coherent and three-demensional than when it was part of a drawing that appeared flat and less unitary. Further, they showed that a line segment was perceived better when it was part of a coherent figure than even when presented alone. Figure 15.23 illustrates their materials. The subject was told that a diagonal line would appear in one of four orientations and locations, relative to a fixation-point, as shown in the top row of Figure 15.23. The subject had to identify which one of the four diagonals had been presented. He was most accurate when the diagonal was part of the figures in row (*b*), next in row (*c*), and least in row (*d*). Accuracy on the diagonal alone [row (*a*)] fell between the accuracy on row (*c*) and that on row (*d*). In other words, the more coherent the figures, the more accurately a part of it could be perceived, and this was true even compared to perceiving the part in isolation.

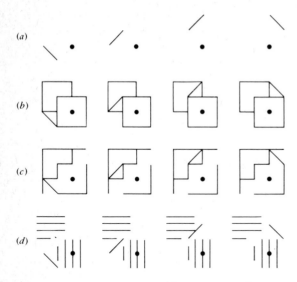

Figure 15.23 The stimuli used by Weisstein and Harris (1974) and Williams and Weisstein (1978) to demonstrate the object-superiority effect.

SUMMARY

Form perception is defined by a pattern of invariant relationships, in which a particular form is specified if no change occurs in our perception even if its elements or components are changed. We applied this to abstract or symbolic forms, and to two-dimensional patterns that represent three-dimensional objects and scenes.

An exception to the interchangability of elements is their orientation, in which a form appears differently when it is inverted or we view it while upside down. It appears as if orientation has to be part of the definition of form.

We then considered evidence of the need for inhomogeneities in stimulation as a prerequisite for form or pattern to be perceived. In the absence of luminance or temporal discontinuities, perception quickly fails. The analysis showed that perception ceases under homogeneous stimulation. This topic led to a discussion of microgenetic development of contours, in which we reviewed evidence that visual edges do not reach phenomenal clarity all at once. Research

on repetition of very dim or brief stimuli supported this view.

Four different determinants of perceived organization or form were discussed. The first was organization in depth, a topic considered at length in Section Two of the text. Depth organization accounts for the most important determinant of form.

The second determinant is segregation of visual edges into figures seen against backgrounds. We noted several implications of this segregation, and discussed in some detail arguments that such segregations normally do not occur in a single glance but are the result of integrations of several fixations over different parts of the figure or scene.

This topic served as an introduction to consideration of the third determinant of figural organization, especially the Gestalt laws of relationships among elements of figures. A number of laws were illustrated, and one line of research by Beck on the law of similarity is discussed in some detail. We noted that the Gestalt laws were not sufficient for a complete understanding of form perception, but applied more to abstract forms than to those representing objects or scenes.

The fourth determinant was the meaning of the form. We first explored several attempts to use informational descriptions of organization; especially by Attneave and by Hochberg. These focused upon the development of measures of redundancy or simplicity—arguing first that information is concentrated on contours, edges, and changes, and second, that what will be seen will be the simplest organization possible from the elements present in the scene.

The most developed work on meaningfulness has been the work of Hochberg on expectancies and schematic maps. He argues that the perception of form is a structure of expectances about what edges go together and what will be seen with eye and body movements. A number of examples of this approach are mentioned, all involving the interplay of visual-feature processing with expectancy testing.

The final topic concerned the recognition or identification of form. We considered a template model, a feature model, and a construction model of recognition, with some examples of each.

SUGGESTED READINGS

The most complete source book on the perception of form is by Zusne (1970). Hochberg (1971a, 1971b) covers a vast range of topics on form and pattern. The original presentation of the Gestalt laws is by Koffka (1935) and it has not been improved upon in over 40 years, although Hochberg (1973) has an excellent discussion. A few more specialized books have appeared. Corcoran (1971) has an excellent introduction to pattern-recognition research, and Kolers and Eden (1968), as well as Dodwell (1971), have collected some important, although usually advanced, research and theoretical articles on this topic. Neisser (1967) has one of the best analyses of the models of pattern recognition. Rock's (1975) book provides an excellent analysis of the problem and a detailed discussion of theory.

Chapter 16

Attention and Visual Search

THE NATURE OF SELECTIVITY

The selectivity of perception has been recognized since the beginning of experimental psychology. This long-standing recognition, however, has not made explanation easier. Part of the difficulty stems from the wide range of phenomena that show some sort of selectivity, and part from the assumption that, for selectivity to occur, all stimuli first have to be identified, and the unwanted ones discarded without their intrusion upon awareness. This assumption has caused more theoretical trouble than any other in perception because it implies a mechanism that acts as a censor in selecting what enters consciousness and what does not.

The very nature of **selectivity** implies information loss. We have already observed that information loss occurs through transduction and recoding of stimulation as it is communicated through the visual system. At every step of the way, beginning with the earliest receptor processes, some aspects of stimulation are transmitted at the expense of others. Those selected are represented in a new form—sometimes enhanced—but often in such a way that recovery of the prior form is impossible. This transformation is ac-

companied by an irreversible loss of information not present in the new representation.

Because selectivity has broad meaning, it must be understood in different ways depending on the particular information involved, and the particular processes and tasks that provide the context. We have already examined those aspects involved in the establishment of a representation of visual stimulation both in terms of its spatial properties (Chapter 4) and its temporal properties (Chapter 6). This chapter focuses on the direction and control of the movements of our eyes to locate stimuli of potential interest. In the next two chapters, we discuss selectivity within a single fixation, and the recognition of objects and features within and across fixations. All these topics are so intertwined that it is difficult to provide explanations for one without referring to the others. For example, if we are searching the environment, our eyes follow one pattern of movements; if we are searching a list for a letter or a word, they follow a different pattern; and if we are scanning a page for meaning, they follow still another pattern. In other words, the movement between fixations is not independent of the information taken in during the fixations—the two aspects of selectivity are closely intertwined.

A number of different visual search tasks have

been intensively studied. In one task, perceivers are asked to search for a target in a large, sometimes cluttered field, a task much like looking for a face in a crowd. Frequently the search is for only one or two targets with little or no concern for nontarget objects. This task requires the selection of one stimulus while ignoring others. An interesting variant of this task is perfomed by the proofreader who must search for errors in spelling as well as erroneous words embedded in a background of continuous correct text. The proofreader's goal is to seach for error, not to read for meaning. The task changes when meaning is involved, as for example, when trying to find your name in a newspaper article.

A number of questions can be asked about visual search. Does search change when the searcher is placed under stress, or when the task is made very difficult, or when the penalty for failure is very severe? We shall see that all these do produce important changes in the strategies employed by searchers and in their success in the search tasks. Can we be trained to be better searchers and, if so, what is that training like?

The examples above are all of active seeking. But seeking often involves more than looking for a specific needle in a specific haystack. Most of the time we visually explore the world around us, not looking for something explicit but rather trying to construct a coherent scene. Because the retinas of human beings have foveas, specialized for representing fine detail in the center of each momentary glance, it is necessary to move our eyes over a scene in order to perceive all of it with clarity. We find that much of our searching activity is for the purpose of integrating successive glances to construct a coherent perception. This may be quite independent of looking for a specific detail in that scene.

A CONCEPT OF VISUAL SEARCH PROCESSES

The movements of our eyes and head provide a mechanism for gross selection among visual stimuli. Clearly the position of the eyes at any moment determines the pattern of stimulation on the two retinal projections and, therefore, the stimuli that are potential objects of interest. In the natural environment, we want to look *at* what we are looking *for*. Thus, the variables that underlie visual search are major determinants of selection in normal perception.

Several common threads run through each of the search tasks. The most important is the distinction between what is in foveal as compared to peripheral vision at any given instant. The objects in central vision can be identified in detail, permitting the perceiver to determine whether any single one is the target being sought. But since that determination usually is negative (otherwise the search ends), the perceiver has to shift his gaze to another part of the visual field. Presumably he decides where to look next largely on the basis of information available in peripheral vision. This information cannot be in fine detail because pattern acuity has dropped 50 percent for an object located only 1 degree from the center of the fovea and, for one 8 degrees from the center, it is only 15 percent of maximum (Riggs, 1965)—see Chapter 4. But different kinds of information can be utilized besides fine detail. For example, an object in motion may draw an eye movement, even when that moving object is seen substantially far out in the periphery, and the object itself cannot be identified. We shall see later how other stimulus dimensions can be noticed even when they occur well into the periphery.

There therefore appear to be two components to the search process occurring at roughly the same time—an identification process of the parts of the retinal projection falling on the fovea, and a decision process concerning the direction of the next eye movement, based on information from the periphery. Can these two tasks be performed at the same time? Do they interfere with one another? How far into the periphery can information be and still be useful? How do we sort out the vast amount of peripheral information available at any given moment?

Preattentive and Focal Attentive Processes

Neisser (1967) has suggested that objects are not identified visually until they are segmented—that is, until the entire visual field is divided into figures on backgrounds. Neisser called this segmentation a **preattentive process,** suggesting that it is global and wholistic, while subsequent processes focus on specific aspects of figures for further analysis. Presumably the preattentive processes are spatially parallel so that the entire visual field is processed simultaneously. These processes are used primarily to direct focal attention, but they are also important in directing or guiding immediate bodily motions such as orienting responses and locomotion. For example, walking or driving an automobile frequently does not require detailed attention to the visual world around us. Instead, we respond to some objects directly, without recognition. It is this type of process to which Beck (1972) referred in his analysis of figural organization based upon similarity (see Chapter 15).

When an important aspect of the environment is segmented, **focal attention** occurs either by a shift in the position of the eyes or by a narrowing of attention. Focal attention operates on the important aspects of the field segregated by the preattentive processes. It is focused because attention is concentrated on only one aspect of stimulus information at a time. As a consequence, analyses may be performed, or figures may be constructed using the information previously extracted. The constructions may result in identification (for example, "It is a circle"), in description of the attributes ("It is green and edible"), or even in a negative statement ("It is not an apple").

Preattentive processes serve to locate and isolate objects in the visual field. There is no further specification of the properties of such objects beyond that given by the visual features themselves. Thus, one region of the field might be segregated according to color (one might be green and another red), but not according to shape (for example, not "One a square and the other a circle"). The latter discrimination requires further processing beyond what the preattentive mechanisms alone can provide. Neisser's distinction between preattentive and focal attention is a useful heuristic device. It permits us to be more explicit in separating some of the control function of eye movements from the identification components of target search. We shall consider some further evidence of this distinction throughout the next few chapters.

THE USEFUL FIELD OF VIEW

Mackworth (1976) defines the size of the **useful field of view** as the area surrounding the fixation point from which the perceiver can detect, discriminate, process, or store information during a given visual task. If this area is determined only by the acuity limit set by the neural coding of the particular visual features in the display, then the useful field of view is always fixed in size for any given set of features. For example, if single letters are to be identified, letter size must be made larger if they are displayed farther from the fovea. We shall see that the size is not fixed at all.

In order to measure the size of the useful field of view, Mackworth asked perceivers to watch a window behind which small figures moved very slowly from top to bottom. Most of the figures were circles, but occasionally a square appeared. At any given time, 10 items were visible—usually 10 circles but occasionally 9 circles and 1 square. The perceiver's task was to detect the square when it was presented. In addition to this task, there was a second window placed beside the first. The subject was required to keep his gaze on the first window, but also to detect any squares that appeared in the second window.

All the squares in the fixated window were detected. Detection of squares in the peripheral window depended on how far into the periphery the second window was placed. Figure 16.1 shows the results. When the windows were 6 degrees apart, 19 of the 20 subjects detected all the squares. But when the windows were 8 degrees apart, half of the subjects began to make errors. Mackworth concluded that the useful field of view was about 6 degrees for targets of this size embedded in similar background items. Had the targets been larger or the context items less simliar, the useful field of view would undoubtedly have been larger.

A number of other factors that have nothing to do with acuity also affect the useful field of view. Although we usually orient our eyes to produce fixation, it is not at all necessary that we do so—that is, it is possible to attend to a part of the visual scene that we are not looking at directly. In other words, the useful

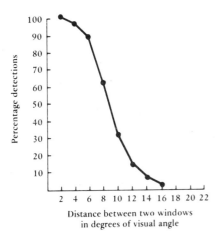

Figure 16.1   The percentage of correct detections of the square in the peripheral window as a function of the distance in visual angle between the two windows. (Mackworth, 1976.)

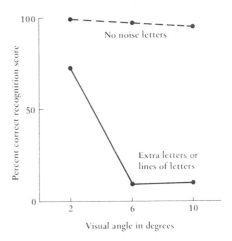

Figure 16.2   Percentage of correct matches between the central and peripheral letters as a function of distance between the peripheral letters. The upper curve is when extra noise letters are absent, whereas the lower curve is accuracy in the presence of noise letters. (Data taken from Mackworth, 1965.)

field of view does not always have to be centered around the fovea, although normally it is so centered.

Tunnel Vision

Mackworth (1965) has measured the size of the field of view by placing several targets in various parts of the periphery and asking observers to indicate whether or not all the targets are the same. For example, he flashed three letters for 100 milliseconds, one on the center of fixation and the other two flanking it equidistant on either side. His results are shown in Figure 16.2. Accuracy was virtually perfect, even when the two flanking letters were as much as 10 degrees apart. Performance deteriorated sharply, however, when 14 irrelevant letters were added on the line, or 20 other lines of 17 letters each were added. When all three targets to be matched were roughly within the fovea, accuracy of matching dropped from 99 percent when no other targets were present, to about 70 percent with the addition of a line or page of irrelevant letters. As soon as the targets were extrafoveal (more than 3 degrees apart), accuracy dropped from over 95 percent to about 10 percent. The difference between a line and a whole page of irrelevant letters was not large.

In a second condition, Mackworth showed that

adding unwanted targets outside the targets was far worse than adding them between the target and the center (Fig. 16.3). Comparing this with the previous condition shows that adding only two unwanted letters drops accuracy from 99 to about 80 percent. However, if they are placed outside the targets, accuracy drops to nearly 40 percent. Mackworth interpreted these results in terms of the size of the useful visual field. Too much information causes this field to constrict so as to prevent overloading the visual processing system. Adding visual noise or unwanted signals can narrow this useful field of view, creating what Mackworth calls **tunnel vision**—a priority given to targets in the fovea. There is even some loss in foveal recognition.

Effects of Context

The narrowing of the field of view is not the only change that occurs when the density of information to be searched increases. Mackworth (1976) asked subjects to search a strip containing lots of dots and one square—see Figure 16.4 for an example. Subjects were instructed to move their eyes from left to right without looking back and, at the end, report whether

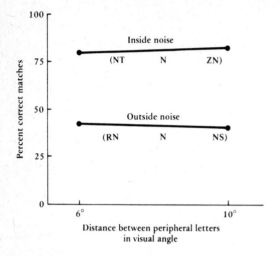

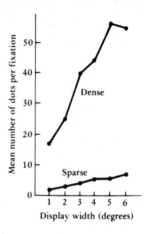

Figure 16.5 The mean number of dots per fixative as a function of the width of the display strip being searched, for both the sparse strips and the dense strips. (Data taken from Mackworth, 1976.)

Figure 16.3 Percentage of correct matches between central and peripheral letters as a function of whether two noise letters were inside or outside the peripheral letters. For example, if the target letters are all Ns, an example of an inside noise display is NT N ZN and an outside noise display is RN N NS. (Data taken from Mackworth, 1965.)

there was a square in the strip or not. The strips could be dense—about ten dots per square degree, or sparse—only about one dot per square degree. All strips were 20 degrees long but could vary in height from 1 to 6 degrees. Figure 16.4 shows a 2-degree dense display containing 270 dots and either one or no squares. The 6-degree wide dense strip had 840 dots. At the other extreme the 1-degree sparse strip had only 16 dots.

Mackworth reported several changes in search strategy as a function of density and width of display. The most impressive change was in the number of dots included in each fixation. This was estimated by dividing the number of dots in the display by the total number of fixations. Figure 16.5 shows that this num-

ber changed little with the sparse displays, but was dramatically affected by the width of the dense display. When looking at dense displays subjects included more content in each glance. No errors were made in locating the target in any of the sparse displays, and errors were significant only for the very widest of the dense displays. These data therefore represent strategy differences within the bounds of effectively errorless performance.

The second change was in the time to search. Three measures are relevant: number of fixations, average duration of each fixation, and total search time (the sum of the other two factors). All three measures showed surprisingly small change, though all increased with density and with width. As the number of dots to be searched increased, searchers took longer, and made more fixations, each of which was a little longer. Subjects therefore did adjust their search time but such adjustment was minor compared to the increase in the number of items included in each fixation.

Mackworth measured the number of times that an observer moved his or her eyes up or down rather than continuing rightward down the display. Figure 16.6 shows an example from one subject searching the 1-degree, 2-degree, and 6-degree wide dense display.

Figure 16.4 An example of one of the stimulus strips used by Mackworth (1976), in which the dots are densely packed in a 2-degree width. The circular area indicates a schematic example of a typical useful field of view.

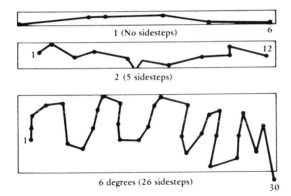

1 (No sidesteps)   6

1   12

2 (5 sidesteps)

1

6 degrees (26 sidesteps)
                                    30

Figure 16.6   An example from one subject showing the relation of forward to side-track eye movements down the strip of dots, as a function of the width of the strip. All three strips are dense.

This subject made no side steps out of 5 eye movements in the narrowest display (side steps are defined as more than a 20-degree deviation from the horizontal axis), but made 5 side steps out of 11 eye movements for the 2-degree display and 26 out of 29 eye movements in the widest displays. Side steps also increased as the sparse display became wider, so that in both cases side steps reflected a change in search strategy as the area of the display was enlarged.

Further, the distance moved by each saccade decreased as the dense displays widened. In general, all eye movements were small—50 percent were less than 2 degrees—so the search was close and precise. This can be contrasted with movements made in a task in which large, well-defined objects are to be located in clear photographs—for example, searching for a fire hydrant in a street scene (Mackworth & Bruner, 1970). In this task, searchers produced a much larger proportion of eye movements greater than 6 degrees. Mackworth (1976) suggested that the ratio of small to large eye movements, a kind of **zoom ratio,** can be used to characterize different tasks. In the circle and square task, a kind of "needle in the haystack" search, the zoom ratio is over ten to one, whereas in looking for a fire hydrant the ratio is almost unity.

The results of these studies can be summarized as follows: The most important effect is that the useful field of view constricts when there are large numbers of potential targets to be perceived and examined. Not only is the area over which the target is to be detected reduced, but the size of eye movements are reduced and the number of side steps increased when the density or width of the display is increased. A second adjustment is to lengthen the processing time for the display by making more fixations and by making each of them longer. In Mackworth's "needle in the haystack" task, this lengthening was not as large, thereby keeping the number of items in each useful field of view constant. In fact, the number of dots included in each field increased dramatically with display density and width, suggesting a third type of strategy, that of including more items to be processed in each fixation as the search becomes more dense.

Attentional Fields

Obviously, information supplied by the stimuli from the periphery of the retina is of great importance in normal perception. How easy is it to detect such stimuli? How quickly can we respond to stimuli that appear in the peripheral retina? Is the response a function of direction of regard, the number of signals present, the amount of practice, or the expectations of the perceiver? These questions have been studied by Sanders (1963) in a series of studies. In these experiments, generally two signals appear, one straight ahead and the other off to the right. The perceiver is usually required to press a telegraph key as quickly as she can to indicate the presence of one, both, or some combination of the two signals. Response latencies (reaction times) may then be compared for the different responses.

Sanders distinguished between three different types of **attentional fields.** The **display field** includes central and peripheral vision of the display as seen during a single glance without any change in fixation. The **eye field** includes all that can be seen with saccadic eye movements. The **head field** has, in addition to the display and eye fields, the field of vision exposed by head movements. In one series of experiments, Sanders mapped the relative sizes of these fields. A perceiver was presented with two patterns, each of which was a column of either four or five lights. She had to press one of four response keys to indicate whether the two stimuli both contained four lights, or both five, or the left one four and the right one five, or vice versa. She had to respond as quickly as possible but, of course, to do so, she had to view both stimuli. She was told to fixate the position where the left-hand stimulus would appear. The right-hand stimulus was from 19 degrees to 94 degrees to the right. Both stimuli appeared simultaneously.

Figure 16.7 shows that, when the head and eyes were both free to move, two discontinuities in performance occurred, one when the patterns were about 30 degrees apart, and the other about 80 degrees apart. When the perceiver's head was fixed so that no head movement was possible, her performance fell off rapidly for the larger display angles (81 to 94 degrees). Sanders suggested that the two dips correspond to the break points between the display and eye fields, and the eye and head fields, respectively. Thus, with relatively large and simple stimuli, peripheral vision is adequate out to about 30 degrees and eye movements extend the visual field out to about 80 degrees. This means that beyond 30 degrees the eye must move, and beyond 80 degrees the head must move.

This hypothesis was strengthened in another study in which the perceiver was told either to remain fixated on the left stimulus or to move her eyes between them. Figure 16.8 shows that when no eye movement was permitted, peripheral vision ended at about 30 degrees. Even before this, reaction time increased exponentially as the visual angle increased from 0 degrees. When the perceiver was permitted to move her eyes, her reaction time was constant out to about 90 degrees, after which it increased rapidly. Notice that even for small angles this condition was slightly slower, suggesting that the perceiver's strategies must have been different in some way when she knew she could move her eyes.

Sanders noted further that these values were dependent on the complexity of the stimuli. The dot task that he used had many cues and did not need acute resolution of fine detail. Although letters are nearly impossible to read at 5 degrees when pulsed briefly (Woodrow, 1938), large block letters displayed for 1500 milliseconds could be discriminated at 30 degrees (Geer & Moraal, 1962).

Sanders reported a further series of studies in which he recorded eye movements and head movements during similar reaction-time tasks. He showed that the decrements in performance seen in Figure 16.7 were not due to the time needed to move the eyes or the head. Those times were a linear function of the distance moved. Consequently, the discontinuity in performance must have been due to some selective

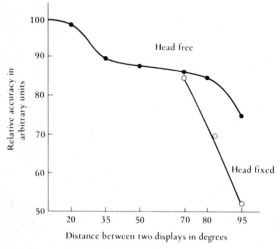

Figure 16.7 Relative accuracy in reporting the number of lights in two columns as a function of the distance between them, when the head is free to move and when it is fixed. (Sanders, 1963.)

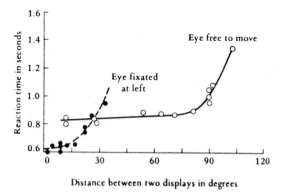

Figure 16.8 Choice reaction time to two stimuli as a function of their separation, when the eyes are fixed on the left stimulus, and when the eyes are free to move. (Sanders, 1963.)

processes. His hypothesis was that within the display field—that is, within a single glance—both stimuli are attended to and processed simultaneously, allowing a more rapid transmission and subsequent processing of the information. Outside the display field, two separate selective acts are needed, and the drop in performance reflects this additional time for the second selective act that is being added. Sanders believes there are actually three stages. In the first, from about 0 degrees to 25 degrees, both stimuli can be adequately discriminated simultaneously without an eye movement. Thus, although the perceiver fixates the left one, he can see enough of the visual features of the right one at the same time to be able to make the discrimination and organize the response. His response is slowed down as the display size approaches 25 degrees, which might imply either a loss in confidence about the right stimulus, or that it takes longer to process a degraded stimulus.

Once the right-hand stimulus is outside the display field, its features are no longer adequate to lead to a decision and response. However, Sanders believed that before an eye movement the perceiver still can get enough information about it to form a hypothesis which can then be tested. Since the perceiver has a hypothesis, less information should be needed for confirmation than if he knows nothing about the right-hand stimulus. Thus, the time to process the right stimulus should be less than that to process an altogether new stimulus. As the angle approaches 80 degrees, however, even the partial information to form a hypothesis is inadequate and an entirely separate process is needed. Therefore another increment of time is added causing the second drop in performance around 80 to 90 degrees.

Sanders verified these predictions in several specific instances. For example, a perceiver was asked to attend and respond to the left stimulus and then to the right one, giving two separate responses. If he can process the right-hand stimulus while fixating on the left, as he should be able to do for small angles, then reaction time to the right should be much shorter than to the left. As the angle increases, forcing him to use two selective acts, the ratio of the two reaction times should decrease until, by the time the eye field is exceeded (that is, around 80 degrees or so), the ratio of the two reaction times should be unity. Sanders found this result, even after he subtracted the eye movement time from the reaction time to the right-hand stimulus. Since this subtraction process runs counter to his prediction, his test is conservative and still supports his interpretation.

Although peripheral information is used to determine the next fixation, the target presently being fixated is also being analyzed. Thus, two tasks are being performed simultaneously. Is this a division of attention or are the two tasks performed independently? If this does represent a division of attention, does one task interfere with the other? Although Sanders did not study interference as such, he clearly showed that the central and peripheral tasks interacted—at least in his experimental situation. When the fixated signal and the peripheral signal were both within the eye field—and especially when they were both within the display field—the time needed to respond to the first signal was increased slightly over that needed when only a single signal was presented and no peripheral processing was needed.

Sanders's theory of selective acts can be reinterpreted in terms of preattentive processes that operate simultaneously over large areas of the retina. Within the display field preattentive processes are capable of locating and segregating all figures and of testing global characteristics. The perceivers in Sanders's experiments only needed information about the height or brightness of the stimulus to tell the difference between four or five lights. When the visual angle between the objects in the field exceeds the limits of the preattentive processes, the spatially parallel nature of the processing is lost and an eye movement is needed to complete testing. One of Sanders's most important findings is that even out to 80 degrees in the periphery, some information is available. This information reduces the amount of time needed to process the stimulus when it is directly fixated after an eye movement. Thus, preattentive processes appear to operate over wide reaches of the peripheral retina. Once a slower head movement becomes necessary, then the preattentive processes have clearly lost their spatially parallel character and two separate glances are needed.

Sanders's notion of selective acts illustrates another interaction between control and identification processes in search. When single targets are not too far into the periphery, it appears that some identification can occur, even while the eye is being directed to move toward them.

One note of caution should be sounded in interpreting Sanders's experiments: he used very large targets and no distracters or nontargets. It is not surprising that the magnitudes of the visual angles over which he found his effects were so large. This does not mean that the eye field is 30° for all target sizes or for all amounts of display clutter or for all search tasks. In fact Sanders's values are probably the largest ones realizable in human vision. However, all the principles he suggested and all the processes he illustrated should be present in all search tasks involving simultaneous peripheral and foveal interactions, whatever the absolute magnitudes are in each situation.

THE FUNCTIONAL FOVEA

When we choose to look at something, we usually do so by directing the line-of-sight of the eyes to the target. This action positions the retinal image of the target over the foveas. But eye movements are not necessary in order to shift attention—perceptual images can be scanned in a manner similar to the way eye movements permit scanning of the physical world. This search-without-eye-movements defines the action of the **functional fovea**.

The operation of a functional fovea was most clearly demonstrated by Zinchenko and Vergiles (1972), using stabilized images. Pictures were presented as stabilized images and were maintained in perception by varying the color. Subjects viewing these stimuli were able to examine the pictures, locate objects in them, and relate different parts of the picture to one another, even for the largest picture covering 30 degrees of the visual field.

Subjects did move their eyes while performing these experiments, but the movements did not shift the image of the picture on the retina. Zinchenko and Vergiles argued that the eye movements reflected the search strategies of the subjects. The strongest evidence for this was the condition in which observers were told not to move their eyes during the stabilized trials. This instruction greatly reduced their performance on the task—the eye movements seemed to be a necessary part of looking and may have been the basis for the scanning by the functional fovea.

Another technique used to demonstrate the operation of the functional fovea measures the improvement in detecting a stimulus presented briefly outside the fovea when subjects know beforehand exactly where it will appear. Normally, of course, observers use the prior knowledge of location to initiate an eye movement, but they can be trained not to do so. Several experiments show positive results in this task. For example, Smith and Blaha (1969) trained observers to maintain fixation on a dot. They were told that a spot would appear in one of eight possible locations around the compass points (north, northeast, east, and so on) during one of two time intervals indicated by a brief click. The subjects had to identify the time interval in which the spot appeared. The results are illustrated in Figure 16.9. The lower curve for the control no-knowledge condition shows that observers were least accurate when the spot was below the fixation point and most accurate when it was to the side. When the subjects were told the location of the spot ahead of time but had to maintain fixation, the same pattern of sensitivity was found (upper curve of Figure 16.9), but there was an overall improvement in sensitivity of about 10 percent. In both conditions, the same areas of the retinas were being stimulated—the only difference was the subjects' expectations about where the stimulus would appear. The expectation produced an advantage as if attention were directed to a location other than the fovea.

Posner, Nissen, and Ogden (1975; see also Posner, 1978) had subjects fixate the center point of a field and monitored their eye movements to be sure that they did not move. The subjects were told to react as quickly as they could to a light that appeared either to the left or to the right of fixation. They had to respond regardless of which light came on. On one-third of the trials, a noninformative plus sign preceded the flash by one second. On another third of the trials, a left-pointing arrow came on, indicating that the light would appear on the left 80 percent of the time, and, on another third of the trials, a right-pointing arrow came on, providing similar information for the right. This procedure permitted the calculation of both the benefit from the cue when it was correct (as it was 80 percent of the time) and the cost of the cue when it was incorrect (as it was 20 percent of the time). Regardless of cue, subjects had to make a single response as soon as they detected the stimulus. Figure 16.10 shows the effect on reaction time of the three types of cues. Clearly the subjects' speed of response was affected by their knowledge of where the stimulus was going to appear. Moreover, responses were faster when the target occurred where expected and slower when the target appeared in the unexpected location.

Zinchenko and Vergiles suggest that the functional fovea is like a zoom lens (see also Gould, 1976), which can be widened or narrowed depending upon

the task. The first few glances of a scene may be made with a wide-angle fovea useful in picking up the prominent features, but not being able to resolve fine detail. After the gist of the scene is acquired, then the foveal field of view narrows and fine detail is examined piece by piece. Notice how close this notion is to Neisser's distinction, described earlier, between global preattentive processing and specific foveal attention to finer detail. Before we can develop this more let us consider some aspects of searching for targets in scenes and the effects of similarity and expectancy.

Searching for Forms

Visual search as a reconnaissance task has received attention both as a theoretical problem and with respect to specific applied tasks. Much of the con-

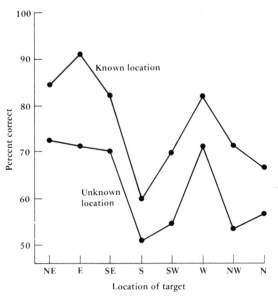

Figure 16.9 Percent correct temporal forced choice detections as a function of the location of the target. The lower curve is when the subject had no prior knowledge of the location of the target whereas the upper curve is when the subject knew the position of the target. (Data taken from Smith and Blaha, 1969.)

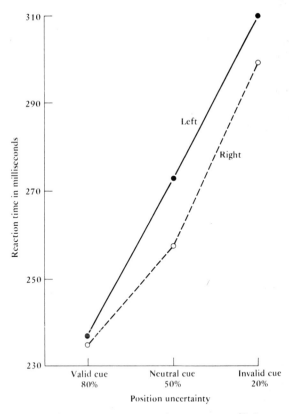

Figure 16.10 Reaction time to detect presence of light as a function of the validity of the preexposure cue indicating the position of the light. (Posner, Neisser, & Ogden, 1975.)

cern has been with the factors that control the position of the next fixation. For example, Williams (1966, 1967) has reported data which suggest that observers use peripheral information to select the position of the next fixation. He presented relatively large fields of nearly 40 degrees containing 100 geometric shapes, each of which was in one of five colors, one of four sizes, and could be one of five shapes (see Figure 16.11 for a schematic example). A two-digit number was in the center of each form. The observer's task was to find the form with a particular number. Trials differed according to the amount of information supplied to the observer about the dimensions and values of the form containing the number—sometimes she was told only the number, and sometimes the specific object containing the number was described. The position and direction of each eye movement was recorded.

When no information other than the number was given, there was no tendency to fixate one type of target more frequently than any other. When informa-

tion was given about a single one of the three dimensions, only color information biased fixation choice. This was shown by a strong tendency to fixate only on the color indicated, permitting search times to drop by nearly 80 percent when the perceiver knew the color of the target. This was less true for size and held only when the size was either the largest or the smallest. Shape information rarely determined fixation choices. When two dimensions were combined (for example, "The number being sought is in a red circle figure"), the percentages of fixations were primarily determined by those of the most powerful cue alone. Hence combining color with shape did not increase the fixations on the particular shapes. Williams's data show that the observers used extrafoveal information to select the object of the next fixation. Search patterns were not random unless the observer had no information about the target. Furthermore, Williams showed that some of the cues were far more important or useful than others.

It is not surprising that shape was not used to select the next fixation point, since differences among the targets were small, and the extrafoveal information available to the viewer probably could not have been used to distinguish among them. Moreover, it is possible that even if the shapes had been more distinguishable, perceivers still would not have used that information in search. If the information from the periphery were based only upon visual features preattentively segmented and organized, specific shape information would not be available. But orientation, movement, and color would be available since, even in the periphery, these could be specified by single feature analyzers. It is possible that reconnaissance might be a device for testing the usefulness of particular visual features in guiding visual search.

Boynton and his co-workers have studied the psychophysical parameters of visual search tasks by evaluating the impact of a large number of variables on the speed of search and on the probability of a successful search. One of their major conclusions is that any variable which reduces visual acuity reduces the likelihood of locating a target by visual information alone. For example, Boynton and Boss (1971) investigated possible trade-offs between luminance, con-

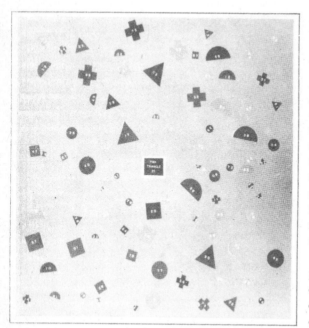

Figure 16.11 A schematic example of a stimulus display used by Williams (1966) in his study of visual search. The center of each geometric shape contained a two-digit number.

trast, and size of target. Such trade-offs are available within limits, but, for example, if contrast is too low, no increase in luminance or target size permits successful search among targets seen in peripheral vision. The target has to be centrally fixated first, and only then might it be identified (assuming that foveal acuity is adequate).

Boynton, Elworth, and Palmer (1958) recorded eye movements during search under a variety of conditions. Of special interest is a subsidiary analysis. They selected two perceivers, one who was very proficient at finding targets, and one who was quite poor at it. The better one had an average duration of fixation of 200 milliseconds, compared with over 330 for the poorer. The better perceiver also made much larger sweeps between fixations, covering nearly 2.5 degrees, compared to 1.5 degrees for the poorer. These differences may reflect better strategies for search or differential acuity. The better perceiver did have better acuity, and he might therefore have needed less fixation time to recognize an item. His better peripheral acuity may permit him to sample information further into the periphery, thereby allowing larger saccadic movements. In this sense the subjects in Williams's experiment may not have been able to use shape information because peripheral acuity for those shapes was not adequate. Boynton has shown in a number of studies that if peripheral acuity is high enough, the shape of the target does appear to stand out, even when viewed peripherally.

We have already mentioned the impact of the number of background items in the peripheral field. Boynton and Bush (1957) varied the number of background curvilinear forms from 8 to 256 in a display in which a single rectilinear target was embedded. In general, the accuracy of finding the target decreased with greater numbers of background items. The decrease was nearly a linear function of the logarithm of the number of items.

Gould and Dill (1969) had subjects look at a standard pattern and then indicate how many of the other eight surrounding patterns were identical to it (Figure 16.12 contains an example). The surrounding patterns were 7–8 degrees from the center of the fovea. Some of the eight patterns were identical to the stan-

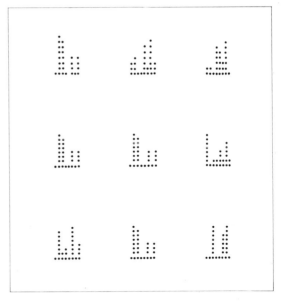

Figure 16.12   A sample display used by Gould and Dill (1969). The subject initially fixated the center pattern, and then had to indicate how many of the patterns were identical to the center standard pattern.

dard pattern, some were very similar to it, and some were dissimilar. The results are given in Figure 16.13—the more similar the standard pattern was to a surrounding pattern, the higher the probability of a subsequent fixation. Thus, even at over 7 degrees, the subject could determine if the pattern was similar enough to be checked directly. Gould (1976) summarized a number of his studies that provide further evidence of this sort about looking at forms.

If a potential target is noticed in peripheral vision, one of the factors that might determine whether a fixation is needed in order to process it fully is the amount of uncertainty the observer has about what the target might be. Consider the case of trying to identify a letter of the alphabet as a function of its size and distance from the fovea. Bouma (1972) has shown that letters have to be larger the farther they are from the center of the fovea in order to hold identification accuracy at some constant level. This relationship is shown schematically in Figure 16.14, where letters are shown of the size necessary for equal identifiability given fixation at the center.

Relative probability of fixation on a pattern

100
90
80
70
60
50
40
30
20

.2 .3 .4 .5 .6 .7 .8 .9

"Similarity" of fixated and standard patterns

Figure 16.13 The relative probability of fixating a pattern as a function of the degree of similarity of the pattern to the center standard pattern. Similarity was a function of the number of common elements in each pair of patterns. (Data taken from Gould and Dill, 1969.)

SEARCHING PICTURES

The discussion thus far has been about looking for targets that have been previously defined and specified. Such studies can tell us something about how we can look at pictures and scenes. However, we do not usually look at pictures and scenes to search for some preidentified detail—we normally search for the global meaning of the stimulus. That is, we are usually interested in what the scene is about rather than whether it contains a particular object.

Research on looking at pictures to obtain global meaning dates back nearly as far as that on text reading. Buswell (1935) provided extensive data on eye fixations while looking at pictures. More recently,

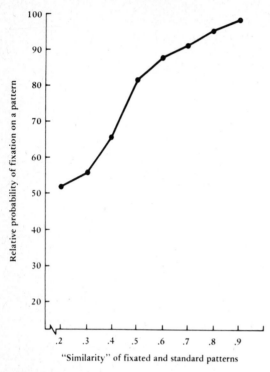

Figure 16.14 A schematic representation of the size of letters necessary for equal recognizability as a function of their distances from fixation. If you fixate on the center and move the page away until the center letter is just identifiable, all the other letters will be equally identifiable. (Bouma, 1971.)

Mackworth has carried out a program with television-recorded eye movements. In Russia, Yarbus (1967) has reported a 20-year program of research in eye movements, including picture viewing.

As one example, Mackworth and Morandi (1967) measured eye fixation choices while the perceiver examined each of two unfamiliar pictures. He was instructed to choose the one he preferred and therefore had no reason to expect to be asked questions about the content. The stimuli were large (16 degrees) square pictures presented for 10 seconds each. To obtain a measure of the information in each part of the pictures, each picture was cut up into 64 squares. A second group of perceivers was asked to rate each little square on informativeness—specifically, how easy it would be to recognize the square on another occasion.

Mackworth and Morandi's findings were quite clear-cut. Fixation choices, which averaged about 300 milliseconds each, were confined primarily to the high-information parts of the picture. Since this was as true within the first two seconds of viewing as within the last two seconds, the viewers did not depend on scanning to find the important parts. Instead, peripheral cues must have been guiding fixation choices from the outset. The authors also found that uniform texture was generally fixated less than contours. However, if the contours were highly predictable and redundant, they did not attract fixations—the eye appeared to be searching for the unusual and irregular.

What is striking about these findings, as well as those of Buswell and Yarbus, is the lack of uniformity in the fixation patterns. There is no broad sweep over the picture, nor any global viewing pattern. Instead, fixations are confined to a few regions, those containing relatively great variation, unpredictability, or a high rate of change. Equally important, the perceiver appeared to know where to look before he completed even a cursory examination of the picture. Thus, peripheral information must have been guiding fixation choices to a location of unpredictable or unusual aspects of the picture. What is even more interesting is the lack of regularity in the order of searching the picture, even in circumstances where the predictability of the fixated parts was impressively high. There did not appear to be any natural order of fixations in viewing a picture. As Kolers (1972) noted, it remains for theory to explain how so many different input sequences can be used to arrive at roughly the same perceptual experience.

Yarbus (1967) reported experiments in which he varied the instruction to the perceiver. In each condition, the viewer knew that she would be asked different kinds of questions after she had looked at the picture for three minutes. Figure 16.15 shows the picture and the eye movements made during the three-minute intervals in each of the instruction conditions. It is clear that the fixation patterns were dramatically altered, both in details and in pattern. It is as if the perceiver concentrated on those parts she expected to use for the task presented to her. In no sense was she stimulus-bound, either in position or sequence of fixations, nor was she response-bound, following some habitual sequence each time.

Loftus (1972) measured eye movements while subjects were looking at pictures which they would have to recognize or describe at a later time. One of his most striking findings was that, in a fixed viewing time, the duration or sequence of fixations did not predict whether a picture was subsequently recognized, but the number of different fixations did. It seemed as if the beginning of each fixation picked up new information that was not further enhanced by extending the duration of the fixation.

Scan Paths

As we have just seen, eye movement records made while examining pictures usually show sequences of fixations containing no pattern; that is, the eye appears to scan the picture helter-skelter. Indeed, even when reading text, the pattern of eye movements is not consistent within or between subjects. Recently, Noton and Stark (1971) have argued for a limited specificity of the sequence of fixation choices—what they call a **scan path**. While they recognize that the sequence of fixations is largely unpredictable before viewing begins, they argue that part of the memory for a picture comprises information about the sequence actually used. Thus, each fixation yields a view, and what is stored is a sequence of pairings of motor commands and views—the scan path. They predict that when a perceiver is asked to recognize a picture he had only recently seen, the re-creation of the scan path used to view the picture initially is a critical component of the recognition process. While Noton and Stark offer some data in support of this hypothesis, it is difficult to see how perceivers store information on the sequence of their eye fixations. Further, even if this information is stored, it would seem to be a very complex way of coding information. As with regressive eye movements in reading, the order of the movements in picture reading—the sequence of inputs—must be relatively independent of the organization we construct from them.

One other possibility is that the scan-path hypothesis is more appropriately applied to perceptual development. Children's recognition memory may be highly dependent upon the specific sequence of eye movements. The sequences themselves might be

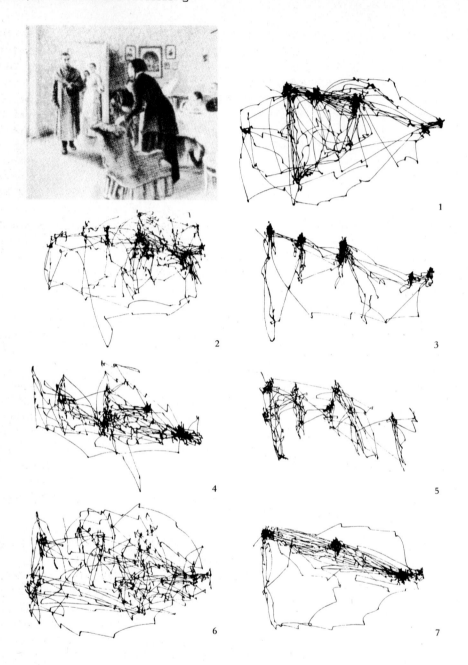

Figure 16.15 Different eye-fixation patterns made to the same picture as a function of instructions to the perceiver. The picture is shown in the upper left panel. (1) Free examination of the picture; (2) "Estimate the material circumstances of the family"; (3) "Give the ages of the people"; (4) "Summarize what they were doing before the arrival of the 'unexpected' visitor"; (5) "Describe the clothes worn by the people"; (6) "Remember the positions of the people and objects in the room"; (7) "Estimate how long the 'unexpected' visitor' has been away from the family."

stored as part of the memory experience, and familiarity might provide greater freedom of search with less dependence on the sequence of looks. Whiteside (1972) provides some data in support of this hypothesis, although the question is far from settled.

INTEGRATING SUCCESSIVE GLANCES

Under normal circumstances what is seen foveally in a particular glance has been seen peripherally in several prior glances. Furthermore, if the glances differed only in eye position, with no intervening head or body motion, the retinal images of the successive glances are all different clear sections of a potentially large image of the scene or picture, with substantial overlap between each momentary image. Under most circumstances the overlap of successive retinal images is very great. If the average distance the eye moves when looking at a scene or picture is 3–5 degrees, and the scene covers 50 degrees, the overlap of successive views is greater than 90 percent. Even with large eye movements, the overlap is rarely less than 50 percent from glance to glance. With head and body motion, or change in the distance into the scene being fixated at proper accommodation, the successive images are also altered in scale, but the overlap of content is still very high indeed. The high degree of overlap between successive glances suggests that the information conveyed by glances is not like independent pieces of a jigsaw puzzle that must be fitted together, but rather nearly identical views of the same scene, with some shifting of the area of maximum clarity, often some rescaling of size and relative position, and some occlusion or addition around the edges.

Hochberg (1968, 1970) argued that mere overlap is not normally sufficient for integration to occur. Instead, he suggested that the perceiver constructs a schematic map (see Chapter 15) that consists of a set of cognitive expectancies about what has already been seen and what will be seen if the fovea is shifted to a new place on the stimulus. Thus, schematic maps are based upon information already picked up from the scene and upon prior knowledge about what to expect

from parts of the scene not yet fixated. For Hochberg, therefore, the schematic map is an integrated perception that transcends specific features or sequences of glances. Passive accumulation of successively overlapping views of a scene without active generation of expectancy and testing would not lead to an integrated panorama of the scene.

The importance of overlap of successive glances per se and of the cognitive construction of expectancies about the content of what we are seeing in each glance has been difficult to demonstrate experimentally. Hochberg (1979) has reported several studies that make a beginning by simulating the process with motion-picture sequences. The viewer was presented with a series of views of a picture in which the overlap from view to view was varied experimentally. Figure 16.16 shows one brief sequence, in which three views of a maze pattern are shown one after the other, each for one fourth of a second. Each view is displaced to the right of the preceding one with an overlap of 50 percent. The amount of overlap was varied experimentally from 25 to 85 percent. When the viewer was

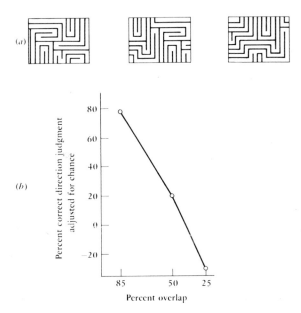

Figure 16.16 A sequence of patterns shown in rapid succession that differ in the degree of overlap between successive ones. (Hochberg, 1979.)

asked to judge whether the successive views were moving to the right or the left, accuracy was much higher, the greater the overlap (see Figure 16.16b). As the degree of overlap decreased, viewers had more difficulty judging the direction of motion because it was more difficult to integrate the successive views. Finally, even with high amounts of overlap, if the succession of views was not orderly, integration did not occur. Since, in these experiments, it is the experimenter that "moves the eye" rather than the observer, the only way the observer could generate expectancies was by predicting the direction of movement. This could be done only if the sequences were orderly. It is this finding that provides some support for the notion of expectancy.

A second factor that seems likely to be included in integration is the perceiver's prior knowledge of where his eyes have been instructed to move from glance to glance. While Gibson has argued that efferent signals should not be necesary in the integration process, there are enough data to show that such signals can be utilized. If they are always used, then the integration that easily occurs with motion picture sequences would be impossible, since the sequence is generated not by the eye movement control system, but externally by the movie maker. Even so, knowing where the eye is going could certainly be helpful in gluing the successive glances together, either by overlap alone or by expectancies.

Perceptual Grammar

While a picture is being examined, there has to be some kind of representation that is being stored, added to, and altered in the course of the looking. We will review evidence in the next chapter about the nature of this representation—that is, about whether it is a visual image, a verbal description, or a more abstract propositional code about the entities and relationships among the entities in the pictures and scenes. But, regardless of the ways in which these various kinds of representations are developed and interact, all of them would seem to be dependent upon and benefit from expectancies about visual scenes being viewed.

In one set of studies, Biederman (1972) has tried to describe a grammar of scenes in pictures—rules that perceivers use in the course of integrating their glances into a coherent representation. His idea is that perceivers use a **visual grammar** in much the same way that listeners use their knowledge of linguistic grammar to help them integrate the sounds they hear into a coherent sequence of meaningful words. In the first study Biederman asked subjects to find an object in either a coherent version or a cut-up version of a picture. It is very difficult to see the cut-up version as a coherent picture. It takes lots of time to figure out how the pieces go together. When asked to pick out one of two brief descriptions for the picture, the accuracy was much lower for the jumbled presentation than for the coherent version even at 100-millisecond exposures. When asked which of four possible objects had to be in a picture, the jumbling also reduced accuracy. This occurred even if the object was shown before the flash—jumbling increased the time to react and produced more failures to identify the presence of the object. Biederman interpreted these effects by arguing that jumbling increased the difficulty and therefore the time it took to construct a schema for the picture.

Biederman (1977) listed five relationships that are normally involved in the schema of a picture (Fig. 16.17). Using this list, he constructed pictures that violated different combinations of these relationships—a kind of visual incongruity—and then measured the time it took to detect the presence of objects and the time it took to detect whether a violation was present. In one task, the subject was told the name of an object beforehand (such as a telephone). A brief flash of the picture was followed by a dot where an object had been. The observer had to decide whether or not the named object was in the position indicated by the dot. Figure 16.18 shows that accuracy was lower when the object previewed violated one or more of the relations, and the more relations violated, the less accurate the recognition. Biederman found no consistent pattern among the five types of violations. They apparently were all equally important.

When the observer was asked to decide whether the object viewed violated any of the relations, Biederman found that the reaction time increased the more

1. *Support* (e.g., a floating fire hydrant). The object does not appear to be resting on a surface.

2. *Interposition* (e.g., the background appearing through the hydrant). The objects undergoing this violation appear to be transparent or passing through another object.

3. *Probability* (e.g., the hydrant in a kitchen). The object is unlikely to appear in the scene.

4. *Position* (e.g., the fire hydrant on top of a mail box in a street scene). The object is unlikely to occur in that scene but it is unlikely to be in that particular position.

5. *Size* (e.g., the fire hydrant appearing larger than a building).

Figure 16.17 A list of relational violations, with an example of each. (Biederman, 1977.)

violations of relations were used in representing that object. In another condition, the subject was asked whether the object violated a particular relation (for example, "was the telephone floating?"). The time it took to make that judgment increased if other viola-

tions were also present for the object, that is, if the floating telephone was also too large for the scene.

It is important to remember that all of Biederman's experiments allowed subjects only a single, brief glance so that there were no eye movements. The

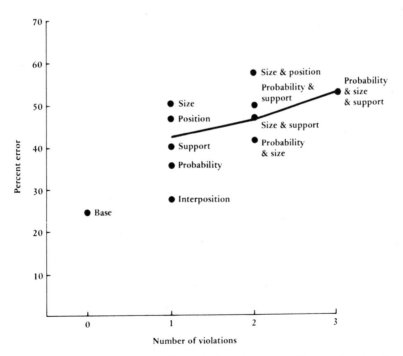

Figure 16.18 Mean percentage of errors in detecting a target object as a function of the number and kind of violations. (Biederman, 1977.)

relevance to this discussion is the importance of Biederman's work in demonstrating the internal relations among the objects—the grammar of the scene that seems to be important in establishing a stable representation.

SUMMARY

Visual search is not usually covered in textbooks on visual perception, even though it represents one of the most important features of selective processes in the extraction of information from visual displays. To illustrate this, a number of examples of search tasks were briefly mentioned, and then used to contrast two different aspects of any search task: perceptual processing to determine both the general features of the display and where to move the eyes for the next fixation; and foveal identification processes to determine what is being looked at, and whether it is the target being sought. Neisser's distinction between preattentive and focal attentive processes was used and elaborated to support these two aspects of visual search.

The first topic we considered concerned the size of the field of view at any one time—the area of the scene over which useful information could be extracted. While visual acuity imposes outside limits, several other factors reduce or enlarge upon these limits. The most important of these is constriction of the field of view, called tunnel vision, which occurs when the amount of information to be processed is too large. We also showed that as the items of information to be processed are spaced further apart, separate attentional acts are needed, which impose a limit on preattentive processing.

It was also shown that attention can be directed to different locations within a field of view without eye movements. This concept of a "functional fovea"

is useful in explaining how we can be sensitive both to the whole field and to only specific parts within each glance.

In the next two sections we considered the variable involved in searching for a particular target form, and in searching pictures for meaning or coherence. We showed that the search patterns of eye movements are sensitive to the information the perceiver has about the target features, as well as the number of targets and the similarity of the nontarget items also present.

Looking at pictures is more complicated because no specific target is being sought. No general or predictable pattern of eye movements occur, even though only high-information parts of pictures are looked at. A critical part of picture or scene looking is the way in which the separate glances are integrated so that we perceive a single picture, not a montage of separate looks. Current work suggests not only that overlap of visual fields between each glance is needed, but also that the perceiver needs to create expectancies about what he will see before he moves his eyes.

As one aspect of the expectations of the perceiver, we considered the notion that a visual grammar or semantics exists—a set of rules known by perceivers about what parts of a scene can go together. Several sets of rules were described, along with some experiments to test their predictability.

SUGGESTED READINGS

The topics in this chapter are treated in Neisser (1967), Yarbus (1967), and Mackworth (see references in text). The volumes edited by Monty and Senders (1976) and by Senders, Fisher, and Monty (1978) contain many papers on visual search and eye movements and are probably the best sources of current literature.

Chapter 17

Visual Representation and Visual Processing

There are a large number of experimental tasks that have been devised to study the nature and use of information in the visual representation. Yet most of them can be understood as involving a comparison or match between two entities—visual features, patterns, letters, letter strings, words, sentences, and so forth—when these entities are presented either simultaneously or successively. When the two entities to be compared are presented simultaneously, correct performance of the task may primarily involve perceptual processes—that is, memory may not be required. We will refer to this case as "visual matching" and will understand it to mean that the match is assumed to be based upon the "physical" characteristics of the stimuli. When the entities to be compared are presented successively, memory of some sort is, by definition, invariably involved. However, since the stimuli may be separated in time by only a few milliseconds or by years, there is a wide variety of processes that can be involved. In the former case, we need think only about a short-term memory, used to store the representation of the initial stimulus until the second becomes available. In the latter case, we must think of long-term memory and all of the concomitant structural features used for storing information over long periods of time. These structures are involved in knowing the names of things and the meanings of words, and in knowledge in general.

Chapters 17 and 18 are organized in such a way as to reflect these differences. Chapter 17 deals with phenomena that are primarily perceptual and with tasks that require as little use of memory as possible, such as visual search and visual matching. Chapter 18 deals with more complex tasks, where memory necessarily plays a role—the recognition and identification of symbolic stimuli such as letters, words, and sentences. These chapters lead directly into Chapter 19 dealing with the comprehension of larger amounts of visual information—the process called reading.

THE NATURE OF THE VISUAL REPRESENTATION

How is information from a stimulus initially represented in the organism? Is the stimulus broken up into bits and pieces—fragments of stimulation that must be put together by the visual system to construct an image—or is their representation wholistic, a complete copy of the stimulus? These are the questions that will occupy us, not only in this section, but throughout the remainder of the book.

Iconic Representation

In the first section of this book we reviewed the various coding processes involved in the transduction of the energy in light into neural signals in the nervous systems. Most of the details of these processes are not critical for the study of information processing, because the latter models are not usually specified by either anatomical locus or neural units. However, since it is necessary in this context to know how the content of the information contained in the pattern of light is initially represented after the transduction process begins, we do need to be concerned with some of these early coding processes.

As we indicated in Chapter 14, information-processing models sometimes refer to the first stage of representation as an icon or as iconic storage. In order to isolate and study the properties of this iconic stage, most researchers have presented information for very brief durations, sometimes followed by a masking stimulus in order to control for the availability of stimulus information. In general, the evidence from this research indicates that information from such brief exposures is available for processing for up to about 250 milliseconds after the presentation begins (see below). In fact, the brief persistence of the icon is undoubtedly related to the method used to produce it. Under normal circumstances of viewing, that is, when the visual display is present continuously and our eyes are fixated on the display for at least a quarter of a second, no persistent mechanism is needed. The iconic representation persists because stable stimulation persists.

There are two principal sources of evidence for the existence of an iconic storage: direct measurements of visual persistence and indirect measurement of information content using partial-report procedures. Virtually all the work has been done with letters and words, so that we must be aware of the possibility that the findings may be limited to this type of information. Visual-persistence studies were reviewed in detail in Chapter 6 when we discussed the apparent duration of a brief visual stimulus. Several different procedures produced estimates of about 250 milliseconds for this duration. If a visual form was painted across the retina by sweeping a narrow slit in

an otherwise opaque surface over a stationary form, perceivers reported that they could see all of the form simultaneously only when the slit traversed it within one-quarter of a second. If the sweep rate was slower, one part of the form had already faded from view while the other end was still being painted on (Haber & Nathanson, 1968; Haber & Standing, 1969). Finally, when perceivers set clicks to occur simultaneously with the onset and offset of brief light pulses, the clicks were set nearly 250 milliseconds apart, even when the pulses were only 10 milliseconds in duration (Haber & Standing, 1970).

Sperling (1960) used a partial-report procedure to assess the amount of information present in the initial representation of the visual display. He exposed displays containing 12 letters, four letters in each of three rows) for brief durations. (Fig. 17.1). When asked to name all 12 letters, perceivers could rarely report more than about four—the capacity of the span of immediate memory for visually presented items (Miller, 1956). This finding by itself could indicate either that all of the letters in the array were not available in the initial representation or, conversely, that all the letters were represented internally but there was insufficient time to name and rehearse all of them before the representation decayed.

The partial-report procedure was designed to permit a choice between these two alternatives. In this procedure, the perceiver was required to report only one of the three rows. After the visual presentation terminated, the perceiver was told which row to report

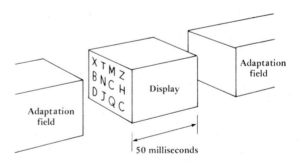

Figure 17.1 Schematic representation of the stimulus sequence in Sperling's (1960) poststimulus indicator experiment.

by the pitch of a tone—high, medium, or low pitched—to indicate that the perceiver should report the top, middle, or bottom row, respectively. The tone occurred either coincident with the offset of the presentation of the letter display or after varying interstimulus intervals up to several seconds.

The report of letters was very good when the tone followed the visual presentation immediately, or by less than about one-quarter of a second. Since the perceiver did not know which row was to be reported until the display had ended, he must have had available all the information from the display (that is, all 12 letters), until the indicator sounded. The number of letters available as a function of delay of the tone indicator is shown in Figure 17.2. The shaded area represents that duration during which visual information from the stimulus was available after stimulation had ended. Since the function levels out after about one-quarter second, Sperling argued that this was the duration of the initial visual storage. This type of evidence also shows rather convincingly that the limitation on report noted by Miller, of about a half-dozen items, could not be an input limitation. It appears as if all the information in the retinal projection

is available for subsequent processing, since the perceiver can extract whichever part is asked for. The limitation must occur after that point in time.

THE USE OF VISUAL INFORMATION

We began this chapter by noting that the major difference between matching two simultaneously presented stimuli and two sequentially presented stimuli was the degree to which memory was involved in the performance of the task. The results of a set of experiments on "character classification" provide an excellent example of the importance of these differences in determining the kinds (or levels) of processes involved in performing different kinds of matches.

Character Classification

The **character classification** experiments of Posner and Mitchell (1967) used identical stimulus–response combinations to produce differences in response latencies as a function of the different matching instructions. The task was very simple—the viewers were required to indicate whether a pair of letters were the same or were different by pressing one of two response keys. They were instructed to make their decisions as quickly as they could. Comparisons were made between the response latencies when instructed to match the letters for their physical characteristics ("Do the two letters look visually the same?"), or on the basis of the letter names ("Do the two letters have the same name, for instance, Bb?"), or on the basis of a higher order rule ("Are the two letters both vowels or not?")

At the simplest level of processing, the match would be based on the physical attributes of the stimulus pair (for example, AA = same; AB = different). At a higher level of processing, the match would be based on the names of the letters so that the stimulus pair "Aa" now would be called "same" instead of "different." The difference between these two tasks is that the physical match could be made solely on the basis of physical attributes of the stimuli and, therefore, without any need to identify the letters based upon

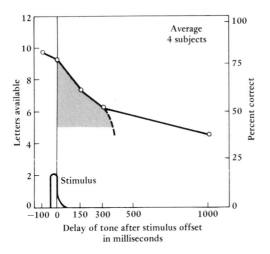

Figure 17.2   Number of letters correctly reported as a function of the delay of the poststimulus indicator (Sperling, 1960). The shaded area represents the visual storage portion.

labels available in memory. The name match requires some memory contact. A match on the basis of a consonant-vowel rule would be at an even higher level of classification (abstraction) since many letters are vowels and many are consonants.

The response latencies obtained from these conditions (Figure 17.3) support the notion that different levels were involved in responding to the three instructions. The depth of processing needed to respond "same" increased from "physical" to "name" to "rule" match. The "same" responses based on physical identity were about 75 milliseconds faster than those based on name identity, and this response was about 180 milliseconds faster than the match based on the rule.

When the response latencies in this experiment are compared with data from experiments in which the instruction was to match only on the basis of phys-

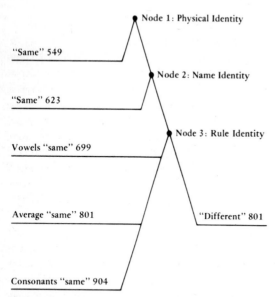

Figure 17.3 Reaction times (milliseconds) for decisions based on instructions to say "yes" if both letters were vowels, arranged in a hierarchy according to whether the stimuli were identical physically (node 1), were identical in their names only (node 2), or whether they could be differentiated only by the vowel–consonant rule (node 3), where vowels were processed faster than consonants. (After Posner & Mitchell, 1967.)

ical identity, or only name identity, the simple tasks were faster. The average physical matches took 420 milliseconds, much less than the 529 for rule matches of stimuli that were physically identical. The average name match took 523 milliseconds, again faster than the corresponding rule match of stimuli with the same name.

These data have been used to argue that when a physical match is permitted by the task demands, then such a match can be made based upon the visual representations alone, without any need to attach names or to carry out any further recognition or identification processing. Presumably, this match involves only information available in early perceptual processes. When the task demands that the items to be classified first be named, then the match must be made on the names, and that would require contact with memory, where the names are stored. Clearly, the higher-level rule match would require contact with rule structures in memory, taking even more time.

A number of experiments introduced a time delay between the two stimuli to be matched in the classification design in order to differentiate among the processes involved. Assuming that a visual representation of the stimulus is available for a limited time, the visual match could be performed only when stimuli are temporally adjacent. If a delay is introduced between the two letters to be matched, the differences in reaction time for the name and physical match should disappear. Figure 17.4 illustrates the differences in reaction time between name and physical identity "same" responses, measured from the onset of the second letter, as a function of the time interval between the two successive stimulus letters. This figure represents a composite of several experiments (Posner, Boies, Eichelman, & Taylor, 1969; Posner & Keele, 1967) in which the viewer was presented with a single letter followed by a second letter with the time interval between them varying from zero to two seconds. The two letters could be either physically identical, have only the same name, or be different. The instructions were to respond "same" if the two letters had the same name, otherwise to respond "different." When the second letter was presented immediately after the first, the match appears to have been made on the basis of the visual characterization of the physical stimuli. In this situation, a physical match was about 90 milliseconds faster than a name match, much like the difference reported earlier. As the delay between the two letters was increased to two seconds, the reaction time difference between the visual and the name match declined almost to zero. Since the information about the first letter must have been retained during this interval in order to make the match when the second letter appeared, it is likely that in this situation the initial visual information was encoded into the letter name. When the second letter was presented, it too could be named and then the names compared. It seems unlikely that the visual matching was carried out in the icon itself since up to two seconds was required before the match could be made and the visual representation was no longer available.

Another line of evidence is derived from the fact that different kinds of similarity have different effects on the time needed to classify two characters. If the visual match is made entirely on the basis of a visual

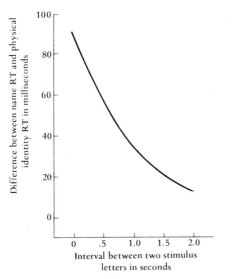

Figure 17.4 Difference in reaction time for name versus physical match as a function of the time interval between the presentation of the two letters to be matched. (Posner & Keele, 1967.)

representation, then the time needed to make a classification of "same" or "different" should not depend on the similarity of the names of the characters, but it might be slowed down if the two forms were visually very similar (for example, on O and Q, or on A and V). On the other hand if a match requires naming the characters, then visual similarity should not matter, but similar sounding names should delay the classification (as with B and T or E and C). Posner and Taylor (1969) verified these predictions and argued that because visual similarity had no impact on name matches, it is unlikely that the perceiver first created a visual image representation and *then* named the letter. Rather, it appears that the visual image and the short-term memory representation were constructed in parallel. The time difference between them suggests that the visual image representation can be initiated or completed faster than the named representation.

Characteristics of Visual Processing

The different outcomes of the character-classification task illustrate the fact that different processes must be invoked to explain even the simple uses of perceptual information. Before presenting some models for information processing in the visual matching task, we should become more familiar with some of the characteristics of visual processing that may be included as components of different theories.

Serial, Parallel, and Configurational Processing

The two major conceptual alternatives for processing any perceptual entity are serial and parallel mechanisms. In parallel processing, all the elements or dimensions of a stimulus are processed simultaneously. This is called **parallel processing** because a number of similar analyses are being performed at the same time. The alternative is **serial processing**, in which one element or dimension of a pattern in processed at a time. A third alternative —**configurational processing**—is frequently thought to be synonymous with parallel processing but is actually very different. Configurational processing denies the existence of the units or elements or dimensions that are assumed to exist in parallel processing. The configurational analysis is carried out directly on larger units or configurations that have properties that are different from the elements. This notion was implicit in the research of Weisstein and Harris cited above. It is also what the Gestalt psychologists meant when referring to the "essential quality" of a form (like "squareness"). This kind of property will become important in understanding perceptual matching (see also Chapter 15 on the perception of "form").

Direction of Processing

The serial processing alternative makes the measurement of response latency a powerful experimental tool. If it is assumed that the processing or comparison of an element or dimension of stimulation takes a unit of time, and that these units are equal for all elements or dimensions of a stimulus, then the manipulation of the number of elements processed should be directly reflected in measures of response latency. If the elements are processed serially, then reaction time should increase linearly with the number of pattern elements or dimensions compared. Therefore, in describing a serial process, the order or sequence of processing becomes important. Moreover, it is not sufficient to assume that processing procedes from left to right simply because we read from left to right. There have been suggestions of "top-down," "bottom-up," and "middle-out" processing (Kinchla & Wolf, 1979). We have already noted evidence for item-by-item processing in Sperling's (1963) experiment. It might be expected that if a perceiver processes the items one by one, he might do so in a consistent direction. Since these are letters, a left-to-right sequence based on reading habits might be expected in this task as well. When Sperling replicated his experiment in 1967, he found a consistent left-to-right superiority. When a perceiver did not have enough time to report all the items correctly, he was always better in reporting the left-hand than the right-hand letters. These data suggest that the perceiver encoded the letter names following an internal left-to-right scan of the icon. Thus the visually coded, spatially stored initial representation was transformed into a linguistically coded, sequentially stored temporal representation. At a rate of one name per 10 milliseconds or less, all the linguistic information in a visual display can usually be extracted in less than one fixation.

But there is evidence from Sperling's experiment as well as from those of others to suggest that this interpretation is too simple. This can be illustrated by one result from Sperling (1967). Figure 17.5 shows the results from a condition in which a five-letter display had been presented. Notice that the accuracy of reporting each of the five letter positions increased as processing time increased. Also, the perceiver appears to begin to process left-hand letters before right-hand ones. But notice that the curves for right-hand letters begin to rise from the baseline before the curves for the left-hand ones have reached maximum, suggesting that the perceiver is processing some aspect of the right-hand letters while he is still continuing to process the left-hand ones. This suggests either some type of parallel processing, transferring more than one letter at a time, or a breakdown in a consistent left-to-right order.

Rate of Processing

If information is processed sequentially, then it should take a fixed amount of time to process similar items. The more time available for processing, the greater the number of items that could be processed. If this description is accurate, then an experiment could be devised to measure the rate of processing—the amount of time necessary to process one item. Sperling (1963) attempted to do this by presenting a display of from two to six letters and asking the perceiver to name all

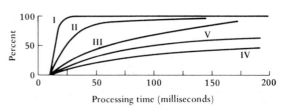

Figure 17.5 Percentage of letters reported from each letter position as a function of processing time, as determined by the delay of the visual noise masking field. (Sperling, 1967.)

of the letters in the display. Immediately following the presentation, a visual noise field was presented to terminate the icon. Sperling reasoned that, at the time of arrival of the visual noise, only those letters already transferred from the icon into short-term memory should be available for report. Those not yet processed would be irretrievably lost. Figure 6.25 (p. 138) presented Sperling's results. As the duration of the display was increased, thereby providing more time to process the content of the icon, the perceiver reported more letters. The rate of extraction was about one letter per 10 milliseconds of processing time. Since Sperling found that the curves for the two-, three-, four-, five-, and six-letter arrays all overlapped, he proposed that the letters were processed serially. In a serial process, the perceiver scans the visual representation, naming the first letter, then the next, and so on until he has named all of the items or run out of time. On the other hand, if the processing were parallel, the perceiver would attend to several or all of the letters at once. In this case, Sperling would have found that more letters were reportable per unit time for larger sized displays. Sperling's data is more consistent with an item-by-item processing model.

A number of other studies have examined the rate of processing using this general procedure, and have tended to find evidence of processing rates around 10 milliseconds per item or less. It is important to note that this manipulation—following the display by a visual noise mask—is designed specifically to assess information extraction from the iconic storage. Thus it would be expected to show very fast rates of processing, much faster than rates based on processing of information within short-term memory, for example.

Parallel Processing: Independence or Interaction

It should be obvious that response latency should be independent of the number of elements or dimensions processed if the processing is occurring in parallel. Moreover, the analysis of processes becomes more complicated if the assumption of uniform processing time per element does not hold, or if performance of a particular task is a result of combination of serial and parallel processes (Townsend, 1971).

A number of information-processing models begin with the assumption that the information presented in a visual stimulus excites parallel input channels to feature detectors. This process has sometimes been called "feature extraction" and is usually identified as a perceptual function as opposed to a memory, decision, or response function. The major differences in these models is whether the parallel channels are viewed as independent or not. An **independent-parallel-channels** model assumes a one-to-one mapping between processing channels and items in the stimulus display. In this view, visual information in different retinal locations is extracted from a stimulus over feature-detection channels that act simultaneously and independently. That is, visual feature information transmitted over one channel does not interact with information transmitted over another channel. Thus, each feature or character of a complex display has a separate input, with the information being transmitted over all channels simultaneously (Eriksen & Eriksen, 1974; Eriksen & Hoffman, 1972, 1973; Eriksen & Spencer, 1969; Gardner, 1973; Schiffrin & Geisler, 1973). In this view, a major component of response latency would be assigned to a central processor that examined the inputs from the various channels. This central "attentional mechanism" would select one of the inputs as a basis for response, depending on the task. Moreover, since all the input information would be entering simultaneously on parallel channels, the perceiver frequently has available more information than is needed to perform the task. Eriksen and Eriksen (1974) modified this model by limiting the input channels described in this way to the central 1 degree of visual angle about the fixation point.

An interactive-parallel-channels model assumes that input channels to feature detectors can inhibit one another (Bjork & Murray, 1977; Estes, 1972). Interaction occurs at the feature-extraction level. Excitation of any input channel excites inhibitory effects on other channels going to the same or other feature detectors. The degree of inhibition is a function of both the similarity or feature overlap of the various stimulus elements involved, and the relative distances in the visual field among the elements. For example, the interactive model predicts that noise affects feature extraction whereas the independent model predicts that it affects decision proccesses.

SELECTIVE ATTENTION

In the previous chapter, we considered some of the processes involved in visual search. In most of these, the perceiver is looking for something in a large display or scene, and has to move his eyes to successive locations in order to find and identify the sought-after target. We showed that to account for performance in this type of task properly we have to distinguish between a general and gross perception of the entire scene, and a detailed, clear view of what is in central vision at any one instant. We reviewed evidence that perceivers must have both kinds of information in order to carry out intelligent search procedures.

Moving our eyes in order to find something is the most typical kind of selectivity in perception. Indeed, we ignore most of the information available in a scene when we search for one aspect. This process is called **selective attention** because some of the information in the display is selected while other information is passed over. In this chapter, we consider selective attention further, but in tasks in which the selection occurs without eye movements. Thus, not only can we select by what we chose to fixate upon, but we can select some of the information within each glance and ignore or reject other information. We shall distinguish three levels of processing at which selective processes can occur: selection of inputs, selection of processes, and selection of outputs. This will not be an exhaustive discussion, but one designed to show how selective mechanisms work. More detailed treatments can be found in Kahneman (1973).

Input Selection

The concept of "attention" in the context of processing information from briefly presented stimuli refers to the fact that analytic processes are usually concentrated on only a small portion of the information available. The proposal that visual information enters on independent parallel channels almost de-

mands the inclusion of a selective process to sort out the wealth of information in the input channels. Many theorists have proposed such a mechanism. For example, Neisser proposed a "preattentive" representation that could be scanned by a mechanism of "focal attention" to select information for use in subsequent processing. But clearly, for this kind of selection to occur, the early stage must be able to register information about the location of stimulus components so that focal attention can be directed to that region of the visual field.

Eriksen and Hoffman (1974) demonstrated the operation of such a spatially directed attentional mechanism. Subjects had to identify letters that were flashed briefly in one of four locations along an imaginary circle whose center was the fixation point. A visual marker indicating the location of the target letter preceded the display by up to 150 milliseconds. The results showed that the response latencies were shorter, the longer the time between the location marker and the display. That is, the subjects could read information out of the initial representation faster when their attention was first directed to the appropriate location. This result is consistent with the findings of Smith and Blahá (1969) and Posner (1975), reviewed on pages 334–335, that providing subjects with location information improves their performance, even when they do not make eye movements.

It therefore appears that an attentional mechanism utilizes information about the location or position of targets. Breitmeyer and Ganz (1976) have suggested that figural and location information is transmitted through parallel and quasi-independent channels. They based this proposal on the evidence that the presence and the location of a briefly presented target can be detected in a metacontrast masking experiment (for example, Fehrer & Biederman, 1962; Fehrer & Raab, 1962; Schiller & Smith, 1966; see Chapter 6), when its figural properties are masked (Breitmeyer, Love, & Wepman, 1974; Weisstein & Haber, 1965). Moreover, Breitmeyer and Ganz propose that these two distinct types of information—figural information and location information—are carried by two different types of channels corresponding to two different types of spatial frequency channels—sustained and transient—that have been discovered in the visual system (see Chapters 4 and 6). Low spatial frequency channels appear to be sensitive to transient stimulation produced by rapid movement, flicker, and abrupt stimulus onset. This would seem to make it appropriate for transmitting information about location or rapid change in location. High spatial frequency channels appear to be more sensitive to slow-moving or stationary stimuli, that is, more appropriate for transmitting figural information. Whether these two independent channels actually exist, however, does not detract from the clear relationship between location information and an attentional mechanism.

Process Selection

Not only are some inputs selected at the expense of others, but that selection may occur at many different points in the information-processing sequence (Erdelyi, 1974). Carr and Bacharach (1976) propose that the very early selection of inputs to the perceptual system is performed by a process called "perceptual tuning," whereas the selection of processes, and of information to be used by the processes, is performed by a process called "conscious attention."

Perceptual tuning is a perceptual control process—it is automatic, dependent upon learning, and independent of the perceiver's intentions. It provides an automatic monitor of conceptually meaningful and ecologically important information. This mechanism is dynamic and task-oriented in the sense that (*a*) it takes into account the perceiver's assumptions about what the nature and organization of the input information ought to be, and (*b*) it is continually involved in the processing of the input. This results in a continuously updated assessment of the sources of information by a continuously updated mechanism (see also Schneider and Shiffrin, 1977).

Conscious attention acts to direct decisionmaking and response systems to particular subsets of the perceptual input. Its primary function is task and process selection, but it can also regulate input as part of this process. Because it can regulate the input to cognitive tasks, conscious attention is seen as a serial process.

According to Carr and Bacharach, the operation of a perceptual tuning mechanism is illustrated by the work of Biederman and his colleagues on the perception of pictures (see Chapter 16, pp. 342–344). They demonstrated that the thematic structure of a picture can facilitate the recognition of the component parts of the picture—performance (both accuracy of identification and reaction time) was poorer when the picture had been jumbled than when it portrayed a coherent scene, even when the perceivers knew before the exposure where the target would appear (Biederman, 1972; Biederman, Glass, & Stacey, 1973; Biederman, Rabinowitz, Glass, & Stacey, 1974). Carr and Bacharach concluded that this evidence indicated that higher-order visual information could be obtained early in processing and that this information guided the identification of scene components via the mechanism of perceptual tuning.

Output Selection

Eriksen and his coworkers have proposed an output selection model to account for many "attentional" effects, especially the effect of spatial proximity (Colegate, Hoffman, & Eriksen, 1973; Eriksen & Eriksen, 1974; Eriksen & Hoffman, 1972, 1973, 1974). They noted that even when the visual search component is eliminated from a task, noise letters or other stimuli impair the processing of a designated target letter. For example, when an indicator is presented as much as 400–500 milliseconds before a target, the presence of noise letters in the display delays correct identification responses. The response is delayed longer when the noise letters are within one-half a degree of visual angle from the target letters, and is negligible when they are separated by more than one degree.

In order to explain these effects, they proposed that, since input selection could not be capable of an infinitely fine degree of selectivity, selection must also occur on the response side. If a minimal amount of information must be processed simultaneously, then the input side of any information-processing system—the visual system, for example—may be said to have a minimal channel size in terms of its capacity to process information. That is, this part of the system will always process *at least* some fixed minimal amount of stimulus information even if that information is not all needed or used in performing the task. In this conception, then, the perceiver cannot shut off the input or close it down below this minimal level—this channel is always filled, at least to the minimal level.

Because the input process will always process some minimal amount of information from the stimulus, the perceiver frequently has available more information than necessary for the production of responses. For example, even with selective attention on a single target letter, a perceiver will process two or three more letters from the target section of a multiletter display. This causes a problem for the response system since it can produce only one response at a time. That is, a person can name only one letter at a time, or move a key in only one direction at a time. Therefore, it is necessary to select among the potential responses to all the information available and to inhibit those that will not be used to produce responses directly. This selection and inhibition takes time and is the reason for the increases seen in reaction time. The effect of spatial proximity is attributed to the properties of spatial discrimination. In selecting which of several available letters to emit as a response, the perceiver must determine which letter came from the indicated position. This is a spatial discrimination and small stimulus differences require longer decision times.

To summarize this view: The perceiver cannot prevent processing noise letters that appear within about 1 degree of visual angle of the target due to the nature of the input channel. Thus, even with selective attention two or more letters will be processed from a display sector. Therefore, the perceiver must inhibit the response until a discrimination is made as to exactly which letter was in the target position. Selection is more rapid if the spatial discrimination is easy.

Eriksen's work has focused on interference created by spatial proximity. Older evidence has demonstrated an even more powerful output interference effect caused by being unable to suppress processing some kind of information. We will review one example of this in Chapter 18 (p. 379), when we consider the Stroop effect. Chapter 18 as a whole focuses on

how familiarity with stimuli affects selective processes.

Visual Processing

Visual Search   One visual processing task that has been used to study early visual processing is the **visual search** task. A perceiver is instructed to look for a particular letter in a large list of letters and to press a button as soon as it is found. (This task may also be thought of as a matching task, where a representation of a sought-for letter is matched with the visual representation of the letters in the list.) A number of experiments using this task have been reported (Neisser, 1963; Neisser & Beller, 1965; Neisser & Lazar, 1964; Neisser, Novick, & Lazar, 1963; Neisser & Stoper, 1965). Typically, 50-line lists that contained a target in unpredictable positions were presented (Fig. 17.6). As soon as the list appeared, the perceivers began to search down the list as rapidly as possible to find the target letter (for example, the letter K in list a). They pressed a button as soon as the letter was found. The processing time per row was computed by dividing the time needed to complete the search by the number of letters in the list. Typical results are shown in Figure 17.7, in which reaction time is plotted as a function of the row of the target letter. The function shows a linear increase in search time with target position. The slope of this line may be taken to represent the average processing time per row, a parameter that should reflect the complexity of the information-extraction process.

In a wide range of experiments, Neisser and his colleagues varied many parameters of this task. They found that looking for the presence of a letter (for example, the letter K in list a) was faster than looking for the absence of a letter that was present in every line but one (for example, looking for the absence of a Q in list b). This finding suggests that relatively little identification of the background letters was needed in list a, thus allowing the scan time to be faster. But it took much longer when the target had to be checked on every line, as in list b. They also found that it was

(a)	*(b)*	*(c)*	*(d)*
EHYP	ZVMLBQ	ODUGQR	IVMXEW
SWIQ	HSQJMF	QCDUGO	EWVMIX
UFCJ	ZTJVQR	CQOGRD	EXWMVI
WBYH	RDQTFM	QUGCDR	IXEMWV
OGTX	TQVRSX	URDGQO	VXWEMI
GWVX	MSVRQX	GRUQDO	MXVEWI
TWLN	ZHQBTL	DUZGRO	XVWMEI
XJBU	ZJTQXL	UCGROD	MWXVIE
UDXI	LHQVXM	DQRCGU	VIMEXW
HSFP	FVQHMS	QDOCGU	EXVWIM
XSCQ	MTSDQL	CGUROQ	VWMIEX
SDJU	TZDFQB	OCDURQ	VMWIEX
PODC	QLHBMZ	UOCGQD	XVWMEI
ZVBP	QMXBJD	RGQCOU	WXVEMI
PEVZ	RVZHSQ	GRUDQO	XMEWIV
SLRA	STFMQZ	GODUCQ	MXIVEW
JCEN	RVXSQM	QCURDO	VEWMIX
ZLRD	MQBJFT	DUCOQG	EMVXWI
XBOD	MVZXLQ	CGRDQU	IVWMEX
PHMU	RTBXQH	UDRCOQ	IEVMWX
ZHFK	BLQSZX	GQCORU	WVZMXE
PNJW	QSVFDJ	GOQUCD	XEMIWV
CQXT	FLDVZT	GDQUOC	WXIMEV
GHNR	BQHMDX	URDCGO	EMWIVX
IXYD	BMFDQH	GODRQC	IVEMXW

Figure 17.6   Portions of lists for visual search. The target is the letter *K* in list *(a)*, the absence of the letter *Q* in list *(b)*, and the letter *Z* in lists *(c)* and *(d)*. (Neisser, 1963.)

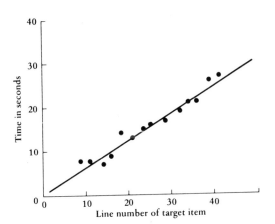

Figure 17.7   Typical results from a visual search experiment. Reaction time is plotted as a function of the row in which the target appeared. (Neisser, 1963.)

easier to find a *Q* among a background of angular letters than round letters, and conversely, a *Z* among round letters than angular letters (see lists *c* and *d* in Figure 17.6, and Figure 17.8). In other words, if the features that discriminated targets from nontargets were easy to differentiate, search was faster than if the targets and nontargets required more complex identification. These results suggest that searching can be performed on the basis of visual-feature characteristics, and therefore that information at this level must have been available.

Rabbitt (1967) has also shown that perceivers are capable of differentiating targets from nontargets on the basis of visual features. He had perceivers sort decks of cards into one of two piles, depending on whether the card contained the letter *O* or *C*. The eight background items were either angular (for instance, *A, E, F, H, I, K, L*) or curved (for instance, *B, D, G, J, P, Q, S*). One of the angular packs was sorted six

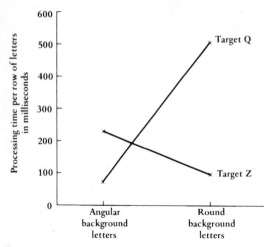

Figure 17.8 Reaction time as a function of angularity of background for angular (Z) and round (Q) targets. (Plotted from data taken from Neisser, 1963.)

times. Then half of the perceivers were switched to another angular pack (for example, with background letters *M, N, T, V, W, X, Y, Z,*), while the remainder were switched to the curved pack. Sorting time for those transferred to the other angular pack did not change, but it increased by 20 percent for the perceivers who were transferred from angular to curved background items. Rabbitt interpreted these results to mean that the perceivers had learned to find those features that differentiated the targets from the background items. The effortless transfer from one angular set to another must mean that the perceivers were not learning anything about the names of the items, but only something about their features. When the names were changed but the features held constant, as from one angular pack to another, no loss in performance was noted. But when those features were changed, the discrimination took longer.

There seems to be ample evidence that perceivers can find a target without having to identify fully each letter encountered. The visual-feature distinctions appear to be sufficient, suggesting at least, that visual features are available as a unit of processing. As additional support for this view, Neisser also found that after a perceiver had searched through many displays, he could not recognize the nontarget background

items in a subsequent recognition test. If all of the features had been fully analyzed to the point of identification, the perceiver should have been able to remember some of the letters. In fact, perceivers from almost all serach tasks of this sort report that the backgrounds looked like a blur—only the targets stood out. Not only were the perceivers unable to remember the background items after the experiment, they were apparently not even aware that they were looking at them. Unfortunately, data on subsequent recognition were not obtained in the experiments in which the features of the targets and the backgrounds were similar. Presumably, the perceiver would have remembered more of the background letters, if he had had to identify them.

Neisser (1963) also examined what happens in the search task when the perceiver has to look for more than one target at a time. Thus, instead of looking just for a *K* in a list *a* of Figure 17.6, he might have to look for a *Q* or a *K,* and respond when he finds an instance of either one. Figure 17.9 shows the results for searches of one, four, or six targets as a function of days of practice. It is clear that without practice, perceivers take longer per row when they have to search for more letters. Searching for an instance of one of six letters takes much longer than a single letter, although not six times as long. However, after many days of practice on this task, perceivers were able to search down the list at the same speed regardless of how many targets they were looking for. Wattenberger (1970) replicated this result, and showed that it holds regardless of whether the perceiver was permitted to make errors in order to go rapidly or was required to hold errors to a bare minimum. Neisser (1967) also noted that searchers in news-clip agencies can look through the newspapers for the names of clients at search rates of 1000 words per minute for over 100 target names. Of course, we have no idea how many targets they miss.

Several explanations have been offered for the improvement with practice in multiple target-search tasks. One possibility is a change from a serial feature-by-feature processing, in which each feature of each target is examined one at a time, to one in which several features or several targets are processed at the same

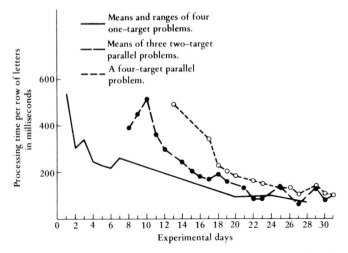

Figure 17.9   Reaction time as a function of days of practice when looking for one, four, or six targets. (After Neisser, 1963.)

time. This might be due to a change in the strategy of the perceiver or to a change in the familiarity of the target items that permits them to be grouped or chunked together into a more meaningful unit, thereby reducing the number of separate items to be processed (see also Schneider and Shiffrin, 1977).

Visual Discrimination
Weisstein and Harris (1974) found that briefly flashed line segments were more accurately identified when they were part of an organized configuration—a drawing that looked unitary and three dimensional—than when the line segments were in any of several less coherent flat designs. Their results suggest that the contents of the visual representation may be more global in nature, that is, more than merely a collection of features. The experimental procedure used by Weisstein and Harris was reviewed in Chapter 15. Target lines were flashed along with different context patterns to produce compound patterns, and the subject had to indicate which one of the four line segments was contained in the stimulus. Because all subjects were more accurate with the organized compounds, Weisstein and Harris concluded that pattern recognition cannot begin with elementary feature detection—there must be some kind of global feature

recognition, or at least a feature-detection process combined with complex pattern detectors. Global figure recognition would occur when the entire pattern is processed simultaneously. The component features would then be analyzed from the total configuration.

The detection of features can also be enhanced by certain kinds of two-dimensional contexts. For example, an element that provides no information but merely supplies context may aid in the detection of another portion of the stimulus array (Pomerantz & Garner, 1973; Pomerantz & Schwaitzberg, 1975). Responses to stimulus pairs such as (), ((,)), and)(showed that subjects attended to the whole pair rather than single elements when discriminating pairs such as () from ((or)) from)(, even when only a single element supplied information relevant to the task. With stimuli like (⌢ , (⌣ ,) ⌣ , or) ⌢ , only single elements occupied attention.

That context can improve discriminability was demonstrated clearly in a series of experiments by Pomerantz, Sager, and Stoever (1977). In one experiment, an oddity task was used to minimize the demands on memory and thereby add weight to the argument that the effect was perceptual. Some of the stimuli used are illustrated in Figure 17.10. The base-

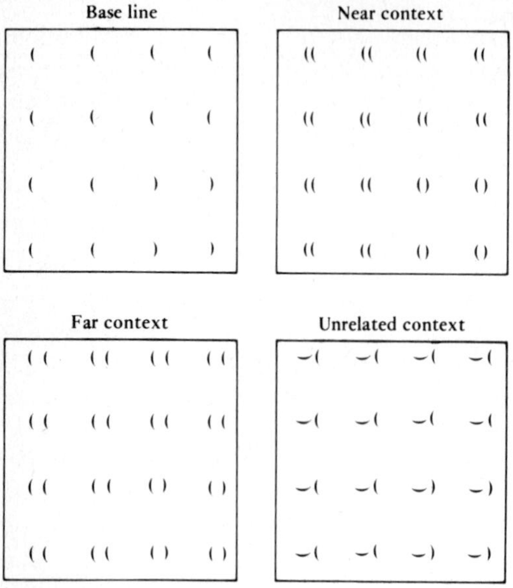

Base line

Near context

Far context

Unrelated context

Figure 17.10 Arrays used to demonstrate a "configural superiority effect." The task was to detect which of the four quadrants in each array was different. In these examples, the lower-right quadrant is different. Response times to the "near"- and "far"-different arrays were shorter than to the baseline arrays—the "configural superiority effect." Responses to near context were faster than to far context, and the responses to the unrelated context control were even slower than to the baseline. (Pomerantz, Sagor, & Stoever, 1977.)

line stimulus consisted of a 4 × 4 array of features. One quadrant was always different and the task was to detect the different quadrant as quickly as possible. The dependent measure was the latency of the response. All other stimuli contained arrays of pairs of features constructed by adding a uniform 4 × 4 array of features to those of the baseline arrays. Figure 17.10 shows examples of arrays with near context, far context, and unrelated context, where "near" and "far" refers to the distance between elements of the stimuli.

Response times to the near- and far-context arrays were shorter than to the baseline arrays. This difference illustrated what the authors called a **configural superiority effect.** The response times were slower to the arrays containing unrelated context than to the

baseline arrays, indicating that more than the mere presence of context features was required for the effect. The authors suggested that the effect of those contexts that improved detection was to permit the subjects to respond to **emergent features**—a concept similar to the notion of a "whole" or a Gestalt. They suggested that the emergent features were functional units to which the subjects responded directly and that wholes were not recognized by prior recognition of their parts.

VISUAL MATCHING

The Same—Different Paradox

Perceptual matching tasks are deceptively simple. A perceiver is shown two patterns, either side by side or one after the other (that is, simultaneously or successively), and must decide as rapidly and accurately as possible whether they are the same patterns or not. If they are identical, then the perceiver must respond by indicating "same"; if they are even the slightest bit dissimilar, the perceiver must respond by indicating "different." The processes involved in the accurate performance of this matching task have the potential of telling us a great deal about perception and the way perceptual processes are involved in the extraction and use of information from visual stimulation. Yet despite the large amount of research devoted to the attempt to understand the mechanisms involved, perceptual matching still presents us with paradoxical results (Nickerson, 1972, 1973, 1979).

The paradox stems from a logical analysis of the task: To determine that two patterns are different requires only that a single difference be discovered, no matter how slight. On the other hand, to determine that two patterns are identical, they must be examined and compared in detail to be certain that slight differences do not exist. Thus, the discovery of a single mismatching element is sufficient to signal a "different" response, whereas, theoretically, a "same" response must await exhaustive comparison of all possible differences (Nickerson, 1965). Theoretically, then, "different" judgments should be faster than "same" judgments. The paradox is that, in general, correct responses to *same* stimuli have been found to be faster than correct responses to *different* stimuli.

Dual-Process Models

As a consequence of this paradoxical result, a simple element-by-element model of visual matching is clearly untenable. Consequently, some investigators have proposed models that include separate processes for producing the "same" and the "different" judgments: a fast, global comparison process to account for the fast "same" responses, and a slower, analytic, element-by-element comparison process to account for the "different" responses (for example, Bamber, 1969; Egeth & Blecker, 1971).

There is another reason for suggesting two independent processes—"same" and "different" judgments are affected differentially by structural variables. For example, Krueger (1973) found that the time it takes to respond "different" was a function of stimulus frequency within a set of trials, whereas the latency to respond "same" was not. Baron (1974), Egeth and Blecker (1971), and Kroll (1977) all reported that the reaction time to *same* stimuli was dependent upon the level of familiarity of the elements of the stimuli whereas the reaction time to *different* stimuli was not. Finally, Klapp (1971) reported that the latency of response to *different* stimuli was a function of the number of syllables in word pairs, whereas the latency of response to *same* word pairs was unaffected by the syllabic structure. There are many more examples of such differences, but these should suffice to illustrate the general conclusion that there were major differences in the processes involved in "same" and "different" responses.

Yet, the dual-process solution has remained unsatisfying. For example, it has been repeatedly pointed out that a two-process model is unparsimonious—using two processes to explain two responses adds little to understanding unless a preprocessor is included to determine which of the two processes should be used. But then there is no need for the two processses, since the decision would already have been made (Kroll & Hershenson, 1980). Indeed, it seems clear that, with respect to the decision mechanism,

"same" and "different" judgments should be alternative outcomes—if one is not indicated, the other must be—unless a "no decision" outcome is to be permitted (Krueger, 1978; Silverman, 1973). Indeed, it is this alternative that provides the direction for the two models to be presented: the two-stage model and the noisy-operator model. Both allow for three alternative outcomes of the initial stage of processing: "same" or "different" responses, or a continuation of processing. The models differ in the subsequent processes—the former procedes to a new process, whereas the latter repeats the first stage. Before presenting these models, however, we shall present evidence from an experimental test of the dual-process theory.

If an "identity processor" assessed *same* stimuli while an independent "feature comparator" processed *different* stimuli, the latency to respond "same" should be independent of the nature of the *different* stimuli. Moreover, if "same" responses were based on a fast, wholistic analysis and "different" responses on a slower, more thorough element-matching process, then limiting exposure duration should have a greater affect on processing *different* arrays than on *same* arrays. Kroll and Hershenson (1980) tested these predictions directly. They used stimuli consisting of pairs of six-letter strings of upper-case letters, exposed in a tachistoscope for either 100 or 1000 milliseconds. The *different* arrays were either easy to discriminate (that is, all of the six letters were different in the two pairs), or hard to discriminate (that is, the strings differed in only one letter).

In one experiment, the stimuli were presented in blocks segregated according to the type of different arrays present (hard or easy). In a second experiment, all stimuli were randomly intermixed. In both experiments, the results were the same—none of the predictions from the dual-process model was supported. The differences in the discriminability of *different* stimuli affected both "same" and "different" responses. Moreover, the limitation of stimulus exposure affected "same" responses at both levels of discriminability and "different" responses only for the hard-to-discriminate arrays. Thus, if anything, "same" responses were more sensitive to changes in stimulus duration than "different" responses.

The Two-Stage Discriminability Model

Kroll and Hershenson (1980) concluded that the dual-process model could not explain their pattern of findings. Instead, they proposed a two-stage model that uses the wholistic and analytic comparison processes of the dual-process model, but arranges them in tandem to form two processing stages. This aspect of the model is similar to one proposed by Atkinson and Juola (1974) for a memory task and to a model for processing dimensional stimuli by Lockhead (1972). A single two-stage sequence was proposed to account for the **"same"**–**"different"** paradox—fast "same" and some fast "different" responses could represent the output of a fast global comparator, but slow "different" responses would also require additional processing through an analytic element-by-element processor. What is required is a decision dimension to determine whether a response is to be made after global comparison or whether further analysis is to be performed. Their experiments suggested that discriminability was one such important dimension.

The specific model proposed by Kroll and Hershenson is presented in the flow diagram in Figure 17.11. It shows a first stage that involves a wholistic or global comparison of the two patterns. A value of overall discriminability is obtained and this value is compared with response criteria values. If the discriminability value is below the criterion for a "same" judgment (C_S), a "same" response is triggered; if the

value is above the criterion for a "different" judgment (C_D), a "different" response is triggered. If a decision cannot be made on the basis of the outcome of the first stage (that is, when ($C_S \leqslant X \leqslant C_D$), a second stage is initiated. In this stage, corresponding elements of the two patterns are compared serially, element pair by element pair, until either a difference is discovered, or all element pairs are exhausted with no difference found. The former case leads to a "different" response; the latter to a "same" response.

The evidence in support of the two-stage discriminability model comes from the experiments designed to test the dual-process model. All the results from those experiments can be explained by this model, and some additional analyses provide further support. First, with respect to the overall findings, the fact that responses to the easy-to-discriminate stimuli were unaffected by stimulus duration could mean that the decision may have been based on information available from the first 100 milliseconds; that is, the first decision stage may use a rough estimate (global comparison) of the difference between the letter strings. The fact that matching latencies were most affected by the short stimulus duration when the discrimination was difficult, whereas easy-to-discriminate arrays were relatively unaffected, suggested that the brief exposure forced the termination of processing prior to completion of the task. This produced fast response latencies but large error rates. On the other hand, the easy-to-discriminate arrays were rapidly and accurately

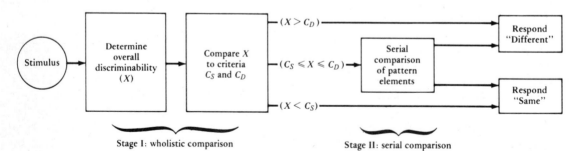

Figure 17.11 Schematic representation of a two-stage discriminability model of perceptual matching. Stage I involves a wholistic comparison of the two patterns that can lead directly to responses in certain cases. If the decision

cannot be made on the basis of the outcomes of the first stage, the second stage is initiated, a serial comparison of the elements of the two patterns. (After Kroll & Hershenson, 1980.)

matched on the basis of an initial, global stage of comparison, for which the 100 milliseconds of exposure provided sufficient information.

The analysis of the response latencies and errors for each of the six possible positions provided further evidence in support of the two-stage discriminability model. These data are shown in Figure 17.12, separately for the 100- and 1000-millisecond durations but combined over mixed and blocked presentation. It is clear that reaction time and errors increased from left to right for stimuli exposed at 1000 milliseconds. For brief-duration stimuli, the response latency was essentially flat, for all positions except the leftmost one. Errors also increased for these stimuli, from left to right. These serial position results also support the two-stage model. For the short-duration stimuli, the second stage would not be involved and the serial comparison would not be performed, and, consequently, the reaction times should be relatively equal. For long-duration stimuli, the hard-to-discriminate arrays would be passed on to a second stage of sequential element-pair processing, producing the increasing left-right function.

There is also another way to test the two-stage hypothesis. If the two stages are distinct, then the time to respond "different" should have been faster when the entire array was different than when the difference occurred only in the first (leftmost) position. That is, the decision about the difference in easy-to-discriminate arrays should be made by the global comparison stage, whereas the hard-to-discriminate arrays should have to be passed along to the serial-comparison stage after first-stage processing. Once again, the results are clear: in both experiments, response times were faster to all-different arrays than to first-position-different arrays—of the 32 comparisons, there was not a single reversal of this direction. The mean reaction times are given in Figure 17.13 separately for the two exposure durations for mixed and blocked presentations. Once again it is clear that a simple serial-comparison process cannot account for these differences, whereas a two-stage theory can. Moreover, Kroll and Hershenson noted that the differences in response latencies between the all-different arrays and the first-position-different arrays may be taken as a rough estimate of the time needed to initiate the second stage and complete one comparison.

Single-Process Iteration: The Noisy-Operator Model

The noisy-operator model proposed by Krueger (1978) attributes the fast responses to *same* stimuli to

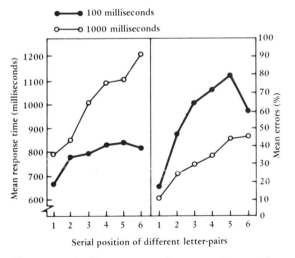

Figure 17.12 Mean response latency and errors for stimulus pairs exposed at 100 and 1000 milliseconds for the serial position of the difference in hard-to-discriminate *different* arrays, combined over mixed and blocked presentations. (Kroll & Hershenson, 1980.)

	Duration	One-different Position one	All-different
Blocked	100	702	574
	1000	860	570
Mixed	100	625	511
	1000	717	593

Figure 17.13 Mean response time in milliseconds for *different* responses to arrays that were all-different or one-different in the first serial position. (Kroll & Hershenson, 1980.)

the affects of internal noise. It rests on the notion that internal noise is more likely to make a *same* pair look different than to make a *different* pair look the same. Furthermore, if pairs that look different must be rechecked, and if rechecking takes time, then those stimuli that are rechecked most will yield the longest processing latencies. *Same* pairs will generate small differences due to noise but different pairs will not, and consequently, the *different* pairs will require rechecking and produce longer latencies.

Krueger's model applies to the single-glance case—that is, the situation in which up to four or five letters could be processed simultaneously. The model assumes that the "dimension" of comparison is not an element of the display, but the entire contents of a single glance. Processing within a single glance is assumed to be configurational, with the two patterns compared wholistically. The outcome of such a comparison could be based upon template matches or overlap measures.

There are three basic assumptions of the model: (*a*) decisions are based upon the number of mismatching features recorded by a "difference counter"; (*b*) internal noise affects the comparison process; and (*c*) if the decision count is not sufficiently high or low to produce a decision, the decision is postponed so that a second glance (or more, if necessary) can be made. Thus, "comparison" consists of a series of successive, independent "looks" or "passes" at the information input. Each pass takes a fixed amount of time—estimated at about 200 milliseconds—and involves a full set of encoding, comparison, and decision operators. The difference-counter cumulates the differences across the independent passes, thereby assuring an eventual response. In other words, the proposal can be characterized as a single-processor accumulative model that allows for rechecking. The "same"–"different" paradox is resolved by the way in which internal noise differentially affects *same* and *different* stimuli.

Therefore, the differential affect of internal noise, while not the essential feature of the processing model, is the factor that makes the model viable. The differential effects seen at the judgmental level are referred back to differential effects at the visual feature

level. Krueger claims that the assumption is reasonable because studies of tachistoscopic identification of letters have reported errors that were related to their physical similarity (for example, Bouma, 1971; Hershenson, 1969b; Townsend, 1971). Moreover, Krueger argues that there is a certain amount of background noise inherent in the feature-detection system, and that the system is just as likely to detect a feature that is not present as it is to miss one that is actually in the stimulus (Massaro & Schmuller, 1975).

Consequently, Krueger assumes that noise serves to "perturb" visual features rather than to delete them; that is, perturbation reduces the fidelity of the trace rather than the strength. Feature perturbation tends to increase the difference count on *same* pairs, since their true difference count is zero, and it tends to increase the difference count on *different* pairs too. But a positive difference counts does not always lead to an immediate "different" decision. For that to happen, the difference count would have to exceed a certain criterion level. Indeed, a low difference count might even trigger a "same" decision since only *same* stimuli can produce very low counts.

If the difference count is not sufficiently high or low, the decision is postponed and a second pass is made. This process of count-and-recheck is continued until a decision can be made (or a deadline of some sort is reached). Most of the decisions will therefore be a result of cumulative difference counts made over a series of passes. These cumulative counts can be represented as relative frequency distributions for *same* and *different* stimuli. Figure 17.14 shows an example of one set of such distributions. The distribution for *different* stimuli is on the right because, generally, it will have a higher difference count than that for the *same* stimuli. There are two criterion points represented: C_S and C_D. These points divide the region into areas of response and no-response. If the count is below C_S, the response "same" is made immediately; if the count is above C_D, the response "different" is made immediately. However, if the count falls between C_S and C_D, the processor goes on to another pass.

The effect of noise must be to increase the count in such a way as to produce a difference either in variability or in skewness between the two distributions.

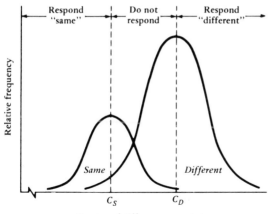

Figure 17.14 Example of one possible set of *same* and *different* distributions on difference count. The distributions illustrated are symmetrical with a greater variance for the *sames*. The criterion for a "different" response is pushed to the right, producing more rechecking for different pairs and, consequently, longer response latencies for "different" responses. (After Krueger, 1978.)

Krueger analyzed all possible combinations of these, each causing differential amounts of rechecking for *same* and *different* pairs. In the case pictured, the *same* distribution is more variable than the *different* distribution: the criterion for "different" has been pushed up to the right, producing more rechecking for *different* pairs and, consequently, longer response latencies.

SUMMARY

The focus in this chapter was on the nature of the first representation of visual information, on the nature of visual processing, and on the use of visual information in visual matching. The evidence suggested that the first representation contains information that is wholistically organized, that is, it is relational or configurational information. The elementary components of visual information such as visual features are probably available at a later stage, or by specific focusing of attention.

A number of different possible characteristics of visual processing was discussed. Serial and parallel processes were contrasted and were shown to be fundamentally different from configurational processssing. Selective attention was described for information presented in a single glance. The possibility of input, output, and process selection was discussed. Our understanding of the characteristics of visual information and of visual processing was applied to the visual matching task. The analysis of the models proposed to explain the data from matching experiments supports the idea that visual information is represented configurationally in the first stage and that element-by-element analysis is a later process involving a focus of attention.

SUGGESTED READINGS

We have already mentioned Moray's (1970) excellent text on attention and Broadbent's (1971) more general statement on information processing. The major part of Kahneman's (1973) book concerns selective attention and it includes an excellent summary of current work on vigilance. Neisser (1967) covers most of the work in this chapter. A collected volume by Mostofsky (1970) contains many fine papers on selective processes in perception.

Chapter 18

Perceptual Recognition and Identification

This chapter will describe research relating to the perceptual recognition and identification of symbolic material. The recognition of forms or configurations has already been introduced in Chapter 15 and some of that knowledge will be applied in this discussion. The major distinction that separates the material in this chapter from that discussed previously is the emphasis on symbolic content. That is, the research to be discussed in this and the next chapter is focused on the relationship between the visual representation of physical symbols and the meaning or knowledge stored in the viewer's memory. Strings of letters, words, phrases, and sentences are all symbols of this sort. Of course, it would be impossible to discuss all of these types of symbols in a single chapter. Therefore, this chapter will describe research on letter strings and words—the simpler sets of symbols—and the next chapter will discuss the extraction of meaning from more complex sets of symbols—the process called "reading."

The processes to be discussed may be termed **visual cognition,** since recognition and identification necessarily involve more than the construction of an internal representation of the world around us. In visual cognition, that internal representation must somehow make contact with memory. That is, contact must be made between the present input and the stored representation of previous inputs. The study of perceptual recognition and identification, therefore, concerns the nature of this contact with memory. This has broad implications for the study of cognition and learning. The nature of the contact with memory will depend not only on perceptual variables and the nature of perceptual processing, but even more on the nature of the representations in memory and the processes that manifest their effect on the input. In many ways, then, the study of visual recognition and identification may be thought of as the study of perception and memory.

The terms "recognition" and "identification" are often used interchangeably despite some important differences between them. **Recognition** describes a sense of familiarity—"I have seen that before"—whereas **identification** requires the production of a specific label or category name—"That is an apple." When reporting our perceptions of words, we identify the visual display, naming the words being read rather than simply noting that we recognize them as being familiar. The difference is important because it is possible to identify words we do not recognize—as when we read a new word—as well as to recognize objects we cannot identify.

The early explanations of perceptual recognition and identification centered around the enhancement or inhibition of perception. For example, it was found that tachistoscopic thresholds were lower for familiar shapes and words (Henle, 1942; Solomon & Howes, 1951; Solomon & Postman, 1952); and it was generally assumed that this occurred because familiar stimuli were perceived better or faster. Proposals that perception can be inhibited (**perceptual defense**) or enhanced (**perceptual vigilance**) were also made for variables related to the motivational and affective state of the perceiver (for example, Bruner, 1957; Bruner & Postman, 1949a, 1949b). This evidence demonstrated that stimuli which were differentially related to internal states of the perceiver produced differential tachistoscopic recognition thresholds. For example, a perceiver who was made anxious by words with sexual connotations might require longer exposure durations than normal to see these words (see "Input-Selection" in Chapter 17).

Although the early experimental findings clearly showed differences in responses as a function of these variables, the explanations were quickly attacked as too simple. One criticism was based on a distinction between "perceptual" and "response" effects; that is, the differences might not reflect perceptual events but events related to response availability or even to a willingness of the perceiver to make a response (Eriksen, 1957; Garner, Hake, & Eriksen, 1956). Indeed, Goldiamond and Hawkins (1958) were able to show that perceivers who expected to see words in a tachistoscope, but were shown fragments, produced a word-frequency effect in their responses. It is now clear that even the perception–response distinction is too simple—that perceivers' responses in recognition experiments can be understood only by reference to much more complex models of the sequence of processes.

One of the difficulties in settling these issues is the fact that an experiment can never demonstrate that an effect did not occur. For example, if a "perceptual effect" is not found in a particular experiment, it may have been because the experiment was not designed appropriately to test for the particular effect—and there is no way to demonstrate conclusively that it was. The alternative to the assertion that a particular variable affects perception is not simply the demonstration that the variable does *not* affect perception in a particular experiment. If one can show, however, that a particular effect can be attributed to another system—the response system, for example—this effect could be removed from the list of perceptual phenomena. We will describe a good example of this in a later section on instructional set. At first glance, it would seem that instructions to pay attention to a particular dimension of stimulation might alter the way the stimulus looks to the viewer. On closer analysis (that is, after careful experimentation), it becomes clear that the differences in response accuracy are probably due to differences in coding strategies used by the subject to remember the various attributes of the stimuli.

What Are the Features of Words?

In previous chapters we presented some data to suggest that the primitive building blocks of form are visual features or edges. We also noted evidence that global configurations formed the content of initial processing, configurations from which individual features could subsequently be derived. The same contrast is present in the research on words as stimuli and, when we examine the different models of word recognition or identification, we will see that some of the differences in the models are on this issue.

But when considering words as stimuli, there are many higher-level variables that may be the basic features used in processing words. All these are related to the rules by which letters are combined and the variables that change with the different combinations. For example, at the simplest level, there are the frequency differences among letters, among combinations of letters, and among words themselves. At the highest level, there are all the possible complicated effects of the meaning of a word or series of words. Woodworth (1938) has an excellent historical review of this work.

The simplest stimulus consisting of letter arrays is one in which each letter is selected independently, and every letter has an equal chance of being selected each time a selection is made. This type of stimulus is frequently called a **"random"** array. In comparison with arrays that differ in the degree to which they approximate statistical properties of letters in English prose, random letter arrays are called **zero-order approximations to English**. In random or zero-order arrays, each letter has 1 chance out of 26 of being selected for each position, and the selection of a letter for any one position is independent of the selection of a letter for any other position. Of course, a sequence of zero-order letters does not resemble English at all. It is zero-order because it does not reflect the different frequencies with which letters actually occur in English nor the typical sequences of letters found in actual words. The first column of Figure 18.1 illustrates some zero-order letter strings constructed in this way.

The first step in approximating some of the statistical properties of English prose is called **first-order approximation to English**. First-order letter arrays are constructed in the same way as zero-order arrays, except that the distribution from which the letters are selected is one in which the letters are represented in the same proportions they would appear in actual English prose. The letters E and T would appear many more times than the letters X and Z and, therefore, the probability of selecing a T would be greater than the probability of selecting an X. First-order arrays approximate the distributional properties of English.

Notice that relatively few infrequently used letters appear in column 2 of Figure 18.1. But the letter sequences are still fairly unlike those found naturally in the language.

Second-order and higher approximations to English come closer and closer to approximating the sequential properties of English. They are all constructed in a similar fashion and we will illustrate it with second-order arrays. Recall that in the previous constructions, letters were selected to fill positions in arrays for each position separately. Now we want to introduce sequential relationships into our selection process; that is, we want the selection of a letter for a particular position to be influenced by the letters in its immediate neighborhood. In second-order arrays, we want the frequency of pairs of letters (digrams) in English prose to be represented in the selection process and therefore in the array. In order to accomplish this, we sample digram frequency in actual written prose passages. For example, in order to select a letter for the first position in the array, we might open an English novel to some page selected at random, randomly select one position on that page as a starting point, and then search along the line for the first space. The letter immediately following the space would be our first letter. Presumably we are selecting randomly from a distribution in which pairs of letters are represented according to

Zero-Order	*First-Order*	*Second-Order*	*Fourth-Order*
YRULPZOC	STANOGOP	WALLYLOF	RICANING
OZHGPMTJ	VTYEHULO	THERARES	VERNALIT
DLEGQMNW	EINOAASE	CHEVADNE	MOSSIANT
GFUJXZAQ	IYDEWAKN	NERMBLIM	POKERSON
WXPAUJVB	RPITCQET	ONESTEVA	ONETICUL
VQWBVIFX	OMNTOHCH	ACOSUNST	ATEDITOL
CVGJCDHM	DNEHHSNO	SERRRTHE	APHYSTER
MFRSIWZE	RSEMPOIN	ROCEDERT	TERVALLE
EJDYOEVZ	ISAAESPW	HEFLINYC	CULATTER
GFXRWMXR	ITYNENEE	EDINGEDL	PREVERAL
BHDTUNQK	OAENSTVT	LIKINERA	FAVORIAL
ANROAHOV	NHIDCFRA	RIPRYPLI	LYMISTIC
HHJHUFSW	YWDNMIIE	UMATSORE	OTATIONS
IJHBWSTT	IODTIRPS	SINEDSIN	INFOREMS
EAPMZCEN	NHGTTEDE	EDESENER	EXPRESPE

Figure 18.1 Pseudowords constructed at different orders of approximation to the statistical properties of letters in English prose. (Miller, Bruner, & Postman, 1954).

their frequency in English. To obtain the second letter, we follow the same procedure. We select a page and starting place at random, search along the line for an instance of the letter we had already picked for the first position, and then select the letter following it in the text as the next letter in the array. The next letter would be filled in by first finding an instance of the second letter and taking the one next to it. Third- and fourth-order arrays are constructed according to the same procedures, except that we sample trigrams or quadrigrams. To sample trigrams, for example, we search for the two letters previously selected and find the third letter from the text.

Another way to think about the **orthographic regularities** of English is in terms of **spelling patterns.** That is, there are certain rules that describe what is permissible and what is not in English spelling. Presumably these rules are known to readers and may affect the way words are perceived and recognized. For example, initial consonants in English words are greatly restricted: initial repeated letters are not allowed; no more than three consonants may precede the vowel (and if there are three, the first must be (*s* or *t* and the second *c, h, t,* or *p*); and of the 441 logically possible combinations of two initial consonants, only 30 are allowed. The same restriction occurs in all positions of words (see Chapter 19 for a more detailed discussion).

The visual shape of a word also provides information about the meaning of the word. Some words are made up of letters of the same size and shape and therefore present a uniform global pattern, some start with tall letters and end with letters below the line, etc. All these differences in the morphological quality of words may play a role in their perception and recognition. Another possible factor is the relationship between the written words and the way they are pronounced. It is clear, for example, that random letter arrays are hard to pronounce, whereas consonant–vowel–consonant trigrams are easy to pronounce. This difference in the degree of pronounceability may affect perception. Clearly, degree-of-pronounceability will be related to the number of syllables in a word or wordlike array. Finally, there is the meaning of words—sometimes called **lexicality** in order to indicate that the meaning of a word in isolation is related to the kind of meanings one finds in a lexicon or dictionary. Words in dictionaries are fundamentally different from ones made up according to any of the above procedures.

Without going into details in this section, we can summarize some of the major conclusions with respect to these variables. It now appears that the only variables that affect perceptual processes are lexical in nature. Almost all other effects have either been shown to be the result of processes occurring subsequent to perception or are still hotly debated. The one generally accepted effect—now frequently called the **word superiority effect**—indicates that there is something about real words that makes them easier to perceive than all other kinds of letter arrays. Most of the recognition models to be presented will attempt to account for this phenomenon.

MODELS OF WORD RECOGNITION AND IDENTIFICATION

As was the case with the perception of space, models of visual word recognition and identification can be categorized according to the size of the unit of perceptual analysis. Some models start with very small units—visual features—and attempt to explain word identification by "constructive" or "integrative" processes. Others start with global representation of the stimulus and explain recognition as a process of differentiation and abstraction. In this section, we present representative models of each of these approaches.

Hierarchical Filter Model

The **hierarchical filter model** for letter and word recognition involves a number of levels or stages of processing that "filter" information by selectively responding to specific aspects of stimulation (LeBerge & Samuels, 1974; Estes, 1975a, 1975b, 1977). It is hierarchical in the sense that some "filter-detectors" feed into other filter-detectors. Figure 18.2 is a flow diagram adapted from a schematic representation of such a system proposed by Estes (1977). Isolated stages of perception and memory are not shown because it is assumed that these processes are not distinguishable, that is, they are either represented by the same process, or they interact in complex ways throughout the succession of stages of visual processing that lead from the original sensory experience to identification and recognition responses.

Estes sees two major tasks for a visual information-processing system that can identify and recognize letters and words. First, since the input during normal reading may be fragmentary, it must be able to process fragments and irregular stimulus patterns—to clean them up, to fill in the gaps in a reasonable way, and to generate a representation of the letter sequence that gave rise to the input at a level more abstract than that of the physical stimulus pattern. Second, the system must include a mechanism whereby information from other sources—context or long-term memory—can interact with the specific stimulus representation to permit recognition and comprehension of words.

The hierarchical filter model processes the input at all possible levels to make use of the past experience of the perceiver. For example, it makes use of the properties of the alphabet by having the visual feature detectors be part of the memory system. Then the frequency properties of the alphabet can be utilized to account for letter and word recognition. In addition, the model assumes that detectors with similar properties are also available to detect letters, letter groups (such as syllables), and words. Figure 18.2 shows how three such sets of trace-detectors and vectors may be hierarchically organized. In other words, the model is

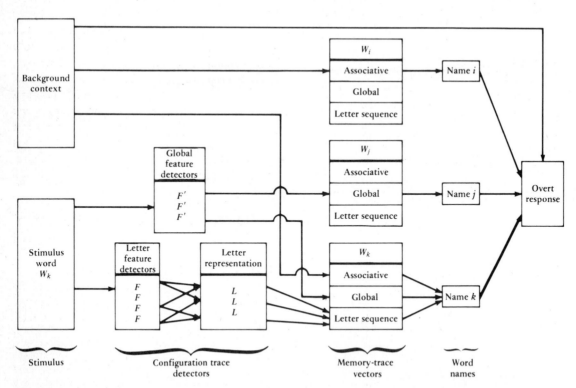

Figure 18.2   Flow diagram showing the schematic representation of the hierarchical filter model for letter and word recognition. Visual input from a stimulus word is filtered through letter feature detectors (F) and global feature detectors (F'). Output of F-combinations activate representations of letters (L), which, in turn, transmit to letter-sequence components of the memory-trace vectors of words (W). All sources of information including background context are filtered through the memory-trace vectors and contribute to the activation of a letter–name response. (Estes, 1977.)

based on the supposition that there are clearly defined levels at which information is integrated and utilized in decision and response processes.

Estes (1975a) has described four such levels of information integration and identification based on features, letters, letters in specific positions, and letter groups. The level of feature-difference detection may be utilized in tasks requiring the detection of differences between pairs of letters. Clearly, in this task, correct responses can be made simply by detecting the feature, or features, that differentiate the two characters. This level of integration appears to be independent of linguistic context effects (Estes, 1975b). The letter-identification level requires a response independent of letter position. Estes assumes, further, that these tasks are also accomplished independently of letter context (Estes, Allmeyer, & Reder, 1974) and, therefore, the "configuration trace detectors" receive no input from "context" in the flow diagram of Figure 18.2. In contrast, the identification of letters-in-position and of letter groups almost always involves the integration of linguistic context information.

A successful model of letter and word recognition, then, must be able to produce accurate responses at each of these levels of processing. To accomplish this, the detectors—the functional units at each level—are regarded as memory traces or **engrams** built up as a consequence of the past experience of each individual perceiver. The frequency of occurrence of each of the patterns and subpatterns will be represented in the detector-memory trace structure. A particular trace would be activated by an incoming pattern of information only if the input pattern matched the one that gave rise to the trace structure. When a match does occur, the detector is activated and transmits a pattern of excitation to the next higher level in the system. When a particular input pattern does not match a particular detector, transmission is blocked through that channel. This process of comparison and selective transmission is assumed to continue through the higher levels of the system—thus the name "hierarchical filter" model. The efficiency of the system arises from the fact that the sensory input pattern need be directed only to a small number of feature detectors in the first stage of processing.

Integration occurs at the higher stages. If the combination of features corresponding to a particular letter is activated by the input on a given trial, then the excitation transmitted from these, in turn, activates the representation of the corresponding letter. Input from the global feature detectors will partially activate the trace vectors of the stimulus word and of other words with similar patterns. Input via the associative pathways represents either immediate context of the stimulus—the other words or letters in the display that are not the focus of attention in the task—or those from past experience that are relevant. These inputs lead to partial activation of the stimulus word and also of other words that overlap with its meaning. The model assumes that the inputs to the word trace vectors—those containing sensory information and those containing associative information—operate independently and with different degrees of specificity.

For a particular stimulus word, only the representation of the letter-sequence component activated by the visual features system will generate input solely to the appropriate memory trace vector. Therefore, there is a convergence of inputs from several sources on the trace vector of the stimulus word. The naming response of this word will be more strongly and quickly activated than those of the other words that share its associative or global attributes. Finally, the multiple effects of context are also represented as playing a role in the ultimate production of the overt response.

Differentiation Model

The **differentiation model** of recognition and identification proposed by Eleanor J. Gibson (1969, 1975, 1977) is a developmental theory because the fundamental mechanisms operate throughout the life of the perceiver. At any point in development, recognition is mediated by the system in a manner consistent with its state at the time of the test. A simplified summary of Gibson's model is illustrated in Figure 18.3. This summary was abstracted from the larger developmental model to eliminate some of the purely developmental aspects not directly relevant to recognition and identification processes.

The starting point of the differentiation model is the same as that of the theory of visual space percep-

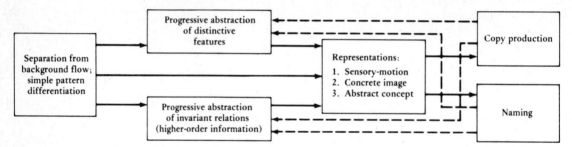

Figure 18.3 Simplified summary of recognition processes and iterations proposed by E. J. Gibson (1969). The mechanisms are continuously operative throughout the life of the perceiver. Recognition at any point in development is me-diated by the state of this system (especially of the representation stage) at the time of test. The feedback loops represent potential sources of information (dashed lines).

tion of James J. Gibson (see Chapter 8): that there is structure in the optical array impinging on the organism. But this structure only represents potential information for the perceiver; it is not necessarily utilized. Not only is the array structured, but there are levels of structure present that vary from differences that are easy to discriminate to highly complex relations that are difficult to discriminate. The potential variables that are not differentiated within the mass of impinging stimulation may be differentiated given the proper exposure and practice. As these variables are differentiated, the resulting perceptions become more specific in the sense that they correspond more closely to the stimulation. The perceiver can then respond in a discriminating manner to the stimulus differences not previously responded to.

The task of the perceiver is not one of construction—the putting together of bits and pieces of stimulation—but that of **differentiation**— the search for aspects of stimulation that reduce uncertainty by finding order. This is accomplished by searching for (*a*) distinctive features to differentiate among objects and events, (*b*) higher-order invariants of stimulus structure, and (*c*) abstract relations to reduce uncertainty. These processes are more like discovery and abstraction than association and integration. They present a picture of the perceiver as an active seeker of information rather than a passive recepticle.

Since the model is really one of continuous perceptual learning, the starting point for our discussion of recognition and identification is shown in Figure

18.3 as an initial or infantile state of representation indicated as "separation from background flow." This label is simply to acknowledge the fact that development must start somewhere and that the newborn infant shows at least a general differentiated responsiveness to stimulation as well as some gross selective responses to stimulus differences (see Chapter 13). It also includes the beginning of simple differentiation of patterns and objects from backgrounds (figure–ground). Obviously, a system whose task it is to recognize differences among objects and events must be able to differentiate those events from background "noise."

Perception is then differentiated in two ways (or by two mechanisms): by the progressive abstraction of distinctive features, and by the progressive abstraction of invariant relations. Both mechanisms continue to operate throughout the life of the perceiver. The abstraction of distinctive features becomes progressively more economical and the abstraction of invariants deals with progressively higher order invariants of stimulation. The consequences of the operation of these mechanisms are manifest in representations in terms of "sensory-motor schemata," or "concrete images" or "abstract concepts," depending on the level of development and the type of stimulation involved. The formation of these representations precedes the ability to produce overt responses such as the production of copies and verbal labels or names. The abstraction and differentiation processes can be accelerated by responses that provide information for monitoring and checking (indicated by the dashed lines in Figure 18.3) and by calling attention to distinctive features and higher-order relations.

As perceptual development proceeds, there is an increasing specificity in the correspondence between information in stimulation and what is perceived. The unique features of stimuli are discovered as a result of changes in stimulation and practice. For example, we can learn to recognize letters by using their unique **distinctive features,** that is, their differentiating, abstract, relational properties that may be represented by a "bundle of features." These features are not constructed (or used in a process of construction), they are discovered. A bundle of distinctive features therefore constitutes a potential set of higher-order relations in stimulation. Figure 18.4 shows a possible list of distinctive features for graphemes. In order for a set of features to be "distinctive," they must meet three criteria: they must be critical, relational, and unique. To be critical means that they must be present in some members of the set to be differentiated and not in others. To be relational means that they must be invariant across brightness, size, and perspective transformations. To be unique means that they should yield a unique pattern for each grapheme. In addition to these requirements, it is also desirable that they be

reasonably economical. Identification of letters, then, would require that these distinctive features be perceived and remembered.

The increase in the economy of information pickup and use is accomplished in two major ways: by detection of the smallest possible distinguishing feature, and by detection and use of superordinate structure to group information into larger units. The smallest possible units can be obtained from a differentiating process where the information is relational—an abstraction of a common contrasting property that divides two sets. In contrast, superordinate structures are the largest units that can be used for accomplishing a task. These units are generated by various rule systems that underlie the particular aspect of perception involved. They are not mere conglomerations of associated parts; they have wholistic properties and resist segmentation. For example, instead of frequency, a wholistic property of words would involve rulelike structures related to allowable positions of consonant clusters, vocalic separation of consonants and clusters of them, and word meaning. It is these superordinate structures that account for the word-superiority effect in perception by providing a unity and coherence to words. They make words easy to recognize and hard to segment.

	A	E	F	H	I	L	T	K	M	N	V	W	X	Y	Z	B	C	D	G	J	O	P	R	Q	S	U
Intersection	+	+	+	+		+	+		.				+			+						+	+	+		
Straight horizontal	+	+	+	+		+	+								+	+			+							
vertical		+	+	+	+	+	+	+	+	+					+	+	+					+	+			
diagonal ⁄	+							+	+		+	+	+	+	+								+	+		
diagonal ⟍	+							+	+	+	+	+	+										+	+		
Curve closed																+		+			+	+	+	+		
open V																			+							+
open H																	+		+						+	
Redundancy cyclic shape		+							+		+					+									+	
symmetry	+	+		+	+	+	+	+	+		+	+	+	+		+	+	+			+					+
Discontinuity vertical	+		+	+	+	+	+	+	+					+									+	+		
horizontal		+	+			+	+								+											

Figure 18.4 A chart of distinctive features for a set of graphemes. (E. J. Gibson, 1969).

The differentiation model, then, can be applied to all aspects of perception. It provides a view of the perceiver as an active seeker of information, and of the perceptual system as an integral part of cognitive functioning. However, perceptual recognition is not due to constructive processes; it is the result of constant seeking and finding higher levels of information in stimulation.

VARIABLES AFFECTING RECOGNITION

As noted at the beginning of this chapter, there are many variables that potentially contribute to recognition and identification responses. These range from simple statistical properties that reflect the frequency and distributional characteristics of letters and letter combinations in English prose to the complexities of meanings associated with words. In this section, we will present some of the experimental research on these variables, starting with the simpler ones and moving to the more complex. This will not be an exhaustive review of the literature. Rather it will attempt to focus on those experiments that supply important information about the role each variable plays in recognition and identification.

Statistical Properties: Redundancy

The statistical properties of letter arrays refer to the frequencies of occurrence of letters and combinations of letters. Clearly a theory of perceptual learning based simply on frequency of occurrence would place great weight on this variable. As noted earlier, stimuli that vary along this dimension are said to be of different approximations to English. The fact that stimulus arrays that approximate the statistical structure of English are reported more accurately in tachistoscopic studies was demonstrated by Miller, Bruner, and Postman (1954), who suggested that the differences were caused by differential perceptual processing. This finding was replicated by Mewhort (1967), using a partial report procedure.

Hershenson (1969a) replicated these results (see the graph for naïve subjects in Figure 18.5), but also found that the accuracy of reporting the letters declined from left to right over the seven letter positions. This pattern suggested that the effect was due to differential forgetting rather than differential perception. Hershenson argued that, if the differences were due to post perceptual events related to the ease with which the different stimulus classes were remembered, the differences in identification of the letters should disappear if all of the stimuli were made easy to remember. This was demonstrated using a group of perceivers who were required to memorize the stimuli to be used. Members of this group studied the lists until they could report correctly over 90 percent of the letters in the arrays when presented with only one or two of the letters. Figure 18.5 shows the effect of this training—a sharp decrease in the effect of approximation to English. Moreover, the trained group did not show the decrease over left–right letter position (Figure 18.6)—their accuracy was an inverted U-shaped function of letter position with the greatest accuracy for those positions near fixation.

To show that the letter-position function for the trained group was due entirely to the relative perceptibility of the letters over retinal position, Hershenson (1969b) repeated the experiment but varied the fixation point. In this way the effects of position with

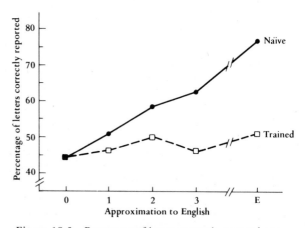

Figure 18.5 Percentage of letters correctly reported as a function of approximation to English for naïve and trained perceivers. (Hershenson, 1969a.)

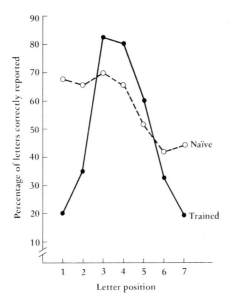

Figure 18.6   Percentage of letters reported as a function of letter position for naïve and trained perceivers. (Hershenson, 1969a.)

respect to fixation point could be separated from left–right position in the sequence. With fixations presented over either the second, fourth, or sixth letter positions, the inverted ∪-shaped functions followed the shifts in the positions of the eyes. For trained perceivers, then, the only differential accuracy that could be demonstrated depended on perceptibility and not on the predictability of the letter sequences. The differences in responses as a function of approximation to English appear to be a manifestation of differential processing during information-extraction from the icon or in subsequent processes. We will return to evaluate another possible role for this type of structure when we describe the redundancy hypothesis as an explanation for the word superiority effect.

Spelling Patterns and Pronounceability

Another major variable that may affect perceptual recognition is the spelling pattern and concomitant level of pronounceability of letter arrays. To study the role of such units in visual recognition, Gibson,

Pick, Osser, and Hammond (1962) varied the degree of pronounceability of stimuli that were exposed in a tachistoscope. Pronounceable arrays consisted of an initial-consonant spelling having a single regular pronunciation, a final-consonant spelling having a single regular pronunciation, and a vowel spelling having a single regular pronunciation when between the consonant sounds. Arrays with low spelling-to-sound correlation were then constructed from these arrays by interchanging the initial and final consonant-spellings. For example, *DINK* became *NKDI,* and *GLURCK* became *CKURGL.* Figure 18.7 shows the percentage of words correctly identified as a function of exposure duration for both pronounceable and unpronounceable arrays. Pronounceable arrays were more easily identified regardless of the duration for which they were presented. Gibson et al. explained this effect in terms of differential sensitivity, suggesting that, in acquiring reading skills, people become sensitive to superforms that are organized according to the auditory-vocal temporal patterns inherent in the relationships between written and spoken English. This sensitivity implies that fewer units need to be processed when such spelling patterns are present, leading to improved accuracy of processing.

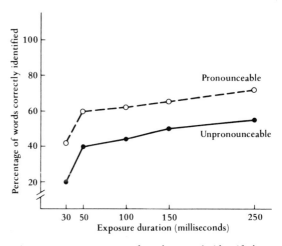

Figure 18.7   Percentage of words correctly identified as a function of exposure duration for pronounceable and unpronounceable arrays of letters (Gibson, Pick, Osser, & Hammond, 1962).

This experiment has recently been replicated with some clarification of the processes involved. Aderman and Smith (1971) showed that the spelling patterns were advantageous only if the perceiver was expecting words that contained such patterns. If they had been looking at words with low correspondence between letter sequences and pronounceability, they performed no better on an unexpected word that had such correspondence. Hershenson (1972) found that a group of perceivers identified more letters from pronounceable arrays than from unpronounceable arrays when the arrays were unfamiliar. However, a second group of subjects who were very familiar with all the stimuli (they had memorized the list), did equally well regardless of the degree of pronounceability. Hershenson concluded that pronounceability plays a role in the retention and report of stimulus information and not in its representation in the icon.

We shall not pursue the spelling-pattern–pronounceability relationship further here, except to note that it has two separable components—the sequential redundancies among the letters in the language and the correspondence of these redundancies to invariant pronunciations. The evidence for the former's importance seems overwhelming, but, as Hershenson (1972) has noted, the role of pronounceability per se in perceptual recognition is still an open question. This is especially true since Gibson, Shurcliff, and Yonas (1970) reported that the same spelling-pattern results are found with deaf perceivers who have never heard an invariant pronunciation of these spelling patterns.

Effect of Letter Context on Acuity and Guessing

Figure 16.14 showed the falloff in visual acuity as a function of distance of the letter from the center of the fovea. We have described how much larger letters have to be when seen farther outside of the fovea in order to be equally discriminable. However, the computations that went into those figures assumed that there was no predictability among the features of each acuity target, and there was no context from other letters. When using real letters, however, the first assumption is clearly incorrect in that not all fea-

tures are equally likely in actual letters. This is one of the reasons why the Snellen eye chart characters are being replaced with Landoldt ⊂ characters (see Figure 4.15, p. 80), because, in the latter, there is no way to predict where the gap is located from detection of any other features of the ⊂.

If a context of other letters is present, acuity limits are altered even more. If the context contains letters that follow the spelling rules of the language, or even comprise an actual word, then the text greatly restricts the alternatives being detected. With an appropriate context, the ability to recognize a letter can be substantially altered. Therefore recognition visual acuity is more properly represented as a family of functions, as illustrated in Figure 18.8.

Figure 18.9. shows how the curves above the "Alpern data" are obtained. On each trial, a letter of some size is presented at a different distance from fixation. The percent correct recognition scores for each size for each distance are used to determine the Alpern curve. The bottom row of the figure shows the task when a context is added. The subject still has to recognize the letter indicated by the arrow, but now the letter is surrounded by other letters. The upper two curves in Figure 18.8 are obtained in this manner. They suggest that recognition accuracy is higher at

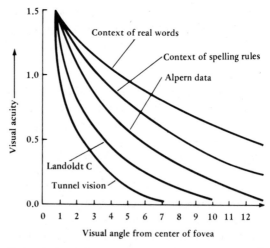

Figure 18.8 Effects of redundancy on visual acuity in peripheral vision.

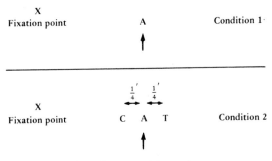

Figure 18.9 Measuring recognition acuity.

each retinal location if there is greater predictability provided by the context. The two lowest curves suggest first, that if predictability among the features is removed altogether, as in using a Landolt C, acuity will diminish slightly. Finally, adding irrelevant context letters narrows acuity, producing what Mackworth (1965) called "tunnel vision" (Chapter 16, p. 329).

Sophisticated Guessing Theory

The effects of context on identifiability of letters has been presented without describing the source of the advantage. One type of explanation that has been advanced for some time is referred to as **sophisticated guessing theory** (see a review by Katlin, 1971; Johnston, 1978). Johnston defines sophisticated guessing theory as follows: "In making perceptual decisions about the identity of a letter in a letter string, people supplement information obtained from that letter itself with contextual information obtained from other letters in the string" (Johnston, 1978, p. 124). The contextual information referred to by Johnston could be constraint based upon spelling rules, lexical constraint because the permissible letters spell a real word, or, with whole sentences as the context, syntactic and semantic constraint because the word has to be one that fits within the context of the sentence.

The implication of guessing is that the effect is not properly a perceptual phenomenon. Subjects might perceive as much of the visual information as they can and then, using the context, simply guess what the letter might be. Such a theory makes no sug-

gestion that they perceive more of the visual features when there is a context that provided the predictability, but, merely that, given whatever visual features they did perceive, they should be more accurate in deciding what letter was actually present. This simple version of the sophisticated guessing theory can be rejected on the basis of experiments by Reicher (1969), described in detail below. Reicher showed that subjects were more accurate in correctly identifying which of two letters had been in a critical position in a four-letter ensemble when the ensemble spelled a word than when it was a random collection. The critical factor in Reicher's experiment was that the two alternatives offered to the subject were both acceptable in that context, that is, the context provided no information about which alternative to choose. For example, "Did you see a D or a K in the fourth position of W O R __ ?"

Thus, it would appear that, in some way or another, having the context increases the availability of the visual features either at the level of the initial encoding of those features, or by preserving the features longer in memory so that they can be processed, or by enabling those features to be combined more effectively with the information given by the context. Johnston (1978) reported two experiments that provide evidence in support of a more perceptual interpretation. However, his experiments do not indicate which of the above possibilities is the correct one. Whatever the explanation, however, having contextual information improves the identifiability of letters on the basis of some stimulus information.

The Word-Superiority Effect

In matching tasks, words are processed faster than strings of unrelated letters (Eichelman, 1970) and, in recognition tasks, perceivers are more accurate in identifying a letter from a word than from an array containing the same letters in scrambled order (Reicher, 1969). These are examples of the superiority often found when studying the processing of words and parts of words. Effects such as these are all parts of the **word-superiority effect**.

Reicher's (1969) experiment provides a clear

demonstration of the effect. He presented a single word followed by a visual noise mask to limit the processing time. When the mask appeared, a pair of letters was presented above one of the letters in the word. The temporal sequence of this display is illustrated in the top row of Figure 18.10. The perceiver's task was to indicate which of the two letters was the same as the letter in the word. Reicher found that perceivers were more accurate in identifying a letter that had appeared in a word than one that had been presented among the same letters scrambled to form a meaningless sequence. Reicher's results cannot be attributed to the information contained in the other letters (for example, in the figure, both *D* and *K* are equally predictable from W̲ O̲ R̲). Since the perceivers did not know until *after* the presentation which position would be probed, theoretically all of the letters in the meaningful word would have produced a higher level of accuracy than those in its anagram. In another condition, depicted in the bottom row of Figure 18.10, only a single letter was presented, again followed by the mask with the two alternatives. Since only a single letter had to be processed, rather than four, it would seem reasonable that this should be an easier task. However, Reicher found it to be more difficult. Perceivers were more accurate in deciding which of two letters was in the display when the letter was part of a meaningful word than when it was presented alone—

the "word-letter-effect." The letter alone and the nonsense anagrams were reported at about the same level of accuracy.

Wheeler (1970) replicated these findings and showed that they could not be accounted for by response bias, difference in word frequencies of the different alternatives, letter frequencies, spatial position uncertainty, or interference between the letters and the alternatives. It appears that when a meaningful word is presented, *all* its letters are processed faster (or at least better) than any single letter when presented alone.

Because the word-letter-effect is counter-intuitive, a number of investigators have attempted to explain it in terms of redundancy. It is possible that the control used by Reicher and Wheeler (and others) depended on the assumption that the viewers could maintain a representation of ambiguous input until the target alternatives were presented. Then a match could be made between the alternatives and the ambiguous representation. But, if the viewer were to synthesize a possible array from the ambiguous input, and keep this in memory until the alternatives were presented, there would be an advantage for the wordlike stimuli. The viewer could synthesize a better representation based on redundancy alone. This possibility has been tested in a number of experiments. When target alternatives were presented before the experiment, thereby equating for redundancy, the advantage of words was eliminated—letters presented alone were detected better than letters embedded in either word or nonword strings (Bjork & Estes, 1973; Estes, Bjork, & Skaar, 1974; Massaro, 1973; Thompson & Massaro, 1973).

Estes (1975) also tested the redundancy hypothesis in a task similar to Reicher's. The stimuli and sequences are illustrated in Figure 18.11. The pretrial adapting field contained four dollar signs marking the positions in which letters could appear. One of three possible stimuli then appeared for 50 milliseconds: a single letter surrounded by "number" symbols in the other locations, a four-letter word, or a four-letter nonword made from the letters of a word. The instruction was to report the stimulus letter that appeared in the position indicated by the poststimulus arrow. On

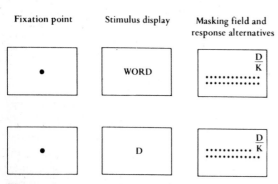

| Fixation point | Stimulus display | Masking field and response alternatives |

Figure 18.10 The display sequence for Reicher's (1969) experiment. The top row shows the sequence when a word was presented, followed by a mask and two alternatives above one of the letter positions. The bottom row is a comparable trial when only a single letter is presented.

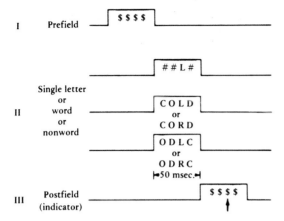

Figure 18.11 Diagram of stimuli and experimental procedure used by Estes (1975) to test the redundancy explanation of the word-superiority effect.

one-fourth of the trials, the probed letter was either an *L* or an *R*; on "word" trials, the displays were so chosen that either an *L* or *R* would produce a word, on "nonword" trials, neither an *L* nor an *R* would produce a word.

The results showed that letters and nonwords did not differ and words were better than both in the percentage of letters reported correctly. The redundancy hypothesis was evaluated directly from an analysis of errors. If the viewers were using redundancy from the context in generating guesses, then they should produce a higher proportion of wrong *L*s and *R*s on "word" trials than on "nonword" trials. That is, the redundancy in the word stimuli would favor these letters. But this hypothesis was not supported by the error analysis—the values obtained (.02 for words and .04 for nonwords) were not very different from what would be expected if the viewers were drawing letters at random from the full alphabet. Estes concluded that there was no evidence that the word advantage was due to redundancy. Instead, he proposed that it was the result of an interaction between linguistic and perceptual processes that could not be accounted for on the basis of inference or response bias based on redundant information from context.

The data from matching experiments are not so clear. Eichelman (1970) compared response latencies for matching words with those for matching letter strings of two, four, and six letters. He found that matching words was a faster process than matching letter strings and that the difference between the words and nonsense strings increased as the number of letters in the stimulus increased (Fig. 18.12). Eichelman also found that the reaction time was a decreasing linear function of the number of letters that were different in the stimuli to be matched. Since this function was not different for the nonsense and meaningful stimulus pairs, Eichelman doubted that the matches were being made on the basis of word names. He suggested that the availability of a name for the words could not account for the faster overall response to the words. This conclusion was supported by the fact that physical identity matches for both types of stimuli were made faster than name matches for these stimuli. He concluded, therefore, that some physical characteristics of words were more salient. Perhaps words were seen as "wholes" while letter arrays remain only strings of letters.

Kroll (1977) explored the nature of the word superiority effect in the matching task using six-letter arrays—the stimuli for which Eichelman found the largest effect. The stimuli were English words, pronounceable nonwords (pseudowords), and consonant

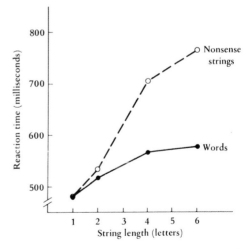

Figure 18.12 Reaction time to indicate whether two strings of letters are physically identical or not, when they are either words or nonsense. (Eichelman, 1970.)

strings. These arrays were easy to discriminate when they were *different* because all of the letters differed. The arrays were flashed in pairs, one above the other, for 100 milliseconds, and the subject had to determine whether they were the same or different. The results showed no differences in response latencies for making "different" responses but words were matched most rapidly and consonant strings least rapidly when the stimulus pairs were the same. Latency responses were equal for "same" and "different" responses when the stimuli were words. A similar pattern was found for errors. In a replication of this design, Kroll had a 1-second visual noise mask follow the stimulus. This time there were no major differences among the response latencies, but the error patterns remained the same. Figure 18.13 shows a composite of the results of the two experiments. Words were still matched slightly faster than other stimuli when they were the same.

Kroll concluded that, since the large differences between consonants and nonwords (the pure measure of structural effects or orthographic regularity) were eliminated by the mask, it probably represented the application of flexible processing strategies by the subjects. The small lexical effect (the difference between words and pseudowords) that remained even with masking was probably related to earlier perceptual processes. But Kroll concluded that the overall pattern of results in the experiments suggested that words were not processed better, or more efficiently. She proposed that the effect was, instead, a result of poorer processing for pseudowords and consonants. That is, the words may be processed normally by a system "tuned" for letter arrays that are words. There is "interference" with this mode of processing when nonwords are presented for processing. Thus, the end result is a delay in processing from the normal rate rather than a speeding up.

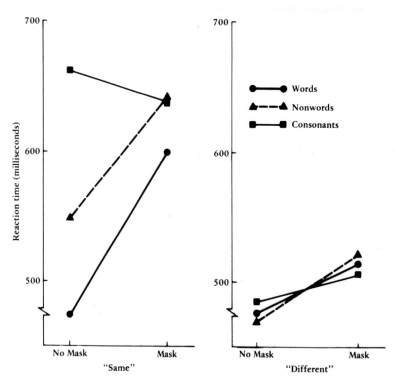

Figure 18.13 Results of matching six-letter arrays of words, nonwords, and consonant strings, with and without a mask. (Kroll, 1977.)

Interference During Encoding

Interference is not a new concept in the information-processing literature. It seems to play a role in visual search tasks when a sought-for stimulus is embedded in irrelevant or unwanted components of stimulation. For example, you can find a target faster if you can learn to ignore (not process) irrelevant background items. See the discussion on Tunnel Vision (p. 329) and Output Selection (pp. 253–254).

Stroop (1935) developed a test, called the **Stroop Effect,** with which to study interference among relevant and irrelevant parts of a visual display. In one form of the test, subjects have to sort cards into different piles depending on the number of words printed on each card (see Figure 18.14 for an example). Interference occurs when the words themselves refer to numbers, which potentially tell the subject to sort the card differently.

Several different types of explanation have been offered to account for this interference effect, explanations that differ with respect to the locus of the effect in the information-processing sequence. One proposed that it was due to interference that occurred at the time of the utterance of the response, but this seems unlikely since the effect is found even when no verbal response is required. To say simply that the perceiver could not suppress the number word because of some prepotency of words is not sufficient,

although it appears as if something of this kind must be involved.

Morton (1969) explained the Stroop effect in terms of interference that occurs when naming one color while ignoring the name of another color, when both names are available after encoding. To test this notion, he used a card-sorting version of this task, in which the perceiver had to sort cards into two piles depending on whether ink used to print a color name at the top of the card was the same color as a patch at the bottom of the card. For example, the word "red" might be printed in green ink at the top of the card and a green patch might be at the bottom. The perceiver had to place this card in a pile in which ink and patch colors were the same, even when the color word at the top did not agree. Cards of this sort took longer to sort than ones that did not have a conflicting color name printed at the top. However, if the perceiver was instructed to look first at the bottom af the card and then at the top (instead of the typical top-to-bottom sequence), the interference disappeared. According to Morton, in this situation the perceiver processed only the color at the bottom, since that was the only information present, and then could easily have developed a strategy to match only the appropriate color at the top. Presumably, color information could be analyzed from the top without any interference. When the processing started at the top, both the ink color and the spelled color get named and are available for comparison. This causes confusion or interference in the comparison step of the processing and, therefore, loss of speed.

According to Morton, the interference can be avoided by chosing an order of processing that delays the availability of the printed color name until the perceiver is ready to match colored inks. At that time, the color word probably gets processed, but it is too late by then—the match has already been made.

Instructional set

Instructional set has similar effects in all kinds of perceptual tasks. Presumably, **set** works to control selectivity in the early processing stages by telling the perceiver that some part, feature, or character of the stimulus is more important than other parts. Since

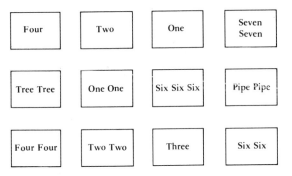

Figure 18.14 Examples of cards that have to be sorted into piles, depending on the number of words written on the card. Thus, a card with one word on it goes into the "1" pile; with two words into the "2" pile, and so on.

this manipulation generally results in a higher accuracy of report for the part emphasized in the instructional set, it suggests that a selective process was initiated. The research on this question has been voluminous, and we shall not attempt to cover much of it here. Haber (1966) offered a general review, and not much new data has been presented since to change the conclusions fundamentally.

A favorite research procedure spanning over 60 years of work has been to present briefly a number of geometric forms, differing in a number of dimensions such as shape, color, size, the number of each type, and so forth. The perceiver would generally be told to report everything that he had been shown, but that one of the dimensions (for example, the colors of each of the objects) was more important so that he should make a determined effort to get the various instances of that dimension correct. The instructional set effect occurs whenever the perceiver is more accurate on the dimension emphasized.

One interpretation of this effect is that the features specifying the emphasized dimension would be represented in iconic storage more vividly. Thus, if colors were more important, then the features specifying the various colors would be stronger or more salient than the features for shape, size, numerosity, and so forth. Stated somewhat more loosely, the colors would stand out. This position has been tested by varying when the instructional set was given to the perceiver. If he does not know what the emphasized dimension is until after the presentation, there would be no way for those features to stand out in the icon—the icon would have decayed by the time the set was given. If the set effect occurs only when the set is given prior to the presentation but not afterwards, then an enhancement in the icon would be supported.

The principle alternative explanation is that there is no enhancement of features in the icon, following the proposition that the content of the icon cannot be manipulated by cognitive factors such as familiarity, expectation, meaningfulness, or, in this case, instructional set. Rather, the facilitation of report of the emphasized dimension occurs because of the way in which the perceiver extracts the information from the icon, and then subsequently organizes and stores that information.

In a series of experiments by Harris and Haber (1963) and Haber (1964a, 1964b) these two types of explanations, plus some variants of each, were compared. Each study used the same stimuli—pairs of concept cards containing two sets of geometric objects. One stimulus card might have three green triangles on the left side and two blue squares on the right side. There were three dimensions (color, number, shape) and each could be one of four different variants. That is, the colors on each side were either red, blue, green, or yellow, the shapes on each side were either triangle, square, star, or circle, and there were either one, two, three, or four instances on each side. A stimulus card was presented for one-tenth of a second, and the perceiver had to describe the card completely in his report. The instructional set manipulation was given only before the presentation (no postpresentation comparison was made in these experiments). On some trials, the perceiver was told that all three dimensions (color, number, and shape) were of equal value in their reports. On other trials, they were told they would earn many more points if they correctly reported one of the dimensions. For example, if the color dimension was emphasized, the perceiver was told he would receive 30 points if he correctly reported the two colors but only 3 points if he correctly named the two shapes or the two numbers. On half of the trials, the perceiver was free to report the dimensions in any order he chose, but on the other half he had to follow a prescribed order, one that he did not know until after the presentation, when he began his report.

The most important manipulation in each of these experiments was the strategy by which the perceivers were trained to encode and remember the stimulus dimensions. Half of the perceivers were trained to use a code that treated the stimulus as two objects, one on the left and one on the right. An "object" code for a particular stimulus might be "one red triangle" (on the left), "three green circles" (on the right). The other half of the subjects were trained to use a code that specified the stimuli in terms of their separate dimensions. The same stimulus in the above example might be encoded in a "dimension" code as "red-green; triangle-circle; one-three." Of course, the order in which the three dimensions were described could be varied without any change in the accuracy of the description. There is only one order possible for the object coders—that given by English syntax.

Those perceivers who were trained to use the "dimensions" coding strategy showed a strong instructional set effect—when one dimension was emphasized, they were more accurate in reporting that dimension. This was due entirely to a loss in accuracy for the unemphasized dimensions, since the emphasized one was not reported any better than the comparable dimension in conditions in which all dimensions were equal in value. Haber (1964b) showed that the coding strategies differed in the order in which the perceiver encoded the dimension—that is, translated the initial representation into the words that he had to use to describe what he saw. Thus, it appears as if the encoding took place from a rapidly fading iconic representation; the parts encoded first were translated relatively accurately, while those aspects left for last were substantially degraded. Since the dimension coders varied the order of encoding as a function of the set instructions given them, they always left the unimportant dimensions for last. The object coders never varied their order of encoding, so no change in performance could be detected, regardless of the instructional set given them.

It is conceivable that these results could be due to order of report and not to order of encoding. If so, it is not the order in which the dimensions were encoded that is important but rather a forgetting process after encoding was completed and the information was being maintained in short-term memory during the process of report. The dimension coders were less accurate on the dimension reported last, so there was probably some forgetting of those parts of the report given last. This was not true for the object coders, presumably because of the greater predictability of the English syntax order, which helps to preserve memory. But more important, the instructional set effect was found for the dimension coders even when the order of report was specified and not left up to the per-

ceiver. Hence, an emphasized dimension is reported best even when the perceiver is forced to report it last.

Another comparison in these data is revealing. In each experiment, the overall accuracy shown by the object coders was higher than that of the dimension coders. Not only were the object coders immune to the instructional sets, and to order of report, but they were generally more accurate in their reports for each comparison made. Haber (1964b) argued that this might be due to their use of the highly overlearned English syntax, which permitted them to begin their encoding faster, complete it more rapidly, rehearse it faster, and make fewer errors during its maintenance in memory. He reported some indirect evidence in support of each of these possibilities, all of which would lead to the findings described.

But it is possible that the difference in accuracy between the two coding strategies was due to a more fundamental property of their respective codes. The dimension coders appeared to concentrate on one dimension at a time, encode its two instances, and then go on to the next dimension, and so forth. The object coders, on the other hand, concentrated on three different dimensions at one time, all in the same spatial location, and then repeated the process on the other side of the stimulus. If one can think of analyzing features represented in the icon (in the same sense as suggested by the visual search work of Neisser) through the use of a set of feature detectors, each of which is tuned to the presence of a particular type of feature, then it is a reasonable prediction that two or more different feature detectors might be used simultaneously over the features in the icon, but that any particular detector, such as for color, might have to be used sequentially, looking first for this color, and then for that one, and so forth. Thus, any task that permits the perceiver to use different feature detectors on the icon would be faster than when he has to use the same detectors over and over. The former is permitted by the object coding strategy, while the dimension code forces processing on a pair of instances of the same feature.

Allport (1968, 1971) has suggested this type of hypothesis, and some earlier data by Lappin (1967) is consistent with it as well. Lappin examined the extent to which perceivers could divide their attention between and among different dimensions of simple geometric forms. In one condition, a simple circular form could vary in color and size, as well as in the direction of tilt of a line bisecting the circle. In a second condition, three circular forms were presented which could vary in each of the three dimensions. However, in this condition, the instructions were to report the value each had on only one of the three dimensions. In the third condition, three circular forms were presented, but the perceiver was required to describe the first circle using one dimension, the second using another dimension, and the third using the third dimension. Lappin found the first condition to be the easiest and the third to be the hardest. He suggested, therefore, that processing could take place faster for different dimensions of the same form, than when the same dimension had to be analyzed over different forms. This would argue that perceivers will be more efficient whenever they can follow an encoding strategy that permits them to use several different feature analyses on each aspect of the stimulus pattern, rather than the same analysis on different aspects.

Several conclusions can be drawn from this group of studies on instructional sets. First, there is no evidence that the instructional set affects anything in the content of the icon itself. The emphasized dimension does not appear to stand out or to be more noticeable. Otherwise we should have found that the first dimension encoded was more accurate when it was emphasized than when it was equal in value to the other dimensions. Second, the instructional set effect does seem to be due to the order of processing of the dimensions, the order in which they are encoded from the iconic representation into a form that can be maintained in short-term memory. Because the dimension coders can vary that order of encoding, they are able to show an effect of instructional set. Third, the differences between the two coding strategies suggests that we can process different features simultaneously but different instances of the same feature only sequentially. In this sense, selective processes can be affected by the order in which we extract information from a briefly held iconic storage, and by the degree to which

the strategy used permits simultaneous attention to more than one dimension at a time.

Motivational and Affective States

Another source of information that has been shown to affect responses in perceptual recognition experiments is the motivational or affective state of the perceiver. The importance of this kind of information is derived from the fact that it reflects input from lasting characteristics of individual perceivers—usually described as the individual's personality—as well as the more immediate and transient states such as hunger and thirst.

At the beginning of this chapter, we discussed the early views of perceptual defense and perceptual enhancement. We noted there the conceptual and methodological difficulties that were immediately apparent. But even if these difficulties were overcome, a logical problem remains for the notion of perceptual defense. How could a perceiver defend himself from perceiving a particular word until he became aware of it and identified it? But if he was aware of it, what could perceptual defense mean? One answer was that we have unconscious perception, that is, we can perceive something without having been aware of having done so. But this explanation simply changes the meaning of our notion of perception and moves the problem back into an earlier perceptual system. Other explanations have also been proposed but the seemingly logical inconsistency of the process of perceptual defense probably was one of the major reasons for the decline of research on this problem.

Erdelyi (1974) has proposed an alternative explanation of perceptual defense and vigilance by reinterpreting them in an information-processing framework. Erdelyi notes that a major premise of the information-processing approach is that the input is sequentially subject to different types of transformations and storages. It would only be natural, therefore, to assume that different selective processes might be operative at different stages of processing. Thus the information-processing approach has within it the implication that selectivity may occur at multiple loci. It is this conception that Erdelyi applies to explain the effects of inputs from motivational and affective systems. It therefore now becomes possible to explain perceptual defense, not merely in terms of a perception–response or visual–verbal distinction but as a fundamental expression of cognitive control processes exercising selective regulation throughout the information-processing sequence. Erdelyi reframes the question of perceptual defense to ask about the locus and mechanisms of selectivity. In this way we can think of bias as part of the processing sequence rather than as artifact.

To illustrate the power of this analysis, Erdelyi catalogued a number of possible selective mechanisms that respond to motivational and affective variables. First, selectivity in looking strategies or in actual peripheral receptor mechanisms may control the information input to the system. These strategies include not only the direction and sequence of fixation, but also the shutting off of the input by closing the eyes. Pupil diameter and accommodation have also been shown to be responsive to internal states and may also be involved in input control. On the output side, selection may occur as a result of reporting strategies, including one of the simplest early explanations for perceptual defense—that the perceiver suppresses his report of troublesome stimuli.

The major contribution of Erdelyi's explanation, however, is the inclusion of processes occurring between input and output. As we noted in our discussion of selectivity earlier, many of the effects produced by instructional sets can be explained by reference to encoding and transfer processes. Erdelyi extends this notion to include "chronic sets" or "personality dispositions" that become part of each individual through years of development. In addition to encoding strategies, the processing of certain material may be interrupted on the basis of partial analysis, or some other information may intrude into the processing sequence causing the original information to be lost. Similar events may take place in a later part of the sequence when information is being transferred to long-term memory. Dixon (1971) has proposed a similar analysis of subliminal perception—the situation in which a perceiver's behavior is modified as a consequence of stimuli he has not yet fully analyzed or iden-

tified. Without going into detail, Dixon sees selective attention and subliminal perception as the end points on a continuum of information handling. This view supports the conception of many theorists that selective processes in attention occur prior to awareness.

The information-processing explanation of perceptual defense makes the paradox of defense a little less paradoxical. If a stimulus fails to be encoded or placed into permanent memory because of its emotional content, it becomes irretrievably lost to the perceiver after the iconic storage and visual image fade. Thus the perceiver can be said to have defended against the input since it is unavailable to him beyond a fleeting moment. Yet, at a different level, he did "perceive" it—after all, it was available, if only for a very short period of time. As Erdelyi notes, the viewer both perceived and defended against perceiving (further) the very same input. The combination of selective and recognitive processes makes many alternative outcomes possible.

SUMMARY

Recognition processes involve some reference to familiarity—a contact between the representation of current stimulation and that of prior stimulation or other aspects of memory. We discussed recognition first by describing the possible features of words, then describing two different approaches to explanation, and finally by reviewing the effects of a number of variables on recognition. The structure of words can be approximated statistically, or can be related to spelling patterns, degree of pronounceability, word shape, or lexicality. Of these variables, it appears that lexicality is the only factor affecting the perception of words.

The two models of recognition discussed represent extreme views. The hierarchical filter model starts with very small units—the visual features—and proposes that perception and memory are constructed simultaneously through experience with words. Recognition represents current contact with structures built from past experience. The differentiation model begins with a visual system prewired to produce the perception of visual space from a highly structured visual input. By progressive abstraction of distinctive features and invariant relations, perceivers are able to make finer and finer discriminations.

Letter context was an important variable. It is clear that perceivers are more accurate in identifying a letter from a word than from an array containing the same letters in scrambled order. This word superiority effect is probably due to lexicality, that is, the knowledge of the meanings of words results in poorer performance in perceptual tasks involving nonwords and pseudowords than in tasks involving real words. Other major factors affecting performance in recognition tasks are instructional set and encoding processes.

However, these variables probably affect coding and retention strategies.

SUGGESTED READINGS

As in the previous several chapters, the best general source of work on perceptual recognition is Neisser (1967). Several of the papers considered in this chapter are also reprinted in Coltheart (1972). For a more detailed discussion of approximations to English, see Attneave (1959) and Garner (1962). Erdelyi's (1973) review of perceptual defense is thorough and wide-ranging, and Dixon (1971), is virtually complete.

Chapter 19

Perceptual Components in Reading

As a skilled cognitive activity, reading has many components in addition to perceptual ones, but the role of vision is certainly a central one in the understanding of the reading process. In this chapter we will concentrate on the perceptual aspects of reading and comment little on the acquisition of reading ability, reading disabilities, or on the testing of reading skills such as comprehension. On the other hand, we will have a lot to say about eye movements during reading, about the size of the visual field during each fixation, about the determination of fixation locations, about the visual features contained in letters, words, and sentences, about the extraction of information from visual features, and about the role of knowledge of features, of the content of the text being read, and of the nature of the language of the text in understanding written text.

Reading is usually defined as extraction of meaning from text (Gibson & Levin, 1975). More specifically, it is the process by which written or printed symbols are translated into a representation in which meaning is already accessible—a translation to a form of language from which the reader is able to derive meaning. This definition makes clear that the reading process is intimately tied to other language processing, especially the ability to extract meaning from speech. But, as we shall see, reading is much more than merely printed speech. The visual components are so different from the auditory ones that reading and listening, while sharing the same language, make very different demands on the information-processing skills of the perceiver (see Clark and Clark, 1977, for a discussion of the perceptual components of listening).

We will not say much about learning to read. Nevertheless, it should be noted that the process of reading as employed by first grade beginners is quite different from that of skilled mature readers. It can even be argued that the beginning process and the skilled process are independent, even though one leads to the other. This relation is similar to that found in many skilled performances, such as driving a car. The perceptual, cognitive, and attentive processes required for beginning performance of the skill bear little resemblance to those used by the skilled driver, even though the skilled driver was a beginner at one time. In any event, our focus is on the components of skilled reading performance and not on how one acquires that skill.

EYE MOVEMENTS DURING READING

Reading requires the active search of a text. Meaning cannot be passively obtained. Eye movements are therefore an integral component of the reading process. Even so, theorists do not agree on the role to assign to eye movements. Some argue that the eye is simply an information pick-up device and its movements do not in themselves enter into the subsequent processing (for example, Kolers, 1976). At the other extreme, theorists like Rayner (1978) argue that eye movements are a central factor in reading and that only by their analysis can we come to understand how reading occurs. We shall treat eye movements as a cen-

tral first step in the extraction of meaning from text thereby permitting discussion of both positions.

Typical Patterns of Eye Movements

Figure 19.1 shows the pattern of movements made while reading a single line of text. There are four principal components of interest in such a record: the distance covered by a saccadic movement, the duration of the fixation pause, the duration of the saccadic movement, and the presence of **regressive** (leftward) **saccadic movements**. In this particular record there are 8 forward saccadic fixations, with an average duration of 29 milliseconds each and an average distance moved of 7.4 character spaces of text.

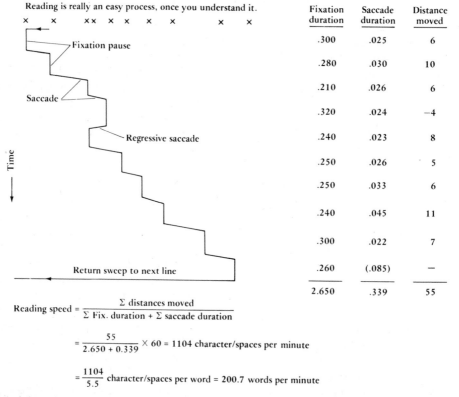

Fixation duration	Saccade duration	Distance moved
.300	.025	6
.280	.030	10
.210	.026	6
.320	.024	−4
.240	.023	8
.250	.026	5
.250	.033	6
.240	.045	11
.300	.022	7
.260	(.085)	—
2.650	.339	55

$$\text{Reading speed} = \frac{\Sigma \text{ distances moved}}{\Sigma \text{ Fix. duration} + \Sigma \text{ saccade duration}}$$

$$= \frac{55}{2.650 + 0.339} \times 60 = 1104 \text{ character/spaces per minute}$$

$$= \frac{1104}{5.5} \text{ character/spaces per word} = 200.7 \text{ words per minute}$$

Figure 19.1 A hypothetical recording of eye movements made while reading a simple sentence. Horizontal position of the line indicates position of the center of the fovea over the text, and the vertical position indicates time. The sentence being read is indicated at the top, with the position of each fixation indicated by the **X**. The values for the fixation duration, saccade duration, and distance associated with each fixation choice are indicated on the right.

There were 9 fixation pauses with an average duration of 268 milliseconds each. There was 1 recessive movement with a fixation duration of 240 milliseconds and a leftward distance of 4 character spaces. The return sweep at the end of the line took 85 milliseconds. All these measures are typical for a college student reading a passage of medium difficulty.

Reading speed in words per minute is calculated by dividing the time it takes to read several passages, of several pages each, by the total number of words read in that time period. For example, the ten words in Figure 19.1 (actually, too short a passage to provide a stable estimate) were read in 2.99 seconds (including the return sweep)—a rate of about 200 words per minute. Because varying difficulty levels also often result in changing word lengths, reading speed is occasionally expressed in character spaces per minute or even syllables per minute (Garver, 1977). For example, 100 words of difficult text may have over 900 character spaces, whereas 100 words of easy text might have only 600 character spaces. In Figure 19.1 reading speed is 1104 character spaces per minute and 320 syllables per minute as well as 200 words per minute. For college students, reading speeds can be as low as 50 words per minute for very difficult technical material, and as high as 500 to 1000 words per minute for easy novels being read for relaxation.

We know there are large individual differences in reading speeds across materials from easy to difficult, across readers from good to bad, and across instructions from skimming to careful attention. Which of the various measures taken from Figure 19.1 contribute to these sources of variability? Saccade duration generally ranges from 25 to 40 milliseconds, and fixation pause durations from 200 to 400 milliseconds. Since the saccade duration accounts for only about 8 to 10 percent of the total time in reading, it is not likely that variation in their durations can account for much of the range of these individual differences. While there is occasionally a correlation between individual differences and saccade duration, they are usually independent. Good readers do not move their eyes more rapidly than poor readers nor is movement speed different for easy as compared to difficult text. Fixation pause duration produces nearly the same re-

sults. It is possible to find correlations between the duration of fixations and the difficulty of text or skill of reader (Roskopf, 1978), but these correlations are low and often absent. How long the eye remains fixated therefore does not seem to account for much of the variation in reading speed and can certainly not account for speed differences of 10 or 20 to 1 when fixation durations rarely vary more than by 2 to 1.

The two remaining variables—distance of forward movement and the time taken up in regressions over a part of the text already examined—account for nearly all of the variation in reading speed. Good readers move their eyes farther than do poor readers between fixation pauses and make fewer regressive eye movements. The same is true when reading easy as compared to difficult text or when reading for relaxation as compared to reading for detailed comprehension and meaning. Most speedreading programs stress instructions that lead to longer saccade distances and inhibition of regressive movements.

Summary statistics of eye movements in reading are often misleading, because summarizing masks the extreme variability in all of these measures. Under no circumstances do we move our eyes the same distance each time, or at a constant rate. Nor do we remain fixated for a constant duration each time. All of these measurements vary, even when the same reader is reading the same type of text for the same purpose.

Most readers hold the page at 30 to 50 centimeters from their eyes, depending on the length of their arm, the height of the table, the size of the print, the weight of the book, and the amount and position of lighting. Most print in books designed for adults is about 3 millimeters high, which makes the typical visual angle of each letter about .25 degree. Thus, a 4-letter word occupies about 1 degree across the retina. If the average distance moved by a particular reader is 8 character spaces, then the average movement is 2 degrees, or slightly more than the width of the fovea.

Position and Duration of Fixations

All the above numbers and rates are useless unless we have some idea of how to interpret the distances, pauses, and locations in the text over which the eye dwells. Even with nearly a century of eye-movement research and speculation, we do not know all the answers to these questions. Information from the text is picked up primarily during fixation pauses and not during the saccades themselves. We know this from the presence of saccadic suppression and from the substantial smear of edges not suppressed. So it seems reasonable to ask how the location of each fixation pause is determined, since it is those locations that limit what is picked up and processed from the text.

Several theories or models of eye movements in reading have been distinguished (see Haber, 1976; Rayner, 1978). The **random model** simply states that the sequence of fixations has nothing to do with the text at all. The eye merely picks up information from an area of the text and moves on—the distance of each movement being determined by some general confidence the reader has in how he is doing but without reference to the particular part of the passage being looked at at the moment. Some movements are large, some small, and some even leftward; some pauses are long, some short, but they also are independent of the text. If confidence is high, distances moved are large and reading speed is high. If confidence is low, so is the speed. With this model the eye is merely the device to bring text into view.

There have been many attempts to discredit the random model. The main basis for rejection has been correlations between some of these eye movement parameters and information-processing variables that suggest at least some internal control over the text. As a simple example, consider the eye movement record in Figure 19.2 from Buswell (1937), in which a college student is reading prose containing some difficult words. If fixations occur randomly, how can the random model explain why each difficult word (which can be defined independently by its frequency of occurrence or prior familiarity to the reader) is fixated several times, yet few of the other words draw multiple fixations?

Even with such data, however, the random model still survives, in part because of its simplicity. The eye is treated simply as a device for bringing the text into the processing system, much as a conveyor

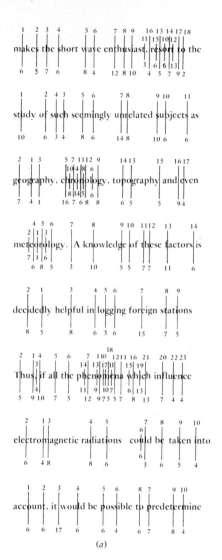

(a)

Figure 19.2 An actual record of fixation choices by a reader over test with a number of difficult (for that reader) words. Each vertical line represents one fixation; with the number at the top of the line indicating the order of the fixation, and the number at the bottom of the line indicating the thirtieths of a second of the fixation pause. (Buswell, 1937).

belt brings materials to be processed into a factory. If the workers in the factory slow down or have trouble, eventually someone has to slow the conveyor belt down, but no moment-to-moment relationship of input along the belt and processing in the factory exists.

This is a poor analogy for the reading process, though it might have some relevance for very skilled, automatic, or perhaps very superficial reading.

The **internal control model** relates the eyes' movements to what the reader is doing at each moment in time. For example, if the eye is fixated on a word that the reader does not know, the duration of fixation is extended, or a second fixation is made on the same word. If a sentence is very difficult, saccades are very small and close together over that sentence. If what is being processed up to the current fixation makes the next few words predictable—say a prepositional phrase—the eye can skip the next word or two, on thereby avoiding the highly redundant preposition. The essence of the internal control model is that a higher level of information processing controls how the eyes move, when they move, and how far.

To support this internal control model we need evidence that the fixation positions and durations are correlated with some aspect of the text being read. The data from Figure 19.2 above are certainly one kind of evidence. Specifically, Buswell shows that if a word is unfamiliar to the reader, the eye remains over the word for longer durations or more fixations. Rayner (1978) has reviewed a number of recent studies that show that unfamiliar words, certain parts of speech, unlikely syntactic forms, or incongruous semantic constructions are all likely to draw extra or longer fixations. These studies show that the processing of a text exerts a specific control over eye movements.

Critics of this model (for example, Kolers & Lewis, 1972) have argued to the contrary that the above results do not tell us anything about eye movements but only about how readers handle difficulty when processing text. Thus, it is possible that when the reader encounters a rare word, extra time is needed to process that word, to fit it into the context, and to continue to construct the meaning of the passage. That extra processing time need not, however, be visual time, so that the eye merely marks time waiting for the internal processor to catch up. The eye is not actively searching for more visual features to help determine the meaning of the passage.

This criticism has been countered by another line of evidence—evidence that the eyes are sensitive to visual features beyond the current center of fixation and that such featural information does affect eye position and duration. This argument assumes that the useful field of view is larger than that of the word currently in the fovea. In other words, the reader is able to pick up visual information from the text that falls outside the fovea. The kinds of information suggested are positions of words (given by detecting the spaces between words), length of words, ends of sentences or clauses (given by detecting punctuation and extra spaces following punctuation), beginnings of sentences (given by detecting capitalization), ends of lines (given by white margin of the printed area of the text), shapes of the words (given by the pattern of ascending or descending letters in the word), and, of course, the actual letters in the words. It is likely that the distance into the peripheral visual field at which each of these sources of information can be picked up depends on the size of the visual feature carrying the information. Hence, resolving individual letters would be difficult in the far periphery, whereas word shape and word length would be easier, and end of line easiest at greater distances. Rayner (1978) considers evidence that shows that the reader is sensitive to information in the text to the right of the current fixation, that is, information that has not yet been fixated.

Reading through a Window

If a reader picks up no information from peripheral vision and uses only the word under the fovea (plus all those previously fixated) to extract meaning from text, then reading performance would not be impaired if the reader is never able to see any of the words to the right of fixation until he actually moves his eyes over them. On the other hand, if he did pick up information from the next few words to the right of fixation, removing them would slow down or otherwise impair performance. Several experiments have examined these possibilities (Bouma, 1971; Newman, 1966; Poulton, 1972). In general, the reader is presented a movie in which a camera with a restricted angle of view moved over the line of print just as the eye would do. The number of character-spaces visible at any time is restricted, so that only part of a line can be seen at any one instant. Using reading performance with no restricted line length as a baseline, all these studies have shown disruption of performance as soon as the visible area of text is restricted to below 25 to 50 character spaces. These studies, while persuasive, have been criticized because some of the disruption could be due to the unusualness of the task. The saccades normally made by a reader are simulated by the camera. Hence, it is not a natural way to read.

McConkie and Rayner (1975) repeated the experiment using a more natural procedure. The text to be read was displayed on a television screen controlled by a digital computer. The reader's eye movements were simultaneously recorded and measured by the same computer, which was programmed to make the appearance of the text contingent upon the position of the eyes while reading. Figure 19.3 illustrates the nature of the task. Part (a) is a sample of the text to be read. The computer displays the text on the television screen so that each letter and space has been replaced by a capital X. When the reader begins and the computer determines that his eye is fixated at the beginning of the first line, all of the Xs around the center of fixation are replaced with the actual letters in the text so that the reader can see them. When he moves his eyes to the next fixation position, the earlier part of the text reverts to Xs and the letters around the new fixation are "uncovered." Part (b) of the figure illustrates how the text would look, for a window size of 17 spaces. The window size—the number of letters uncovered in each glance—is determined by the computer. In addition, the window was centered either on the area of fixation, or to the right of fixation, or to the left of fixation.

Figure 19.4 shows the results of several experimental conditions. In general, restricting viewing to less than three or four words (actually less than about 30 spaces) disrupted performance, in that distance moved decreased.

McConkie and Rayner also manipulated the text information not in the window. In general, the greater the amount of information contained outside the window area, the less important the size of the window was. For example, Figure 19.4 contrasts the results

from the displays shown in Figure 19.3 (b) and (c). Figure 19.4 shows that saccade distance is greater when word length information is preserved outside of the window (Fig. 19.3c) as compared to when the spaces are filled in so that the position of the words cannot be seen in peripheral vision (Fig. 19.3b). Notice, however, that word length information seems to be effective only for windows of 25 spaces or less— about 12 spaces from the center of fixation, or 2–3 words, as shown by the difference between the two curves in Figure 19.4

The same effect occurs when word shape information is preserved outside the window. Specifically, when outside of the window, ascenders are replaced with ascenders, descenders with descenders, and so

Normal Text

By far the single most abundant substance in the biosphere

is the familiar but unusual inorganic compound called water. In

nearly all its physical properties water is either unique or at the

extreme end of the range of a property. It's extraordinary

(a)

XXXXXXXXXXXXXXXXXXXXXXXXXXXXXXXXXXXXXXXXX

XXXXXXXXXXXXXsual inorganic coXXXXXXXXXXXXXXX

XXXXXXXXXXXXXXXXXXXXXXXXXXXXXXXXXXXXXXXXXX

XXXXXXXXXXXXXXXXXXXXXXXXXXXXXXXXXXXXXXXXX

(b)

Xx xxx xxx xxxxxx xxxx xxxxxxxx xxxxxxxxx xx xxx x

xx xxx xxxxxxxx xxxsual inorganic coxxxxxx xxxxxx xxx. Xx

xxxxxx xxx xxx xxxxxxxx xxxxxxxxxx xxxxx xx xxxxxx xxx

xxx xxxxxxx xxx xx xxx xxxxx xx x xxxxxxxxxx. Xx'x xxxxx

Note. In all cases, the window size is 17 character spaces. The subject's fixation point is on the letter r in *organic* and there are 8 characters spaces to the left and right containing readable text.

(c)

Figure 19.3 Examples of the materials used by McConkie and Rayner (1975). In (a), part of the normal text is shown. In (b), all characters and spaces are replaced by **X**, except for the 17 character spaces around the center of fixation. In (c), the space character is preserved outside the 17-character "window."

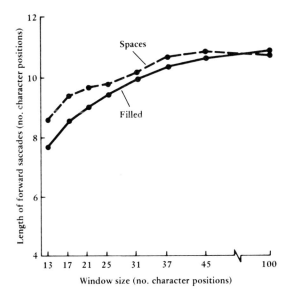

Figure 19.4 The length of forward saccades (vertical axis) is shown for each window size (horizontal axis), when the space character is filled by the X (filled) or left as a space (space).

forth, saccade distance is greater, showing that readers are sensitive to shape information beyond the word on the center of fixation. Word shape information is only effective for about 1–2 words beyond the center.

These studies provide strong evidence that the reader does attend to information well to the right of the center of the current fixation and that the distance over which information is attained can be as large as a number of words.

Rayner (1974) reported a different type of experiment which also used a gaze-contingent display system. Several lines of text appeared on a screen, under computer control. The computer also monitored eye movements and was programmed to change one word in the text when the reader's eyes were fixated at some point on the text that preceded that word. An example of one of the brief passages is shown in Figure 19.5. Rayner's argument was that, if the reader has not picked up any information about the word to be changed prior to the change, then after it was changed, it would take no longer to read that part of the text than if the word was originally in its changed

A.   The robbers guarded the pcluce with their guns.

B.   The robbers guarded the palace with their guns.

Figure 19.5 An example of one sentence from Rayner (1974). A is the sentence originally presented on the computer display. The arrow indicates the predetermined eye position that will trigger the change. B is the replacement sentence with the one word changed. The replacement occurred when the eye positions crossed the boundary marked by the arrow.

form. If, on the other hand, the reader had picked up some information, then when he encountered the new word it should slow him down, cause extra fixations, or in some other way disrupt the normal reading process. To test this, Rayner made several types of changes, including ones that preserved word shape and length (such as changing police to palace), length but not shape (palace to hostel), or neither length nor shape (palace to home). He also varied the semantic meaning of the sentence. For each variation, he manipulated the distance from the to-be-changed word at which eye position was changed. The change occurred during the saccade that carried the eye over the trigger position so that the reader could not notice the actual change in the display as it occurred.

Rayner's results are plotted in Figure 19.6. They show that reading is affected when the change is from nonsense to sense only if the change is made no more than about five spaces or one word away. If the original word was a real word, no effect on reading was detected. Rayner also demonstrated (but does not show in Figure 19.6) that if the change was from nonsense to sense but of a different length or shape, the distance over which the effect occurred was larger. For example, if this change altered shape, then it was noticed no more than two words away, and changing length was noticed no more than three words away. Again, these results show that readers do pick up information beyond the center of the current fixation. If the change preserves shape and length then the change can be determined only by noticing the changes in the individual letters and this can be only done one word away. Letter information is picked up just from the next word beyond the fixation but not farther. We pick up

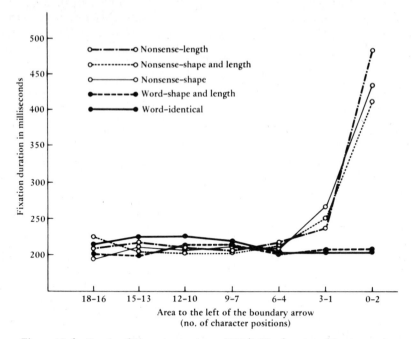

Figure 19.6   Results of Rayner's experiment (1974). The duration of fixation on the last word prior to crossing the boundary (vertical axis) is plotted as a function of the distance of the boundary arrow from the changed word (horizontal axis). Five different conditions are plotted. For three of them (when the change was from a nonsense word to a real word of the same length L, the same shape S, or the same length and shape SL), fixation duration increased only when the boundary was closer than 5 spaces — that is, about one word. If the change was from a real word to another one of the same length or shape, or to the same word, no changes occurred in fixation duration.

shape information from about two words away because when shape is changed it is noticed in that range but no farther. Word length is being picked up as far as three words away. Rayner did not test for punctuation changes, sentence boundaries, or length of lines, but presumably these could be noticed even farther than letter shape and length information.

One last study also bears on this question. Haber, Haber, and Furlin (1980) presented part of a passage that ended in midsentence. The reader had to guess the next word. Then some more of the text appeared, again ending in the middle of another sentence and the subject had to guess what the next word was. Sometimes the word to be guessed was merely indicated by blank spaces, sometimes by the number of letters in the correct word and sometimes by both the number of letters and the shape of the word. Re-

gardless of the difficulty of the text, letting the reader know the correct number of letters improved his guessing accuracy by about 10 percent, and if he also knew the shape of the word, accuracy increased another 10 percent. From these results the authors argued that readers usually and typically are able to make use of word length and word shape information in helping them extract the meaning of the text.

All this evidence suggests that the eye picks up information beyond the center of the current fixation. This information is used in the processing of the text and also affects subsequent eye positions and durations. This provides support for an internal control model of eye movements.

There is also a third type of eye movement model—called the **external control.** If visual information is being taken in well to the right of the center of the current fixation, maybe the eye-movement control system uses that information to plan the position of the next fixation. We have already reviewed evidence to show that when searching for a target, peripheral vision is used to pick up information about likely places to which to move the eyes. Is there any evidence that this also applies to eye movements during reading? Do we skip over some words because peripheral vision shows that they were short and unimportant? The evidence in reading is scanty and equivocal. The problem is that nonvisual information such as syntactic structure, can also predict which word might be skippable without any visual information about size or shape. Typically, experiments cannot determine which source of information is used by the visual system in determining fixation position. Therefore, at present, peripheral guidance for fixation presentation, while a possibility, has yet to be demonstrated. So far, all of the data from eye movement records can be accounted for by the internal control model. Even so, support for the internal control model means that the eye-movement positions can be quite revealing of the information pickup stage of reading.

Eye–Voice Span

One very interesting measure of the information-processing aspects of reading is the **eye–voice span** in oral reading. The span is an index of how far the eyes are ahead of the voice. It can be measured either in number of words or number of milliseconds. The eye–voice span is considered an index of the amount of material the reader must perceive, process, and retain from the time his eyes fixate until his voice pronounces the words. The size of the eye–voice span has been used as a measure of ongoing short-term processing and storage.

In one study of reading, Morton (1964) had students read nonsense and meaningful passages that differed in their statistical resemblance to English prose. He recorded the voice of the reader on a tape recorder that was synchronized with an eye-movement recorder. In this way, Morton could tell where the eye was fixating on the line and what word was being uttered at each instant in time. Figure 19.7 shows a typical record. The upper part contains the eye fixations, and the lower part the voice track. Morton found that the duration of fixations was about 240 milliseconds and was constant over different kinds of materials ranging from random words to continuous meaningful text. This was the case even though reading speed increased from just over 80 to nearly 230 words per minute and the eye–voice span increased from about one to nearly three words. In the latter cases, this represented a span of 640 milliseconds in length.

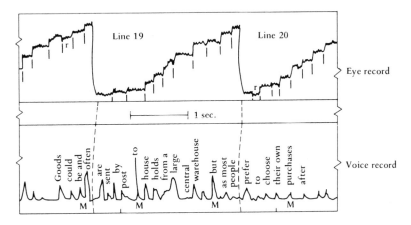

Figure 19.7 An eye movement record and a voice record taken simultaneoulsy by an oral reader. Notice that the voice does not pronounce a word until the eye is well beyond it in the text. (Morton, 1964.)

Geyer (1968), using meaningful texts of varying difficulty, also found fixation time to be constant. His measurement of the eye–voice span ranged from about 800 milliseconds for difficult material to nearly 1200 milliseconds for easy material. Neither Geyer nor Morton could discover any regularities in the pattern of fixations, although Geyer did attempt to examine the kinds of errors readers made. He classified corrected errors into those in which the reader misperceived the word and those in which he merely mispronounced or misspoke his oral response. When misperceptions occurred, the voice usually would stop, the eye would return to the misperceived word and reread the text out to the size of the span. Then the voice would pick up again. When mispronunciations occurred, only the voice would return to the error, the eye retreating enough only to maintain the span. Geyer also noted that when the voice had to pause for punctuation or emphasis, the eye also paused. But, of course, the eye was looking at a word unrelated to the pause, farther down the text, and often even on the next line.

Redundancy in Text and Reading

One of the great failures of research on reading has been its lack of attention to the nature of language and of language processing. Since reading is the extraction of meaning from text, the structure of the text itself must be described before we can even begin to understand how the reader processes it. We need to know the ways in which readers make use of the structural characteristics of the text in order to translate the visual representation of the text into a language whose meaning is known to the reader. This means that we must understand the processes and strategies by which readers carry out the translation process.

There are models of the processes involved in reading that start with the smallest visual elements and construct letter names, words, phrases containing those words, sentences, paragraphs, and finally whole passages (for example, Gough, 1972). There are also models of reading that suggest that processing is directed or guided by expectations based upon the knowledge the reader already possesses about the structure of the language and the content of the passage being read (for example, Hochberg, 1976). We have already discussed one of the former models—the hierarchical filter model—in Chapter 18. This section will discuss the redundancies in print that form the basis for expectancies. In Chapter 14 we described the concept of redundancy and, in Chapter 18 we showed how knowledge of the spelling rules of English increased the redundancy, and hence the predictability, of letter sequences drawn from real words. Such redundancy is present at all levels of language, not just those relating to letter sequences. The usefulness of redundancy is that, in the process of reading, the reader can attend to the visual features of the text—the black marks of various kinds on the page—while she can also predict what some of these visual features will be even before she has picked them up with her eyes. The prediction does not have to be perfect and often is not. Information theory defines redundancy as the reduction in the number of alternative possibilities of which the message is actually composed. Knowledge about language increases the redundancy of the message and therefore its predictability. This implies that less stimulus information is needed in order to determine the content of a message when the redundancy of the message is high. The reading process can be characterized as one of constant interplay between information extracted from visual features on the one hand and from the prediction based on redundancy—another form of analysis.

Before we can show in detail how this occurs, we shall consider the major sources of redundancy available to readers. We shall discuss this for reading English, though, of course, the presentation applies in principle to any language being read by a fluent reader or speaker of that language. We shall consider redundancies that refer to the marks on the page of print, redundancies that refer to the structure of the language, and redundancies that refer to the content of the passage.

Redundancy on the Printed Page.

Figure 19.8 lists some examples of various kinds of printing conventions used in English prose. As can be seen, even if all the individual letters were replaced by a common symbol (such as the Xs in Figure 19.3),

PRINTING CONVENTIONS

End of Line Conventions:	Right and left justified Hyphen indicates word division
Paragraph Conventions:	Indentation Skip a line Bold face, initial character enlarged, etc.
Sentence Boundary Conventions:	Initial capitalization Final punctuation marks Extra space
Phrase Boundary Conventions:	Punctuation Extra space
Transformation Conventions:	Question has question mark at end (some languages at beginning) Imperatives and exclamations have exclamation mark. Statements have periods. Emphatics have italics or boldface.
Direct Speech Conventions:	Quotation marks Paragraphing for change of speaker
Word Conventions:	Space before and after Initial capitalization for proper nouns

Figure 19.8 Some different printing conventions used by typesetters and typists. Nearly all of these generate syntactic rules.

the reader can extract a great deal of information about the locations of words, sentences, paragraphs, and even the structure of sentences from punctuation. Of course, if the reader is unfamiliar with the way books are printed, none of this information is available. Similarly, if prose is printed so that every word is given a single line (as in a list), only the word boundaries are visually defined.

Redundancy among Letter Features
Regardless of typeface, once you know the names for the letters of the alphabet, you know, in effect, the general rules for how the letters are shaped. This means that, given partial visual features, we can predict the rest of the features and be able to recognize the letter. There are several different

ways of describing this type of redundancy. Figure 19.9 shows one example, in which a brief paragraph is printed with either all the tops of the letters removed or all the bottoms. It is clearly easier to read the passage when the bottoms of letters are missing than the tops, which suggests that more information (that is, less redundancy) is contained in the tops. (These passages, of course, are in context so many other redundancies are present besides just the information from the visual features. The top–bottom difference occurs even for isolated letters.)

There have been many attempts to describe the visual features that compose letters. Gibson and Levin (1975) review a number of such attempts. Most of them have looked at different kinds of line elements in terms of their length, orientation, degree of closure or circularity, general size, and position in relation to the

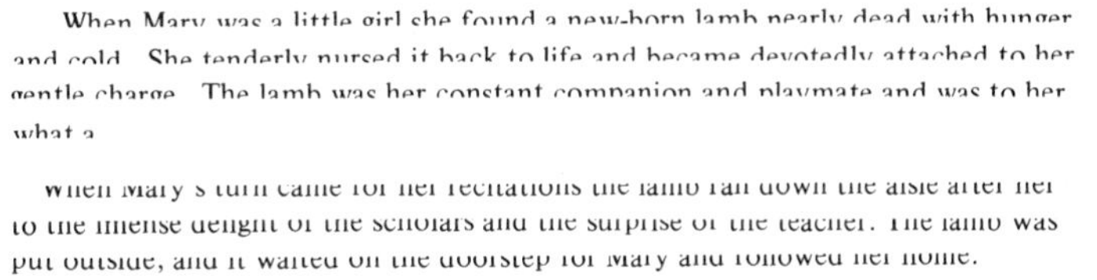

When Mary was a little girl she found a new-born lamb nearly dead with hunger and cold. She tenderly nursed it back to life and became devotedly attached to her gentle charge. The lamb was her constant companion and playmate and was to her what a

When Mary's turn came for her recitations the lamb ran down the aisle after her to the immense delight of the scholars and the surprise of the teacher. The lamb was put outside, and it waited on the doorstep for Mary and followed her home.

Figure 19.9 An example of the difference in ease of reading that occurs when the bottoms or the tops of letters are removed. (Huey, 1908.)

line and to other letters (see Figure 18.4: Gibson's list. Figure 19.10 shows a visual-feature list for upper-case letters in English. A slightly different featural set is necessary for lower-case letters. The 26 letters, each of which can appear in upper and lower case, plus ten numbers, as well as the standard punctuation marks, make about 75 characters. If a feature set is created that uniquely distinguished these 75 characters with a minimum number of features, 7 features are needed. The estimate from current research (Gibson & Levin, 1975) is that about 20 binary features (features that are either present or absent in each character) are used to differentiate among the 75 characters. The independent combination of 20 different features specify slightly over one million letters if there is no redundancy. Thus, it is clear that the features characterizing English letters are highly redundant.

Figure 19.11 provides examples of a number of typefaces of English. While superficially different from each other, the features that comprise each of the the typefaces are virtually identical. There are several letters, such as a lower case *a* or lower case *g,* that have different features but other than those, nearly all the visual-feature sets handle almost all the common typefaces in English. A few typefaces are difficult to read (see the last two lines of Figure 19.11), but those use a different set of visual features.

The implication of the very high redundancy among the visual features is that relatively little visual information is necessary from a letter in order to determine its name. Picking up only one or two features is usually all that is necessary. For example, if all that has been detected of a capital letter is a diagonal, from that one feature alone, you can eliminate from the 26 possible alternatives all but the 11 capital letters: *A, K, M, N, Q, R, V, W, X, Y,* and *Z.* If all you pick up is a horizontal line at the bottom of the letter, then you can eliminate all alternatives except *E, L,* and *Z,* and so forth. If you see both a diagonal and a lower horizontal, it has to be *Z.* Although each letter may be made up of 5 or 6 features drawn from a set of as many of 20, it usually is necessary to detect only two or, at most, three of those features in any single letter to determine its name. As we will see below, when

combined with knowledge of spelling rules, only one feature of a letter is sufficient to determine its name.

Redundancy in the Shapes of Words

If an envelop is drawn around the outline of a lower-case word, different words have characteristic **shapes** and lengths. This profile is independent of the particular letters and, as such, provides visual information as to what the word is without having to process the individual letters. Figure 19.12 is a passage in which every instance of any of the 95 commonest words in English has been replaced simply by its outline shape. As you can see, this passage is relatively easy to read and, in fact, with a little practice at this task, most readers can proceed at an almost normal rate of reading.

Figure 19.13 provides the profiles for these 95 most frequent words. It is interesting that these words account for almost 50 percent of all of the words that appear in normal print. That is, they account for half the words in this book. This list contains virtually no nouns or verbs. It is mainly a list of what is loosely called **functors.** Because these words appear so frequently in print, it seems quite likely that readers have learned the shapes of these words rather early in their reading experience and are able to recognize them partially by their shape alone. The redundancy of shape is by no means perfect, however. As can be seen from Figure 19.13, there are 41 different shapes represented by these 95 most frequent words, and for nearly all these shapes there is more than one word that possesses that shape. Thus, while knowing the shape reduces the number of alternatives, thereby increasing the redundancy, it does not eliminate all alternatives. Hence, for many words this source of redundancy cannot predict exactly which word it is without other information such as context. The reason it is possible to read the passage in Figure 19.12 so easily is that, in addition to shape, the full context is available.

We have already reviewed some evidence to show that readers can attend to word shape and, in fact, they do use it. The McConkie and Rayner (1975) experiment shows that, when the text outside the window preserves word-shape information, subjects are able to

	Vertical lines	Horizontal lines	Oblique lines	Right angles	Acute angles	Continuous curves	Discontinuous curves
A		1	2		3		
B	1	3		4			2
C							1
D	1	2		2			1
E	1	3		4			
F	1	2		3			
G	1	1		1			1
H	2	1		4			
I	1	2		4			
J	1						1
K	1		2	1	2		
L	1	1		1			
M	2		2		3		
N	2		1		2		
O						1	
P	1	2		3			1
Q			1		2	1	
R	1	2	1	3			1
S							2
T	1	1		2			
U	2						1
V			2		1		
W			4		3		
X			2		2		
Y	1		2		1		
Z		2	1		2		

Figure 19.10 The visual features that can uniquely describe and differentiate the 26 capital letters of English in the type style illustrated. This is not a binary feature list, since each feature can take printed values from 0 to 4. (Lindsay & Norman, 1977.)

perceive farther into the periphery. The Haber, Haber, and Furlin (1980) study shows that when words to be guessed have their shape preserved, accuracy of guessing is improved substantially. Reading teachers often refer to most of these 95 words as **sight words**, for the reader is able to recognize the word from the pattern alone without having to process the individual letters.

An example of various type styles.

An example of various type styles.

An example of various type styles.

An example of various type styles.

An example of various type styles.

An example of various type styles.

An example of various type styles.

An example of various type styles.

An example of various type styles.

An example of various type styles.

An example of various type styles.

An example of various type styles.

𝔄n example of various type styles.

𝕳n example of various type styles.

𝕬n example of various type styles.

Figure 19.11 Examples of different typefaces for the English alphabet.

The three sources of redundancy discussed so far: those from printing conventions, those from the features within letters, and those from the shape of whole words, each provides substantial sources of information about letters, words, and structure of the text. With this redundancy, the reader is not entirely dependent on visual information to identify letters, words and structure.

Redundancies in the Structure of the Language

We shall now consider several sources of knowledge that readers have when they know the language they are reading. These include spelling rules, which restrict the combinations that letters can take, and syntax rules, which restrict sequences of words.

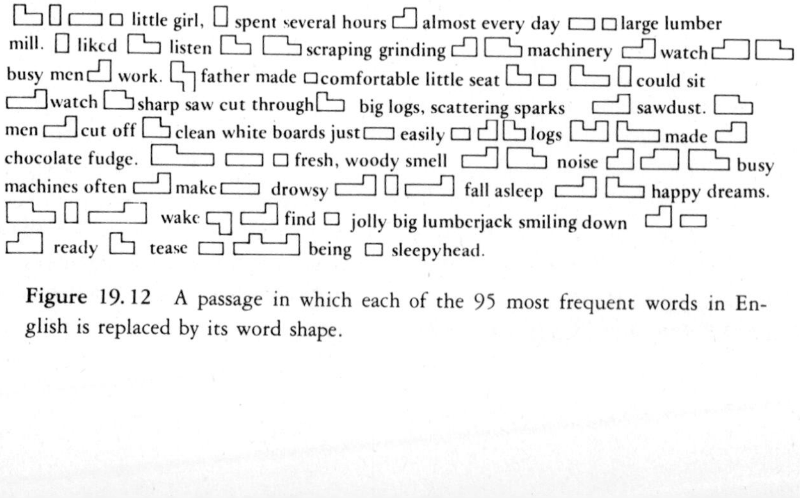

⬜⬜⬜⬜ little girl, ⬜ spent several hours ⬜ almost every day ⬜⬜large lumber mill. ⬜ liked ⬜ listen ⬜ ⬜scraping grinding ⬜⬜ machinery ⬜watch⬜⬜ busy men⬜ work. ⬜father made ⬜comfortable little seat ⬜⬜ ⬜⬜ could sit ⬜watch⬜sharp saw cut through⬜ big logs, scattering sparks ⬜ sawdust. ⬜ men⬜cut off ⬜clean white boards just⬜ easily ⬜⬜⬜logs ⬜⬜ made ⬜ chocolate fudge. ⬜ ⬜⬜ fresh, woody smell ⬜⬜⬜ noise ⬜⬜⬜⬜ busy machines often ⬜make⬜ drowsy ⬜⬜⬜⬜ fall asleep ⬜⬜⬜ happy dreams. ⬜⬜⬜ wake⬜⬜find ⬜ jolly big lumberjack smiling down ⬜⬜ ⬜ ready ⬜ tease ⬜⬜⬜ being ⬜ sleepyhead.

Figure 19.12 A passage in which each of the 95 most frequent words in English is replaced by its word shape.

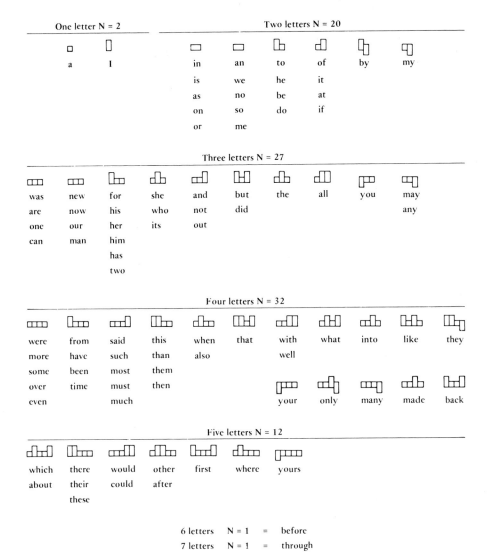

Figure 19.13 Word profiles for the 95 most frequent words of English, taken from the Kucera and Francis (1967) word count. These 95 words, which represent only 0.2 percent of all types in the word count, account for 50 percent of all tokens in English print.

Spelling Rules Although a fluent speaker of the language who does not know how to read knows nothing about **spelling rules,** several theories about reading have linked the letter restrictions to phoneme restrictions that exist for speech (Gibson & Levin, 1975). As an alphabetic language, English has a very small number of separate letters that can be combined in a relatively large number of ways to make up an enormously large set of words. However, if it were permissible to combine the 27 characters (including the space character) randomly (that is, if any character could follow or precede any other character), there would be no redundancy in a letter sequence. To decode the sequence would require specific identification of each character in the sequence. English, however, has very specific rules that restrict the combinations of letters. When these rules are known, having identified one or several letters of a word the letters that can follow are not all the possible letters of the language, but, in fact, only a very small subset of them.

Because English is an Indo-European language, spelling rules apply within a single **syllable**. While syllables are more properly defined for speech rather than for print, in print a syllable can be loosely defined as a **nuclear vowel** made up of 1 or 2 spelled vowels, preceded by 0, 1, 2, or 3 consonants, and followed by

0, 1, 2, 3, or 4 consonants. Words, of course, can be single syllables or combinations of several syllables. When in combination, the spelling rules apply to each syllable separately. Figure 19.14 lists all the consonant combinations that can precede the nuclear vowel in an English syllable. There are no instances in which four consonants can precede a nuclear vowel and there are only 9 instances of combinations in which three consonants can precede a nuclear vowel. Since there are over 9,000 possible ways to combine the 21 consonants in all possible combinations of 3 and yet only 0.1 percent of those are permissible, the redundancy is impressively large. There are 441 possible combi-

Letter sequence restrictions for English words
Initial consonant clusters

Four initial consonants – none allowed – <u>0</u> out of <u>193,481</u> alternatives

Three initial consonants – <u>9</u> combinations allowed out of <u>9261</u> alternatives

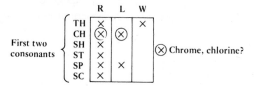

Two initial consonants – <u>28</u> combinations allowed out of <u>441</u> alternatives

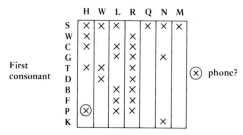

One initial consonant – all <u>21</u> combinations allowed out of <u>21</u> alternatives

Figure 19.14 Initial component cluster combinations found for English words, for three-, two-, and one-letter sequences. (Haber & Haber, 1980.)

nations of 2 consonants, and yet only 30 of those are found in English words. All 21 consonants can appear singly.

A few letter combinations found in an English dictionary are absent from Figure 19.14. For example, the initial *cz,* as in *czar,* or the initial *ps* as in *psychology,* or the initial *ph,* as in *phone,* do not appear. It is not clear what to do with such combinations psychologically. The letter combinations themselves have come into English from other languages, and, in some cases, represent non-English spellings and non-English pronunciations. In a few cases, the words appear very frequently, such as the *ps* combination in this book. On the other hand, psychologically, such spelling combinations are not considered productive in that, if you were asked to spell the initial consonant in the pronounced word *sigh* it would be a rare English speller who would use an initial *ps.* It is on these grounds that such spelling combinations are not included. Even if they were, however, they might add only another dozen or so entries to the table.

Figure 19.15 includes all the combinations of vowels in the nuclear vowel. The five vowels (plus *y* when it follows a consonant) can all occur by themselves. Some of them can occur in two-letter combinations (*eau* is the only three-letter vowel combination found in English, though it is imported from the French, and is not used productively). Six vowels, taken one or two at a time, could be combined theoretically, in 42 different ways, and over half of those can be found in English spellings. Thus, the amount of redundancy in the spelling of nuclear vowels is much less than for initial consonants. Since there are

many multisyllabic words in English there are also rules for combining separate syllables and separate morphemes into larger units. Some of those rules require slight changes in the configurations so that the final consonants in some cases are doubled, a silent *e* is deleted, and so forth.

It is clear, then, that being familiar with the spelling rules for the letter combinations in the language provides a tremendous amount of redundancy in being able to predict letter sequences. Thus, if you are told that the initial letter of a word is a *t,* you can tell by reference to Figure 19.14 (or the equivalent knowledge that adult readers carry around in their heads) that all six vowels can follow or the consonants *h, r,* and *w.* If Figure 19.14 also included the frequencies with which each of these combinations occurred, it would be obvious that the most likely alternative is *h.* Of all nine combinations of initial *t* followed by any other letter, *th* accounts for 65 percent of the words in English (Haber & Haber, 1980).

Syntax   Syntax is a description of the structural regularities of the language. In most circumstances it is identical for printed and spoken forms of the language. Figure 19.16 provides one example of syntactic redundancy given simply by the identification of each class of functors. Thus, whenever you encounter one of these functors in a sentence you can

DETERMINERS (a, an, the) and quantifiers (some, all, many, two, six, etc.) begin a new *Noun Phrase.*

PREPOSITIONS (to, at, in) begin a new *Prepositional Phrase.*

DEFINITE PRONOUNS (I, you, he, she, it, etc.) begin a new *Noun Phrase.*

VERB AUXILIARIES WITH TENSE (is, are, was, have, can, etc.) begin a new *Verb Phrase.*

RELATIVE PRONOUNS (that, which, who, when) begin a new *Clause.*

COMPLEMENTS (for-to, that, etc.) begin a new *Clause.*

SUBORDINATING CONJUNCTIONS (because, when, since, if, etc.) begin a new *Clause.*

COORDINATING CONJUNCTIONS (and, or, but, nor) begin a new *Constituent* similar to preceding one.

Figure 19.16 Some examples of syntactic redundancy stemming from functors, adapted from Clark and Clark (1977).

Nuclear vowel clusters in English syllables

A	E	I	O	U	Y
AI	EA	IE	OA		
AU	EG		OI		
	EI		OO		
	EU		OU		

Figure 19.15 Nuclear vowel clusters found in English syllables. (Haber & Haber, 1980.)

predict the class of word (and often the class of the entire clause) that follows it. Figure 19.17 provides an example, based upon more general rules. If you have identified the syntactic form of the words up to each point in a sentence, there are great restrictions on the syntactic class of the words to come.

Figure 19.18 provides a list of another category of syntactic restrictions. In fact, some of these are not merely syntactic but also involve the meaning of words. But in each case the use of a particular kind of word or class of word places restrictions on the way the rest of the sentence can be constructed.

It is possible to construct sentences in which the sequence of words lead us to expect one particular syntactic structure but a different one is actually used. What is printed violates our syntactic expectation. These have been called "garden path" sentences (Fodor, Bever, & Garrett, 1974), and are examples where the initial syntactic structure forces one interpretation, so that it is oten very hard to reorganize the sentence into the proper one. Figure 19.19 provides three examples of "garden path" sentences.

Redundancies Based upon Knowledge of the Content

It is clearly comparatively easy to read text on a topic with which you are familiar. Indeed, there are several different kinds of redundancies that the reader is using in such circumstances.

Semantic Relations among Words

The effects of the semantic relations among words have not been studied nearly as intensively in the context of reading as some of the redundancies listed earlier. It seems reasonable, however, that when you know something about the topic, the likely choice of vocabulary items is more predictable; the purpose that the writer has in communicating is more predictable; and so forth. In one empirical study of this type of redundancy (Haber, 1980), two types of sentences were used (see Figure 19.20). Subjects were presented with these sentences and asked to read them and press a button if they detected any misspellings in the sentences. Each sentence appeared in one of two versions: one in which the word that might be

---

THIS SHORT SENTENCE DEMONSTRATES SYNTACTIC REDUNDANCY

A. If restrictions are only from the left side:

_____ can be anything

THIS _____ can be adjective, noun, or quantifier (adverb)

THIS SHORT_____ can be noun or adjective

THIS SHORT SENTENCE _____ can be verb, time adverb, or new clause

THIS SHORT SENTENCE DEMONSTRATES_____ can be noun phrase, adverb, or new clause

THIS SHORT SENTENCE DEMONSTRATES SYNTACTIC _____ must be noun or adjectival phrase

B. If restrictions are in both directions:

_____ SHORT SENTENCE DEMONSTRATES SYNTACTIC REDUNDANCY. Must be *article*

THIS_____ SENTENCE DEMONSTRATES SYNTACTIC REDUNDANCY. Must be *adjective*

THIS SHORT _____ DEMONSTRATES SYNTACTIC REDUNDANCY. Must be *noun*

THIS SHORT SENTENCE _____ SYNTACTIC REDUNDANCY. Must be *verb*

THIS SHORT SENTENCE DEMONSTRATES_____ REDUNDANCY. Must be *article* or *adjective*

THIS SHORT SENTENCE DEMONSTRATES SYNTACTIC _____ . Must be *noun*.

Figure 19.17 An example of syntactic restrictions. The sentence analyzed is at the top. In *A*, the restrictions on each word are based only on the words that come before it. In *B*, the restrictions take into account words before and after each one, and therefore are much more extensive. (Haber & Haber, 1980.)

Examples of co-occurrence restrictions

Grammatical

Plurals: The cat climbing my leg has <u>20</u> sharp └────┘s

Past: Yesterday he └────┘ and └────┘ something
              unprintable.

Functional

Verbs requiring 2 following NPs:
<u>Put</u> └────┘ └────────┘
     object   location
Put the salt in the cellar.

Verbs requiring 1 following NP:
<u>Close</u> └────┘
      object
He closed ⌊the safe.⌋

Verbs obligatorily without following object NP
He <u>died</u>.

Categorical

Animate verb requires animate subject
   The man walked
   *The table walked

Adjective of measure requires measurable noun
   Tall building
   *Tall democracy
   Green wall
   *Green ghost

Semantic

Noun: <u>son</u> requires a NP with person old enough
Adverb: <u>quickly</u> requires a verb of action, movement
Verb: <u>waltz</u> requires a subject NP with legs

Fixed phrases

To tell the └────┘
He hit the nail on the └────┘

Figure 19.18 Some selected examples of syntactic and semantic restrictions on word choices.

misspelled was semantically constrained by the preceding context and the other in which the constraint was minimal. Haber predicted that subjects would be faster at detecting the presence of a misspelling when constraint was high, since, with the high redundancy, they would anticipate the word. Reaction time differences strongly supported this hypothesis. It should also be noted that if redundancy was sufficiently high, the subject might assume that the word followed and not notice the misspelling. This prediction also was supported. Virtually all the errors in which the subject failed to notice the misspelling were on the high-redundancy forms. This experiment demonstrated what

1. The horse raced past the barn fell.
2. The pitcher pitched the ball pitched the ball.
3. The porter carried in a trunk died.

Figure 19.19 Three examples of garden path sentences (Fodor, Bever, & Garrett, 1974), in which syntactic redundancy is very low and the reader is led down the garden path of expectation.

anyone who has ever done any proofreading knows: the more familiar you are with the topic being read (especially if you have written it yourself), the more difficult it is to find any errors in it. Thus, in general, as the meaning of the sentence becomes available to the reader through his initial processing, the alternative possibilities for subsequent words are greatly restricted.

Redundancies Given by the Genre of the Text

Once a writer commits himself to a particular form, the structure of that form greatly limits alternatives at all levels of text. For example, one can describe a murder in the form of a detective story or in the form of a newspaper article. One can describe a loan as a legal document or as an I.O.U. One can relate an improbable happening as a fairy story, or as a story in a first-grade reading book. One can write a sonnet or a nursery rhyme, and so forth. In each case, the form chosen places restrictions on the structure of the text. For example, Figure 19.21 shows the kinds of restrictions that are placed on a fairy tale in terms of the structure of the story, the choice of words, grammar, the format, its length, the way it is printed, the types of characters, and so forth. If the reader is familiar with the genre and therefore with these restrictions, the redundancies that the restrictions create substantially reduce alternatives at all levels of language processing.

A related source of redundancy is knowledge of the author's style. A short story by Hemingway shares very few characteristics with a short story by Mark Twain. This is true even where the contents of the stories are similar. Obviously, this type of redundancy is of no use if you are not familiar with the different stylistic qualities of authors. But if these are familiar to the reader, then those are severe restrictions on the alternatives that can occur.

Strong Semantic Constraint	*Weak Semantic Constraint*
He sat reading a vook until it was time to go home.	He sat reading a vill until it was time to go home,
Passing overhead was a dird which stood out starkly against the sky.	Passing overhead was a dall which stood out starkly against the sky.
Quickly he ate his ceal, which all spies have to do at some time.	Quickly he ate his cessage, which all spies have to do at some time.
He gave his wife a set of wine plasses for her birthday.	He gave his wife a set of fine plasses for her birthday.
After checking his equipment, the parachutist gumped out of the plane.	After checking his equipment, the psychologist gumped out of the plane.
The crowd stood watching the fire hurn after the explosion.	The crowd stood watching the tire hurn after the explosion.

Figure 19.20 Examples of some sentences used by Haber (1980). Those in the left column provide a strong semantic constraint on the misprinted word, whereas those in the right column provide a far weaker constraint.

In this discussion we have distinguished three sources of redundancy: those that regulate the rules for placing marks on the page, those that stem from the language system being used, and those that stem from the content of the text. These redundancies are useful, however, only if they are known by the reader. Thus, implicit in this description is the assumption that one of the things that is being acquired with the skill of reading is the knowledge of these variables. There is evidence to support this assumption for a few of the redundancies, but not for the others. For example,

A.	Opens:	"Once upon a time . . ."
		"Long, long ago there lived . . ."
	Closes:	"And they lived happily ever after."
B.	Characters:	Stereotyped as particular extremes: good/wicked, kings/paupers, beautiful/ugly.
C.	Normal rules of reality are suspended.	
		There are impossible beings (dragons and witches), impossible places (ice palaces and gingerbread cottages), impossible objects (magic swords), and impossible events (people turn into toads).
D.	Time:	Remote.
E.	Place:	Remote or unreal (never-never land, deep forest).
F.	Language:	Coordinate. This *and* this, *then* this happened. Events unfold, but do not cause each other, so *because* (subordination) is rare. Little conversation. Often meter is poetic as in nursery rhymes: "And over the bridge and up the hill and under the deep green wood . . . we wove."

Figure 19.21 Examples of some of the distinctive features of the genre for fairy tales.

several studies (Haber & Haber, 1979; Lefton, 1977) have shown that children constrain their guesses of letter sequences by the rules of spelling as a function of their age, little constraint is found in the first grade, and heavy constraint by the end of elementary school. Unfortunately, we need good developmental evidence for these kinds of redundancies, particularly since some of them would not be expected to be important until much later ages.

VISUAL FIELD SIZE

As we showed in the previous chapter (pp. 374–375), redundancy increases visual acuity at each distance from the fovea. In effect this means that the same-sized feature can be detected farther into the periphery if it is made more redundant. In this sense, then, redundancy increases the size of the effective field of view. That is, we can see the same level of detail farther into the periphery as redundancy increases.

Figure 19.22 illustrates the possible effects of these changes. It also suggests that the size of the visual field can be changing from moment to moment in reading, rather than being fixed by characteristics of retinal sensitivity or neural coding. In general, the amount of redundancy is lower at the beginning of a paragraph than in the middle, and this implies that the size of the effective field of view is going to be

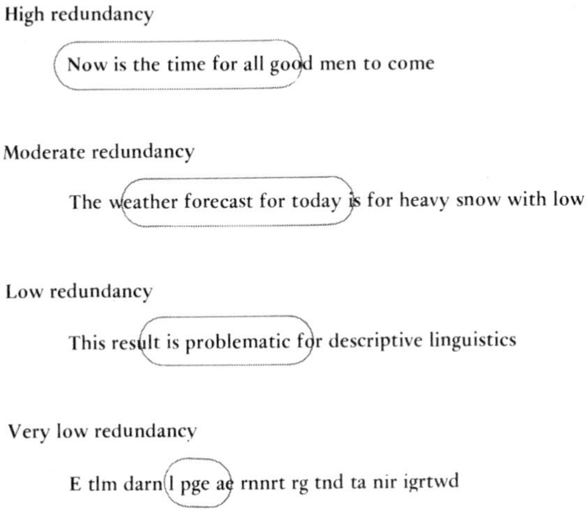

High redundancy

Now is the time for all good men to come

Moderate redundancy

The weather forecast for today is for heavy snow with low

Low redundancy

This result is problematic for descriptive linguistics

Very low redundancy

E tlm darn l pge ae rnnrt rg tnd ta nir igrtwd

Figure 19.22 A schematic example of the range of the effective field of view in which letter features could be analyzed, as a function of the redundancy available in the line of print. Haber & Haber, 1980.)

smaller. There already is evidence (Busswell, 1922) that fixations are closer together at the beginning of a paragraph than they are in the middle. A reasonable corollary to this is that if the size of the effective field of view is large, then so are the saccade distances. Thus, with large effective fields of view reading speeds can be higher.

We have already reviewed a substantial amount of evidence to suggest that readers do attend to information beyond the center of the fovea. What has not been studied in the experimental literature is how those distances vary as a function of redundancy of the text. In his work on eye–voice span, Geyer (1968) did show that the eye–voice span was larger for easy as compared to difficult text. While difficulty of text is a crude way of expressing redundancy, Geyer does have some evidence of a changing effective field of view size with redundancy.

SUCCESSIVE FIXATION AREAS

When eye movements are measured as a reader reads a passage, we can determine the average distance

moved by each saccade. In the example in Figure 19.1 the average distance was about 7 character spaces per movement. Since this is so easy a statistic to calculate, it has usually been assumed that it also provides a measure of the size of the effective field of view. But the data on acuity just reviewed suggest that the effective field of view is much larger. This means that the successive effective fields of view overlap from movement to movement. Figure 19.23 illustrates what this must mean. In our discussion of eye movements while exploring pictures and in visual search, we assumed that successive eye movements produced overlapping fields of view, but there has been relatively little attention paid to the implications of overlap in reading. It is unfortunate that the units on graphs specified in character spaces per fixation fool us into thinking that this is the unit of the size of the effective field of view.

The implications of overlap mean that each area of the text is looked at several times, initially by the peripheral retina, then by the parafoveal retina, then the fovea itself, and then by the parafoveal retina on the other side. Recognizing this multiplicity of views helps to understand three critically important theoretical problems underlying the reading process. First, overlapping fields of view promote a perceptual integration of the whole line of print in the same way as

Successive overlap of effective field of views

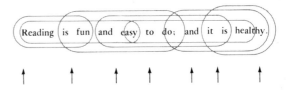

Reading is fun and easy to do; and it is healthy.

Arrows indicate the fixation centers
Average distance move = 7 character spaces
Effective field fo view = 25 character spaces
Each area of text seen 25/7 = 3½ times

Figure 19.23 A schematic example of the successive overlap of the effective field of views of successive fixations on a line of print. In this example the arrows indicate the center of each fixation. If the average distance moved is 7 character spaces, and the average effective field of view is 25 character spaces, then each area of the text is seen 25/7 or about 3.5 times.

integrating all of the views in a picture can lead to a constructed picture. Most readers report introspectively that they "see" a whole line even though their acuity would never permit that kind of clarity. As noted in Chapter 16, Hochberg (1979) has data to show that integration in pictures cannot occur unless it is cognitively guided, that is, unless the viewer has expectations of what he will see before he moves his eyes. Obviously, redundancy is the cognitive guidance to create this integration in reading.

Second, successive overlap provides the basis for peripheral vision to work. Parts of the sentence first come into view peripherally, then more centrally. This permits a time sharing of different levels of processing from different parts of the phrase or to different depths. When a part of the text first comes into view in the periphery only the most general and higher-level redundancies can be used. We certainly cannot see letter features or even whole letters at those distances. But we can be testing out semantic and syntactic hypotheses. What kind of a phrase are we in? Where are the punctuation marks located? How long is the phrase? Where are the sentence boundaries? And so forth. With the next fixation, this same area of text can now be seen with greater clarity and we can pick up word length and word shape so that we can acquire some general idea of the nature of the words. Syntax is going to be very powerful in isolating the functors from the content words. With those high-frequency words, particularly the functors, the shape and length are probably sufficient to provide exact identification. If the functors can be identified the syntactic information that follows from them provides us with even further information about what is coming in the text. The next fixation will bring that portion of the text directly over the fovea and now letter features themselves can be processed if needed, but in many cases there is already sufficient information. Some of Rayner's data (pp. 389–393) has already shown this happening.

Obviously none of this is useful if there is no context available or if the redundancy is very low because the text is difficult or is on a topic unfamiliar to the reader.

A third benefit of successive overlap is particu-larly important for English. English is notoriously difficult to process word by word, for each word has many alternative meanings and pronunciations. You can verify this in even the simplest of dictionaries if you try to find a word that has only one meaning. Consequently, when you encounter a word it is not always possible to determine which meaning is the appropriate one unless you have the context, that is, some of the text to the right of the word. Some of the ambiguity disappears if you only know the words to the left of the one you are trying to identify. But if you have the full syntax of the phrase, extending beyond the center of the fovea, it is a rare English sentence in which any ambiguity is left.

To delay the final assignment of meaning until the entire phrase is available, we need a way to pick up information from the right side of the phrase without losing what has been seen on the left side. One way of doing this is simply to take in all the words in a phrase and hold them in some unprocessed buffer storage until the entire phrase has been looked at. Then the phrase can be examined as a whole and meanings assigned to each of the words. But if the words in the phrase are picked up and stored in unprocessed form—unrelated to each other—as soon as a phrase exceeds several words, the short-term memory is overloaded and some of the phrase is forgotten. Successive overlap, however, provides a different technique. We do not have to depend on an uncoded memory; rather the successive overlap allows us to see the whole phrase. This notion is consistent with the large eye–voice spans that occur with high redundancy. It is a technique of getting lots of text to look at before final processing and pronunciation of it is completed.

This general discussion of redundancy has attempted to show how knowledge of the structure of the language, of the conventions of the way marks are put on the paper, and of the topic being read all have direct perceptual implications for the reading process. They improve effective acuity; they enlarge the effective field of view; they create successive overlap, all of which are direct aides in extracting meaning from reading text.

SUMMARY

Reading is defined as extraction of information from printed text, in which printed symbols are translated into a representation in which meaning is already accessible. The process requires active search of the text, carried out by saccadic movements of the eyes, in which most of the variation in reading speed is due to how far the eye moves between each fixation, rather than to the duration of each fixation or the speed of the movements.

Three models to describe the patterns of eye movements in reading were examined. The random model argues that the fixation choices are independent of both the text and the processing strategies of the reader, but are adjusted only by the overall level of difficulty of the text. The internal control model argues that the reader's processing of the text determines when and how far the eye moves.

Substantial evidence is reviewed to support the internal control model, thereby rejecting the random model. This includes evidence that readers pick up information ahead of the center of fixation, that difficult words cause extra fixations, and that correlations exist between eye movement patterns and features of the text. The external control model argues that in addition to internal control by the reader's processing, features of the text determine the positions of fixation. The difficulties of distinguishing this model from the internal control one were pointed out.

When reading orally, the eye is fixated on words ahead of those being pronounced by the voice. This eye–voice span changes as a function of overall difficulty level of the text, as well as with specific problems with individual words or structures.

The processing of text information is considered to be a form of analysis-by-synthesis, in which the reader extracts features from the page of print and organizes these according to predictions he makes based upon his prior knowledge of the redundancies among those features, in the language itself, and in his knowledge of the topic being read. We discussed each of these three sets of redundancies in detail.

Redundancies among the printed features of the text include the printing conventions used by typesetters and typists, the features comprising each letter of the alphabet, and the overall shape feature of very frequent words. In each case, knowing conventions, letters, or words means that partial visual features permit the reader to predict information without needing to identify each visual feature completely.

The second set of redundancies comes from the reader's knowledge of the language itself. These include the spelling rules that specify allowable combinations of word sequences. The third source of redundancy includes semantic relations among the words based upon the reader's knowledge of the meaning of words and of the topic, plus knowledge of genre, style, and author.

In the final section of the chapter we considered some of the perceptual consequences of an analysis-by-synthesis based upon available redundancies. The first of these is that the size of the field of view—the amount of the text that can be processed—varies with redundancy. The second is that there is substantial overlap of successive fields of view, so that each part of a line of text is seen several times, rather than once. Overlap makes perceptual integration of the line of text easier, provides a way for peripheral vision to pick up information, and makes it possible to avoid deciding what each word means in isolation, since with overlap, a number of words can be seen together.

SUGGESTED READINGS

A number of recent books have appeared that include material on the perceptual components of the reading process. These include relevant chapters in Gibson and Levin (1975), Reber and Scarborough (1977), Pirozzolo and Whitrock (1980), Levin and Williams (1970), and Kavanagh and Mattingly (1972). A number of the papers in Monty and Senders (1976) and Senders, Fisher, and Monty (1978) concern eye movements in reading, with Rayner (1978) providing an excellent summary.

References

Aderman, D., & Smith, E. E. Expectancy as a determinant of functional units in perceptual recognition. *Cognitive Psychology*, 1971, *2*, 117–129.

Aguilar, M., & Stiles, W. S. Saturation of the rod mechanism at high levels of stimulation. *Optica Acta*, 1954, *1*, 59–65.

Allport, D. A. The rate of assimilation of visual information. *Psychonomic Science*, 1968, *12*, 231–232.

Allport, D. A. Parallel encoding within and between elementary stimulus dimensions. *Perception and Psychophysics*, 1971, *10*, 104–108.

Alpern, M. Metacontrast. *Journal of the Optical Society of America*, 1953, *43*, 648–657.

Alpern, M. Muscular mechanisms. In H. Davson (Ed.), *The eye*. Vol. 3. New York: Academic Press, 1962.

Alpern, M. Effector mechanisms in vision. In J. A. Kling & L. A. Riggs (Eds.), *Woodworth and Schlosberg's experimental psychology*. (3rd ed.) New York: Holt, Rinehart and Winston, 1971. Pp. 369–394.

Alpern, M. Eye movements. In D. Jameson & L. M. Hurvich (Eds.), *Handbook of sensory physiology*. Vol. VII/4. *Sensory psychophysics*. Berlin: Springer-Verlag, 1972.

Aronson, E., & Tronick, E. Perceptual capacities in early infancy. In J. Eliot (Ed.), *Human development and cognitive processes*. New York: Holt, Rinehart and Winston, 1970.

Atkinson, R. C., & Juola, J. F. Search and detection processes in recognition memory. In D. H. Krantz, R. C. Atkinson, R. D. Lucek, & P. Suppes (Eds.), *Contemporary developments in mathematical psychology*. Vol. 1. San Francisco: Freeman, 1974.

Atkinson, R. C., & Shiffrin, R. M. Human memory: A proposed system and its control processes. In G. H. Bowen & J. T. Spence (Eds.), *The psychology of learning and motivation*. Vol. 2. New York: Academic Press, 1968.

Attneave, F. Some informational aspects of visual perception. *Psychological Review*, 1954, *61*, 183–193.

Attneave, F. *Application of information theory to psychology*. New York: Holt, Rinehart and Winston, 1959.

Attneave, F., & Olson, R. K. Inferences about visual mechanisms from monocular depth effects. *Psychonomic Science*, 1966, *4*, 133–134.

Ball, W., & Tronick, E. Infant responses to impending collision: Optical and real. *Science*, 1971, *171*, 818–820.

Bamber, D. Reaction times and error rates for "same–different" judgments of multi-dimensional stimuli. *Perception and Psychophysics*, 1969, *6*, 169–174.

Banks, M. S., Aslin, R. N., & Letson, R. D. Sensitive period for the development of human binocular vision. *Science*, 1975, *190*, 675–677.

Banks, M. S., & Salapatek, P. Contrast sensitivity function of the infant visual system. *Vision Research*, 1976, *16*, 867–869.

Barlow, H. B. Summation and inhibition in the frog's retina. *Journal of Physiology*, 1953, *119*, 69–88.

Barlow, H. B. Single units and sensation: A neuron doctrine for perceptual psychology. *Perception*, 1972, *1*, 371–394.

Baron, J. Successive stages in word recognition. In S. Dornic & P. M. A. Rabbitt (Eds.), *Attention and performance*. Vol. 4. New York: Academic Press, 1974.

Barrow, H. G., & Tenenbaum, J. M. Recovering intrinsic scene characteristics from images. In A. Hansen & E. Riseman (Eds.), *Computer vision systems*. New York: Academic Press, 1978.

Battersby, W. S., Oesterreich, R. E., & Sturr, J. F. Neural limitations of visual excitability: VII. Nonhomonymous retrochiasmal interaction. *American Journal of Physiology*, 1964, *206*, 1181–1188.

Beck, J. Perceptual grouping produced by line figures. *Perception and Psychophysics*, 1967, *2*, 491–495.

Beck, J. Similarity grouping and peripheral discriminability under uncertainty. *American Journal of Psychology*, 1972, *85*, 1–20.

Benson, C. W., & Yonas, A. Development of sensitivity to static pictorial depth information. *Perception and Psychophysics,* 1973, *13,* 361–366.

Berkeley, G. *An essay towards a new theory of vision.* Dublin: Jeremy Pepyat, 1709. Reprinted: New York: Dutton, 1922.

Berlyne, D. E. Attention. In E. Carterette & M. Friedman (Eds.), *Handbook of perception:* Vol. 1. *Historical and philosophical roots of perception.* New York: Academic Press, 1973.

Berry, R. N. Quantitative relations among vernier real depth and stereoscopic depth acuities. *Journal of Experimental Psychology,* 1948, *38,* 708–721.

Biederman, I. Perceiving real-world scenes. *Science* 1972, *177,* 77–79.

Biederman, I., On processing information from a glance at a scene: Some implications for a syntax and semantics of visual processing: In S. Treu (Ed.), *User-oriented design of interactive graphic systems.* New York: ACM, 1977, pp. 75–88.

Biederman, I., Glass, A., & Stacey, E. W. Searching for objects in real-world scenes. *Journal of Experimental Psychology,* 1973, *97,* 22–27.

Biederman, I., Rabinowitz, J., Glass, A., & Stacey, E. W. On the information extracted from a single glance at a scene. *Journal of Experimental Psychology,* 1974, *103,* 597–600.

Bjork, E. L., & Estes, W. K. Letter identification in relation to linguistic context and masking conditions. *Memory and Cognition,* 1973, *1,* 217–223.

Bjork, E. L., & Murray, J. T. On the nature of input channels in visual processing. *Psychological Review,* 1977, *84,* 472–484.

Blackwell, H. R. Psychophysical thresholds: Experimental studies of methods and measurements. *Bulletin of the Engineering Research Institute,* University of Michigan, 1953, No. 36.

Blake, R., & Camisa, J. Is binocular vision always monocular? *Science,* 1978, *208,* 1497–1499.

Blakemore, C., & Campbell, F. W. On the existence of neurons in the human visual system selectively sensitive to the orientation and size of retinal images. *Journal of Physiology,* 1969, *203,* 237–260.

Bloch, A. M. Expériences sur la vision. Paris: *Society Biologie Memoriale,* 1885, 37, 493–495.

Bond, E. K. Perception of form by the human infant. *Psychological Bulletin,* 1972, *77,* 225–245.

Boring. E. G. *Sensation and perception in the history of experimental psychology.* New York: Appleton-Century-Crofts, 1942.

Bornstein, M. H., Kessen, W., & Weiskopf, S. Color vision and hue categorization in young human infants. *Journal of Experimental Psychology: Human Perception and Performance,* 1976, *2,* 115–129.

Bouma, H. Visual recognition of isolated lower case letters. *Vision Research,* 1971, *11,* 459–474.

Bouma, H., & de Voogd, A. H. On the control of eye saccades in reading. *Vision Research,* 1974, *14,* 272–284.

Bower, T. G. R. Discrimination of depth in premotor infants. *Psychonomic Science,* 1964, *1,* 368.

Bower, T. G. R. Stimulus variables determining space perception in infants. *Science,* 1965, *149,* 88–89.

Bower, T. G. R., Broughton, J. M., & Moore, M. K. The coordination of visual and tactual input in infants. *Perception and Psychophysics,* 1970, *8,* 51–53.

Bower, T. G. R., Broughton, J. M., & Moore, M. K. Infant responses to approaching objects: An indicator of response to distal variables. *Perception and Psychophysics,* 1970, *9,* 193–196.

Boynton, R. M. Some temporal factors in vision. In W. A. Rosenblith (Ed.), *Sensory communication.* New York: Wiley, 1961. Pp. 739–756.

Boynton, R. M. Color vision. In J. A. Kling & L. A. Riggs (Eds.), *Woodworth and Schlosberg's experimental psychology.* (3rd ed.) New York: Holt, Rinehart and Winston, 1971. Pp. 315–368.

Boynton, R. M. Discrimination of homogeneous double pulses of light. In D. Jameson & L. M. Hurvich (Eds.), *Handbook of sensory physiology.* Vol. VII/4. *Sensory psychophysics.* Berlin: Springer-Verlag, 1972.

Boynton, R. M. *Human color vision.* New York: Holt, Rinehart and Winston, 1979.

Boynton, R. M., & Boss, D. E. The effect of background luminance and contrast upon visual search performance. *Illuminating Engineering,* 1971, *66,* 173–186.

Boynton, R. M., & Bush, W. R. Laboratory studies pertaining to visual air reconnaissance. Wright Air Development Center, Technical Report 55-304, Part 2, 1957. Pp. 1–46.

Boynton, R. M., Elworth, C., & Palmer, R. M. Laboratory studies pertaining to visual air reconnaissance. Wright Air Development Center, Technical Report 55–304, Part 3, 1958, Pp. 1–61.

Boynton, R. M., & Seigfried, J. Psychophysical estimates of on-responses to brief light flashes. *Journal of the Optical Society of America,* 1962, *52,* 720–721.

Boynton, R. M., Sturr, J. F., & Ikeda, M. Study of flicker by increment threshold technique. *Journal of the Optical Society of America,* 1961, *51,* 196–201.

Braunstein, M. L. *Depth perception through motion* New York: Academic Press, 1976.

Braunstein, M. L., & Payne, J. W. Perspective and form ratio as determinants of relative slant judgements. *Journal of Experimental Psychology,* 1969, *81,* 584–590.

Breitmeyer, B. G., & Ganz, L. Implications of sustained and transient channels for theories of visual pattern masking, saccadic suppression, and information processing. *Psychological Review,* 1976, *83,* 1–36.

Breitmeyer, B., Love, R., & Wepman, B. Contour suppression during stroboscopic motion and metacontrast. *Vision Research,* 1974, *14,* 1451–1456.

Brindley, G. S. Afterimages. *Scientific American,* 1963, *209* (Oct.), 84–93.

Brindley, G. S., & Merton, P. A. The absence of position sense in the human eye. *Journal of Psyiology,* 1960, *153,* 127–130.

Broadbent, D. E. *Perception and communication.* London: Pergamon, 1958.

Broadbent, D. E. *Decision and stress.* New York: Academic Press, 1971.

Bronson, G. The postnatal growth of visual capacity. *Child Development,* 1974, *45,* 873–890.

Brown, K. T., & Wanatabe, K. Isolation and identification of a reception potential from the pure cone fovea of the retina. *Nature* (London), 1962, *193,* 958–960.

Bruner, J. S. On perceptual readiness. *Psychological Review,* 1957, *64,* 123–152.

Bruner, J. S., & Postman, L. Perception, cognition and behavior, *Journal of Personality,* 1949, *18,* 14–31. (a)

Bruner, J. S. & Postman, L. On the perception of incongruity: A paradigm. *Journal of Personality*, 1949, *18*, 206–223. (b)

Buswell, G. T. Fundamental reading habits: A study of their development. *Education Monograph Supplement*, 1922, *21*.

Buswell, G. T. *How people look at pictures*. Chicago: University of Chicago Press, 1935.

Buswell, G. T. How adults read. *Supplementary Educational Monographs*, 1937, *45*.

Campbell, F. W., & Robson, J. G. Application of Fourier analysis to the visibility of gratings. *Journal of Physiology*, 1968, *197*, 551–566.

Carlson, V. R. Overestimation in size-constancy judgments. *American Journal of Psychology*, 1960, *73*, 199–213.

Carlson, V. R. Size constancy judgments and perceptual compromise. *Journal of Experimental Psychology*, 1962, *63*, 68–73.

Carr, T. H., & Bacharach, V. R. Perceptual tuning and conscious attention: Systems of input regulation in visual information processing. *Cognition*, 1976, *4*, 281–302.

Chapanis, A., & McCleary, R. A. Interposition as a cue for the perception of relative distance. *Journal of General Psychology*, 1953, *48*, 113–132.

Charnwood, J. R. B. *Essay on binocular vision*. London: Hutton, 1951.

Chase, W. G., & Simon, H. A. The mind's eye in chess. In W. G. Chase (Ed.), *Visual information processing*. New York: Academic Press, 1973. Pp. 215–282.

Cheatham, P. G. Visual perceptual latency as a function of stimulus brightness and contour shape. *Journal of Experimental Psychology*, 1952, *43*, 369–380.

Cheatham, P. G., & White, C. T. Temporal numerosity: I. Perceived number as a function of flash number and rate. *Journal of Experimental Psychology*, 1952, *44*, 447–451.

Clark, H. H., & Clark, E. V. *Psychology and language: An introduction to psycholinguistics*. New York: Harcourt, Brace, 1977.

Clark, W. C., Smith, A. H., & Rabe, A. Retinal gradients of outline distortion and binocular disparity as stimuli for slant. *Canadian Journal of Psychology*, 1956, *10*, 1–8.

Cohen, A. I. Vertebrate retinal cells and their organization. *Biological Reviews*, 1963, *38*, 427–459. Figure 2, p. 435.

Cohen, W. Spatial and textural characteristics of the Ganzfeld. *American Journal of Psychology*, 1957, *70*, 403–410.

Colegate, R. L., Hoffman, J. E., & Eriksen, S. W. Selective encoding from multielement visual displays. *Perception and Psychophysics*, 1973, *14*, 217–224.

Colthart, M. Iconic memory: A reply to Professor Holding. *Memory and Cognition*, 1975, *3*, 42–48.

Cooper, R. The development of recursion in pictorial perception. Paper presented at Conference on Picture Perception, Center for Research on Human Learning, University of Minnesota, July, 1975.

Corcoran, D. W. J. *Pattern recognition*. Baltimore: Penguin, 1971.

Coren, S. Subjective contours and apparent depth. *Psychological Review*, 1972, *79*, 339–367.

Coren, S., & Girgus, J. S. Illusions and constancies. In W. Epstein (Ed.), *Stability and constancy in visual perception*. New York: Wiley, 1977. Pp. 255–284.

Cornsweet, T. N. Stabilized images techniques. In M. A. Whitcomb (Ed.), *Recent developments in vision research*. Washington:

National Academy of Science—National Research Council Publication No. 1272, 1966.

Cornsweet, T. N. Information processing in the human visual system. *Stanford Research Institute Journal*, 1969 (Jan.), Feature Issue No. 5.

Cornsweet, T. N. *Visual perception*. New York: Academic Press, 1970.

Craik, F. I. M., & Lockhart, R. S. Levels of processing: A framework for memory research. *Journal of Verbal Learning and Verbal Behavior*, 1972, *11*, 671–684.

Craik, K. J. W. Origin of visual afterimages. *Nature*, 1940, *145*, 512.

Crawford, B. H. Visual adaptation in relation to brief conditioning stimuli. *Proceedings of the Royal Society* (London), Series B, 1947, *134B*, 283–300.

Dainoff, M., & Haber, R. N. How much help do repeated presentations give to recognition processes? *Perception and Psychophysics*, 1967, *2*, 131–136.

Davey, E. The intensity-time relation for multiple flashes of light in the peripheral retina. *Journal of the Optical Society of America*, 1952, *42*, 937–941.

Day, R. H., & McKenzie, B. Perceptual shape constancy in early infancy. *Perception*, 1973, *2*, 315–320.

de Groot, A. D. *Thought and choice in chess*. The Hague: Mouton, 1965.

Deregowski, J. B. Pictorial perception and culture. *Scientific American*, 1972, *227* (Nov.), 82–88.

DeValois, R. L. Processing intensity and wavelength information. *Investigative Ophthalmology*, 1972, *11*, 417–427.

DeValois, R. L., Abramov, I., & Mead, W. R. Single cell analysis of wavelength discrimination at the lateral geniculate nucleus in the macaque. *Journal of Neurophysiology*, 1967, *30*, 415–433.

DeValois, R. L., & DeValois, K. K. Neural coding of color. In E. C. Carterette & H. Friedman (Eds.), *Handbook of perception*. Vol. 5. New York: Academic Press, 1975. Pp. 117–166.

DeValois, R. L., & Marrocco, R. T. Single cell analysis of saturation discrimination in the macaque. *Vision Research*, 1973, *13*, 701–711.

Ditchburn, R. W., & Ginsburg, B. L. Vision with a stabilized retinal image. *Nature*, 1952, *170*, 36–37.

Dixon, N. F. *Subliminal perception: The nature of a controversy*. London: McGraw-Hill, 1971.

Dobson, V. Spectral sensitivity of the two-month infant as measured by the visually evoked cortical potential. *Vision Research*, 1976, *16*, 367–374.

Dodwell, P. C. *Visual pattern recognition*. New York: Holt, Rinehart and Winston, 1970.

Dodwell, P. C. *Perceptual processing: Stimulus equivalence and pattern recognition*. New York: Appleton-Century-Crofts, 1971.

Dodwell, P. C., & Engel, G. R. A theory of binocular fusion. *Nature*, 1963, *198*, 39–40, 70–74.

Doherty, M. E., & Keeley, S. M. On the identification of repeatedly presented brief visual stimuli. *Psychological Bulletin*, 1972, *78*, 142–156.

Doris, J., Casper, M., & Poresky, R. Differential brightness thresholds in infancy. *Journal of Experimental Child Psychology*, 1967, *5*, 522–535.

Doris, J., & Cooper, L. Brightness discrimination in infancy. *Journal of Experimental Child Psychology*, 1966, *3*, 31–39.

Dow, B. M. Functional classes of cells and their laminar distribution in monkey visual cortex. *Journal of Neurophysiology,* 1974, *37,* 927–946.

Dowling, J. E., & Boycott, B. B. Organization of the primate retina: Electron microscopy. *Proceedings of the Royal Society* (London), Series B, 1966, *166,* 80–111.

Dunker, K. Uber induzierte Bewegung. *Psychogische Forshung,* 1929, *12,* 180–259.

Ebenholtz, S. The constancies in object orientation: An algorithm processing approach. In W. Epstein (Ed.), *Stability and constancy in visual perception.* New York: Wiley, 1977. Pp. 71–90.

Efron, R. The duration of the present. *Annals of the New York Academy of Science,* 1967, *138,* 713–729.

Egeth, H., & Blecker, D. Differential effects of familiarity on judgments of sameness and difference. *Perception and Psychophysics,* 1071, *9,* 321–327.

Eichelman, W. H. Familiarity effects in the simultaneous matching task. *Journal of Experimental Psychology,* 1970, *86,* 275–282.

Enroth-Cugell, C., & Robson, J. G. The contract sensitivity of retinal ganglion cells of the cat. *Journal of Physiology,* 1966, *187,* 517–552.

Epstein, W. *Varieties of perceptual learning.* New York: McGraw-Hill, 1967.

Epstein, W. The process of "taking-into-account" in visual perception. *Perception,* 1973, *2,* 267–285.

Epstein, W. *Stability and constancy in visual perception.* New York: Wiley, 1977.

Epstein, W., & Park, J. Examination of Gibson's psychophysical hypothesis. *Psychological Bulletin,* 1964, *62,* 180–196.

Epstein, W., Park, J., & Casey, A. The current status of the size–distance hypothesis. *Psychological Bulletin,* 1961, *58,* 491–514.

Erdelyi, M. H. A new look at the New Look: Perceptual defence and vigilance. *Psychological Review,* 1974, *81,* 1–25.

Eriksen B. A., & Eriksen, C. W. Effects of noise letters upon the identification of a target letter in a nonsearch task. *Perception and Psychophysics.* 1974, *16,* 143–149.

Eriksen, C. W. Unconscious processes. In M. R. Jones (Ed.), *Nebraska symposium on motivation.* Lincoln: University of Nebraska Press, 1957.

Eriksen, C. W. Temporal luminance summation effects in backward and forward masking. *Perception and Psychophysics,* 1966, *1,* 87–92.

Eriksen C. W., & Hoffman, J. E. Temporal and spatial characteristics of selective encoding from visual displays, *Perception and Psychophysics,* 1972, *12,* 201–204.

Eriksen, C. W., & Hoffman, J. E. The extent of processing of noise elements during selective encoding from visual displays. *Perception and Psychophysics,* 1973, *14,* 155–160.

Eriksen C. W., & Hoffman, J. E. Selective attention: Noise suppression or signal enhancement. *Bulletin of the Psychonomic Society,* 1974, *4,* 587–589.

Eriksen, C. W., & Spencer, T. Rate of information processing in visual perception: Some results and methodological considerations. *Journal of Experimental Psychology Monograph,* 1969, *79* (2, Pt. 2).

Eriksson, E. S. The shape-slant in variance hypothesis in static perception. *Scandanavian Journal of Psychology,* 1967, *8,* 193–208.

Estes, W. K. Interactions of signal and background variables in visual processing, *Perception and Psychophysics,* 1972, *12,* 278–286.

Estes, W. K. Memory, perception, and decision in letter identification. In R. L. Solso (Ed.), *Information processing and cognition: The Loyola Symposium.* Hillsdale, N.J.: Lawrence Erlbaum Associates, 1975. P. 3030. (a)

Estes, W. K. The locus of inferential and perceptual processes in letter identification. *Journal of Experimental Psychology: General,* 1975, *104,* 122–145. (b)

Estes, W. K. On the interaction of perception and memory in reading. In D. Le Berge & S. J. Samuels (Eds), *Basic processes in reading: Perception and comprehension.* Hillsdale, N. J.: Lawrence Erlbaum Associates, 1977. Pp. 1–25.

Estes, W. K., Allmeyer, D. H., & Reder, S. M. Serial position functions for letter identification at brief and extended exposure durations. *Perception and Psychophysics,* 1976, *19,* 1–15.

Estes, W. K., Bjork, E. L., & Skaar, E. Detection of single letters in words with changing versus unchanging mask characteristics. *Bulletin of the Psychonomic Society,* 1974, *3,* 201–203.

Euchid *Optics* c. 300 B.C.

Fagan, J. F. Infant color perception. *Science,* 1974, *183,* 973–975.

Fain, G. L., & Dowling, J. E. Intracellular recordings from single rods and cones in the mud-puppy retina. *Science,* 1973, *180,* 1178–1181.

Fantz, R. Visual perception from birth as shown by pattern selectivity. *Annals of the New York Academy of Science,* 1968, *118,* 793–814.

Fantz, R. L. Ordy, J. M., & Velelf M. S. Maturation of pattern vision in infants during the first six months. *Journal of Comparative and Physiological Psychology,* 1962, *55,* 907–917.

Farber, J., & Rosinsla, R. R. Geometric transformation of pictured space. *Perception,* 1980, *1,* 269–282.

Fechner, G. *Elements of psychophysics,* 1860. English ed. of Vol. 1, edited by H. E. Adler, D. H. Howes, & E. G. Boring. New York: Holt, Rinehart and Winston, 1966.

Fehrer, E., & Biederman, I. A comparison of reaction time and verbal report in the detection of masked stimuli. *Journal of Experimental Psychology,* 1962, *64,* 126–130.

Fehrer, E., & Raab, D. Reaction time to stimuli masked by metacontrast. *Journal of Experimental Psychology,* 1962, *63,* 143–147.

Festinger, L., & Canon, L. K. Information about spatial location based on knowledge about efference. *Psychological Review,* 1965, *72,* 373–384.

Flock, H. R., & Moscatelli, A. Variables of surface texture and accuracy of space perception. *Perceptual and Motor Skills,* 1964, *19,* 327–334.

Fodor, J. A., Bever, T. G., & Garreth, M. E. *The psychology of language: An Introduction to psycholinguistics and generative grammar.* New York: McGraw-Hill, 1974.

Forsyth, D. M., & Chapanis, A. Counting repeated light flashes as a function of their number, their rate of presentation, and retinal location stimulated. *Journal of Experimental Psychology,* 1958, *56,* 385–391.

Fraisse, P. *The psychology of time.* New York: Harper, 1963.

Friedman, S. L., & Stevenson, M. Perception of movement in pictures. In M. A. Hagen (Ed.), *The perception of pictures.* Vol. 1. New York: Academic Press, 1980.

Frisby, J. P. Real and apparent movement—same or different mechanisms? *Vision Research,* 1972, *12,* 1051–1056.

Fuchs, A. F. The neurophysiology of saccades. In R. A. Monty & J. W. Senders (Eds.), *Eye movement and psychological processes.* Hinsdale, N. J.: Lawrence Erlbaum Associates, 1976. Pp. 39–54.

Ganz, L. Temporal factors in visual perception. In E. C. Carterette & H. Friedman (Eds.), *Handbook of perception.* Vol. 5. New York: Academic Press, 1975. Pp. 169–231.

Gardner, G. T. Evidence for independent parallel channels in tachistoscopic perception. *Cognitive Psychology,* 1973, *4,* 130–155.

Garner, W. R. *Uncertainty and structure as psychological concepts.* New York: Wiley, 1962.

Garner, W. R., Hake, H. W., & Eriksen, C. W. Operationism and the concept of perception. *Psychological Review,* 1956, *63,* 317–329.

Geer, J. P., & Moraal, J. Peripheral pattern identification: An experiment on dynamic vision. *I.Z.F. Report,* 1962, Number 18.

Geyer, J. J. Perceptual systems in reading: The prediction of a temporal eye-voice span. In H. K. Smith (Ed.), *Perception and reading.* Newark, Del.: International Reading Association, 1968

Gibson, E. J. *Principles of perceptual learning and development.* New York: Appleton-Century-Crofts, 1969.

Gibson, E. J. How perception really develops: A view from outside the network. In D. Le Berge & S. J. Samuels (Eds.), *Basic processes in reading: Perception and comprehension.* Hillsdale, N.J.: Lawrence Erlbaum Associates, 1977. Pp. 155–173.

Gibson, E. J. & Levin, H. *The psychology of reading.* Cambridge, Mass.: MIT, 1975.

Gibson, E. J., Pick, A. D., Osser, H., & Hammond, M. The role of grapheme-phoneme correspondence in the perception of words. *American Journal of Psychology,* 1962, *75,* 554–570.

Gibson, E. J., Shurcliff, A., & Yonas, A. Utilization of spelling patterns by deaf and hearing subjects. In H. Levin & J. P. Williams (Eds.), *Basic studies in reading.* New York: Basic Books, 1970. Pp. 57–73.

Gibson, J. J. *The perception of the visual world.* Boston: Houghton Mifflin, 1950.

Gibson, J. J. Visually controlled locomotion and visual orientation in animals. *British Journal of Psychology,* 1958, *49,* 182–194.

Gibson, J. J. *The senses considered as perceptual systems.* Boston: Houghton Mifflin, 1966.

Gibson, J. J., & Dibble, F. N. Exploratory experiments on the stimulus conditions for the perception of visual surface. *Journal of Experimental Psychology,* 1952, *43,* 414–419.

Gibson, J. J., & Gibson, E. J. Perceptual learning: Differentiation or enrichment? *Psychological Review,* 1955, *62,* 1–32.

Gilchrist, A. L. Perceived lightness depends on perceived spatial arrangement. *Science,* 1977, *195,* 185–187.

Gilchrist, A. L. Color perception without contrast. Paper presented at the Lake Ontario Vision Establishment Conference, February, 1978.

Gilchrist, A. L. The perception of surface blacks and whites. *Scientific American,* 1979, *240* (March), 112–125.

Gilinsky, A. S., & Cohen, H. H. Reaction time to change in visual orientation. *Perception and Psychophysics,* 1972, *11,* 129–135.

Gogel, W. C. Equidistance tendency and its consequences. *Psychological Bulletin,* 1965, *64,* 153–163.

Gogel, W. C. The metric of visual space. In W. Epstein (Ed.), *Stability and constancy in visual perception.* New York: Wiley, 1977. Pp. 129–182.

Goldiamond, I., & Hawkins, W. I. Vexierversuch: The log relationship between word-frequency and recognition obtained in the absence of stimulus words. *Journal of Experimental Psychology,* 1958, *56,* 457–463.

Goldman, M., & Hagen, M. A. *The forms of caricature psysiognomy and political bias.* 1980, in press.

Goldwater, B. C. Psychological significance of pupillary movements. *Psychological Bulletin,* 1972, *77,* 340–355.

Gough, P. B. One second of reading, In J. P. Kavanagh & I. G. Mattingly (Eds.), *Language by ear and by eye.* Cambridge: MIT, 1972. Pp. 331–358.

Gould, J. Looking at pictures. In R. A. Monty & J. W. Senders (Eds.), *Eye movements and psychological processes.* Hillsdale, N.J.: Lawrence Erlbaum Associates, 1976. Pp. 323–346.

Gould, J. D., & Dill, A. Eye movement parameters and pattern recognition. *Perception & Psychophysics,* 1969, *6,* 311–320.

Graham, C. H. (Ed.), *Vision and visual perception.* New York: Wiley, 1965.

Green, D. M., & Swets, J. *Signal detection theory and psychophysics.* New York: Wiley, 1966.

Gregory, R. L. Visual illusions. In B. Foss (Ed.), *New horizons in psychology.* Baltimore: Penquin, 1966.

Gregory, R. L. *Eye and brain.* New York: McGraw-Hill, 1969.

Gregory, R. L. *The intelligent eye,* London: Weidenfeld and Nicholson, 1970.

Grimsdale, R. L., Sumner, F. H., Tunis, C. J., & Kilburn, T. A system for the automatic recognition of patterns. *Proceedings of the Institute of Electrical Engineers,* 1959, *106,* 210–221.

Gruber, H. E., & Clark, W. C. Perception of slanted surfaces. *Perceptual and Motor Skills,* 1956, *6,* 97–106.

Gulick, W. L., & Lawson, R. B. *Human stereopsis.* New York: Oxford, 1976.

Guzman, A. Computer recognition of three-dimensional objects in a visual scene. Unpublished Ph.D. dissertation, MIT, 1968.

Gyr, J. W. Is a theory of direct visual perception adequate? *Psychological Bulletin,* 1972, *77,* 246–261.

Haber, L. R., & Haber, R. N. Acquisition of spelling rules. Paper presented at the Psychonomics Society Convention, November, 1979.

Haber, L. R., & Haber, R. N. The spelling canon for English monosyllabic words. Unpublished paper, 1980.

Haber, R. N. A replication of selective attention and coding in visual perception. *Journal of Experimental Psychology,* 1964, *67,* 402–404. (a).

Haber, R. N. The effects of coding strategy on perceptual memory. *Journal of Experimental Psychology,* 1964, *68,* 257–262. (b).

Haber, R. N. Effect of prior knowledge of the stimulus word on word-recognition processes. *Journal of Experimental Psychology,* 1965, *69,* 282–286.

Haber, R. N. (Ed.), *Information processing approaches to visual perception.* New York: Holt, Rinehart and Winston, 1969.

Haber, R. N. Information processing. In E. Carterette & M. Friedman (Eds.), *Handbook of perception*. Vol. 1. New York: Academic Press, 1973.

Haber, R. N. Control of eye movements during reading. In R. A. Monty & J. W. Senders (Eds.), *Eye movements and psychological processes*. Hillsdale, N.J.: Lawrence Erlbaum Associates, 1976. Pp. 443–451.

Haber, R. N. Leonardo: Our first theorist on the perception of pictures. In C. F. Nodune & D. F. Fisher (Eds.) *Perception and pictorial representation*. New York: Holt, Rinehart and Winston, 1979. Pp. 84–99.

Haber, R. N. Detection of misprint errors: Evidence of semantic control over reading. Unpublished paper, 1980.

Haber, R. N., Haber, L. R., & Furlin, K. Word length and word shape as sources of information in reading. Unpublished manuscript, 1980.

Haber, R. N., & Hershenson, M. The effects of repeated brief exposures on the growth of a percept. *Journal of Experimental Psychology*, 1965, 69, 40–46.

Haber, R. N., & Hershenson, M. *The psychology of visual perception*. (1st ed.) New York: Holt, Rinehart and Winston, 1973.

Haber, R. N., & Nathanson, L. S. Post-retinal storage? — Parks' camel as seen through the eye of a needle. *Perception and Psychophysics*, 1968, 3, 349–355.

Haber, R. N., & Standing, L. G. Clarity and recognition of masked and degraded stimuli. *Psychonomic Science*, 1968, 13, 83–84.

Haber, R. N., & Standing, L. G. Direct measures of short-term visual storage. *Quarterly Journal of Experimental Psychology*, 1969, 21, 43–54.

Haber, R. N., & Standing, L. G. Direct estimates of apparent duration of a flash followed by visual noise. *Canadian Journal of Psychology*, 1970, 24, 216–229.

Hadad, G. M., & Steinman, R. M. The smallest voluntary saccade: Implications for fixation. *Vision Research*, 1973, 13, 1075–1086.

Hagen, M. A. The development of sensitivity to cast and attached shadows in pictures as information for the direction of the source of illumination. *Perception and Psychophysics*, 1976, 20, 25–28. (a).

Hagen, M. A. Influence of picture surface and station point on the ability to compensate for oblique view in pictorial perception. *Developmental Psychology*, 1976, 12, 57–63. (b).

Hagen, M. A. (Ed.). *The perception of pictures*. New York: Academic Press, 1980, 2 volumes.

Hagen, M. A., & Elliott, H. B. An investigation of the relationship between viewing condition and preference for true and modified perspective in adults. *Journal of Experimental Psychology: Human Perception and Performance*, 2, 479–490.

Hagen, M. A., Glick, R., & Morse, B. The role of two-dimensional surface characteristics in pictured depth perception. 1980, in press.

Hagen, M. A., & Jones, R. K. Cultural effects in pictorial perception: How many words is one picture really worth? In R. Walk & H. Pick (Eds.), *Perception and experience*. New York: Plenum, 1978. Pp. 171–212.

Haith, M. M., Bergman, T., & Moore, M. J. Eye contact and face scanning in early infancy. *Science*, 1977, 198, 853–855.

Haith, M. M., & Campos, J. J. Human infancy. In M. R. Rosen-zweig & L. W. Porter (Eds.), *Annual review of psychology*, 1977, 28, 251–294.

Hanson, A., & Riseman, E. (Eds.), *Computer vision systems*. New York: Academic Press, 1978.

Harris, C. S. Perceptual adaptation to inverted, reversed, and displaced vision. *Psychological Review*, 1965, 72, 419–444.

Harris, C. S., & Gibson, A. R. Is orientation-specific color adaptation in human vision due to edge detectors, afterimages, or "dipoles"? *Science*, 1968, 162, 1506–1507.

Harris, C. S., & Haber, R. N. Selective attention and coding in visual perception. *Journal of Experimental Psychology*, 1963, 65, 328–333.

Harter, M. R., & White, C. T. Perceived number and evoked cortical potentials. *Science*, 1967, 156, 406–408.

Hartline, H. K., & Ratliff, F. Inhibitory interaction of receptor units in the eye of *Limulus*. *Journal of General Physiology*, 1957, 40, 357–376.

Hay, J., & Pick, H., Jr. Visual and proprioceptive adaptation to optical displacement of the visual stimulus. *Journal of Experimental Psychology*, 1966, 71, 150–158.

Hayek, R. A. *The sensory order*. Chicago: University of Chicago Press, 1952.

Haynes, H., White, B. L., & Held, R. Visual accommodation in human infants. *Science*, 1965, 148, 528–530.

Hebb, D. O. *The organization of behavior*. New York: Wiley, 1949.

Hecht, S. Vision: II. The nature of the photoreceptor process. In C. Murchinson (Ed.), *A handbook of general experimental psychology*. Worcester: Clark University Press, 1934. Pp. 704–828.

Hecht, S., & Mintz, E. U. The visibility of single lines at various illuminations and the retinal basis of visual resolution. *Journal of General Physiology*, 1939, 22, 593–612.

Hecht, S., Peskin, J. C., & Patt, M. Intensity discriminations in the human eye: II. Relationship between $\Delta I/I$ and intensity for different parts of the spectrum. *Journal of General Physiology*, 1938, 22, 7–19.

Hecht, S., Shlaer, S., & Pirenne, M. H. Energy, quanta, and vision. *Journal of General Physiology*, 1942, 25, 819–840.

Heckenmuller, E. G. Stabilization of the retinal image: A review of method, effects and theory. *Psychological Bulletin*, 1965, 63, 157–169.

Heinemann, E. G. Simultaneous brightness induction as a function of inducing - and test-field luminances. *Journal of Experimental Psychology*, 1955, 50, 89–96.

Held, R. Plasticity in sensory motor systems. *Scientific American*, 1965, 211, 84–94.

Held, R., & Bossom, J. Neonatal deprivation and adult rearrangement: Complementary techniques for analyzing plastic sensory-motor coordination. *Journal of Comparative and Physiological Psychology*, 1961, 54, 33–37.

Held, R., & Freedman, S. J. Plasticity in human sensorimotor control. *Science*, 1963, 142, 455–462.

Held, R., & Gottlieb, N. A technique for studying adaptation to disarranged hand-eye coordination. *Perceptual and Motor Skills*, 1958, 8, 83–86.

Held, R., & Hein, A. V. Adaptation of disarranged hand-eye coordination contingent upon re-afferent stimulation. *Perceptual and Motor Skills*, 1958, 8, 87–90.

Helmholtz, H. von. *Physiological optics*, 1850. (J. P. C. Southall, Ed.) Optical Society of America, 1925.

Helmholtz, H. von. *Treatise on physiological optics.* Vol. III. (Translated from the 3rd German ed., 1867, J. P. C. Southall, Ed.) New York: Dover, 1962.

Henle, M. An experimental investigation of past experience as a determinant of form perception. *Journal of Experimental Psychology,* 1942, *30,* 1–22.

Hering, E. *Outlines of a theory of the light sense,* 1877. Cambridge, Mass.: Harvard University Press, 1964.

Hershenson, M. Visual discrimination in the human newborn. *Journal of Comparative and Physiological Psychology,* 1964, *58,* 270–276.

Hershenson, M. Development of the perception of form. *Psychological Bulletin,* 1967, *67,* 326–336.

Hershenson, M. Stimulus structure, cognitive structure, and the perception of letter arrays. *Journal of Experimental Psychology,* 1969, *79,* 327–335. (a).

Hershenson, M. Perception of letter arrays as a function of absolute retinal locus. *Journal of Experimental Psychology,* 1969, *80,* 201–202. (b).

Hershenson, M. The development of visual perceptual systems. In H. Moltz (Ed.), *The ontogenesis of vertebrate behavior.* New York: Academic Press, 1971. Pp. 29–56.

Hershenson, M. Verbal report and visual matching latency as a function of the pronounceability of letter arrays. *Journal of Experimental Psychology,* 1972, *96,* 104–109.

Hershenson, M., & Haber, R. N. The role of meaning in the perception of briefly exposed words. *Canadian Journal of Psychology,* 1965, *19,* 42–46.

Hirsh, I. J., & Sherrick, C. E. Perceived order in different sense modalities. *Journal of Experimental Psychology,* 1961, *62,* 423–432.

Hochberg, J. E. The psychophysics of pictorial perception. *Audio-Visual Communication Review,* 1962, *10,* 22–54.

Hochberg, J. In the mind's eye. In R. N. Haber (Ed.), *Contemporary theory and research in visual perception.* New York: Holt, Rinehart and Winston, 1968. Pp. 303–331.

Hochberg, J. Attention, organization and consciousness. In D. I. Mostofsky (Ed.), *Attention: Contemporary theory and analysis.* New York: Appleton-Century-Crofts, 1970. Pp. 99–124.

Hochberg, J. Perception: I. Color and shape. In J. A. Kling and L. A. Riggs (Eds.), *Woodworth and Schlosberg's Experimental Psychology.* (3rd ed.) New York: Holt, Rinehart and Winston, 1971. Pp. 395–474. (a)

Hochberg, J. Perception: II. Space and movement. In J. A. Kling and L. A. Riggs (Eds.), *Woodworth and Schlosberg's Experimental Psychology.* (3rd ed.) New York: Holt, Rinehart and Winston, 1971. Pp. 475–550. (b)

Hochberg, J. The representation of things and people. In E. H. Gombrich, J. Hochberg, & M. Black (Eds.), *Art, perception and reality.* Baltimore: John Hopkins University Press, 1972. Pp. 47–94.

Hochberg, J. Organization and the Gestalt tradition. In E. Carterette & M. Friedman (Eds.), *Handbook of perception.* Vol. 1. New York: Academic Press, 1973. Chapter 10.

Hochberg, J. Toward a speech-plan eye-movement model and reading. In R. A. Monty & J. W. Senders (Eds.), *Eye movements and psychological precesses.* Hillsdale, N.J.: Lawrence Erlbaum Associates, 1976. Pp. 396–416.

Hochberg, J. E. Art and perception. In E. C. Carterette & H. Friedman (Eds.), *Handbook of perception,* Vol. 10. New York: Academic Press, 1978.

Hochberg, J. Perception of successive views. *Science,* 1980, in press.

Hochberg, J. Some of the things that pictures are. In C. F. Nodine & D. F. Fisher (Eds.) *Perception and pictorial representation.* New York: Holt, Rinehart and Winston, 1979. Pp. 17–41.

Hochberg, J., & Brooks, V. The psychophysics of form: Reversible-perspective drawings of spatial objects. *American Journal of Psychology,* 1960, *73,* 337–354.

Hochberg, J., & Brooks, V. Pictorial recognition as an unlearned ability: A study of one child's performance. *American Journal of Psychology,* 1962, *75,* 624–628.

Hochberg, J., & Brooks, V. The perception of motion pictures. In E. C. Carterette & M. P. Friedman (Eds.), *Handbook of perception.* Vol. 10. New York: Academic Press, 1978.

Hochberg, J., & McAlister, E. A quantitative approach to figural "goodness." *Journal of Experimental Psychology,* 1953, *46,* 361–364.

Hochberg, J., Triebel, W., & Seaman, G. Color adaptation under conditions of homogeneous stimulation (Ganzfeld). *Journal of Experimental Psychology,* 1951, *41,* 153–159.

Hoffman, K. P., & Stone, J. Conduction velocity of afferents to cat visual cortex: A correlation with receptive field properties. *Brain Research,* 1971, *32,* 460–466.

Holst, E. von. Relations between the central nervous system and the peripheral organs. *British Journal of Animal Behavior,* 1954, *2,* 89–94.

Holst, E., von, & Mittelstaadt, H. Das Reafferenz-princip. *Die Naturwissensdraften,* 1950, *20,* 464–467.

Holway, A. H., & Boring, E. G. Determinants of apparent visual size with distance variant. *American Journal of Psychology,* 1941, *54,* 21–37.

Howard, I. P., & Templeton, W. B. *Human spatial orientation.* New York: Wiley, 1966.

Hubel, D. H., & Wiesel, T. N. Receptive fields, binocular interaction, and functional architecture in the cat's visual cortex. *Journal of Physiology,* 1962, *160,* 106–154.

Hubel, D. H., & Weisel, T. N. Binocular interaction in striate cortex of kittens reared with artificial squint. *Journal of Neurophysiology,* 1965, *28,* 1041–1059.

Hubel, D. H., & Wiesel, T. N. Receptive fields and functional architecture of monkey striate cortex. *Journal of Physiology,* 1968, *195,* 215–243.

Hubel, D. H., & Wiesel, T. N. Stereoscopic vision in macaque monkey. *Nature,* 1970, *225,* 41–42.

Hudson, W. Pictorial depth perception in subcultural groups in Africa. *Journal of Social Psychology,* 1960, *52,* 183–208.

Huey, E. B. *The psychology and pedagogy of reading.* New York: Macmillan, 1908. Republished by MIT Press, 1968.

Hyman, R. Stimulus information as a determinant of reaction time. *Journal of Experimental Psychology,* 1953, *45,* 188–196.

Ittelson, W. H. *Visual space perception.* New York: Springer-Verlag, 1960.

Jakobson, R., & Halle, M. *Fundamentals of language.* 's-Gravenhage:Mouton, 1956.

James, W. *The principles of psychology.* New York: Holt, Rinehart and Winston, 1890.

Johansson, G. Visual perception of rotary motion as transformations of conic sections. *Psychologia,* 1974, *17,* 226–237.

Johansson, G. Spatial temporal differentiation and integration in visual motor perception. *Psychological Review,* 1976, *35,* 379–393.

Judd, D. B. Chromaticity sensibility to stimulus differences. *Journal of the Optical Society of America,* 1932, *22,* 72–108.

Judd, D. B., & Wyszecki, G. W. *Color in business, science, and industry.* (2nd ed.) New York: Wiley, 1963.

Julesz, B. *Foundations of cyclopean perception.* Chicago: University of Chicago Press, 1971.

Kahneman, D. Time intensity reciprocity under various conditions of adaptation and backward masking. *Journal of Experimental Psychology,* 1966, *71,* 543–549.

Kahneman, D. Method, findings and theory in studies of visual masking. *Psychological Bulletin,* 1968, *70,* 404–425.

Kahneman, D. *Attention and effort.* New York: Prentice-Hall, 1973.

Kandel, G. L. A psychophysical study of some monocular and binocular factors in early adaptation. Unpublished doctoral dissertation, University of Rochester, 1958.

Karmel, B. Z., & Maisel, E. B. A neuronal activity model for infant visual attention. In L. B. Cohen & P. Salapatek (Eds.), *Infant perception: From sensation to cognition.* New York: Academic Press, 1975. Pp. 78–131.

Katz, D. *The world of color.* London: Kegan Paul, 1935. Translated by R. B. MacLeod & C. W. Fox.

Kaufman, L. On the nature of binocular disparity. *American Journal of Psychology,* 1964, *77,* 373–402.

Kaufman, L., & Pitblado, C. B. Further observations on the nature of effective binocular disparities. *American Journal of Psychology,* 1965, *78,* 379–391.

Kavanagh, J. P., & Mattingly, I. G. *Language by ear and by eye.* Cambridge: MIT, 1972.

Keesey, U. T. Effects of involuntary eye movements on visual acuity. *Journal of the Optical Society of America,* 1960, *50,* 769–774.

Keller, E. L., & Robinson, D. A. Absence of a stretch reflex in extraocular muscles of the monkey. *Journal of Neurophysiology,* 1971, *34,* 908–919.

Kelly, D. H. Effects of sharp edges in a flickering field. *Journal of the Optical Society of America,* 1959, *49,* 730–732.

Kelly, D. H. Visual responses to time-dependent stimuli. *Journal of the Optical Society of America,* 1961, *51,* 422–429.

Kelly, D. H. Theory of flicker and transient responses: I. Uniform fields. *Journal of the Optical Society of America,* 1971, *61,* 537–546.

Kelly, D. H. Flicker. In D. Jameson & L. M. Hurvich (Eds.), *The handbook of sensory physiology.* Vol. VII/4. *Sensory psychophysics.* Berlin: Springer-Verlag, 1972.

Kennedy, J. M. Picture perception and phantom contours. In C. F. Nodine and D. F. Fisher (Eds.) *Perception and pictorial representation.* New York: Holt, Rinehart and Winton, 1979. Pp. 167–195.

Kessen, W., Salapatek, P., & Haith, M. M. The visual response of the human newborn to linear contour. *Journal of Experimental Child Psychology,* 1972, *13,* 9–20.

Kinohla, R. A., & Wolfe, J. M. The order of visual processing: "Top-down," "bottom-up," or "middle-out." *Perception and Psychophysics,* 1979, *25,* 225–231.

Klapp, S. Implicit speech inferred from response latencies in same–different decision. *Journal of Experimental Psychology,* 1971, *91,* 262–267.

Klein, G. S. Semantic power of words measured through the interference with color naming. *American Journal of Psychology,* 1964, *77,* 576–588.

Knudsen, E. I., & Konishi, M. A neural map of auditory space in the owl. *Science,* 1978, *200,* 795–797.

Koffka, K. *Principles of Gestalt psychology.* New York: Harcourt Brace, 1935.

Kohler, I. *The formation and transformation of the perceptual world.* (Tr. by H. Fiss.) International Universities Press, 1964. Originally *Über Aufbau and Wandlungen der Wahrnehmungswelt.* Vienna: R. M. Rohrer, 1951.

Kolers, P. A. Some differences between real and apparent movement. *Vision Research,* 1963, *3,* 191–206.

Kolers, P. A. Three stages of reading. In H. Levin & J. P. Williams (Eds.), *Basic studies in reading.* New York: Basic Books, 1970. Pp. 90–118.

Kolers, P. A. Reading pictures: Some cognitive aspects of visual perception. In T. S. Huang & O. J. Tretiak (Eds.), *Picture bandwidth compression.* New York: Gordon Beach, 1972. (a)

Kolers, P. A. *Aspects of motion perception.* New York: Pergamon, 1972. (b)

Kolers, P. A. Buswell's discoveries. In R. A. Monty & J. W. Senders (Eds.), *Eye movements and psychological processes.* Hillsdale, N. J.: Lawrence Erlbaum Associates, 1976. Pp. 373–395.

Kolers, P. A., & Eden, M. *Recognizing patterns: Studies in living and automatic systems,* Cambridge, Mass.: MIT, 1968.

Kolers, P. A., & Lewis, C. Bounding of letter sequences and the integration of visually presented words. *Acta Psychologica,* 1972, *36,* 112–124.

Kopfermann, H. Psychologische Untersuchungen uber die Wirkung zweidimensionaler Darstellungen korperlicher Gebilde. *Psychologische Forschung,* 1930, *13,* 293–364.

Kornheiser, A. S. Adaptation to laterally displaced vision: A review. *Psychological Bulletin,* 1976, *83,* 783–816.

Kristofferson, A. B. Attention and psychophysical time. *Acta Psychologica,* 1967, *27,* 93–100.

Kroll, J. F. Familiarity and expectancy in the perception of words and letter arrays. Unpublished doctoral dissertation, Brandeis University, 1977.

Kroll, J. F., & Hershenson, M. Two stages in visual matching. *Canadian Journal of Psychology,* 1980, *33,* in press.

Krueger, L. Effect of irrelevant surrounding material on speed of "same"–"different" judgments of two adjacent letters. *Journal of Experimental Psychology,* 1973, *98,* 252–259.

Krueger, L. E. A theory of perceptual matching. *Psychological Review,* 1978, *85,* 278–304.

Kuffler, S. W. Discharge patterns and functional organization of mammalian retina. *Journal of Neurophysiology,* 1953, *16,* 37–68.

Kypriotaki, L. There came a wind like a bugle: From linguistic analysis to literary criticism. Paper presented at the Southeastern Conference on Linguistics. Athens, Georgia. April, 1972.

Lackner, J. A. A device for investigating adaptation to sensory arrangement. *Journal of Psychology,* 1973, *85,* 137–141.

Lackner, J. A. Adaptation to displaced vision: Role of proprioception. *Perceptual and Motor Skills,* 1974, *38,* 1251–1256.

Lackner, J. R. Adaptation to visual and proprioceptive rearrangement: Origins of the differential effectiveness of active and passive movements. *Perception and Psychophysics,* 1977, *81,* 55–59.

Lappin, J. S. Attention in the identification of stimuli in complex visual displays. *Journal of Experimental Psychology*, 1967, *75*, 321–328.

Latour, P. L. Visual threshold during eye movements. *Vision Research*, 1962, *2*, 261–262.

LeBerge, D., & Samuels, S. J. *Basic processes in reading: Perception and comprehension.* Hillsdale, N. J.: Lawrence Erlbaum Associates, 1977.

Lee, D. N. Visual information during locomotion. In R. B. MacLeod & H. L. Pick, Jr., *Perception: Essays in honor of James J. Gibson.* Ithaca, N. Y.: Cornell University Press, 1974. Pp. 250–267.

Lee, D. N. The functions of vision. In H. L. Pick & E. Saltzman (Eds.), *Models of perceiving and processing information.* New York: Lawrence Erlbaum Associates, 1977. Pp. 159–170.

Lee, D. N., & Aronson, E. Visual proprioceptive control of standing in human infants. *Perception and Psychophysics,* 1974, *15*, 529–532.

Lee, D. N., & Lishman, J. R. Visual proprioceptive control of stance. *Journal of Human Movement Studies,* 1975, *1*, 87–95.

Lee, D. N., & Lishman, R. Visual control of locomotion. *Scandinavian Journal of Psychology,* 1977, *18*, 224–230.

Lefton, L. A. Guessing and the order-of-approximate effect. *Journal of Experimental Psychology,* 1973, *101*, 401–403 (a)

Lefton, L. A. Metacontrast: A review. *Perception and Psychophysics,* 1973, *13*, 161–171 (b).

Leibovic, K. N. *Information processing in the nervous system.* New York: Springer-Verlag, 1969.

Leibowitz, H. W., & Harvey, L. O., Jr. Size matching as a function of instructions in a naturalistic environment. *Journal of Experimental Psychology,* 1967, *74*, 378–382.

Leibowitz, H. L., & Harvey, L. O., Jr. Effect of instructions, environment, and type of test object on matched size. *Journal of Experimental Psychology,* 1969, *81*, 36–43.

Levin, H., & Williams, J. P. *Basic studies in reading.* New York: Basic Books, 1970.

Lindsay, P., & Norman, D. *Human information processing.* (2nd ed.) New York: Academic Press, 1977

Linksz, A. *Physiology of the eye.* New York: Grune and Stratton, 1952.

Liss, P. Does backward masking by visual noise stop stimulus processing? *Perception and Psychophysics,* 1968, *4*, 328–330.

Lockhead, G. R. Processing dimensional stimuli: A note. *Psychological Review,* 1972, *79*, 410–419.

Loftus, G. R. Eye fixations and recognition memory for pictures. *Cognitive Psychology,* 1972, *3*, 525–551.

Long, G. E. The effect of duration of onset and cessation of light flash on the intensity-time relation in the peripheral retina. *Journal of the Optical Society of America,* 1951, *41*, 743–747.

Ludvigh, E. Extrafoveal visual acuity as measured with Snellen test-letters. *American Journal of Ophthalmology,* 1941, *24*, 303–310.

Lythgoe, R. J., & Tansley, K. The relation of the critical frequency of flicker to the adaptation of the eye. *Proceedings of the Royal Society* (London), *1929, 105B*, 60–92.

Mach, E. *The analysis of sensations.* Chicago: Open Court, 1914.

Mackay, D. M. Elevation of visual threshold by displacement of retinal image. *Nature,* 1970, *225*, 90–92.

Mackay, D. M. Visual stability and voluntary eye movements. In R. Jung (Ed.), *Handbook of sensory physiology.* Vol. 7, Part 3. Berlin: Springer-Verlag, 1973, Pp. 307–331.

Mackworth, N. H. Visual noise causes tunnel vision. *Psychonomic Science,* 1965, *3*, 67–68.

Mackworth, N. H. Stimulus density limits the useful field of view. In R. A. Monty & J. W. Senders (Eds.), *Eye movements and psychological processes.* Hillsdale, N. J.: Lawrence Erlbaum Associates, 1976. Pp. 307–322.

Mackworth, N. H., & Bruner, J. How adults and children search and recognize pictures. *Human Development,* 1970, *13*, 149–177.

Mackworth, N. H., & Kaplan, I. T. Visual acuity when eyes are pursuing moving targets. *Science,* 1962, *136*, 387–388.

Mackworth, N. H., & Morandi, A. J. The gaze selects informative details within pictures. *Perception and Psychophysics,* 1967, *2*, 547–552.

MacLeod, R. B., & Pick, H. L., Jr. *Perception: Essays in honor of James J. Gibson.* Ithaca, N. Y.: Cornell University Press, 1974.

Marks, L. E. *Sensory processes: The new psychophysics.* New York: Academic Press, 1974.

Marks, W. B., Dobell, W. H., & MacNichol, E. F. Visual pigments of single primate cones. *Science,* 1964, *143*, 1181–1182.

Massaro, D. W. Perception of letters, words, and nonwords. *Journal of Experimental Psychology,* 1973, *100*, 349–353.

Massaro, D. W., & Schmuller, J. Visual features, preperceptual storage, and processing time in reading, In D. W. Massaro (Ed.), *Understanding language: An information-processing analysis of speech perception, reading, and psycholinguistics.* New York: Academic Press, 1975.

Matin, L. Eye movements and perceived visual direction. In D. Jameson & L. M. Hurvich (Eds.), *The handbook of sensory physiology.* Vol. VII/4. *Sensory psychophysics.* Berlin: Springer-Verlag, 1972.

Matin, E., Clymer, A., & Matin, L. Metacontrast and saccadic suppression. *Science,* 1972, *178*, 179–182.

Maurer, D. Infant visual perception: Methods of study. In L. B. Cohen & P. Salapatek (Eds.), *Infant perception: From sensation to cognition.* Vol. 1. New York: Academic Press, 1975. Pp. 1–76.

Maurer, D., & Salapatek, P. Developmental changes in the scanning of faces by infants. *Child Development,* 1976, *47*, 523–527.

McCollough, C. Color adaptation of edge detectors in the human visual system. *Science,* 1965, *149*, 1115–1116.

McConkie, G. W., & Rayner, K. The span of the effective stimulus during fixation in reading. *Perception and Psychophysics,* 1975, *17*, 578–596.

McFarland, J. *Perception of line forms.* Chicago: University of Chicago Press, 1973.

McKenzie, B. E., & Day, R. H. Object distance as a determinant of visual fixation in early infancy. *Science,* 1972, *178*, 1108–1110.

McKinney, J. P. Disappearance of luminous designs. *Science,* 1963, *140*, 403–404.

Meltzoff, A. N., & Moore, M. K. Imitation of facial and manual gestures by human neonates. *Science,* 1977, *198*, 75–78.

Melvill-Jones, G. The vestibular system for eye movement control. In R. A. Monty & J. W. Senders (Eds.), *Eye movement and psychological processes.* Hinsdale, N. J.: Lawrence Erlbaum Associates, 1976. Pp. 3–18.

Melvill-Jones, G., and Gonshor, A. Goal-directed flexibility in the vestibulo-ocular reflex arc. In P. Bach-y-rita & G. Lennerstrand, *Basic mechanisms of ocular motility and their clinical implications.* New York: Pergamon, 1975. Pp. 227–245.

Mewhort, D. J. K. Familiarity of letter sequences, response uncertainty, and the tachistoscopic recognition experiment. *Canadian Journal of Psychology*, 1967, *21*, 309–321.

Miller, G. A. The magical number seven, plus or minus two. *Psychological Review*, 1956, *63*, 81–97.

Miller, G. A., Bruner, J. S., & Postman, L. Familiarity of letter sequences and tachistoscopic identification. *Journal of General Psychology*, 1954, *50*, 129–139.

Mitchell, D. E. Effect of early visual experience on the development of certain perceptual abilities in animals and man. In R. D. Welk & H. L. Pick, Jr. (Eds.), *Perception and experience*. New York: Plenum, 1978. Pp. 7–36.

Monty, R. A., & Senders, J. W. *Eye movements and psychological processes*. Hinsdale, N. J.: Lawrence Erlbaum Associates, 1976.

Moray, N. *Attention: Selective processes in vision and hearing*. New York: Academic Press, 1970.

Morton, J. The effects of content upon speed of reading, eye movements and eye-voice span. *Quarterly Journal of Experimental Psychology*, 1964, *16*, 340–355.

Morton, J. Categories of interference: Verbal mediation and conflict in card sorting. *British Journal of Psychology*, 1969, *60*, 329–346.

Mueller, C. G. Frequency of seeing functions for intensity discriminations at various levels of adapting intensity. *Journal of General Physiology*, 1951, *34*, 463–474.

Neisser, U. Decision-time without reaction-time: Experiments in visual scanning. *American Journal of Psychology*, 1963, *76*, 376–385.

Neisser, U. *Cognitive psychology*. New York: Appleton-Century-Crofts, 1967.

Neisser, U., & Beller, H. K. Searching through word lists. *British Journal of Psychology*, 1965, *56*, 349–358.

Neisser, U., & Lazar, R. Searching for novel targets. *Perceptual and Motor Skills*, 1964, *19*, 427–432.

Neisser, U., Novick, R., & Lazar, R. Searching for ten targets simultaneously. *Perceptual and Motor Skills*, 1963, *17*, 955–961.

Neisser, U., & Stoper, A. Redirecting the search process. *British Journal of Psychology*, 1965, *56*, 359–368.

Nelson, K., & Kessen, W. Visual scanning by human newborns: Responses to complete triangle, to sides only, and to corners only. Paper presented at the meeting of the American Psychological Association, Washington, D. C., September 1969.

Newman, E. B. Speed of reading when span of letters is restricted. *American Journal of Psychology*, 1966, *79*, 272–278.

Nickerson, R. S. Response times for "same"–"different" judgments. *Perceptual and Motor Skills*, 1965, *20*, 15–18.

Nickerson, R. S. Binary-classification reaction time: A review of some studies of human information processing capabilities. *Psychonomic Monograph Supplements*, 1972, 4 (17; Whole No. 65), 275–318.

Nickerson, R. S. The use of binary classification tasks in the study of human information processing. In S. Kornblum (Ed.), *Attention and performance. Vol. 4.* New York: Academic Press, 1973.

Nickerson, R. S. On the time it takes to tell things apart. In J. Requin (Ed.), *Attention and performance. Vol. 7.* Hillsdale, N. J.: Lawrence Erlbaum Associates, 1978.

Nodine, C. F., & Fisher, D. F. (Eds.) *Perception and pictorial representation*. New York.: Holt, Rinehart and Winston, 1980.

Norman, D. A. *Models of human memory*. New York: Academic Press, 1970.

Norman, R. A., & Werblin, F. S. Control of retinal sensitivity: I.

Light and dark adaptation of vertibrate rods and cones. *Journal of General Psychology*, 1974, *63*, 37–66.

Noton, D., & Stark, L. Scanpaths in saccadic eye movements while viewing and recognizing patterns. *Vision Research*, 1971, *11*, 929–942.

O'Brien, B. Vision and resolution in the central retina. *Journal of the Optical Society of America*, 1951, *41*, 882–894.

Ogle, K. N. On the limits of stereoscopic vision. *Journal of Experimental Psychology*, 1952, *44*, 252–259.

Ogle, K. N. The optical space sense. In H. Davson (Ed.), *The eye*. New York: Academic Press, 1962. Pp. 211–417.

Ogle, K. N. *Researches in binocular vision*. New York: Hafner, 1964 (originally published in 1950).

Panum, P. L. *Physiological investigations concerning vision with two eyes*. Keil: Schwering's Bookstore, 1858. Translated by C. Hubscher, Dartmouth Eye Institute, Hanover, N. H., 1940.

Pastore, N. *Selective hisotry of theories of visual perception: 1650–1950*. New York: Oxford, 1971.

Peeples, D. R., & Teller, D. Y. Color vision and brightness discrimination in two-month-old human infants. *Science*, 1975, *189*, 1102–1103.

Phillips, R. J. Stationary visual texture and the estimation of slant angle. *Quarterly Journal of Experimental Psychology*, 1970, *22*, 389–397.

Piaget, J., & Inhelder, B. *The child's conception of space*. New York: Norton, 1967.

Pirenne, M. H. *Vision and the eye*. London: Chapman and Hall, 1948. (Second edition, 1967.)

Pirenne, M. H. *Optics, painting, and photography*. New York: Cambridge University Press, 1970.

Pirozzolo, F. J., & Wittlock, M. C. *Neuropsychological and cognitive processes in reading*. New York: Academic Press, 1980.

Polyak, S. L. *The vertebrate visual system*. Chicago: University of Chicago Press, 1957.

Pomerantz, J. R., & Garner, W. R. Stimulus configuration in selective attention tasks. *Perception and Psychophysics*, 1973, *14*, 565–569.

Pomerantz, J. R., Sager, L. C., & Stoever, R. J. Perception of wholes and their component parts: Some configurational superiority effects. *Journal of Experimental Psychology: Human Perception and Performance*, 1977, *3*, 422-435.

Pomerantz, J. R., & Schwaitzberg, S. D. Grouping by proximity: Selective attention measures. Perception and Psychophysics, 1975, *18*, 355–361.

Posner, M. I. Abstraction and the process of recognition. In G. H. Bower & J. T. Spence (Eds.), *The psychology of learning and motivation*. New York: Academic Press, 1969. Pp. 44–100.

Posner, M. I. Psychobiology of attention. In M. Gazzaniga & C. Blakemore (Eds.), *Handbook of psychobiology*, New York: Academic Press, 1975.

Posner, M. I. Chronometric analysis of abstractism and recognition. In W. K. Estes (Ed.), *Handbook of learning and cognitive processes*. Vol. 5. Hillsdale, N. J.: Lawrence Erlbaum Associates, 1977.

Posner, M. I., Boies, S. J., Eichelman, W. H., & Taylor, R. L. Retention of visual and name codes of single letters. *Journal of Experimental Psychology*, 1969, *79*, (Monograph Supplement 1), 1–16.

Posner, M. I., & Keele, S. W. Decay of visual information from a single letter. *Science,* 1967, *158,* 137–139.

Posner, M. I., & Mitchell, R. F. Chronometric analysis of classification. *Psychological Review,* 1967, *74,* 392–409.

Posner, M. I., Nissen, M. J., & Ogden, W. Attending to a position in space. Paper presented to the Psychonomic Society Convention, November 1975.

Posner, M. I., Nissen, M. J., & Ogden W. C. Attended and unattended processing modes: The role of set for spatial location. In H. L. Pick, Jr. & E. Saltzman (Eds.), *Modes of perceiving and processing information.* Hillsdale N. J.: Lawrence Erlbaum Associates, 1978. Pp. 137–158.

Posner, M. I., & Taylor, R. L. Subtractive method applied to separation of visual and name components of multiletter arrays. *Acta Psychologica,* 1969, *30,* 104–114.

Poulton, E. C. Peripheral vision: Refractoriness, and eye movements in fast oral reading. *British Journal of Psychology,* 1962, *53,* 409–419.

Pritchard, R. M. Stabilized images on the retina. *Scientific American,* 1961, *204* (June), 72–78.

Purdy, W. C. The hypothesis of psychophysical correspondence in space perception. Unpublished Ph.D. dissertation, Cornell University, 1958. University Microfilms No. 58–5594.

Purkinje, J. *Beobachtungen and Versuche zur Physiologie der Sinne.* Zweiter Bachchen. Berlin: G. Reimer, 1825.

Rabbitt, P. M. A. Learning to ignore irrelevant information. *American Journal of Psychology,* 1967, *80,* 1–13.

Rappoport, J. L. Attitude and size judgement in school age children. *Child Development,* 1967, *38,* 1187–1192.

Ratliff, F. *Mach bands.* San Francisco: Holden-Day, 1965.

Ratoosh, P. On interposition as a cue for the perception of distance. *Proceedings of the National Academy of Science,* 1949, *35,* 257–259.

Rayner, K. The perceptual span and peripheral cues in reading. Unpublished doctoral dissertation, Cornell University, 1974.

Rayner, K. The perceptual span and peripheral cues in reading. *Cognitive Psychology,* 1975, *7,* 65–81.

Rayner, K. Eye movements in reading. *Psychological Bulletin,* 1978, *85,* 1–50.

Reber, A. S., & Scarborough, D. L. *Toward a psychology of reading.* Hillsdale, N. J.: Lawrence Erlbaum Associates, 1977.

Reicher, G. M. Perceptual recognition as a function of meaningfulness of stimulus material. *Journal of Experimental Psychology,* 1969, *81,* 275–280.

Reisen, A. H. Plasticity of behavior: Psychological aspects. In H. F. Harlow & C. N. Woolsey (Eds.), *Biological and biochemical bases of behavior.* Madison: University of Wisconsin Press, 1958. Pp. 425–472.

Reisen, A. H. Electrophysiological changes after sensory deprivation. In A. H. Reisen (Ed.), *The developmental neuropsychology of sensory deprivation.* New York: Academic Press, 1975. Pp. 153–164.

Ricco, A. Relazione fra il minimo angolo visual e l'intensita luminosa. *Memorie della Regia Academia di Scienze, lettere edarti in modera,* 1877, *17,* 47–160.

Richter, J. P. *The notebooks of Leonardo da Vinci.* Vol. 1. New York: Dover, 1970.

Riggs, L. A. Visual acuity. In C. H. Graham (Ed.), *Vision and visual perception.* New York: Wiley. 1965. Pp. 321–349.

Riggs, L. A. Saccadic suppression of phosphenes: Proof of a neural basis for saccadic suppression. In R. A. Monty & J. W. Senders (Eds.), *Eye movements and psychological processes.* Hinsdale, N. J.: Lawrence Erlbaum Associates, 1976. Pp., 85–100.

Riggs, L. A., Armington, J. C., & Ratliff, F. Motions of the retinal image during fixation. *Journal of the Optical Society of America,* 1954, *44,* 315–321.

Riggs, L. A., Merton, P. A., & Morton, H. B. Suppression of visual phosphenes during saccadic eye movements. *Vision Research,* 1974, *14,* 977–1011.

Riggs, L. A., Ratliff, F., Cornsweet, J. C., & Cornsweet, T. N. The disappearance of steadily fixated visual test objects. *Journal of the Optical Society of America,* 1953, *43,* 495–501.

Robinson, D. A. The mechanics of human smooth pursuit eye movements. *Journal of Physiology,* 1965, *180,* 569–591.

Robinson, D. A. The physiology of pursuit eye movements. In R. A. Monty & J. W. Senders (Eds.), *Eye movements and psychological processes.* Hinsdale, N. J.: Lawrence Erlbaum Associates, 1976. Pp. 19–32.

Robson, J. G. Receptive fields. In E. C. Carterette & M. P. Friedman (Eds.), *Handbook of perception.* Vol. 5. New York: Academic Press , 1975. Pp. 81–116.

Rock, I. The orientation of forms on the retina and in the environment. *American Journal of Psychology,* 1956, *69,* 513–528.

Rock, I. *The nature of perceptual adaptation.* New York: Basic Books, 1966.

Rock, I. *Orientation and form.* New York: Academic Press, 1973.

Rock, I. *An introduction to perception.* New York: Macmillan, 1975.

Rock, I. In defense of unconscious inference. In W. Epstein (Ed.), *Stability and constancy in visual perception.* New York: Wiley, 1977. Pp. 321–373.

Rock, I., & Ebenholtz, S. Stroboscopic movement based on change of phenomenal rather than visual location. *American Journal of Psychology,* 1962, *75,* 193–207.

Rosinski, R. R. *The development of visual perception.* Santa Monica, Calif.: Goodyear, 1977.

Rothbalt, L. A. & Schwartz, M. L. Altered early environment: Effects on the brain and visual behavior. In R. D. Walk & H. L. Pick, Jr. (Eds.), *Perception and experience.* New York: Plenum, 1978. Pp. 37–76.

Rothkopf, E. Z. Writing to teach and reading to learn: A perspective on the psychology of written instruction. In N. L. Gage (Ed.), *The psychology of teaching methods. The 75th yearbook of the National Society for the Study of Education,* Part I. Chicago: National Society for the Study of Education, 1976.

Roufs, J. A. Dynamic properties of vision: I. Expected relationships between flicker and flash thresholds. *Vision Research,* 1972, *12,* 261–278.

Rubin, E. *Visuell wahrgenommene Figuren.* Copenhagen: Glyndendalske, 1921.

Rushton, W. A. H. Visual pigments in the colour blind. *Nature,* 1958, *182,* 690–692.

Rushton, W. A. H. A foveal pigment in the deuteranope. *Journal of Physiology* (London), 1963, *168,* 345–359.

Rushton, W. A. H., Campbell, R. W., Hagins, W. A., & Brindley, G. S. The bleaching and regeneration of rhodopsin in the living eye of the albine rabbit, and of man. *Optica Acta,* 1955, *1,* 183–190.

Ryan, J. A., & Schwartz, C. Speed of perception as a function of mode of presentation. *American Journal of Psychology,* 1956, *69,* 60–69.

Sackett, G. P. Monkeys reared in isolation with pictures as visual input: Evidence for an innate releasing mechanism. *Science*, 1966, *154*, 1468–1473.

Sackitt, B. Locus of short-term visual storage. *Science*, 1975, *190*, 1318–1319.

Sackitt, B. Iconic memory. *Psychological Review*, 1976, *83*, 257–276.

Sakitt, B. Psychophysical correlates of photoreceptor activity. *Vision Research*, 1976, *16*, 129–140.

Salapatek, P. Visual scanning of geometric figures by the human newborn. *Journal of Comparative and Physiological Psychology*, 1968, *66*, 247–258.

Salapatek, P. Pattern perception in early infancy. In L. B. Cohen & P. Salapatek (Eds.), *Infant perception: From sensation to cognition*. Vol I. New York: Academic Press, 1975. Pp. 133–248.

Salapatek, P., Bechtold, A. G., & Bushnell, E. W. Infant visual acuity as a function of viewing distance. *Child Development*, 1976, *47*, 860–863.

Salapatek, P., & Kessen, W. Visual scanning of triangles by the human newborn. *Journal of Experimental Child Psychology*, 1966, *3*, 155–167.

Sanders, A. *The selective process in the functional visual field*. Institute for Perception, RVO-TNO, Soesterberg, The Netherlands, 1963.

Schiff, W., Caviness, J. A., & Gibson, J. J. Persistent fear responses in rhesus monkeys to the optical stimulus of "looming." *Science*, 1962, *136*, 982–983.

Schiffrin, R. M., & Geisler, W. S. Visual recognition in a theory of information processing. In R. L. Solso (Ed.), *Contemporary issues in cognitive psychology: The Loyola Symposium*. New York: Wiley, 1973. Pp. 53–101.

Schiffrin, R. M., & Schneider, W. Controlled and automatic human information processing: II. Perceptual learning, automatic attending, and a general theory. *Psychological Review*, 1977, *84*, 127–190.

Schiller, P. H. Single unit analysis of backward visual masking and metacontrast in the cat lateral geniculate nucleus. *Vision Research*, 1968, *8*, 855–866.

Schiller, P. H., & Smith, M. Detection in metacontrast. *Journal of Experimental Psychology*, 1966, *71*, 32–46.

Schindler, R. M. The effects of prose context on visual search for letters. *Memory and Cognition*, 1978, *6*, 124–130.

Schlosberg, H. Stereoscopic depth from single pictures. *American Journal of Psychology*, 1941, *54*, 601–605.

Schmidt, M. W., & Kristofferson, A. B. Discrimination of successiveness: A test of a model of attention. *Science*, 1963, *139*, 112–113.

Schneider, W., & Schiffrin, R. M. Controlled and automatic human information processing: I. Detection, search, and attention, *Psychological Review*, 1977, *84*, 1–66.

Schuller, M. J. Chromatic vision in human infants: Conditioned operant fixation to "hues" of varying intensity. *Bulletin of the Psychonomic Society*, 1975, *6*, 39–42.

Sekuler, R. Spatial vision. In M. R. Rosensweig & L. W. Poster (Eds.), *Annual review of psychology*, 1974, *25*, 195–232.

Sekuler, R. W., & Ganz, L. Aftereffect of seen motion with a stabilized retinal image. *Science*, 1963, *139*, 419–420.

Sekuler, R. W., & Pantle, A. A model for aftereffects of seen movement. *Vision Research*, 1967, *7*, 427–439.

Selfridge, O. G. Pandemonium: A paradigm for learning. In *The mechanization of thought processes*. London: H. M. Stationery Office, 1959.

Shannon, C. E. A mathematical theory of communication. *Bell System Technical Journal*, 1948, *27*, 379–423; 623–656.

Shebilske, W. Visuomotor coordination in visual direction and position constancies. In W. Epstein (Ed.), *Stability and constancy in visual perception*. New York: Wiley, 1977. Pp. 23–70.

Shlaer, S. The relation between visual acuity and illumination. *Journal of General Physiology*, 1937, *21*, 165–188.

Singer, W., & Bedworth, N. Inhibitory interaction between X and Y units in cat lateral geniculate nucleus. *Brain Research*, 1973, *49*, 291–307.

Slater, A. M., & Findlay, J. M. Binocular fixation in the newborn baby. *Journal of Experimental Child Psychology*, 1975, *20*, 248–273.

Sloan, L. L. Measurement of visual acuity. *Archives of Ophthalmology*, 1951, *45*, 704–725.

Smith, S. W., & Blaha, J. Preliminary report summarizing the results of location uncertainty: Experiments I–VII. The Ohio State University, 1969.

Solomon, R. L., & Howes, D. H. Word frequency, personal values, and visual duration threshold. *Psychological Review*, 1951, *58*, 256–270.

Solomon, R. L., & Postman, L. Frequency of usage as a determinant of recognition thresholds for words. *Journal of Experimental Psychology*, 1952, *43*, 195–201.

Sperling, G. The information available in brief visual presentations. *Psychological Monographs*, 1960, *74* (11, Whole No. 498).

Sperling, G. A model for visual memory tasks. *Human Factors*, 1963, *5*, 19–31.

Sperling, G. Successive approximation to a model for short-term memory. *Acta Psychologica*, 1967, *27*, 285–292.

Spigel, I. Relation of movement aftereffect duration to interpolated darkness intervals. *Life Science*, 1962, *6*, 239–242.

Spigel, I. (Ed.), *Visually perceived movement*. New York: Harper & Row, 1965.

Steinman, R. M. Oculomotor effects. In P. Bach-y-rita & G. Lennerstrand (Eds.), *Basic mechanisms of ocular motility and their chemical implications*. New York: Pergamon, 1975.

Steinman, R. M. Role of eye movement in maintaining a phenomenally clear and stable world. In R. A. Monty & J. W. Senders (Eds.), *Eye movement and psychological processes*. Hinsdale N. J.: Lawrence Erlbaum Associates, 1976. Pp. 121–150.

Stevens, S. S. Issues in psychophysical measurement. *Psychological Review*, 1971, *78*, 426–450.

Stiles, W. S., & Crawford, B. H. The luminous efficiency of rays entering the eye pupil at different points. *Proceeding of the Royal Society (London)*, Series B. 1933, *112*, 428–450.

Stroop, J. R. Studies of interference in serial verbal reactions. *Journal of Experimental Psychology*, 1935, *18*, 643–662.

Stroud, J. The fine structure of psychological time. In H. Quastler (Ed.), *Information theory in psychology*. New York: Free Press, 1956. Pp. 174–207.

Sukale-Wolf, S. The prediction of the metacontrast phenomenon from simultaneous brightness contrast. Unpublished doctoral dissertation, Stanford University, 1971.

Sutherland, N. S. Object recognition. In E. Carterette & M. Friedman (Eds.), *Handbook of perception*. Vol. 3. *Biology of perceptual systems*. New York: Academic Press, 1973. Pp. 157–186.

Swets, J. A., Tanner, W. P., & Birdsall, T. G. The evidence for a decision-making theory of visual detection. University of Michigan: Electronic Defense Group, Technical Report No. 40, 1955.

Swets, J. A., Tanner, W. P., & Birdsall, T. G. Decision processes in perception. *Psychological Review*, 1961, *68*, 301–340.

ten Doesschate, J., & Alpern, M. The effect of photo-excitation of the two retinas on pupil size. *Journal of Neurophysiology*, 1967, *30*, 562–576.

Thiery, A. Über Geometrische-optische Tauschungen. *Philosophische Studiern*, 1896, *12*, 67–126.

Thomas, J. P. Spatial resolution and spatial interaction. In E. C. Carterette & M. P. Friedman (Eds.), *Handbook of perception*. Vol. 5. New York: Academic Press, 1975. Pp. 233–264.

Thompson, M. C., & Massaro, D. W. Visual information and redundancy in reading. *Journal of Experimental Psychology*, 1973, *98*, 49–54.

Townsend, J. T. Theoretical analysis of an alphabetic confusion matrix. *Perception and Psychophysics*, 1971, *9*, 40–50.

Tronick, E. Stimulus control and the growth of the infant's effective visual field. *Perception and Psychophysics*, 1972, *11*, 373–376.

Tronick, E., & Clanton, C. Infant looking patterns. *Vision Research*, 1971, *11*, 1479–1486.

Tronick, E., & Hershenson, M. Size-distance perception in preschool children. *Journal of Experimental Child Psychology*, 1979, *27*, 166–184.

Tulanay-Keesey, U. The role of eye movements in maintenance of vision. In R. A. Monty & J. W. Senders (Eds.), *Eye movements and psychological processes*. Hinsdale, N. J.: Lawrence Erlbaum Associates, 1976, 101–112.

Turvey, M. T. Contrasting orientations to the theory of visual information processing. *Psychological Review*, 1977, *84*, 67–88.

Turvey, M. T., & Remez, R. Visual control of locomotion in animals: An overview. In L. Harmon (Ed.), *Interrelations of the communicative senses*, 1979. Pp. 275–295.

Uhlarik, J., & Johnson, R. Development of form perception in repeated brief exposures to visual stimuli. In R. D. Walk & H. L. Pick, Jr. (Eds.), *Perception and experience*. New York: Plenum, 1978.

Volkmann, F. C. Vision during voluntary saccadic eye movements. *Journal of the Optical Society of America*, 1962, *52*, 571–578.

Volkmann, F. C. Saccadic suppression: A brief review. In R. A. Monty & J. W. Senders (Eds.), *Eye movements and psychological processes*. Hinsdale. N. J.: Lawrence Erlbaum Associates, 1976. Pp. 73–84.

Volkmann, F. C., Schick, A. M. L., & Riggs, L. A. Time course of visual inhibition during voluntary saccades. *Journal of the Optical Society of America*, 1968, *58*, 362–369.

Wald, G. Human vision and the spectrum. *Science*, 1945, *101*, 653–658.

Wald, G. The receptors of human color vision. *Science*, 1964, *145*, 1007–1017.

Wald, G., & Brown, P. K. Human color vision and color blindness. *Cold Spring Harbor Symposia on Quantitative Biology*, 1965, *30*, 345–361.

Wallach, H. Brightness constancy and the nature of achromatic colors. *Journal of Experimental Psychology*, 1948, *38*, 310–324.

Wallach, H., & O'Connell, D. N. The kinetic depth effect. *Journal of Experimental Psychology*, 1953, *45*, 205–217.

Wallach, H., O'Connell, D. N., & Neissen, O. The memory effect of visual perception of three-dimensional form. *Journal of Experimental Psychology*, 1953, *45*, 360–368.

Walls, G. *The vertebrate eye*. Bloomfield Hills, Mich.: Cranbrook Institute of Science, 1942.

Wattenbarger, B. L. The representation of the stimulus and character classification. Human Performance Center Technical Report #22, University of Michigan, Ann Arbor, August 1970.

Weisstein, N. Backward masking and models of perceptual processing. *Journal of Experimental Psychology*, 1966, *72*, 232–240.

Weisstein, N. Metacontrast. In D. Jameson & L. M. Hurvich (Eds.), *The handbook of sensory physiology*. Vol. VII/4. *Sensory psychophysics*. Berlin: Springer–Verlag, 1972.

Weisstein, N., & Haber, R. N. A U-shaped backward masking function in vision. *Psychonomic Science*, 1965, *2*, 75–76.

Weisstein, N., & Harris, C. S. Visual detection of line segments: An object-superiority effect. *Science*, 1974, 186, 752–755.

Werner, H. Studies on contour. *American Journal of Psychology*, 1935, *47*, 40–64.

Werner, H., & Wapner, S. Toward a general theory of perception. *Psychological Review*, 1952, *59*, 324–338.

Wertheimer, M. Experimentelle Studien über das Sehen von Bervegung. *Zeitschrift für Psychologic*, 1912, *61*, 161–265.

Westheimer, G. H. Eye movement responses to a horizontally moving visual stimulus. *Archives of Ophthalmology*, 1954, *52*, 932–943.

Westheimer, G. Oculomotor control: The vergence system. In R. A. Monty & J. W. Senders (Eds.), *Eye movements and psychological processes*, Hinsdale, N. J.: Lawrence Erlbaum Associates, 1976. Pp. 55–64.

Westheimer, G., & Campbell, F. W. Light distribution in the image formed by the living human eye. *Journal of the Optical Society of America*, 1962, *52*, 1040–1044.

Wheatstone, C. Contributions to the physiology of vision: Part I. On some remarkable, and hitherto unobserved, phenomena of binocular vision. *Royal Society of London Philosophical Transactions*, 1938, *128*, 371–394.

Wheeler, D. D. Processes in word recognition. *Cognitive Psychology*, 1970, *1*, 59–85.

White, C. T., Cheatham, P. G., & Armington, J. C. Temporal numerosity: II. Evidence for central factors influencing perceived number. *Journal of Experimental Psychology*, 1953, *46*, 283–287.

Whiteside, J. A. Eye movements of children, adults and elderly persons during inspection of simple dot patterns. Unpublished doctoral dissertation, University of Rochester, 1972.

Wiesel, T. N., & Hubel, D. H. Spatial and chromatic interactions in the lateral geniculate body of the rhesus monkey. *Journal of Neurophysiology*, 1966, *79*, 1115–1156.

Williams, A., & Weisstein, N. Line segments are perceived better in a coherent context than alone: On object-line effect in visual perception. *Memory and Cognition*, 1978, *62*, 85–90.

Williams, L. G. The effect of target specification on objects fixated during visual search. *Perception and Psychophysics*, 1966, *1*, 315–318.

Williams, L. G. The effects of target specification on objects fixated during visual search. In A. F. Sanders (Ed.), *Attention and performance*. Amsterdam: North Holland Publishing Co., 1967. Pp. 355–360.

Winston, P. H. *The psychology of computer vision*. New York: Mc-Graw-Hill, 1975.

Winston, P. H. *An introduction to computer vision*. Cambridge, Mass.: MIT, 1977.

Woodrow, H. The effect of pattern upon simultaneous letter span. *American Journal of Psychology*, 1938, *51*, 83–96.

Woodworth, R. S. *Experimental psychology*. New York: Holt, Rinehart and Winston, 1938.

Worrall, N. A test of Gregory's theory of primary constancy scaling. *American Journal of Psychology*, 1974, *84*, 505–510.

Wulff, V. J., Adams, R. G., Linschitz, H., & Abrahamson, E. W. Effect of flash illumination on rhodopsin. *Annals of the New York Academy of Science*, 1958, *74*, 281–290.

Wurtz, R. H. Extraretinal influences of the primate visual system. In R. A. Monty & J. W. Senders (Eds.), *Eye movements and psychological processes*. Hinsdale, N. J.: Lawrence Erlbaum Associates, 1976. Pp. 231–244.

Yarbus, A. L. *Eye movements and vision*. New York: Plenum, 1967.

Yonas, A., & Hopen, M. A. Effects of static and kinetic depth information on the perception of size by children and adults. *Journal of Experimental Child Psychology*, 1973, *15*, 254–265.

Young, F. A., & Lindsley, D. B. *Early experience and visual information processing in perceptual and reading disorders*. Washington: National Academy of Science, 1970.

Young, L. R., & Sheena, D. Survey of eye movement recording techniques. *Behavioral Research Methods and Instrumentation*, 1975, *7*, 397–429.

Zakia, R. D. *Perception and photography*, New York: Prentice Hall, 1975.

Zeigler, H. P., & Leibowitz, H. Apparent visual size as a function of distance for children and adults. *American Journal of Psychology*, 1957, *70*, 106–109.

Zeki, S. M. Color coding in rhesus monkey prestriate cortex. *Brain Research*, 1973, *53*, 422–427.

Zinchenko, V. P., & Vergiles, N. Y. *Formation of visual images*. New York: Consultants Bureau, 1972.

Zusne, L. *Visual perception of form*. New York: Academic Press, 1970.

Index of Names

Index of Subjects

Boldface folios indicate pages on which the terms are defined.

Acknowledgments (continued)

Figure 15.5: I. Rock, The orientation of forms on the retina and in the environment. *American Journal of Psychology,* 1956, *69,* 516.

Figure 15.15: J. Beck, Similarity grouping and peripheral discriminability under uncertainty. *American Journal of Psychology,* 1972, *85,* 3.

Figure 15.21: J. Hochberg and V. Brooks, The psychophysics of form: Reversible-perspective drawings of spatial objects. *American Journal of Psychology,* 1960, *73,* 340.

Figures 17.14 and 17.16: U. Neisser, Decision-time without reaction-time: Experiments in visual scanning. *American Journal of Psychology,* 1963, *76,* 337. 385.

Figure 18.17: E. J. Gibson, A. A. Pick, H. Osser, and M. Hammond, The role of grapheme-phoneme correspondence in the perception of words. *American Journal of Psychology,* 1962, *75,* 562.

Vision Research

Figure 6.6: J. A. Roufs, Dynamic properties of vision: 1. Expected relationships between flicker and flash thresholds. 1972, *12,* 261–278. Copyright 1972 by Pergamon Press, Ltd.

Figure 6.7: D. N. Whitten and K. T. Brown, Slowed decay of the monkey's cone receptor potential by intense stimuli, and protection from this effect by light adaptation. 1973, *13,* 1659–1662. Copyright 1973 by Pergamon Press, Ltd.

Figure 6.17: P. H. Schiller, Single unit analysis of backward visual masking and metacontrast in the cat lateral geniculate nucleus. 1968, *8,* 855–866. Copyright 1968 by Pergamon Press, Ltd.

Figure 1.15: R. W. Rodick, *The vertebrate retina.* Copyright 1973 by W. H. Freeman and Company.

Figure 10.17: R. Held and A. V. Hein, Adaptation of disarranged hand–eye coordination contingent upon re-afferent stimulation. *Perceptual and Motor Skills,* 1958, *8,* 87–90.

Metropolitan Museum of Art

Music and Good Luck by William Harnett.